Using Ventura Publisher®

2nd Edition

Diane Burns
S. Venit
Linda J. Mercer

que®
CORPORATION
LEADING COMPUTER KNOWLEDGE

Using Ventura Publisher®

2nd Edition

Library of Congress Catalog No.: 88-63851
ISBN 0-88022-406-1

93 92 91 90 89   8 7 6 5 4 3 2 1

Interpretation of the printing code: the rightmost double-digit number is the year of the book's printing; the rightmost single-digit number, the number of the book's printing. For example, a printing code of 89-1 shows that the first printing of the book occurred in 1989.

Using Ventura Publisher, 2nd Edition, is based on Ventura Publisher Versions 2.0 and earlier.

ABOUT THE AUTHORS

Diane Burns
S. Venit

Diane Burns and S. Venit own and operate TechArt, a graphic design and production shop in San Francisco, where they use PageMaker as one of their primary tools. At TechArt, they designed and developed *The Page-Maker Classroom*, training material for Aldus Corporation.

Burns and Venit have coauthored 9 books and over 50 articles about microcomputer applications in the business environment and have trained hundreds of users in hands-on computer classes for business applications. Their articles have appeared in national magazines, including *PC Magazine*, *PC Week*, and *Publish!* Their articles include reviews of laser typesetters, page composition systems, and desktop publishers. Both are experienced in training the staffs of large corporations in the use of microcomputers and in developing written training materials. Their books integrate text and graphics to provide practical applications for new users.

Linda J. Mercer

Linda J. Mercer, CSP, is the product manager for software and image-processing products at Tab Products of Houston, where she uses Ventura to produce marketing materials.

In 1982, Mercer founded Information Network, a Houston-based information management company. Today the firm develops curriculum for desktop publishing programs and uses Ventura and PageMaker to produce ads, newsletters, manuals, directories, and catalogs. Other divisions of the company maintain databases, process mail, and provide records-management advice and assistance. Mercer has been working with computer-assisted systems for more than 11 years, helping vendors develop and clients implement systems to expedite the production, storage, and delivery of corporate information.

Publishing Manager

Lloyd J. Short

Production Editor

Jeannine Freudenberger

Editors

Kelly Currie
Kelly Dobbs
Greg Robertson
Alice Martina Smith
Steven Wiggins

Technical Editors

Richard and Sally Clements

Indexer

Sharon Hilgenberg

Book Design and Production

Dan Armstrong
Brad Chinn
Cheryl English
Lori A. Lyons
Jennifer Matthews
Dennis Sheehan
Louise Shinault
Peter Tocco

Composed in Times Roman and Excellent No. 47
by Que Corporation

CONTENTS AT A GLANCE

TABLE OF CONTENTS

I   The Production Process with Ventura Publisher

II Designing and Producing Different Types of Publications

13   Designing and Producing Newsletters, Magazines, and Newspapers 475

▼ ACKNOWLEDGMENTS

This edition of *Using Ventura Publisher* drew on the involvement of several individuals who use Ventura daily. Jane Hudson (Docuset Houston); Jennifer Nech (Systems Software Support, Houston); and Derrick Booth (Subsea Data Services and president of the Ventura Publisher Users Group of Houston) depend on Ventura as an essential production tool to create their products—their client's printed pages. Their practical tips, illustrations, and descriptions of new program operations bring to the manuscript experience that no single individual could accomplish in such a short time.

Other individuals have given a great deal of help managing the details that surround writing and illustrating a manuscript of this scope. Thanks to Ventura experts Reyna Cowan (Berkeley, California) and Doug Jumper (Docuset, Houston) for participating with the authors in the development of the first and second editions. Thanks to Carroll Hanks (Xerox, Houston) and Brenda Beck (Hill and Knowlton) for providing information about the new versions of the program. Thanks to Sharron Murphy and Micki Mastin for making the facilities of Information Network constantly available. Thanks to the literary and technical editors at Que for salient critiques and helpful suggestions. Thanks to James Reid Jr. (Houston) for providing invaluable support throughout the development of both editions.

Thanks also is due the following individuals and organizations for contributing examples and illustrations presented in Part III: Phil Schaefer (Tab Products of Houston); Gordon Mercer (Diamond G/M Beefmasters, Sheridan, Texas); Pete Mercier (Intech Automated Systems, San Antonio); Mavis Eppes (1987-89 Houston Chapter Newsletter Editor, Association of Records Managers and Administrators); John Paul Richards (graphic designer, Houston); Carl Rose (Design Automation, Houston); Jane Holsten (Smart Moves, Houston); Donna Kelley with Christopher Glazek and Lisa LaBreque (ZetaType Desktop Publishers, San Francisco); Emily Rosenberg (Venture Development Services, Oakland, California); *PC Magazine* (Ziff-Davis Publishing Company); Hilton Trevis (Punch Line House, Sandton, South Africa); Gary Shepherd (Sandia National Laboratories, Albuquerque); Art Berliner (Walden Capital Partners); Kevin Price and Jolene Overbeck (Orrick, Herrington & Sutcliffe); United Way on the Bay Area; Jerry Murphy (Survey Research Associates); Gail Ferrari (Pacific Presbyterian Medical Center); Stephen Buss & Associates; Jeff Yerkey Design (San Francisco); Charles Heineke and Jim Nech (Houston Area League of PC Users, Inc.); Paul Ford and David Davis (Davis Ford Agency) with Barbara Heglund, Susie Rich, and Scott Wald (*LaserJet Journal*); Ballet Fantasque Company; and Arvind Kumar (India Currents).

Finally, we appreciate all the valuable time and willing help offered by John Meyer, President of Ventura Software, in explaining new enhancements to Ventura and in finding contributors for Part III of the book.

TRADEMARK
ACKNOWLEDGMENTS

Que Corporation has made every effort to supply trademark information about company names, products, and services mentioned in this book. Trademarks indicated below were derived from various sources. Que Corporation cannot attest to the accuracy of this information.

Adobe Illustrator is a trademark of Adobe Systems Incorporated.

Apple, LaserWriter, LaserWriter Plus, and MacPaint are registered trademarks of Apple Computer, Inc.

AST TurboLaser is a registered trademark of AST Research, Inc.

AutoCAD is a registered trademark of Autodesk, Inc.

Bitstream is a registered trademark of Bitstream Inc.

Cricket Draw is a trademark of Cricket Software, Inc.

DXF is a trademark of Autodesk, Inc.

Dr. HALO is a registered trademark of Media Cybernetics, Inc.

Epson MX-80, Epson FX-80, Epson RX-80, and Epson LX-80 are trademarks of Epson America, Inc.

GEM, GEM Draw, and GEM Paint are trademarks of Digital Research Inc.

Hercules Graphics Card is a trademark of Hercules Computer Technology.

IBM is a registered trademark and IBM ProPrinter, IBM PC XT, PS/2, and DisplayWriter are trademarks of International Business Machines Corporation.

JLaser is a registered trademark of Tall Tree Systems.

LaserJet is a trademark of Hewlett-Packard Co.

Linotronic is a trademark of Allied Corporation.

Lotus and 1-2-3 are registered trademarks of Lotus Development Corporation.

Manager Mouse is a registered trademark of The Torrington Company.

MS-DOS and Microsoft 3COM LAN Manager are registered trademarks and Microsoft is a trademark of Microsoft Corporation.

MultiMate is a registered trademark of Multimate International, an Ashton Tate Corporation.

Novell is a registered trademark of Novell, Inc.

PC Mouse is a trademark of Mouse Systems Corporation.

PC Paintbrush+ is a registered trademark of ZSoft Corporation.

PostScript is a registered trademark of Adobe Systems, Inc.

SAMNA Word IV is a trademark of SAMNA Corporation.

SideKick is a registered trademark of Borland International, Inc.

TIME is a registered trademark of Time, Inc.

X-ACTO is a registered trademark of Hunt Manufacturing Co.

Ventura Publisher is a registered trademark of Ventura Software, Inc.

WordPerfect is a registered trademark of WordPerfect Corporation.

WordStar and WordStar 2000 are registered trademarks of MicroPro International Corporation.

Xerox is a registered trademark and Interpress is a trademark of Xerox Corporation.

XyWrite is a trademark of XyQuest, Inc.

CONVENTIONS USED IN THIS BOOK

The conventions used in this book have been established to help you learn to use the program quickly and easily. As much as possible, the conventions correspond with those used in the Ventura Publisher documentation.

Commands and menu names are written with initial capital letters exactly as they appear on-screen. Names of dialog boxes are written in all capital letters. Words and letters that the user types are written in *italic* or set off in a separate line. Options in dialog boxes and on-screen messages are written in a special typeface and capitalized exactly as they appear on-screen.

Introduction

Xerox® Ventura Publisher®, created by Ventura Software and marketed and supported by Xerox Corporation, is one of the most sophisticated desktop publishing programs for IBM® XTs, ATs, PS/2s, and compatibles on the market today. Ventura lets you compose pages on a screen and see the pages as they will be printed. Because of the program's power and sophistication, you can learn to produce publications that rival the quality of professionally typeset and printed documents—with a minimum investment in equipment and software.

Desktop publishing uses personal computers to produce typeset-quality text and clean graphic images, merge them on the same page, arrange the elements in an effective design, and then print finished pages on a high-resolution laser printer or typesetter. Desktop publishing techniques lessen the need for rulers, pens, blue-line boards, wax, tape, screens, and X-ACTO® knives in the production of camera-ready pages for offset printing or photocopier reproduction. Desktop publishing, when appropriately implemented, can reduce the amount of time and money spent producing communications for which quality in presentation counts.

Why a Book about Ventura?

Because of the scope of the tasks undertaken with desktop publishing systems, Ventura is a complex program. The program's large number of options make it versatile, but they also present to the user a formidable number of commands, options, and alternative ways to accomplish production tasks. Because of this complexity, without the type of guidance offered in this book, learning to use Ventura is not as easy as learning to use other programs. If you are just starting with Ventura, you will continually be finding new tasks that Ventura can do as you learn to use Ventura for new types of projects.

Even through the program can produce beautiful publications, *you* may not be able to produce beautiful documents without getting some helpful advice from professional designers. *Using Ventura Publisher*, 2nd Edition, offers production tips that are useful to designers and gives design principles for less experienced users. The material gives these tips and principles while detailing the steps you take to complete a variety of projects—from short ads, forms, brochures, and fliers to full-length books and reports. This book is a practical guide that goes beyond the Ventura manuals to give examples and hints on using the program's features in a production environment.

1

Who Should Use This Book?

No matter what your background and experience, you will need to learn new methods and new terms when you enter the world of desktop publishing. This book brings together the vocabularies of the typesetter, designer, word processor, and computer operator to explain clearly the concepts from these many disciplines, which are merged in desktop publishing applications.

This book is intended for professional desktop publishers, as well as for people who use Ventura to produce only occasional documents. The numerous examples demonstrate the wide range of possibilities with Ventura. By studying these examples and tips, you will be able to improve the appearance of your documents and reduce your overall production time.

What Is New in Version 2.0?

In the fall of 1988, the Ventura development team introduced a new version, 2.0, as the base product. Ventura 2.0 builds on the capabilities of earlier versions and offers users a natural, nearly painless transition into the more powerful program. A complementary product, called the Professional Extension, was also announced at the same time. As you can see by the features covered in Chapter 10, the Professional Extension guarantees that Ventura will continue to dominate the DOS-compatible desktop marketplace. With the announcement of these products, Xerox also released information about the network versions of each. Today these four products offer a Ventura solution for a wider variety of users than ever before.

The improvements to Ventura fall into many categories because the programming team managed to simplify techniques and dialog boxes but still add dozens of new features. (To help readers who have been using Ventura's earlier versions, enhancements unique to Version 2.0 are flagged with a graphic icon like the icon next to this paragraph.) Learning to use Version 2.0 after learning Version 1.1 warrants spending enough time to find out whether a particular technique or project has changed because of innovations in the new version. You don't want to overlook the new features, because they provide many shortcuts and extend the capabilities of the program.

Some changes are subtle enough that users of earlier versions might first let the differences go undetected. For instance, once you start the program, Ventura now lets you type on a page just as though you had inserted paper into a typewriter. Before you quit, you are prompted to name the chapter file, and then Ventura names the source text file with the same name.

Other improvements are more immediately obvious and are loudly applauded by users of earlier versions. For example, now you can find the frame that controls a graphic simply by selecting the graphic. When you need help understanding the options in a dialog box, you can click the ? (question mark) to read Ventura's Help notes. And you can print a style file and compare typographic settings in designs you create. Furthermore, Version 2.0 takes more advantage of the PostScript language for printing than did earlier versions. In short, if you have never used Ventura before, by starting with Version 2.0 you get a head start because the Ventura development team had the good sense to listen to early Ventura users.

What Is in This Book?

Part I of *Using Ventura Publisher* (Chapters 1–8) addresses Ventura's basic features and describes the steps involved in producing a document. Part II (Chapters 9–11) offers specific advice about defining the type specifications and designing and producing different kinds of publications. This part also includes a chapter devoted to the Professional Extension. Part III (Chapters 11–16) presents examples of publications produced by using Ventura and highlights specific design and production tips. If you are already using Ventura, you may want to skim Part I, looking for the tips; read Part II; and use Part III as a reference source when you have a specific production problem.

Part I

The information in Part I lays a foundation. Chapter 1 defines desktop publishing and describes Ventura's basic functions. After comparing Ventura's features with word processing programs and with graphics programs, the material describes the final form of a page created in Ventura and gives an overview of the production process.

Chapter 2 discusses the equipment required to run Ventura and compares the capabilities of the base, professional, and network versions of the program. Chapter 3 takes you through the steps of starting Ventura and gives a detailed description of Ventura's opening screen and menu commands. This chapter also provides a summary of the steps involved in producing a complete document in Ventura.

Chapter 4 discusses the three methods of placing text on a page in Ventura (typing, loading, or pasting) and compares formatting in a word processing program and formatting in Ventura so that you can choose the best procedure for your project. Chapter 5 covers the techniques used to format text once it is in Ventura, including changing paragraph formats (alignment and spacing) and character formats (font, leading, and kerning).

Chapter 6 describes Ventura's built-in graphics tools and tells you how to bring in graphics created in other programs. You will learn how to scale and crop graphics, how to position them on a page, and how to create lines, boxes, and circles. The differences between vector and bit-mapped graphics are also shown.

Chapter 7 presents page-by-page and step-by-step instructions and tips for laying out a document after you have prepared your text and graphics files in other programs. This chapter includes discussions and illustrations of how to use Ventura's frames to define the document's basic grid and how to position text and graphics on the page. Chapter 8 takes you through the steps involved in printing with different printers, including Apple®'s LaserWriter®, Hewlett-Packard®'s LaserJet™, and Allied's Linotronic™ typesetters.

Part II

In Part II the discussion focuses on design decisions. Chapter 9 begins with a discussion of the typographer's view of a document—specifically, how to select fonts for a document. This chapter also discusses which fonts are available for each printer, how the fonts are installed, and how new fonts are created. You learn how to determine which fonts, sizes, and styles are available for your printer before you start the design process and how to work with a limited font selection. Definitions and illustrations of different leading and kerning are given, along with special tips on copy fitting.

Chapter 10 explains how to use the Professional Extension to create tables from spreadsheets and databases and to process technical documents that are longer and more complicated than any you can handle with the base product alone. You see each feature of the Professional Extension and learn how to use these features for cross-referencing chapters and pages, creating mathematical and scientific formulas and equations, and applying instructions for vertical justification of elements on pages.

Chapter 11 explores ways to use Ventura as a design tool and offers advice to designers who are planning layouts for Ventura production. You learn how to use Ventura's style files and chapters to serve as design templates, and you see how to set up design elements on a page you add to the chapter. Attaching a copy of these elements to pages where they are needed aids the Ventura team during production and helps preserve design consistency.

Part III

Part III (Chapters 11 through 16) offers many examples of different types of documents, illustrating specific design principles and production tips. These examples include books, reports, manuals, magazines, newsletters, brochures, fliers, ads, slides, and overhead transparencies. These examples provide you with the tips and techniques you need to become a skilled desktop publisher.

Appendix and Glossary

The Appendix includes an extensive categorized list (with sources) of monitors, printers, and software components that are compatible with Ventura.

The Glossary includes terms used on Ventura's menus and dialog boxes, as well as terms used in traditional typesetting, design, and printing.

We hope that you enjoy *Using Ventura Publisher*, 2nd Edition, and that you profit from the many useful tips offered in this book.

The Production Process with Ventura Publisher

Includes

Overview of Xerox Ventura Publisher and Desktop Publishing

Configuring Your System for Ventura Publisher

Using Ventura

Loading, Typing, and Generating Text

Formatting Text, Tables, and Lists

Creating and Importing Graphics

Creating Full-Page Layouts

Printing

Overview of Xerox Ventura Publisher and Desktop Publishing

X erox Ventura Publisher is a page-layout application that runs on IBM and compatible MS-DOS® systems. With Ventura, you can create illustrated documents that are assembled from a variety of text and graphics sources, and you can preview full pages on-screen before printing on a high-resolution printer or typesetter. When combined with text and graphics from other software programs, Ventura's features automate many of the tasks of layout artists' tools and materials: typeset galleys of type, photographic reproductions of line art, halftones of photographs, pens, pressure-sensitive tapes, knives, wax, blue lines, boards, and acetate overlays.

Created by Ventura Software, Inc., and marketed by Xerox Corporation, Ventura has played a major role in bringing the PC-compatible world into the desktop publishing revolution. With the release of Ventura Publisher 2.0, Xerox Corporation has also made available a separate product called the Professional Extension. Both products offer similar text and graphics capabilities. The Professional Extension, however, offers features that more readily produce equations and tables and can handle documents that are long enough to warrant the use of extended computer memory. The Professional Extension also offers an automatic feature that causes text to reach a uniform length on pages. Although many publishers will find the features of Ventura Publisher comprehensive enough to handle all their publishing requirements, professional typographers and departments responsible for the production of long documents may want to use the Professional Extension.

This book tells you how to use both Ventura Publisher 2.0 and the Professional Extension on the IBM XT, AT, PS/2™, and compatibles. The features common to both programs are covered in Chapters 3–9, and those that are unique to the Professional Extension are covered in Chapter 10. Throughout the book, you also will find tips and suggestions for using the programs with compatible printers, scanners, and software programs in order to add speed, quality, and dimension to a program that can be used to produce a wide variety of publications.

In this chapter, you see how desktop publishing has evolved from technological breakthroughs in a number of different fields. And you see how desktop publishing is changing the way printed pages are produced in many communications areas. You learn about Ventura's basic capabilities by examining a page produced by using Ventura with several other programs, and you get an overview of the production process.

Desktop Publishing: An Evolving Technology

The term *desktop publishing* did not exist a few years ago. But the term quickly caught on as a way to describe the combined results of recent changes in personal computer and microcomputer technology. Desktop publishing is the use of personal computers to produce typeset-quality text and clean graphics images, merge the text and graphics on the same page, and then print the pages on a high-resolution laser printer or typesetter. Ventura Publisher rightly falls under the category of desktop publishing, although the term is often applied to a wide variety of applications, including some that do not offer Ventura's page composition and typesetting features.

The cost of microcomputer equipment for on-screen graphics processing has dropped, and improved laser technology also has reduced the price of high-resolution printers and typesetters. Manufacturers of type began designing new typefaces or adapting traditional typeface designs to take advantage of new printer capabilities. Software developers realized that hardware breakthroughs opened the way for the development of programs that merge text and graphics directly on-screen (see fig. 1.1).

This combination of hardware and software capabilities (embodied in Ventura Publisher) is having a dramatic impact on typesetters, designers, publishers, corporate publications departments, small businesses, and individuals who dream of producing their own great novels. To understand the significance of these capabilities, you need to understand something about the elements that form the foundation of desktop publishing.

Using Low-Cost Equipment

Not surprisingly, you need a hard disk, a graphics card and monitor, and at least 640K of conventional computer memory to run Ventura Publisher. (The program comes on fifteen 5 1/4-inch or eight 3 1/2-inch disks, including drivers and utilities.) The Professional Extension version of Ventura Publisher supports—but does not require— extended memory. (The Professional Extension requires at least 144K beyond 640K in order to recognize the extended memory. If you intend to use the optional EDCO hyphenation dictionary, however, 1.5M of extended memory is required.) See Chapter 2 for a more detailed explanation of hardware requirements.

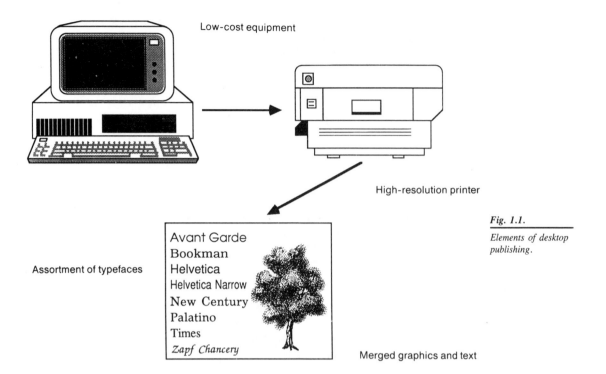

Low-cost equipment

High-resolution printer

Assortment of typefaces

Avant Garde
Bookman
Helvetica
Helvetica Narrow
New Century
Palatino
Times
Zapf Chancery

Merged graphics and text

Fig. 1.1.

Elements of desktop publishing.

The cost of computers has decreased dramatically during the past few years. Owning a personal computer once meant a $5,000 investment in a computer with little memory and no software. Now many PCs priced under $2,000 include the storage memory and graphics components required for desktop publishing tasks.

Today, you can select a fast, powerful desktop publishing system from a single vendor, or you can assemble the components yourself by choosing products offered by a growing number of vendors who are competing for their niche in the desktop publishing marketplace. As you add memory and high-resolution or full-page monitors to your system configuration, your computer investment will rise from $2,000 toward $4,000 to $6,000. If you intend to publish often and under rigorous deadlines and schedules, however, the investments you make in extended memory and full-page monitors will be quickly rewarded.

Using High-Resolution Printers

Low-cost laser printers can produce high-resolution output that previously was available only from typesetting equipment. *Resolution* is an indication of the sharpness of the edges of printed characters and graphics. Resolution is commonly measured by the number of dots per inch. For example, dot-matrix printers print both text and graphics by pushing pins against a ribbon that strikes paper and leaves an imprint. The resolution of the imprint is determined by the number of thin metal pins the manufacturer puts in the print head. The resolution common to most dot-matrix printers is 120 dots per inch. This resolution is considered coarse when compared to the resolution produced by typesetting equipment, which uses a different technology to print images at 1,200 or 2,400 dots per inch (see fig. 1.2). Typesetting equipment, however, can cost from $20,000 to $100,000.

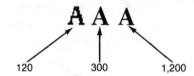

Fig. 1.2.

Characters printed at 120, 300, and 1,200 dots per inch.

The revolution in printing came when Canon® introduced the 300-dots-per-inch laser printer engine that is used in many printers now available for less than $5,000. Printers such as the Apple LaserWriter (used to print the example shown in fig. 1.2) and Hewlett-Packard's LaserJet use Canon technology. Other manufacturers make laser printers with different laser engines that print 400 or 600 dots per inch. Allied's Linotronic typesetters use the same laser technology to phototypeset images at 1,200 or 2,400 dots per inch. Ventura is designed to take full advantage of these printers' capabilities.

To the untrained eye, documents printed at 300, 600, 1,200, and 2,400 dots per inch may appear to be of the same quality—the text looks typeset at all these settings. Professional typesetters and designers can see the differences among these resolutions, but the average reader does not unless the results are compared side by side. With Ventura Publisher and a printer that costs as little as $3,000, you can achieve results that previously required an investment of more than $20,000.

Using Different Typefaces

The transition to laser printers led to changes in printer typefaces. A *typeface* is a collection of characters (alphanumerics, punctuation, and symbols) that share a common design. Courier and Helvetica are two different typefaces (hundreds of typefaces are available). The letter *A* in Courier typeface has a design different from the letter *A* in Helvetica typeface. Desktop publishing introduces a broader range of typefaces than ever was possible outside of most printing shops.

Not so long ago, a typewriter had only one typeface—either pica or elite. More recently, you could change the typeface in your typewriter or printer by changing the daisywheel or type element. But each document usually showed only one typeface throughout—Courier, for example. Although you could mix boldface and regular characters on a page, you couldn't mix normal characters and italic. With dot-matrix printers, you could mix regular, boldface, italic, and different font sizes; but the low resolution of the output was considered inferior to the output of letter-quality printers (see fig. 1.3).

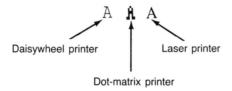

Daisywheel printer   Laser printer

Dot-matrix printer

Fig. 1.3.

*Typefaces from a
daisywheel printer, a
dot-matrix printer,
and a laser printer.*

With desktop publishing (and all its software and hardware components), you can combine a variety of typefaces, type styles, and type sizes within a single document and print or typeset full pages. These features may vary among printers, but any laser printer offers more than two options. (Most letter-quality printers are limited to normal and bold.) Desktop publishing still does not offer the typeface variety that professional typesetting does, but new typefaces are added to the list daily. Ventura Publisher supports many new typefaces and provides a means for you to use them on a laser printer.

Merging Text and Graphics

One result of these recent technological changes is the availability of new software programs that can combine text and graphics. But merging text and graphics on-screen is not new; professional page-composition systems have been merging text and graphics for years. TIME® magazine, for example, started composing pages on a computer more than 15 years ago. Time, Inc., however, paid more than $250,000 for that system. Most publishers continued to use X-ACTO knives and wax to paste up text and art on boards—slow and tedious work (see fig. 1.4).

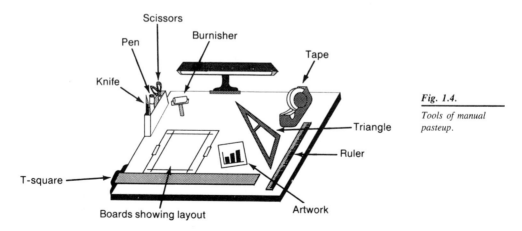

Scissors

Pen

Burnisher

Tape

Knife

Triangle

Ruler

T-square

Boards showing layout

Artwork

Fig. 1.4.

*Tools of manual
pasteup.*

Before the advent of desktop publishing software, microcomputer users were able to produce text with word processing programs and produce graphics with their spreadsheets or drawing programs. But the output from these various programs rarely was merged—either on-screen or on paper. Instead, reports were assembled with all the graphics relegated to an appendix, or the graphics were printed on separate pages and merged with the text pages later. Users with adventurous spirits left spaces in the text and inserted the graphics later, using scissors and glue. Now, personal computer users can merge text created from a word processor with graphics drawn in Ventura or loaded from other programs.

Ventura is one of the first page-composition packages that actually eliminates pasteup. With Ventura, microcomputer users can merge text from a word processor with graphics from a drawing program and print fully composed documents in one step. The basic tools of on-screen pasteup are the computer with its various programs and a high-resolution printer. Ventura incorporates the text and graphics from other programs. The graphics then can be copied and scaled directly on the screen. After the layout of all the pages is finished, any changes made on one page cause linked text on following pages to shift automatically.

With Ventura, you actually can see on the screen what the page will look like. Ventura is a *WYSIWYG* system (pronounced "wizzy-wig"), and WYSIWYG means that "what you see is what you get." In other words, you see the graphics and the text on the screen as they will appear on the printed page (with slight variations due to the difference in resolution between the screen and the printer).

As you can see, desktop publishing has emerged as a result of technological breakthroughs in several fields. The fact that desktop publishing programs are personal computer applications means that many individuals and businesses already have desktop publishing facilities. Even though these users may not consider themselves publishers, they are beginning to realize that these new capabilities have the potential of making all printed communications more effective.

Desktop Publishing: A Blend of Tradition and Knowledge

Desktop publishing blends the skills associated with four crafts: typesetting, graphic design, printing, and computing. Because each discipline has its own set of technical terms and standards, professionals in all these fields must add new terms to their vocabularies in order to "speak" desktop publishing. Users, too, are discovering that terms such as *spot*, *dot*, and *pixel* may refer to similar concepts and that each discipline has something to share with the others.

Typesetting Traditions

Typesetters work with codes: one code sets the typeface, another sets the style, another sets the size, and so on. One distinct advantage of coded typesetting is the precision of the measurement with which type can be set. The disadvantage of the code-based system is that codes are difficult to learn. Furthermore, many typesetting machines lack the capacity to permit previewing the text as it will look when printed. In order to locate and correct coding errors, typesetters must print the text by means of the photochemical typesetting device—thereby adding to both the time and the cost of production.

Ventura Publisher's features rival many features found in the most sophisticated typesetting systems, including permitting the user to select fine units of measurement to determine the space between lines and letters. Furthermore, with the Professional Extension, vertical justification of text on pages can be controlled by setting measures for space to be added between text and illustrations, text and tables, and between or within paragraphs. Although typesetters may need to adjust their demands and expectations slightly to match the capabilities of desktop publishing systems, desktop publishing does not have to mean typography of poorer quality.

Menu-driven systems like Ventura Publisher can be slower than code-based typesetting machines, but many typographers are willing to trade a measure of speed for desktop publishing's low-cost WYSIWYG screens, short learning curve, and economical printing options. Besides, you still can enter Ventura's formatting as codes in the text files if you prefer.

Design Traditions

Professional designers take pride in their ability to take a client's ideas and create dramatic functional products. The process of translating design ideas into concrete results is painstaking and time-consuming, as is reflected in the fees charged for design services.

Initially, some professional designers may balk at the idea of using a computer for such creative tasks, and they may resist because of reduced billing amounts that result from the time saved by using a computer as a primary design tool. These designers quickly learn, however, that the economies realized by using a desktop publishing system result in increased demand for design services at all levels because of lower costs passed on to clients.

With Ventura Publisher, designers can rough out ideas quickly and deliver to clients a design that looks more like finished work than the traditional penciled sketches in the preliminary stages. Designers can store the file and fine-tune the design later for final production. Furthermore, the same files can be duplicated and modified for other documents in the same design project series or for similar documents in another design series.

Graphic design amateurs can produce nice-looking publications with Ventura Publisher—a fact that may be a bit disconcerting to professionals. But the best designs still require the knowledge and skills learned as part of the designer's trade. With desktop publishing, designers have acquired another tool that can support their tradition of excellence and help meet the business community's demand for economy in the production of printed communications.

Printing Traditions

Not so long ago, you had to take your original work to an offset printer to make multiple copies of your document. More recently, copying equipment has been improved so that good-quality reproductions are inexpensive and easy to produce. In either case, the final result depends on the condition of the original page. You need clean, clear, black images on white paper.

Now, laser printers print the entire image, including gray scales, directly on any color paper you choose, and you can print in color on some systems. You can easily and quickly print hundreds of "originals" for immediate distribution. If you take the same image to an offset printer, however, you may find that the camera which makes plates does not see the image the same way you do. In later chapters in this book, you learn how to prepare your master copy for offset printing. You also learn the vocabulary you need in order to communicate with the printer, who is accustomed to dealing with graphics professionals.

Computing Traditions

The final ingredient in blending tradition and knowledge comes from the computer industry. Pixels, screen fonts, ports, baud rates, icons, and menus all are terms born of a technology with which you will become familiar as you move into desktop publishing.

Throughout this book, you will find production tips that will help you get the most out of your Ventura Publisher desktop publishing system. You will come to understand, for example, the importance of developing good housekeeping habits for your disk files, just as many designers practice good housekeeping with the paper and precision hand tools that they use in their studios.

Desktop Publishing with Ventura Publisher

Desktop publishing has been discussed in general terms, sometimes using Ventura Publisher as an example. But what about Ventura Publisher itself? How is the program similar to and different from other software programs that you may be using on your computer?

Ventura Publisher is a page-composition program. Ventura enables you to compose pages by using elements (text and graphics) that you created previously in other programs, as well as elements created in Ventura. Figure 1.5 shows some examples of the types of publications that you can produce with Ventura.

Ventura Publisher is one of the first personal computer page-composition programs that addresses the tasks associated with producing long documents. Ventura can handle long documents such as reports, books, and manuals; in addition, the program is a highly effective tool for producing short documents, including newsletters, brochures, forms, display ads, and presentation materials.

You can use Ventura Publisher to set up the basic grid of the page layout for the document and then to funnel the assorted text and graphics into place. Ventura provides features to allow you to make an index and to place headers, footers, and footnotes where you want them in a publication. Ventura assembles the text and graphics

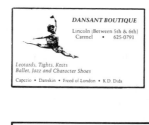

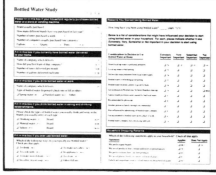

Fig. 1.5.

Publications produced by Ventura Publisher.

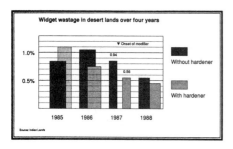

from other programs and provides tools to crop, copy, enlarge, and reduce the graphics from other programs. Ventura's graphics features also can be used to create new images by using five drawing tools (as described in Chapter 6).

After you finish the layout of all the pages, you easily can change the copy, picture sizes, numbers of illustrations, or other elements that make up the publication and reprint the full page layout. You can let Ventura Publisher automatically place text throughout a publication, or you can control page layouts individually and arrange and rearrange elements on each page. In either case, you actually can see on-screen very nearly how the page will look.

Using Ventura and Word Processors

You can type text into Ventura Publisher much the way that you type text with your word processor. On the Ventura screen, though, the text looks almost as it will look when you print the page. For example, you can see the difference between 12-point Times italic and 14-point Helvetica boldface. Although a few word processors let you mix limited type selections, few match Ventura's capability to mix type styles and sizes and display different typefaces on the screen.

Ventura Publisher is a graphics-oriented program with a display of menus and pages on the screen (even if you don't incorporate graphics on the pages themselves). As a result, Ventura tends to be slower for word processing than a true word processing program, which is designed for speed. Furthermore, Ventura does not have some of the functions that most word processing programs incorporate, such as global searches or spell checkers. For these reasons, you will be wise to prepare and edit long documents with your word processing program before you load the text into Ventura.

Once you load a word processing file into a Ventura publication, you can make any needed text changes from within Ventura Publisher. The changes can be saved into the original word processing file when you anticipate revising or reusing your work. Ventura's capacity to read, update, and write files in many compatible formats sets the program apart from other desktop publishing programs. Because you can use Ventura Publisher to assemble files from many different word processing software packages, you can use work stations equipped with word processing software to prepare files for quick publishing turnaround.

Using Graphics with Ventura

You can draw simple graphics—such as lines, boxes, and circles—in Ventura Publisher, or you can import graphics created by other programs. Graphics images that have been loaded into Ventura can be scaled and cropped to fit the space available. Illustrations created by layering Ventura's drawn graphics can be scaled to different sizes and cut and copied into place in different publications. Like most drawing programs, Ventura also offers a variety of lines and fill patterns for graphics objects created with Ventura'a graphics drawing tools. By mixing cyan, magenta, yellow, and black in percentages, you can define custom colors (or shades of gray) for displaying Ventura-drawn graphics on color monitors. Overlays can be printed from black-and-white laser printers for color reproduction during offset printing, or compatible color printers can be used to create each original on demand.

Most drawing programs accommodate some form of text entry, but they do not handle text formatting, such as columnar layouts and tabular data, the way Ventura does. Furthermore, most graphics programs do not handle multiple pages. By working directly with a drawing or painting program, however, you can use some of the more sophisticated features—such as rotation, airbrush effects, and pixel-by-pixel image manipulation—that are not offered directly by Ventura. You also can use a paint program to touch up images that have been digitized through a scanner.

Creating the Final Ventura Page

A Ventura publication can be composed of text and graphics created entirely in Ventura Publisher or created from elements brought in from other programs. Examine figure 1.6. First, the text was typed, using two different word processing programs. Then the text was transferred into Ventura with the program's Load Text/Picture command. The graphics logo was created with a drawing program, Dr. HALO®. A scanned image was modified, using PC Paintbrush Plus®, before the image was placed on the page in Ventura. The text of the banner was typed directly into Ventura and kerned to tighten letter spacing. Hairline rules and boxes were added with Ventura's page-layout and graphics tools. Running footers and automatic page numbering were set up by using Ventura's Headers & Footers command. Gray bars at the top and bottom of each page were drawn once and repeated on every page. All these concepts are explained later in this book.

Fig. 1.6.

A page created by Ventura Publisher.

Figure 1.6 illustrates just one sample of what is possible with Ventura. The rest of this book shows you how to create a page like this one and a variety of other publications.

How Ventura Affects the Publishing Process

Ventura Publisher brings together functions that once were divided among different people at different locations. Here is an example of the publishing process before desktop publishing. A typist typed the text of a newsletter and sent the file—either on paper or on disk—to the typesetter for formatting and typesetting. Meanwhile, the graphics department used a computer or pens and ink to create the graphics images for an outside service to photostat to the correct size. Eventually, the galleys of type and the reproductions of the figures landed on a drafting table, where the layout artist trimmed the paper and pasted it down on boards, which were then used to produce the final pages.

With Ventura Publisher, one person can type the text, draw the graphics, and compose the pages on-screen. But just because one person is performing all the steps does not mean that the steps in the publishing process are much different.

You can assume, of course, that if one person is responsible for an entire production process, that person probably is strong in some areas and weak in others. For that reason, many desktop publishing departments still divide the tasks of desktop publishing among different people. Nevertheless, when the production team is small (as is common in desktop publishing environments), weak spots can develop in the production cycle—areas in which no one on the team has expertise. This book provides tips in areas where you and your team may be lacking.

Dividing Tasks and Responsibilities

Even if only one person ultimately produces the document, the associated tasks and responsibilities still can be divided conceptually among typical publishing roles: production manager, author, editor, copy editor, designer, illustrator, and production crew.

The *production manager* oversees the entire project, coordinating tasks and efforts to be sure that everyone involved meets the schedule. The production manager adjusts the schedule as needed.

The *author* delivers complete, accurate text, probably on disk. An author may format the text if he or she is familiar with final design specifications.

An *editor* then reviews the text and graphics to make sure that the document is organizationally sound, clear, and complete. The editor also may be responsible for tone and content. The *copy editor* reads the text and reviews graphics for grammatical, typographical, and formatting errors and makes sure that all references to figures or other sections or pages of the document are accurate.

The *designer* determines the overall appearance of the pages: paper size and orientation, margins, and basic grid structure. The designer also specifies the typefaces, sizes, and styles to be used in the document and also may specify fill patterns or treatments for all illustrations. The *illustrator* produces the graphics files that will be placed on the page. In some cases, the illustrator may be the author or the designer.

Finally, the *production crew* includes anyone who actually uses Ventura to assemble the pages. The production crew also may format the text with a word processor if the formatting has not been done by the author.

These responsibilities may be performed by one person or divided among several (depending on the situation). Being aware of the different "publishing hats" you may have to wear may help you more easily produce high-quality work with Ventura Publisher.

Understanding the Steps in the Production Process

Whether you produce a document from start to finish on your own or work as a part of a team, you can set up an efficient production schedule if you recognize the steps involved in a typical production cycle. Some of these steps take place simultaneously, and some projects may demand that steps be eliminated or may call for a slightly different sequence. A typical production schedule showing relationships among the following steps is shown in the GANTT chart in figure 1.7. (A *GANTT chart* is a graphic representation of tasks scheduled along a time line, showing task duration, dates, and status.)

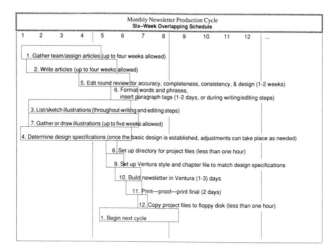

Fig. 1.7.

A typical production schedule.

A typical production schedule includes these tasks:

1. Gather the team, identify the division of responsibilities, and prepare the production schedule. In this case, the team may include the client ordering the work as well as the production group. Or a ''team'' may be simply one individual who sketches a single timetable.

2. Write the text with a word processor. Even if the authors are not using the same type of computer that you will be using with Ventura Publisher, almost any text can be converted or telecommunicated before the final Ventura stage.

3. Sketch or list illustration ideas.

4. Determine the design specifications, including all the following:

   • Determine typefaces, sizes, and styles for different elements within the text and decide on the basic text format. Ask questions such as these: Will the paragraphs have a first-line indentation? What space will be left between paragraphs? Will the text be justified? Will headings be flush left or centered?

   • Determine the basic page layout—the grid set by margins and columns; include page size, margins, orientation, number of columns, and positions and sizes of intercolumn rules.

   • Specify final (maximum) size of illustrations, as well as typefaces, sizes, and styles to be used within the illustrations and in the captions.

- Establish the final page count or the range of pages expected to be filled. This count will help you decide whether to divide a long publication into smaller documents or sections, determine how to divide the publication, and estimate the printing costs. The page count traditionally has been performed after the text is written because the design itself may be affected by the content and structure of the text. If, however, authors know the design specifications while writing the text, authors using compatible word processors can expedite the project by inserting tab signs and formatting words and phrases within paragraphs for special emphasis as the publication develops.

5. Let one or more editors read the text: one reading for accuracy and completeness of the content, one reading for grammar and consistency of usage, and one reading to mark the text according to the design specifications. Most professionals find that one person cannot read on all these levels in one round. If you have only one reader, make sure that these readings are done separately.

6. Edit and format the text with the word processor. Do as much of the editing as possible in the word processing program before you place the text into Ventura.

7. Create the illustrations by using the graphics program best suited for each. Remember the following points:

   - Some illustrations or graphic elements can be added by using Ventura's graphics features.

   - Clip-art from electronic collections can be used to add display type fonts, maps, or symbolic illustrations in line-art and bit-mapped formats.

   - Scanners can digitize photographs and line drawings that would otherwise be difficult to reproduce.

   - Paint-type programs are best suited for working with digitized images and for making original artwork for graphics and illustrations.

   - Drafting-type packages are best suited for line art and technical illustrations.

   - Spreadsheets or graphing programs are most efficient for graphs that are derived from tables of numbers.

8. Set up a directory on the hard disk to hold the files needed to assemble the publication. Keeping a set of files on a floppy disk during production is also a good safeguard.

9. Use Ventura to create and save the basic design of the publication in a style file. When the basic design is overridden on individual pages, the remaining design elements are controlled by the chapter file. Chapter files serve the purpose of binding together the separate source files (both

text and graphics) that complete the publication. In many cases, when you want to re-use a design, you start by using the chapter file as a template. You will learn more about the role of each of these types of files in Chapters 3 through 7.

10. Use the Ventura tools to insert the text and graphics files created in other programs. Add new elements.

11. Print the documents. (This step will occur many times during the production cycle because of repeated editing and fine-tuning.)

12. When the project is finished, copy all files related to that publication to one or more floppy disks. Store the backup disks in a safe location.

Some of these steps are essential to any Ventura production cycle. But other steps, such as designing a publication from scratch, are considered advanced skills. *If you are new to design, start with small projects that mimic other document designs.* After you have learned how to use Ventura's basic features (described in Chapters 3 through 8) and have tried designing a few pages, you can tackle the advanced topics covered in Chapters 9 and 11. Table 1.1 describes the levels of the steps and lists which chapters provide information about each step.

Table 1.1
Where To Find More Information

Step	Level	Chapter
1	Basic	Chapter 1 (this section)
2	Basic	Chapter 4
	Advanced	Chapter 5
3	Basic	Chapter 6
	Advanced	Chapter 11
4	Basic	Chapter 5
	Advanced	Chapters 7, 9, 11
5		-(not covered in this book)-
6	Basic	Chapters 4, 5, 9
	Advanced	Chapters 7, 11, Part III
7	Basic	Chapter 6
8	Basic	Chapter 3
	Advanced	Part III
9	Basic	Chapters 3, 7
	Advanced	Chapter 11, Part III
10	Basic	Chapters 4–7
11	Basic	Chapter 8
12	Basic	Chapter 3
	Advanced	Part III

Meeting Deadlines

Publishing often is ruled by deadlines—probably more than any other business or activity. You cannot, after all, send out a June newsletter in July. And when the publication is part of a larger product package, the marketing or distribution group needs the documents finished as soon as the product itself is ready for shipment, even though writing the text is often difficult until the product is available in final form. In every case, publishing professionals must struggle to meet deadlines and still maintain the highest quality in their productions.

Chapter Summary

The process of combining text and graphics on a page continues to change, in large measure because of rapid change in converging technologies. Some people believe that desktop publishing in the twentieth century is revolutionizing communications as significantly as Gutenberg's press did in the fifteenth century. Others claim that desktop publishing is more renaissance than revolution. And—believe it or not—still others are already calling for the end of the desktop publishing era and heralding the beginning of electronic publishing. Whether revolution, renaissance, or just another layer in the software that we adopt to provide business solutions, Ventura Publisher and the Professional Extension hold a central position in the development of cost- and quality-effective business communications.

In the end, of course, the real impact of these innovations will not be on the production methods as much as on the readers, who will benefit from clearly formatted, dramatically illustrated publications produced in a timely fashion at an affordable cost.

Configuring Your System for Ventura Publisher

Deciding which components to include in your desktop publishing system deserves careful consideration. This chapter describes the basic components needed to use Ventura Publisher or the Professional Extension and suggests ways to enhance your basic system to use the program more efficiently. The chapter also introduces special terms and alternatives for your monitor, mouse, and printer.

The appendix contains a list of vendors offering products that you can add to your system to better meet your publishing needs. Announcements of new products and improvements to existing products appear almost every day, but the appendix gives you an introduction to the array of products that turn ''bare-boned'' desktop publishing systems into faster, more sophisticated systems.

Deciding Which Ventura Product To Use

Xerox offers two separate products for composing text and graphics from disparate sources: Ventura Publisher 2.0 and the Professional Extension. Both operate similarly, but the Professional Extension adds features that prove beneficial in certain publishing environments. Table 2.1 compares the Professional Extension and Ventura Publisher 2.0.

Ventura 2.0 uses a 350-word file of exceptions to the rules established by the hyphenation algorithms (USENGLSH.HY1 and USENGLSH.HY2) and also checks a custom user dictionary. The Professional Extension uses a 130,000-word file, the EDCO hyphenation dictionary. With the Professional Extension, you can specify the length of words that can be hyphenated and set a minimum number of characters before or after the hyphen. To use the utility that is provided to update the dictionary, you need to have available about 2.5M of EMS.

Table 2.1
Comparing the Professional Extension and Ventura Publisher 2.0

Task	Professional Extension	Ventura
Rotate text for column labels	Yes	Yes
Create fractions and simple formulas	Yes	Yes
Create complex equations	Yes	No
Import spreadsheets and tables of imported text	Yes	Yes
Import data files into automatically ruled row and column formats	Yes	No
Automatically track page numbering for cross-references tied to other pages or chapters in the complete publication	Yes	No
Replace variables embedded in source text files	Yes	No
Provide ways to make forms	Yes	Yes
Create custom hyphenation dictionaries	Yes	Yes
Create custom hyphenation rules	Yes	No
Automatic vertical justification of frames and text on pages	Yes	No
Process source files larger than 500K	Yes	No
Use memory beyond 640K to speed document processing tasks	Yes	Yes
Use EMS to hold text files	Yes	No
Use EMS to hold program code and screen fonts	Yes	Yes

The Professional Extension automatically adjusts the white space between elements on the page to achieve a uniform baseline at the bottom of each page. With Ventura Publisher, you can force vertical justification by using the Column Balance command or by adjusting the fit of copy and illustrations page-by-page.

Most of what you can accomplish with the Professional Extension you also can do with Ventura Publisher. But when your publications include equations, long documents, or frequent tables with varying formats, you may decide that the additional dollars spent for the Professional Extension software and recommended memory components are well worth the investment.

Compatibility between Ventura's Versions and Products

You can use Ventura Publisher Version 1.1 style and chapter files in Version 2.0, but not vice versa. Xerox reports, however, that you may need to reinstall Ventura to add EGA screen fonts if you get an error message when you are loading into V2.0 a style file that was created with V1.1. Fortunately, this problem is not always encountered.

You can trade chapters between Ventura 2.0 and the Professional Extension, but tables and equations appear as text coded with angle brackets in V2.0 and as formatted tables and equations when you open Ventura with the Professional Extension batch file. Because the Professional Extension is actually an add-on program (making a total of twenty 5 1/4-inch installation disks), you can start by typing either *VP* or *VPPROF* once you complete the installation.

Ventura on Networks

Ventura 2.0 and the Ventura Publisher Professional Extension are compatible with 3Com®, PC Network, Novell®, and other networks. With a single copy of either program's network version, one person at a time can access the file server from a station on the network. In this type of shared resource environment, the network file server saves display and default preferences for each individual. To add simultaneous access for multiple users, you need to install a copy of the base program or the Professional Extension for each work station. Then the program on the network server manages the use of shared files and printers through a variety of techniques:

- Locking chapters to prevent more than one user at a time from changing a chapter (and its related files)

- Browsing chapters to permit simultaneous access to the latest edited version of a chapter

- Protecting style sheets as read-only files, which help to ensure that corporate standards are not altered inadvertently during document production

- Informing you when a source document used in a Ventura document has been edited by another program during Ventura operations

- Sending a command to the network server's spooler to release the printer at the end of a job

Chapters 3 through 9 explain how to use the features found in both the Professional Extension and Ventura Publisher 2.0, and Chapter 10 discusses the Professional Extension's unique features.

Selecting the Other System Components

A basic Ventura system includes a computer, a monitor, a draft-quality printer, and the Ventura program itself. Before installing Ventura on your system, be sure that your equipment meets Ventura's minimum requirements:

- IBM XT or compatible personal computer with at least 640K (Ventura uses 520K to start)

- Hard disk drive with at least 3M free space

- MS-DOS® or PC DOS Version 2.10 or higher

- Graphics board/monitor: Color Graphics Adapter (CGA) is minimum acceptable resolution (Enhanced Graphics Adapter [EGA], Video Graphics Array [VGA], or Hercules Graphics Card™ recommended).

Your desktop publishing system may include a computer with extended or expanded (EMS) memory, a draft-quality dot-matrix printer, a full-page high-resolution monitor, a laser printer or typesetter for final copies, a scanning device, a library of software, and the Ventura program. You easily can start with a minimum system and later add a new monitor, printer, scanner, computer, or other improvements as you progress with Ventura. To give you an idea of the types of possible configurations for running Ventura (many other combinations are possible), figure 2.1 shows three sample configurations.

The Computer

Ventura runs on an IBM PC XT™; a Personal Computer AT; or a PS/2 model 50, 60, or 80 and compatible systems. Your computer system must have a minimum of 640K, a graphics card, a monitor, and 3M of hard disk space. Sample files to produce letterhead, books, newsletters, directories, presentation materials, and brochures are automatically copied into the TYPESET directory, which is created during program installation. Once you have installed Ventura, you can erase the sample files to free approximately 500K of space, if necessary. As you need each sample file, you can load the appropriate chapter from the copy of the example disk provided with your program.

You should plan to leave several megabytes free on your hard disk to hold publication files, including text, graphics, page layouts (CHP), and style files and related font width tables. Ventura may need as much as 500K of hard disk memory for these files during production. Although you can read files from any drive and directory, operations are faster when the files reside on the hard disk. The Ventura program and the hyphenation dictionaries need about 1M of disk space, and the drivers and font files you need for printing require an additional 1M to 3M of storage, depending on your printer. Ventura lets you access multiple hard disk drives after you start the program.

After you install Ventura, you start the program by typing *VP* or *VPPROF*, depending on which product you installed. Each set of letters is the name of a batch (BAT) file Ventura creates in the root directory of the hard disk drive you designate during program installation. Batch files are made up of a series of commands, options, and

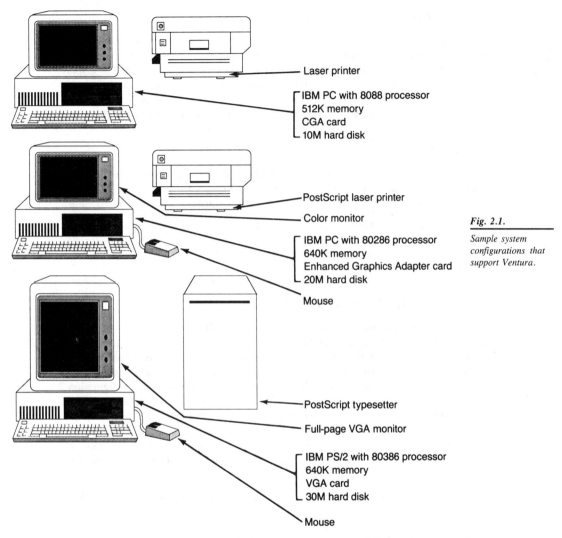

Laser printer

IBM PC with 8088 processor
512K memory
CGA card
10M hard disk

PostScript laser printer

Color monitor

IBM PC with 80286 processor
640K memory
Enhanced Graphics Adapter card
20M hard disk

Mouse

Fig. 2.1.

Sample system configurations that support Ventura.

PostScript typesetter

Full-page VGA monitor

IBM PS/2 with 80386 processor
640K memory
VGA card
30M hard disk

Mouse

switches written in a syntax DOS understands. The batch file Ventura creates designates the directory where the program is stored, specifies the monitor you selected, sets the screen fonts that are initially loaded (you have an option to change them after you start Ventura), and sets the mouse port.

To make Ventura better fit your system configuration, you can edit the start-up batch file with special instructions called switches. (Be sure to use a word processor that saves files in an unformatted ASCII text file.) For example, you can use a word processor to add /X switches at the ends of the batch-file lines. Add an /X switch for every drive you want to display in the item selector lists that Ventura displays when you load and save files. A batch-file command edited to include /X switches for drives D and E looks like this:

DRVRMRGR VP %1 /S = SD_X6655.EGA/M = 32/X = D:/X = E:

As you progress with Ventura and undertake more and more types of projects, you may want to add an /I switch to the batch file to help you enable custom defaults at program start-up. By adding an /I switch, you establish where to store the display default (INF) files Ventura creates each time you quit the program. (You can always change defaults during program operations.) The /I switch permits you to save a unique set of defaults to a designated directory. To add an /I switch, follow this pattern:

/I = D:\DIRECTORY

D stands for the drive letter, and *DIRECTORY* stands for the name of the directory where you intend the file to reside. When you start Ventura with the edited batch file, Ventura reads the default display options from the designated directory.

In Chapter 3, you learn how to set up the display options to create custom batch files for individual projects and users. If you add a different /I switch to every batch file you create, each custom batch file initiates the defaults found in the directory you designate with the /I switch.

The Operating System and Memory

Your computer system must run under MS-DOS or PC DOS Version 2.10 (or higher) and must have available at least 640K of random-access memory (RAM). If you plan to run Ventura from a 640K system that loads programs into the conventional memory (memory-resident programs) at start-up, you should restart the computer without loading the RAM programs to optimize the speed of processing with your configuration. After you start Ventura without loading the RAM programs, between 100K and 150K of conventional memory is left available to handle the documents and graphics included in a publication. Operations like turning from page to page will be noticeably slower once the size of these source files exceeds the amount of conventional memory available, because Ventura must read and write the files to and from the hard disk rather than from RAM.

Ventura uses your computer's memory beyond 512K in designated sections called buffers. You can reallocate memory from the graphics and screen font buffers to the text buffer by editing the batch file, and you can remove memory from the screen font buffer to increase performance without altering the graphics buffer. The Ventura Publisher reference manual includes an installation supplement to Appendix A, which describes how to modify all the switches in the batch file and makes recommendations about settings.

You can configure 80286 and 80386 and compatible computers with more than 640K of random-access memory by adding extended memory or expanded memory specification (EMS) boards or chips. If at least 128K of EMS memory is available, Ventura 2.0 uses 108K of the additional memory for storing system software and screen buffers, thereby freeing more of the conventional memory for storing source files.

A smaller quantity of EMS memory (64K) can be configured to hold about 58K of Ventura 2.0 program code if you are using Microsoft® Windows on a 286 or 386 computer. You cause the computer to recognize the additional memory by adding a line about the device to your CONFIG.SYS file, which is stored in the root directory of your hard disk. Changes to the CONFIG.SYS file are not enabled until you edit and save the file (as an unformatted ASCII file) and then restart the computer.

Xerox advises that if you install a disk cache program to segment part of the additional memory for use with Ventura, you can often eliminate the BUFFERS statement in the CONFIG.SYS file created during program installation. Removing the BUFFERS statement makes more conventional memory available for handling multiple fonts and long documents. You also can use a disk cache when a system on a network has less than 640K available. Because some of the program files reside in the cache, more conventional memory space is left open for documents.

Although disk caching is the recommended technique for maximizing the use of extended or EMS memory with Ventura 2.0, you can use a RAM disk when you cannot use a disk cache. Ventura will write all overflow files to the RAM disk, which yields faster access to information than the hard disk does. You create a RAM disk in the additional memory with the DOS VDISK command or with a separate utility. You add an /O switch to the batch file Ventura creates in order to designate the overflow drive.

The Professional Extension Memory Requirements

The Ventura Professional Extension operates on systems equipped with 640K but requires that you add EMS memory to support the hyphenation dictionary and to take advantage of the product's capability to use EMS memory when publishing long documents or complex tables. If you intend to use the EMS memory only for screen fonts and program code, you need at least 144K of EMS memory available when you start the Professional Extension. Ventura will use more memory if it is available. You need at least 256K available at start-up if you want to process documents larger than 500K. If you intend to use the EDCO hyphenation dictionary and to publish long documents, you need at least 1.5M of EMS memory available at start-up.

The Professional Extension uses EMS memory for storing documents rather than system files. Thus, you can handle long documents faster and do not have to split long tables, lists, and documents into segments, as Ventura Publisher requires. As a general guide, Ventura Publisher can readily handle documents from 1 to 50 pages in length. (The faster and more capable computer components yield satisfactory performance with more pages.) If the document is tabular or heavily formatted, however, you may need to split a page into framed areas into which you pour segments of the text file. Chapter 3 shows how to access Ventura's DIAGNOSTICS dialog box, where a running count of elements per frame is displayed.

Xerox reports that the Professional Extension eliminates the all too familiar message `Frame Too Complex`. Those of you who use Ventura Publisher to publish directories and catalogs without the benefit of the additional room now offered by EMS memory will no longer need to add frames to pages for the continuation of long documents that contain tabs and other types of formatting instructions. But you will need to add EMS memory to realize the full benefits. The LIM 3.2 EMS standard supports up to 8M of

◆ **2.0**

additional memory, enabling you to load both the EDCO hyphenation dictionary and a chapter file of 6.5M. The LIM 4.0 EMS standard supports up to 32M of EMS memory. Check the documentation you receive with the EMS product to determine whether you need to add a device driver instruction to the CONFIG.SYS file used to configure your system for operation with the Professional Extension.

The Monitor

Your computer system requires a graphics card and monitor, which let you see your work on a screen. The higher your monitor's screen resolution, the more accurately your monitor displays text and graphics. As you will see when you use Ventura, the results on any monitor only *closely approximate* how a page will look when you print it. You should choose your display configuration according to your need. The results produced by your current CGA (Color Graphics Adapter) card and monitor may be adequate.

The more you work with Ventura, the more demanding you will become of the quality of the image shown in Ventura's work area. If you intend to use Ventura often, you deserve better resolution than is possible with a CGA board. The Enhanced Graphics Adapter (EGA), the Hercules Graphics Card, and the Video Graphics Array (VGA) configurations offer better resolution on partial page displays.

All monitors can show the full page when you use the Reduced View command in Ventura. When you work in Reduced view on an ordinary 13-inch monitor, however, seeing the text and graphics clearly enough to edit may be difficult or impossible. With standard monitors you would therefore use Normal view or Enlarged view for most editing and fine positioning of frames and graphics. These views allow you to see only part of the page at once. You need to change frequently to Reduced view to see the full page and make adjustments to frames and margins, and then return to a closer view for finer edits. You can eliminate the time lost for screen refreshes between view changes if you upgrade to a full-page display system, using a monitor that displays the full page on a larger screen. This type of monitor makes all edits easy in one view.

With higher-resolution full-page displays, however, you may lose monitor compatibility with other programs you use. Full-page monitors that are compatible with popular business and graphics programs may use only part of the display with another program, such as your word processor. Generally, the higher the resolution and the bigger the page, the more memory your computer needs.

To display color, you must use a VGA, an EGA, a Display Enhancement Board (DEB), or a multifunction card. Ventura enables you to mix and name up to six unique colors by combining percentages (from 1 to 100 percent in increments of .2 percent) from the basic palette, which is composed of cyan, magenta, yellow, and black. You also can define and name any of 500 shades of gray as custom colors. The colors and shades of gray used in a layout will display on a VGA or a multisync monitor.

On your monitor, you can color text, areas, or graphic shapes you place in the publisher's window, but Ventura does not use color in the menus, sidebars, dialog boxes, or icons. With a noncolor printer, you have the options of printing projects designed for color printing in shades of gray or as color separations that can be combined during the offset printing process. Compatible color printers, on the other hand, print color originals. Using color during the Ventura design process can help you visualize how a final product will look. You should not expect the colors you see on the screen, however, to match the color in the printed product. The color of the paper as well as the toner in your printer create the hues on the printout.

Although color displays help you determine how to use color in layouts, especially when you use your laser printer to prepare the camera-ready pages for offset printing, bear in mind that using color also slows processing. To overcome this problem, you may need to add EMS memory to your system. You need the additional memory to accommodate instructions for color and to allow space for the publications you create.

Clearly, choosing the most suitable monitor has a significant impact on your productivity. The many available display systems are different in shape and resolution, in compatibility with programs and screen fonts, and in choices of color or monochrome (amber, white, black, gray, and green). And monitors vary considerably in price. You should research carefully before you buy.

Table 2.2 shows product names and display resolutions for monochrome and two-color monitors that Ventura lists as available for selection during program installation.

The sixteen-color or gray-level EGA and VGA monitors included in table 2.3 are also available for selection during program installation. Gray-level VGA monitors display shades of gray in TIFF images and improve screen redrawing performance. You may need to add extra memory to support these displays, however. If you use one of the 800×600 resolution monitors listed in table 2.3, make sure that you select an analog monitor, which you connect to the card and monitor with a 15-pin-to-9-pin cable.

After you choose a monitor, the installation program copies the appropriate drivers and expands the screen font files on your hard disk. (Screen fonts shape the letters you see on-screen.) The higher the resolution of the monitor you select, the greater the number of screen fonts Ventura copies to your hard disk. As you learn in Chapter 9, you can add, remove, and rename screen font files after installation. Adding EGA screen fonts (by rerunning part of the installation program) to systems originally installed with VGA monitors can shorten the time needed to display a screen by as much as 40 percent to 60 percent, but you sacrifice clarity in the definition of fonts on-screen.

The Mouse

To access Ventura, you can use a mouse, the keyboard, or one of SummaSketch's cursor or stylus models #1812, 1201, or 961. If you choose a Summagraphic tablet, normal operations may not permit the active tablet area to extend to all four corners of the tablet.

Table 2.2
Two-Color and Monochrome Monitors

Name	Type	Resolution
AT&T® 6300	Monochrome	640×400
Hercules card/compatible	Monochrome	720×348
IBM CGA or compatible	Color	640×200
IBM EGA or compatible	2-color	640×200
IBM EGA or compatible	Enhanced 2-color	640×350
IBM EGA or compatible	Monochrome	640×350
IBM VGA or compatible	2-color	640×480
IBM PS/2 Model 30	MCGA or compatible	640×480
MDS Genius™ Full Page	Monochrome	720×1000
Wyse WY-700 Display	Monochrome	1280×800
Xerox 6065	Monochrome	640×400
Xerox Full Page Display	Monochrome	720×992

Table 2.3
16-Color and Gray-Level Monitors

Name	Type	Resolution
Amdek AM132 VGA	16 colors or grays	800×600
AST-VGA, AST-VGA PLUS	16 colors or grays	800×600
ATI VGA WONDER, WONDER-16	16 colors or grays	800×600
AT&T DEB Board	16 colors	640×400
Genoa SuperVGA/HiRes	16 colors or grays	800×600
IBM EGA or compatible	16 colors	640×200
IBM EGA or compatible	Enhanced 16-color	640×350
IBM VGA or compatible	16 of 256K colors/grays	640×480
Paradise VGA PLUS, PLUS 16, PROFESSIONAL	16 colors or grays	800×600
Sigma VGA H	16 colors or grays	800×600
STB VGA Extra/EM	16 colors or grays	800×600
Tecmar VGA, VGA/AD	16 colors or grays	800×600
Tseng Labs VGA	16 colors or grays	800×600
Video 7 VEGA VGA, VRAM VGA, FASTWRITE VGA	16 colors or grays	800×600
Wyse WY450 VGA	16 colors or grays	800×600

A mouse is not required to operate Ventura, but one is essential if you want to be efficient and productive. Without the mouse, you must use the arrow keys to move the pointing cursor to open menus. With the mouse, you can open menus and access tools much more quickly by sliding the mouse across the screen and either clicking or releasing the mouse button to select options. Ventura uses only the left button on a two- or three-button mouse.

Two basic types of mouse are available: optical and mechanical. The *optical mouse* requires a special pad. Although you can use the *mechanical mouse* with an optional rubber pad for better control, a special pad isn't necessary. Most users like the mouse they use most often. In other words, once you become accustomed to using a certain type of mouse, becoming familiar with the shape of another takes a while.

The following are acceptable:

- Microsoft serial or bus mouse

- IBM serial or bus mouse

- Xerox 6065 mouse

- PC Mouse™ or one of the following equivalents:
  - Summa™ Mouse
  - Logitech Mouse
  - Manager Mouse®
  - Microage Mouse

Although many brands and varieties of mice are available, they all fall into two categories: those that need a port to attach to the computer and those that bring their own port (called a *bus mouse*). A *port* is a cable outlet in the back or side of the computer through which you can connect the computer with peripherals, such as a printer, a modem, or a mouse. If your ports are filled, you can add more ports by adding a serial or parallel card to your computer. To use a bus mouse, you *must* add a card. (The mouse cord plugs into the card.) If you plan to use Ventura with Microsoft Windows, you should use a bus mouse to avoid potentially erratic effects.

Printers and Printer Connections

You can print draft-quality Ventura documents on some dot-matrix printers, but for best quality, you should produce final copy on a laser printer or typesetter. The printers that Ventura currently supports include

- Any PostScript®-compatible printer or typesetter (Apple, NEC, TI, IBM, and others market PostScript-compatible products.)

- LaserJet Plus, LaserJet Series II or 2000

- LaserJet with 92286F font cartridge

- JLaser™ printer card and compatible printer

- Tall Tree Systems, JLaser printer card and compatible printer

- LaserMaster controller card

- Xerox 4045 Laser Printer

- Xerox 4020 Color Ink Jet Printer

- IBM ProPrinter™

- Epson, NEC, and Toshiba dot-matrix printers

The most current list of supported printers appears on your monitor when you install the program.

You can install up to six printers for use with Ventura, and you can install the program on workstations that are not directly connected to a printer. In both cases, you should select the printer type you intend to use for final printing before you install other types of printers you may use for drafts. (As further described in Chapter 3, Ventura establishes a default printer width table based on the first printer you install.)

If you are configuring a workstation to access more than one printer of the same type, you install the printer only once. Ventura lets you choose alternative printer ports during publishing operations. If you are installing an HP LaserJet Plus, install both the 150-dpi and the 300-dpi drivers as separate printers. Then you can switch to the 150-dpi driver to overcome printer memory errors.

Your choice of printer(s) affects your choice of fonts when you use Ventura. Because each printer's files take up disk space, install only the printers you plan to use. If you use a PostScript printer, some fonts that you can see on-screen will not print unless you buy additional fonts from a font vendor. If you are using a non-PostScript printer, you cannot print illustrations made from scanned artwork that contain shades of gray or print outlined rather than solid fonts by using the font library delivered with Ventura.

Some printers may require special start-up commands or even special cables in order to work with your computer. Currently, two printers (the AST TurboLaser® and the Cordata printers) require that you place special instructions in the files Ventura uses. When you install a new printer, you should follow the instructions in the printer's manual to test the printer in a self-test mode and then test the printer with your computer. The Ventura Publisher reference guide includes batch-file commands, switch-setting diagrams, and pin assignments in the printer information appendix.

Speeding Your Printing

If your printer's built-in fonts don't meet your needs, you can add fonts by storing them in the printer's memory—a process called *downloading*. You can shorten printing time by downloading fonts and page-description commands to your printer at the start of each Ventura session rather than at the start of each print request (see Chapter 8). You can initiate these techniques any time after you install Ventura. For example, if you routinely use a logo or other graphic characters, you can program these custom characters as downloadable characters. The appendix includes vendors of font generators as well as custom programming services.

Another way to reduce print processing time is by adding a different kind of printer port and processor to your computer. Several printers and printer add-on products use a card and processor installed in the computer (rather than the printer's built-in processor) to translate the page layout from the page description language into instructions similar to a map, where each point in the map is described by its coordinates.

The printer then compiles the individual bit-mapped instructions into a page. These add-on processors communicate to the printer's engine directly through a high-speed port, bypassing the printer's slower processor. Many of these products add PostScript capabilities to non-PostScript printers.

The type of printer port, serial or parallel, also affects printing speed, as described in the next section.

Assigning Printer Ports

The computer communicates to each printer through a cable, which is connected to a port that is usually located on the back panel of your computer. Serial and parallel communication ports send a set of instructions for each page. Parallel ports send and receive information simultaneously; they can get messages *from* the printer while they send page information *to* the printer. Thus parallel ports are usually faster than serial ports, which cannot send and receive simultaneously.

During Ventura's installation, you can guess at the number (usually 1 or 2) and type of port. If you enter the wrong port number or port type, you can select an alternative port in the SET PRINTER INFO dialog box, opened from the Options menu, after you start Ventura.

The Scanner

Existing pieces of artwork can be digitized so that they appear as illustrations in your Ventura publications. A *scanner* creates a *digitized image* by converting a paper copy into a file in one of the Ventura-supported paint-type formats: GEM Paint™ (IMG), PC Paintbrush® (PCX), Macintosh Paint® (PNT), or TIFF (TIF, which is short for Tagged Image File Format). Each change between black and white on the original artwork is mapped out in the scan file. In the case of TIF images, however, changes from white to black are recorded as levels of gray, which can be printed when you use a printer that simulates printing levels of gray. PostScript printers print TIF images, as do HP printers that have been equipped with gray-scale printer controllers.

Gray-scale images are made up of gray dots, rather than just black dots. *Halftoning*, or *dithering*, is the process of modifying a gray-scale image to print from a device that prints just black dots. All laser printers dither, or halftone, scanned images instead of printing dots of gray. But many new high-resolution typesetters and new laser printers print a halftone image that may be suitable for a high-quality publication. The results are at least as good as you have come to expect from newsprint.

You can reproduce photographs in 64 levels of gray, with accuracy of 1/300 inch. If you start with a high-contrast photograph, you can get an extremely accurate laser-printed reproduction, as the image in figure 2.2 shows. If you use a scanner to create an image, you can vary the number of gray levels and the resolution to create the optimum file for manipulation with Ventura.

You can enlarge, reduce, or crop digitized images by using Ventura's frame function. You can obscure part of the image by laying shapes over the frame, and you can add text or arrows to emphasize a section of an illustration in a frame. You can edit the image, however, only by using a painting program like Dr. HALO or Publisher's Paintbrush to add to or subtract from the scanned artwork. Many times, lines and shapes in scanned images need cleaning up to render the effect you intend. You must use a painting program compatible with the scanned file format to correct imperfections or alter the scanned file. You cannot use Ventura's graphics tools to edit the illustration that was scanned.

Fig. 2.2.

Scanned images can look like halftones.

Before you count on the results from scanned illustrations, be sure to test your scanner's optional settings for resolution, brightness, and contrast. Print the test results on the printers you have available. Different printers present dramatically different results from the same files. Both flatbed and sheet-feed scanners can be used successfully to create image files for use with Ventura. When you use a sheet-feed scanner, you may need to fasten small pieces of artwork to larger pages so that the paper moves through the feeder smoothly. You learn more about scanning, loading, and printing images in Chapter 6.

Scanning documents with an optical character reader offers you an alternative way to capture text in ASCII format. Some scanners can be programmed to capture ASCII formats (OCR) and image formats. Although desktop scanners have been used for several years to convert text to digital storage, only recently have scanners handled the problems associated with scanning typeset fonts and multiple column formats and with segregating text and image areas into separate files to permit later editing.

Including a scanner and a scanning program as components of your desktop publishing system increases your opportunity to include *any* text, photograph, or illustration as a source file for your publications. You also can use a video input device (camera or monitor) to digitize images, but these systems work best with three-dimensional scenes rather than flat art. If you do not have scanning equipment connected to your system, you can have outside service bureaus digitize files in Ventura-compatible formats.

Graphics Software

You can build a library of images from digitized clip-art vendors. Alternatively, you can create illustrations in drafting and drawing programs and import the illustrations into Ventura to be used as graphics source files. Ventura supports the following image file formats:

- GEM™
- CGM
- DXF™
- EPS (Encapsulated PostScript)
- HP 7470 and HP 7475 HPGL
- Macintosh® PICT
- Macintosh Paint
- TIFF (Tagged Image File Format)
- Video Show™
- AutoCAD® (.SLD)
- Lotus® (.PIC)
- PC Paintbrush (.PCX)
- Microsoft Windows Metafile

The Ventura utility disk contains a conversion program that enables you to convert files captured with a background utility like SideKick® into a PCX file compatible with Ventura. In many cases you can load shots of screens captured with other programs directly into Ventura without first executing a utility conversion. The appendix includes information about sources of compatible scanners and software programs that enable you to modify scanned images, create new images, and access libraries of digitized clip art.

GEM (from Digital Research Inc.), a graphics front-end interface program for MS-DOS, supports Ventura. Once you start Ventura, a run-time version of GEM acts as the graphics environment manager and sets the way you send instructions and commands to Ventura. You cannot access other GEM applications or commands through Ventura under the run-time version; but if you install the full GEM system, you can run other applications that are compatible with Ventura, such as GEM Paint and GEM Draw™. Graphics file formats are further discussed in Chapter 6.

Chapter Summary

Setting up your desktop publishing system can be as simple as adding Ventura to an existing configuration or as involved as selecting each component to complement and enhance the other components in ways that tailor the system's capabilities to your publishing needs. After you have selected your hardware configuration, you must install Ventura on your hard disk, using the program named VPPREP on Disk 1 to start the process. Whenever you add components, you need to reinstall Ventura only if you add to or change the components that make up your system. You do not need to reinstall Ventura if you add only software or scanners.

This chapter introduces the alternatives in system components. In Chapter 3, you will begin using Ventura and learn how to manage the files that Ventura needs to produce publications. In Chapters 4, 5, and 6, you will discover how much you can accomplish with Ventura's text, graphic, and formatting capabilities. And Chapter 7 illustrates how the individual capabilities come together during the layout and production processes.

Using Ventura

This chapter provides an overview of Ventura and attempts to give you an idea of the myriad tasks you can accomplish with this powerful program. Many of the topics in this chapter are covered in more detail elsewhere in the book. But after reading this chapter, you will be able to use Ventura to start, save, and back up a publication.

Starting Ventura

Once you have installed Ventura, you can start the program directly from DOS and run Ventura independently, or you can start through Microsoft® Windows Executive and run Ventura as an application. If you experience problems starting Ventura with either of the two methods described in this chapter, review your installation procedure as described in the Ventura documentation.

Starting Ventura from DOS

If you set up your version of Ventura with all the same directory names and file organization assumed by the Ventura installation program, start Ventura by typing *vp* at the C› prompt and pressing Enter. If you have the Professional Extension, type *vpprof* at the C› prompt and press Enter. (The capabilities of the Professional Extension are summarized in Chapter 10.)

Troubleshooting Tip

If the Publisher's Window Doesn't Open

If Ventura does not open into the publisher's window when you start the program from DOS, erase the INF files in the VENTURA directory and then restart Ventura. If the window still doesn't open, you may need to reinstall the program.

Starting Ventura from Windows

Beginning with Patch 2 to Ventura's Version 1.1, you can run Ventura under Microsoft Windows Executive. This feature enables you to access Metafiles cut to the Clipboard with other Windows programs. (In general, clipboards keep sections of text or

39

images in memory and transfer them from one file or page to another. You will learn more about clipboards as you proceed through this chapter. For more information, refer to Chapters 4 and 6.)

Starting Ventura from Windows Executive is possible only after you have completed the installation procedures. You then can double-click the VP.PIF file name in the WINDOWS\PIF directory to start Ventura. (See your Windows documentation for more information.)

Examining the Publisher's Window

When Ventura loads successfully, a graphics screen containing many elements appears. These elements represent tools that you can use to complete many publishing tasks. Figure 3.1 shows the publisher's window as it displays the first time you load the program. Each time you start Ventura, the window reflects how the last session of Ventura ended.

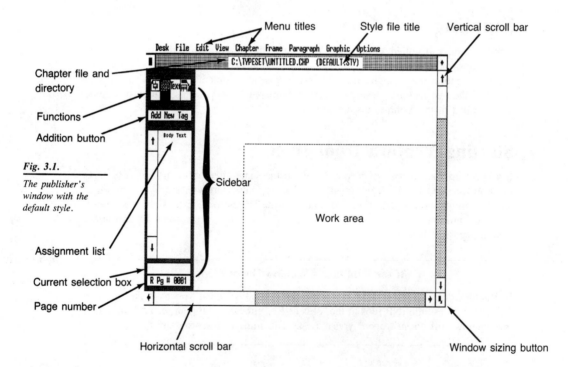

Fig. 3.1.

The publisher's window with the default style.

Menu titles · Style file title · Vertical scroll bar

Chapter file and directory

Functions

Addition button

Sidebar

Work area

Assignment list

Current selection box

Page number

Horizontal scroll bar

Window sizing button

Along the top of the publisher's window, you see the names of Ventura's nine menus. The second line of the window shows the titles and locations of the chapter and style files. The largest section of the publisher's window is the work area, where the pages carrying text and illustrations display. To the left of the work area is an area called the sidebar that contains four publishing function icons, an addition button, an assignment list, and two rectangular boxes providing information about where you are in the publication. These two boxes are called the current selection box and the page indicator. (In the Professional Extension, an addition button labeled Table Edit displays beneath the publishing function icons. Table Edit allows you to edit tables, import text to long tables, and repeat column headings from page to page. This feature is detailed in Chapter 10.) The scroll bars, located at the bottom and right borders of the work area, let you move different portions of the page into view.

In figure 3.1, the size and location of the opaque portion of the scroll bars indicates that only the top left portion of the page is in view. The sidebar covers a portion of the available work area and shows that the second function, the Paragraph function, is active. The tag name Body Text appears in the assignment list, and the title bar indicates that the currently untitled chapter will store in the TYPESET directory, using Ventura's default style file. (Style names are shown in parentheses in the title line. The name of the directory in which the style file resides, however, does not display in the title line.) Later in this chapter, you learn how to find the location of the style file named at the top of the work area.

Figure 3.2 shows how Ventura's opening screen appears when the last session ended with a view one page chosen for a chapter styled by the file &BOOK-P1. Because the sidebar is suppressed from view, the work area is wider than in figure 3.1, and the rulers are set to display in inches. In figure 3.3, graphic tools display in the sidebar. You can also see two vertical rules in the work area, indicating that &NEWS-P3 styles the page with lines drawn between columns. Note that the rulers in this window are set in picas and points.

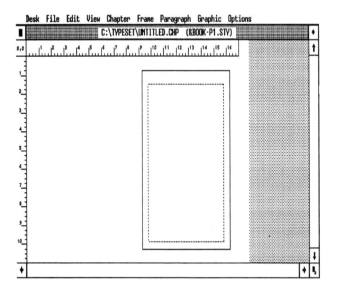

Fig. 3.2.

The publisher's window with book style.

You can use either the mouse or the keyboard to select menus, commands, features, and elements on the page or in the work area. Although Ventura does not require a mouse, operating without one is difficult. If you plan to use Ventura, you should

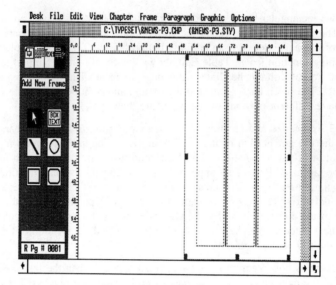

Fig. 3.3.

The publisher's window with newsletter style.

equip your system with a mouse. The speed gained in publication preparation will return your investment quickly. This book was written with the assumption that most readers would use a mouse, but keyboard input alternatives are also explained in tables 3.2 and 3.3.

Using the Mouse

If you are a touch typist, you may initially find using a mouse awkward. But after a little practice, you will find that the mouse provides the quickest access to many of Ventura's features.

First-time mouse users should take a moment to move the mouse on the desk surface. Make a small circular movement and observe the corresponding action of the mouse cursor on the monitor. Then pick up the mouse and place it at a different spot on your desk. Notice how the mouse cursor's movement originated in the same point both times. The mouse can be positioned on either the left or right of your keyboard and does not require a large area. (If you accidentally opened a menu as you practiced moving the mouse, move the pointer outside the menu and click the left button to close the menu.)

Efficiency Tip

Repositioning the Mouse

First-time mouse users tend to run the mouse off the edge of the work surface. By lifting the mouse, you can reposition it on the table or pad without repositioning the cursor on-screen.

To use a mouse as an input device, you need to become familiar with several terms that describe mouse operations:

Point	Position mouse pointer over object
Click	Point at object; click left button
Double-click	Click left button twice in quick succession
Slide	Move the mouse cursor across the desk
Drag	Point at object and hold down left button as you move mouse; release mouse button when object or pointer is in appropriate location (used to move and resize elements on the page)

Ventura uses only the left button on any mouse. Table 3.1 summarizes basic mouse operations.

Table 3.1
Basic Mouse Operations

Action (any cursor shape)	Result
With drop-down menus	
Point to menu	Opens menu
Slide	Highlights commands
Click	Selects a command on an open menu
With pull-down menus	
Point to menu and press and hold the left mouse button	Opens menu
Release the mouse button	Selects a command on an open menu
Click outside menu or on gray commands	Closes menu
Click ellipsed commands shown in black	Opens dialog box
Click nonellipsed commands shown in black	Words or check marks indicate change in status of selected command, command is executed, and dialog box closes
In the sidebar	
Click publishing icons	Changes publishing task and sidebar items

Table 3.1—*Continued*

Action (any cursor shape)	Result
Click addition button	Enables activity
In the scroll bars	
Click any arrow	Moves list or page in work area in small fixed increments
Click patterned areas between arrows	Moves list or page in larger fixed increments
Drag white bar between arrows	Moves list or page in requested increments
In the work area	
Position any mouse cursor in Reduced or Facing Pages View and press Ctrl-E or Ctrl-N	Zooms that position of the page into the work area, in the chosen size view

Figure 3.4 illustrates the publisher's window after being shrunk into a different area on the monitor. Practice the movements so that you can observe how the mouse performs when you click rather than drag the diagonal arrow at the lower right corner of the publisher's window.

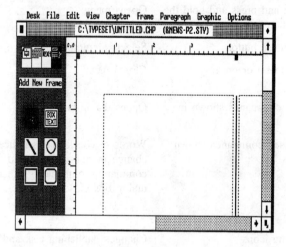

Fig. 3.4.

Moving the publisher's window with the mouse.

After positioning the mouse pointer on the screen, you slide the mouse to drop down the menus, and point and click to select commands or change publishing functions.

Working without a Mouse

Even if your computer is not equipped with a mouse, you can still access all Ventura's features. You can use the keys from the numeric keypad and certain Ctrl-key sequences. Once you install the program without a mouse, the arrow keys on the numeric keypad become active. If you installed Ventura with a mouse, you can switch out of mouse mode if you have problems with your mouse. Here are the keyboard equivalents to Ventura's mouse operations:

Mouse Operation	Keyboard Equivalent
Point or slide	Up, down, left, and right arrows
Click	Home and End
Drag	End, arrows, and Home

Table 3.2 lists keys you can use to perform a variety of tasks.

Table 3.2
Working without a Mouse
(^ represents the Ctrl key)

Task	Keys	Description of Activity
Add frame (or add graphic control frame by starting with ^P)	^U	Select Frame function
	^2	Select Add Frame
	Arrows	Position tool in work area at upper left corner of frame to draw
	End, right and down arrows, Home	Start, define, and complete a frame
Resize a frame	^U, arrows, Home	Select frame to resize (frame handles display)
	Shift and arrows	Position cursor on a handle
	End, arrows, Home	Start, define, and complete resizing
Move a frame	^U, arrows, Home	Select frame to move (frame handles display)
	End, arrows, Home	Start, define, and complete move

Table 3.2—*Continued*

Task	Keys	Description of Activity
Draw a graphic	^P	Select Graphic function
	Arrows	Position cursor over the graphic tool to use
	Home	Select graphic tool
	Arrows	Position tool in work area at upper left edge of graphic to draw
	End, right and down arrows, Home	Start, define, and complete graphic
Resize a graphic	^P	Select Graphic function
	Arrows, Home	Select graphic
	Shift and arrows	Position cursor on a handle
	End, arrows, Home	Start, define, and complete resizing
Move a graphic	^U, arrows, Home	Select frame that controls graphic
	^P	Select Graphic function
	Arrows	Position cursor within graphic shape
	Home	Select shape to display graphic handles
	End, arrows, Home	Start, define, and complete move
Add new tag	^I	Select Paragraph function
	^2	Select Add New Tag
Select Text	^O, arrows	Select Text function; move cursor to beginning of selection

Table 3.2—*Continued*

Task	Keys	Description of Activity
	End, arrows	Start and define selection
Set font for selected text	^2	Enable Set Font activity
Reposition text edit cursor	Right Shift-Ctrl, then arrows	

Each successive tap on one of the arrow keys moves the work-area cursor one line up or down, or one character to the left or right, depending on which arrow key you use. To move in finer increments, press Shift and an arrow key simultaneously. You can open a menu by pointing to the name with the up-, left-, or right-arrow key if you are using drop-down menus. If a menu does not open when you point to it, press the End key to ''pull down'' the menu into view. Then use the down-arrow key to highlight the appropriate command, and press Home to activate that command. To cancel a menu without choosing a command, move the cursor outside the menu and press Home. To cancel a dialog box without changing the settings, press Ctrl-X.

When you work without a mouse, you will find that the most time-consuming task is scrolling the view in the work area. To scroll through a page, you must first move the cursor to the arrows in the scroll bars on the right side of the work area and then repeatedly press the Home key. As an alternative, you can position the cursor on an arrow and then press the End key to start a scroll and the Home key to stop the scroll.

To turn pages, use the PgDn and PgUp keys. You also can use the GO TO PAGE dialog box, which you open by pressing Ctrl-G.

This book is sprinkled with Efficiency Tips, many of which provide shortcuts to help you overcome the difficulties of working without a mouse. If you're a touch typist or word processing operator who is already skilled at using keys in coded combinations, you may find these shortcuts to functions and menus as convenient to use as the mouse. (Most of the shortcut keys are also listed next to their corresponding commands in the menus.)

If you install Ventura without a mouse and then decide you want to add one, you must reinstall Ventura. And if your system is configured with a mouse, you can always switch to keyboard mode by pressing the right Shift key and the Ctrl key simultaneously. (Note: You may have to press right Shift-Ctrl twice to switch from mouse mode.) As you change modes, Ventura beeps to alert you of the new input mode. To exit keyboard mode, press Shift-Ctrl again.

Using the Menus and Commands

The nine menus, which display along the top of the window, provide copyright and diagnostic information and allow you to import and edit files, design layouts, and attach typographic and graphic characteristics. You set the method for accessing menus and commands with Set Preferences command. The default setting is for drop-down menus. With this option set, you point to the menu, and the menu opens or "drop down" on the screen. You then move the pointer and click to choose from the list of items. As you move the cursor through the menu items, the active commands (those shown in black) display highlighted in reverse video. To close a drop-down menu, move the icon outside the menu and click the mouse button.

Alternatively, you can elect to set the menus as pull-down menus. With this option set, you point to the menu title and then hold down the left mouse button to open the menu. To select a command, you drag the cursor through the menu items and release the mouse button when the command is highlighted. When you release the button, the choice is made. Depending on the command you've selected, either the menu closes or a dialog box opens.

To change the method for selecting menus and commands, open the Options menu and select the Set Preferences command, opening a dialog box. In the SET PREFER-ENCES dialog box, position the mouse cursor on the Menu Type option and click. A pop-up menu displays, as shown in figure 3.5. Drag the cursor in the pop-up menu to the alternative option. When you release the mouse button, the Menu Type option displays the new method in use.

Fig. 3.5.

Changing the method for choosing menus and commands.

To find Ventura's description of the menu types, click the question mark near the top right corner of the SET PREFERENCES dialog box, drag the cursor to the Menu Type option, and release the mouse button to read the note that displays (see fig. 3.6). The question marks in dialog boxes offer notes or help messages. Click OK to close the note box.

You can select one of two menu types. [OK]
Drop-down menus appear and remain on the
NOTE screen when the mouse touches the menu
selection. Pull-down menus appear only
as long as you hold the mouse button.

Fig. 3.6.

The help message for the Menu Type *option.*

As you view each menu, notice that some commands display in black, others in gray. Only the commands shown in black letters beneath each menu title are available for selection with the current function. (Don't worry about memorizing the commands on the menus. Finding the command you want is easy once you learn how Ventura organizes elements under each menu title.)

Choosing a command that is followed by ellipses (...) displays a dialog box, where you make additional selections or entries. If you open a dialog box while you're exploring the menus, click Cancel to close the dialog box without making any changes to the options. (For more on dialog boxes, see this chapter's section entitled ''Using Dialog Boxes.'') When you click a menu command that does not include ellipses, the command executes and the menu closes.

Some commands are ''toggles'' that simply turn on and off when you choose them. When a toggle command is active, a check mark displays in front of the command in the menu, or the wording in the command changes to show the current setting (see fig. 3.7).

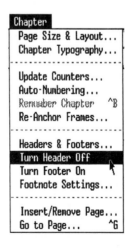

Fig. 3.7.

Toggle commands that change wording to display status.

You can execute many commands with keyboard shortcuts. In most cases, these shortcuts are shown on the menu with the respective commands. Figure 3.7 shows two shortcuts to Chapter menu commands (Ctrl-B and Ctrl-G). Many shortcuts involve holding down the Ctrl key while typing the letter displayed on the command line. (The caret [^] symbol on the menu represents the Ctrl key.) For your convenience, table 3.3 shows the Ctrl-key shortcuts to Ventura's features.

Table 3.3
Table of Keyboard Shortcuts
(^ represents the Ctrl key)

Action	Keyboard Shortcut
Changing the view in the work area	
Go to page	^G
Change to Enlarged View	^E
Change to Normal View	^N
Change to Reduced View	^R
Show/hide tabs, returns, and end-of-file symbols	^T
Widen the work area (show/hide sidebar)	^W
Changing functions and related operations	
Change to Frame function	^U
Change to Paragraph function	^I
Change to Text function	^O
Insert special item	^C
Edit special item	^D
Change to Graphic function	^P
Fill graphic shape	^F
Define line attributes	^L
Bring graphic to front	^A
Send graphic to back	^Z
Select all graphics	^Q
Selecting commands	
Assign function keys to tag paragraphs	^K
Enable addition button	^2
Recall last dialog box	^X
Renumber chapter	^B
Save	^S

The Edit menu shows a different type of shortcut to the cut, copy, and paste features. Once you have selected text, graphics, or frames, you can use the Del and Ins keys on the numeric keypad. Use Del to cut the selection and Ins to paste it into a new position, either in the same or in a different chapter. The keyboard shortcut to copy a selection is to press Del and one of the Shift keys simultaneously.

The contents of the Edit menu change as you choose three of the publishing functions. In figures 3.8 and 3.9, notice how the commands on the Edit menu reflect the items associated with the current publishing function. Figure 3.8 shows the Edit menu when the Text function is active, and figure 3.9 shows the Edit menu for the Frame and Graphic functions.

Although you can store only one set of items from the Frame, Text, and Graphic functions to the Clipboard at a time, you can have a selection for each function. For example, you can have in the Clipboard's memory both a selection of text and a

Fig. 3.8.

The Text Edit menu to copy and paste text.

Fig. 3.9.

The Frame Edit menu.

framed illustration that you're moving to new locations. As Chapters 4 and 6 reveal, you can also cut and copy frames that contain text and graphics.

Using Dialog Boxes

As mentioned in the preceding section, when you select from any menu a command that is followed by ellipses (. . .), a command dialog box opens. Dialog boxes display the names of the options that define the specific effects of each command. Dialog boxes can include lines for text entry, selection boxes that you click to activate, scrolling lists from which you choose alternate settings, buttons to click for an immediate effect, and prompts for the pop-up menus of responses and notes. Some dialog boxes offer just a couple of options, but others include many options, one of which may even open another related dialog box.

To experiment with the movements in a dialog box, select the Footnote Settings command in the Chapter menu. Once the FOOTNOTE SETTINGS dialog box is open, try some of the movements described in table 3.4. Figure 3.10 shows the FOOTNOTE SETTINGS dialog box as it appears when the Usage & Format option is turned off. Click the alternative answers to this option and notice how the related commands and values in the box display as active commands, ready for use. As you proceed through this book, the options in each dialog box are explained.

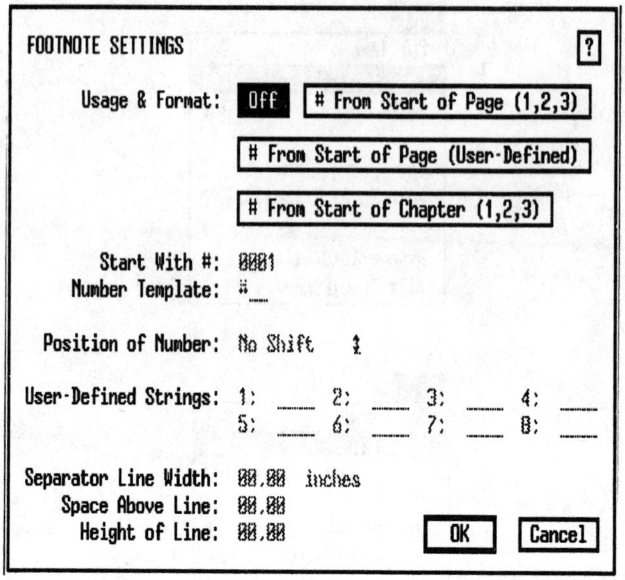

Fig. 3.10.

The FOOTNOTE SETTINGS dialog box.

Table 3.4
Dialog Box Operations

Task	Operation
To read the notes about the box and its options	Click the question mark and then drag and release to select the option from the pop-up menu
To choose alternative settings	Click within boxes outlined in black
	Click a setting for an option (or the symbol following it) to open the pop-up menu, drag the cursor to new setting, then release to choose the setting
To move text-entry cursor (when visible) forward one option	Press Tab
To move text-entry cursor (when visible) backward one option	Press Shift-Tab
To reposition text-entry cursor beside an option	Click to the right of the option's value

(Depending on your configuration, you also may be able to move the text-entry cursor in the dialog box by pressing the left-, right-, up-, and down-arrow keys.)

Table 3.4—*Continued*

Task	Operation
To erase a value	Backspace over the value
To erase the contents of a line in which the text-entry cursor displays	Press Esc
To see items in lists for selection	Drag the scroll bars
To select items from lists	Double-click name in list or click name and click OK
To choose an alternative type of measurement system	Click any measurement term
To close a dialog box and change the settings	Click OK or Done or press Enter
To close a dialog box and cancel the changes	Click Cancel or press Ctrl-X
To reopen last dialog box used	Press Ctrl-X

Whenever a measurement term appears in a dialog box, you can click the term to convert the units into another measurement system, including fractional points, inches, centimeters, or picas and points. Fractional points offer the most precise system of measurement but have a maximum value of 99.99. Here's how 99.99 fractional points translate (approximately) to the other measurement systems:

99.99 fractional points ≈ 1.39 inches

3.53 centimeters

8 picas and 4 points

The other measurements equal each other (roughly) in the following ways:

1 inch ≈ 2.54 centimeters, 6 picas and points, 72 fractional points

1 centimeter ≈ 2.04 picas and points, 28.32 fractional points, .39 inch

1 point ≈ 1.02 fractional point, .014 inch, .036 centimeter

1 pica ≈ 12.00 fractional points, .167 inch, .423 centimeters

Suppose that the current system measures in inches and you want to convert to the fractional point system. If the measurement value you select is greater than 1.39 inches, Ventura displays four tildes (˜˜˜˜) rather than a fractional point measurement.

Click OK, Cancel, or Done to close a dialog box. (Pressing the Enter key has the same effect as clicking OK or Done.) When you choose OK to close a dialog box, Ventura searches through the file to find other text affected by the change. While you learn to use Ventura's typographic, page design, and Graphic menus and commands, you will find yourself opening dialog boxes often to check command settings. If you don't want to keep any changes you've made, or if you've made no changes, click Cancel (or press Ctrl-X) to close the box and return to the work area quickly.

Efficiency Tip

Shortcuts to Dialog Boxes

Although Ventura offers many keyboard shortcuts to commands (see table 3.3), only a few shortcuts to dialog boxes are available:

Ctrl-C	Opens the pop-up menu of special items to insert boxed characters, footnotes, index entries, fractions, frame anchors, and chapter and page number references at the point where the text edit cursor is positioned
Ctrl-D	Opens the EDIT SPECIAL ITEM dialog box for the item in text at the cursor
Ctrl-G	Opens the GO TO PAGE dialog box
Ctrl-K	Opens the UPDATE TAG LIST box in Paragraph function and the ASSIGN FUNCTION KEY box in the other functions
Ctrl-S	Opens the ITEM SELECTOR box the first time you save the chapter or updates the disk files once you name a chapter
Ctrl-X	Reopens the last dialog box opened from a menu (when similar functions and selections are active) or cancels current dialog box
Esc	Erases the contents of a text-entry line

Controlling the Display

Ventura offers you several options for changing the work-area display:

- You can use the View menu commands to enlarge and reduce the size of the image in view.

- You can use the scroll bars to move different portions of the page onto the screen.

- You can set default preferences by changing the settings in the Options menu.

Enlarging and Reducing the View

The first four commands in the View menu—Facing Pages View, Reduced View, Normal View, and Enlarged View—affect the size of the pages shown in the work area. Figure 3.11 compares the different views on a system configured with a full-page monitor. If you work on a system with a partial-page monitor, your views will

Normal view

Enlarged view

Reduced view

Facing Pages view

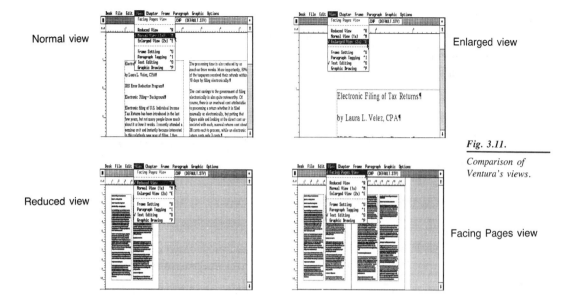

Fig. 3.11.

Comparison of Ventura's views.

look similar to those illustrated in the figure. Chapter 2 includes a discussion of the alternatives available when choosing monitors.

Changing the scale of a view enables you to work more comfortably during different phases of the publishing process. As you place files, the Reduced view allows you to see how text and images fill the page. Working in the Normal and Enlarged views allows you to edit and format text and images more accurately.

The Facing Pages View command is available only when you use the Page Size & Layout command of the Chapter menu to open the PAGE LAYOUT dialog box and select Double as the Sides option. Facing pages always display in Reduced view and offer a quick way to turn through the pages in a chapter. You can use the Facing Pages view to check the layout of design elements on pages that will face each other in final form. Later in this chapter, you see how to widen the work area, allowing Ventura to enlarge slightly the text and graphics seen in the Normal and Enlarged views.

With Ventura, what you see in the work area is representative of what appears on the printed page. In many cases, the printed results look better than the window's representation because laser printers have better resolution than screens. Ventura's capability to display so that "what you see is what you get" depends on the capabilities of the monitor, graphics card, screen fonts, and printer used in your system.

Using the Scroll Bars

Ventura's scroll bars let you scroll pages and lists into view in the work area. To move a different section of the page into view, use the scroll bars and arrows positioned along the right and lower borders of the publisher's window. You will also find

Efficiency Tip

Shortcuts to Views

The shortcuts to the View commands are easy to remember. You simply use the Ctrl key with the first letter of the view name:

View	*Shortcut*	*Task*
Normal	Ctrl-N	Editing text
Reduced	Ctrl-R	Placing files and positioning frames
Enlarged	Ctrl-E	Editing small text, graphics, and frames

No shortcut is available for the Facing Pages View.

---

scroll bars in the sidebar when the Frame, Paragraph, or Text function is active. These scroll bars serve the purpose of moving a list rather than the page into view. The third place you find scroll bars is in some of Ventura's dialog boxes. Figure 3.12 includes examples of each type of scroll bar.

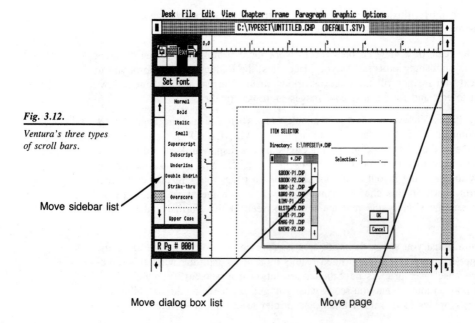

Fig. 3.12.

Ventura's three types of scroll bars.

Move sidebar list

Move dialog box list   Move page

For each type of scroll bar, the technique for using the bars is the same. The vertical scroll bar begins at the up arrow near the top right corner of the screen and ends at the down arrow near the base of the screen. When you position the mouse cursor on an arrow and click, you scroll the page up or down slightly. The horizontal scroll bar runs along the bottom of the screen. The arrows at the corners of the base of the screen let you move the page left and right in small increments. Each time you click an arrow on either scroll bar, a different portion of the page displays in the view.

The area between the end arrows of each scroll bar is divided into two parts. The opaque section represents the portion of the page you have in view; the textured section represents the portion of the page not in view. When you click within the textured area, Ventura moves the next screen of the page into view. When you drag the opaque section with the mouse, your movement determines the depth or width of the scroll. Because each scroll causes the screen to redraw, you will find that dragging the scroll bar moves the page into view faster than repeatedly clicking the end arrows. With practice you will learn how far to drag before releasing the mouse button to achieve the result you want.

You can avoid using the scroll bars by using the mouse to zoom an area into view. To zoom to a position with the mouse (rather than scroll to that position), follow these three basic steps:

1. Press Ctrl-R to change to Reduced view.

2. Place the icon at the position to which you want to scroll.

3. Press Ctrl-N for a zoom to Normal view, or press Ctrl-E for Enlarged view.

These basic steps work if you're using the Frame, Paragraph, or Graphic function when you position the mouse. If you have the Text function active when you position the icon, you must click the mouse to activate the text I-beam on the page, and then press Ctrl-N or Ctrl-E to zoom to the position in the text.

Notice that the scroll bars change to indicate the location of the segment of the page you are viewing. This technique is particularly helpful when you're working with facing pages, because you can zoom from one page to another without waiting for Ventura to draw the screen for the next page.

Choosing Display Defaults

The Options menu contains 13 commands, 8 of which influence the display in the publisher's window. What you see as you start Ventura depends in part on the Options menu settings that were in effect at the close of the last Ventura session. Ventura stores the active settings in an information file called VP.INF, which the program re-creates each time you choose Quit from the File menu. As you will see in the section on "Saving Custom Defaults," you can create and save alternative custom default files to match project requirements or accommodate different users' preferences.

Six of the display-type commands (the six in the second section of the menu) operate as toggles to either hide or show elements in the work area. The other two display-type commands, Set Preferences and Set Ruler, open dialog boxes in which you choose settings and options. See figure 3.13 to locate the commands that influence the work area's display.

```
┌─────── Options ───────┐
│ Set Preferences...     │
│ Set Ruler...           │
│ Set Printer Info...    │
│ Add/Remove Fonts...    │
│ ---------------------- │
│ Hide Side-Bar      ^W  │
│ Hide Rulers            │
│ Show Column Guides     │
│ Hide All Pictures      │
│ Hide Tabs & Returns ^T │
│ Show Loose Lines       │
│ ---------------------- │
│ Turn Column Snap Off   │
│ Turn Line Snap Off     │
│ ---------------------- │
│ Multi-Chapter...       │
└────────────────────────┘
```

Fig. 3.13.

The Options menu.

First study the largest group of commands, the show-and-hide commands, which are listed under the first dotted line in the Options menu. Each of these commands toggles between Show and Hide as you select the command. You can show or hide the sidebar, rulers, column guides, pictures, tabs and returns, and loose lines. The sidebar, ruler, and column-guide commands *always* affect the display; the other commands affect the display only when your view includes pictures or text. For example, you can hide the sidebar by clicking Hide Side-Bar, thus increasing the work area.

This chapter covers the commands that hide and show the sidebar, rulers, and column guides. In Chapters 4, 5, and 6, you learn when to use the Pictures, Tabs & Returns, and Loose Lines commands as you format and size text and illustrations.

Showing and Hiding the Sidebar

When you're working in Normal or Enlarged View, hiding the sidebar (clicking Hide Side-Bar in the Options menu) widens the work area and enlarges the image on the page by a small percentage. Projects in which the width of columns, images, or graphics exceeds 5 inches may require you to widen the work area often as you fine-tune copy and page composition.

When you suppress the sidebar from view, you cannot see the page number or the current selection box, or draw with the Graphic tools. You can move and resize graphics that are already drawn, however, because the Graphic selection tool is active when you choose the Graphic function. (To learn more about selecting graphics, see Chapter 6.)

Showing and Hiding the Rulers

Ventura has two rulers that you can use to help position and align elements on the page. The rulers display along the top and left borders of the work area (refer to fig. 3.12). When the rulers are in view, a third tool, called the ruler's crosshairs, is also

Shortcuts to the Sidebar Features

When working with a widened view, you can use several shortcuts to access most of the sidebar features you need during production.

Shortcut	*Task*
Ctrl-U	Change to the Frame function
Ctrl-I	Change to the Paragraph function
Ctrl-O	Change to the Text function
Ctrl-P	Change to the Graphic function
Ctrl-2 with Frame function	Add a new frame
with Paragraph function	Add a new tag
with Text function	Set font attribute for selected text
with Graphic function	Add a new graphic control frame
Ctrl-W	Return the sidebar to view
Ctrl-K	Update tag list

available to help check the alignment of elements, whether they are on one page or on facing pages. To display the rulers, select Show Rulers in the Options menu. For more information on rulers, see the section called "Setting Rulers."

Showing and Hiding Column Guides

Ventura's column guides display along the margins and columns of the page as defined in the Frame menu's MARGINS & COLUMNS dialog box. The guides display as dashed lines on the monitor and serve as a visual reference tool while you design and complete layouts. Although you can set column guides and margins for areas you define on the pages (frames), only the column guides and margins set for pages display on the screen. Because column guides do not print, Ventura offers other methods, described in Chapter 5, to lay printed rules between columns and around all or part of a page.

Setting Rulers

The measurement systems you see on the rulers are controlled by the choices you make in the SET RULER dialog box (accessed from the Options menu). You can choose different measurement systems to set the increment for the horizontal and vertical rulers: inches, centimeters, or picas and points. Inches increment in eighths (8 eighths = 1 inch); centimeters increment in tenths (10 centimeters = 1 decimeter); and picas and points increment in twelfths (12 points = 1 pica). Figure 3.14 shows the SET RULER dialog box with the ruler set in inches.

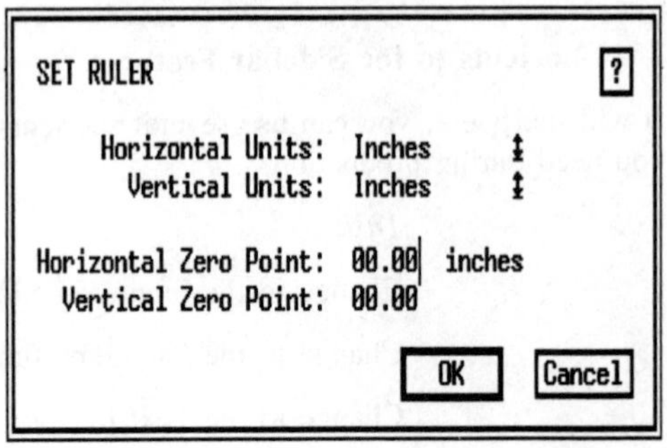

```
┌─────────────────────────────────────────────┐
│  SET RULER                              [?]   │
│                                               │
│        Horizontal Units:  Inches        ↕     │
│          Vertical Units:  Inches        ↕     │
│                                               │
│     Horizontal Zero Point:  00.00| inches     │
│       Vertical Zero Point:  00.00             │
│                                               │
│                           ┌────┐ ┌──────┐     │
│                           │ OK │ │Cancel│     │
│                           └────┘ └──────┘     │
└─────────────────────────────────────────────┘
```

Fig. 3.14.

The SET RULER dialog box with the ruler set in inches.

Tick marks on the rulers divide the space into the specified increments. As you enlarge the view, the distance between the tick marks increases, enabling you to pinpoint a location more precisely. Rulers in Enlarged and Normal views show more tick marks than rulers in Reduced view. The resolution and screen driver of the monitor also affect the precision of the grids on the Ventura screen.

The Zero Point options in the SET RULER dialog box refer to the starting points of the rulers shown in the work area (see fig. 3.14). The Horizontal Zero Point and Vertical Zero Point options offer the most exact method of setting a ruler's starting position. You can set the starting positions for the rulers by typing values in the SET RULER dialog box.

You also can set the zero point from the work area by dragging the 0,0 point displayed at the intersection of the rulers. Each time you drag the zero point, two dashed lines (crosshairs) follow your movement (see fig. 3.15). When you release the mouse button, the crosshairs disappear, and the zero (starting) point for each ruler changes to that point.

Figure 3.16 shows a horizontal ruler with a starting point equal to the margin. This setting is helpful when you need to assign positions for tabs, because Ventura starts at the left margin of the active frame when measuring tabs. The rulers and crosshairs may be all you need in order to check the accuracy of alignment or to choose which measurements to set in some of the commands that affect the page design. Other tools are available, however, to help you position elements mathematically (and therefore more precisely than you can see on most monitors). Techniques for setting text locations at measured positions, placing page elements along column guides, and aligning graphics to measured positions from the edge of the printed page are demonstrated in Chapters 6 and 7.

Setting Preferences

The Options menu's SET PREFERENCES dialog box (refer to fig. 3.5) has two options that affect the display of text in the work area: Text to Greek and On-Screen Kerning. Greeking and kerning are graphic art terms and are used here to instruct Ventura how to display text on the screen.

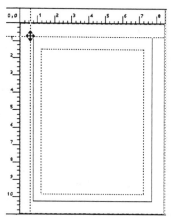

Fig. 3.15.

Dragging the 0.0 point in the work area.

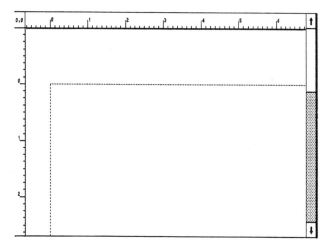

Fig. 3.16.

The ruler with the zero point equal to the margin.

Traditionally, *greeking* is the technique artists use to illustrate a page design quickly, with horizontal lines drawn to approximate the type. With Ventura, you can use the same method to draw a page rapidly in both the Reduced and Facing Pages views. The Text to Greek value you choose in the SET PREFERENCES dialog box relates to the size of the letters on the screen in each view. For example, on an EGA monitor, 12-point type greeks when you select 6 as the size to greek. (12-point type is only 6 pixels high in Reduced view.) When you click None as the answer to the Text to Greek option, Ventura takes longer to display a page than if you had chosen All, because greeked text displays faster than nongreeked text.

Although Ventura's greeked lines do not individually estimate type size as do many artist's renderings, a group of greeked lines in the work area approximates the amount of space the type will take. The resulting view gives you a good idea of the basic page design. Like the artist making a layout, you can use the Reduced and Facing Pages views to see how well page elements are balanced and to preview the results of alternative options for commands that affect the page design.

Kerning is a term used to define fine adjustments to the amount of space between typeset characters. The On-Screen Kerning option in the SET PREFERENCES dialog box affects only those paragraphs that carry kerning instructions in their respective tag settings. (Only those printer width tables that define which pairs of letters to kern support automatic kerning.) On-screen kerning slows the display process because Ventura must interpret a more complex set of mathematical instructions to format all the paragraphs that you set to kern automatically. Unless you are using large fonts (18-point) or have a high-resolution monitor, you will not be able to see the effects of on-screen kerning.

In Chapters 5 and 9, you can read more about kerning and will see that you have two ways to set kerning values: one for predetermined pairs of letters within tagged paragraphs (which you can turn on and off globally with the Chapter Typography command) and another for selected letters. When you kern selected letters (with the Set Font command), what you see on your monitor always represents, as closely as your display allows, the space that will appear between the kerned letters when you print.

You also can use the Set Preferences command to hide the pop-up menu symbols from display by setting Pop-Up Menu Symbols: Hidden rather than Shown. Hiding the symbols does not inhibit your ability to open the menus, because a click and drag anywhere on the option setting yields the same effect.

Saving Custom Defaults

The settings you choose for the Show/Hide, Set Ruler, and Set Preferences commands save as display defaults in the VP.INF file when you choose Quit from Ventura's File menu. In addition to these commands that affect the display, the active function and the last style file in use also save as defaults in the INF file. Most important though, the defaults set in the dialog boxes you access to load the chapter, style, and source files save as new default values to be used the next time you start Ventura from DOS.

For this reason, if you work on several projects at once, you may want to save a custom default file for each project. This technique not only can save time by eliminating the steps required to reestablish a project's display defaults at start-up but also helps you load and save files to the directories established for that project.

You can use the following procedure to customize the defaults for the display-type commands as well as for the ITEM SELECTOR dialog boxes opened with the File menu's Save and Load commands. (Refer to this chapter's section on ''Loading Chapter, Style, and Source Files'' to learn how to use the ITEM SELECTOR dialog boxes.) The procedure lists the names of the commands that save as INF defaults and explains how to copy the defaults into a file referenced by a custom batch file. You need to know how to use Ventura to choose the new defaults, how to use DOS to copy files, and how to use a word processor to edit and save the new batch file as an unformatted ASCII file.

1. Start Ventura and customize the options for the following commands:

   Options menu
     Set Preferences

Set Ruler
Set Printer Info
All six Show/Hide commands
Turn Column Snap
Turn Line Snap

File menu
All Save and Load commands (Save, Save As, Load Text/Picture, Load Diff Style, Save As New Style) to set the defaults in the ITEM SELECTOR dialog boxes (Choosing Load Diff Style also sets the default style file name.)

(After you select each command, load or save each type of file.)

Edit menu
File Type/Rename

2. Quit Ventura.

3. Use DOS commands to change to the Ventura subdirectory and to copy the VP.INF file to a custom information file. For example, if MANUALS.INF is the name of your custom file, type these commands:

   CD C:\VENTURA
   COPY VP.INF MANUALS.INF

4. Use DOS commands to change to the root directory and to copy the VP.BAT file to a custom batch file. For example, if VPM.BAT is the name of your custom file, type these commands:

   CD C:\
   COPY VP.BAT VPM.BAT

5. Edit the custom batch file (VPM.BAT) with a word processor that offers you an option to save a file as an unformatted ASCII file. The custom batch file already contains the following instructions (the contents of the second line differ with each configuration):

   CD C:\VENTURA
   DRVRMRGR VP %1 /S=SD_X6655.EGA/M=32

   You need to add two lines between these two instructions. If MANUALS.INF is the name of your custom INF file, type

   ERASE VP.INF
   COPY MANUALS.INF VP.INF

   between the two lines. Save the batch file as an ASCII file and return to the DOS prompt at the root directory.

6. To start Ventura and use the custom defaults, type the custom batch file name at the DOS prompt.

7. As you choose alternative settings for commands while you work, you are not changing the defaults in the custom batch file. To do so, repeat steps 1 through 3.

You can change many command defaults during a publishing session. To set an alternative default, you simply need to choose an alternative option during production. The new setting prevails until you change it. Even if you quit Ventura and subsequently restart the program, that alternative option will still be in effect as the new default.

Understanding Ventura's Files

Every Ventura project you undertake is defined by a collection of files—a chapter file, a style file, and at least one source file. Both of these files reference other files that are needed to complete the design and composition of each project. The organizational chart in figure 3.17 illustrates how Ventura assembles each chapter.

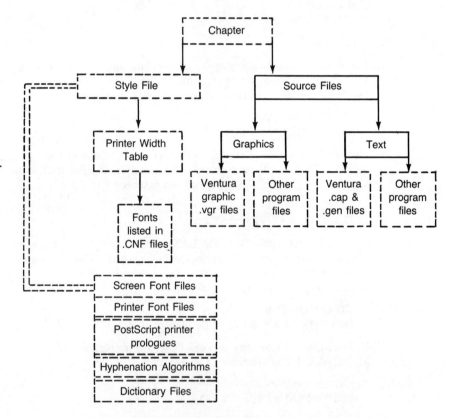

Fig. 3.17.

Ventura collects the names and locations for a project's files in the chapter file.

At first, the term *chapter* may seem inappropriate when you are producing business cards or forms. Consider, however, that Ventura's definition of a chapter is a collection of elements that share similar page sizes and numbering schemes through a portion of a publication. Therefore, you might combine, create, and file several forms in one chapter or make individual chapters for each form.

To open a previously saved project, you need to know only the name and location of the *chapter file*. Ventura's default location for chapter files is the TYPESET directory, which Ventura creates during program installation. The default file extension for chapter file names is CHP.

The first purpose of a chapter file is to list the names and locations of the style and source files used in the project. The first file referenced by the chapter file is the *style file*. Each chapter file uses a style file to interpret the typographic effect of the tag names assigned to paragraphs of text, to define the size of the page, and to define the number and measure of the margins, columns, and rules set for the page. You name the style file and can designate where to file it, but style files, like chapter files, default to the TYPESET directory.

Ventura updates the active style file (named at the top of the publisher's window) when you choose alternative settings for several commands, including Page Layout, Margins & Columns (when the page is selected as the active frame), Sizing & Scaling, Set Printer Info, and all the Paragraph menu commands. To learn the location of the style file you are using, check the Directory setting in the dialog box for the Save As New Style command (under the File menu). The role of the style file in formatting is discussed fully in Chapter 5.

The style file also references a file used to complete the assembly of a project. The file name of the *width table* is stored in the style file to indicate which type of printer you will be using for the current project. The various types of printers supported by Ventura form characters, spaces, and graphics in unique ways. As discussed in Chapter 8, you can successfully change from one type of printer to another when you know which width table to use.

The width table applies instructions to the fonts your printer supports. Each printer uses unique file names and extensions for font files, and each font has its own file. If you add fonts to the collection delivered with your printer, you collect the new font names in a CNF file. You also can use the CNF file to specify the name of the directory where the collection of printer fonts resides. Screen fonts, like printer fonts, are also stored in individual files. You select a collection of screen fonts when you type the extension as the Screen Fonts option in the SET PRINTER INFO dialog box.

Screen fonts are also stored one font per file. You collect screen fonts for use by establishing a convention for naming file extensions. Then you can change to a set of screen fonts that matches the printer fonts you will be using by typing the extension for the screen font collection in the SET PREFERENCES dialog box. Screen fonts are discussed further in Chapter 9.

Source files contain the text and graphics you use in a project. You can use Ventura to create source document files and then save the files to formats compatible with your word processor. Most often, though, the bulk of text and graphics included in a publication consists of files created in other programs and loaded into Ventura.

As you load a source document into a Ventura chapter, any formatting instructions set in the original file are either interpreted or stripped from the file. Many times, Ventura interprets bold, italic, tabs, and underscore formats correctly but strips centering, indents, and page breaks. (See Chapter 4 to learn more about what to expect.) When you load into a chapter any files containing illustrations or photographs created by other programs, however, you do not change the original files as you crop and size the image in the work area. (See Chapter 6 for more on graphic sources.)

As you edit a source document shown in Ventura's work area, your text edits are stored in the original file. Any typographic tags you attach are stored at the beginning of the affected paragraph in the source file. Both these features make switching between word processing and desktop publishing software easy, which expedites editing and formatting tasks during production. For example, if you place a source file in a Ventura chapter and notice that a word used many times is spelled incorrectly, you can quit Ventura and edit the file with your word processor or spelling program. When you start Ventura and open the chapter, the updates display in the source file.

If you want to use Ventura to create a source document file rather than import a document from another program, simply begin typing on the first blank page in a Ventura chapter you have named. When you do so, Ventura automatically stores the text to a source file with the same name as the chapter but with an extension matching the default extension of the last word processor accessed. As discussed in Chapter 4, you can rename or convert these source text files to file formats other than ASCII.

Besides referencing the source files you load to a project, the chapter file references CAP and VGR files—files that Ventura creates, names, and stores as you use the Frame, Text, and Graphic functions during production. Essentially, the CAP and VGR files serve a purpose similar to that of other source files loaded to Ventura after they're created in other programs.

The CAP file stores text you type in empty frames, text you type in boxes drawn with the box text tool, and text you type in the frames created by the Anchors & Captions command. (The text you type in the ANCHORS & CAPTIONS dialog box stores in the CHP file, however, not in the CAP file.) You can convert the contents of CAP files to compatible word processing file formats, as is discussed in Chapter 4. A chapter's CAP file has the same name as the chapter, stores to the same directory, and is an ASCII file that you can spell-check with external programs.

The VGR file stores the elements you draw with Ventura's graphic tools. Like the CAP file, the VGR file has the same name as the corresponding chapter file and stores to the same directory. But Ventura cannot convert the VGR file into a file format that is compatible for editing with other programs. You can have many source files for each project but only one STY, VGR, and CAP file per chapter.

In addition to tracking the names of files related to the project, the CHP file stores the text you type in dialog boxes opened from the Page menu's Headers & Footers command and the Frame menu's Anchors & Captions command. (You learn how to use these commands in Chapter 7.) Because the text and settings for headers and footers are stored in the chapter file, if you intend to use the same settings in separate projects, you can start the second project by saving the first project under a new name.

Although the chapter file assembles the files for a chapter, a separate file called the *publication file* assembles the related chapters into a publication. When you are producing books or lengthy documents, you use Ventura to create a publication file

(PUB) that stores the name and location of each chapter you include in the publication. You use the publication file to print and perform certain processes (like generating tables of contents and indexes and renumbering) for several chapters. To work on an individual chapter referenced in a PUB file, you load the chapter file just as you would any chapter file. When you want to print or organize a table of contents or an index for several chapters, you use the Multi-Chapter command from the Options menu.

Note: You use the Save As command to create a copy of the CHP, CAP, and VGR files. To create a copy of all files associated with a project, you use the Copy All command from the Options menu's MULTI-CHAPTER OPERATIONS dialog box. The section "Duplicating and Archiving Projects" in this chapter explains how to duplicate a project's files.

When you use the Multi-Chapter command to create indexes or tables of contents, Ventura generates a file that you name and save to a directory. The default extension for such a *generated file* is GEN. Generated files are used in the same ways as source files loaded from other programs. You can generate a table of contents and index for just one chapter or for several chapters, as you learn in Chapter 4. In Chapter 5, you learn how to generate a file containing design and typography settings for the style file in use.

The two other types of files to which Ventura refers in order to assemble a publication are the *hyphenation algorithms* (HY1 and HY2) and the *dictionaries* (DIC). These files determine where words may be automatically hyphenated when source text files are loaded onto the pages of a chapter. The hyphenation files are different from all the other files used to assemble a publication. The names of the files are not referenced in the chapter or style files but are automatically recognized by Ventura when you retain the default extensions. Therefore, if you need to change hyphenation algorithms for publishing materials in different languages or need to establish custom dictionaries for specific projects, you must change the extensions of the hyphenation and dictionary files in the VENTURA subdirectory before you start Ventura. These files are discussed further in Chapter 5.

In summary, you can see that you need at least a style file and a chapter file to define a project. Style files set the basic design, and chapter files make the pages unique by calling in the source files, headers and footers, frames (with their respective columns and margins), and graphics found on the pages of a publication. You may create source files in numerous other programs or with Ventura's text and graphic tools. The default extensions for compatible source files are shown in Chapters 4 (text) and 6 (graphics). The default extensions for the other files Ventura uses to assemble a publication are shown in table 3.5.

Table 3.5
Files Used To Assemble a Project

Type of File	Default Extension
The Controlling Files for Each Project	
Startup default information	INF
Chapter	CHP
Chapter information	CIF
Hyphenation	HY1 or HY2
Dictionaries	DIC
Publication	PUB
Style	STY
Width table	WID
The Source Files Created with Ventura	
Caption text	CAP
Generated text	GEN
Graphics	VGR

Note: The CIF files capture the creation date, the date last saved, and the date last archived in a format usable by external document management programs.

Loading Chapter, Style, and Source Files

All the Open, Save, and Load commands open similar dialog boxes. Once you choose one of these commands from the File menu, an ITEM SELECTOR dialog box opens (see fig. 3.18). You use this dialog box to designate the name and location of the file you are opening, saving, or loading. The instructions for using the ITEM SELECTOR dialog box are consistent for all the File menu commands. In the case of the Load Text/Picture command, however, you first choose the type of file you want to load and the format for the file, and then you choose the file, using the ITEM SELECTOR dialog box.

The Directory line at the top of each dialog box shows the default location and extension for the type of file selected with the File menu command. A list of files that match the Directory setting appears in the list beneath the file specification (see fig. 3.18). The information shown in the Directory line is familiar to those of you who are accustomed to working with DOS to manage directories on floppy and hard disks. The Directory option, known in DOS terms as the path, tells Ventura where to look for the files you want to retrieve and where to store the files you want to save. The Directory setting consists of four parts:

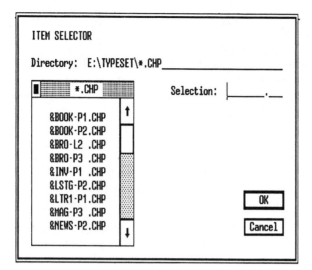

Fig. 3.18.

The ITEM SELECTOR dialog box.

1. The *drive* is followed by a colon, as in C:.

2. The *directory name* is preceded and followed by backslashes (\). For example \TYPESET\ indicates that the file you are looking for is in a directory named TYPESET.

3. The *file name* follows the last backslash and can be up to eight characters long. You end a file name with a period. Ventura does not recognize spaces and capitalization.

4. The *file extension* follows the file name and can be up to three characters long.

Ventura uses the DOS conventions to insert wild cards in file names and file extensions. For example, Ventura's default response to the Open Chapter command is to fill the Directory option with

C:\TYPESET*.CHP

To minimize the number of files displayed in the list (making finding a particular file easier), you can add DOS wild cards to the file filter. Use the asterisk (*) as a wild card when you want to search for any series of characters in a name or extension. Typing *88*.CHP*, as the file name in the Directory option, for example, tells Ventura to display in the assignment list all the files that begin with *88* and end with *CHP*.

To match any one character, you can use the question mark (?). For example,

C:\TYPESET\89??CAT.CHP

causes Ventura to display such files as 8901CAT.CHP, 8902CAT.CHP, and 8903CAT.CHP.

Whenever you change the default value in the Directory option for the chosen command and select a file from the new location, the new value prevails until you change it again. Each File menu command has its own default location and file extension. You should refrain from renaming file extensions unless you intend to follow a well-defined pattern for your Ventura projects. Once you open an ITEM SELECTOR dialog box, the extension shown in the Directory option is the only clue to knowing which dialog box you have opened. Here are the default extensions for the File menu commands:

Command	Extension
Open	CHP
Save and Save As	CHP
Save As New Style	STY
Load Diff Style	STY
Load Text/Picture	Changes extension defaults as you select from the available file formats. Ventura creates a copy of graphic files, saving line art formats as GEM and image formats as IMG.

Each ITEM SELECTOR dialog box responds to the same mouse and keyboard operations, enumerated in table 3.4. Although you can use the text tool to enter drive and directory names in the Directory option, you can use the mouse to click through the directories and drives without worrying about typing drives, colons, directory names, and backslashes in the necessary sequence.

To use the mouse to change the Directory option, click the rectangular button displayed at the top left corner of the assignment list. This button is known as the backup button. Drive and directory names display in the assignment list with a diamond-shaped button in front of each name (see fig. 3.19). The Directory setting changes as you click the backup button.

Ventura beeps if more than 100 file names (the most that can be displayed) match the criteria you set in the Directory option. If you hear a beep, reduce the number of files listed by typing a part of the file name in the Directory option, using one of the DOS wild cards.

You can use the scroll bars to display more of the names in the assignment list. Or when you know the name of the file you want to load, open, or save, you can type the specific file name in the Selection option. If you're loading or opening a file that is named in the assignment list, click the name to fill the Selection option. If you're saving a file, type the name of the file and a period. Once you type a period to indicate the end of the file name, Ventura provides the default file extension when you click OK.

When you try to load a file that is not in the proper format, a warning message displays in a note box. If Ventura gives you this type of message when you are using the Load Text/Picture command, check the Directory option line to make sure that you've chosen the correct file format to complete the intended open, load, or save instruction. See the section on "Saving Files" to learn more about the File menu's Save commands.

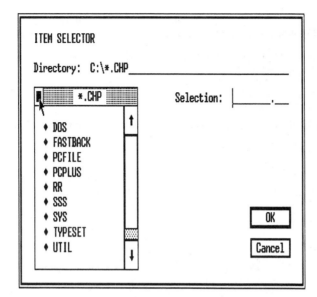

Fig. 3.19.

Choosing drives and directories.

Efficiency Tip

Selecting a File Name Quickly

Double-clicking a file name in an assignment list causes Ventura to fill the Selection option and close the dialog box with OK. (Double-clicks must occur within a certain time frame. You select this time frame by choosing a value for Double Click Speed in the Options menu's SET PREFERENCES dialog box. You have four choices: Slow, 2, 3, 4, and Fast. If you never use double-clicks, set the option to Fast. If you're learning to use a mouse, experiment with the other values to find the one that matches the speed with which you can double-click.)

Troubleshooting Tip

If You Select a Drive You Don't Have

Be careful when you choose which disk drive to use. If you don't have a B drive but accidentally select drive B, wait for Ventura to prompt you. Then click Cancel in the prompt box that appears, and select the correct drive when the ITEM SELECTOR dialog box reopens. If Ventura will not cancel the request, you may be forced to reboot the computer, losing any changes you did not save.

Starting a New Chapter

The Ventura program arrives stocked with several sample chapter and style files that are available for you to use and modify. All the samples are stored in the TYPESET directory, which Ventura creates during the installation process. Rather than modify the contents or commands of those sample publications, you can borrow a copy of a sample style file to begin a project.

Efficiency Tip ─────────────────────────────────────

Opening a Specific Ventura Project Directly from DOS

The fastest way to start Ventura and open a previously created chapter is to include the path and file names of the chapter when you type VP:

VP *drive:\directory\filename.chp*

For example, to start Ventura and display a chapter called &BOOK-P1, type

VP C:\TYPESET\&BOOK-P1.CHP

at the C› prompt. Because the command uses DOS syntax, you can put the path and file name in a custom batch file between VP and the % sign of the DRVRMRGR line in the VP.BAT file. (See ''Saving Custom Defaults'' in this chapter.)

Before starting a new chapter, you should first decide which style file to use and what to call the new chapter. It is also a good idea to copy source files for the project from floppy disks to the hard disk to make processing faster. (Don't plan to load source files from more than one floppy disk in the same drive.)

Once you start the Ventura program, the names and locations of the active chapter file and style file display beneath the menu titles in the publisher's window. When you start Ventura, the UNTITLED chapter displays in the work area. To start a new chapter when a chapter is in view, click New in the File menu.

Although you can always change a chapter's style file, check the name of the title in parentheses at the top of the work area to determine whether the active style file is the one you intend to use. (To find the location of the style file, check the Directory option under the Save As New Style command ITEM SELECTOR dialog box.)

Using a Sample Style File

Ventura's reputation for efficiently dealing with multipage publications was earned, in part, because of the way Ventura handles the many files that make up a publication. Rather than store all the contents in one large file, Ventura captures the names and locations of source files and keeps those addresses in a file called the chapter file. To give you a glimpse of the process and some practice at creating a simple project, let's use one of Ventura's sample style files as a layout and design tool to produce some personalized stationery like that shown in figure 3.20. Follow these steps:

1. Open the File menu and select Load Diff. Style.

2. Select &LTR-P1 from the list in the dialog box. (Use the scroll bar to move the name into view, and click the backup button to change to the TYPESET directory if necessary. All the names starting with & are example files provided with the Ventura program. If you did not install or keep the example files in the TYPESET directory, insert the example disk in drive A, and change to that drive to select the sample style file.)

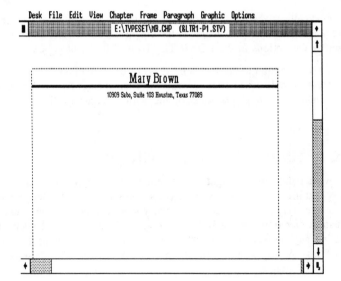

Fig. 3.20.

Personalized stationery created using a sample style file.

3. Select the Text function and move the I-beam into a Reduced view of the work area.

4. Click to position the editing cursor, type your name, press Enter, type your address, and press Enter.

5. Change to the Paragraph function; move the tagging cursor into the work area and on your name, and click to select the one-line paragraph containing your name.

6. Move the tagging cursor to the assignment list in the sidebar and click Name.

7. Move the tagging cursor into the work area and on your address, and click. Shift-click the next paragraph of the address to select it at the same time.

8. Move the tagging cursor to the assignment list in the sidebar and click Address.

9. To print the stationery, open the File menu and select To Print. Press Enter to select the default print options.

10. To save the stationery, press Ctrl-S. Notice the path and file extension set as the Directory option. Type your initials as the name of the chapter. Do not type an extension for the file name. Press Enter to start the save process. As you save the chapter of stationery, Ventura displays the names of the chapter, style, and source files that are updated in the process.

Ventura automatically saves the text you type on the base page of a chapter, in the same directory and with the same name as the chapter. The extension and format for the file is set by the options in the LOAD TEXT/PICTURE dialog box.

[I]

Even when you use Ventura to produce a business card or small ad, you may find that Ventura assembles a half-dozen files to print the final piece. To use Ventura effectively, you should understand the roles of the various types of files in publishing projects.

Naming a Style File for the Chapter

Sometimes, what seems like a slight adjustment to the design specifications in one project has a significant and surprising effect in another project. Because changes store in the active style file automatically when you save a chapter, new users often make the mistake of modifying the style file defaults. To avoid this problem, make a habit of starting any project by using the Save As New Style command *before* you select Save or Save As to name the chapter in view. A discussion of these commands appears later in this chapter.

Fortunately, until you choose the Save or Save As command, Ventura's ABANDON dialog box (accessed from the File menu) lets you forgo any unintentional changes to the active style file. If the Abandon command is not available for selection, you have made no changes that you can abandon.

You create new style files by saving an active style file under a new name. To get you started, Ventura copied at least one sample style file to the TYPESET directory during program installation. (In Chapter 7, you see the naming conventions Ventura uses for all the sample style files.) Using the file named DEFAULT is like starting fresh because it contains only one tag and standard settings for an 8.5-by-11-inch page with one-inch margins (unless you have modified DEFAULT since you installed Ventura).

To maintain consistency for similar types of projects (such as proposals, reports, or manuals), you start each project by using the Load Diff. Style command to retrieve the style file set for each type of project.

To preserve the settings of the active style file yet use a copy of it to begin a new project, open the File menu and click Save As New Style. The ITEM SELECTOR dialog box opens to a list of file names that match the specifications set in the Directory option at the top of the dialog box. The text cursor is positioned at the Selection line, ready for you to type the new style file name. If you want to overwrite an existing name in the list, click that name and then click OK.

Once you have named a style file for the project, you can set up the basic elements of the page design in the chapter. You can share style files (and therefore page and typographic designs) between projects. And with a little planning, you can change style files during production to see the effect of alternative page designs.

You have several options for overriding the basic page design to accommodate exceptions, whether on one or on several consecutive pages. Although Chapter 7 explains in detail how you can mix page designs within a project, the basic principle of setting a page design is fundamental to using Ventura.

You set the size, margins, columns, and features of chapter pages when you select page one as a frame and then establish design settings. This page is known as the *base* page. You can override the design of the base page (and those pages created from it for multiple-page source text files) in two ways:

1. By inserting new pages where you initiate design changes

2. By placing frames on a page and establishing new settings for the frame

To customize a new page design within a chapter, you select the new page as an active frame and then modify the settings you want to appear differently. The new settings prevail for that page and for any pages that are automatically created when you load a source file onto the new page. The settings for the frames and pages you add are saved as settings in the chapter file, whereas base page settings are stored in the style file.

You cannot, however, establish more than one setting within a chapter for each command that affects the elements contributing to the design of a page. Several page elements are controlled by the CHP file, in which Ventura will not support more than one selection for the following:

- Any of the PAGE LAYOUT dialog box options

- The text and format of automatic headers and footers (although you can individually suppress them on selected pages and have alternating right and left pages with different text)

- The format for footnotes and footnote numbering

Any changes you make to these features prevail throughout the chapter, regardless of how many custom page designs you define in the chapter. As you use Ventura, however, you will learn how to organize projects or devise manual techniques to override (when you need to) most of the default values set for the chapter.

Setting Page Size, Margins, and Columns

Ventura has a reputation for handling designs so that documents flow from page to page. But you can use Ventura also to design individual, or free-form, pages composed of juxtaposed text and graphics. To set the design of any page, first establish the size and orientation of the paper for printing and then set the number and measure for the margins and columns to display in the view.

The PAGE LAYOUT dialog box, shown in figure 3.21, offers seven alternative paper sizes (referred to as Paper Type) that you can print in either portrait or landscape orientation. When the width of the paper is greater than the length, you choose Landscape for the Orientation option. In Chapter 7, the alternative options for each Page Layout command are discussed in detail, as is also a method of printing on custom paper sizes other than those listed in the dialog box.

To set the size and number of margins and columns on the page, you first must select the page in the work area as the active frame, which often requires merely selecting the Frame function. If other frames were more recently chosen as the active frame,

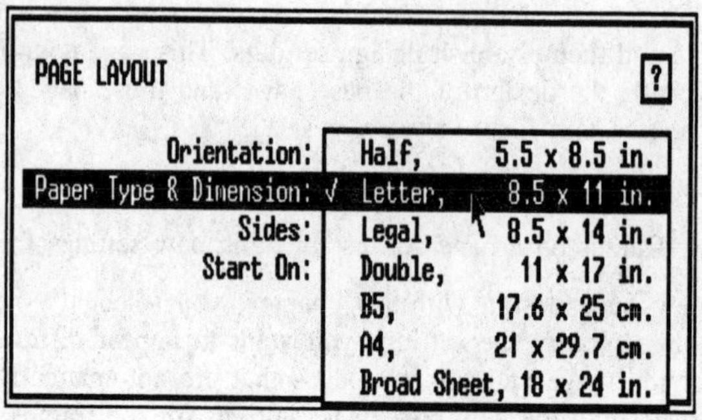

```
 PAGE LAYOUT                                    [?]

                  Orientation:   Half,        5.5 x 8.5 in.
 Paper Type & Dimension:  √  Letter,      8.5 x 11 in.
                        Sides:   Legal,       8.5 x 14 in.
                     Start On:   Double,       11 x 17 in.
                                 B5,          17.6 x 25 cm.
                                 A4,          21 x 29.7 cm.
                                 Broad Sheet, 18 x 24 in.
```

Fig. 3.21.

The PAGE LAYOUT dialog box.

you must choose the Frame function, move the cursor onto the page, and click. Eight black handles display around the perimeter of the active frame.

When you select the page as the active frame and then open the Frame menu, the menu displays with several of the commands enabled, as shown in figure 3.22. You use the first command, Margins & Columns, to set the margins and columns. (No commands are available if you have not selected an active frame. If you select as active a frame drawn on the page, the Anchors & Captions command is also available.)

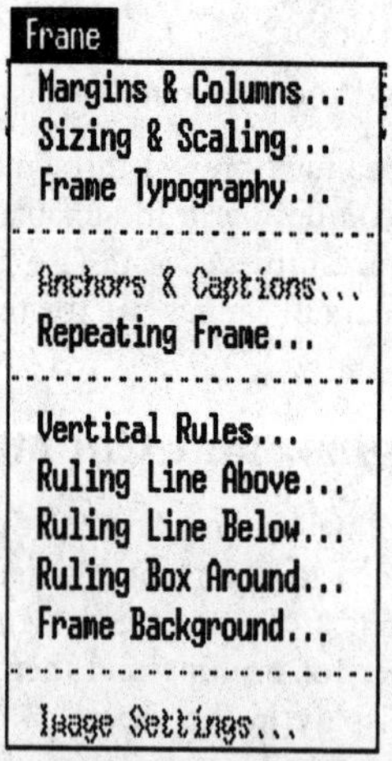

```
 Frame

 Margins & Columns...
 Sizing & Scaling...
 Frame Typography...
 - - - - - - - - - - - - - - -
 Anchors & Captions...
 Repeating Frame...
 - - - - - - - - - - - - - - -
 Vertical Rules...
 Ruling Line Above...
 Ruling Line Below...
 Ruling Box Around...
 Frame Background...
 - - - - - - - - - - - - - - -
 Image Settings...
```

Fig. 3.22.

The Frame menu with several commands enabled.

When you select a frame holding a source file, the name of the source file displays in the current selection box at the base of the sidebar (refer to fig. 3.1). Figure 3.23 shows a page set with margins and columns different from those shown in the frame placed in the center of the page. (You can set different margins and columns for each frame. The basic design is set on the base page and is saved in the style file.)

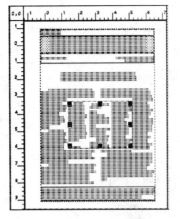

Fig. 3.23.

A page with margins and columns different from the frame's margins and columns.

Setting Rules and Patterns on the Page

The style file also controls the number and measure of rules you set for the base page and the choices you make for the page background. You can set both of these design elements by selecting the page as the active frame and then choosing the appropriate commands from the Frame menu.

To cause vertical rules to appear between columns or at specific locations on the page, you choose the Vertical Rules command from the Frame menu. When you want to set a background pattern other than white for the page, open the FRAME BACK-GROUND dialog box to choose from the colors and patterns displayed as alternative options. As you learn to use frames to reserve space on the page, you can also choose to set those frames with vertical rules or background patterns different from those set for the page.

Using the Publishing Functions

Ventura uses four publishing functions to control the placement and content of typographic and graphic elements included in a project. These functions—Frame, Paragraph, Text, and Graphic—are represented by the four adjacent symbols, or icons, located at the top of the sidebar. As you activate one of the icons with a click of the mouse, the icon displays in reverse video, and the cursor shape changes to symbolize the active publishing function. Table 3.6 lists the four publishing functions and their corresponding icons, cursor shapes, and purposes.

Table 3.6
The Publishing Functions

Function Name	Icon	Cursor Shape	Purpose
Frame		**+**	Selecting a frame to redefine boundaries or establish border treatments and backgrounds for areas where you place text and graphics source files
Paragraph			Tagging paragraphs with typographic instructions
Text		I	Typing and editing text; attaching character attributes to selected text within paragraphs
Graphic			Drawing arrows, lines, and circular, rectangular, and rounded rectangular shapes (The box text tool is extremely useful for creating complex layouts that include relatively small quantities of text.)

As you change publishing functions, the sidebar changes to offer tools to help you load source files, add typographic instructions, enter text and text attributes, and create graphics and boxes of text (see fig. 3.25).

The publishing functions are described fully in Chapters 4 through 6, but here's a summary of the basic operations of each function. The *Frame function* is used to reserve space for source files and to load them into place on the pages. You can use this function also to select the page as the active frame when you want to establish settings for commands that affect the basic design of a page. The Frame function works with commands located on the Edit, Frame, and Page menus.

The *Paragraph function* is used to set the typographic characteristics for paragraphs of text included in the publication. You can also accomplish the task with word processing software (as described in Chapter 4) by typing tag names in source files. Here are the basic steps to tagging a paragraph in Ventura:

1. Choose the Paragraph function.

2. Click the tagging cursor on a paragraph to select the paragraph.

3. Click a tag name from those shown in the assignment list.

Shortcuts to the Publishing Functions

The Ctrl-key shortcuts shown on the View menu make changing publishing functions fast and convenient, with or without a mouse. In figure 3.24, notice the correspondence between the arrangement of the U, I, O, and P keys and the order of the function icons:

Frame function	Ctrl-U
Paragraph function	Ctrl-I
Text function	Ctrl-O
Graphic function	Ctrl-P

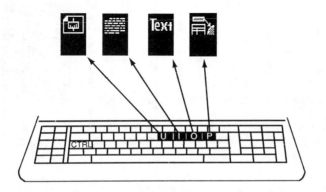

Fig. 3.24.

UIOP keys corresponding to the function icons.

The name of the tag displays in the current selection box to indicate which paragraph tag you've selected. You change the settings established for all paragraphs tagged with the same name by choosing from the available options for any of the Paragraph menu commands. To add new tag names to the assignment list, you use the Add New Tag button in the sidebar (or use the Paragraph function's shortcut, Ctrl-2). You can change and define settings for tags when you first select a paragraph and then choose the alternative commands and options accessed from the Paragraph menu. Ventura interprets any untagged paragraph as a paragraph that should be set with the characteristics of the default values set for body text. You can change those values to create custom defaults for each project (discussed further in Chapter 5).

With the *Text function*, you can type text directly into Ventura. Before you type new text, you use the text cursor to establish the text insertion point. As Chapter 4 describes, you can type text on a blank page or type text in a frame. If you type text in a source file, however, you update the contents of the source file with your edits.

You use the Text function to enable several Edit menu commands to cut, copy, and paste text; to insert reference points for footnotes and index entries; and to tie an illustration to a point in text. You also can use the Text function to format, within paragraphs, phrases to carry special typographic attributes. Chapter 5 discusses how to use the Text function to set formatting attributes for selected text within paragraphs.

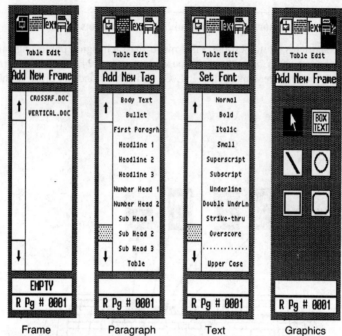

Fig. 3.25.

*The sidebar of each
function.*

The *Graphic function* provides six tools with which you can create various graphic elements and boxes of text. Any graphics created will be attached to a frame. The Add New Frame button enables you to add frames while the Graphic function is active. You also can select a frame while you're using this function. This way you can create groups of graphic elements and move, cut, copy, and paste them, using the frame to which they are attached. For example, you can attach a frame to a section of text, and the frame will follow the text when the text moves. You can then tie graphic elements to frames that are attached to areas of text. You can create a graphic that prints on every page, just left pages, just right pages, or alternating pages. Chapter 6 explores the use of the graphic tools and the Graphic and Edit menu commands for building simple illustrations.

Using Frames To Reserve Space for Text and Graphics

As mentioned previously, you use the Frame function to place text, images, and graphics files on pages within defined areas. If you choose the Frame function and see eight handles displayed along the perimeter of the page, the page is selected as the designated area (see fig. 3.26). To add a frame to a page, choose the Frame function and then click Add New Frame. When you move the mouse into the work area, the cursor shape changes to represent the corner of a rectangle (again see fig. 3.26).

As you drag the mouse in a diagonal direction, the cursor changes to a pointing hand. The frame increases in size until you release the mouse button (see fig. 3.27).

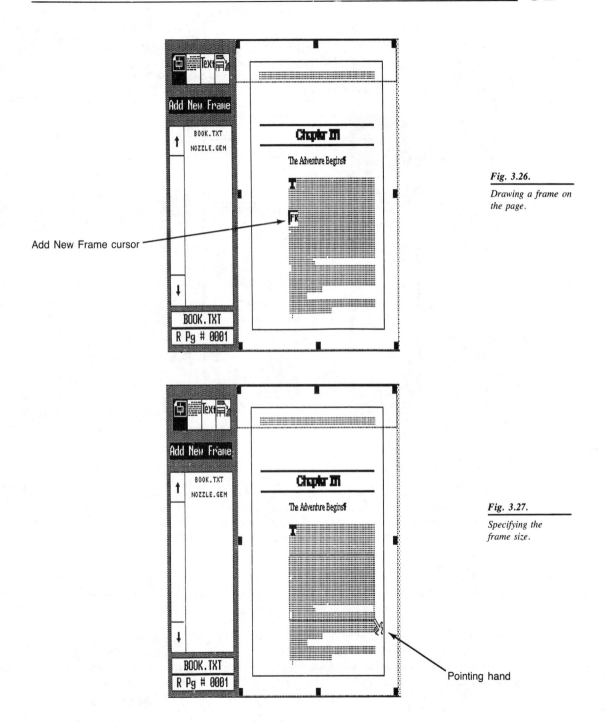

Add New Frame cursor

Fig. 3.26.

Drawing a frame on the page.

Fig. 3.27.

Specifying the frame size.

Pointing hand

Immediately after you add a frame to the page, the graphic handles display to indicate that the frame you just drew is selected as the active frame. Until you type text or place a source file in the frame, the current selection box displays EMPTY to describe the contents of the selected frame (see fig. 3.28).

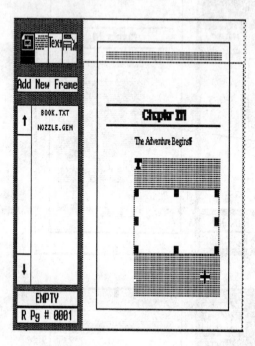

Fig. 3.28.

A page and a selected empty frame.

Placing Text and Graphics

To place a source file on a page or frame, you must first load the file using the Load Text/Picture command. The dialog box that opens next shows the formats for the type of file that is selected (see fig. 3.29). From the available choices for the Type of File option, select whether you intend to load Text, Line-Art, or Image files. Then choose the Text Format, the Line-Art Format, or the Image Format. (To learn more about the various file types and formats, see Chapters 4 and 6.)

Once you have selected the file type and format, you can click One to load one file or Several to load more than one file in succession. You then choose the Destination option. The choices are List of Files, Text Clipboard, and Text Cursor. Choose List of Files and the file or files are loaded into the assignment list for use in the chapter. Choose the Text Clipboard option when you want to paste the file or files (with the Paste command or the Ins key) into position after you select the edit point. Selecting Text Cursor tells Ventura to place the files automatically at the point of the cursor. To enable this option, you must set the cursor location before choosing Load Text/Picture from the File menu.

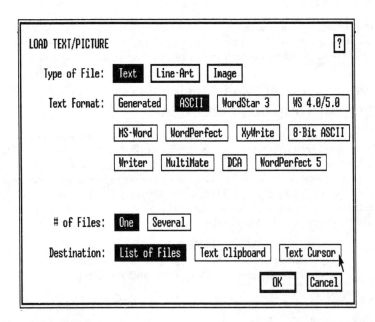

Fig. 3.29.

The LOAD TEXT/ PICTURE dialog box.

When you have made all the choices, close the LOAD TEXT/PICTURE dialog box by clicking OK. The ITEM SELECTOR dialog box then opens. You can either select the name from the list or change the Directory option so that you can filter through the matching files on a different drive or directory. When you're using the Text Clipboard option or the Text Cursor option, multiple files will be merged in the order you select them (concatenated). If you don't have EMS memory, concatenate large files with care (see Chapter 2). Both these options use the memory allocated for the text Clipboard.

When you find the file you want to load, click the name and then click OK (or double-click, as described in the Efficiency Tip in the section on "Loading Chapter, Style, and Source Files") to place the name of the file in the Selection option. Close the dialog box by clicking OK to cause Ventura to load the name of the file to the destination you have chosen.

When you begin a Load/Text Picture operation by first choosing the frame where you intend to place the source file, Ventura automatically fills the selected frame when you click OK to close the ITEM SELECTOR dialog box. If the entire contents of the source file do not fit in the selected frame, Ventura continues the file the next time you select a frame and click the file name. If you selected the page as the active frame, Ventura adds as many pages as are required to hold the contents of the file (for the base page as well as any pages you have added using the Insert/Remove Page command). If you did not select a frame when you began loading a source file, select the frame with a click of the Frame function cursor once you're positioned inside the frame. Then slide the mouse to the sidebar and select the file name from those shown in the assignment list.

You can place a graphics source file more than once in a chapter but must copy a text source file to use it more than once. In Chapter 7 you learn how to cut, copy, paste, and repeat frames and their contents on successive and selected pages.

Selecting, Changing, and Moving Text, Paragraphs, Graphics, and Frames

Like most computer programs, Ventura requires that before an operation can be performed you must select something on which to work. You must select a section of text, a paragraph, a graphic or set of graphics, or a frame before you can change that element's appearance or location. The method you use to select items in the work area depends on the type of item you want to select. Before you select an item (or items), click the publishing icon that represents the type of element. Table 3.7 summarizes the keys and mouse operations used to select elements in the work area.

Table 3.7
Mouse and Keyboard Operations To Select
Frames, Graphic Shapes, Text, and Paragraphs

Task	Operation
To select a paragraph, frame, or graphic	Click within the element
To add to the selected set	Shift-click another element of the same type
To select a graphic, paragraph, or frame beneath a selected element of the same type	Ctrl-click the selected element.
To add an element beneath others to a selected set	Ctrl-Shift-click the element
To select all graphics associated with the selected frame	Press Ctrl-Q (the shortcut to the Graphic menu's Select All command)
To deselect a selected element	Shift-click the selected element
To deselect all selected elements	Click away from a selected element but within the work area
To select text	Click, slide, Shift-click
	Click, drag, release
To extend a selection of text	Shift-click where you want the selection to end

Once the element is selected (by one of the methods listed in tables 3.2 and 3.7), the menus offer several commands to change the appearance of the element. You use the menu commands and the sidebar features to define how you want to change the selected element.

Note that table 3.7 lists two ways to select text. If you drag rather than slide the text cursor, you select the text in your path of movement until you release the mouse button. You also can position the edit cursor with a click and then Shift-click at the opposite end of the text you want to select. The selected text displays in reverse video. Which method works best for you depends on the resolution of your monitor. Once text is selected, you attach custom attributes by selecting from the available choices in the Text function sidebar or by using the Set Font button.

To select a paragraph with the tagging cursor, choose the Paragraph function and click the mouse on a paragraph of text. The selected text displays in reverse video, in the same way that a selection of text within a paragraph displays in reverse video. Once you have selected a paragraph, you can choose from the available commands in the Paragraph menu. (Chapter 5 covers this menu's commands in detail.) Using the Paragraph menu commands, you set the format for all paragraphs tagged with the same name as the selected paragraph. Changing the size of type in the body text tag, for example, causes every untagged paragraph in the chapter to reformat according to the new setting. (As mentioned previously, Ventura interprets untagged paragraphs to be body text.)

In comparison to the other page elements, paragraphs are unique. When you're using the Paragraph function, you cannot cut, copy, or paste into position on other pages those paragraphs that you select with the tagging cursor. But you *can* cut, copy, and move frames that contain paragraphs. And you can use the Text function to select up to a full page of text for cutting or copying. When you cut and copy frames of text, the typographic qualities accompanying the text when you place the frame in a new chapter will be interpreted properly only if the style file for the chapter contains the same tag names.

Efficiency Tip

Cutting, Copying, and Pasting Text

To cut, copy, and paste paragraphs of text, select the text with the Text function and then choose from the available commands on the Edit menu. To insert the text in the new position, click the text cursor at the point where you want to insert the text and press the Ins key. Be sure to select the paragraph return following a paragraph if you want the paragraph's tag to follow to the new position.

To select a Ventura-drawn graphic, change to the Graphic function, move the cursor into the work area on the graphic, and click. Ventura displays the graphic handles and the graphic control handles around the perimeter of the frame to which the graphic is attached. Both types of handles are shown in figure 3.30. As is emphasized in Chapter 6, Ventura attaches graphics to the last selected frame if you do not change the selection before you use the graphic drawing tools.

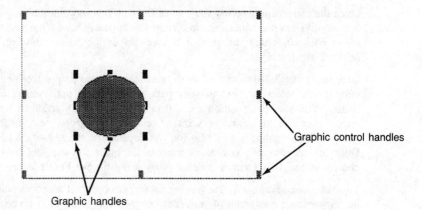

Fig. 3.30.

Graphic handles and graphic control handles.

Graphic control handles

Graphic handles

Depending on the size of the object you are selecting, you may need to change to Reduced view to see all the handles that define the boundary of the selected element. Small frames and shapes, however, may display all their handles only when you look at the element in Enlarged view. You don't have to see all the handles to work with the element, but you may need to change views or scroll the element into view when you want to choose a particular handle.

Once you have selected a frame or (graphic), you can use the handles to size the selected element. To change the size of a frame you have drawn, select the frame with a click of the mouse anywhere within the frame or graphic. The handles appear around the frame. Place the cursor directly on a handle and then press and hold the mouse button to change the cursor to the sizing cursor, which is represented as a pointing finger. If you choose a corner handle, you can change the proportion of the shape in two directions simultaneously. With the other handles, you can change the proportion of the shape in only a single direction. Drag the mouse to size the frame, and release the mouse button when the frame is properly sized. Figure 3.31 illustrates how to use the mouse to change the size of the selected frame: position the cursor on a handle, resize the frame, and release the mouse button.

To move a selected frame or graphic, position the mouse cursor within the frame or graphic and drag the element to another position. When you press and hold the mouse button, the cursor changes to a four-arrow diamond shape. Do not place the cursor directly on a handle or you will size the frame rather than move it. (see fig. 3.32).

If the new position for the graphic is on another page, use the Edit menu commands to cut (or copy) the selected element and then insert it after you've turned to and selected the new page.

Graphics source files placed in frames also can be moved within the frame, which enables you to crop the picture after you place it. Chapter 6 shows you how to use the mouse and the Frame menu's SIZING & SCALING dialog box to move graphics source files within frames. The techniques to select, change, and move text, paragraphs, graphics, and frames are covered in more detail as each function is explained in Chapters 4 through 7.

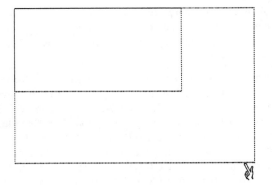

Fig. 3.31.

Using the mouse to resize a selected frame.

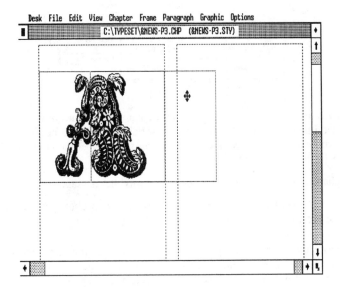

Fig. 3.32.

Using the mouse to move a graphic.

Saving and Copying Files

The File menu offers several commands to save files:

- The *Save command* updates the chapter, style, and source files, leaving the current project in view so that you can continue working. This command is the only Save command with a Ctrl-key shortcut (Ctrl-S).

- The *Save As command* makes a copy of the chapter in view, letting you choose a new location and name for the copy. Once named, the copy of the chapter and the new title display in the work area. The source files used in the original chapter are not moved or copied when you use a Save As command.

- The *Save As New Style command* makes a copy of the active style file, letting you choose a new location and name for the copy. Once named, the new style file is saved with any changes you make when you choose the Save or Save As command.

The Save command saves the chapter and style named at the top of the work area, with any changes you have made. Once you choose either of the Save As commands, however, Ventura provides an ITEM SELECTOR dialog box in which you can change the location for the new file in the Directory option. You name the new file in the Selection option. (The ITEM SELECTOR dialog box operations are discussed in more detail in the section on "Loading Chapter, Style, and Source Files.") If you type or select a file name shown in the assignment list, Ventura prompts you, to make sure that you intend to overwrite that file with the file in the work area (see fig. 3.33).

Fig. 3.33.

The Overwrite Existing File prompt.

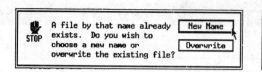

Select the Overwrite option to use the same file name as the one you selected. If you want to select a new name for the file, click New Name. If you did not intend to create a new file, you can still click New Name. You can then cancel the command or name the new file in the Selection option.

When the chapter file name you have chosen returns the message

Renaming the base pages text files to match this chapter name leads to a conflict with a file name that already exists

you can choose Overwrite to replace the text file in the directory with the one in view. To rename the chapter (and therefore the file for the base page) select New CHP Name and type in a new name. As with the Overwrite prompt, you can cancel the command after you select New CHP Name.

Choosing the New or Open Chapter command invokes prompts that ask whether you want to save changes to the active chapter and style in view and continue working in Ventura. Figure 3.34 shows the first of the two prompts. The prompts give you two choices: Save and Abandon. By starting a save process with one of these commands, you can choose whether to update the chapter and style files individually (if you have made changes). You can update the style and not the chapter file by using the New or Open Chapter command and then choosing to abandon changes to the chapter file. If you choose to save the changes to the chapter file, the style file is updated automatically.

Changes are saved to the style file when you select either the Save or the Save As New Style command from the File menu, or when you select Save in the prompt box that appears after you select to abandon the changes to the chapter.

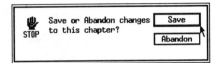

Fig. 3.34.

Saving or abandoning changes to the chapter.

After you answer the inquiries to save or abandon the changes to the files named at the top of the work area, either the UNTITLED chapter or an ITEM SELECTOR dialog box opens, depending on whether you used New or Open Chapter to clear the work area of the preceding chapter in view. Before you begin making changes to page design and typographic styles for the new project, remember to determine whether you intend to load a different style file, use the style file named at the top of the window, or save the active style file to a new style name.

Choosing Quit from the File menu displays a prompt that offers three options: Save, Abandon, and Don't Quit. You have the choice of saving or abandoning the changes to the chapter and style files, or you can resume operations by choosing Don't Quit.

Abandoning changes by choosing the File menu's Abandon command causes Ventura to reload into memory—and therefore into view—the last versions of the files saved on disk. When you choose OK at the prompt to revert to the last issue saved, you abandon changes to both the chapter and style in view. You must learn to save the work in progress to disk often, for two reasons:

- You can then freely use the Abandon command to ''undo'' changes that you decide not to keep.

- You need to update the disk files for the active project. In the event of a power or program failure, the version last saved to disk will be available when you select Open Chapter and establish the proper path to the chapter in the Directory option.

Efficiency Tip

Save Your Work Often

You should use the File menu's Save command (or the shortcut Ctrl-S) to update the disk files for the chapter in view at the following times:

- Every 5 to 15 minutes during a work session, depending on the amount of progress you've made

- When you finish a page and before turning to another page

- When you finish placing, sizing, or cropping an image

- Before you change command settings that have a far-reaching effect

Choosing Quit from the File menu also offers the opportunity for you to Save or Abandon changes to the files you have in view (see fig. 3.35).

Fig. 3.35.

Choosing Quit from the File menu.

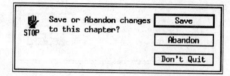

Later in this chapter, you will see how to save copies of all the files in a project by using the Options menu's Multi-Chapter command. Like New and Open Chapter, the Multi-Chapter command also prompts you to save changes to a chapter in view before you can proceed with Multi-Chapter operations.

Here's a summary of Ventura copying and saving procedures:

- To make a copy of an entire project, use the Copy All command, which becomes available once you open the Options menu's MULTI-CHAPTER OPERATIONS dialog box.

- To make a copy of a chapter or style file (without copying the source files), use the Save As and Save As New Style commands from the File menu.

- To save changes to the style file and not the chapter file, choose New or Open Chapter from the File menu and abandon the changes to the chapter.

- To make a copy of a source text file with Ventura, use the Edit menu's File/Type Rename command, as discussed in Chapter 4. You cannot use this command to rename or convert source graphics files.

You need to pay attention to the paths displayed in the ITEM SELECTOR, DOS OPERATIONS, COPY ALL, and FILE TYPE/RENAME dialog boxes. Failure to notice Ventura's path assumptions can cause you to save documents in unintended directories, because once you change the defaults and use the new ones, they prevail until you change them again. See the procedure on "Saving Custom Defaults" if you want to keep a copy of a batch file that initiates custom project defaults each time you start Ventura.

Caution: Always check the Directory option when saving or loading any type of file. Although you establish custom defaults while you use Ventura, the program reverts to the original defaults provided with the program when a Ventura session ends without your executing the Quit command. The defaults are saved in the VP.INF file, but when a VP.INF file is not found, Ventura opens to the UNTITLED chapter with the style file named DEFAULT shown in view. Any custom file defaults are erased, and the initial defaults delivered with Ventura prevail when you restart the program.

Backing Up Files during Production

Ventura offers an option to let you update backup files automatically every time you choose the Save command. To keep backup files of work in progress, choose Yes for the Keep Backup Files option in the Options menu's SET PREFERENCES dialog box. Ventura then creates and updates backup files for the CHP, VGR, and CAP files with each Save. A production backup of this type may help you recover a file that became lost or corrupted because of an operator, system, or disk error during production. If you are keeping production backups on-line for certain projects and not others, change the Keep Backup Files option appropriately as you start working on each project. Ventura maintains only one setting for backups and adheres to the new default each time you change the setting.

You cannot, however, choose where these automatic backups store. Ventura names and files them to the directory chosen for the chapter file. To indicate that the file is a backup file, Ventura replaces the first character in the file extension with a $. When you need to retrieve and use a backup file, you open or load the file just as you would any other file of the same type, but you must change the first letter in the file extension shown in the Directory option to a $. If you want to change the extension for the chapter back to CHP, use Save As and rename the extension. The next time Ventura saves the chapter, it overwrites the old backup files.

You should also make backups of the entire hard disk regularly—every day, week, or month, depending on the activity of your system. Keep the backup disks in a safe place, preferably away from the computer. You create system backups with DOS or other programs that are external to and independent of Ventura's operations. In the section ''Duplicating and Archiving Projects'' you learn how to remove files associated with a project.

Organizing Your Projects

Good file management is an important element in any project, especially if more than one person is involved in the production process. Managing Ventura project files seems somewhat complicated, however, because of the fact that every single project is composed of many files, and some files are shared among many projects. This section shows you how to use Ventura's features to adopt filing schemes that let you share resources between related projects and isolate those projects that are separate. In short, if you adopt a logical file plan for storing files, managing Ventura's files can be relatively easy.

Keeping your projects in order is not the only reason for having a good organizational plan. As you know, Ventura runs only on computers equipped with a hard disk. If you are accustomed to working only on floppy disks, you've probably experienced the problem of running out of space. You can encounter the same situation when working with a hard disk, although much less quickly. Organizing projects helps you manage hard disk space effectively. Adopting practices to help free disk space from completed projects keeps space available for new projects and can help to minimize time spent backing up active projects.

When you use Ventura to produce lengthy documents, you may need to concern yourself also with organizing projects into segments that Ventura can expediently handle. The section called ''Understanding Ventura's Minimums and Maximums'' discusses the file and memory size limitations Ventura imposes when loading lengthy chapter files.

Creating Directories for New Projects

Ventura creates the TYPESET directory during program installation to hold the source, chapter, and style files for the sample publications provided with the program. If you let Ventura's initial defaults prevail, the files Ventura creates for new chapters and styles are automatically saved to the TYPESET directory. Any imported text and graphics files remain in the directories from which they were imported. Although you can use these defaults when you work with a limited number of small projects, if you use Ventura often you should establish a plan for the types of projects you undertake. Your system of organization should be uniquely tailored to the types of publications you produce, but here are a few general guidelines:

- To preserve the contents of the sample files delivered with Ventura, make a directory called VPTRAIN into which you can copy selected chapters (using the Multi-Chapter Copy All command) as samples for experimenting and use.

- Do not plan to load source files from more than one disk in a single floppy drive unless you plan immediately to use File Type/Rename to copy the file to the hard disk. Otherwise, Ventura will save any source file edited during the session to the floppy disk inserted in the drive when you save the chapter file.

- To publish newsletters or other similar periodicals, keep the source text files, style file, and chapter file in a directory for each issue. If you have more than one issue in production at a time, make a directory for each issue. You can use the same directory for all issues when you don't have simultaneous production efforts in progress. Archive to a floppy disk each completed issue and remove the directory if you will not reuse it.

- To publish a book or manual in which one style is shared throughout several chapters, keep the style file and the chapter template in a directory separate from the directories that store the individual chapter and source files for each segment of the publication. If an individual chapter has a custom style, keep the unique style in the directory for that chapter.

- When several publications can share source files (which conserves disk space and expedites updates), keep the shared files in one directory and make a directory to hold each similar group of projects.

For example, if you use Ventura to make forms, brochures, and newsletters for a company, you might make a directory called ARTWORK and then make one directory called FORMS and another called BROCHURE. If a newsletter is produced one issue at a time, call the newsletter directory NEWSLETT.

Subdirectories stem from a directory that begins at the root directory of your system. In the example in the preceding paragraph, if you create the three project directories as subdirectories of ARTWORK, you see only the directory called ARTWORK (along with other root-level directories) when you view the contents of the root directory in the ITEM SELECTOR dialog box. The other three directory names display when you change the Directory option to include the name of the shared directory (see fig. 3.36). Ventura will save and load files to and from any subdirectory on your system so long as the path name to the directory does not exceed 41 characters.

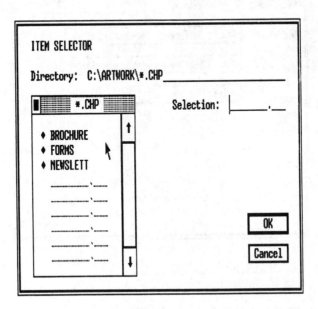

Fig. 3.36.

Accessing a subdirectory with the ITEM SELECTOR *dialog box.*

To make a directory,

1. Click the DOS File Ops command in the File menu to open the DOS FILE OPERATIONS dialog box (see fig. 3.37).

2. Type the drive and name for the new directory in the File Spec option, using DOS syntax. For example, type

   C:\ARTWORK

   to make a directory called ARTWORK under the root directory.

3. Click Make Directory as the Operation option. The command blinks to indicate that action was taken.

4. Click Done to close the dialog box.

If Ventura responds with a message that you cannot make the directory because of limited disk space, you may need to remove other files and directories to free space on the hard disk. Later in this section, you learn to use Ventura to archive and remove projects—important procedures when you depend on a computer equipped with a hard disk.

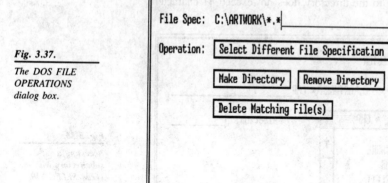

Fig. 3.37.

The DOS FILE OPERATIONS dialog box.

Troubleshooting Tip

When Ventura's DOS File Ops Commands Don't Work

The successful completion of a DOS File Ops command is contingent on two factors: the amount of available disk space, and the contents of the batch file that is automatically executed when you start your computer. The AUTOEXEC.BAT file must include access to DOS commands, which are frequently stored in a separate directory.

To make a subdirectory, type, in the File Spec option of the DOS FILE OPERATIONS dialog box, the name(s) of the directories that precede the directory. For example, to make a project directory called FORMS that is a subdirectory of ARTWORK, type

    C:\ARTWORK\FORMS

in the File Spec option of the dialog box. Then click Make Directory to complete the instruction.

Keeping projects in separate directories is not a requirement, but the method yields several benefits. For one thing, the rosters of files in assignment lists are shorter, allowing you to choose files quickly without scrolling through lengthy lists of files. (The assignment list cannot show more than 100 files.) Keeping projects in separate directories also helps to avoid confusion when different members on the production team need to update or use the files related to the project in progress. Perhaps the most important reason for keeping projects in separate directories is that you can expedite erasing files related to a specific project once the project is complete.

Duplicating and Archiving Projects

Once you make a directory or format a floppy disk, you can save to the directory or disk any style, chapter, or source text file you have in view. You have already seen how to use the Save As and Save As New Style commands to create copies of chapter and style files you intend to use for new projects. And in Chapter 4, you learn how to use the File Type/Rename command to make copies of source documents. When you want to duplicate a project for use on another system, or back up a project's files to floppy disks during or after production (a process commonly referred to as *archiving*), however, you should use the Copy All command from the MULTI-CHAPTER OPER-ATIONS dialog box to create copies of all the files Ventura uses to assemble the project in view.

Archiving a completed project can help reserve for current projects hard disk space that you need to keep on the computer. Because the width table and all the source files copy to the designated disk and directories, the backup file on disk is frozen in time. Even though you may later remove shared source files from the hard disk or add printers or fonts that change your configuration, you will still be able to print the chapter as it appeared when archived.

As a chapter loads into the work area, several messages display that relay the path and file names of the source files and the files Ventura uses to control the appearance of text on the page. After loading a chapter, you can see a list of some of the file names and locations associated with that project by opening the Options menu, choosing Multi-Chapter to open the MULTI-CHAPTER OPERATIONS dialog box, and clicking the Open command (see fig. 3.38).

The names and locations for the VGR, CIF, CAP, and WID files do not display in the list shown in the MULTI-CHAPTER OPERATIONS dialog box. The VGR, CIF, and CAP files have the same name as the chapter and reside in the same directory named in the title line of the publisher's window. The location and name of the width table in use is shown as the Width Table option in the SET PRINTER INFO dialog box opened from the Options menu.

Caution: Do not use DOS commands to move or duplicate publications unless you understand thoroughly how Ventura uses the files needed to assemble a publication (see table 3.5).

Efficiency Tip

Changing the Pointer in a Chapter File

You can edit chapter files with a word processor but only with extreme caution. To change the paths or names of files used in the project, you can use a word processor to edit the chapter file and correct the drive, directory, or file name locations shown at the top of the file. When editing, never remove the space at the end of each line, and be certain to save the file as an unformatted ASCII file.

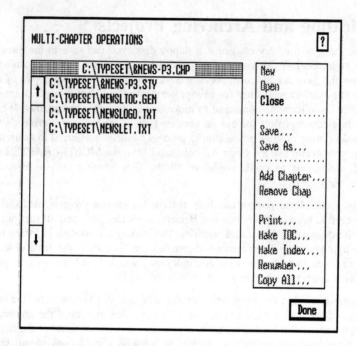

Fig. 3.38.

Listing a chapter's files with the MULTI-CHAPTER OPERATIONS dialog box.

You can use the Copy All command to move a project from one location to another, whether the location is on a different computer or just a different directory on the system where the chapter was created. When you use the Copy All command, Ventura finds and relocates all the files that are needed to assemble the chapter, or a set of chapters whose names are listed in a publication file. All the files listed in table 3.5 and each of the text and graphics source files you load to each chapter are copied. To copy all the files associated with a chapter to a single directory on the hard disk or to a floppy disk, follow these steps:

1. Open the chapter you want to copy into the work area, using the File menu's Open Chapter command.

2. Choose the Multi-Chapter command from the Options menu. If you made any changes, Ventura prompts you to save the changes to the files in view before you can proceed.

3. Choose the Copy All command from the list of commands shown in the MULTI-CHAPTER OPERATIONS dialog box.

4. Type the drive and directory names in the first DESTINATION option, which designates your preferred destination for the project's files (see fig. 3.39). The final backslash is required. Be careful not to make a "typo" in the directory name or Ventura will create a new directory and copy files into it.

5. If each destination will be the same as the first, click Make All Directories the Same As the First. Ventura then duplicates the destination for each type of file.

6. Click OK to begin the copy process. (The COPY ALL dialog box does not respond when you press Enter as OK.)

7. After the copy process is completed, click Done to close the MULTI-CHAPTER OPERATIONS dialog box.

```
┌─────────────────────────────────────────────────────┐
│ COPY ALL                                             │
│                                                      │
│                  SOURCE (from this file)             │
│                                                      │
│      PUB or CHP:  C:\1511\JULY\JULY.CHP_____  │
│                                                      │
│                                                      │
│                DESTINATION (to these directories)    │
│                                                      │
│        PUB & CHPs:  B:\JULY_____  │
│        STYs & WIDs: B:\JULY_____  │
│         Text Files: B:\JULY_____  │
│      Graphic Files: B:\JULY_____  │
│        Image Files: A:\ARTWORK|_____  │
│                                                      │
│           Command: [ Make All Directories the Same As the First ] │
│                                                      │
│                              [   OK   ]  [ Cancel ]  │
└─────────────────────────────────────────────────────┘
```

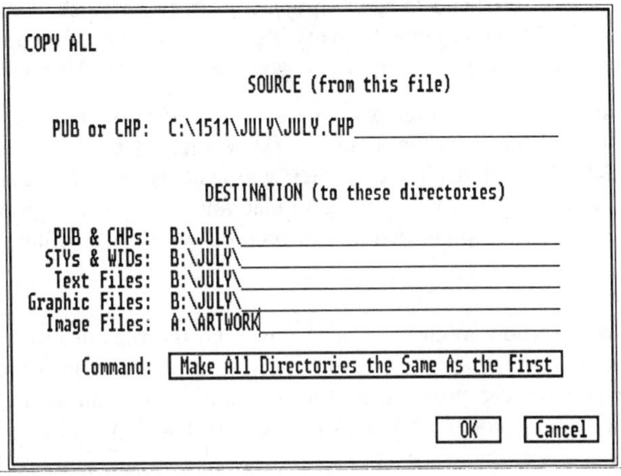

Fig. 3.39.

Duplicating a project with the COPY ALL dialog box.

Ventura makes a directory on the target disk if you include a directory name in the DESTINATION option. After Ventura builds an archive list of the files, the copying process begins. If additional disks are needed to hold the files, Ventura asks whether you intend to continue the archiving process. Insert another disk to store the files each time Ventura prompts you to do so, and click Continue. Ventura also gives you the choice of canceling the archive process at that point. When you cancel an archive process after the program has copied some files to disk, Ventura does not remove or erase from the disk the files that have already been copied.

If you copy files to disks that contain files with the same names as those you're copying, Ventura prompts you to choose whether to Overwrite or Keep Old versions on disk or cancel the archive process.

Once a copy process completes, click Done to close the MULTI-CHAPTER OPERATIONS dialog box. Notice that the chapter shown in the work area is the one with which you began, not the copy you just prepared. To work on the copy, use the File menu's Open Chapter command, changing the Directory option to access the new files.

You follow steps 1–7 in this section to copy a chapter from the floppy to the hard disk. In Chapter 4 you learn how to use the Multi-Chapter command to assemble a collection of chapter files into a publication. Remember to begin the process with the File menu's Open Chapter command and to use the COPY ALL dialog box to make a directory for the project you are loading to the hard disk.

Reducing the Space Required for Projects Loaded from Archives

Ventura writes the width table file to disk every time you use the Copy All command. The width table is often the largest file in any archive set of files. Although having a copy of the table used to produce a project is essential when you reload the chapter, if you use the Copy All command to move projects from floppy disk to hard disk, you end up with a copy of a width table on every archive disk. (Ventura copies style files and width tables to the same directory when you use the Copy All command.)

If you keep in the VENTURA directory a master copy of all width tables in use, you can delete the width table from the archive disk. Ventura defaults to find the named width table in the VENTURA directory when you load the archived chapter file into the work area. When deleting files, make sure that you specify the appropriate file and location in the File Spec option before you proceed with the deletion process.

See Chapter 8 to learn how to create a print file of all the files needed to assemble a chapter. A print file, which is a composite copy of all the files in a project, can be quite large. Because you can print a print file by using DOS commands, you can print a Ventura project from a computer that is not equipped with Ventura.

Removing Files and Directories

Once a project is complete and you have created an archive set of floppy disks, you can free hard disk space by removing the files for that project. Ventura does not provide any automatic procedure for deleting all the files associated with a project. But when you have used a file-naming convention that includes starting all a project's files with the same numbers or letters, you can use DOS wild cards to devise a File Spec for the DOS FILE OPERATIONS dialog box. (See the discussion of DOS wild cards in this chapter's section "Loading Chapter, Style, and Source Files.") When you then click Delete Matching File(s) in the DOS FILE OPERATIONS dialog box, Ventura asks whether you intend to delete all the matching files found (refer to fig. 3.37). Make certain that you are deleting files from the proper directory before you choose the option to proceed, because this operation erases all the files that match the filter shown in the File Spec option.

The Delete Matching File(s) option deletes from only one directory at a time. If you want to delete files stored in separate directories, you must complete the File Spec option for each directory and choose Delete Matching File(s) each time.

You cannot remove a directory until the directory is empty. Once you have erased all the files from a directory, you can remove the directory by typing the name of the drive and directory in the File Spec option and then clicking Remove Directory. After the command blinks, click Done to close the dialog box and resume operations.

The operations to delete matching files and remove directories perform only when the named files and directories do exist and when the files are not write-protected.

Understanding Ventura's Maximums and Minimums

Although you can organize chapters into publications spanning several hundred pages, Ventura's limits can restrict the size and complexity of your publications.

Paragraph length in Ventura 2.0 and the Professional Extension is limited to 8,000 characters, or approximately 1,600 words typed on 8 pages. If you need to overcome this maximum, see Chapter 5 to learn how to use the Breaks command from the Paragraph menu to make paragraphs print adjacent to one another. When you are using line endings rather than paragraph endings (as explained in Chapter 4) to publish lists or tabular material, remember to insert at least one paragraph return every few pages or so, to prevent exceeding the 8,000-characters-per-paragraph limit.

In a 640K system with Ventura 2.0, a chapter can contain up to 48,000 paragraphs (representing as much as 500K of text) depending on the version of DOS you are running, the type of screen driver (EGA color drivers reduce the amount of text), the size of the width table, and the number of tags in your text. When you count tags, remember to count the tags Ventura generates along with the tags you add and any tags you may have in the source files, that are not defined in the style file. With the Professional Extension, you can have more paragraphs per chapter when you include EMS memory in your system configuration.

Because Ventura uses hard disk space when you are working on projects, you must have enough room on the hard disk for Ventura to access. Make it a habit to always leave at least 2M of disk space open, to prevent running out of space when you are working on a project.

The lists in the Item Selectors cannot display the names of more than 100 files at a time. The computer will beep to indicate when more than 100 files meet the criteria you have typed in the Directory option. If you hear a beep and the file names you want to use don't display, change Directory to match more specifically the names of the files you need to find.

Several other types of maximums are evident when you open a dialog box that only reports information. Ventura's Desk menu has a well-concealed command that opens the VENTURA PUBLISHER DIAGNOSTICS dialog box. When you open the Desk menu, click the mouse on the word Ventura in the left-hand box on the page. The settings shown in the dialog box (see fig 3.40) change to reflect the current status of your system.

The first set of statistics in the dialog box define how Ventura allocates the memory in your system for processing text, paragraphs, and line elements. The first three settings display numbers that are unique to your configuration. Text Memory in Use, Paragraphs in Use, and Line Elements in Use indicate how much space is used by the chapter you have in view.

The line element count is not the same as the number of lines of text, however, because one line of text can represent several types of elements. For example, each tab counts as two elements, and each attribute change (such as bold or italic) counts as

```
VENTURA PUBLISHER DIAGNOSTICS

Internal Memory in Use:      4109 /    25000 bytes
External Memory in Use:     54536 /    94152
    EMS Memory in Use:      98304 /   278528
   Text Memory in Use:      28016 /    36832
    Paragraphs in Use:       415 /     1024 paras
  Line Elements in Use:      945 /     1533 elements


 Ext. Mem. Swapped Out:         0
Text Mem. Swapped Out:         0


      Width Table Size:     4557 bytes
   Graphics Buffer Size:    48000
      Screen Fonts Size:    68000
      Hyphenation Size:     10244
     Perm. Strings Size:    10057
   FARCODE Overlay Size:    61776

                                          OK
```

Fig. 3.40.

The VENTURA
PUBLISHER
DIAGNOSTICS
dialog box.

three line elements. A change in font between paragraphs is one element, but each line of text is counted as two. One line with two tabs in a directory, then, might count as six line elements. The maximum number of lines of text in one frame is actually 362 lines if you do not have a tab, an attribute, or a change of font within those lines of text. Exceeding the number of line elements per frame causes Ventura to display a Frame Too Complex message before you can continue working. If you frequently must exceed the number of line elements per frame, consider upgrading to the Professional Extension and adding additional internal memory to your system configuration.

The second set of statistics in the dialog box reports how external memory is being used. As you open different chapters into view, the statistics change to reflect the current load.

In the last group of statistics, you can cause two settings to change. Width Table Size reports the amount of space used by the printer width table you are using. You can make printer width tables smaller or larger by removing or adding printer fonts. Small width tables leave more space available for other publishing tasks. In Chapter 8 you learn how to create width tables that contain only the fonts you need to use. In addition, Hyphenation Size changes when you use Ventura's alternative hyphenation algorithms. In Chapter 5, you learn more about using the draft and final versions (for English) that are delivered with the program.

Ventura also has three important minimums. It takes more than one file to complete any project, as you have seen throughout Chapter 3. Each printer width table must include at least one font, and you should never remove all Ventura's screen fonts. (Adding and removing printer and screen fonts are covered in Chapters 8 and 9.)

Consult in Chapter 2 the table that compares the different features and maximum file sizes for Ventura Publisher and the Professional Extension. In general, if you frequently publish long documents, you may want to consider adding memory and upgrading to the Professional Extension to expedite document processing.

Chapter Summary

The best way to learn Ventura is to use it. This chapter provides an overview of the program so that you can do just that. Initially, you will probably start Ventura simply to explore the program. The sections of this chapter that describe the publisher's window and its tools will be helpful at that stage. When you begin to make full use of Ventura for your publishing tasks and find yourself working on more than one project at a time, you will want to use some of the commands described in this chapter to set up project directories and save text and graphics source files. In Chapter 4, you will learn much more about typing and editing text with Ventura.

Loading, Typing, and Generating Text

In most projects, you begin a publication with word processing. Although most page-composition programs allow you to import text from word processing programs, Ventura offers several unique benefits:

- You can read and write files to many file formats and can combine several files into one file.

- You can automatically update source files with the production edits made during page composition.

- You can tag text for page composition and formatting and can insert anchors to tie illustrations and footnotes to text.

- You can create a table of contents and an index for source files assembled in a chapter.

- You can print spot-color separations as camera-ready artwork for mass production by an offset printer.

- You can rotate text in increments of 90 degrees or print outlined letters if you have a PostScript printer.

In text-based publishing projects, Ventura's capability to handle picture placement, fractions, and folio and footnote text expedites technical document production. Methods to import these types of text from word processing files are introduced in this chapter; Chapter 7 explains how to incorporate the elements into the design of a publication. This chapter also discusses how to use Ventura to create and update tables of contents and indexes as page numbers change during the production stages.

Ventura's page-composition features also enable you to design and write copy for ads, forms, or presentation materials directly in Ventura. The WYSIWYG display, although slower than the display for some word processing programs, lets you see immediately how the page elements look in combination. You can make changes to the copy, adjust font sizes, or rearrange the various page elements until you arrive at a desirable balance. In short, depending on the type of projects you undertake, you may find that you routinely use Ventura to design ad and form layouts as you write copy, without first preparing source text files with a word processing program.

103

In this chapter, you learn how to use Ventura to type and edit text on a page, and you learn when to use your word processor to prepare text for Ventura. The steps preceding the placement of text into Ventura—such as setting up pages, columns, and framed areas—are presented in Chapter 3. In Chapter 5, you learn to format paragraphs of text with paragraph tags and format phrases in paragraphs with attribute settings. If you have never used Ventura, read both this chapter and the next. After you see what you can do with Ventura and know the capabilities of your word processor, you can decide how to make the best use of your time in a publishing project.

You have five ways to include text in a Ventura publication:

- Type text using Ventura's text tool, creating new source files as you type

- Import source text typed in other programs, using the Load Text/Picture command

- Cut or load text to the Clipboard to paste into place

- Type caption, folio, and constant text in Ventura's dialog boxes

- Generate files of text by using Ventura's Make TOC and Make Index commands

Most text printed in a publication is imported to Ventura from a word processing program rather than typed directly in Ventura. Word processing programs offer features that Ventura lacks, like spell checkers, macros, and search-and-replace functions. Database and spreadsheet programs serve purposes distinct from those of Ventura; yet files created by these programs may also be used as source files for publications. Ventura lets you edit imported files or create new files as you need them. In the next section, you see how the text tool operates as an input and editing device on all the types of text in a publication. The use of the text tool for formatting is described in Chapter 5.

Typing and Editing Text in Ventura

Every time you start Ventura, the publisher's window opens to the first page (known as the base page) in an untitled chapter. To type text on a Ventura page, choose the Text function icon (the third from the left at the top of the sidebar). Then move the cursor into the work area. Notice that the pointer changes to resemble an I-beam.

After you click the I-beam on the first page of an untitled chapter, the text edit cursor, which looks like a vertical line, appears in front of an end-of-file marker at the top of the page (see fig. 4.1). Now you may begin typing. Ventura automatically names a document file with the same name assigned to the chapter when you select Save or Save As from the File menu. The document extension for the file name corresponds to the file format default in the current settings in the LOAD TEXT/PICTURE dialog box.

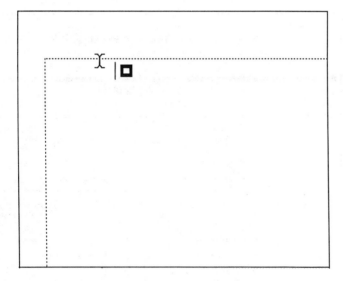

Fig. 4.1.

The Text function I-beam, Text edit cursor, and end-of-file marker.

Look for the End-of-File Marker

To see the end-of file marker, activate the Show Tabs & Returns command on the Options menu. Then when you place the edit cursor next to an end-of file marker, the current selection box displays END OF FILE.

The active style file named in the title line of the window sets the base page design and establishes the typographic qualities of the text typed as body text. Each style file can have different default settings for body text, but you may find that using Ventura's default style file is useful when you want to start a new document to meet custom specifications. The settings for body text in Ventura's default style file are shown in figure 4.2.

Once you begin to build a chapter in Ventura (or when you open a previously stored chapter), *where* you click the I-beam to position the edit cursor determines how Ventura responds. You can click the I-beam to respond in one of four ways:

- If you click the I-beam within text, the edit cursor displays at the position of the click and is ready for you to make changes (see fig. 4.3). As you type, changes take on the format of the surrounding text.

- If you click the I-beam on a page that you added using the Insert/Remove Page command, the edit cursor does not display immediately. Instead, an inquiry box prompts you to cancel the request or click New File to continue. If you select New File, you are then given the opportunity to name the new file and select a file format (see fig. 4.4).

Fig. 4.2.

Body Text defined by the default style file.

C:\TYPESET\DEFAULT.STY

Tag Settings

Body Text

■ Font	Face:	Times
	Size:	12 points
	Style:	Normal
	Color:	Black
	Overscore:	Off
	Strike-Thru:	Off
	Underline:	Off
	Double Underline:	Off
■ Alignment	Horz. Alignment:	Justified
	Vert. Alignment:	Top
	Text Rotation:	None
	Hyphenation:	USENGLSH
	Successive Hyphens:	2
	Overall Width:	Column-Wide
	First Line:	Indent
	Relative Indent:	Off
	In/Outdent Width:	00.00 inches
	In/Outdent Height:	1
	In From Right to Decimal:	00.00 inches
■ Spacing	Above:	13.98 fractional pts
	Below:	13.98 fractional pts
	Inter-Line:	13.98 fractional pts
	Inter-Paragraph:	00.00 fractional pts
	Add in Above:	When Not at Column Top
	In From Left (Left Page):	00,00 picas & points
	In From Right (Left Page):	00,00 picas & points
	In From Left (Right Page):	00,00 picas & points
	In From Right (Right Page):	00,00 picas & points
■ Breaks	Page Break:	No
	Column Break:	No
	Line Break:	Before
	Next Y Position:	Normal
	Allow Within:	Yes
	Keep With Next:	No

■ Tab Settings	Leader Char:	46
	Leader Spacing:	2
	Auto-Leader:	Off
■ Special Effects	Special Effect:	None
■ Attribute Overrides	Line Width:	Text-Wide
	Overscore Height:	0.009/0.139 inches
	Strike-Thru Height:	0.009/0.052 inches
	Underline 1 Height:	0.009/0.014 inches
	Underline 2 Height:	0.009/0.035 inches
	Superscript Size:	10 points/0.078 inches
	Subscript Size:	10 points/0.018 inches
	Small Cap Size:	10 points
■ Paragraph Typograpy	Automatic Pair Kerning:	Off
	Grow Inter-Line To Fit:	On
	Letter Spacing:	0.100 Ems
	Tracking:	0.000 Ems Looser
	Minimum Space Width:	0.600
	Normal Space Width:	1.000
	Maximum Space Width:	2.000
	Vert. Just. At Top of Para:	0.194 inches
	At Bottom of Para:	0.194 inches
	Between Lines of Para:	0.000 inches
■ Ruling Line Above	Width:	None
■ Ruling Line Below	Width:	None
■ Ruling Box Around	Width:	None

Tab Settings

■ Body Text

Tab Number 1:	Left, 00.50, 32		Tab Number 9:	Left, 04.50, 32
Tab Number 2:	Left, 01.00, 32		Tab Number 10:	Left, 05.00, 32
Tab Number 3:	Left, 01.50, 32		Tab Number 11:	Left, 05.50, 32
Tab Number 4:	Left, 02.00, 32		Tab Number 12:	Left, 06.00, 32
Tab Number 5:	Left, 02.50, 32		Tab Number 13:	Left, 06.50, 32
Tab Number 6:	Left, 03.00, 32		Tab Number 14:	Left, 07.00, 32
Tab Number 7:	Left, 03.50, 32		Tab Number 15:	Left, 07.50, 32
Tab Number 8:	Left, 04.00, 32		Tab Number 16:	Left, 08.00, 32

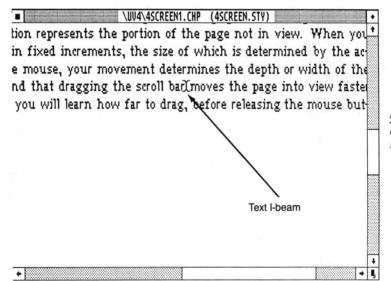

Fig. 4.3.

Click the I-beam to select the edit point.

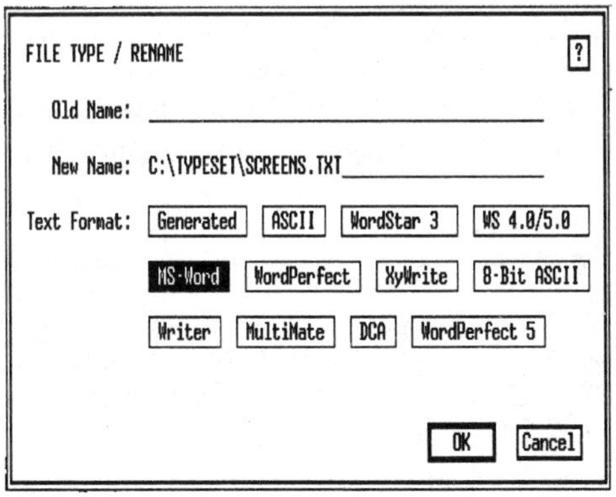

Fig. 4.4.

The FILE TYPE/ RENAME dialog box.

- If you click the I-beam within a blank frame or graphic box drawn on the page, the edit cursor displays at the upper left margin of that area, ready for you to type text (see fig. 4.5). When you type in one of these defined areas within a chapter, the text is stored in an ASCII file. Ventura automatically names this file with the same name as the chapter and adds the extension CAP. You can convert text stored in frames into individual documents with specific word processing formats. (You cannot convert text entered in graphic boxes.) This procedure is discussed in ''Converting Documents to Different File Formats,'' in this chapter.

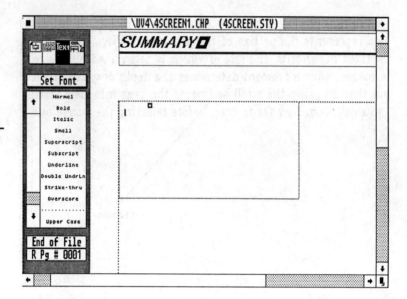

Fig. 4.5.

The edit cursor in a blank frame.

• If you position the cursor and click on text that was stored by one of Ventura's dialog boxes, you see a message indicating that you cannot directly edit this text (see fig. 4.6). Editing this type of text is discussed in "Typing and Editing Text in Generated Tags," in this chapter.

Fig. 4.6.

The generated tag message.

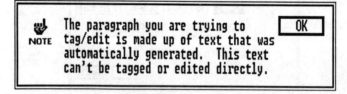

Most of the time, to edit text displayed on the page, first choose the Text function. Then move the text I-beam into the work area and click to select the edit point. When the edit cursor displays, you are ready to edit text. Remember that text from generated tags can be edited only by opening the dialog box where that text was stored.

Once you set or use the edit cursor in a frame, you can move the mouse and click to select the Frame function and see the name of the text file just edited. Check the current selection box at the bottom of the sidebar. Frame handles automatically display around the perimeter of the named frame (see fig. 4.7).

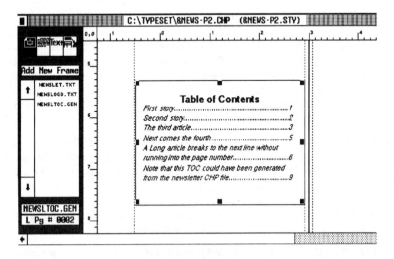

Fig. 4.7.

The current selection box showing the name of the document stored in the selected frame.

To reposition the edit cursor in a frame, use the arrow keys to move the cursor within the boundaries of the frame where you clicked the Text I-beam. To move to another frame, move the mouse cursor into the desired frame and then click the I-beam to activate the edit cursor in the new frame.

When FRAME TEXT displays as the current selection, the contents are saved to the CAP file for that chapter. Text typed in graphic boxes is edited in the same way as framed text and is also saved to the CAP file for that chapter. The current selection box does not display BOX TEXT as the selection until the box is selected with the Graphic selection tool. You will learn more about the use of the box text tool in Chapter 6, when you learn to use the alternative graphic grids Ventura provides to help align elements at regular intervals on the page.

Efficiency Tip

Choosing an Edit Position Quickly

Instead of using the scroll bars to view text on a different part of the page, you can position the edit cursor in Reduced view and press Ctrl-N to display that edit position in Normal view. Then use the arrow keys to position the cursor more precisely. This zoom technique works only when you leave the I-beam and edit cursor positioned at the edit point and use the keyboard shortcuts (Ctrl-N or Ctrl-E) to change views.

Text edits made to the documents within a chapter are saved to disk when you save the chapter file. Make a habit of saving the chapter file by pressing Ctrl-S as soon as you are satisfied with a series of edits.

Creating New Document Files with Ventura

The best way for you to create long documents is with a compatible word processing program. However, Ventura does offer a way for you to create documents that you can later edit with a word processor.

Typing Text on a Blank Page

The file you begin is automatically named when you click the edit cursor on a blank base page. The file is named immediately but is saved to disk only when the chapter file is saved with the Save command on the File menu. Ventura automatically names and saves a file created this way, using the text format option that was last used. The default format is ASCII, but you change the default when you load a source text file from a compatible word processor.

For example, if the chapter file name is INVITE and a Microsoft Word file was the last file loaded with the Load Text/Picture command, the source document file created with Ventura is named INVITE.DOC (Word files have the extension DOC). The source document name displays in the assignment list and in the current selection box when you select the page as the active frame. You can change the file name and format, if necessary, using the FILE TYPE/RENAME dialog box explained in "Converting Documents to Different File Formats," in this chapter.

When you add a page after the base page by using Insert/Remove Page and click the Text function I-beam to begin typing, Ventura responds with a NEW FILE inquiry box. Click New File. The FILE TYPE/RENAME dialog box opens, and you can name the file and select the file format. You can press Esc to clear the entry provided by Ventura, use the backspace key to erase characters, or the left- and right-arrow keys to position the edit cursor. Once you complete the file name, select the format and click OK to accept the new settings. If you don't want to name a new file, you can click Cancel in the FILE TYPE/RENAME dialog box and return to the current page.

After you close the FILE TYPE/RENAME dialog box by clicking OK, the edit cursor in the work area blinks at the left margin. The small hollow-square end-of-file marker appears immediately after the cursor.

The end-of-file marker is only one of many special symbols that are displayed in the work area. When you edit text, you should display all the symbols in the work area to

Efficiency Tip

Displaying Format Symbols When Editing Text

Use the Show/Hide Tabs & Returns command on the Options menu to display or hide the different symbols indicating where special types of characters are embedded in the text.

Think of this command as a question: "Show Tabs & Returns?" Adding the question mark makes it apparent that the symbols are hidden when the command says *Show* and displayed when the command says *Hide*. Show the symbols when editing text to avoid inadvertently deleting them with the backspace key.

avoid inadvertently deleting instructions embedded in text. Table 4.1 shows the symbols in the work area for each embedded instruction Ventura uses. If you do not see the symbols shown in table 4.1, choose Show Tabs & Returns from the Options menu to display the symbols. When you review page composition or the content of text, you may prefer a less cluttered, more WYSIWYG view, so you can select Hide Tabs & Returns from the Options menu. To help you avoid inadvertently deleting a special instruction, the current selection box always shows you the name of each instruction found in the text.

Table 4.1
The Show Tabs and Returns symbols

Symbol	Purpose	\<Code\>	Keyboard and Menu Command
→	Tab	9	Tab
▪	Discretionary hyphen	-	Ctrl-hyphen
␣	Nonbreaking space	N	Ctrl-space bar
	Thin space	|	Ctrl-Shift-T
	Em space	_	Ctrl-Shift-M
	En space (1/2 em)	˜	Ctrl-Shift-N
	Figure space (1/4 em)	+	Ctrl-Shift-F
↵	Line break	R	Ctrl-Enter
¶	Paragraph	no code	Enter
□	End-of-file marker	no code	no code
	Footnote and frame anchors, index markers	$code	Edit menu Ins Special Character

As you add text to files placed on the pages of a chapter (either by typing or by using the Clipboard as described later in this chapter), Ventura automatically adds pages to the chapter to hold the text you are adding. If you add another page with the Insert/ Remove Page command and type text on the inserted page, you are starting a new file to include in the chapter.

Typing Text in an Empty Frame

If you click the I-beam in an empty frame and type text, Ventura automatically stores the text in a file with the chapter name plus the extension CAP. The CAP file, which is explained in Chapter 3, holds all the text you type in empty frames, caption frames, and in boxes drawn with the Graphic box text tool. (The CAP file does not hold the text you type in CAPTION dialog boxes—that text is stored in the CHP file.) When you select a frame that contains text stored in the CAP file, Ventura displays FRAME TEXT as the frame name in the current selection box of the sidebar (see fig. 4.8).

Fig. 4.8.

FRAME TEXT *in the current selection box.*

You will learn more about the kinds of text stored in the caption (CAP) file as you read through this chapter and Chapters 6 and 7. You can use your word processor to edit CAP files and use spelling programs on them to check for misspellings. The text entries accumulate in the file in the sequence in which they are made. When you access a CAP file with another program, be careful not to remove any of the return symbols in the file and be sure to save the file as an ASCII file. You can use Ventura to convert framed text from a CAP file to a word processing format and then reload the file. This procedure is described in "Converting Documents to Different File Formats," in this chapter.

Adding Text to a Document File

When you want to add text to a document file, you must first place the document on the page or in a frame before you can edit the text. If you type text into an empty frame and then try to place a document file into the same frame, Ventura warns you that your actions will cause the caption text for the current frame to be overwritten (see fig. 4.9).

Fig. 4.9.

Warning before overwriting a caption frame.

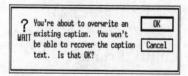

If you click OK when you see this warning message, the CAP file for the active frame is overwritten with the text imported to the frame. You can recover the overwritten text only by using the Abandon command from the File menu to reload the last saved version of the files into memory.

As you might expect, typing text into a blank frame is occasionally desirable. In cases where you have only a few words on the page, you may find it expedient to start a new project directly in Ventura. In general, however, the better policy is to load document files into frames and avoid cluttering caption files with lengthy text segments. As you learn in Chapter 5, you can frame headlines with rules without placing the text in separate frames.

Editing Text

As discussed in Chapter 1, you can edit text better using the features of a word processor than using the features of a WYSIWYG program. Although this statement is true, Ventura offers some editing features that your word processor may not:

- You can move text files between different word processors.

- You can insert reference points for footnotes, illustrations, figures, tables, captions, and index items.

- You can reference the current page or chapter number anywhere on the page.

- You can label illustrations.

- You can view on-screen a close representation of what will print on paper.

You still will want to use your word processor and spelling programs to prepare long source files before publication.

Once you position the Text edit cursor within text on a page, you can begin to edit the text. Type to insert new characters; use the backspace key to erase characters. You can use the arrow keys to reposition the cursor within the frame or reposition the mouse cursor to move the I-beam from one frame to another (see fig. 4.10). The editorial changes made are saved to the source files when you save the chapter.

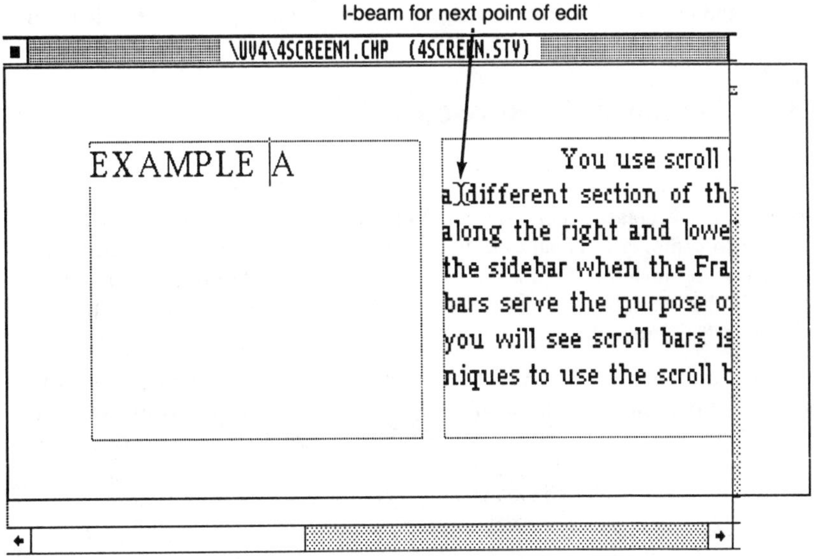

I-beam for next point of edit

\UV4\4SCREEN1.CHP   (4SCREEN.STY)

EXAMPLE A

You use scroll
a different section of th
along the right and lowe
the sidebar when the Fra
bars serve the purpose o
you will see scroll bars is
niques to use the scroll t

Fig. 4.10.

Moving the cursor from frame to frame.

You can use Ventura's editing tools to rearrange sections of text. Suppose that you want to move words from the end to the beginning of a sentence. The procedure is to select the words, remove the words, then reinsert the words.

To select the words, click the I-beam to mark the beginning of the phrase. Then position the mouse cursor at the other end of the phrase and hold the Shift key while you click the mouse button. The selected characters are displayed in reverse video. You can change the length of the selected text by repositioning the cursor and then holding the Shift key while clicking the mouse button (see fig. 4.11).

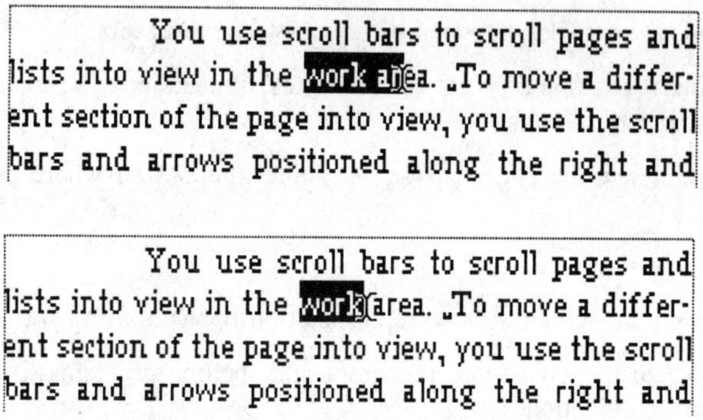

Fig. 4.11.

Selecting text to cut, move, or change length.

> You use scroll bars to scroll pages and lists into view in the work area. To move a different section of the page into view, you use the scroll bars and arrows positioned along the right and

> You use scroll bars to scroll pages and lists into view in the work area. To move a different section of the page into view, you use the scroll bars and arrows positioned along the right and

Dragging the mouse is the alternative way to select text. Position the text I-beam, click, and then press and hold the mouse button while you drag the mouse to the end of the desired text (again see fig. 4.11). The selected characters are displayed in reverse video. You can change the selection by repositioning the mouse and holding the Shift key while you click. You also can select text backwards—that is, go to the end point first and click; then move the I-beam to the beginning of the selection and click.

Using the Clipboard To Revise Text

Ventura provides a Clipboard feature that you can use to move text from one place to another. The contents of the Clipboard can be moved into different chapters, but the Clipboard contents are erased when you quit Ventura. If you have separate disk files you would like to combine to create a source document, you can use the File menu's Load Text/Picture command to load a file directly to the Clipboard (discussed later in this chapter). In this section you learn to use the edit cursor to cut and paste text on the page through the Clipboard.

After you select a portion of text, you can use the cut, copy, and paste features to move the words from one place to another. The maximum amount of text you can

[I]

select or move is the amount you can see on one page when you are working in Reduced view. You save this text to the Clipboard by using the Cut or Copy command on the Edit menu (see fig. 4.12). Then you use the Paste command to retrieve text from the Clipboard. In order for this command to be available, the Text function must be active and the edit cursor must be positioned at an edit point. You can store only one selection of text at a time on the Clipboard.

Suppose that you start with the page shown in figure 4.13. You want to copy a section of text to the Clipboard and then paste that text onto a page in the same chapter. Follow these steps:

1. Select the text to be copied (see fig. 4.13).

2. Choose the Copy command from the Edit menu (again see fig. 4.12). Ventura copies the selected text to the Clipboard.

Fig. 4.12.

The Edit menu with active commands to cut and copy text.

3. Open the GO TO PAGE dialog box from the Chapter menu (see fig. 4.14). The Relative to: File option indicates that the last edit point was in a frame placed on the page. Relative to: Document is displayed if the edit point was in text placed on the page. Change the Which Page option to Selected so that you can type the Selected Page number. You also can choose to set Which Page as First, Previous, Next, or Last.

4. Position the edit cursor at the point to edit.

5. Choose the Paste command from the Edit menu.

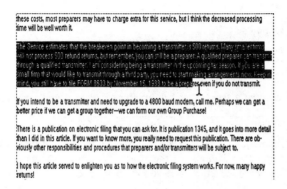

Fig. 4.13.

Selecting text to copy.

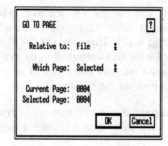

Fig. 4.14.

Turning to a selected page.

Efficiency Tip ──

Using Shortcuts To Cut, Copy, and Paste Text

To rearrange segments of text, use the following procedure:

1. Select text using either method described in the preceding section.

2. Press Del to cut or erase the selection or Shift-Del to copy the selection.

3. Open the GO TO PAGE dialog box with Ctrl-G; then select the options you need to use to turn to the edit point.

4. Reposition the I-beam at the edit point and click.

5. Press the Ins key to paste the text into the spot marked by the edit cursor.

Efficiency Tip ──

Using the Clipboard

The Clipboard can carry as much text as can be selected from a page in view. All text is erased from the Clipboard (memory) when you quit Ventura.

To load files of text to the Clipboard, use the File menu Load Text/Picture command, and set the Destination option to Text Clipboard. Source files loaded to the Clipboard overwrite text selections cut or copied there.

The Clipboard can carry three selected items at a time:

- One selection of text
- One set of graphics
- One set of frames

The Clipboard cannot carry dialog box text (generated tags).

The Clipboard can carry a frame that has graphics tied to it and text stored in it.

You can put text, graphics, or entire frames in the Clipboard and then open a Ventura chapter to paste the selected items on the page. You can pick and mix frames and graphics in one Clipboard selection, but you cannot make more than one selection of text at a time. Graphics selections are discussed in Chapter 6; in Chapter 7, you see how to take full advantage of the Edit menu's Cut, Copy, and Paste commands.

Typing and Editing Text in Generated Tags

In Ventura, the term *generated tags* is used to describe text stored in dialog boxes. The features designed to help you create folios, page headers and footers, footnotes, and picture captions are all known as generated tags. When you use Ventura's features to create these types of text, you use commands from the Chapter, Frame, and Edit menus to open dialog boxes and store reference points in the text.

The text elements you type in a header, footer, or caption frame created by using the Chapter menu commands are all examples of generated text. Generated text is displayed in a frame at the position where the text will print on the page. When you click on the text with the I-beam, a message is displayed indicating that you cannot edit that text directly.

To know which dialog box stored the generated text, you need to know the frame type. To determine the type of frame, choose the Frame function and click within the frame to check the current selection box. In Chapter 7, you learn how to use the Headers & Footers and Anchors & Captions commands on the Chapter menu.

To edit header text, select the Headers & Footers command from the Chapter menu. When you use this feature to set headers or footers in a chapter, you can place text at three column positions on two lines at the top and bottom of a page (see fig. 4.15). You can insert chapter, page, and text attribute codes on the lines designated to hold text for the Left, Right, and Center positions.

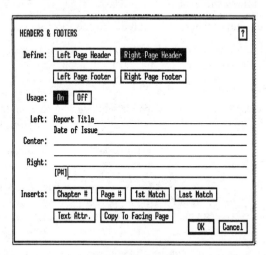

Fig. 4.15.

The HEADERS & FOOTERS dialog box.

Illustration captions are another type of text that can be stored in dialog boxes. With illustration captions, you can take advantage of Ventura's automatic numbering features. Captions that are longer than the length of the line provided in the dialog box can be typed into the caption frame on the page. You position the edit cursor before the end-of-file marker and type. You can resize the frame with the frame cursor if you want to enlarge the size of the caption frame. (Using the mouse to resize a frame is covered in Chapter 3.)

Text typed directly in the caption frame is stored in the CAP file for the chapter. For this reason, if you click the cursor to edit text in a caption frame, you can directly edit any text entered into the frame. Remember to return to the dialog box to edit text stored there. You cannot import captions for illustrations in a source text file. You can, however, use Ventura to start the caption and then extend the length of the caption, using word processing software.

You can set an anchor to tie illustrations to a specific point in text, as described in "Importing Formatted Text," in this chapter. Inserting anchor reference points with your word processor can greatly speed the page production process if your publications often include drawings and photographs. Chapter 7 discusses how to handle figure or table captions at the page-layout stages of production.

Typing and Editing Footnotes

Ventura's footnote feature enables you to mark reference spots in text and then store up to one-half page of text (per page) for footnotes. You number footnotes and set the style for the chapter, as described in "Setting Up Footnotes," in this chapter. The footnote features, however, work only with text placed on the page (not in a frame placed on the page), and footnotes print on the page on which they are referenced. Before you can see footnotes, you must select Footnote Settings from the Chapter menu and click any Usage & Format option except Off.

To insert footnotes, follow these steps:

1. Click the edit cursor where the reference to the footnote occurs.

2. Move the mouse cursor to the Edit menu and click Ins Special Item (or press Ctrl-C) to pop up the Ins Special Item menu.

3. Click Footnote (or press the F2 key).

After you complete these steps and the screen is redrawn, you see the footnote symbol in the text and the footnote frame at the bottom of the page (see fig. 4.16).

4. Position the cursor in the footnote frame and type over the words Text of Footnote with the text of the footnote.

After you position and type the text of a footnote, you can customize the display and numbering sequence by using Ventura's Footnote Settings command. To delete the footnote, position the edit cursor on the reference point and delete as you delete any other text character.

Footnote text and reference points can be imported with source files at the same time as the referenced text, because Ventura uses < > codes to identify footnotes. Ventura numbers and positions the footnote and reference point when you load the source file to a chapter. In "Setting Up Footnotes," in this chapter, you learn how to number, format, and edit footnotes.

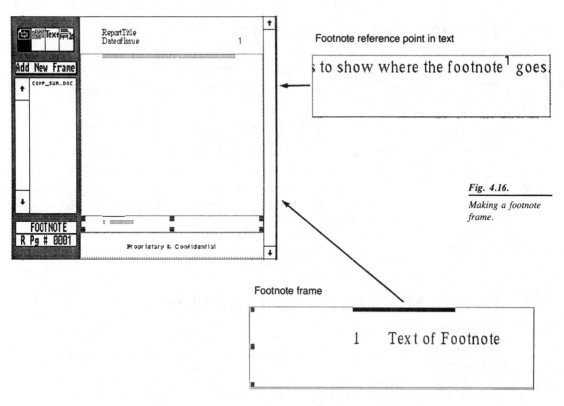

Footnote reference point in text

s to show where the footnote[1] goes

Fig. 4.16.

Making a footnote frame.

Footnote frame

1   Text of Footnote

When you create headers, footers, footnotes, and captions by using dialog boxes, you use commands from two Ventura menus:

Chapter menu
   Auto-Numbering
   Headers & Footers
   Footnote Settings

Frame menu
   Anchors & Captions

Ventura automatically provides frames on the page where the text is displayed. In the case of footnotes and captions, you can directly edit the text stored in the generated frame without returning to the dialog box. In all other cases, you must open the dialog box where the text is stored in order to change the text shown in the frame.

Although each command generates text for a different purpose, generated tags have several things in common: The format for each type of generated tag can be changed by selecting a paragraph and changing the settings through the Paragraph menu. You can change formats for generated tags, and you can assign different tags to the paragraphs within frames. In Chapter 5, you learn how to use generated tags to apply typographic settings to text.

Loading Source Text Files

Using Load Text/Picture from the File menu, you can combine many different source files into a single Ventura chapter. The source files can be in different word processor formats. The files may flow from page to page, be inserted within other pages, or be placed in specific locations reserved with a frame.

When you place a source file in a frame drawn on the page, the file fills the frame. Any text that does not fit in the frame can be continued to another frame drawn on the page or on another page in the chapter. Once a file is placed on a page, however, Ventura automatically adds as many pages as required to hold the remainder of the file.

A page may contain frames for separate articles or may reserve space for illustrations and callouts. In Chapter 7, several of the designs presented use frames that reserve space on the page for artwork and illustrations; other designs use frames drawn on the page to hold text files. In either case, the frames placed on the page save space where different margins, columns, and rules can be set.

Loading Files with the Load Text/Picture Command

You select the Load Text/Picture command from the File menu to load source files of text and graphics into a Ventura chapter. To import source text files, select Text from the Type of File options (see fig. 4.17). Chapter 6 discusses the Line-Art and Image format options from the LOAD TEXT/PICTURE dialog box. One of the Text Format options automatically fills the box with black. To select a different Text Format, move the mouse pointer and click on the desired box. Most options in this dialog box are versions of word processing programs. Four options, though, are different from the rest of those offered in the dialog box:

Fig. 4.17.

The LOAD TEXT/ PICTURE dialog box.

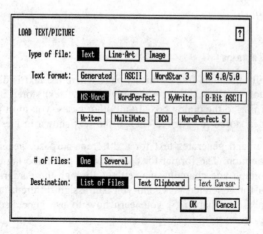

- Generated

- ASCII

- 8-Bit ASCII

- DCA

Click `Generated` when you load table-of-contents, index, or style files generated by using Ventura's commands. Click `ASCII` when you import text. (Most spreadsheet and database files should be printed to a file and then loaded as WordStar files.) The `8-Bit ASCII` option enables you to load ASCII text from many foreign languages. You can use this option to import decimal values above 128 to Ventura as international characters (more information on international character sets is given later in this chapter). Click `DCA` to load files with a defined document-content architecture (DCA)—for example, files created by the IBM DisplayWriter™, SAMNA Word IV™, and WordStar 2000®.

Once you choose the format of the text to be loaded, you can specify the `# of Files`. Click `One` to load a single file or click `Several` to load more than one file. Then choose the destination from the active options. The source file or files can be loaded into the `List of Files`, into the `Text Clipboard`, or directly onto the page at the point of the edit cursor.

Choosing `Text Cursor` as the destination allows you to merge files of text with source files already loaded and referenced in the assignment list. If you do not position the cursor before you select the load command, the `Text Cursor` option is not available. Remember that the text you load to the Clipboard overwrites any other text you may have placed in the Clipboard.

After selecting the number of files to load and the destination, click OK to open the ITEM SELECTOR dialog box. You use the ITEM SELECTOR dialog box to name, find, save, and retrieve source and chapter files to and from disks. The full operation is discussed in Chapter 3, but here is a summary:

- You can type a new drive, directory, and file extension filter in the `Directory` line of the dialog box.

- You can click the backup button to move through the drives.

- You can click the directory name to see the contents of each directory and drag the scroll bars to view more files on the list.

The files listed in the selection box match the path and file-name extension shown in the `Directory` line. You can click the backup button to change directories and drives, scroll through the lists displayed, and click the file names you want to select. Double-clicking a file name selects the file and closes the dialog box with OK or (if you selected `# of Files: Several`) displays the list again.

If you know the name of a file you want to load, you can type the name as the `Selection` option and select OK by clicking or pressing Return. Ventura finds the files that match the filter typed in the `Directory` option. You can add DOS wild cards or the letters in the file name to narrow the number of file titles that are displayed in the ITEM SELECTOR list (see fig. 4.18).

Fig. 4.18.

*Using a filter to find
a file.*

Some word processing programs attach file extensions automatically and load only files that carry the proper extension. In contrast, Ventura accepts files named with extensions different from the source program's default. Maintaining Ventura's default extensions as part of your filing discipline, however, is a good idea because using this convention enables you to identify groups of files quickly. Table 4.2 lists the default extensions used by programs listed in the LOAD TEXT/PICTURE dialog box.

To select the desired file from the assignment list, click the name and then click OK to close the dialog box and load the file into the chapter (remember that you can double-click on the name to select the name and OK at once). The name of the file is displayed in the Frame function assignment list if you have chosen Destination: List of Files. If you selected an empty frame as the active frame before executing the Load Text/Picture command, the file also appears on the page (see fig. 4.19).

Table 4.2
Compatible Word Processing Programs' File Extensions

Program Name	Ventura's Default Extension
MultiMate	· MMT
Microsoft Word	DOC
ASCII files	TXT
WordStar 3.0	WS
WordStar 4.0, 5.0	DOC
WordPerfect 5.0	WP
Writer	XWP
XyWrite	TXT

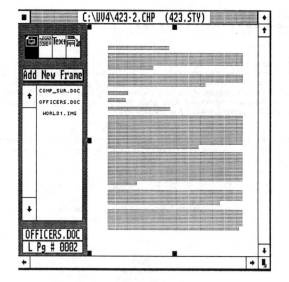

Fig. 4.19.

A source file fills the selected frame.

Letting Ventura Name Chapters and Documents

Ventura automatically names a chapter the same name as the first source document you load to the base page of a displayed untitled chapter, unless another chapter already uses the same directory location and name. In that case, Ventura leaves the chapter untitled until you name it.

When you save and name an untitled chapter that has a source document placed on the base page, Ventura renames the source document to match the chapter. If Ventura finds in the same directory another document with the same name, you are given the options of overwriting the file or selecting a new name for the chapter.

As long as you select one of the word processing programs listed in the dialog box, Ventura preserves some of the character formatting of the imported text—for example, boldface, italic, and underline. Ventura does not preserve indentations, margins, columns, or typeface styles or sizes.

Ventura's Load Text/Picture command checks the requested file to verify that the chosen file format matches the file type option selected in the dialog box. As Ventura imports compatible word processing files, the program removes formatting codes that it doesn't understand. When you reopen the file with your word processor, you will have to reset the instructions for headers, footers, spacing, font sizes, and styles (as well as for column alignment, centering, and justification). For this reason, if you intend to preserve all the formatting and coding set by the word processing program, make a copy of the file before loading it with Ventura's Load Text/Picture command. The examples in figures 4.20 and 4.21 illustrate how Ventura preserves some of the text attributes you set with compatible word processing programs.

Report Title
Report Date - D R A F T   I N   P R O G R E S S
Page 1 of 10

This is a sample Microsoft Word 4 file. During the early draft and edit stages or report writing, Word's formatting commands were used to format the text, before loading the file to Ventura. Headers were set to appear on every page, by using the Running head commands the WP program offers. Space between paragraphs was set in the Space above option of Paragraph formatting. One space was left after the period at the end of sentences. (This paragraph was set as justified text.)

A Centered Heading

The Table below was typed with tabs for the column heads set as center tabs, and tabs for the items set as decimal tabs. This paragraph is set as Left aligned. The item lines were set to indent one-half-inch.

	1988	1989	1990	1991
Item	30.	15	10	7
Item	30.789	15.89	10.987	7.66

This paragraph was set to indent an inch and a half on both sides. Character formats are illustrated below:

Bold
Italic
<u>Underline</u>
~~Strikethru~~
<u>Double Underline</u>
Superscript
Subscript

Fig. 4.20.

A Word file before being imported to Ventura.

```
This is a sample Microsoft Word 4 file. During the early
draft and edit stages, Word's formatting commands were used
to format the text, before loading the file to Ventura.
Headers were set to appear on every page, by using the
Running head commands the program offers. This paragraph was
set as justified text.
@CENTER HEAD = A Centered Heading
@BODY LEFT = The Table below was typed with tabs for the
column heads set as center tabs, and tabs for the items set
as decimal tabs. This paragraph is set as Left aligned. The
item lines were set to indent one-half-inch.
@TABLE HEADS =      1988 1989 1990 1991
@TABLE ITEMS = Item 30.  15.  10.  7.
@TABLE ITEMS = Item 30.789    15.89     10.987     7.66
@BODY INDENT = This paragraph was set to indent an inch and
a half on both sides. Character formats are illustrated
below:
@CENTER HEAD = Bold
@CENTER HEAD = Italic
@CENTER HEAD = Underline
@CENTER HEAD = Strikethru
@CENTER HEAD = <M=>Double Underline<D>
@CENTER HEAD = Superscript
@CENTER HEAD = Subscript
```

Fig. 4.21.

A Word file after being imported to Ventura.

If you want to test character-formatting commands for your own word processor, make a sample file to load into a test chapter. You place coded formatting instructions into the word processing file (see "Importing Formatted Text," in this chapter).

Removing Text Files

You use the Remove Text/File command from the Edit menu to remove files from pages, frames, and the Frame function assignment list. You can remove a file from its location on the page, or you can remove the file name from the list of files and the location at the same time.

If you first select the frame holding the source document, the `File Name` option displays the current file name (see fig. 4.22). If you want to reuse the same file in another place in the chapter, click `Frame` and `OK` to remove the selected file. To remove the file from the list of files and the location at the same time, click `List of Files`. When you open the dialog box with a Frame text file selected, the only available options are to remove the text or cancel the request (see fig. 4.23).

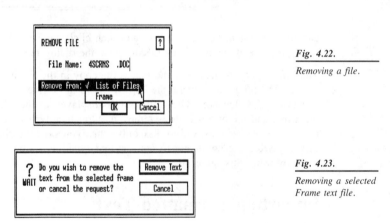

Fig. 4.22.

Removing a file.

Fig. 4.23.

Removing a selected Frame text file.

To delete a file placed or typed into a frame, select the frame and press Delete. This method of removing a file from the page leaves the name of the source available in the assignment list for subsequent placements. Once you delete a Frame text file, you cannot retrieve the text unless you abandon the changes made since the last save.

Converting Documents to Different File Formats

Because Ventura can work with different types of word processing files, the program can read and write different types of files. When you exchange documents between word processing systems, Ventura transfers documents from one format to another. Line endings transfer as soft and hard returns where appropriate, but only a few of the character-format codes transfer correctly between different programs.

Use Ventura to convert a file to another file format by following this procedure: place the file in a frame, select the frame as the active frame, and open the Edit menu. Then choose the File Type/Rename command to open the dialog box (see fig. 4.24).

The FILE TYPE/RENAME dialog box is the same dialog box that opens when you start a new file on a page. In this case, however, the `Old Name` option shows the name of the file in the active frame, which is the file you are copying. You can type a name

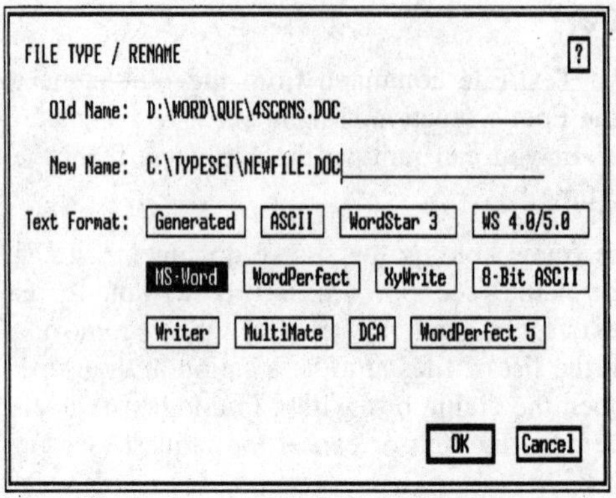

Fig. 4.24.

*Converting a file by
using the FILE
TYPE/RENAME
dialog box.*

and location for the new document and then click the Text Format option you want
to use to store the copy. Click OK to close the dialog box.

The File Type/Rename command places the copy in the file indicated in the New Name
option. The program converts the copied file to the format of the word processor you
chose in the dialog box. The new copy is displayed as the file named in the assignment list, and the original file is removed automatically from the assignment list. The
new file, however, is saved to disk only when you save the chapter. You can use the
File Type/Rename command to convert text typed as frame text (these are the CAP
files) by using this same procedure.

Importing Formatted Text

Format refers to both the format of a file and the format of text. Earlier in this chapter, you saw how to load source text files from a variety of programs that use different
file formats. Converting files from one format to another also has been covered in this
chapter. Importing formatted text involves a different meaning of the word *format*.
This section discusses how you can use a word processor to prepare source files with
format instructions to define the appearance of text on the pages. Formatted text is
displayed in the defined formats in Ventura's WYSIWYG view when you place the
file.

You can create source files with a word processor and then send text format instructions to Ventura in three ways:

- As paragraph formats set by tag names
- As character attributes set during word processing
- As codes typed in angle brackets

In all three cases, you type characters in specific sequences to send the formatting
instructions to Ventura. With character formats like boldface, italic, and underline,
you often can use your word processor's features to format the text, and then Ventura

can use those codes without altering them. The following sections further describe how you can use a word processor to send text format instructions to Ventura. Chapter 5 covers setting and defining format instructions in Ventura.

Efficiency Tip

Word Processing Habits To Develop when Importing Compatible Files

Develop good word processing habits when you import compatible files to Ventura. Some of these good habits are

- Use one tab between columns of numbers.

- Do not indent paragraphs with tabs.

- Use only one space at the end of every sentence and after every colon.

- Don't leave any blank lines between paragraphs.

- Format characters and phrases in paragraphs with the features of compatible word processors.

- Suppress hyphenation and justification.

Develop the good habit of typing one space instead of two at the end of each sentence and after every colon in text. Typing two spaces causes Ventura to interpret the second space as a nonbreaking space, which leaves extra space during hyphenation and justification. You can use your word processor to search for and replace occurrences of a period or a colon followed by two spaces to ensure that Ventura does not leave large gaps between sentences in text.

Remember that when you load files, Ventura strips out some of your word processor's formatting and replaces it with instructions that more precisely define for Ventura the appearance of text on the page. If you want to keep a copy of the word processed format, copy the file and save it under a different name. Any text edits that you make to the document copy during production are made only to the source file used during production; you will have to duplicate text changes in the word processed file to keep that file updated.

Paragraph Formats

One planning step in a publishing project is to determine what you will call the types of paragraphs in your text. Although you must define the settings for each type of paragraph in Ventura (as detailed in Chapter 5), you can embed the names of the paragraph types during the word processing stage, using your word processing software's glossary or macro features.

Each unique paragraph format is referred to as a *tag* by Ventura. A tag consists of five components (the "at sign" @, the tag name, a space, an equal sign, and another space). The tag name can be up to 13 characters in length and can include any keyboard character. To Ventura, the capitalization of tag names in source files is irrelevant. A tag name in a word processing file can look like any of these examples:

@tag name =

@Tag Name =

@Tag name =

@tag Name =

@TAG NAME =

In Chapter 5, you are encouraged to use either lowercase or initial capital letters, as shown in the first three versions of the tag in the preceding example. You can keep tag names short and use the search-and-replace feature to help insert tag names consistently. When you load a source file with tags that have not been named or defined in Ventura, the tags in the assignment list are displayed in all uppercase.

Earlier in this chapter, you saw how text typed in Ventura automatically takes on the default characteristics of the Body Text tag. When you tag sources of text, you tag only the paragraphs that you want to set differently from the settings customized as body text. All untagged paragraphs default to body text, and every project can have different default settings for body text. Refer to figure 4.2 for the values established by Ventura's default style file.

Efficiency Tip

Removing Blank Lines from Word Processing Files

If you need to remove blank lines (extra paragraph marks) from word processing files to be loaded into Ventura, you can place the following phrase on the first line of the file to be imported:

@PARAFILTR ON =

Any occurrence of two carriage returns is changed to a single return. After you import and save the file with Ventura's commands, remove the filter command from the word processing file, or Ventura refilters the file each time you choose the Open Chapter command.

If you are planning a project that can use Ventura's table-of-contents, automatic-numbering, or bullet features, tagging text in the source file can save time and also save you from typing text that you may not need to type. For instance, if you want to number (and renumber automatically after edits or text rearrangement) section headings or items in a list, you can type a tag name that references the numbering instructions which you set in Ventura, instead of typing numbers in the text. The same is true for bullets or other symbols normally used to emphasize items in a table or list. You do not type bullets; you tag the paragraph, defining the characteristics of the bullet you want used, and Ventura displays and prints the character automatically. To learn more about inserting bullets, see Chapter 5; the other features mentioned here are covered later in this chapter.

Character Attributes

Ventura uses the term *attributes* to refer to treatment of any characters, words, or phrases that are in any way different from the rest of the paragraph. Boldface, italic, and underlined words in paragraphs are all examples of attributes set with the text.

Test the compatibility of the attributes your word processor offers with the attributes Ventura offers. Sometimes, the technique you use in your word processor produces codes that are recognized by Ventura. In such cases, loading the file into Ventura does not change the way the text with attributes is displayed in your word processing program. When attributes are encountered in a form that Ventura does not support, the attributes are either removed from the file or translated into an angle-bracket code, depending on the type and version of word processing software you use.

Coded attributes consist of letters enclosed by angle brackets (greater-than and less-than signs) positioned at the beginning and end of the characters with the special attribute. For example, if your word processor's attribute codes are not compatible with Ventura's, the attribute codes stored in the source file look like this:

<Start Attribute>Attributed Text<End Attribute>

Choose the starting code from those shown in table 4.3. The ending code for attributes is always <D>, but the ending codes for font, color, size, shift, and kerning vary as shown in table 4.3. The Set Font commands in the table, however, end with a number that is unique for the various settings. The numeric ending codes also are shown in table 4.3.

Table 4.3
Character Attributes To Type in Angle Brackets

Assignment List Attributes	<Code>
Light	L
Medium	M
Bold	B
Italic	1
Small	S
Underline	U
Double Underline	=
Overscore	O
Superscript	^
Strike-thru	v
Reset to Tag's Setting	D

Table 4.3—*Continued*

Set Font Command Attributes	<Code>	
Color	Cn	n = 0 white, 1 black, 2 red, 3 green, 4 blue, 5 cyan, 6 yellow, 7 magenta
End Color	C255	Reset to the color set for the paragraph
Typeface	Fnnn	nnn = the number assigned to the typeface (a table of Ventura's typeface IDs is provided in Chapter 5)
End Typeface	F255	Reset to the paragraph's typeface
Point Size	Pnnn	nnn = point size
End Point Size	P255	Reset to the paragraph's point size
Base Line Jump	Jnnn	nnn = vertical shift measured in 1/300 of an inch; maximum amount approximately 1/2 inch
End Jump	J0	Reset to the base line of the paragraph
Begin Kerning	B%-n	Replace n with the number of ems to add or subtract; maximum amount approximately 1/2 inch
End Kerning	D%0	Reset to the normal position for the next character

You can see the effect of the attributes you set in Ventura because the program's WYSIWYG capability displays text as it will print. You can edit text that carries attributes, but be careful when you are editing the beginning or end of the sequence. If you erase the ending angle-bracket code without erasing the beginning, the attribute carries to the end of the paragraph. Attributes are reset to normal when another attribute code is encountered. For that reason, when you want to start a new attribute after another attribute, you don't have to reset the first attribute to normal by typing <D>. For example, a publication named the ARMAdilla always carries this style in the text:

ARMA*dilla*

The attribute codes that produce the effects are seen as three bracketed codes if Ventura does not support your word processor's text attributes:

<B>ARMA<BI>dilla<D>

Because attribute codes are distinguished by angle brackets, you must type *two* brackets when you use your word processor to enter angle brackets in a text file. For example, to type a greater-than or less-than sign, you need to type *two* greater-than or less-than signs:

>> or <<

If you want to enclose text within angle brackets, you type two brackets at each end:

<<text in brackets>>

Otherwise, Ventura thinks that anything within two single angle brackets is a formatting code.

Efficiency Tip

Figuring Out the Sequence of the Angle Brackets

If you use a complex angle-bracket code repeatedly, use Ventura the first time to create the sequence. When you combine several attributes, the codes in the text file are combined in the brackets. When you access the text file with your word processor, you can copy and repeat the coded sequence as needed.

Special Symbols

The font libraries delivered with Ventura enable you to print (and see) symbols that you cannot make by pressing keyboard characters. To access the characters in Ventura's default library (the international font set), press and hold the Alt key and type three numbers from the numeric keypad (not the numbers on the top of the keyboard). For example, rather than insert two hyphens to create a dash between words, you insert a typographic dash by holding down the Alt key and typing *197*.

Several codes have keyboard shortcuts you can use to add the character in Ventura because the codes represent symbols that are used often in publishing. Table 4.4 shows the Ventura shortcuts to codes that have equivalent angle-bracket codes you can type in the source document. If you add the symbol by using Ventura, you can use either the shortcut or the Alt-key numbers to insert the code.

Efficiency Tip

Adding Typographic Quality to Dashes and Quotation Marks

The typographic characters for dashes (Alt-197) and quotation marks (Alt-169, Alt-170) can be converted automatically from two hyphens (--) and " " marks typed from the keyboard. To do this, open the Options menu and select the Set Preferences command. Then choose ", --, or Both from the Auto Adjustments line. The algorithm for the quotation mark conversion works on a per-paragraph basis. In a paragraph, the first quotation mark that either starts the paragraph or is preceded by a space is converted to an opening quotation mark (''). The next quotation mark is converted to a closing quotation mark (''). If the quotation mark is preceded by a numeral, however, the quotation mark is not converted. This feature allows you to use quotation marks as inch marks.

Table 4.4
Ventura Keyboard Shortcuts to Typographic Characters

Character	VP Shortcut	Alt-Numeric Key or <WP Decimal Code>
" Opening quotation marks	Ctrl-Shift-[	169
" Closing quotation marks	Ctrl-Shift-]	170
© Copyright symbol	Ctrl-Shift-C	189
® Register mark	Ctrl-Shift-R	190
™ Trademark	Ctrl-Shift-2	191
– En dash	Ctrl-[	196
— Em dash	Ctrl-]	197
▢ Hollow box	Ctrl-C F1	$B0
■ Solid box	Ctrl-C F1	$B1

To embed a special character in text (one you cannot make with the keyboard), first find the character you want to use in table 4.4 or 4.5. (All printers support the international character set; PostScript printers also support the Symbol character set). For instance, you can make a cent sign appear in the text by holding the Alt key and typing *155* from the numeric keypad. If your word processor cannot display the symbol, you see another symbol (or perhaps <155>) in the text file when it is accessed with your word processor. In Ventura, you will see a ¢ sign. Table 4.4 shows just the symbols that have shortcuts in Ventura. However, you can choose from almost 200 symbols, as illustrated in table 4.5.

Efficiency Tip

Adding Box Characters

Hollow and filled boxes can be added to text files as special symbols that are printed in the type size set for the paragraph.

To insert boxes in text with Ventura, perform three steps:

1. Place the cursor in the text at the point where you want the box to print.

2. Open the Edit menu and then choose Ins Special Items or press Ctrl-C to pop up the menu.

3. Click Box Char (or press F1) and choose Solid or Hollow.

The box is inserted at the cursor and flows with the text like any other character. You can mark the box and use the Set Font command to change its size or to shift its vertical position. The code to use with your word processor to insert a box character is <$B0> for a hollow box and <$B1> for a solid box.

Table 4.5
Printout of CHARSET.CHP

Alt-	Int'l	Symbol		Alt-	Int'l	Symbol		Alt-	Int'l	Symbol
1–31	not used			63	?	?		95	_	_
32	space	space		64	@	≅		96	`	⎯
33	!	!		65	A	A		97	a	α
34	"	∀		66	B	B		98	b	β
35	#	#		67	C	Χ		99	c	χ
36	$	∃		68	D	Δ		100	d	δ
37	%	%		69	E	E		101	e	ε
38	&	&		70	F	Φ		102	f	φ
39	'	∍		71	G	Γ		103	g	γ
40	(	(		72	H	H		104	h	η
41	)	)		73	I	I		105	i	ι
42	*	*		74	J	ϑ		106	j	φ
43	+	+		75	K	K		107	k	κ
44	,	,		76	L	Λ		108	l	λ
45	–	–		77	M	M		109	m	μ
46	.	.		78	N	N		110	n	ν
47	/	/		79	O	O		111	o	o
48	0	0		80	P	Π		112	p	π
49	1	1		81	Q	Θ		113	q	θ
50	2	2		82	R	P		114	r	ρ
51	3	3		83	S	Σ		115	s	σ
52	4	4		84	T	T		116	t	τ
53	5	5		85	U	Y		117	u	υ
54	6	6		86	V	ς		118	v	ϖ
55	7	7		87	W	Ω		119	w	ω
56	8	8		88	X	Ξ		120	x	ξ
57	9	9		89	Y	Ψ		121	y	ψ
58	:	:		90	Z	Z		122	z	ζ
59	;	;		91	[	[		123	{	{
60	<	<		92	\	∴		124				
61	=	=		93	]	]		125	}	}
62	>	>		94	^	⊥		126	~	~

Table 4.5—*Continued*

Alt-	Int'l	Symbol		Alt-	Int'l	Symbol		Alt-	Int'l	Symbol
127				159	ƒ	↵		191	™	⇓
128	Ç			160	á	ℵ		192	„	◊
129	ü	ϒ		161	í	ℑ		193	…	⟨
130	é	′		162	ó	ℜ		194	‰	®
131	â	≤		163	ú	℘		195	•	©
132	ä	∕		164	ñ	⊗		196	–	™
133	à	∞		165	Ñ	⊕		197	—	Σ
134	å	ƒ		166	ª	∅		198	°	
135	ç	♣		167	º	∩		199	Á	
136	ê	♦		168	¿	∪		200	Â	
137	ë	♥		169	"	⊃		201	È	
138	è	♠		170	"	⊇		202	Ê	
139	ï	↔		171	‹	⊄		203	Ë	
140	î	←		172	›	⊂		204	Ì	
141	ì	↑		173	¡	⊆		205	Í	
142	Ä	→		174	«	∈		206	Î	
143	Å	↓		175	»	∉		207	Ï	
144	É	°		176	ã	∠		208	Ò	
145	æ	±		177	õ	∇		209	Ó	⟩
146	Æ	″		178	Ø	®		210	Ô	∫
147	ô	≥		179	ø	©		211	Š	⌠
148	ö	×		180	œ	™		212	š	
149	ò	∝		181	Œ	∏		213	Ù	⌡
150	û	∂		182	À	√		214	Ú	
151	ù	•		183	Ã	·		215	Û	
152	ÿ	÷		184	Õ	¬		216	Ÿ	
153	Ö	≠		185	Ş	∧		217	ß	
154	Ü	≡		186	‡	∨		218		
155	¢	≈		187	†	↔		219		
156	£	…		188	¶	⇐		220		
157	¥	|		189	©	⇑		221		
158	¤	—		190	®	⇒		222		

If you want to use the Symbol set shown in table 4.5 rather than the International set, you must include a Font instruction with the code. For example, to print a division mark in a mathematical statement, you type a code in the source file that is a combination of the Alt key plus the decimal value from table 4.5 and Ventura's numeric code *128*, which identifies the typeface as Symbol.

To embed a special symbol in a word processing file to be imported into Ventura, include all the necessary instructions in angle brackets. For example, to make a division mark, first type the Font instruction *<F128>*, type *<152>* (the International representation of the division mark), and then end the font setting by typing *<F255>*. Your word processing file should look like this:

<F128><152><F255>

In Ventura, you set the same code by following these two steps:

1. Press the Alt key while you type the decimal value from the keypad.

2. Select the character that Ventura displays with the text tool and click Set Font to set the typeface to Symbol. When you look at the source text file in a word processor, you see <F128M>ÿ<F255D>.

Both sets of codes have the same effect in this example because the medium-weight font style (indicated by the *M*) is the default style for the typeface. You can use the Text function's Set Font button to choose the Symbol font and change the size of the font. Whether you insert angle-bracket codes or use Alt-key combinations to include a special character in text, you must set the Font as Symbol if you have chosen a character from the Symbol columns in table 4.5.

You can use other symbol sets (many PostScript printers also support ITC Zapf Dingbats), but the symbols do not appear on the screen unless you have a matching screen font. The symbol prints if your printer supports it even though it does not appear on the screen.

Efficiency Tip

Inserting Text Attributes and Special Symbols in Dialog Boxes

In many Ventura dialog boxes where you store sequences of text that are repeated in a publication, such as headers and footers, an option called Text Attr. is displayed. In each instance, you use this option to embed the ending attribute codes in the dialog box and then use the option again to establish a pattern for the starting attribute code. (You can embed any angle-bracket codes shown in tables 4.4 and 4.5 in Ventura's dialog boxes.) When a dialog box is not long enough to let you complete the ending attribute codes, however, remember this point: any attribute that is started continues only to the end of the paragraph.

Illustration Anchors, Footnote Text, and Index Terms

Although you can use Ventura to insert references to describe where illustrations, footnotes, fractions, and index terms tie to a position in text, you also can embed the codes during word processing. Ventura also can import footnote text from a word processor's source file (see fig. 4.25).

Table 4.6 shows the codes and the syntax used to type these codes in text files. If you use Ventura to define the position and text for these text elements, you see the coding in the source file as it is displayed in figure 4.25 when you access the file with word processing software. If you need to change the position of the reference points with word processing, move all the codes and text displayed within the brackets.

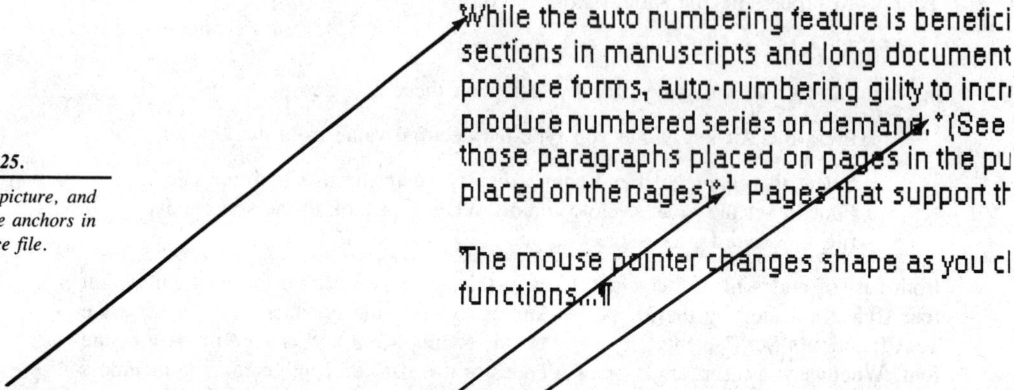

Fig. 4.25.

Index, picture, and footnote anchors in a source file.

While the auto numbering feature is benefici
sections in manuscripts and long document
produce forms, auto-numbering gility to incr
produce numbered series on demand.*(See
those paragraphs placed on pages in the pu
placed on the pages)*[1] Pages that support th

The mouse pointer changes shape as you cl
functions...¶

<$AAuto Numbering;Chapter Numbering>
<$SIllustration captions;Captions>

<$IAuto Numbering;forms><$IForms;auto-numbering>While the auto numbering feature is beneficial for numbering sections in manuscripts and long documents, if you use Ventura to produce forms, auto-numbering gives you the ability to increment the counter and produce numbered series on demand. <$&Numbered Form[v]>(See fig 4.52) As with the Footnote feature, only those paragraphs placed on pages in the publication, (not frames placed on the pages)<$FThe page is often referred in the Xerox documentation, as the underlying page> Pages that support the use of the

<$IChanging;appearance of mouse pointer><$Ichanging;borders around boxes>The mouse pointer changes shape as you change publishing functions...

<$ICaptions;labels><$ICaptions;text>Illustrations imported to Ventura's chapter files, often need a caption to label the illustration and a line or two or text....

Efficiency Tip ─────────────────────────────────────

Cutting and Pasting Footnotes, Index References, and Picture Anchors

When you want to move a footnote, picture anchor, or index reference point to another location, you can use Ventura's Clipboard. Position the Text cursor beside the desired attribute in the text. The current selection box indicates that the cursor has encountered the instruction you want to move. Then press the Del key, reposition the cursor, and press the Ins key.

Inserting Fractions into Text

The Fraction option under the Edit menu's Ins Special Item command lets you insert fractions in text, setting the numerator over the denominator in one of two ways. In figure 4.26, you see the two types of fractions Ventura offers, and you see how they use space in a paragraph. As you type a fraction, you select the type of setting you want to use.

Table 4.6
Text File codes

Type these $ instructions within angle brackets in source files and replace the text shown in italics with the text used for the feature: footnotes, anchors, indexes, fractions, and page and chapter numbers.

Feature	*<Code>*
Footnote	$F*text*
Picture anchor (same page)	$&*anchor name*
Picture anchor (below)	$&*anchor name[v]*
Picture anchor	$&*anchor name[^]*
Picture anchor, automatic	$&*anchor name[-]*
Index entries	$>I*Primary term[Primary Sort key];* *Secondary[Secondary Sort Key]*
Index See entries	$S*See Term*
Index See Also entries	$A*See Also Term*
Hidden text	$!*text*(Hidden text will not display in Ventura.)
Chapter number	$R[C#]
Page number	$R[P#]
Fraction	$e*numerator* over *denominator*
Fraction	$e*numerator/denominator*

To insert a fraction, first position the edit cursor at the point in text where you need a fraction. Then select the Edit menu Ins Special Item command to open the pop-up menu from which you select the Fraction command. Ventura responds by opening a special editing window, reserved for working with fractions (see fig 4.27). To use the shortcut to the fraction editing window from the publishing work area, position the edit cursor in text and press Ctrl-C and then F4.

Fig. 4.26.

Comparing how fractions affect spacing.

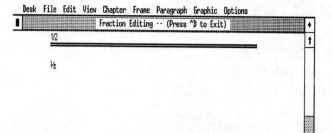

Setting fractions as ½ maintains uniform line spacing in a paragraph. By comparison, $\frac{1}{2}$ uses more vertical space between lines. Once Ventura displays the fraction in the publishing window (not the fraction window), you can select the fraction to change the point size and vertical shift. For example, $\frac{1}{2}$ was changed from 12 to 6 points, and the fraction was shifted up by $^{32}/_{1000}$ of an inch.

Fig. 4.27.

Typing and displaying fractions.

Desk File Edit View Chapter Frame Paragraph Graphic Options

Fraction Editing -- (Press ^D to Exit)

1/2

½

The Text cursor appears at the top left corner of the window above the double rules. Type the fraction as either *1/2* or *1 over 2* (leaving a space before and after *over*). Once you type enough numbers to complete a fraction, Ventura displays the fraction beneath the ruled lines. To close the fraction editing work area, press Ctrl-D. The fraction displays in text as it will in print, but it is preceded by the same nonprinting symbol (a small O) that precedes anchors for footnotes, anchors, and index points.

You do not need to press the Return key after you complete a fraction in the fraction editing window. You can type more than one fraction on the same line in the window by inserting a space between the fractions. When you set fractions with diagonal slashes, Ventura takes care of adjusting the font sizes and superscripts. When you set the numerator over the denominator, Ventura adjusts the vertical spacing if you enable Grow Inter-Line To Fit in the Paragraph menu's TYPOGRAPHY SETTINGS dialog box for the tag used to format the paragraph where the fraction occurs.

In figure 4.26, you see how diagonal fractions take more horizontal space than do fractions placed over and below a horizontal rule. The illustration also shows that you can reduce the amount of vertical space a fraction takes by changing the point size for the fraction and by shifting the fraction up. To make these types of adjustments to a fraction, select the fraction with the Text I-beam and open the FONT SETTINGS FOR SELECTED TEXT dialog box. Set the font to a smaller size and shift the fraction up. If you are working in a paragraph set in 12-point type, set the fraction as 6-point and then look at the results in an enlarged view. Because Ventura provides 12-point screen fonts for all monitors, what you see on-screen closely represents the alignment and size of the type as it will print.

Efficiency Tip

Shortcuts to the Fraction One-Half

Ventura provides two shortcuts to the fraction one-half, one for each style shown in figure 4.28. First, position the edit cursor where you want the fraction; then press the keys in the order they are listed in the figure.

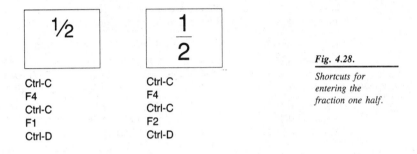

Ctrl-C
F4
Ctrl-C
F1
Ctrl-D

Ctrl-C
F4
Ctrl-C
F2
Ctrl-D

Fig. 4.28.

Shortcuts for entering the fraction one half.

To edit a fraction, you position the edit cursor immediately preceding the fraction. The current selection box displays the word FRACTION when you place the edit cursor at a fraction's edit point. After the cursor is positioned, press Ctrl-D. Ventura opens the fraction editing window, where you edit the numbers, letters, or spaces as needed.

When you use Ventura to type fractions, codes are embedded in the source text file. This fact means that you can format word processing files for setting fractions. Simply adopt a practice of including the codes in the word processing file as you approach the final edit rounds of a project. As with any complex series of angle-bracket codes, use Ventura to make a pattern that you can copy and insert by using word processing features. Figure 4.29 shows the text file used to create figure 4.26; note how Ventura's coding appears in the source text file.

Setting fractions as <$E1/2 > maintains uniform line spacing in a
paragraph. By comparison, <$E1 over 2 > uses more vertical space
between lines. .... to change the point size and vertical shift
<P6MJ246><$E1 over 2 ><J248> <P255DJ0> was changed from 12 to
6 points, and the fraction was shifted up by <$E32/1000 > of an inch.

Fig. 4.29.

Fraction codes in a word processing file.

Importing Unformatted Text

Always try to do as much character formatting and tagging as possible in the word processing stage. Sometimes, though, your only sources of text are unformatted files. You can load unformatted text into Ventura, format it with Ventura's tools, and then save the file in a format compatible with your word processor. Three common sources of unformatted text are discussed in this section. These sources are ASCII files from any word processor, data saved in ASCII format from a spreadsheet or database program, and telecommunicated text.

ASCII Files

ASCII stands for American Standard Code for Information Interchange and is a "generic" way that text files can be saved. Many word processors provide ways to read, edit, and write ASCII files. If the name of your word processor is not listed in Ventura's LOAD TEXT/PICTURE dialog box, you can still load your text files into Ventura if the files have been saved with the text-only option that most word processors offer. If your word processor doesn't offer this option, you may need to transfer the text to a compatible format through a telecommunication session.

To load unformatted text files, click the Text option from the LOAD TEXT/PIC-TURE dialog box. Then choose the desired format for the file. To select the correct file format from those listed in the dialog box, you need to know how many carriage returns represent a paragraph in the unformatted ASCII source file. For files with one carriage return (like those made by the 1-2-3 /Print File command), use the WordStar option. For files with two carriage returns for each paragraph, use ASCII. In an ASCII file, Ventura waits for two hard carriage returns before ending a paragraph. You can use the Edit menu File Type/Rename command to convert ASCII files into word processing file formats. Then insert character attributes and tag names in that file with your word processor.

The 8-Bit ASCII option lets you load ASCII text from many foreign languages. You can use this option to import the decimal values above 128 to Ventura as the characters shown in the International character set column of table 4.5.

Spreadsheets and Databases

Most PC programs that manage numbers and data offer an ASCII print option or a print-to-file feature with which you can create a source document Ventura can load. If the print file has two carriage returns between paragraphs, you use the File menu's LOAD TEXT/PICTURE dialog box's Text Format: ASCII option to load the source file to Ventura. If the file has only one paragraph return between paragraphs, select the WordStar option. (In WordStar® files, Ventura treats single carriage returns as paragraph breaks.)

Usually, you must do a certain amount of preparation after you make the print file and before you load the file to Ventura. The print file may separate columns with field delimiters or commas that need to be converted into tabs if you want to use Ventura's proportional fonts and decimal alignment capabilities. Because Ventura interprets <9> as a tab symbol, you can use a word processing or report writing program to replace each space with a tab or with <9>. You also can format the print file with paragraph tags and any of the symbols, attributes, and instructions shown in tables 4.3 through 4.6.

When loading lists into Ventura from databases where several hundred paragraphs constitute the list, keep in mind that Ventura supports a maximum of 8,000 paragraphs in a single chapter. You can overcome the 8,000-paragraph limit in two ways: split the publication into several chapters or use <R> (commonly referred to as a newline code) to end the lines instead of using paragraph symbols. If you use the latter technique, you should insert a paragraph return every 4,000 or 5,000 characters.

Database publishing projects are often long; require tabs and tab leaders; and use format changes to separate headings, summary, and detailed information. As discussed in Chapter 3, some formatting elements (for example, tags and tabs) count as more than one line element and therefore reduce the number of lines of text you can have in a frame. For this reason, Ventura may warn you during processing that the project cannot be completed because the frame is too complex. To avoid this problem, design database layouts with these guidelines in mind:

- Minimize the use of leader tabs.

- Minimize the number of tags you use.

- Use line breaks rather than paragraph returns between items in a long list.

- Make sure that you are using the smallest printer width table possible (see Chapter 8 to learn about width tables).

- Load source files on the base page and then into repeating frames drawn on the page.

The technique illustrated in figure 4.30 shows how to use repeating frames for producing directories, catalogs, lists, and labels. Ventura automatically makes as many pages as needed to hold the contents of the source file, once you set up the first page in the sequence described in the text of the figure. Follow the sequence indicated for drawing the frames, designating the frames as repeating frames that show on all pages, and loading the source file to the page and frames. If you do not follow this sequence, the information will not display in sequential order. See Chapter 7 to learn more about using the Frame menu's Repeating Frame command.

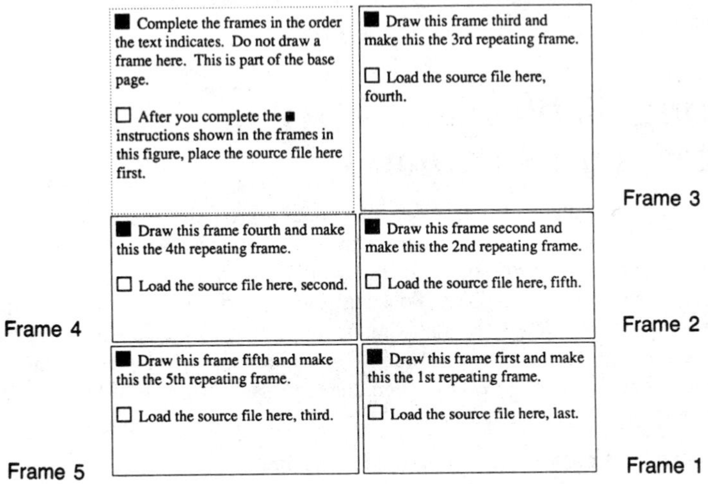

■ Complete the frames in the order the text indicates. Do not draw a frame here. This is part of the base page.

☐ After you complete the ■ instructions shown in the frames in this figure, place the source file here first.

■ Draw this frame third and make this the 3rd repeating frame.

☐ Load the source file here, fourth.

Frame 3

■ Draw this frame fourth and make this the 4th repeating frame.

☐ Load the source file here, second.

■ Draw this frame second and make this the 2nd repeating frame.

☐ Load the source file here, fifth.

Frame 4

Frame 2

■ Draw this frame fifth and make this the 5th repeating frame.

☐ Load the source file here, third.

■ Draw this frame first and make this the 1st repeating frame.

☐ Load the source file here, last.

Frame 5

Frame 1

Fig. 4.30.

Using repeating frames to avoid the problem of a frame too complex to process.

You also can plan a layout strategy using the Paragraph menu Breaks command. To see this technique, load Ventura's sample chapter (&PHON-P2.CHP) and note how the tags set phone numbers adjacent to company names without using tabs.

The Professional Extension version of Ventura enables you to undertake large publishing projects with complex formatting, if you have EMS memory in your system configuration. The Professional Extension also offers a print-to-table feature that speeds publishing spreadsheets. When you use Prn to Table to load a spreadsheet file, Ventura makes a copy of the file and then displays the copy as formatted data in ruled columns and rows. Edits made during Ventura production are stored in the copy of the source file (see Chapter 10 to learn more about the Professional Extension).

Telecommunicated Text

You can transfer text from one computer to another through connecting cables or through modems and telephone lines. Text received through a communication session can be edited and formatted with any word processor that reads ASCII files. You also can use Ventura's tools to edit ASCII files.

Some communication programs let you transfer your files intact with the word processing formatting codes. Instead of choosing ASCII as the protocol for transmission, choose a binary format and protocol. (See your communication program's documentation for more information.) If you are sending your text through a mailbox facility or communication program that does not relay binary files, character attributes and line endings may change during the communication session.

When communicating from mainframe computers, set the communication parameters to send [CR][LF][CR][LF] at the end of every paragraph ([CR] = decimal 10 and [LF] = decimal 13). Sending carriage returns without line feeds (or vice versa) causes erratic results.

Creating Tables of Contents, Indexes, and Footnotes

Creating tables of contents and indexes always poses a problem: you need to know the page number of the final publication before the publication is actually final. Ventura has features that permit you to build both types of files and automatically update page numbering as your work progresses. You can track up to 10 types of paragraphs as table-of-contents entries. With the indexing feature, you can index by primary and secondary terms and create *See* and *See Also* references. Tables of contents and indexes then can be regenerated easily when changes affect pagination in a publication including single or multiple chapters.

You create a table-of-contents file or an index file after you indicate where the entries for each file are to appear in the source file. In both cases, you can use your word processor to prepare the source text files.

Making a Table of Contents

If you use Ventura's Make TOC command, you can provide content tables with production drafts as the project proceeds. At the outset, all you must do is decide which tag names are used to format paragraphs of text representing headings in the table of contents. For example, the tags to generate a table of contents for this book might be set as follows:

Head-Chp

Head-Mai

Head-Maj

Head-Min

Head-Sub

The tag names all begin with *Head* so that they are displayed together in the Paragraph function assignment list. The abbreviations after the hyphen were chosen to create an alphabetical sequence that duplicates the hierarchy of the headings. (Ventura organizes tag names in alphabetical order in the assignment list.) You can include up to 10 tag names when you instruct Ventura to build a table-of-contents file.

The first step in creating a table-of-contents file is to tag the paragraphs in the chapter file. You can add the names of paragraph tags in source text files, as explained in "Importing Formatted Text." You also can use Ventura's Paragraph function to tag the paragraphs used as headings.

You can make a table of contents for a single chapter or for many related chapters by using the same convention. You simply tell Ventura which tags are being used to format headings that should appear in the table of contents. To do so, you use the Multi-Chapter command from the Options menu.

When you click Multi-Chapter from the Options menu, Ventura asks you to save or abandon any changes made in the work area if you have a chapter in view. Click Save in the prompt box to update the chapter file in the work area if you have made changes you want saved.

Once you save the active chapter files in the work area, the MULTI-CHAPTER dialog box opens (see fig. 4.31). To make a table of contents, you use four of the commands shown in the list on the right side of the dialog box:

- New
- Add Chapter
- Save or Save As
- Make TOC

You first choose the New command to clear the list of files shown under the title bar of the dialog box (unless those files are the chapters you want to use). Then click Add Chapter and select the names of the chapters you want in the table of contents. As you

Fig. 4.31.

Creating a table of contents.

add chapters to the list, the name of the most recent selection is added to the bottom of the list. You can rearrange the order by dragging files from one position to another with the mouse cursor (again see fig. 4.31).

After all the chapters are in the list (even if it is only one chapter), click Save or Save As. In the ITEM SELECTOR dialog box that opens, type a name for the publication. The name you choose is displayed in the title bar with the extension PUB.

Now click Make TOC to open the GENERATE TABLE OF CONTENTS dialog box. The top line of the box shows the generated file's location and title. Ventura names the table of contents file with the first five characters of the PUB file name, adding TOC before the extension GEN (see fig. 4.32). The next line shows the title string that appears at the top of the table of contents. You can change either of these defaults by using the Text cursor.

```
GENERATE TABLE OF CONTENTS                              [?]

     TOC File:  D:\WORD\QUE\SCREETOC.GEN_____
 Title String:  Table of Contents_____
      Level 1:  [C#] · [*HeadChp]→[P#]_____
      Level 2:  [*HeadMaj]→[P#]_____
      Level 3:  [*HeadMaj]→[P#]_____
      Level 4:  [*HeadMin]→[P#]_____
      Level 5:  [*HeadSub]→[P#]_____
      Level 6:  _____
      Level 7:  _____
      Level 8:  _____
      Level 9:  _____
     Level 10:  [_____]

      Inserts:  [Tag Text]  [Tab]  [Chapter #]  [Page #]

                [Text Attr.]

                                      [OK]  [Cancel]
```

Fig. 4.32.

The GENERATE TABLE OF CONTENTS dialog box.

Next, tell Ventura which tags are used for each level of the table of contents. To type the names of the tags into the text file, position the Text cursor and then click Tag Text from the list of Inserts options for each level that you want to use. Type over the words [*tag name] with the names of the tags you are using. You can insert a tab, a chapter number, and a page number on each level. When the list of tag names is complete, click OK to close the dialog box. Ventura processes the file and then asks whether you want to save the changes. If you intend to update the source files and use Make TOC again, save the changes. Putting a chapter into a publication does not change the way you work on it as an individual chapter.

Ventura makes a table-of-contents file by copying every paragraph tagged with the names typed in the GENERATE TABLE OF CONTENTS dialog box. To see the file, use the Load Text/Picture command from the File menu and click GEN as the file type. Select and place the file on the page in the same way that you place any text file on a page. You can edit that file with Ventura's Text function or with a word processor.

Attached to every paragraph in a Ventura table-of-contents GEN file is a numbered Z_TOC tag. You use these tags to set the format for each type of heading in the table of contents. The tags are numbered in the same sequence as the tag levels in the GENERATE TABLE OF CONTENTS dialog box. As with all automatically generated tags, you can change the default formats. (Using tags to format text is covered in Chapter 5.) When formatting table-of-contents entries, though, do not change the names of the tags because Ventura will use the same tag names the next time you choose Make TOC.

To update a table of contents that was saved previously, choose Multi-Chapter from the Options menu and click Open to see the list of publication files in the ITEM SELECTOR dialog box. Select the PUB file from the assignment list and then click Make TOC. If you don't want to make any changes in the GENERATE TABLE OF CONTENTS dialog box, click OK. When the process is complete, click Save to keep the settings in the dialog box so that you can use them again.

Setting Up an Index

Indexing is a combination of both art and discipline. Ventura helps you make a good index *look* good. The quality of the index depends on how consistently and thoroughly you build the reference terms and concepts in the text. Because you can import index reference points and text to Ventura from the word processing text files, you may want to make a draft index to evaluate the quality of your index before you print the final copy.

Ventura can capture, sort, and paginate indexes that are two levels deep and help you overcome many tedious production details associated with producing an index. You can insert primary, secondary, and cross-reference terms (*See* and *See Also*) into an index. (Ventura's *See* and *See Also* terms do not refer the reader to a page in the chapter but to another item in the index.) When additions, revisions, and changes occur in the text, you can generate an updated index by using the Renumber command in the MULTI-CHAPTER OPERATIONS dialog box.

To make an index with Ventura, complete these three steps:

1. Insert the index reference point in the text.

2. Insert the terms and the instructions about the terms into the text.

3. Generate the index file by using the Make Index command from the MULTI-CHAPTER OPERATIONS dialog box.

The first two steps can be completed in Ventura or in your word processor. Adding index reference points and index terms to source files is discussed in "Importing Formatted Text." This part of the chapter shows how to use Ventura's features to complete these tasks.

To insert an index reference point using Ventura's commands, choose the Text function and position the edit cursor where you want to insert the reference in the work area. Open the Edit menu and select Ins Special Item to access the Index Entry option from the pop-up menu. Alternately, you can press Ctrl-C to pop up the Insert/Special Item menu and then press F3 to mark the index reference symbol. After you mark the point to reference, the INSERT/EDIT INDEX ENTRY dialog box appears (see fig. 4.33).

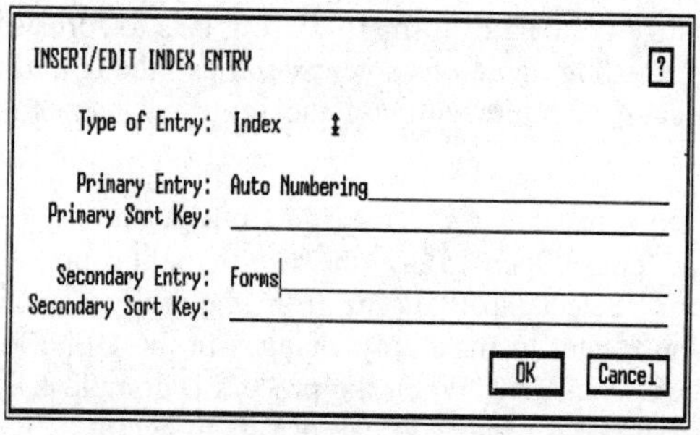

Fig. 4.33.

The INSERT/EDIT INDEX ENTRY dialog box.

```
┌─────────────────────────────────────────────────┐
│ INSERT/EDIT INDEX ENTRY                      [?] │
│                                                  │
│     Type of Entry:  Index    ↕                   │
│                                                  │
│    Primary Entry:  Auto Numbering_____ │
│  Primary Sort Key: _____ │
│                                                  │
│  Secondary Entry:  Forms|_____ │
│ Secondary Sort Key: _____ │
│                                                  │
│                            [  OK  ] [Cancel]     │
└─────────────────────────────────────────────────┘
```

The Type of Entry option offers three choices:

Index
See
See Also

The purpose of the Primary Entry and Secondary Entry options changes as you choose the different types of entries:

- If you choose Index, use the Primary Entry for the major headings and the Secondary Entry line for optional headings that appear under a primary entry.

- If you choose See, use the primary entry to type the term that is *not* used in the index and use the secondary entry for the preferred term. Ventura provides the word *See* before the secondary entry when you generate the index.

- If you choose See Also, use the primary entry for the index item and the secondary entry for the related item. In this case, Ventura inserts *See Also* before the secondary term when you generate the index.

Page numbers and chapter numbers for index entries are generated when you make the index. To include page or chapter numbers for *See* or *See Also* entries, however, you must use the technique described in the Efficiency Tip "Inserting Page and Chapter References in *See* and *See Also* Entries."

Both the primary and secondary index entries have optional sort keys for all three types of entries. These are used to sort the term differently from the way it is entered in the index. You may find that these sort keys are helpful when you begin terms with articles, as in the following example:

The Last Picture Show

You sort this term by *Last* rather than *The*.

The sort keys also are helpful when terms begin with numbers but should be sorted in alphabetic sequence. Here is an example:

3-D

Three

You use *3-D* as the primary entry and *Three* as the primary sort key.

Efficiency Tip

Inserting Page and Chapter References in *See* and *See Also* Entries

See and *See Also* entries do not permit Ventura to supply page or chapter number references. If you need to refer to pages or chapters for *See* and *See Also* entries, specify Type of Entry: Index. Type *See* or *See Also* in the Primary Entry and Secondary Entry options (if you use both) followed by the term. Then retype the term (without *See* or *See Also*) in the sort key options.

Generating an Index

You are ready to generate an index after you have set the index reference points and terms through the INSERT/EDIT INDEX ENTRY dialog box. When you click Multi-Chapter from the Options menu, Ventura asks you to save or abandon any changes made in the work area. Click Save to update the chapter file in the work area if you have made changes you want saved.

After you save the active chapter files in the work area, the MULTI-CHAPTER OPERATIONS dialog box opens. To generate an index, you use four of the commands shown in the list on the right side the dialog box:

- New

- Add Chapter

- Save/Save As

- Make Index

The first three commands are the same as those described in "Making a Table of Contents." Choose the New command to clear the list of files shown under the title bar of the dialog box (unless those chapters are the ones you want to index). Click Add Chapter to begin building a new set of chapter titles in the list or to add a chapter to the list. As you add chapters, the name of the most recent selection is added to the bottom of the list. You can rearrange the order by dragging files from one position to another with the mouse cursor.

Once all the chapters to index are listed, click Save and select a name for the publication. The name you choose is displayed in the title bar with the extension PUB.

Click Make Index to open the GENERATE INDEX dialog box (see fig. 4.34). The top line of the box shows the generated file's location and title. The next line is a title string that appears at the top of the index. You can change either of these defaults with the Text cursor. As the default name, Ventura uses the first five characters of the publication name, followed by IDX.GEN.

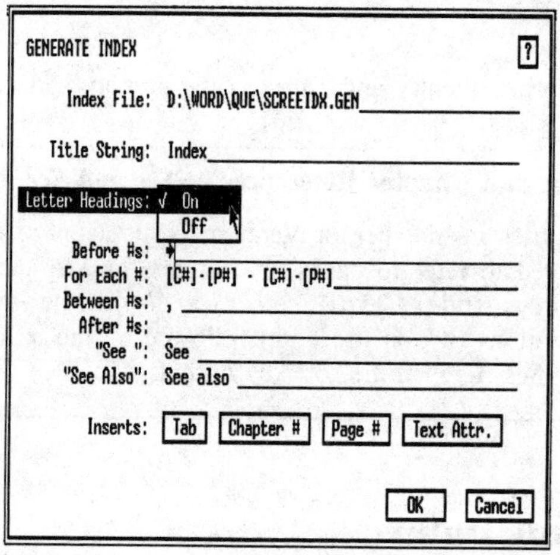

Fig. 4.34.

The GENERATE INDEX dialog box.

Click On from the Letter Headings options when you want to separate the groups of index entries with letters (A, B, C) or numbers (1, 2, 3). If you index terms that start with a character other than a letter or a number, the terms are grouped under an exclamation mark (!) in the generated index.

You use the next four options in the dialog box to specify whether to include chapter numbers with page numbers, and you define what to put between these numbers by using Before #s, For Each #, Between #s, and After #s. You can embed attribute codes and save custom defaults for each publication. Ventura's default values produce the format illustrated in figure 4.35.

The Inserts options at the bottom of the dialog box are used to insert some of the coding for tabs and page and chapter numbers. You complete the dialog box entries by using the Text cursor. If you click the Text Attr. option, Ventura inserts an

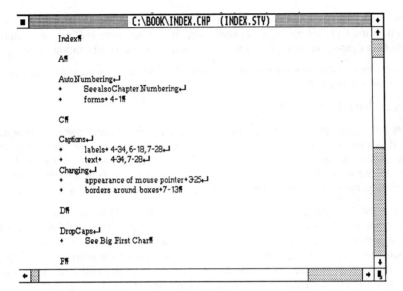

Index¶

A¶

AutoNumbering↵
   ♦   See also Chapter Numbering↵
   ♦   forms♦ 4-1¶

C¶

Captions↵
   ♦   labels♦ 4-34, 6-18, 7-28↵
   ♦   text♦   4-34, 7-28↵
Changing↵
   ♦   appearance of mouse pointer♦ 3-25↵
   ♦   borders around boxes♦7-13¶

D¶

DropCaps↵
   ♦   See Big First Char¶

F¶

Fig. 4.35.

Sample index produced with Ventura default values.

ending code <D> for character attributes at the Text cursor's location. As discussed in the Efficiency Tip "Inserting Text Attributes and Special Symbols in Dialog Boxes," you can use angle-bracket attribute codes to set text different from the default established by the paragraph's tag. Each attribute change requires a starting and an ending code.

Before #s defines what comes between the index term and the page-number reference. A tab is inserted as the default; but you can override the default with a comma and a space in order to maximize the use of space on a line in the index. If you place an attribute code in the Before #s option, you must place the ending code for the attribute in the After #s option. You might embed angle-bracket codes in Before #s and After #s, for example, to change the font size for the chapter and page numbers to a point size smaller than the text of the entry.

You use the For Each # option to specify whether to include chapter and page numbers and to define what to put between them. The default setting includes two sets of numbers separated by hyphens so that references to contiguous pages appear as

Index Entry 4 - 1 - 4 - 3

You can use character attributes to distinguish chapter numbers from page numbers. You add the attribute settings as angle-bracket codes in the For Each # option. For example,

<B>[C#]<D> - [P#] - <B>[C#]<D> - [P#]

results in

Index Entry **4** - 1 - **4** - 3

In this case, you must insert two ending codes because you want the page numbers printed in the style set by the paragraph's tag. If you are indexing just one chapter, delete both chapter number [C#] references and the hyphens that follow them.

Between #s sets the punctuation between sets of references. For example, the default settings of a comma and a space separate noncontiguous entries as

Index Entry 4 - 1 - 4 - 3, 4 - 5

After #s sets the punctuation after each index entry. The default value is no punctuation. If you use a starting angle-bracket code in Before #s, you must enter the appropriate ending angle bracket code in this option. Character attributes (like bold and italic) all end with <D>. If you change the font face, size, or color in Before #s, be sure to type the appropriate ending code (from table 4.3) in the After #s option.

The *See* and *See Also* options define the text and attributes that will be used to set these types of cross-references to primary and secondary index entries. You can replace words, change the capitalization of words, and embed angle-bracket code attributes to differentiate *See* and *See Also* from the text of the entry. Remember to place the ending attribute code after *See* or *See Also*, or the entire cross-reference entry will reflect the character attribute coding you initiate in these options.

Once you have changed the default values, click OK to close the dialog box and start the index process. Ventura makes an index by copying every term you referenced using the Edit menu's Ins Special Item and Index Entry commands. Once the terms are collected into the IDX.GEN file, Ventura sorts the terms and cross-references and then inserts the page references. To access the index file generated by the program, use the Load Text/Picture command from the File menu and click GEN as the file type. Select and place the file on the page in the same way you place any text file on a page.

Each entry ends with a line return, except the last entry in an alphanumeric group, which is followed by a paragraph return. Ventura inserts Z tags (generated tags) for each paragraph of text in the file: Z_INDEXLTR for the group separators, Z_INDEXMAIN for main entries, and Z_INDEXTITLE for the title string.

To update an index, choose Multi-Chapter from the Options menu and click Open to see the list of publication files in the dialog box. Select the name of the desired publication file and then select the Renumber command from the MULTI-CHAPTER OPERATIONS dialog box. Renumber updates the chapter, page, figure, and table numbers across chapters. To let Ventura take care of numbering across chapters, you must use the UPDATE COUNTERS dialog box, as described in Chapter 7, to set the initial chapter, page, table, and figure counters in each chapter to Previous Number + 1. Then click Make Index, click OK, and click Overwrite in the box that is displayed, in order to save the updated file over the old one. When the process is complete, click Done to complete the process.

The Index Doesn't Generate Properly

If the index does not generate, check the number of files set in the FILES statement of the CONFIG.SYS file used to configure your system. For Ventura operations, this number should be at least 15.

Also check the number of entries filed under a single index letter. The maximum number of entries under an index letter is approximately 3,000 bytes. If you exceed this maximum, you may lose some entries. For example, if you have more than 3,000 bytes under the index letter *A*, you may lose some entries. Remember that Ventura counts formatting and tabs as elements along with the text. The number of items you can include diminishes if you have tabs, font changes, or tab leaders in indexes.

Setting Up Footnotes

Ventura's footnote feature is designed to number and position footnotes automatically on the same pages as their reference points in text. For the feature to work, you must place text files on the pages instead of in frames placed on the pages. If you intend to group footnotes at the end of a chapter or want to footnote text in frames, you must position and number the footnotes manually.

The techniques used to establish a reference point and to type the text of footnotes during word processing are covered earlier in this chapter. The syntax used to embed reference points and related text in source files is shown in table 4.6. The text of the footnotes is saved in the source text files at the point where you insert the footnote reference, but the settings for footnotes are stored with the style file.

To enable the footnote feature, click Footnote Settings from the Chapter menu to open the FOOTNOTE SETTINGS dialog box. Then choose the Usage & Format option that matches the numbering system you want to use (see fig. 4.36). You can choose to number the notes on each page separately or in sequence with the other footnotes in the chapter. If you do not want to number footnotes but intend to use special symbols to introduce each footnote, choose the user-defined numbering option. You can have only eight unique footnote symbols per page, but you can establish unique values for each by typing keyboard characters as new defaults for the user-defined strings.

Use the Start With # option to establish the first number of the footnote in the chapter. The Number Template option lets you embed characters to be printed around the footnote number. For example, to enclose a footnote number in parentheses, type (#) in the Number Template option. The number sign (or pound sign) reserves the position between the parentheses for the footnote number. Footnote numbers and symbols displayed in text can be superscript or subscript when you choose the corresponding option as the position of the number.

The three commands at the bottom of the FOOTNOTE SETTINGS dialog box are used to establish the width and height of the line that Ventura automatically draws

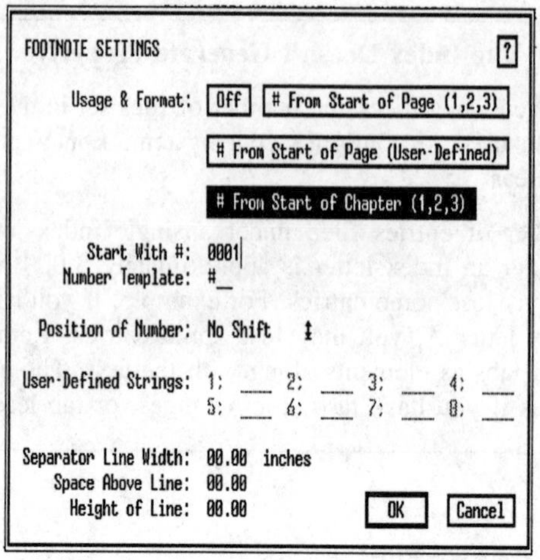

Fig. 4.36.

*The FOOTNOTE
SETTINGS dialog
box.*

```
┌──────────────────────────────────────────────────────┐
│ FOOTNOTE SETTINGS                                  [?] │
│                                                        │
│   Usage & Format:  [Off] [# From Start of Page (1,2,3)]│
│                                                        │
│                    [# From Start of Page (User·Defined)]│
│                                                        │
│                    [# From Start of Chapter (1,2,3)]   │
│                                                        │
│      Start With #:  0001|                              │
│   Number Template:  #_                                 │
│                                                        │
│ Position of Number: No Shift   ↕                       │
│                                                        │
│ User·Defined Strings:  1: ___  2: ___  3: ___  4: ___  │
│                        5: ___  6: ___  7: ___  8: ___  │
│                                                        │
│ Separator Line Width:  00.00  inches                   │
│     Space Above Line:  00.00                           │
│       Height of Line:  00.00         [ OK ] [Cancel]   │
└──────────────────────────────────────────────────────┘
```

to separate the footnote text from the text on the page. The value you type in the Separator Line Width option defines the length of the line *from the edge of the page rather than from the margin of the page or the footnote frame.* Setting the Space Above Line option as a value greater than zero causes space to be left between the separator line and the top of the footnote frame. You set the thickness of the line by typing a measurement in the Height of Line option.

You use Ventura's Text function to embed reference points for footnotes in the text on the page. Click to position the Text cursor where you want the reference number to appear and then open the Edit menu to select Ins Special Item and then Footnote. If Show Tabs & Returns is enabled, a small letter O is displayed in the position where you inserted the footnote reference. If the Usage & Format option has been defined in the FOOTNOTE SETTINGS dialog box, you see the number of the footnote in the text. The current selection box indicates that the cursor is positioned at a footnote reference. When you have a footnote reference point in the text and have enabled the footnote feature, a frame for the footnote is displayed at the base of the page.

The size of the footnote frame is influenced by the values set in the Above and Below space in the Body Text tag. (These spacing values are set in the SPACING dialog box from the Paragraph menu.) The size of the frame expands and contracts as you add to and edit the text of the footnote. You cannot resize the footnote frame with the frame handles because Ventura resizes the footnote frame automatically based on the quantity of text in the footnote.

To make the separator line that Ventura draws automatically between page text and footnote text start at the same margin as the text on the page, select the footnote frame with the Frame cursor and then open the MARGINS & COLUMNS dialog box from the Frame menu. Footnote frames can have only one column, and the length of the column is adjusted as you set the left and right margins. In the example shown in figure 4.16, the margins of the footnote frame have the same values as those of the page. The separator-line width is set one inch longer than the margins, which results in a line drawn inside the left margin for a length of 1 inch.

To format the text and numbers in a footnote frame, you use the Spacing, Alignment, and Breaks commands as described in Chapter 5. Ventura generates a Z_FNOT# tag for every footnote number and tags the text of the footnote with Z_FNOT ENTRY. Because each element of the footnote is separately tagged, you can establish individual formats for the numbers and text.

When you click Usage & Format: Off in the FOOTNOTE SETTINGS dialog box, footnote numbers and footnote text are not displayed. Any references or text that has been set in the source file, however, is not erased. When you enable a Usage & Format option other than Off, the footnotes are displayed in Ventura's work area. You can see the references to footnotes in the current selection box whether or not the Usage & Format option is enabled. To avoid erasing footnotes, always enable Show Tabs & Returns when editing files that contain footnotes. To erase a footnote from the source file, simply delete the reference to the footnote.

Efficiency Tip

Keyboard Shortcuts to the Edit Menu's Special Items

You can quickly access any of the six items displayed in the Ins Special Item pop-up menu displayed from the Edit menu:

1. Position the edit cursor in text where you want the special item to appear.

2. Press Ctrl-C.

3. Press the appropriate function key:

F1	Box characters
F2	Footnote references
F3	Index entries
F4	Fractions
F5	Frame anchors
F6	Cross-references

Setting Up Automatic Numbering

Ventura has several automatic-numbering features that manage page and chapter numbers as well as numbers for figures, tables, captions, and footnotes. The Chapter menu's Auto-Numbering command can be used to number items in lists, sections in manuals, or paragraphs in an outline. The command also can be used to include (with or without numbering) text or rules to be printed consistently with designated paragraphs. By using the Auto-Numbering command, you can eliminate the need to type numbers or repeating text in source files.

The automatic-numbering features are beneficial for numbering sections in manuscripts and long documents. If you use Ventura to produce forms, automatic numbering gives you the capability to increment a counter and produce a numbered series of forms. As with the footnote feature, only paragraphs placed on pages in the publication (not frames placed on the pages) can be tagged for automatic numbering. Some potential uses of the automatic-numbering command are listed here:

- Numbering outlines, lists, tables of contents, and manuals

- Creating a numbered series of forms

- Inserting short lines of constant text

When you tag a paragraph in a source file with one of the names referenced in Ventura's AUTO-NUMBERING dialog box, Ventura inserts another tagged paragraph when the file is loaded into a Ventura chapter. The second tag, called a Z_SEC tag, controls the sequence and format of the numbering and repeating text. You see only the second paragraph and tag when you view the file in Ventura's work area. The outline numbering in figure 4.37 was generated by setting automatic numbering with the names of five tags. In figure 4.38, a tag was set to number the form and another tag was set to provide the line numbers beside the items in the form.

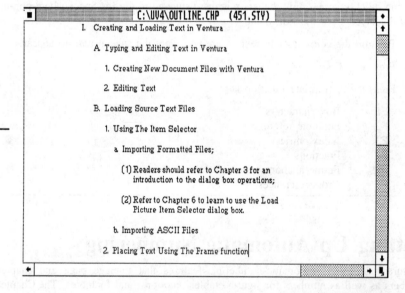

Fig. 4.37.

An automatically numbered outline.

```
 ■ ░░░░░░░░░░  C:\UV4\OUTLINE.CHP  (451.STY) ░░░░░░░░  ◆
                                                          ↑
      I. Creating and Loading Text in Ventura

         A. Typing and Editing Text in Ventura

             1. Creating New Document Files with Ventura

             2. Editing Text

         B. Loading Source Text Files

             1. Using The Item Selector

                 a. Importing Formatted Files;

                     (1) Readers should refer to Chapter 3 for an
                         introduction to the dialog box operations;

                     (2) Refer to Chapter 6 to learn to use the Load
                         Picture Item Selector dialog box.

                 b. Importing ASCII Files

             2. Placing Text Using The Frame function|
                                                          ↓
 ◆ ░░░░░░░░░░░░░░░░░░░░░░░░░░░░░░░░░░░░░░░░░░░░░░  → ▌
```

In Chapter 5, you see how to set custom formats for generated tags and the tags used to name paragraphs. You make the two paragraphs print adjacent to one another by using the Alignment, Breaks, and Spacing commands from the Paragraph menu. You define any text attributes for the numbers or constant text, however, by using the method described in the Efficiency Tip "Inserting Text Attributes and Special Symbols in Dialog Boxes," in this chapter.

To open the AUTO-NUMBERING dialog box, click Auto-Numbering on the Chapter menu. Click the Usage: On option to enable the Level and Inserts options (see fig. 4.39). The cursor is displayed in position to edit the Level 1 option. The selections made in this dialog box are saved as defaults for the style file. You can turn off

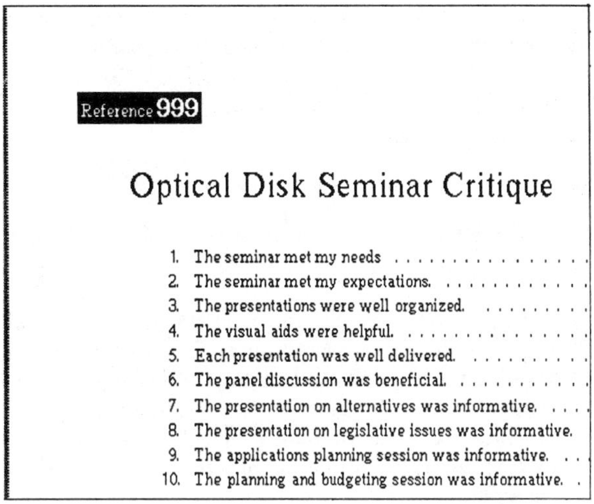

Reference **999**

Optical Disk Seminar Critique

1. The seminar met my needs . . . .
2. The seminar met my expectations. . . . .
3. The presentations were well organized. . . . .
4. The visual aids were helpful. . . . .
5. Each presentation was well delivered. . . . .
6. The panel discussion was beneficial. . . . .
7. The presentation on alternatives was informative. . . . .
8. The presentation on legislative issues was informative. .
9. The applications planning session was informative. . . .
10. The planning and budgeting session was informative. .

Fig. 4.38.

A numbered form with numbered lines.

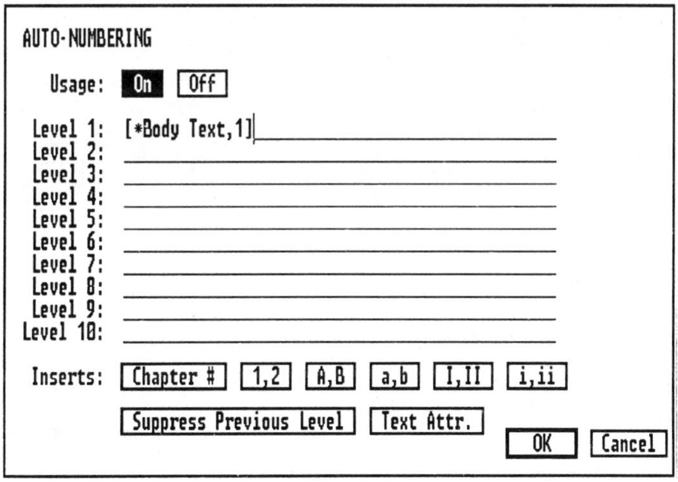

AUTO-NUMBERING

Usage: On   Off

Level 1: [*Body Text,1]
Level 2:
Level 3:
Level 4:
Level 5:
Level 6:
Level 7:
Level 8:
Level 9:
Level 10:

Inserts: Chapter #   1,2   A,B   a,b   I,II   i,ii

Suppress Previous Level   Text Attr.

OK   Cancel

Fig. 4.39.

Automatic numbering with Ventura's default style file.

the settings when you do not want to use the feature. The only paragraphs affected are those named in the dialog box.

Each entry you make in the AUTO-NUMBERING dialog box must be inserted in a specific format. Ventura provides a pattern for you to follow when you click to select the style of number from the Inserts option. The five numbering options follow:

1   A   a   I   i

You can combine the five styles to accommodate Roman numeral outlines as well as Arabic numbering schemes that repeat each number's level with the next (for example, 1, 1.1, 1.1a).

As you click each numbering option, Ventura displays a different prompt on the line in the dialog box where the cursor was positioned. For example: [*tag name,1,1] appears when you click 1,2 from the Inserts options. These elements must be placed in brackets in the order listed. The commas separate the bracketed elements, which represent three types of information:

- The tag name
- The style of numbering
- The starting number for this tag

Customize the tag-name prompt by leaving the bracket and asterisk in place and striking over tag name with the name you want to use. The first number indicates which Inserts option was chosen and is followed by the starting number for the tag. Ventura defaults to the equivalent of *1* for each Inserts option when you erase the starting number. If you erase the style of numbering, Ventura does not number the paragraph at all. Any text you type outside the brackets is displayed and printed each time the tag is encountered.

Ventura also defaults to display all previous level numbers when each successive level is encountered. In figure 4.40, the presence of [-] on every Level option shows that the display of the preceding Level option has been suppressed. Unless you need to print the hierarchy of each number as each level is encountered, suppress the preceding level from printing by adding the [-] code to each tag; you add this code by clicking the Suppress Previous Level option for each entry. Place the code at either the beginning or the end of the other commands defined in each Level option.

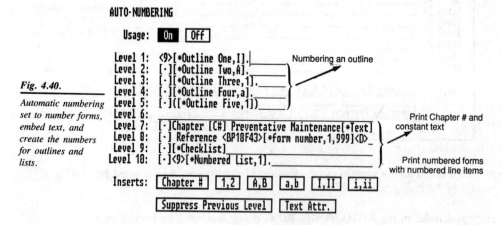

Fig. 4.40.

Automatic numbering set to number forms, embed text, and create the numbers for outlines and lists.

Each of the 10 Level options can be used independently or with another level. For example, you can use all the levels for one numbering system, or you can use part of the dialog box for numbering and part of the dialog box for inserting constant text.

In the AUTO-NUMBERING dialog box, the only named paragraph that is stored with Ventura's default style file is Body Text. If you enable automatic numbering and leave

Body Text named in the dialog box, every untagged paragraph in the source file is displayed under a number when you close the dialog box by clicking OK. To eliminate the numbers and all the tags associated with the numbers, open the AUTO-NUMBERING dialog box again and click Usage: Off. You may find that including the Body Text tag in the dialog box is useful in two situations:

- To cause numbers to start counting over again in the same source file when body text is encountered

- To number every untagged paragraph in the source file

You do not have to use the Body Text tag to reset the counter. (If you do, every untagged paragraph has two paragraph symbols and tags when viewed in a chapter.) In figure 4.40, the dialog box contains all the commands needed to do the following:

- Number a five-level outline using I.A.1.a.(1) as the counting style

- Insert the chapter number and the words *Preventative Maintenance* at paragraphs that are formatted with a tag named Text

- Number items incrementally in separate lists in the chapter using 1,2,3 as the counting style

- Start a form-numbering series at 1,999 (the number prints larger than the word *Reference*, which is constant text)

Level 6, shown in the middle of the dialog box in figure 4.40, is left blank so that the end of the outline-numbering series is easier to see. The counter for the numbered list is reset when any other tag in the box precedes the Numbered List tag in the source file. To ensure that each list begins with *1*, however, the Checklist tag was added to the dialog box. Make sure that each list starts with *1* because you have no guarantee that a tag named in the dialog box always precedes the beginning of a new numbered list. The Checklist tag resets to *0* the counter for each numbered list and allows a unique format for the title of each numbered list.

You include the chapter number in a numbering system when you choose Chapter # from the Inserts options (see fig. 4.40, level 7). The Text Attr. option is used to embed character formatting around numbers and constant text. You also can embed angle-bracket codes for the special symbols listed in tables 4.2 through 4.5 before or after the square-bracket codes inserted in this dialog box. Position these codes in the sequence in which you want to display them (see fig. 4.40, levels 1 and 10).

Once you learn to use the automatic-numbering feature, you will observe that the source files use fewer tags, are easier to read as source files, and are easier to keep updated. In figure 4.41, the source file contained one tag and one line of text:

@Text = Do not mix lubricant with other fluids

In comparison, without automatic numbering, the source file would look like this:

@Head = Chapter 13 Preventative Maintenance

@Text = Do not mix lubricant with other fluids

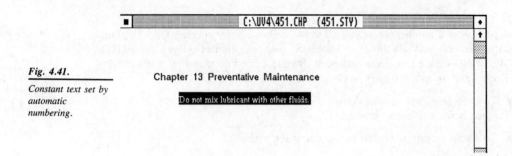

Fig. 4.41.

Constant text set by automatic numbering.

To make changes that affect how a paragraph is numbered, simply move the paragraph with word processing and change the tag name if you are changing the numbering level for that paragraph.

Efficiency Tip

Editing Automatically Numbered Source Files with a Word Processor

The fastest way to reorganize items in source files referenced in the AUTO-NUMBERING dialog box is to edit the text with a word processor. Move the items into the new sequence and change the name of the paragraph tag if you want to number the item at a different level. (You do not see the Ventura Z_SEC tags in word processing.) The next time you load the chapter file into Ventura's work area, the changes are numbered according to the new sequence.

The tags generated by Ventura to control automatic numbering look like any other paragraph symbols in the work area, but the text and numbers shown by the tags' settings cannot be edited. You can see the name of the tag when you select the paragraph with the tagging cursor. The number of the Z_SEC tag displayed corresponds to the Level option you assigned the tag in the AUTO-NUMBERING dialog box. Although you do not edit the content of Z_SEC tags, you may need to edit or delete the content of the text in the corresponding paragraphs.

When you edit and move items in paragraphs that have a corresponding Z_SEC tag, follow these steps:

1. Select the text with the Text cursor.

2. Cut the text to the Clipboard.

3. Insert the text into position.

4. Renumber the chapter using Ctrl-B (or using the Renumber Chapter command from the Page menu).

To delete the text in a paragraph named in the AUTO-NUMBERING dialog box, you must work through several steps. (Refer to the Efficiency Tip ''Editing Automatically Numbered Source Files with a Word Processor'' if you have several of these types of changes to make). This procedure follows:

1. Turn on Show/Hide Tabs & Returns in the Options menu.

2. Position the Text I-beam immediately after the paragraph symbol for the Z_SEC tag and select that symbol and the text to delete.

3. Press the Del key to erase the highlighted text.

4. Press Ctrl-B to renumber the chapter.

Chapter Summary

The process of placing text into Ventura is relatively straightforward. You use the Load Text/Picture command to bring in files from other programs. You use the Paste command to insert up to a page of text that was cut or copied from another chapter. You use the Text function to type short segments of text.

Use the Load Text/Picture command to import text typed in a word processor or any data saved as a text-only ASCII file from a spreadsheet or database program. If the text has been formatted in a word processing program Ventura supports, Ventura preserves some of that formatting and allows you to convert source files from one format to another. You can choose to list the file as a separate file or merge files with one another.

Text typed directly into Ventura takes on the characteristics of the surrounding text. The characteristics are set by the tag name that is attached to the paragraph—unless you define special attribute settings for a word or section of text within a paragraph. You can set or change both types of text characteristics during word processing by using the procedures discussed in the section "Importing Formatted Text" or using Ventura features described in Chapter 5, "Formatting Text, Tables, and Lists."

5

Formatting Text, Tables, and Lists

The word *format* can mean many things. You can use *format* to describe a type of text file, as in Chapters 4 and 6. You also can use *format* to describe the general design of a brochure, newsletter, or book. In that context, formats for different projects are illustrated in Chapters 12 through 16. Ventura provides 20 sample formats in the style sheet files written to the TYPESET directory during program installation. This chapter discusses how to set up your own style files as you develop format settings for projects. The goal is to learn how to use the Ventura tools that affect the appearance of text on the page.

Ventura's formatting features give you the ability to position, size, rotate, and align text within the margins of pages, columns, and frames. You can format paragraphs with the same type specifications and assign special treatment for words or phrases within paragraphs. When formatting paragraphs, you can determine whether to allow hyphenation within the paragraph, and you can define ruled lines to set apart selected paragraphs for emphasis.

You also may select a color from the default palette of eight colors or mix custom colors to display and print text, graphics, and patterns on the page. Users of systems configured with what-you-see-is-what-you-get (WYSIWYG) color monitors, but not color printers, can use color formatting to see whether color complements the design. Subsequent mass production of the color page by an offset printer matches the colors on the monitor only if the color of stock and inks used in printing match the mix on-screen. Although an exact match is unlikely for most projects, you may find color WYSIWYG helpful in evaluating alternative color schemes. Configuring a color system is discussed in Chapter 2.

In this chapter, you see how to use Ventura's style file feature (*tags*) to format paragraphs and the Text function to format words and phrases in paragraphs. Formatting text is closely related to the page-layout process covered in Chapter 7. You learn to use the style file to define the size of the pages, margins, and columns that hold text and graphics. Several typographic techniques and design principles, explained in Chapter 9, help you decide how to choose fonts to complement the design of a page. Understanding the techniques in those chapters also helps you to format text.

The Role of the Style File in Formatting

As discussed in Chapter 3, Ventura uses a chapter (CHP) file to assemble all the files related to a project. One of those files is a *style file* (STY). When a series of chapters is referenced by a publication (PUB) file, each CHP file references the STY file for the chapter. You can load an existing chapter file to use previously developed patterns or templates (for example, when working on repetitive projects). You can start new projects by modifying an existing style file or developing a new style file. The style file defines the size, margins, columns, and position of the base page of a chapter and stores the list of tags that label the different format and typography settings for text.

Ventura's use of style files to control the overall page and typography characteristics of each project offers several benefits. You can ''borrow'' a copy of the samples provided with the program to get a quick start on a project. You can create custom designs for different projects and establish a series of designs for related projects. Several chapters or projects can share a common design, perhaps developed according to the specifications of a professional designer. You can use different style files to evaluate the effects of dramatic or subtle changes in the design specifications. With Ventura's network Version 2.0, each licensed user can reference and use read-only style files from a common library. Page production, therefore, is simplified for individual users, and design consistency is maintained.

The following design elements are controlled by the style file:

- Paper size and orientation
- Measure and number of margins on the base page
- Width and number of columns on the base page
- Footnote and automatic numbering settings
- Placement of vertical rules on the base page
- Background pattern of the base page
- Format instructions for tagged paragraphs of text

Every time you start Ventura, the name of the active style file appears in parentheses beneath the menu titles. When you select Show Column Guides from the Options menu, the design of the base page set by the active style file is outlined with margin and column guides (see fig. 5.1). Text, when typed or loaded into the chapter named in the title line, displays according to the settings established for the tags named in the sidebar. Typed text defaults to the settings for body text. Later in this chapter, you learn to modify the default settings and add new tags to store typographic instructions for paragraphs in the text.

The base page establishes a design pattern for pages created when a multipage source text file is placed on the base page. You can have more than one page design in a chapter, but only the settings established for the base page are saved as settings in the style file associated with that chapter. Whenever you insert a new page by using the Insert/Remove Page command from the Chapter menu, you can set new margins or

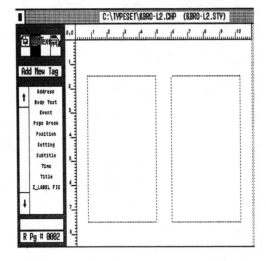

Fig. 5.1.

A two-column brochure designed for landscape printing.

columns that will prevail for each page created from the pattern of the new page. This capability accommodates changes in page design within a chapter and enables you to paginate more than one source file in a chapter. As you learned in Chapter 4, you also can override the settings of a page by placing frames on the page to accommodate specifications differing from the overall design.

To define the settings for the design elements set by the style file, use commands from four of Ventura's menus. The menus and commands stored by the style file are listed in table 5.1. Other commands appearing in these menus are not stored as settings in the style file.

Table 5.1
Style File Contents

Menu	*Command*	*Option**
Chapter	Page, Size, and Layout	
	Chapter Typography	Column Balance
		Move Down to 1st Baseline
		By Pair Kerning
		Vert Just Within & Around Frame
	Auto-Numbering	
	Footnote Settings	
Frame	Margins & Columns	(for the base page)
	Sizing & Scaling	Flow Text Around
		Frame X Y, Width, Height,
		Horizontal & Vertical Padding

Table 5.1—Continued

Menu	Command	Option*
	Vertical Rules	
	Ruling Line Above	
	Ruling Line Below	
	Ruling Box Around	
	Frame Background	
Paragraph	Font	
	Alignment	
	Spacing	
	Breaks	
	Tab Settings	
	Attribute Overrides	
	Special Effects	
	Paragraph Typography	
	Ruling Lines Above, Below, and Around	
	Define colors	
	Update tag list	Assign Func Keys
Options	Set Printer Info	Width Table

*This column only shows individual names of options when all the options for a command are not stored in the style file. If all the options are stored in the style file, they are not listed in this column.

You override the style file's page-design settings when you place frames on pages or create new pages with individual margin and column settings. (Additional instructions are stored in the chapter file.) In both cases, however, the format of the text is influenced by the measures of the margins and columns defined for the area in which you place the text.

Besides defining the boundaries of the page in the work area, the style file contains the names of all the tags used to format paragraphs. In Ventura, a *paragraph* is any segment of text ending with a hard carriage return (when loaded from compatible word processors) or two consecutive carriage returns (when loaded as an ASCII file). Figure 5.2 shows an ASCII file in a word processing program and in Ventura; the ¶ symbol represents a carriage return. Ventura 2.0 imposes a limit of approximately 48,000 paragraphs per chapter and 8,000 bytes per paragraph. You can build chapters nearly 10 times larger with the Professional Extension and EMS, described in Chapter 2. In Chapter 4, you learn how to use line breaks rather than paragraph returns to overcome the bytes-per-paragraph limit.

You can choose unique formats for up to 128 types of paragraphs. Identify each type of paragraph with a name, called a *tag*. For example, the tags shown in the Paragraph function assignment list in figure 5.3 are used to identify types of copy in a newsletter.

Ventura inserts two paragraph returns when you press the¶
ENTER key in an ASCII file. You can edit ASCII¶
files in Ventura, letting Ventura handle word¶
wraps within paragraphs. Though the ASCII.TXT¶
file will display carriage returns at the¶
end of every line in the file when you acess the¶
file using a word processing program, Ventura¶
only interprets two consecutive returns as the end of a paragraph.¶

¶

Ventura inserts two
paragraph returns when
you press the ENTER key
in an ASCII file. You can
edit ASCII files in Ven-
tura, letting Ventura handle word wraps within
paragraphs. Though the
ASCII.TXT file will dis-
play carriage returns at the
end of every line in the
file when you acess the
file using a word processing program, Ventura only
interprets two consecutive
returns as the end of a
paragraph.¶

¶

Fig. 5.2.

*An ASCII file in a
word processing
program and in
Ventura.*

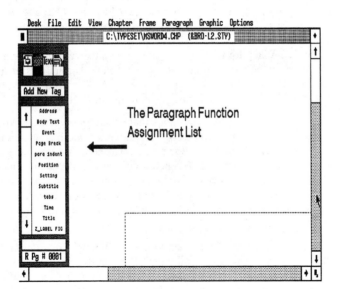

Fig. 5.3.

*The Paragraph
function assignment
list.*

Add and name tags by using the Paragraph function's Add New Tag button. Define
the settings for each tag by using the first 12 commands on the Paragraph menu (see
fig. 5.4). The dialog boxes associated with these commands are covered in "Setting
Paragraph Formats" in this chapter. You use the last command in the Paragraph
menu, Update Tag List, to manage the list of tags you create.

With Ventura, you can customize a default tag, called Body Text, for each style file.
Paragraphs that use the values established for the Body Text tag do not need individual tags. You cannot change the name of the default tag, and you cannot remove the
tag from the style file. In "Managing Tags in the Style File," you learn more about
naming, removing, and converting paragraphs from one format to another.

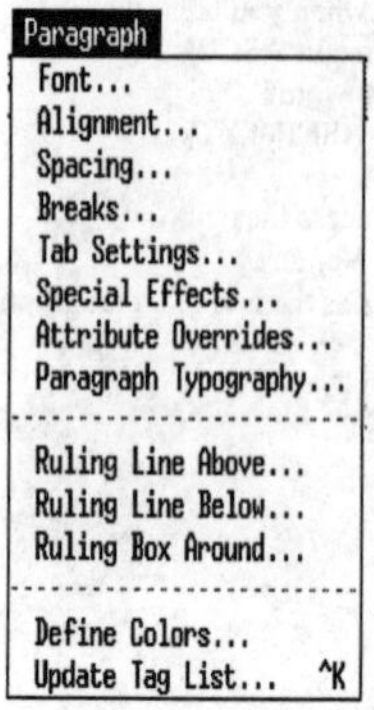

Paragraph
- Font...
- Alignment...
- Spacing...
- Breaks...
- Tab Settings...
- Special Effects...
- Attribute Overrides...
- Paragraph Typography...
- - - - - - - - - - - - - - - - -
- Ruling Line Above...
- Ruling Line Below...
- Ruling Box Around...
- - - - - - - - - - - - - - - - -
- Define Colors...
- Update Tag List...   ^K

Fig. 5.4.

The Paragraph menu text format commands.

Using tags is not the only way to format text. You also can format individual characters, words, phrases, and paragraphs by using the Text function. Character formatting overrides the values set by the paragraph's tag. In contrast to tagging, character formatting is not stored as a setting in the style file but is stored in the text file as a code (or sequence of codes). When formatting characters, you attach attributes by using the Text function to select text and sidebar options. The Set Font button accesses the same type of dialog box used to select the typeface of text. The section "Formatting Phrases in Paragraphs" explains how to use Ventura to emphasize words.

The paragraph and character format instructions that define the typefaces, sizes, and styles have to be sent to the printer. To do so, Ventura uses a width table that matches the selected fonts with those supported by the printer. The style file stores the name of the width table selected for the project. When you change to a different printer width table, you enable fonts and format capabilities unique to individual printers. If you use one printer and have never added any fonts, use the same width table all the time. You can see the name of the width table in use when you open the Options menu's SET PRINTER INFO dialog box.

You need not change width tables if you want to use a different printer during production. For example, you can design, set, and proof an annual report on a 300-dots-per-inch printer, but you can use a higher resolution printer to create the final camera-ready pages—using the same width table. If you change width tables during a project, you do not see the same line or pagination breaks in the printed copies. For more on width tables, see Chapters 3 and 8.

Efficiency Tip

Using a Single Style File with Two Printers

The style file establishes which width table is used. The width table determines the fonts available. When you use two types of printers during the production phase, always leave the width table you use for the *final printer* in the Width Table option of the SET PRINTER INFO dialog box, accessed from the Options menu. What you see on the draft printout duplicates the line and paragraph endings as they appear on the final version, but the draft version does not properly shape each letter.

As noted in table 5.1, several commands from the Frame and Chapter menus also are set by the active style file. In Chapter 3, you learned to use the Frame menu's Margins & Columns command and the Chapter menu's Page Size & Layout command to establish the size and characteristics of the page. This chapter discusses the relationship between the settings when commands from those menus affect commands in the Paragraph menu. In Chapter 7, you learn how to use commands from the Frame and Chapter menus to override a default setting defined by the style file.

Chapter 4 covers the guidelines for preformatting text files with paragraph tags and character codes. Using the glossary or macro features of a compatible word processor, you can insert tag names and character formats more quickly than you can with Ventura. Even if you have a compatible word processing program, however, there are at least four good reasons to format in Ventura:

- You can develop designs on-screen with Ventura as you create a reusable project style.

- Although you can preformat text by typing tag names into text files in a word processor, you must define the settings for each tag in Ventura.

- Ventura's character formatting is more comprehensive than that of any word processing program, but figuring out which codes to type into the text files for character attributes different from those of your word processor can prove more cumbersome than using Ventura to attach the attributes.

- Fine-tuning a design and making subtle format adjustments is easier with Ventura's realistic WYSIWYG display than with a less graphic word processing screen.

Any text you place or type into the work area is formatted as specified by the settings for the Body Text tag until you override the default and attach a different tag to the text. To override the paragraph settings for selected letters or phrases within a paragraph, use the Text function's character-formatting features. See Chapter 11 for instructions on quickly evaluating the effect of alternative design specs.

The look of the text you see depends on which style file is active. When you choose the Load Diff. Style command from the File menu, the appearance of the pages in the work area changes to reflect the page margins, column settings, and paragraph tags in the newly loaded style file. Figure 5.5 shows a formatted chapter file. In figure 5.6, the tag names for the paragraphs are identical, but the newly selected style file is reflected in the page design and typographic settings.

When you installed Ventura, 20 sample style files were copied into a directory named TYPESET (unless you chose not to copy the example files to disk). These designs for brochures, manuals, newsletters, tables, graphs, and books are used by the sample chapter files also stored in the same directory. The default style file that appears when you first start Ventura also is stored in the TYPESET directory. In Chapter 3, you saw how to use a sample style file without changing the settings. Leaving Ventura's sample style files unchanged is a good idea. Start a new project by making a copy of a sample style file, renaming it, and placing the copy in the directory of your choice. Customize the copy rather than the original.

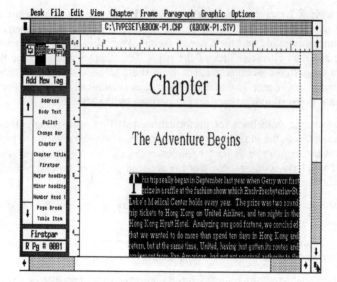

Fig. 5.5.

A formatted chapter file using the &BOOK-P1.STY style file.

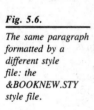

Fig. 5.6.

The same paragraph formatted by a different style file: the &BOOKNEW.STY style file.

Accidentally changing a style file is an easy mistake to make. To avoid modifying a style file unintentionally, use the commands from the File menu in this sequence:

1. To start a new project, choose New when any chapter other than UNTITLED is in view.

2. To use a style file other than the active one, choose the Load Diff. Style command.

3. To make a copy of the active style file, choose Save As New Style and rename the new style file.

4. To name the chapter file, choose Save As.

Figure 5.7 shows the File menu; figure 5.8 shows the ITEM SELECTOR dialog box. The techniques used to load and save files with the ITEM SELECTOR dialog box are detailed in Chapter 3. Remember to look at the name of the directory and path shown at the top of the dialog box. Ventura's default extension for style files (STY) is shown after the asterisk. As with all file names, if you let Ventura provide the extension when you name a new style file, you won't have to type *STY* when you load the file.

Fig. 5.7.

Start a new project by using the File menu commands.

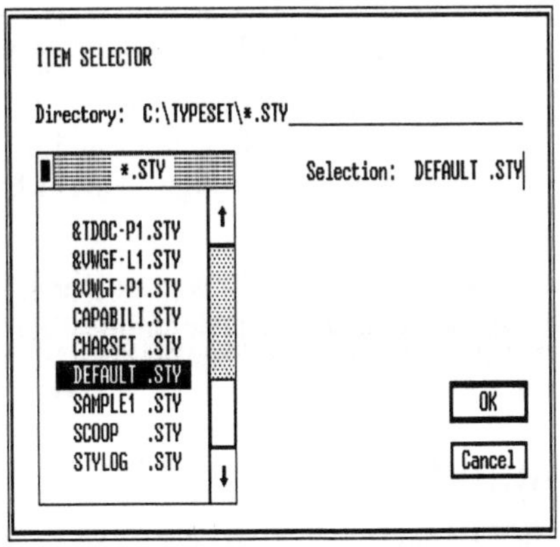

Fig. 5.8.

The ITEM SELECTOR dialog box.

You can make a different style file for each chapter, or you can use the same style file for chapters with the same basic design specifications. Any changes you make to the design elements set by the style file apply to all the chapters using that file. See Chapter 3 for a discussion of the alternatives in project file organization.

When you retrieve a chapter with the Open Chapter command from the File menu, Ventura retrieves the chapter's style file as the program assembles the related files in the work area. When you save a chapter file, Ventura saves and updates the active style file with any changes you have made. Always make sure that you are using a style file you intend to update before choosing the Save or the Save As command. If you need to abandon all changes, click Abandon on the File menu; Ventura reloads the chapter and style files as they were when last saved.

Setting Paragraph Formats

You define the format of a paragraph with the commands in the Paragraph menu. Type style and size, margin justification, horizontal and vertical spacing and alignment, ruling lines, and hyphenation are choices that you can make on a paragraph-by-paragraph basis. When a paragraph does not have a tag name, Ventura assumes that you want the Body Text settings to define the format of that paragraph. In many publishing projects, most text is formatted by the Body Text settings, and only a few paragraphs in the text file need a tag.

Attaching a tag to a paragraph is a two-step process. First, you select the paragraph; then you tag it. "Attaching Tags to Paragraphs" in this chapter shows you alternative ways to tag paragraphs. Before you can define paragraph formats, however, you need to know the basic steps to select a paragraph and attach a tag:

1. Click the Paragraph function.

2. Leave the paragraph cursor over a paragraph in the work area and click, selecting the paragraph. The selected paragraph is displayed in reverse type.

3. Click a tag name in the assignment list, tagging the selected paragraph.

When you select a paragraph, the name of the active tag is displayed in the current selection box at the bottom of the sidebar (see figs. 5.5 and 5.6). Selected paragraphs display in reverse video as illustrated in the figures by white text on a black background.

The Paragraph menu commands are active only when a paragraph is selected. The following sections describe the commands available on the Paragraph menu (refer to fig. 5.4).

The Font Command

The Font command from the Paragraph menu sets the typeface, size, style, and color of the text. If you first select a paragraph and click Font, the FONT dialog box opens (see fig. 5.9). The name of the tag for which you are specifying font options appears in the upper left corner of the FONT dialog box.

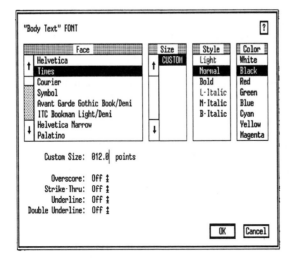

Fig. 5.9.

The FONT dialog box.

Face

You change the font for the tag named at the top of the dialog box when you select another name from the list of typefaces. The selected paragraph and all other paragraphs tagged with that same name change to reflect the new setting. The list you use in the Face option depends on the type of printer you use.

PostScript® printers print only the typefaces supported by your printer; they do not necessarily support all the names shown in the list in the FONT dialog box. See Chapter 8 for a comparison of the built-in printer fonts on PostScript printers and to learn how to add fonts.

Ventura comes with a width table containing information for 42 typefaces, identified by name in the FONT dialog box if you have a PostScript printer. Table 5.2 lists all the typefaces available. See Chapter 9 to learn how to add screen fonts purchased separately from Ventura.

Table 5.2
Typefaces in Ventura

Typeface	ID Number	Typeface	ID Number
American Typewriter	100	*Helvetica Narrow	50
*ITC Avant Garde	51	ITC Korinna	54
ITC Benguiat	26	Letter Gothic	105
Bodoni	36	Lubalin	24
Bodoni Poster	37	ITC Machine	101
*ITC Bookman	23	Melior	31

Table 5.2—_Continued_

Typeface	ID Number	Typeface	ID Number
Century Old Style	38	New Baskerville	33
Cheltenham	39	*New Century Schoolbook	20
*Courier	1	Optima	52
Franklin Gothic	56	Orator	104
Franklin Gothic Heavy	57	*Palatino	21
Friz Quadrata	28	Park Avenue	35
ITC Galliard	32	Prestige Elite	103
ITC Garamond	22	Sonata	130
Glypha	27	ITC Souvenir	25
Goudy	34	*Symbol	128
*Helvetica (Swiss)	2	*Times (Dutch)	14
Helvetica Black	55	Trump Mediaeval	30
Helvetica Condensed Lt.	58	*Zapf Chancery	29
Helvetica Condensed	59	*Zapf Dingbats	129
Helvetica Condensed Black	60	Reset to Tag Font	225
Helvetica Light	54		

*These faces are available with most printers supporting Adobe PostScript and compatibles.

You can override the paragraph default setting for selected characters within the paragraph by using the Text function's Set Font button. When you do this, Ventura inserts the ID number of that typeface into the text file; Ventura does not insert this number into the text file when you select a font for tagged paragraphs.

Size

If you have a non-PostScript printer, select the type size from the list of sizes in the FONT dialog box. If the word CUSTOM appears, your PostScript printer prints any point size between 1 and 254 in half-point increments when you type a value in the Custom Size field.

Type sizes are measured in units called _points_. There are 12 points in a pica and approximately 6 picas in an inch (72 points to the inch). Not all printers use all the possible sizes of every typeface. If the Auto-Adjustments: Styles option is set in the Options menu's SET PREFERENCES dialog box, changing the size of a font increases the value set in the Inter-Line option of the SPACING dialog box by 1.2 percent. As you increase or decrease the font size, the space between lines of text adjusts proportionately. Permitting Ventura to adjust spacing values can create unevenly aligned multicolumn and facing-page layouts. The alignment of text on uniform baselines is discussed later in this chapter. This alignment can serve as a production aid, however, only when you are working on a single column layout.

When you choose Grow Inter-Line To Fit: On in the PARAGRAPH TYPOGRA-PHY dialog box, interline spacing adjusts to accommodate changes in the size of selected text within paragraphs. This setting enables you to increase the font size for selected text without having to adjust the paragraph's interline spacing.

Style

You can print the tagged paragraph with light, normal, bold, or italic when these options are displayed in the FONT dialog box. If the options appear gray, the font is not available with the printer width table you have chosen.

Color

In addition to choosing the typeface, size, and style, you can select a color from the list displayed in the FONT dialog box.

Ventura prints color separations when you select Spot Color Overlays: On in the File menu's TO PRINT dialog box. A separate page prints for every enabled color. Use the Define Colors option in the Paragraph menu (described later in this chapter) to enable and create custom colors. (See Chapter 8 for more information on printing colors).

As discussed in Chapter 9, selecting colors with a PostScript printer enables you to print text as shades of gray and as outlined and rotated text. On non-PostScript printers, colors print as 100 percent black.

Overscore, Strike-Thru, and Underline

Change the defaults for Overscore, Strike-Thru, Underline, and Double Underline from Off to On to print lines, respectively, over, through, or under all the text in a paragraph. To apply the same treatment to phrases within paragraphs, see ''Formatting Phrases in Paragraphs'' later in this chapter.

Efficiency Tip

Opening the FONT Dialog Box

You can open the FONT dialog box in four ways, because Ventura allows you to treat all of a paragraph, part of a paragraph, or the first character in a paragraph with distinct format instructions. The four sets of instructions for opening the FONT dialog box are given here:

- To set the font of a selected paragraph, use the Font command on the Paragraph menu. This command affects the tag settings for that paragraph and all other paragraphs tagged similarly.

- To set the first character in a paragraph differently from the rest of the paragraph, open the SPECIAL EFFECTS dialog box from the Paragraph menu and click Big First Char. Then choose the Set Font Properties option to open the FONT SETTING FOR BIG FIRST CHAR dialog box.

- To add a bullet at the beginning of each paragraph, open the SPECIAL EFFECTS dialog box from the Paragraph menu and click Bullet. Choose Set Font Properties to open the FONT SETTING FOR BULLET CHARACTER dialog box.

- To set the font of selected characters, words, or phrases, use the Set Font button of the Text function.

The Alignment Command

Font specifications define the appearance of each character; alignment settings position the text within the page, column, and frame boundaries. The ALIGNMENT dialog box from the Paragraph menu contains 12 options that affect the alignment of text (see fig. 5.10). To change settings for the first eight options, click the displayed setting. When the pop-up menu appears, drag the cursor to the setting you want and release the mouse button. To change settings for the next four options, enter values. These options are described in the following sections.

Fig. 5.10.

The ALIGNMENT dialog box.

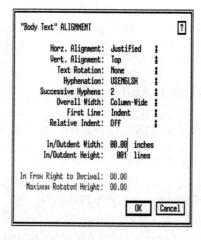

```
"Body Text" ALIGNMENT                          [?]

              Horz. Alignment:  Justified    ‡
              Vert. Alignment:  Top          ‡
               Text Rotation:   None         ‡
                 Hyphenation:   USENGLSH     ‡
           Successive Hyphens:  2            ‡
               Overall Width:   Column-Wide  ‡
                  First Line:   Indent       ‡
              Relative Indent:  Off          ‡

             In/Outdent Width:  00.08| inches
            In/Outdent Height:  001  lines

    In From Right to Decimal:  00.00
       Maximum Rotated Height:  00.00

                                   [ OK ] [Cancel]
```

Horizontal Alignment

When you select Alignment from the Paragraph menu, the first option you can specify in the ALIGNMENT dialog box is the horizontal alignment of the tagged paragraph. Left, Right, Center, Justified, and Decimal options are available in the pop-up menu. Figure 5.11 shows these five types of paragraph alignment. *Left-aligned* text is flush with the left margin, leaving a ragged right margin. *Right-aligned* text is flush with the right margin, leaving a ragged left margin. *Centered* text means that each line is centered within the margins. *Justified* text aligns text flush with left and right margins. If you want to set tabs in a tag, choose any alignment other than justified.

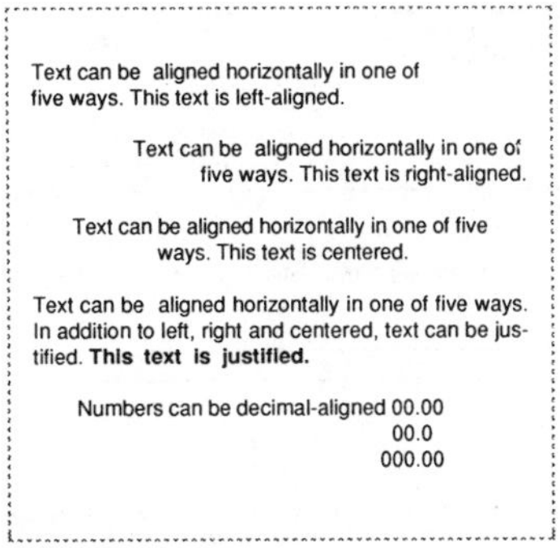

Text can be aligned horizontally in one of five ways. This text is left-aligned.

Text can be aligned horizontally in one of five ways. This text is right-aligned.

Text can be aligned horizontally in one of five ways. This text is centered.

Text can be aligned horizontally in one of five ways. In addition to left, right and centered, text can be justified. **This text is justified.**

Numbers can be decimal-aligned 00.00
00.0
000.00

Fig. 5.11.

Five types of paragraph alignment.

Decimal alignment places the first decimal point (or period) in a line at a specified distance from the right margin. You set the measurement in the In From Right to Decimal option that becomes available when you choose Decimal as the Horz. Alignment option. With this new feature, you can quickly align a numbered list on a decimal or align numbers in a column following a single line of text. Because word wrap is disabled when tabs are present in a tag, you must force line breaks (using Ctrl-Enter) if the tagged items are longer than one line in length. To align multiple-line paragraphs, use the technique illustrated in figures 5.20 through 5.23.

To remove automatic tab signs inserted when you tag a paragraph with the Decimal option, change the Horz. Alignment option to another setting. If you try to backspace over inserted tab signs, you remove the tab sign and the paragraph return at the end of the preceding line. The current selection box does not show a name for this type of tab, and you cannot move the text cursor in front of this tab.

The decimal character on which the paragraphs are aligned can be changed from a decimal point to any other character by typing the ASCII value of the desired character in the SET PREFERENCES dialog box opened from the Options menu. Alternate ways to look up the character values are discussed in ''The Special Effects Command'' later in this chapter.

Vertical Alignment

You also can specify how you want the tagged paragraph to be aligned vertically on the page. In the Vert. Alignment option in the ALIGNMENT dialog box, you can specify Top, Middle, or Bottom to position paragraphs placed in frames and in box-text graphics (see fig. 5.12). If the frame contains other text above this tag, vertical alignment is calculated from the bottom of that text to the bottom of the frame. If other text in the frame is below this tag, vertical alignment is calculated from the top of the frame to the top of that text. The Vert. Alignment options make positioning text in tables and forms easy because Ventura calculates the spacing based on the size of the frame you draw or resize.

This text is horizontally center-aligned and vertically top aligned.

This text is horizontally center-aligned and vertically middle aligned.

This text is horizontally center-aligned and vertically bottom aligned.

Fig. 5.12.

Top, Middle, and Bottom vertically-aligned text that also is centered.

Text Rotation

Rotated text can be useful for labeling headings for tables, crediting illustrations, annotating graphs, or varying the design element in layouts. Ventura posts a measurement to the Maximum Rotated Height option in the ALIGNMENT dialog box when you choose 90, 180, or 270 from the pop-up menu. You can change the default setting Ventura provides to set the text's starting position. Ventura measures from the opposite edge of the frame where the degree setting starts the text, illustrated by the text in the frames in figure 5.13. Because rotated text displaces other text on the page, rotated text should be placed within frames or box-text graphics.

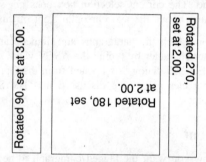

Fig. 5.13.

Text rotated to 90, 180, and 270 degrees.

The Top and Bottom margins of these frames are set to 0. The text was moved away from the rules around the frames, by adding 6 points as In From Left and In From Right spacing values in the SPACING dialog box opened from the Pargraph menu.

Hyphenation

Ventura hyphenates text as you open chapters, load files, and type text. The hyphenation decisions Ventura makes are based on two types of files: rules (or algorithm) and dictionary files. You specify these files in the Hyphenation option in the ALIGN-MENT dialog box.

Several rules files are delivered with Ventura: two for American English (USENGLSH.HY1 and USENGLSH.HY2) and one each for Spanish, French, Italian, and British English. Two rules files can be installed at once and appear as choices in the Hyphenation option in the ALIGNMENT dialog box. During program installation, Ventura sets up USENGLSH.HY1 as the hyphenation file. If you want to use any other rules file, copy the file from the Utilities disk to the VENTURA directory using the DOS Copy command. Rules files have the extension HY2. Change the extension to HY1 if you want the file to appear first in the Hyphenation pop-up menu.

The USENGLSH.HY1 file misses some opportunities to hyphenate words. The USENGLSH.HY2 file is more capable, larger, and slower. See Chapter 10 for information about the 130,000-word EDCO hyphenation dictionary, if you are not satisfied with the results from the dictionaries supported by Ventura. 1.2M of disk space and 1.2 bytes EMS memory are required to support the EDCO dictionary that comes with the Professional Extension.

If you want to use the slower but better USENGLSH.HY2 hyphenation file, copy the file from the Utilities disk to your Ventura directory. You can use the faster (less accurate) USENGLSH.HY1 file for working drafts and the more capable USENGLSH.HY2 file for final drafts. Use DOS to rename each file with the HY1 extension before you start Ventura. All tags set with the draft hyphenation file, HY1, will hyphenate according to the active rules file without changing any tags when you use the final hyphenation file. If you are producing a bilingual publication, use the extension HY1 for one language and HY2 for the other.

During program installation, two dictionary files also are copied to assist in making hyphenation decisions. The first is called HYPHEXPT.DIC and contains about 350 words that don't follow hyphenation rules. The second dictionary, called HYPHUSER.DIC, enables you to enter words requiring custom hyphenation. To add words, use your word processor to access the file named HYPHUSER.DIC in the VENTURA directory. Add the words in all lowercase and insert hyphens where needed. You can suppress hyphenation by typing a word in this file without hyphens. Remember to save the file as an ASCII file, or the hyphenation results are erratic.

You can maintain several user dictionaries if needed, although you can use only one at a time. To keep separate project dictionaries, use DOS to copy the HYPHUSER.DIC to a file named for the current project. When you want to use the alternative dictionary, use DOS again: once to rename the original HYPHUSER.DIC to a temporary name and again to rename the custom dictionary as HYPHUSER.DIC. Ventura looks for the HYPHUSER.DIC file in the VENTURA directory when you start the program.

If you rename the HY1, HY2, and DIC files to other file extensions before you start Ventura, you increase the amount of memory available for processing files. This technique is somewhat awkward, but you can set up a batch file to rename the files for specific projects. If you forget to rename the files, Ventura reminds you in a warning box that the dictionaries or algorithms are unavailable to make hyphenation decisions.

Successive Hyphens

You can control the number of consecutive lines ending with hyphens by selecting 1, 2, 3, 4, 5, or Unlimited in the Successive Hyphens option of the ALIGNMENT dialog box.

To modify Ventura's hyphenation decisions, position the cursor where you want the word to be hyphenated and press Ctrl-hyphen to insert a *discretionary hyphen* that prints only if the word breaks over a line. The Show Loose Lines command from the Options menu identifies where inserting discretionary hyphens can improve the appearance of justified text (see fig. 5.14). Sometimes you can correct loose lines by typing a discretionary hyphen in the first word beneath the loose line.

To suppress hyphenation for a word, insert a discretionary hyphen in front of the word.

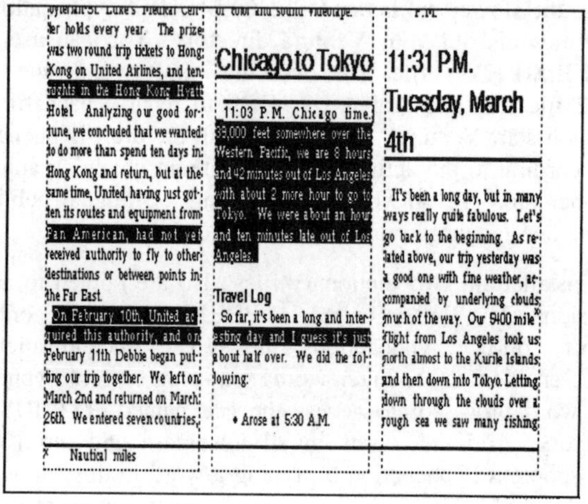

Fig. 5.14.

Controlling loose lines.

Overall Width

The horizontal alignment you select (left-aligned, right-aligned, centered, justified, or decimal) adjusts to the width of the column or the frame, depending on the width you select in the Overall Width option. If you have a two-column page and you tag a paragraph in a right-hand column with Overall Width: Frame-Wide, you also must choose Column Balance: On in the CHAPTER TYPOGRAPHY dialog box. Otherwise, the text overlaps text in the left-hand column.

You can override the default setting for the chapter by selecting a frame and installing a unique Column Balance setting for text in the selected frame.

First Line, In/Outdent Width, and In/Outdent Height

The margins of the page or frame where you place text determine the starting position for text paragraphs. You indent from those margins by using the ALIGNMENT dialog box's First Line and In/Outdent Width options. You can choose to *indent* text (move it inside the left margin) or *outdent* text (move it outside the left margin) for a specific number of lines.

For example, instead of tabbing a paragraph to indent at 0.25 inch, click First Line: Indent and type the value you want in In/Outdent Width; for example, *0.25* inch. When you want to move the line outside the margin to create a hanging indent, choose First Line: Outdent and enter the desired measurement in In/Outdent Width. Figure 5.15 shows how you use the outdent setting to create hanging indents.

Though PC users are still buying dot-matrix printers, the laser printer is giving them an alternative to think about, according to industry observers.

Laser printers, though relatively expensive, are being used more in networked environments where the distributed use of the printer justifies the expense, several analysts said. The non-impact printers also catch user interest because they are less noisy, offer sharper graphics (commonly 300-by-300 dots per inch) and can produce from eight to ten pages per minute.

Fig. 5.15.

Hanging indents.

The In/Outdent Height option specifies how many lines of the paragraph to indent or outdent. Generally, only the first line of a paragraph is affected by an indent or outdent; this option is therefore usually 001.

To position a paragraph of more than one line outside the right margin, use the Relative Indent option with the Breaks command, as described in the following section.

Relative Indent

You can use the length of the preceding line as the measurement for a flexible indentation: one that changes with the length of the preceding paragraph's last line (see fig. 5.16). To add a fixed value to the relative indentation, select Relative Indent from the ALIGNMENT dialog box, choose Indent or Outdent for the First Line option, and type a value in In/Outdent Width.

Usually when you format text, you leave Relative Indent set to None so that the indentation for each paragraph is the specific value you set. Use the Relative Indent option when you want to set a paragraph with one format next to a differently formatted paragraph. You can create the effect of a lead-in by using relative indent when you also choose Line Break: No in the BREAKS dialog box for the paragraph. You also can use this technique to create a paragraph that hangs in the right margin.

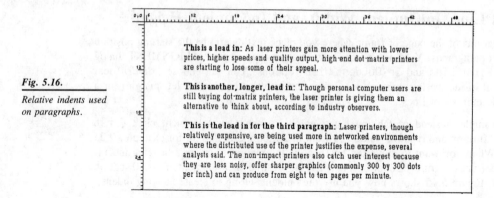

Fig. 5.16.

*Relative indents used
on paragraphs.*

The Spacing Command

With the Spacing command, you can define the vertical spacing before, after, within, and between paragraphs, as well as paragraph indentations from the margins. The first five options in the SPACING dialog box affect vertical spacing inside the top and bottom margins; the remaining options add or subtract from the margins as you set them using the Margins & Columns command from the Frame menu.

Above, Below, Inter-Line, and Inter-Paragraph

The values set for the first four options in the SPACING dialog box are part of the formula Ventura uses to position paragraphs vertically on the page. Typographers and designers use the word *leading* to describe the measurement from the base of one line of text to the base of the next line of text. Ventura calls leading *interline spacing*.

If you choose Auto Adjustments: Styles in the SET PREFERENCES dialog box of the Options menu, Ventura adjusts spacing whenever you change font sizes in the FONT dialog box. The values you set for the Above, Below, and Inter-Line options in the SPACING dialog box increase or decrease by 20 percent (1.2 times the last setting) when the Auto-Adjustment: Styles option is enabled. To let Ventura set the values for the Inter-Line option as you select the font sizes, make sure that you click Auto-Adjust: Styles in the SET PREFERENCES dialog box before you choose the font size. For example, a 10-point typeface receives 12-point leading. Figure 5.17 shows how different leading affects the look of sample text.

Fig. 5.17.

*Sample text with
different leading.*

This is
sample text
with nine
point
leading.

This is
sample text
with 10
point
leading.

This is
sample text
with 11
point
leading.

This is
sample text
with 12
point
leading.

If you increase the point size of the type to more than 12 points, you may want to override the calculated default to reduce the leading. Conversely, if you are working with line lengths greater than five inches, try increasing the interline spacing by 0.33 fractional points (1/3 of a point) to improve the readability of the text.

Any value you type in the SPACING dialog box overrides the calculated default. To turn off the automatic adjustment feature, click Auto Adjustments: None in the SET PREFERENCES dialog box. All automatic settings made previously are unaffected, but Ventura does not make further adjustments. Chapter 9 includes a discussion of leading and font selection and offers tips on how to use leading and other techniques to make copy fit in a specified space. If you are using the Professional Extension, the following section on the use of the spacing values in multicolumn layouts applies to the vertical justification features found in the Chapter, Frame, and Paragraph menus' TYPOGRAPHY dialog boxes.

In the Professional Extension you can control how much space is added between frames and paragraphs of text, between paragraphs, and between lines in a paragraph. This feature, *Vertical Justification*, is described in Chapter 10.

Aligning Text Evenly across Columns

Keeping text aligned evenly across columns requires that you set spacing values as the Body Text tag (see fig. 5.18).

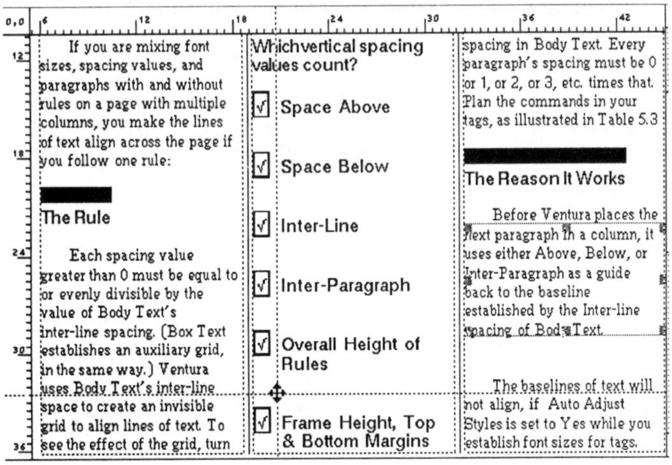

Fig. 5.18.

Aligning text evenly across columns.

If you are mixing font sizes, spacing values, and paragraphs with or without rules on a page with multiple columns, you can make the lines of text align across the page if you follow one rule:

Each spacing value greater than 0 must be equal to or evenly divisible by the value of the Body Text's interline spacing.

You apply this rule to these commands:

Spacing

Ruling Lines

Margins & Columns

Sizing & Scaling

Table 5.3 lists the menus and commands that affect vertical spacing and shows the spacing values corresponding to those in figure 5.18. The alignment of baselines across the page should be uniform even when font sizes and paragraph spacing change. You cannot align across columns on the page if you change the vertical spacing values in increments other than integer multiples of the Body Text tag's interline spacing.

In the Professional Extension, the spacing values chosen for vertical justification settings also must be zero or equivalent to an integer multiple of the Body Text tag's interline spacing value. As you develop tags with varying font sizes (or paragraph rules) for multicolumn layouts, choose any setting but Styles for the Auto Adjustments option in the pop-up menu opened from the SET PREFERENCES dialog box. You can control the leading by typing values in the Paragraph menu's SPACING dialog box for each tag.

Table 5.3
Commands That Affect the Even Alignment of Text

	Tag Names and Values			
Command and Option	Body Text	Ruled Head	Check Box	Checked Items
Paragraph menu				
Font				
Size	12	15	16	14
Spacing (in fractional points)				
Above	13.98	13.98	13.98	13.98
Below	27.96		13.98	13.98
Inter-Line	13.98	13.98	13.98	13.98
Inter-Paragraph	13.98		13.98	13.98
Ruling Lines and Ruling Box				
Space Above Rule 1				
Height of Rule 1		10.98	0.66	
Space Below Rule 1		3.00		
Height of Rule 3				
Space Below Rule 3		0	−0.66	
Overall Height		13.98	0	

Table 5.3—*Continued*

	Tag Names and Values			
Command and Option	*Body Text*	*Ruled Head*	*Check Box*	*Checked Items*
Frame menu				
Sizing & Scaling (in picas and points)				
Frame Height	66,00			
Margins & Columns (in picas and points)				
Top Margin	05,10			
Bottom Margin	29,10			

To make text align, you may need to set several spacing values, depending on how many paragraph formats are on the page. Follow these steps to achieve an even text alignment:

1. Establish the size of the frame as a multiple of the value of interline spacing of the Body Text tag.

2. Establish the interline spacing (or leading) of Body Text using the fractional-point measuring system. Every paragraph's spacing must be an integer multiple of that value or zero.

3. Set Auto-Adjustments: None in the SET PREFERENCES dialog box of the Options menu.

4. Set the font sizes and the spacing options as even multiples of the Body Text's interline spacing for every type of paragraph that appears on the page. (Body Text does not have to be used on the page.)

5. Look at the results and set Above, Below, Inter-Paragraph, and ruling lines as needed, making sure that the total of any spacing value is zero, equal to, or evenly divisible by the value of Body Text's interline spacing. You can suppress the Above space at the tops of columns by choosing Add in Above: When Not at Column Top.

You cannot align text across columns if leading breaks the spacing value rule. Remember that if you have Grow Inter-Line To Fit: On, the spacing in a paragraph may change. In the Professional Extension, Ventura cannot align and justify vertically unless you follow the same rule when you set vertical spacing values in the TYPOGRAPHY dialog boxes.

Efficiency Tip

Aligning Text in Frames with Text on the Page

Ventura uses Body Text's interline spacing value to establish an invisible grid for the page. Follow these steps to align text in frames:

1. Choose the Turn Line Snap On command from the Options menu. If you are placing frames on pages and want even text alignment across the page, any frame you add aligns along the invisible grid.

2. Follow the rule for spacing values for all paragraphs and all margins in frames where you place text.

Calculating the Space between Paragraphs

Ventura does not use every measurement set in the Above, Below, and Inter-Paragraph options of the SPACING dialog box as the program determines how much space (or *leading*) to leave between paragraphs on the page. The amount of space left between paragraphs is conditioned by the adjacent paragraphs' settings. The conditions are as follows:

- If the Below space in one tag is greater than the Above space in the next tag, Ventura uses the Below value.

- If the Above space in one tag is greater than the Below space in the preceding tag, Ventura uses the Above value.

- If ruling lines are used, Ventura adds Overall Height to the Above or Below value chosen. (You learn about setting rules in the discussion of ruling lines commands later in this chapter.)

- If Inter-Line space is equal in two adjacent paragraphs, Ventura uses the Inter-Paragraph value to add space between paragraphs.

After Ventura determines which conditions exist, the amount of spacing is totaled and increased by the value of the first paragraph's interline spacing.

Troubleshooting Tip

Getting Rid of Troublesome Tags

If you accidentally set in the spacing commands a value that exceeds the page length, turning to another page causes the page counter to add blank pages to the chapter. To remove those pages, reopen the SPACING dialog box and change the setting in the tag or use the Remove Tag command from the Paragraph menu to convert the incorrect tag to Body Text. If the tag's name is not in the current selection box, or if you are unsure of the name, use your word processor to edit the text file and remove the reference to the tag. Remember to remove the tag from the style file when you start Ventura again.

Add in Above

The Add in Above option in the SPACING dialog box tells Ventura when to add the Above spacing. Add in Above: Always adds the specified spacing whenever the tag is encountered (if the Above space matches the conditions stated in the preceding list). Add in Above: When Not at Column Top adds the spacing only for tagged paragraphs located within rather than at the top of a column.

Settings For, In From Left, In From Right, and Inserts

The last four options in the SPACING dialog box affect the horizontal placement of text within the margins set by the MARGINS & COLUMNS dialog box's Left Margins and Right Margins options. These four options enable you to set temporary margins for an entire paragraph of text, as illustrated in figure 5.19. Select the paragraph for which you are making the settings and type a value for In From Left, In From Right, or both. With the Settings For: Left Page and Settings For: Right Page options, you can set different measurements for the designated page. When you use Ruling Lines commands on the Paragraph menu for a tag set at Overall Width: Margin in the ALIGNMENT dialog box, the ruling lines follow the temporary margins set with the Spacing command for the tag. Any indent values set in the ALIGNMENT dialog box are added to the value set in In From Left.

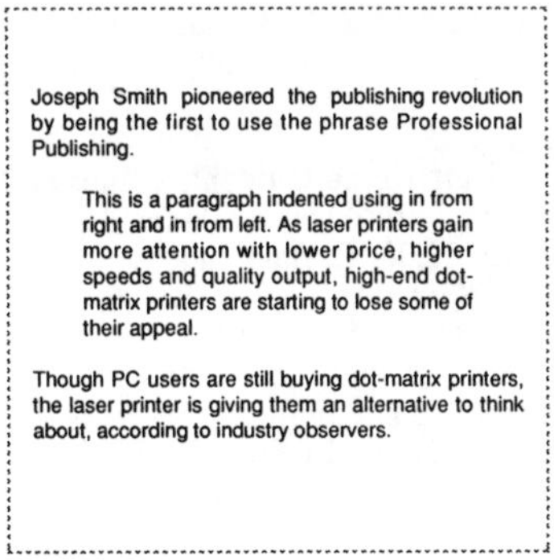

Joseph Smith pioneered the publishing revolution by being the first to use the phrase Professional Publishing.

This is a paragraph indented using in from right and in from left. As laser printers gain more attention with lower price, higher speeds and quality output, high-end dot-matrix printers are starting to lose some of their appeal.

Though PC users are still buying dot-matrix printers, the laser printer is giving them an alternative to think about, according to industry observers.

Fig. 5.19.

A paragraph set inside the margins.

Use the Inserts: Copy To Facing Page option to duplicate the In From Left and In From Right settings for paragraphs positioned on the facing page.

The Breaks Command

You use the BREAKS dialog box, accessed from the Paragraph menu, to establish where a paragraph begins. Usually, you think of a paragraph beginning below another paragraph. Ventura enables you to set breaks for paragraphs and define whether the position of the paragraph is at the top of a column or page or on the same line as the first line or the last line of the preceding paragraph. With Ventura, you can set breaks between paragraphs to print paragraphs side by side (see fig. 5.20).

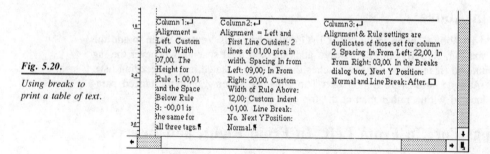

Fig. 5.20.

Using breaks to print a table of text.

With a typewriter, you create tabular data and tables by tabbing to each position and typing. This task is tedious because you must plan the length of each column and manually wrap each column of text. Word processors have a variety of ways for indenting paragraphs and placing them side by side. If you are using a word processor to prepare tables of text for use with Ventura, type only one column of text so that the paragraphs in the text file occur in the same sequence as they are read: left-to-right on the page (see fig. 5.21).

Fig. 5.21.

A text file for a table of text.

```
@C1 = Column 1:⏎
Alignment = Left. Custom Rule Width 07,00. The Height for Rule
1: 00,01 and the Space Below Rule 3: -00,01 is the same for all
three tags.⏎

@C2 = Column 2: ⏎
Alignment = Left and First Line Outdent: 2 lines of 01,00 pica in
width. Spacing In from Left: 09,00; In From Right: 20,00. Custom
Width of Rule Above: 12,00; Custom Indent -01,00. Line Break:
No. Next Y Position: Normal.⏎

@C3 = Column 3: ⏎
Alignment & Rule settings are duplicates of those set for column
2. Spacing In From Left: 22,00, In From Right: 03,00. In the
Breaks dialog box, Next Y Position: Normal and Line Break:
After. ⏎
```

Page Break, Column Break, and Line Break

The simplest use of the Breaks command is to set a tag always to print at the top of a page or column. In this case, choose the Before setting for the Break option that suits your purpose (see fig. 5.22). Using page breaks, you can use Before & After to place a tag alone on a page, Before/Until Left to place a tag on the next left page, or Before/Until Right to place a tag on the next right page. However, the most common settings used in Body Text are Page Break: No, Column Break: No, and Line Break: Before.

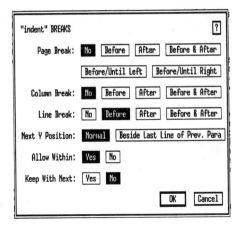

Fig. 5.22.

*The BREAKS
dialog box.*

You can set each of the first three options in the BREAKS dialog box. Ventura follows the instructions in the same order as presented in the dialog box. If you select No for all three options, be sure to set an indent by using In From Left and In From Right in the SPACING dialog box. Or, you can change the Next Y Position option to Beside Last Line of Prev. Para (follow the procedure described in the following section) to keep the paragraphs from overlapping. When you are positioning multiple paragraphs in a columnar format, set the last paragraph in the column with Line Break: After and Next Y Position: Normal.

Next Y Position

The optional break points enable you to employ a technique commonly referred to as *vertical tabbing*, although you set margins rather than tabs to position the paragraphs. Using breaks, temporary margins, and the Next Y Position option, you can set paragraphs of text adjacent to single-line items as illustrated in figure 5.20. (The *Y position* refers to the vertical position of the text on the page.) You set the position for each column with the In From Left and In From Right options in the SPACING dialog box.

Choose Normal for the Next Y Position option when you want a paragraph to start on the same line as the first line of the preceding paragraph. To create the effect shown in figure 5.20, choose No in all three break options and set temporary margins for the second paragraph (so that the paragraph doesn't overlap the preceding paragraph) with the In From Left and In From Right options in the SPACING dialog box. Repeat the process for each column of text, but in the last column's tag, set Line Break: After.

When you want a paragraph to start on the last line of the preceding paragraph, choose Next Y Position: Beside Last Line of Prev. Para; choose Line Break: After, and then decide whether you want the indent to be relative to the length of the last line in the preceding paragraph. If yes, choose Relative Indent: Length of

Previous Line in the ALIGNMENT dialog box. If you want to set the indentation at a precise location, use the SPACING dialog box In From Left option. Figure 5.23 shows how two paragraphs were used to format each heading in an outline. The only line breaks are after each paragraph of text.

I. Creating and Loading Text in ⅂

A. Typing and Editing Text in

1. Creating New Document

2. Editing Text¶

B. Loading Source Text Files¶

1. Using The Item Selector¶

Fig. 5.23.

Formatting an outline.

Allow Within and Keep With Next

Paragraphs that should not split across columns or pages can be tagged as Allow Within: No. Choosing Keep With Next: Yes on the BREAKS dialog box forces two paragraphs to print on the same column or page.

Efficiency Tip

Controlling Paragraph Splits

Allow a paragraph to split by specifying Yes for the Allow Within option of the Paragraph menu's BREAKS dialog box. Click No when you want a paragraph to end in the same column in which it starts.

The TYPOGRAPHY dialog boxes accessed from the Chapter and Frame menus control where a paragraph splits if the text spans columns and margins. You set the default for the chapter; the default is overridden when you select a frame and set different values in the Frame TYPOGRAPHY dialog box. To set the defaults, choose the minimum number of lines for the widow and orphan of the paragraph. A *widow* is the number of lines printed after the break; an *orphan* is the number of lines printed before the break. (Remember that orphans are those left behind.) See Chapter 7 for more on widows and orphans.

The Tab Settings Command

Choose the Tab Settings command from the Paragraph menu to access the TAB SET-TINGS dialog box (see fig. 5.24). With the options in this dialog box, you can format lists and single-line tables of text. You can set the format for up to 16 tabs per tag, choosing from four types of alignment. Ventura also enables you to align text on a custom character (set with the SET PREFERENCES dialog box on the Options menu.). *Tab leaders* are used to place dots or lines that guide the eye across the page. Tab leaders can be customized for each tag in the style file.

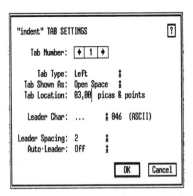

Fig. 5.24.

The TAB SETTINGS dialog box.

Before starting any tabular project, test a text file containing tabs. If you use a word processor whose tabs appear as right arrows in Ventura's work area, the table or list is formatted by Ventura when loaded, using the values set by the style file's default tag, Body Text. To see the tab signs in the work area, choose Show Tabs & Returns from the Options menu. Figure 5.25 shows the symbols that may appear when you choose this command. When editing and formatting, display the symbols to avoid adding and removing instructions you otherwise would not see. The name of the symbol (the only exception is automatic tabs) appears in the current selection box when the text cursor encounters each symbol.

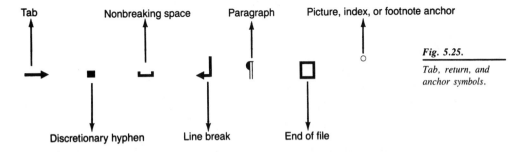

Fig. 5.25.

Tab, return, and anchor symbols.

Some word processing programs change with each version. One version, therefore, may save tabs as signals that Ventura can interpret, but another version of the same program may not. You can force a tab sign to import to Ventura in text files created with incompatible programs by typing <9> wherever you intend to use a tab. If you want angle brackets to surround the number 9 as an item in your text, type <<9>> to keep Ventura from interpreting the characters as a tab. Chapter 4 includes further discussion of importing formatted and unformatted text.

To set tabs, select a paragraph with the Paragraph cursor and choose the tag name you want to format with tabs. You can use the Body Text tag if two conditions exist:

- Alignment: Justified is not chosen for the tag. With Ventura, you can establish tab settings with justified alignment, but the tabs are not read until the alignment is changed.

- The interline spacing values for Body Text in the selected list or table are appropriate for Ventura to use as the foundation for the baseline grid of the entire chapter. (See ''Aligning Text Evenly across Columns'' in this chapter if you are mixing font sizes, spacing values, and ruling lines in multicolumn layouts.)

To type tabs in Ventura, select the Text function, position the text cursor in the text, and then press the Tab key. Remove a tab from the text file by deleting the tab symbol. Remove automatic decimal tabs (described in ''The Alignment Command'' earlier in this chapter) by choosing another type of paragraph alignment. The options in the TAB SETTINGS dialog box are described in the following sections.

Tab Number

The TAB SETTINGS dialog box displays the settings for Tab Number. Click the scroll arrow on either side of Tab Number to access settings for other tabs. You can overcome Ventura's 16-tab restriction by positioning the first column flush left, decimal-aligned or indented with the Alignment command, and setting a 17-column table. Or you can combine use of the Breaks and Alignment commands to position two paragraphs on the same line, allowing more than 16 tabs on a line (see ''Next Y Position'' in this section). Another way to overcome the default limit of 16 tabs is to place two frames side by side on a page.

Tab Type

The Left, Right, Center, and Decimal settings for the Tab Type option in the TAB SETTINGS dialog box enable you to choose the type of alignment for each column set at a tab location:

- Left tab—the tab setting is the left margin of new text.

- Right tab—the tab setting is the right margin of new text; text is to the left of the tab setting.

- Center tab—the tab setting is the center of each line of new text; text centers at the tab setting.

- Decimal tab—the tab setting is a decimal point often used to align numbers in columns.

In figure 5.26, two tabs are used to align the entries in the three-column directory; because the names are flush left with the margin, no tab is needed before each name. The first tab is a right tab set to position the dot leaders and addresses. The second tab aligns the phone numbers at the right of the column.

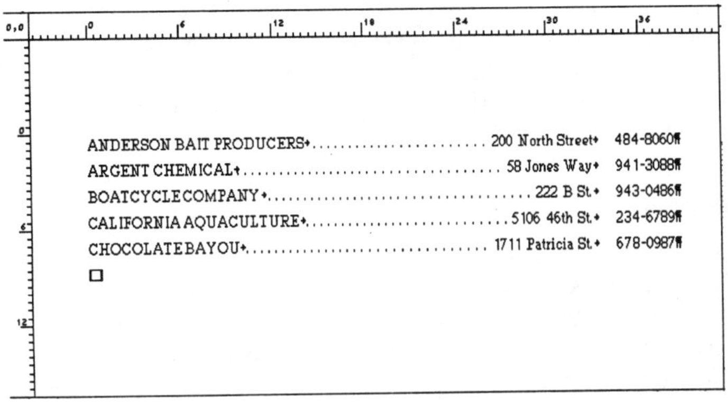

ANDERSON BAIT PRODUCERS•......................200 North Street• 484-8060¶
ARGENT CHEMICAL•................................58 Jones Way• 941-3088¶
BOATCYCLECOMPANY•................................222 B St.• 943-0486¶
CALIFORNIA AQUACULTURE•............................5106 46th St.• 234-6789¶
CHOCOLATE BAYOU•............................1711 Patricia St.• 678-0987¶
□

Fig. 5.26.

A directory set with tabs.

Efficiency Tip

Making a Directory Look Like It Is Aligned with Tabs

Tabs consume more memory than most other instructions in Ventura. As a result, you may encounter the `Frame Too Complex` message when projects include tabs and lengthy source text files. When you can, use the Breaks command rather than the Tab Settings command and you may avoid the problem. (Other alternatives are presented in Chapter 7.)

Ventura provides a sample chapter file named &PHON-P2.CHP that illustrates the creation of a two-column telephone directory without any tabs. Load the sample chapter file and look at the Breaks set for the Body Text and Phone tags. (See ''The Breaks Command'' earlier in this chapter for a description of the technique used.) The sample file also shows the placement of automatic headers on the directory pages using the HEADERS & FOOTERS dialog box's `Left` and `Right` options. The pages end at a uniform length in both columns because the chapter default for `Column Balance: On` is set in the TYPOGRAPHY dialog box accessed from the Chapter menu.

A layout for publishing directories planned with the Breaks command contributes to faster production than layouts planned with tabs or multiple frames. The key is labeling the source file with the appropriate tag name or names. Make your own sample file, following the example set by Ventura's &PHON.CHP, remembering that extra carriage returns in the source text file (&PHON.TXT) are used only in ASCII file formats.

The phone numbers in figure 5.26 can be set to align on the hyphens by setting a custom value for a decimal tab. When you select Tab Type: Decimal in the TAB SETTINGS dialog box, you can choose to align the information on any Ventura character symbol. You can find a table of the character sets and codes in Chapter 4 or by printing CHARSET.CHP in the TYPESET directory. When you know the value to which to change the decimal default value, open the SET PREFERENCES dialog box from the Options menu and type the ID number of the desired symbol for the Decimal Tab Char option. The value you select remains the custom decimal alignment character until you change the value again. You cannot store the value with the tag; instead, the value is stored in the VP.INF file that Ventura re-creates each time you end a publishing session. See Chapter 3 to learn how to store custom INF files to save frequently used settings.

Tab Location

When positioning tabs, Ventura measures from the margin of the left column established by the Margins & Columns command. As with all dialog box measurements, you can click the Tab Location option in the TAB SETTINGS dialog box to convert to equivalent values. You can estimate a tab location by setting the ruler's zero points even with the column's left margin. To change the ruler's system of measurement and the zero points, choose Set Ruler from the Options menu. You can set the rulers and the zero points in the system of measurement that matches your specifications: in inches, centimeters, or picas.

Chapter 3 explains how to set the zero points by dragging 0,0 from the upper left corner of the work area. A quick summary of this process is given here:

- Choose Show Column Guides from the Options menu, if you are setting tabs for a page rather than a frame drawn on the page. (Column guides do not display in drawn frames.)

- Choose Show Rulers.

- Drag 0,0 from the upper left corner of the work area and release the mouse button when the crosshairs are positioned to match the column guides.

Tabs are measured from the left margin of the column in which they appear. Columnar text tagged in a frame set with deep left and right margins starts at a different location than similarly tagged text placed in a frame with narrow margins. You can set temporary margins with the In From Left option in the ALIGNMENT dialog box to indent the first column before the first tab location.

You can place text files with tabs on the page or in frames drawn on the page. If you want to use Ventura's footnote feature to annotate financial tables, plan a layout strategy that enables you to place the tables on the page rather than in a frame drawn on the page. Ventura's footnote features do not work with text placed in frames on the page. Use of the automatic numbering feature also necessitates placing text on the page and not in frames.

Tab Shown As: Leader Char, Leader Spacing, and Auto Leader

Tab leaders are a convention used to guide a reader's eye from one column to another. Tables of contents, directories, catalogs, and listings often use leaders. One way to set a column to accept tab leaders is to choose Tab Shown As: Leader Char and set the Leader Spacing value to 2. These options are in the TAB SETTINGS dialog box. Right-aligned, underlined leaders are illustrated in figure 5.27.

◊◊◊◊◊◊◊◊◊◊◊   **Custom Tab Leaders**

Tab leaders can be used to create a graphic effect, as well as draw lines from variable starting positions to a right-aligned tab stop.

Fig. 5.27.

Leaders set as diamonds and underlines.

Last month: _____   Last year: _____

First through fifteenth:_____   First six months: _____

Ventura enables you to set custom leaders when you choose Leader Char: Other. This option has four available settings, spaces, periods, underlines, and custom. You can choose any value from Ventura's character sets and type the ID number of that character. (A table of the character sets and codes is in Chapter 4.) In contrast to customizing decimal alignment characters, the custom Leader Char option affects each tag's leader individually instead of every leader in the file. If you need more than one custom leader, create a tag for each one. The Leader Spacing option enables you to adjust the number of spaces between leader characters from 0 to 8; the higher the number, the greater the space. Use 0 with Underline for a solid rule.

After you use a leader tab, however, you may have to use several frames on a page to place a list of more than a couple of pages in order to minimize the number of line elements Ventura calculates per frame. See Chapters 7 and 11 through 16 to learn about alternative layout and design strategies.

Set Auto Leader: On to create leader characters from the end of text to the right as set by the tab location. You can set the Leader Char option to create solid, dashed, or dotted lines from margin to margin when you tag paragraphs without text. Although Auto Leader works without inserting a tab sign in text, Ventura informs you that automatic leaders (like tabs) are not displayed with justified alignment.

The Special Effects Command

The Special Effects command is located on the Paragraph menu. You format two types of special effects with the SPECIAL EFFECTS dialog box: bullets and big first characters (see fig. 5.28). To turn off either Special Effects character, click None. The Bullet and Big First Char (often referred to as *dropped cap* options) use the Commands: Set Font Properties option to set the face, size, and style of the first character in a paragraph. Bullets also use the Show Bullet As, Bullet Char, and Indent After Bullet options.

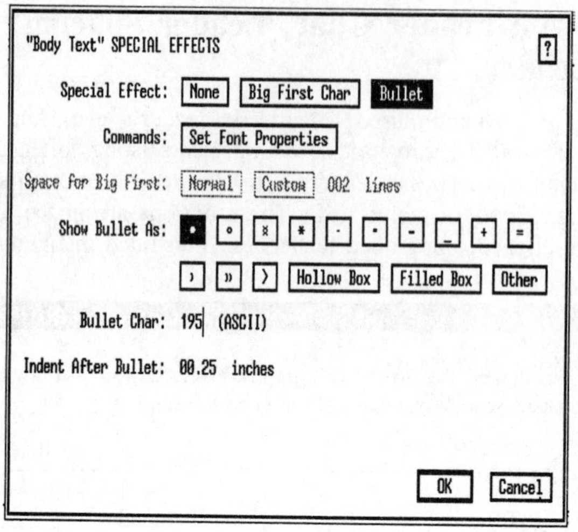

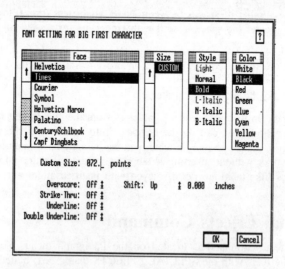

Fig. 5.28.

The SPECIAL EFFECTS dialog box opened from the Paragraph menu.

Big First Char, Commands, and Space for Big First

Dropped caps are a convention used by designers to emphasize the first letter in a paragraph. To set dropped caps with Ventura, click Special Effect: Big First Char in the SPECIAL EFFECTS dialog box. To set the font type and size differently from the rest of the paragraph, click Set Font Properties to open the FONT SETTING FOR BIG FIRST CHARACTER dialog box, shown in figure 5.29.

Fig. 5.29.

Setting a custom font size for a drop cap.

You can choose a type face, size, style, and color for the first letter of the paragraph, using the FONT SETTING FOR BIG FIRST CHARACTER dialog box. This dialog box works the same as the FONT dialog box described in "The Font Command" in this chapter. If you select Space for Big First: Normal, Ventura aligns the top of the big character with the top of the first line of text and calculates the number of lines to indent. If you select Custom, you enter the number of lines to indent, and Ventura aligns the baseline of the big character with the baseline of the last line of indented text.

The FONT SETTING FOR BIG FIRST CHARACTER dialog box offers one more option: You can shift the first character up or down from the baseline selected in the Space for Big First option of the SPECIAL EFFECTS dialog box. To choose the way you want to shift the character, click Shift: Up or Shift: Down and type the desired measurement to the right.

Bullet, Show Bullet As, Bullet Char, and Indent After Bullet

Using the SPECIAL EFFECTS dialog box, you can define bullets to appear as the first character in a paragraph, without typing a bullet. Click Special Effect: Bullet to enable the Show Bullet As settings. Each setting's ASCII value is displayed in the Bullet Char option as you click the available symbols. Click Show Bullet As: Other when you want to choose an ASCII decimal value not displayed (see the Efficiency Tip, "Looking Up Alternative Character Sets").

Besides the special characters Ventura displays as Show Bullet As options, you also can choose Hollow Box or Filled Box as the bullet option.

In the SPECIAL EFFECTS dialog box, specify an amount to indent the text after the bullet, or the text in the paragraph overlaps the bullet. If you want to fill a hollow box with the first letter in the paragraph, do not set an indent. The default is 0.25 inches.

After you have chosen a bullet character, you can specify font properties of the character using the FONT SETTINGS FOR BULLET dialog box. Access this box by clicking the Commands: Set Font Properties option. You can select a font different from the rest of the paragraph for the bullet, as well as set a custom size and style. The Shift option on the FONT SETTINGS FOR BULLET dialog box is available to adjust the position of the bullet up or down a maximum of just under 0.5 inch. You can create custom bullets by combining a symbol from the SPECIAL EFFECTS dialog box with the Over-score, Strike-thru, Underline, and Double Underline options in the FONT SETTINGS FOR BULLET dialog box. To change the height or position of these options, open the ATTRIBUTE OVERRIDES dialog box on the Paragraph menu and adjust the settings.

The Attribute Overrides Command

The Attribute Overrides command is available on the Paragraph menu. The ATTRIBUTE OVERRIDES dialog box includes eight options that enable you to override Ventura's defaults for the height (thickness), spacing, and size of text attributes: Line Width, Overscore Height, Strike-Thru Height, Underline 1 Height, Underline 2 Height, Superscript Size, Subscript Size, and Small Cap Size. Because these adjustments are usually slight, made in fractional points, the changes probably do not appear accurately on-screen. Print the page to check the results.

Looking Up Alternate Character Sets

To customize tab leaders, tab decimal alignment, and bullets, you can use Ventura's SPECIAL EFFECTS dialog box to learn the ASCII value of several symbols from Ventura's character set. Select a paragraph with the paragraph cursor, open the SPECIAL EFFECTS dialog box from the Paragraph menu, click `Special Effect: Bullet`, and click the various `Show Bullet As` settings. As you click the symbols, the decimal value of each character is shown in the `Bullet Char` option.

In figure 5.27, the tab leader is set as `Custom` with a value of 192 and the leaders that display on-screen are selected. The text function's SET FONT dialog box was used to change the face to Symbol.

To see the full character set delivered with Ventura, print CHARSET.CHP from the TYPESET directory in the work area. (The reference guide includes the same list as CHARSET.CHP and the Dingbat symbols that some printers support separately.) The first column in CHARSET shows the decimal value you should type whenever you are prompted to specify a custom ASCII symbol; the second column shows the international set. The third column shows the equivalent in the symbol font set, but you must set the font as Symbol to access these characters. If you have installed other fonts, check the supplier for a table of the equivalent ASCII values. Chapter 4 includes the international and symbol font columns of CHARSET.CHP.

The `Line Width: Text Wide` and `Line Width: Margin Wide` options on the ATTRIBUTE OVERRIDES dialog box refer to the attribute's length. `Margin-Wide` sets the attribute from margin to margin. This setting is useful for the lines above or below entries in a table. `Text-Wide` sets the `Line Width` equal to the length of the attributed text. (Remember that you select the attribute using the Text function sidebar for phrases and the FONT dialog box for paragraphs.)

You can adjust the amount that lines are shifted up or down for overscores, strikethroughs, and underlines. The size of a superscript or subscript character and the amount of shift above or below the baseline can be fine-tuned. You also can set the `Small Cap Size` for any tag.

The Paragraph Typography Command

The Paragraph Typography command is available on the Paragraph menu. The TYPOGRAPHY SETTINGS dialog box controls the space between letters and words with one command that controls vertical spacing (see fig. 5.30). Setting `Grow Inter-Line To Fit: On` causes Ventura to increase the amount of space between lines in a paragraph where a selection of text has a font size larger than the rest of the text. This vertical-spacing feature can be useful when creating technical documents and manuscripts.

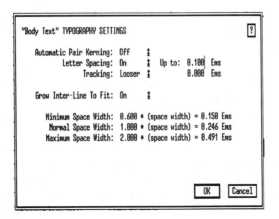

```
"Body Text" TYPOGRAPHY SETTINGS                        [?]

    Automatic Pair Kerning:  Off      ‡
             Letter Spacing:  On       ‡   Up to:  0.100  Ems
                  Tracking:  Looser   ‡           0.000  Ems

    Grow Inter-Line To Fit:  On       ‡

        Minimum Space Width:  0.600 * (space width) = 0.150 Ems
         Normal Space Width:  1.000 * (space width) = 0.246 Ems
        Maximum Space Width:  2.000 * (space width) = 0.491 Ems


                                           [  OK  ]  [ Cancel ]
```

Fig. 5.30.

The TYPOGRAPHY SETTINGS dialog box.

The TYPOGRAPHY SETTINGS dialog box options share one common characteristic: each controls precise adjustments to space. The Automatic Pair Kerning, Letter Spacing, Tracking, and Space Width options enable you to modify the horizontal increments of spaces between letters and words. The Grow Inter-Line To Fit option changes the vertical or interline spacing for lines containing different size typefaces.

- Automatic Pair Kerning controls the space between selected letters. You choose Automatic Pair Kerning to improve spacing (normally on type larger than 12 points) between *certain* letters.

- Tracking also controls spacing between letters, but does so throughout the entire paragraph. You choose Tracking to tighten or loosen the space between *all* letters in a paragraph.

- Letter Spacing inserts the space between letters up to the value specified if the space between words is not enough to justify a paragraph.

- Grow Inter-Line To Fit adjusts the space only for a line that contains a larger character without changing the values set in the SPACING dialog box.

With the options in the TYPOGRAPHY SETTINGS dialog box, you can improve the appearance of headlines and justified text in narrow columns. See Chapter 9 to learn more about using these features as copy-fitting aids and to learn more about tracking, kerning, and letter spacing.

The options in the TYPOGRAPHY SETTINGS dialog box are described in the following sections.

Automatic Pair Kerning

Kerning refers to the fine adjustments made to the space between pairs of letters to achieve a balanced look, although kerning usually is not obvious in text smaller than

10 points. To see the effects of automatic kerning on-screen, use the SET PREFER-ENCES dialog box opened from the Options menu to select the minimum point size to display as kerned.

You can use Ventura's automatic kerning feature only if you have a PostScript printer in your system configuration or have acquired fonts with kerning tables compatible with other printers. Manual kerning, however, is supported by all printers. As explained in the "Quick Manual Kerning for All Printers" Efficiency Tip, you can kern selected text quickly and see the results on-screen.

For example, in figure 5.31, the space between the characters *AV* is smaller than the space between the characters *VE* to compensate for the shapes of the letters. If the space between the letters is not adjusted or kerned, the *A* and the *V* appear farther apart than the *V* and the *E*. Kerned text generally looks better than text that is not kerned, especially as you increase the point size of fonts. Automatic kerning, how-ever, slows down the formatting process slightly.

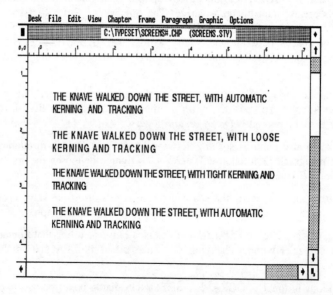

Fig. 5.31.

The effects of kerning.

Chapter 9 discusses kerning and adding fonts in greater detail. Manual kerning, as described in the section "Formatting Phrases in Paragraphs" in this chapter, works on all printers for every font you can print.

Automatic Pair Kerning uses information stored in the width table to adjust the space between these pairs. To improve the appearance of headlines and text for an entire chapter, select Automatic Pair Kerning: On in the CHAPTER TYPOGRAPHY dialog box. Use the Automatic Pair Kerning option in the FRAME TYPOGRA-PHY or Paragraph TYPOGRAPHY SETTINGS dialog box to override the chapter setting, turning off kerning for Body Text, for example. You cannot turn on automatic

pair kerning for a frame or paragraph if the option is Off in the CHAPTER TYPOG-
RAPHY dialog box. On-Screen Kerning from the Options menu enables you to see
the effects of automatic kerning in the work area but slows screen redrawing. Manual
kerning is shown on-screen at all times.

Efficiency Tip

Quick Manual Kerning for All Printers

You can kern selected text to move letters closer together or farther apart and see the
results as you do so. Select the letters you want to kern with the text tool, hold the
Shift key, and press the left (for tighter) or right (for looser) arrow key. Notice that
you can see the measurement Ventura accumulates when you open the FONT SET-
TINGS FOR SELECTED TEXT dialog box. See Chapter 9 for a detailed discussion
of kerning.

Letter Spacing

Ventura provides an option for you to see whether changing the amount of space between letters improves the format of text on the page. Letter spacing is the space
added between letters if space added between words does not force a line to justify.
The Show Loose Lines command from the Options menu displays the lines that can
benefit from adjustment in reverse type, like selected text. *Loose lines* are lines of text
with more space than allowed by the Maximum Space Width setting on the Paragraph
TYPOGRAPHY SETTINGS dialog box, because of the length and order of the words
in the line.

To adjust loose lines, choose Letter Spacing: On in the Paragraph TYPOGRAPHY
SETTINGS dialog box. (The ''Controlling Loose Lines'' Efficiency Tip in this chapter covers alternative ways of eliminating loose lines.) When you decrease the Up to
ems value in the Letter Spacing option, Ventura adds no more space between letters than the amount of space specified. (One *em* is the amount of space occupied by
the capital letter *M* in that font). If you increase the em value, the amount of space
added between letters increases. The amount of space between words on the line is
reduced, therefore, resulting in narrower gaps of white space between words. Ventura
reduces the space between words only to the specified Minimum Space Width.

Tracking

Tracking contracts the space between all characters—in contrast to letter spacing,
which adjusts the space only in loose lines and justified text. Choose Tracking:
Looser to widen the spaces between letters. Choose Tracking: Tighter to narrow
the spaces between letters. Tracking can be used to make a headline fit into a space
and also can be with kerning. Changing the tracking for body copy by the smallest
fractions can eliminate loose lines and reduce the space the copy requires. In figure
5.32, the top line of the heading is set for Tracking: Tighter and the bottom line is
set for Tracking: Looser to force the lines to fit in the same amount of space. The
value is a percentage of an em space and takes hundredths of thousandths of an em,
depending on point size, to adjust.

Fig. 5.32.

Tracking a logo.

COLLEGEAGE

MAGAZINE

Minimum, Normal, and Maximum Space Width

The three space widths options—Minimum, Normal, and Maximum—define the amount of space allowed between words in justified text (unjustified text uses only the Normal option). You insert Minimum and Maximum values as percentages of the Normal space width and let Ventura calculate the setting in ems.

The Normal Space Width option is the basis for comparing the Minimum and Maximum option values. If you set Normal Space Width to 1, the Minimum Space Width is a value less than 1 (usually .600) and the Maximum Space Width is a value greater than 1 (usually 2.000). To double the space allowed between words, change Normal to 2 and adjust the other space widths accordingly. (Remember that 1 is the highest minimum value that can be set.) Each value you set is calculated and displayed in em values.

Efficiency Tip

Controlling Loose Lines

If the words in justified text are displayed with too much space between them, creating *rivers* (gaps of white) in the text, you can try several techniques to improve the text's appearance:

- Adjust hyphenation manually with Ctrl-- (hyphen).

- Edit the text. A slight change in words or in word order may solve the problem.

- Change the hyphenation authority. USENGLSH, Ventura's hyphenation dictionary, misses some opportunities to hyphenate words. USENGLSH2 is slower but more accurate.

- Allow more consecutive lines to end with hyphens by choosing a larger number in the ALIGNMENT dialog box Successive Hyphens option.

- Tighten tracking by 1 or 2 thousandths of an em. This adjustment affects all similarly tagged paragraphs and can reduce the total page count.

- Change the Letter Spacing option on the Paragraph TYPOGRAPHY SETTINGS dialog box.

The Ruling Lines Commands

As you use Ventura, you begin to recognize dialog boxes opened with other commands. The RULING LINES dialog box, opened with any of the Ruling Line commands from the Paragraph menu, is the same box that appears with the Frame menu's Ruling Line commands. From the Paragraph menu, however, you have more available options. When you choose a Ruling Line command from the Paragraph menu, you can set rules over, under, and around paragraphs. The top line in the box indicates which command you have chosen. If you want to remove that rule, click None. Any values set in the dialog box remain so that you can select a width later to reinstate the rule. Figure 5.33 shows the dialog box that appears when the Ruling Line Above command is selected from the Paragraph menu.

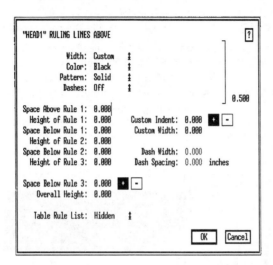

Fig. 5.33.

The RULING LINES ABOVE dialog box accessed from the Paragraph menu.

The measurement term, shown to the far right of Dash Spacing, can be changed by clicking the measurement displayed. In most instances, the unit should be set as fractional points when defining rules. The unit of measurement to the left of the term, however, is constant and converts into the equivalent values. When you see the height of the rules in the top right area of the dialog box, you are actually seeing lines and spaces at twice the size they appear in the work area. The maximum rule width that can be displayed in the dialog box is 0.5-inch thick, because only 1 inch of space is available where the rules appear.

The Ruling Line Above, Ruling Line Below, and Ruling Box Around commands on the Paragraph menu have individual dialog boxes. Each dialog box is similar in terms of setting width; color, pattern, and dashes; and height, space above, and space below rules.

Width

When you click one of the five available Width settings from the RULING LINES dialog box, the related options for color, pattern, space, and height become available for selection. Text-wide rules are as wide as the first line of text in that paragraph. Margin-wide rules are as wide as the column, less any In From Left or Right indents in effect. Column-wide rules are as wide as the column, and frame-wide rules are as wide as the frame if Overall Width: Frame is set for that tag in the

ALIGNMNENT dialog box of the Paragraph menu. If you select Custom, the Custom Width, Custom Indent, Dash Width, and Dash Spacing options become available.

To create rules of a specific width, type that measurement as the Custom Width. (You may want to change the measurement term to picas or inches for this setting.) Any temporary indents in effect for the tag also affect ruling lines. The Custom Indent option enables you to position a custom rule to the right (click +) or to the left (click −) of the active left margin. To use Custom Indent to override a 3-pica In From Left setting, set Custom Indent: 03.00 picas and points and click − (minus).

Each RULING LINES dialog box opened from the Paragraph menu operates in the same way but with different effects. Figure 5.34 shows how rules are used to emphasize headlines, create dashed lines, and create boxes. You can use Ruling Line Above and Ruling Line Below commands in a paragraph tag, but if you use the Ruling Box Around command, the Width option in the other dialog boxes defaults to None. Any values set when this conflict occurs remain in the dialog box so that you can decide to change the Width option.

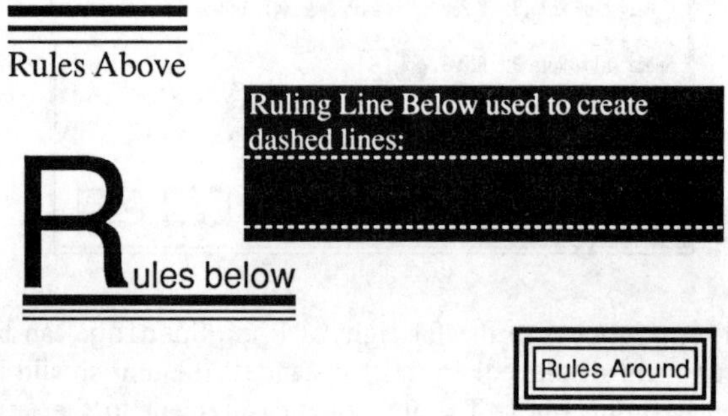

Fig. 5.34.

Rules above, rules below, and ruling box around.

Height, Space Above, and Space Below Rules

For the first ruling line in a tag (called *Rule 1*), you have three options. You can set the space above the rule, set a height (*thickness* or *weight*) for the rule, and set the space below the rule. These settings are all specified in the RULING LINES dialog box. To see how Ventura displays the value of the overall height, enter values for these three options. The Overall Height (at the bottom of the dialog box) is the sum of the space values set for the first settings; this sum is the amount of space required to position the rule.

With Rule 2, you can set values for the height of the rule and the space below the rule. If you define Rules 1 and 2, the Overall Height value equals the amount of space required to position both rules.

Rule 3 is different than the other two and can play an important role even if you do not select a height for it. You can shift all the ruling lines up or down by the amount you specify as Space Below 3. Click the plus sign (+) to add space and the minus sign ($-$) to subtract space. The shift value you apply to Rule 3 affects all three rules. By shifting the line, you overlap the rules with text in the paragraph above or below them, enabling you to print reverse type if your printer supports printing white text.

Every time you change a value in any of the rule options, Ventura retotals the Overall Height value. If you are working on a multicolumn layout, this value should be equal to or an even multiple of the Body Text tag's Inter-Line value in the SPACING dialog box. Ruling lines become part of the tagged paragraph and increase the amount of space set between the last and first lines of successive paragraphs. The overall height of any rule adds to the space Ventura calculates for leading between paragraphs. If you are concerned with the uniform alignment of text on pages, you can combine Overall Height of a ruling line with the value set as the Above or Below option in the SPACING dialog box. The result should be a value of zero or an integer multiple of the Body Text tag's Inter-Line value.

Rules play an important part in the design of most publications. See Chapter 7 for a comparison of Ventura's alternative techniques to add horizontal and vertical rules.

Color, Pattern, and Dashes

You can set three weights of rules for each Ruling Line command, although you may use only one color and pattern for all three. When defining rules, select the width of the rule from the available Width options. Set the ruling height. When you have established a value for Height of Rule 1, set the Color and Pattern. An enlargement (twice the size) of the rule appears in the work area. Adjust the spacing above and below the rule to match your intentions. If you have chosen Width: Custom, you can add or subtract the values set for Custom Indent and Custom Width, discussed previously.

Dashes: On enables you to create horizontal dashes and vertical dashes. To make horizontal dashes, keep the Height of Rule and Dash Spacing values nearly equal. For the logo in figure 5.35, three paragraphs are tagged with different rule settings; the Color is Black and the Pattern is Solid for each. (See the Efficiency Tip "Using White Type on Black Rules" in this chapter.) The first tag uses dashes to create vertical rules, setting the Height of Rule 1 greater than the value of Dash Spacing. The tag for "Covers" creates a rule that prints adjacent to the rule created by the last line's tag. The font color selected for the text in the second two paragraphs is white (set in the FONT dialog box accessed from the Paragraph menu). Not all printers print white text on black rules. To check the capability of your printer, print the chapter called CAPABILI.CHP in your TYPESET directory.

If you do not have a color printer, you can use the Color settings to print color separations for spot-color copy for the print shop. The palette provided with Ventura can be customized as described in "Defining Custom Colors" later in this chapter.

The Dashes option toggles between Dashes: Off and Dashes: On as you click the option. You can specify a custom dash width and dash spacing if you set Dashes: On. Set Dash Width wider than Dash Spacing when you want to create a horizontal dashed line. Dashes are good for creating data-entry and typewriter forms. You also can use dashes to give headlines graphic strength by adding horizontal or vertical rules to a tagged paragraph.

Fig. 5.35.

Logo with dashes.

Efficiency Tip

Using White Type on Black Rules

If your printer supports reverse type, you can print white type on black rules as shown in figure 5.35. To set up white type, follow these steps:

1. Click the Ruling Line Above command from the Paragraph menu, opening the RULING LINES ABOVE dialog box.

2. Set Height of Rule 1 as the size of the white text you are using plus the amount of black you want above and below the text.

3. Click beside the Space Below Rule 3 option and enter a value half the total of the size of the rule and the size of the text.

4. Click the minus sign beside Space Below Rule 3.

5. Change the Color setting in the FONT dialog box to White.

Increase the Space Below Rule 3 value to move the text up; decrease the Space Below Rule 3 to move the text down.

If your printer supports white characters on a black background, the effect of reverse type is created because you shifted the Space Below Rule 3 option up so that the text prints on the rule.

The Define Colors Command

The Define Colors command on the Paragraph menu enables you to define new colors and create shades of gray. You can store six colors or shades of gray per style sheet. If you have a color monitor, you can see the effect of the colors and shades of gray on-screen. Other monitors display patterns of black that represent shades of gray for the colors. Ventura also supports color printers.

With Ventura, you can design a project for color printing. You can print in color on a color printer or in shades of gray on a black-and-white printer. (See Appendix F of the Xerox Reference Guide for limitations for your printer.) You can print color separations for spot-color printing. To enable the colors you want to use—or define new colors—choose the Define Colors command from the Paragraph menu. The DEFINE COLORS dialog box appears, as shown in figure 5.36, with the Screen Display pop-up menu open.

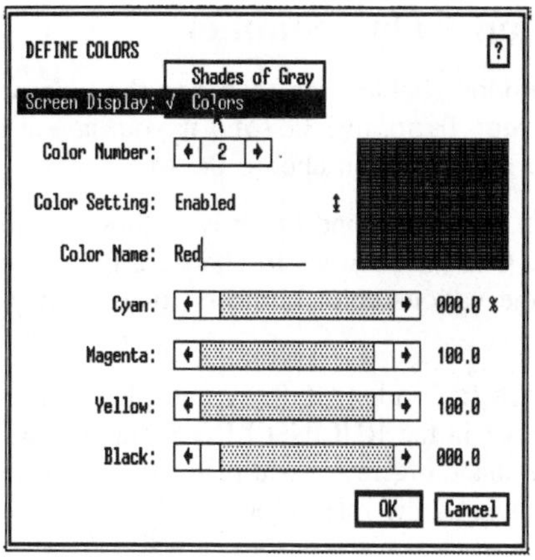

```
DEFINE COLORS                          [?]
                    Shades of Gray
 Screen Display: √  Colors
    Color Number:  [◆] 2 [◆] .
   Color Setting:  Enabled        ↕
     Color Name:  Red
          Cyan:  [◆]            [◆]  000.0 %
       Magenta:  [◆]            [◆]  100.0
        Yellow:  [◆]            [◆]  100.0
         Black:  [◆]            [◆]  000.0
                              [ OK ] [Cancel]
```

Fig. 5.36.

The DEFINE COLORS dialog box.

After you define the colors to be used in a project, Ventura displays the color names in all dialog boxes with a color setting option. You can define a color for a frame or frame background, a paragraph or selected phrase, a rule above, below, or around a paragraph, a Big First Character, or a bullet.

When you complete a project using several colors or shades of gray and want to print it, set Spot Color Overlays: On in the PRINT dialog box, accessed from the File menu, so that Ventura prints a separate page for each color used. Otherwise, all enabled colors print together on the same page. At print time, Ventura asks whether you are sure you want color-spot overlays so that you have the chance to print all the colors on a single page. If you respond YES, Print Spot Color Overlays, each color prints in solid black on a separate page with the name of the color represented at the top of each page.

You can define the exact color you want to print to a color printer by mixing percentages of cyan, magenta, yellow, and black. This procedure is described in "Customizing Colors." The following sections explain the options on the DEFINE COLORS dialog box.

Efficiency Tip

Using the Colors Option To Create a Blue-line Proof with PostScript Printers

Many offset printers provide a blue-line of multicolor projects for client approval before printing. This one-color proof shows all pages as they appear when printed. Black appears solid and other colors are differentiated by different shades of gray (or screens). Define the appropriate color for each tag in a multicolor project and print a copy with Screen Display set as Shades of Gray in the DEFINE COLORS dialog box and Spot Color Overlays: Off in the PRINT dialog box. After approval, set Spot Color Overlays: On to print each color as solid black on a separate page to deliver to the printer.

Screen Display and Color Number

The Screen Display option enables you to define the type of environment you are working in. Choose Screen Display: Colors if you have a monochrome monitor. Shades of gray are shown even if you choose Color.

Choose a color number. White is 0 and black is 1; these are the only color numbers that cannot be changed. Click the arrows to choose a higher or lower color number. As you move through the various color numbers, the Color Name and Color Setting options change.

If you set Screen Display: Shades of Gray and plan to use the enabled color for rules, set Pattern: Solid in the RULING LINES dialog box. Do not use the Pattern option to choose a shade of gray if you plan to use a shade of gray created with the Define Colors command as the rule color.

Color Setting and Color Name

If you want to print a spot-color overlay for a color on the palette, set Color Setting: Enabled. If you do not use the color in your project, set Color Setting: Disabled so that Ventura does not print a blank overlay page for that color. If you disable a color used in your project, the name is removed from the list in every dialog box in which color options are displayed.

As you move through the various color numbers, notice that the Color Name option changes to reflect the current color number. The ''mix'' of the four basic colors also changes to show the composition of that color.

If you want to define a new color, you can assign the color a new name by typing this name on the Color Name option. If you have not given the color a new number, you ''override'' the existing color with that number. The following section explains how custom colors are mixed.

Customizing Colors

To customize a color, select a color number, enable the color (if it is used in your project), and provide a name for the color. You may want to choose one of the existing colors and change the percentages of cyan, magenta, yellow, and black to alter the appearance of that color. To change the percentages, click the arrows or drag the scroll bar. Each of these colors can be set to intensities between 0 and 100 percent in increments of 2 percent. Using these four colors—and variations of them in 2 percent increments—you can create over 125 million colors. The colors you create print to any color PostScript printer, such as the QMS ColorScript. All colors you enable are listed in every dialog box offering a color setting.

The gray scale works like color, except you create colors using just the black color bar. Choose a color number and set the cyan, magenta, and yellow color bars to 0. Use the black color bar to create the desired shade of gray. You can name the color based on the percentages of black selected. For example; move the black color bar to 10 percent and name the color *10*. That name appears in all dialog boxes with a color setting. Remember to set `Screen Display: Shades of Gray` when defining a gray scale.

You can create a shade of gray even if you set `Screen Display: Color`. When you print, the colors print as shades of gray.

If you have defined a scale of gray, you can print spot-color overlays for the various shades of gray just as you can for colors. If you set `Spot Color Overlays: On` in the Print menu, each shade of gray is printed as solid black on separate pages. If you set `Spot Color Overlays: Off`, each shade of gray is printed as the appropriate shade of gray.

If you try to print colors on a black-and-white PostScript printer, the colors are printed as shades of gray.

--- *Efficiency Tip*

Eliminating Blank Pages for Unused Colors

Ventura prints all seven layers of color separately when you request spot-color overlays, whether or not you have used all the available colors. Disable the colors you do not use in the project before you print to eliminate blank pages being printed.

After you mix a custom color, Ventura retains the color mixes until you change or disable them. You must remix custom colors when you enable that color again. You can reset to Ventura's default value (red, green, blue, cyan, yellow, or magenta) using the pop-up menu for Color Setting.

--- *Efficiency Tip*

Using Gray Scales and Patterns with Rules

You can use the `Pattern` option on the RULING LINES dialog boxes as another way to set a gray scale. When you create a shade of gray using the Define Colors command, set `Pattern: Solid` in the RULING LINES dialog box if you plan to use your defined shade of gray for the rule. Do not mix the gray settings you can specify in the `Pattern` option with those you create, or you may get undesirable results.

Summary of Setting Paragraph Formats

To format text, lists, and tables, combine options from the first 12 commands in the Paragraph menu. The methods you use to format paragraphs of text also apply to formatting footnotes, headers, outlines, tables of contents, indexes, and advertisements. Each style file maintains a list of tags and settings as you design and modify the settings in each tag. Make sure that your text file's tag names match those in the various style files you want to use so that you can see the effects of alternative designs.

As you can see, tagging is the key to most of the formatting you do. If you plan a project carefully, most text-based publishing assignments should use the default Body Text tag to set the majority of copy so that only a small number of paragraphs need tagging. In any case, tagging is easy when you use the techniques described in the following section.

Attaching Tags to Paragraphs

Most of the format associated with text is defined by the instructions stored with the tag name in the style file. As this chapter explains, special words and phrases in paragraphs are formatted through instructions written to the text file instead of through an attached tag. The previous sections in this chapter cover the Paragraph menu commands that you use to choose and define tags. This section shows you alternative ways to select paragraphs and attach tags.

You can attach tags in three ways:

- Select the paragraph(s) and click the desired tag in the assignment list.

- Select the paragraph(s) and press the function key assigned to the desired tag.

- Embed tags in text files using a word processor or another program.

Selecting a Paragraph

To see or change the format settings associated with a paragraph, choose the Paragraph function, position the cursor in a paragraph, and click. The selected paragraph is displayed in reverse, and the name of the tag attached to the paragraph appears in the current selection box in the sidebar (see fig. 5.37). When you select a paragraph with the paragraph cursor, the Paragraph menu's format commands are enabled.

Selecting More than One Paragraph

You can select all the similar paragraphs on a page and attach the tag names at once, speeding the formatting process greatly. To select multiple paragraphs, move the paragraph cursor over each paragraph and hold the Shift key while you click the mouse button. If you click with the Shift key on a selected paragraph, you deselect the paragraph. When you select more than one paragraph, the word MULTIPLE appears in the current selection box.

You can tag all selected paragraphs with a new tag name. You can see and change the settings for only the first tag selected, however. Any paragraph in a selected set can be deselected with a Shift-click on the paragraph. Remember that Ventura sets all untagged paragraphs with the characteristics of the Body Text tag when you first type or import text.

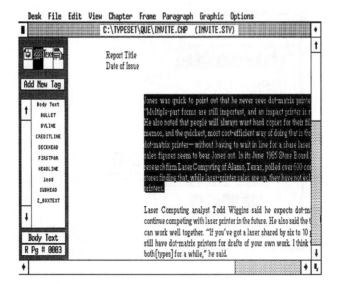

Desk File Edit View Chapter Frame Paragraph Graphic Options

C:\TYPESET\QUE\INVITE.CHP (INVITE.STV)

Add New Tag

Body Text
BULLET
BYLINE
CREDITLINE
DECKHEAD
FIRSTPAR
HEADLINE
lead
SUBHEAD
Z_BOXTEXT

Body Text
R Pg # 0003

Report Title
Date of Issue

Jones was quick to point out that he never sees dot-matrix printer "Multiple-part forms are still important, and an impact printer is r He also noted that people will always want hard copies for their fil memos, and the quickest, most cost-efficient way of doing that is the dot-matrix printer—without having to wait in line for a share laser sales figures seem to bear Jones out. In its June 1985 Store Board research firm Laser Computing of Alamo, Texas, polled over 600 com stores finding that, while laser-printer sales are up, they have not ecl printers.

Laser Computing analyst Todd Wiggins said he expects dot-m continue competing with laser printer in the future. He also said the t can work well together. "If you've got a laser shared by six to 10 still have dot-matrix printers for drafts of your own work. I think both [types] for a while," he said.

Fig. 5.37.

A selected paragraph with the Body Text tag.

Assigning Function Keys to Tags

The Update Tag List command is available on the Paragraph menu. The keyboard shortcut, Ctrl-K, opens the ASSIGN FUNCTION KEYS dialog box when the Frame, Text, or Graphic function is active. Ctrl-K opens the UPDATE TAG LIST dialog box when you have a paragraph selected (see fig. 5.38). Click Assign Func Keys. When you open the dialog box, you can assign a tag name to the keys F1 through F10 by typing the names of the tags next to the function-key label (see fig. 5.39). Ventura assigns the Body Text tag to F10, but you can override that assignment by typing a different tag name.

When function keys have an assigned tag and you are using the Text or the Paragraph function, simply press the function key to attach that tag to the selected paragraph(s).

Efficiency Tip

Tagging While Editing

You can use the text cursor to select a paragraph to tag if the function keys are set with the tag names you want to use. To tag a paragraph while editing, click the text cursor within the paragraph and press the function key assigned to the desired tag.

Tagging Text Files

When you use your word processor (or another program) to prepare text files with tag names, precede each tag name with an at sign (@) and follow each tag name with a space, an equal sign, and another space (see fig. 5.40). Any difference in this syntax

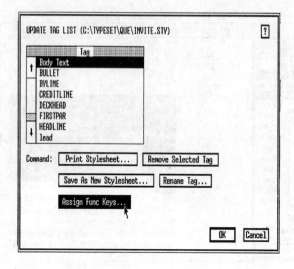

Fig. 5.38.

The UPDATE TAG LIST dialog box.

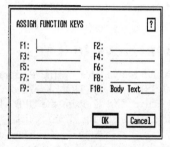

Fig. 5.39.

The ASSIGN FUNCTION KEYS dialog box.

causes the tag name to be read as text when loaded into a Ventura chapter. Tag names in the text file that do not correspond to tag names in the style file are displayed in all uppercase in the assignment list and are set with the characteristics of the Body Text tag. When you start a new chapter by importing a file with tags for which no style file exists, all tag names appear in uppercase. Also, if you misspell the name of a tag, the name appears in uppercase. If you load a tagged file for which a style file should exist but the tags appear in all uppercase in the list, be sure that you have loaded the correct style file.

Managing Tags in the Style File

Although most well-planned publications use only a few tag names, you invariably develop custom tags as you fine-tune the pages in a publication. Ventura enables you to use up to 128 tag names per style file to specify different paragraph formats and provides ways for you to add, remove, and convert tags from one to another. You may use Ventura's features to generate a copy of the instructions stored in the style file, including the settings for the base page and the list of tag names. The following sections explain how to add, remove, and rename tags, and print the contents of a style file.

```
@HEADLINE TOP = The Rule
Each spacing value greater than 0 must be
equal to or evenly divisible....(Body Text
again)
@HEADLINE TOP = The Spacing Values To
Consider
@CHECK BOX =
@CHECKED ITEM = Space Above
@CHECK BOX =
@CHECKED ITEM = Space Below
@CHECK BOX =
@CHECKED ITEM = Inter-Line
@HEADLINE TOP = Applying the Rule
First, look at the inter-line spacing in
Body Text....(Body Text Again)
```

Fig. 5.40.

Tag names in a word processing file.

Adding Tags

When you want to add a tag name to the assignment list, select a paragraph with a tag with similar settings and click the Add New Tag button in the Paragraph function sidebar. The ADD NEW TAG dialog box opens for you to type the name of the new tag (see fig. 5.41).

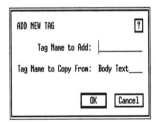

Fig. 5.41.

The ADD NEW TAG dialog box.

Tag names can be up to 13 characters in length, including spaces, numbers, and symbols. Tag names can include uppercase and lowercase letters, although changing just the case in a tag name does not create a unique tag name. You can have up to 128 tag names, including Ventura's general tags (for headers, footers, tables of contents, indexes, captions, footnotes, and automatic numbers); tag names found in the text file but not found in the style file; and tags you make.

Efficiency Tip

Change Body Text Attributes Temporarily When Creating a New Style File

Untagged text imported into Ventura has the characteristics of Body Text. You can save formatting time by temporarily changing Body Text settings to those needed for other tags before adding those tags. Body Text may be justified, with hyphenation on and no ruling lines, for example, but the project has several levels of flush-left heads with no hyphenation and ruling lines. To avoid changing alignment, adding rules, and turning off hyphenation for each new tag, define Body Text with those settings before adding new tags. After the other tags are added, set the Body Text characteristics.

Don't Use All Uppercase Tag Names

When naming tags, avoid using all uppercase letters. When Ventura finds tag names in text files that do not match the tag names in the active style file, the unused names appear in the assignment list in all uppercase. Tag names with capital letters have the same settings as the Body Text tag unless the capital-letter tag has been changed with the commands of the Paragraph menu. You can rename tags with uppercase names to uppercase and lowercase using the Update Tag List command from the Paragraph menu.

Removing Tags

With Ventura, you can remove individual tags and convert tagged paragraphs to another tag. Use the `Remove Selected Tag` command in the UPDATE TAG LIST dialog box accessed from the Paragraph menu (see fig. 5.42). Before you can proceed however, Ventura requires that you save the chapter file in view. By default, the Remove Selected Tag command changes all paragraphs with the removed tag to Body Text tags. If you convert the tag to Body Text, the paragraphs in the text file no longer have a tag. However, you can override the default and convert a removed tag to another tag.

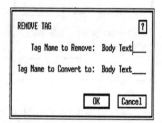

Fig. 5.42.

The REMOVE TAG dialog box.

To remove a tag name, select the tag from the Tag list shown in the UPDATE TAG LIST dialog box, and select the Remove Selected Tag command. Ventura supplies the removal and default conversion tag names in the dialog box that opens. You can type in new names, or click OK to accept the names Ventura provides.

Renaming Tags

You rename tags using the Rename Tag command on the UPDATE TAG LIST dialog box. To do so, select Update Tag List from the Paragraph menu and select the tag to rename from the Tag list (after you respond to Ventura's request to update the chapter file on disk). With a tag name selected, click `Rename Tag`. Type the new name of the tag in the RENAME TAG dialog box, shown in figure 5.43. Ventura updates the new tag name in the text file and the assignment list.

Too Many Tags

Ventura allows only 128 tags in one style file and displays a message when you exceed this maximum. Most often, the reason is that you have loaded a text document tagged with names matching another style's tags, and the Assignment List contains both sets of tag names. If you loaded the wrong text file, click the Frame function, select the frame containing the text file, and choose Remove Text/File from the Edit menu. After you remove the file from the list of files, choose Load Diff. Style from the File menu to reload the original style or a different style file name. Removing a text file does not remove tags added to the Tag List.

Fig. 5.43.

The RENAME TAG dialog box.

Creating a Style File Printout

The UPDATE TAG LIST dialog box offers a Print Stylesheet option. When the command is selected, an ITEM SELECTOR dialog box opens to the Selection option where you can type the name of the style file you want to print. The default extension GEN is set in the Directory option in this dialog box. When you name the file, close the box with OK, and wait for Ventura to finish processing. After generating the file, you can load the text file to a page just as you would any other file. Select Text Format: Generated. Ventura provides STYLOG.STY in the TYPESET directory for formatting generated style sheets. Print the style file so that you have a master copy of the style file for repetitive projects and so that you can document complicated techniques. Tag values in the style file print only if they are different from the values set for the Body Text tag.

Formatting Phrases in Paragraphs

Words, phrases, and names within paragraphs sometimes need a different emphasis from the rest of a paragraph. To format a phrase within a paragraph, select the text you want to format and select the attribute to attach. Ventura offers three features affecting the format of selected text:

- The Text function assignment list

- The FONT dialog boxes opened from the Font and Special Effects commands on the Paragraph menu

- The ATTRIBUTE OVERRIDES dialog box

Chapter 3 explains how to select the text to which you want to apply a new format. In the following sections, you learn how to use each of the features listed.

Changing the Typeface of Selected Phrases

The Text function offers two ways to format phrases within paragraphs:

- The sidebar attributes

- The Set Font button

As in paragraph tagging, you must select the text to format and attach the attributes from the sidebar as you point and click the mouse. Attributes selected from the sidebar often appear in the text file as though the attribute is coded there. When you click the Set Font button, the FONT SETTING FOR SELECTED TEXT dialog box appears, as shown in figure 5.44.

Fig. 5.44.

The FONT SETTING FOR SELECTED TEXT dialog box.

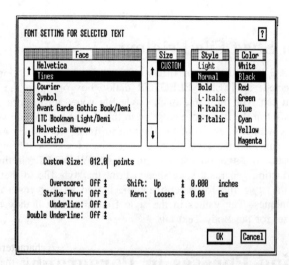

When the word processing program does not support an attribute, you see bracketed codes in the word processing file. All the bracket codes used by Ventura are presented in the tables in Chapter 4.

The first attribute listed is not actually an attribute but represents the normal format for the paragraph. Click Normal to cancel any attribute settings in the Text function sidebar and in the SET FONT dialog box. Figure 5.45 shows results of several sample attribute settings. All attribute settings are reset to Normal when a paragraph return or another code is encountered.

Bold

Italic

Small

Superscript

Subscript

Underline

Double UndrLn

~~Strike thru~~

O̅v̅e̅r̅s̅c̅o̅r̅e̅

Fig. 5.45.

Results of sample attribute settings.

In Ventura, attribute codes have a starting position and an ending position. To see where the attribute code is attached, move the text cursor near the position and use the right-arrow and left-arrow keys to move the I-beam until Attrib Setting appears in the current selection box. The fastest way to remove attribute coding is to select the text and click Normal in the assignment list. You can erase individual attribute codes by using the Text function, but you must erase the beginning and the end of the code. Attributes cut to the Clipboard with the Del key can be inserted in a new place with the Ins key as long as you cut and insert the beginning and end of the attribute code.

The assignment list includes options that position superscripted and subscripted text. If your printer doesn't support Ventura's automatic superscript and subscript sizes, use the Set Font button in the Text function sidebar to change the size and position of the selected characters.

Underlining, Striking Through, and Overscoring Text

To format a phrase with underline, strike-through, or overstrike characteristics, select the character(s) you want to emphasize. Click the desired attribute in the assignment list. Figure 5.46 shows examples of these attributes.

The Attribute Overrides command from the Paragraph menu enables you to change the thickness and position of underlines, overscores, and strike-throughs set for the selected text. To change the height or position of the attribute, do the following:

1. Click the Paragraph function.

2. Select the entire paragraph with the Paragraph cursor.

3. Open the ATTRIBUTE OVERRIDES dialog box and change the default values for the height, size, and position of the attribute.

Because you changed the defaults through the command on the Paragraph menu, all paragraphs tagged with that name emphasize selected text in this new way. Attributes for large font sizes increase size and spacing when you select Auto-Adjustments: None in the SET PREFERENCES dialog box, accessed from the Options menu. For underlined text, you may want to add space between the underline and the following text.

Fig. 5.46.

Underlines, strike-throughs, and overstrikes.

This is a sample of underlined text.

This is a sample of text that has been striked thru.

This is a sample of text that has been overscored.

Changing the Case of Selected Text

When you need to change the capitalization in a section of text, select the text and click the appropriate command in the Text function assignment list. The Upper Case command changes all selected text to capitals; the Capitalize command affects the first character of paragraphs and letters preceded by a space; the Lower Case command changes all uppercase letters to lowercase. Changing the case of selected text causes the text in the source file to change accordingly. With the case attribute commands, codes are not embedded in the text.

Shifting and Kerning Text

You can select text, click the Set Font button from the Text function sidebar, and use the FONT SETTINGS FOR SELECTED TEXT dialog box to adjust a character in text up or down from the baseline by using the Shift By options in the dialog box. You can shift selected letters up or down in increments of 1/300 inch (up to a maximum of 0.5 inch). Interactive kerning using the Shift key and the arrow keys after you select text is discussed in the Efficiency Tip "Quick Manual Kerning for All Printers," in this chapter. You can kern a selected letter to the left, moving in increments of 1/700 inch up to a maximum of about 0.5 inch. To use either of these options, click to change the measurement unit to fractional points. Seeing the effect on low-resolution and medium-resolution monitors is more difficult than on the printed page. Manual kerning and shifting are supported by all printers. The values and codes are embedded in the text file. For more on manual kerning, see Chapter 9. See Chapter 4 to learn more about using your word processor for formatting attributes in text files.

Chapter Summary

Now that you have seen the ways to format text on the page, you can compare Ventura's features with the capabilities of your word processing program and decide how to approach any large publishing project. Remember that the goal is to do as much formatting as possible in your word processor, because Ventura's WYSIWYG display slows the display of pages in the work area.

In this chapter, you saw how Ventura uses the style file and coded types in the text to establish the format of characters on pages. Chapter 7 provides more tips about efficient methods of applying these settings in the page-layout stage. Before you move to the multifaceted design and layout steps, read Chapter 6 to learn about the sources of graphics for a Ventura publication.

Creating and Importing Graphics

A characteristic of Ventura and other new page-composition programs is their capability to combine graphics and text on a page. Ventura contains some built-in graphics tools and also imports graphics created from other programs. As a result, you have two ways to generate graphics:

- Use Ventura's Graphic drawing tools

- Import graphics with the LOAD TEXT/PICTURE dialog box

This chapter discusses both techniques. First, you learn how to create graphics with Ventura's tools and how to include the graphics in layouts. You also see how to use Ventura's box text tool to create forms and other types of layouts with limited amounts of text on the page. In the second half of the chapter you see how to load, size, and embellish graphics source files. The differences among various source graphics files are explained.

Chapters 4 and 5 point out that Ventura provides text and formatting tools you can use to lend graphic emphasis to a page. Special character sets, ruling lines, and patterned backgrounds can be used to develop logos or headlines, and a variety of other ''graphic'' elements that you add to the page by tagging or typing bracketed codes. Tags and angle-bracket codes are interpreted and the results displayed when Ventura reads the instructions embedded in the source text file. Ventura-drawn graphics, on the other hand, are stored in a source file that Ventura creates when you use the Graphic tools. You can copy graphics from one chapter to another using the Graphic and Frame Clipboards.

Chapter 7 combines the features presented in Chapters 3 through 6 to show you how to lay out style and chapter files to produce different types of publications. To exploit fully the graphics potential of Ventura, expect to use features from all four publishing functions and related menus.

219

Drawing Graphics with Ventura's Tools

Creating an illustration in Ventura is different from sketching an illustration on a page. With Ventura, you create figures by laying lines, ellipses, and rectilinear shapes on the page. Although you may use just one graphic shape (when you add an arrow between the callout and a point in an illustration, for instance), you may also create shapes by overlaying lines, circles, rectangles, and boxes of text. The first illustration shown in figure 6.1 was made with a fat line and a box of text. The pointing symbols were made with two rectangles, a line, and a box of text.

Fig. 6.1.

Using a collage of shapes to create an illustration.

The collage technique lets you create simple crisp figures. You benefit from Ventura's capability to change the position, order, attributes, and sizes of the graphic shapes you draw. Ventura's grids and rulers can help you achieve precise alignment and match scale specifications. You can resize one graphic or all the selected graphics in a group; you can move them into new positions using the pointer tool and the Graphic Clipboard. You should first experiment by drawing with Ventura's tools on a blank page. In "Working with Graphics Drawn in Ventura," you see how to select, layer, scale, and repeat the graphics you draw.

Six Graphic tools are displayed in the sidebar when the Graphic function is selected. Four are drawing tools: the line tool, the rectangle tool, the ellipse tool, and the rounded rectangle tool. The box text tool draws boxes that hold text; the sixth tool is a pointer used to select graphics in the work area. Figure 6.2 shows the Graphic sidebar, and figure 6.3 shows the cursor shapes of the Graphic tools.

The box text tool is unique among Ventura's graphics tools: you can type text into a box placed on the page. The text you type in a box-text graphics box is stored in the chapter CAP file as is the text typed into empty frames on the page. Box text is different from frame text because it overlays all other text on the page. (Frames, by contrast, maintain the order in which they were laid. To re-layer frames, you cut and reinsert them; the last frame inserted is on top of the other frames.) You can wrap text around box text or around Ventura-drawn graphics by adding blank frames where you do not want text to appear. The steps to wrap text around frames are given in Chapter 7. "Using Box Text," in this chapter, shows how to create forms and illustrations for callouts with box text.

Use commands on the Graphic menu to manipulate selected graphics on-screen (see fig. 6.4). The first three commands (Show On All Pages, Send to Back, Bring to Front) let you repeat or rearrange graphics once they are drawn. The Line Attributes

Fig. 6.2.

The Graphic sidebar.

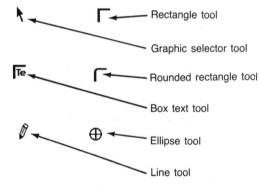

Rectangle tool

Graphic selector tool

Rounded rectangle tool

Box text tool

Ellipse tool

Line tool

Fig. 6.3.

Cursor shapes of the Graphic tools.

and Fill Attributes commands set the color, pattern, and thickness of Ventura-drawn graphics. Both attributes have default settings that can be overridden after you draw a graphic. You also can set custom defaults for each Graphic tool. The Select All command is used to select all the graphics associated with a frame. Grid Settings lets you set horizontal and vertical grids (which can have different units of measurement) for every set of graphics on a page. As you read through this chapter, you find practical ways to use all these commands.

Fig. 6.4.

The active Graphic menu.

To add graphics to a page, position the cursor on the Graphic function and click. Notice that eight gray handles display around the perimeter of the frame that Ventura assumes you want to use to control the graphics to be drawn (see fig. 6.5). By comparison, frame handles that are used to cut, copy, size, and embellish frames are solid black squares, not gray. Later in this chapter, you learn how and when to add frames to serve as graphic control frames. If you do not have a frame drawn on the page, Ventura uses the page as the graphic control frame. You can select an alternative frame as the graphic control frame by clicking the Graphic selector in the desired frame.

Fig. 6.5.

Graphic control handles outlining the frame most recently selected.

To select a Graphic tool, position the Graphic selector over the desired tool in the Graphic sidebar and click. Then move the cursor into the work area. The appearance of the cursor changes to resemble the tool you have chosen (refer to fig. 6.3).

All the drawing tools work similarly. After you select the shape you want and move the cursor into the work area, hold the mouse button as you drag the cursor to the opposite end of the desired area, drawing the shape from top left to bottom right. (Only lines can be drawn in any direction). As long as you hold the mouse button, you can keep adjusting the size of the object. Once you release the mouse button, the size is set, and the Graphic selector is displayed again.

Notice that as soon as you release the mouse button (and any time you select a drawn object), handles frame the graphic. Lines have a handle at each end, but other shapes have from two to eight handles, depending on the size of the shape. You can change the proportion and size of a graphic by using the pointer tool to select the object and then dragging one of the handles. Drag the corner handles in any direction to change both dimensions of a graphic. Drag the handles in the middle of each side of the graphic "box" horizontally or vertically to change one dimension only. To move the graphic on the page, click in the area surrounded by the handles. Hold the mouse button until the cursor changes to a cross with arrows on each end. As long as you hold the mouse button, you can move the graphic.

The following sections explain how to use the Graphic tools and related commands from the Graphic and Edit menus to create simple figures. When you draw graphics using the Graphic tools, Ventura creates a VGR file with the same name as the chapter and saves the file in the same directory as your chapter file. Ventura displays the name of the file when you use the load, save, and copy commands but does not list the VGR file in the CHP file or in the OPEN dialog box accessed from the Multi-Chapter command on the Options menu.

Drawing with the Line Tool

To experiment with drawing features, first select a frame as the graphic control frame. (If you do not want to use the frame Ventura has selected, click the Graphic selector in any other frame on the page. Graphics do not have to be within or touching their graphic control frame.) Click the line tool from the Graphic sidebar when you are ready to begin drawing.

Use the line tool to draw a figure with perpendicular or diagonal lines or lines with different shapes at each end of the line. You cannot draw arcs with the line tool.

To draw a line, follow these steps:

1. Click the line tool. Notice that the cursor shape changes to a pencil as you move the mouse cursor into the work area.

2. Position the pencil point where you want to start the line.

3. Hold the mouse button and drag the cursor as far as you want the line to extend. Then release the mouse button. The cursor becomes a pointer when you release the mouse button.

When you complete a graphic, the handles display, indicating that the graphic is selected. The name of the tool used to create the graphic appears in the current selection box. The handles must display if you want to change a graphic after it has been drawn. To select a graphic, click the selector tool on the desired graphic. To select a graphic near other graphics, hold the Ctrl key and click the graphic. Each time you click, handles appear on an adjacent graphic. In "Selecting Graphics To Change Them," you learn an alternative method of displaying handles on graphics that are difficult to select with Ctrl-click.

Changing the Length and Position of a Line

To change a line's length or angle, first select the line with the selector tool. (The handles around the graphic control frame display when you select the graphic.) Then click a handle at the end of the line, hold the mouse button, and drag the handle until the line is the desired length or angle. As you change a line's length or angle, the cursor is displayed as a pointing hand. Notice also that the old line stays on-screen as a reference until the procedure is completed. If you press Alt while changing a line, the line snaps to the closest 45-degree axis (refer to fig. 6.6).

Efficiency Tip

Drawing Straight Lines with the Alt-key

To draw a straight line, click the line tool and press the Alt key as you draw. Ventura snaps the line straight horizontally or vertically in 45-degree increments (see fig. 6.6).

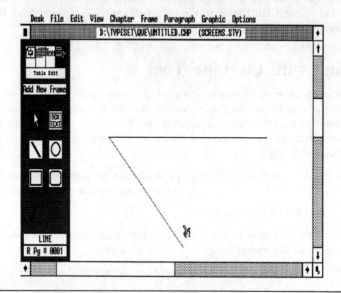

Fig. 6.6.

The angles to which the Alt key snaps lines.

To move the line to another position on the page, click the middle of the line (away from the handles) and hold the mouse button. When the cursor changes to a cross with arrows on each end, you can drag the line anywhere in the work area (see fig. 6.7).

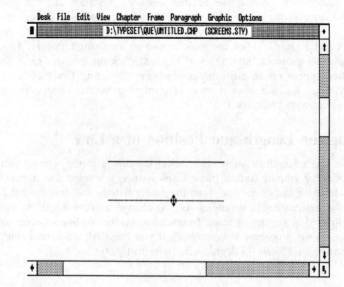

Fig. 6.7.

Moving a line.

Changing the Appearance of Lines

You can change the thickness, color, and end style of any line drawn with the line tool. First, select the graphic to display the line handles; then open the Graphic menu and select the Line Attributes command. The LINE ATTRIBUTES dialog box options are the same for all four drawing tools (see fig. 6.8). Shapes drawn with the line tool have only one dimension; shapes drawn with the other graphics tools are two dimensional. All shapes use the Line Attributes command to set the thickness, color, and end style of lines or outlines around shapes, as explained in the following sections.

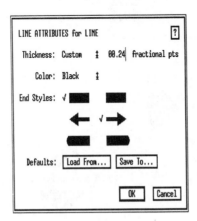

Fig. 6.8.

The LINE ATTRIBUTES dialog box.

Thickness

The options on the top line of the LINE ATTRIBUTES dialog box let you change the thickness of a line from None to any of five preset values. The dialog box displays the actual measurements for these preset values in the measurement system you choose. (To change the measurement system, click the unit of measurement to the right of Thickness.) When you select each option from the Thickness pop-up menu, the chosen width—varying from 1/1000 to 1/4 inch (or the equivalent)—displays. The width of the line, however, is not reflected in the dialog box samples.

You cannot change the preset values, but you can set a custom line width. When you select Thickness: Custom, a text cursor appears next to the measurement. Type over the value Ventura provides (or press Esc to erase the value and move to the first digit in the option). The value you type can be set as the new default for Custom if you click Save To before closing the dialog box.

Color

Printers supporting white-and-black text also can print white-and-black graphics. With such a printer, you can use white shapes, which are like opaque paint. Use the shapes to obscure parts of shapes and create new shapes from the parts that remain uncovered.

Using Thick Lines as Shapes

You can make triangles and boxes laid on a diagonal by using thick lines. Although Ventura does not display a line more than 0.5 inch wide in Normal view, you can print lines up to 9.999 inches wide. The images in figure 6.9 were drawn by overlaying custom width lines drawn on the diagonal with other lines and shapes.

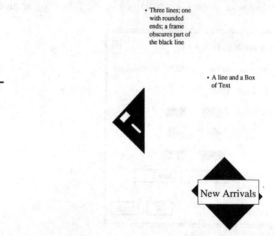

- Three lines; one with rounded ends; a frame obscures part of the black line

- A line and a Box of Text

Fig. 6.9.

Shapes laid on a diagonal.

New Arrivals

Use the Color option in the LINE ATTRIBUTES dialog box to print color graphics if your desktop publishing system includes a color monitor (other than CGA) and a color printer. You mix new colors with the Define Colors command from the Paragraph menu, as described in Chapter 5. Lines drawn with Ventura's line tool may be colored only with solid shades. (Ventura's other graphics shapes and frame backgrounds also let you set the density and pattern of a color.)

If you are using a black-and-white PostScript printer and PS2.EFF as your prologue file, selecting a color for a line produces a patterned shade of gray when you print (see Chapter 9 for more information). To preview how a black-and-white print will look when you use alternative color names to produce gray, click through the alternative color numbers in the DEFINE COLORS dialog box and notice how the results display. The patterns shown in the dialog box approximate the shades of gray that print for colored lines.

Ends of Lines

Three types of end styles are available for lines: flat, arrow, and rounded. You set the end styles with the Graphic menu LINE ATTRIBUTES dialog box (again see fig. 6.8). To change the style of the beginning of a line, position the pointing cursor to the left of the end styles shown in the left column, and click. To change the style of the end of a line, use the end styles in the right column. A check mark appears to the left of the selected style. If you select white as the color of the line and you have a mono-chrome monitor, the end style options in the dialog box are not displayed, but the check marks are.

Custom Line Defaults

The Defaults options—Load From and Save To near the bottom of the LINE ATTRIBUTES dialog box—let you set and use custom line attributes for each draw-ing tool. Every time you use the same tool, the custom defaults take effect. To change the default options, select Thickness, Color, and End Styles for the lines around the graphic and click Save To to save the settings as defaults. When you want to change a selected graphic to the default style for that type of graphic, click the Load From button. The default options blink when selected to indicate that action was taken.

Drawing Shapes with Lines

You can create hollow geometric figures or other simple shapes in Ventura with the line tool (see fig. 6.10). If you use the line tool to create a shape, however, you cannot fill the shape with a pattern; you can, however, choose different weights and line endings for each line segment. If patterned geometric shapes are required, how-ever, you may need to create them in another program and load them as graphic source files.

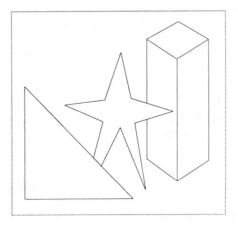

Fig. 6.10.

Hollow shapes drawn with the line tool.

Thick lines can also be used to create graphic shapes. See the Efficiency Tip "Using Thick Lines as Shapes" for a description and illustration of using lines to create solid shapes.

Efficiency Tip

Reusing the Same Graphic Tool Quickly

When you draw more than one graphic of the same type, don't return to the Graphic sidebar every time to reselect the tool. Instead, hold the Shift key when you start drawing. Each time you start using the same tool, press the Shift key. When you release the mouse button, the drawing cursor appears, ready to draw the next graphic. To return to the standard cursor, don't hold the Shift key when you draw the last graphic or click the pointer tool or another Graphic icon in the sidebar.

Drawing with the Two-Dimensional Tools

When you use Ventura's Graphic tools to draw rectangles, ellipses, rounded rectangles, and boxes of text, you can fill the shapes with colors and patterns, as well as define the outline of the shape. The Graphic menu LINE ATTRIBUTES dialog box controls the appearance of the outline, as discussed in the section ''Changing the Appearance of Lines.'' Filling the shapes with the FILL ATTRIBUTES dialog box is described in ''Filling Two-Dimensional Shapes'' later in this chapter.

Drawing Rectangles and Rounded Rectangles

Both the rectangle and rounded rectangle tools draw four-sided shapes. All rectangles drawn with these tools have horizontal and vertical edges. (See the Efficiency Tip ''Using Thick Lines as Shapes,'' which illustrates using lines to lay four-sided shapes on the diagonal.) Once you select either tool, the shape of the cursor in the work area changes to resemble the upper left corner of the selected Graphic tool. Using the rectangle tools, you can draw boxes in any proportion.

As soon as you create a rectilinear shape, and any time you select one with the pointer tool, up to eight handles frame the shape. The handles must be displayed before you can use Ventura's features to change a graphic, but you do not have to be able to see all the handles to work with the graphic.

You can change the shape and size of a rectangle by using the pointer tool to select the object and then dragging one of the handles. You can drag the corner handles in any direction to change both dimensions of the shape. If you drag one of the handles in the middle of the side of the shape, you change only one dimension. You cannot, however, change rounded corners to square corners or vice versa.

To move a rectangle, position the mouse pointer in the center of the area surrounded by the handles and hold the mouse button. When the cursor changes to a cross with arrows on each end, hold the mouse button and move the graphic.

Efficiency Tip

Making a Small Box

Although you can draw ballot boxes (small boxes used to check items) with the Graphic tools, Ventura offers two other techniques that make adding ballot boxes adjacent to text easy. To start a paragraph with a ballot box, select the paragraph with the Paragraph cursor and then open the SPECIAL EFFECTS dialog box from the Paragraph menu. Set Special Effect: Bullet; set Show Bullet As to either Hollow Box or Filled Box. (Chapter 5 discusses how to format bullets set with this command.)

If you need a small box between words in a line, position the text cursor and then open the Edit menu to select Ins Special Character. (You can use the keyboard shortcut Ctrl-C after positioning the Text cursor.) From the pop-up menu, select Box Char (or press F1) and choose either Hollow or Filled.

Efficiency Tip

Drawing a Perfect Square with the Alt-Key

To draw a perfect square, press the Alt key while pulling the drawing tool straight down. Although the Graphic grid is disabled while you are using the Alt-key, you can set either the horizontal or vertical grid to draw the square to size without the Alt-key. Then press the Alt-key as you click on the bottom right graphic handle, and the graphic snaps to a perfect square.

Drawing Circles and Ovals

Use the ellipse tool to draw circles and ovals. When you click the ellipse tool in the sidebar and move the cursor into the work area, the cursor shape changes into a circle divided into quarters. Position the cursor, using the horizontal line in the circle as the top of the shape. Then press the mouse button and drag the pointing hand diagonally down and to the right to make the circle the correct size. You can draw circles in only one direction, from top left to bottom right. If you move the cursor in any other direction, the circle looks like a line; when you click the graphic, however, the word CIRCLE displays in the current selection box (see fig. 6.11).

When you first create a circle or oval, and any time you select it with the pointer tool, up to eight handles frame the graphic. When you click a circle's handles, you can use the pointer to enlarge, reduce, and reshape the circle.

All circular shapes drawn with the ellipse tool have horizontal and vertical axes. If you want a circle to have a diagonal axis, you can create a circle by laying a short fat line with rounded ends on the page as illustrated in the Efficiency Tip "Using Thick Lines as Shapes." You cannot draw arcs with the line tool; but if your printer allows overlays, you can overlay an ellipse with another opaque ellipse to create a semicircle (see fig. 6.12).

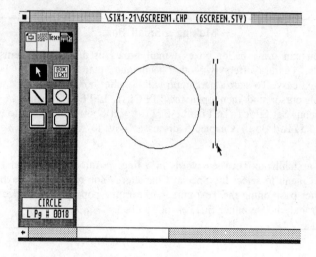

Fig. 6.11.

*Two circles: one
circle looks like a
line.*

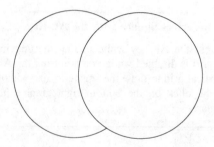

Fig. 6.12.

*Creating an arc by
layering circles.*

Two layered circles

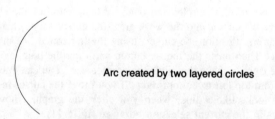

Arc created by two layered circles

Circular shapes take on the default line style and fill shade, but you can change these
settings for selected objects with the Line Attributes and Fill Attributes commands on
the Graphic menu. The LINE ATTRIBUTES and FILL ATTRIBUTES dialog boxes
for circles are the same as those for rectangular and linear shapes.

Circles can be made to look like a pie graph by adding lines to segment the shape. In
figure 6.13, both circles were segmented with the line tool. You cannot pattern the
segments uniquely, however, because Ventura treats the whole circle as a shape.

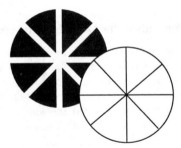

Fig. 6.13.

Two circles segmented with lines.

Filling Two-Dimensional Shapes

The Graphic menu contains commands that allow you to change the outline, color, pattern, and density of graphics drawn with Ventura's two-dimensional tools. When you draw or select a graphic, you can change the settings of the commands for the active graphic or graphics. First, select the graphic, then open the Graphic menu to select the command you want to use.

You can change the style of the border around the shapes with the Line Attributes command, as described in the discussion of drawing lines. You can select one of Ventura's defined colors or mix a custom color (see Chapters 5 and 8 for more information). You also can fill a shape with your choice of nine options, including Hollow (no pattern), Solid, and seven variations of patterns (see fig. 6.14).

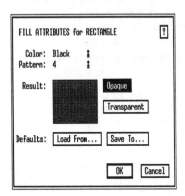

Fig. 6.14.

The FILL ATTRIBUTES dialog box.

The selected pattern is displayed in the Result box below the pattern options in the FILL ATTRIBUTES dialog box. To the right of the Result box are two more options: Opaque and Transparent. An opaque pattern completely covers any graphics below it. Any graphics below a transparent pattern are visible through the pattern unless you chose Solid. See ''Layering Graphics'' in this chapter for an example of the uses of opaque and transparent patterns.

If the Commands in the Graphic Menu Are Gray

Most of the commands in the Graphic menu are available for use only if one or more graphic shapes are selected. To choose a graphic, select the Graphic function and then select a shape in the work area with the selector tool. To select all the graphics attached to a frame, first select the frame, then press Ctrl-Q. You can add any graphic tied to the same control frame to the selected set with Shift-click. You deselect a graphic from the selected set when you Shift-click it.

The default commands in the FILL ATTRIBUTES dialog box operate in the same way as the commands in the LINE ATTRIBUTES dialog box. By overlapping opaque and transparent rectangular shapes, you can create shapes that are not complete rectangles or that have drop shadows. "Layering Graphics" later in this chapter describes the techniques used to create multiple overlaying shapes.

Working with Graphics Drawn in Ventura

Three new features make using Ventura's Graphic tools to create symbols and figures much easier. The Alt-key line constraint described in the first part of this chapter makes drawing straight lines and perfect squares and circles a snap. At least as helpful is the new feature that causes the frame handles for a selected graphic to display automatically. Earlier versions of Ventura defaulted to repeat any graphics drawn on the base page on every clone of that page in the chapter. Now you can designate which, if any, graphics automatically repeat. In addition, you should know how to collect graphic "sets" and use Ventura's grids for alignment if you intend to use Ventura's tools to their full potential.

Often, one or two shapes are enough to create the graphic you need. When you need to produce figures, logos, or symbols with Ventura, however, you may need to lay several graphics shapes on a page. You can create charts and simple illustrations with Ventura's Graphic tools and then overlay shapes to make new shapes. In this part of the chapter, you learn how to group graphics with a controlling frame to expedite selecting, moving, copying, and placing graphics. You also see ways to use Ventura's grids and baselines to control the position and size of graphic shapes on the page.

Creating a Graphic Control Frame

All graphics are attached to a frame. Even when you draw just one graphic on a page, Ventura attaches the graphic to the page or to the frame selected as the graphic control frame.

Ventura designates the last frame that was active as the graphic control frame, unless you select a different one before you begin drawing (refer to fig. 6.5). You can attach more than one graphic to a frame, and several graphic control frames can exist on each page. Each frame can be used to establish a horizontal and vertical grid to help quickly achieve precise alignment and uniform sizing of graphic shapes. Ventura shows the frame associated with a graphic when you display the graphics handles.

Using the Page as the Graphic Control Frame

When you pour text onto pages with the Load Text/Picture command, Ventura opens and fills as many pages as needed to hold the file. Ventura creates these pages automatically, defining the new pages with the same margins, columns, and graphics established for the first page. You can insert a new page in a chapter and load another multiple-page source file into the chapter. The pages holding each file can have different margins, columns, and graphic features. Use the Show On All Pages command on the Graphic menu to designate whether selected graphics drawn on a page in a set should display on all the pages in that set. You cannot use the Repeating Frame command on the Frame menu to control placement of graphics attached to the page.

If you designate a graphic drawn on a page created by Ventura to show on all pages and then use the Insert/Remove Page command on the Page menu to create new pages, the graphic appears on every inserted page. If you delete or change the graphic on the original page, however, you must delete or change it individually on each inserted page. If you change the graphic on the first inserted page, the change is reflected on each page inserted at that time (see fig. 6.15). A graphic drawn on a page in a set of pages does not appear on inserted pages if you insert the pages before you draw and designate the graphics to show on all pages.

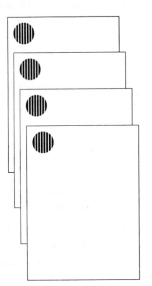 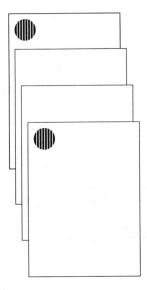

Fig. 6.15.

A chapter with different page graphics.

Adding a Frame as the Graphic Control Frame

Any frame drawn on the page can serve as a graphic control frame. Use the Add New Frame button from the Graphic function or Frame function sidebars to add a new graphic control frame to the page. If you start with the Frame function Add New Frame command, you select the frame as the graphic control frame when you click the Graphic function immediately after adding the frame.

The graphics you associate with a frame do not have to be within or touching the frame, but the graphics move when you move the frame. If you create a callout for a figure, for example, you can attach the callout to the figure using the frame that holds the illustration as the graphic control frame. When you cut, copy, delete, or move the figure, the attached callout follows it.

Adding a frame to serve as a graphic control frame is also helpful when you create an illustration with Ventura's Graphic tools. You can select the graphics as a group by selecting the frame, and you can add or subtract individual graphics from the selected set as needed. You can move graphics independently of the frame, but if you move or size the frame, you move the graphics.

You can copy, cut, and paste graphics tied to the same frame with the Edit menu Frame commands, leaving the Graphic Clipboard open to carry other graphics. Because you can copy more than one frame to the Clipboard (by selecting more than one at a time), you can paste several figures into a chapter by copying the graphic control frames to the Clipboard.

Another advantage of using a frame rather than the page to control graphics is that you can designate the frame as a repeating frame to mirror and maintain the correct layering of graphics on facing pages. To create a graphic control frame, follow these steps:

1. Select the Graphic function.

2. Click Add New Frame from the sidebar.

3. Move the cursor into the work area. The cursor changes to a cornered FR.

4. Click and drag the cursor to form a four-sided frame.

5. Release the mouse to complete the frame. The frame handles display as graphic control handles (see fig. 6.16).

Efficiency Tip

Changing the Frame that Controls a Graphic

You can change the frame associated with a graphic by selecting the graphic, cutting it, selecting the intended frame, and then pasting the graphic into that frame.

When you want to move the shapes on the page as a group, move them by moving the frame. (You also can select the frame and press Ctrl-Q to select all the graphics associated with that frame.) If you move the frame, Ventura does not show that the

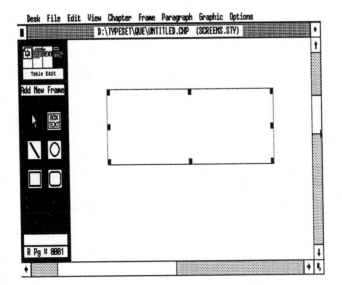

Fig. 6.16.

A new graphic control frame.

graphics are moving—only that they have moved. If you want to see outlines of the graphics as they move, press Ctrl-Q to select all the graphics attached to the frame and move the cursor between handles displayed in the set of graphics. Then click to drag the shapes into place. The frame stays in the original position when you move the graphics this way.

Efficiency Tip

Enlarging the View To Select the Right Tool or Graphic

If the shapes you have drawn are too small to display all the handles in Normal or Reduced view, you may need to change to Enlarged view to be able to move, size, or select the correct graphic. The pointing hand used to size and reshape appears when not enough space exists between handles to position the crossbar cursors. Remember that you can zoom a point into view by positioning the Graphic selector over the point you want to see and then pressing Ctrl-N (for Normal view) or Ctrl-E (for Enlarged view). Press Ctrl-R to return to Reduced view.

Changing the size of the frame does not change the position of the graphics. If you want to change the size of selected graphics relative to one another, select the set of graphics and pull a corner or side handle of the selected set to resize all the graphics.

Selecting Graphics To Change Them

You select a graphic by clicking the Graphic selector tool over the shape in the work area. Selecting one graphic is easy when no other graphics are nearby. Selecting one shape from many graphics or selecting a specific set of shapes is more complicated when many graphics handles are displayed on the page. Fortunately, you can use one of two approaches when selecting graphics: you can select each shape, or you may have better luck deselecting from the set tied to the active graphic control frame. Both techniques are explained here.

To select a graphic or set of graphics by selecting each one, follow these steps:

1. Select the Graphic function.

2. Move the cursor into the work area, and click within or along the perimeter of the shape you want to select. When you select a shape, its handles appear.

3. To keep selecting shapes, Shift-click each additional shape. You also can Shift-click to deselect one already selected.

4. To select shapes buried beneath others, press Ctrl-Shift.

An easier approach to selecting several graphics associated with a frame is to select the frame and then press Ctrl-Q. Eliminate graphics from the selected set by pressing Shift-click on shapes. Click outside all the selected shapes to remove all the handles at once.

Cutting, Copying, and Pasting Graphics Drawn in Ventura

After using Ventura's tools to draw or select graphics, you can cut, copy, or paste a graphic from frame to frame or chapter to chapter. You perform these actions with the Edit menu. When you use the Cut or Copy command, Ventura stores the graphic in a temporary memory area, referred to as the Clipboard. The Graphic Clipboard is separate from the Text and Frame Clipboards but works in the same manner. Each graphic you cut or copy replaces the previous contents of the Graphic Clipboard. The only way to see what's on the Clipboard is to paste the contents on a page.

Efficiency Tip

Collect Graphics in a "Clipboard" Chapter

Ventura saves the contents of all three Clipboards when you close and open chapters but erases the contents when you use the Quit or Abandon command. As you develop artwork you want to use, you can collect the graphics in a "Clipboard" chapter. Open that chapter before you open the project you want to work on and select the graphic control frames you want to use. If you need artwork from more than one page, collect the selections on a page inserted at the front of the file.

Once you have collected the graphics, select each frame individually using the Frame cursor and Shift-click. (You do not need to select the graphics.) Then press Shift-Del to copy the selection of frames to the Clipboard. You can use the Insert/Remove Page command to delete the page from the chapter after you have copied the selection to the Clipboard memory. You must save the changes to the Clipboard chapter if Ventura is to retain the selections in memory when you open a new chapter file.

The Cut command removes the graphic from the screen and places it on the Graphic Clipboard. The Copy command places a copy of the graphic on the Clipboard and leaves the original graphic on the screen. The Paste command inserts a copy of the graphic directly on top of the original image, unless you select another page as the active frame before pasting. You can repeatedly paste the same graphic in place and then move each copy into position with the Graphic pointer.

If you position a graphic at the top left corner of a frame, for example, you can quickly place the same graphic in the other three corners. First, using Reduced view, select the graphic and choose the Copy command from the Edit menu. This command leaves the graphic on-screen and also places it on the Clipboard. Choose the Paste command from the Edit menu and move the inserted graphic into place. Each time you paste the shape on the page, the copy appears in the original location. Move each copy into place. (If you paste a copy on top of another, you can move each one into place because Ventura automatically selects the top graphic to move.)

Troubleshooting Tip

A Graphic Has Been Deleted but Still Appears On-Screen

When you select a graphic, black handles appear around the graphic. If you choose the Cut command from the Edit menu and the graphic still appears on-screen, you may have more than one graphic in the same position. Select the graphic and choose the Cut command again.

Efficiency Tip

Cleaning Up the Image When Editing Graphics

After each edit, Ventura repaints the screen. Sometimes black spots (or "noise") are left from graphics in spaces that are now blank. Press the Esc key to reformat the page and make the spots disappear.

Layering Graphics

You can stack or overlay shapes with other shapes to create simple drop shadows and more complicated illustrations. (First, however, print the CAPABILI.CHP file from the VENTURA directory to make sure that your printer supports layered graphics.) As you add shapes to a page, the most recently drawn graphic appears on top of the other graphics. You can dig out the graphics underneath others by pressing Ctrl-click in the area of the graphic until the appropriate handles are displayed. Although you can layer objects as you design an illustration, you may need to re-layer shapes moved into place using the Graphic Clipboard. The Send to Back and Bring to Front commands in the Graphic menu work only with graphics shapes tied to the same frame.

The most common use of layered graphics is to obscure part of shape in order to create another shape. As mentioned earlier in this chapter, you can make an arc by layering a white opaque circle on an outlined circle. The illustrations in figure 6.1 are graphic shapes laid in three layers. You can also create a drop-shadow effect by layering graphics. Drop shadows add dimension to objects by creating the illusion of depth.

The following steps show you how to create a drop-shadow effect by layering graphics, using the Graphic menu and the Clipboard:

1. Draw the graphic that is to form the top layer, using one of Ventura's tools.

2. Choose Fill Attributes (or press Ctrl-F) to create a fill pattern of solid white or opaque for the top layer.

3. Use Copy (or Shift-Del) to place a duplicate of the newly created graphic on the Clipboard.

4. Use Paste (or Ins) to place the duplicate back on the same Ventura page. The second graphic appears on top of the original graphic.

5. Use Fill Attributes to change the fill pattern of the second graphic to the color black. (Press Ctrl-F or Ctrl-X because FILL ATTRIBUTES was the last dialog box opened.) Click the pattern of your choice. This block is to form the drop shadow.

6. Hold the mouse button until the cross with arrows appears. Move the black box—the shadow—to an offset position against the white box (see fig. 6.17).

7. Use Send to Back (or Ctrl-Z) to move the dark box behind the white box (see fig. 6.18).

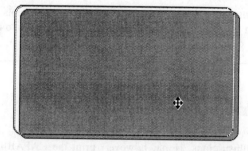

Fig. 6.17.

Creating a drop-shadow effect.

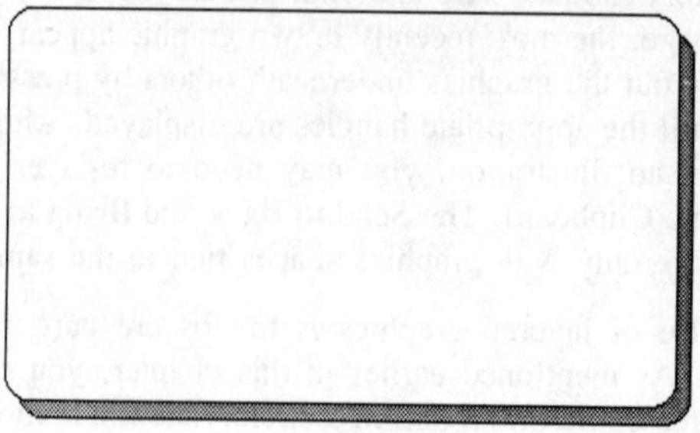

Fig. 6.18.

Finished box with drop shadow.

Shortcuts for Graphics

Following are shortcuts that you can use when working with graphics.

Drawing

Shift-click keeps selected the drawing tool in use.

Press the Alt key as you draw a line (or after selecting a line's handle) to straighten the line on the closest 45-degree axis.

Layering

Ctrl-Z sends the selected shape to the back of several stacked images.

Ctrl-A brings the selected shape to the front of several stacked images.

Selecting graphics

Ctrl-Q selects all the graphics associated with the active control frame.

Shift-click adds a graphic to a set of selected images.

Ctrl-click selects another graphic in a group of images that are close together.

Ctrl-Shift-click adds adjacent graphics to the set of selected images.

Changing the appearance of lines and fillings

Ctrl-L chooses Line Attributes from the Graphic menu.

Ctrl-F chooses Fill Attributes from the Graphic menu.

Ctrl-X opens the last dialog box used or repeats the last command.

Changing the function

Ctrl-I enables the Text function for typing box text.

Ctrl-P enables the Graphic function.

Cut, Copy, and Paste with keys from the numeric pad

Del cuts the selected shapes from the page.

Shift-Del copies the selected shapes to the Clipboard.

Ins pastes the shapes on the Clipboard to the page.

Positioning and Sizing with Grids and Rulers

Several features help you position shapes precisely on the page:

- Changing views
- Using rulers

- Establishing grids
- Using column and margins as guides

You can choose Enlarged from the View menu to zoom into an area. Because Enlarged view doubles the size of all elements on the page, this option is useful for exact placement or cropping of graphics. You also can use the Grid Settings command from the Graphic menu to select the increments for an invisible alignment grid on the page (see fig. 6.19). The grid works only in the Graphic function. Grid Settings is similar to the Column Snap and Line Snap commands on the Options menu: when you create or move a graphic, it snaps to fit the grid. If you must move a shape after it is drawn, you can use the column guides or the rulers to see the measurements from the top and sides of the page.

Fig. 6.19.

The GRID
SETTINGS
dialog box.

Efficiency Tip

Drawing a Perfect Circle with the Alt-Key

To draw a perfect circle, press the Alt key while pulling the ellipse tool straight down. Although the graphic grid is disabled while you are using the Alt-key, you can set either the horizontal or vertical grid to draw the circle to size without the Alt-key. Then press the Alt-key as you click on the bottom right graphic handle; and the graphic snaps to a perfect circle.

You can change the grid settings to size and position shapes precisely. In figure 6.20, the grids for a 2-inch circle were changed to .10 inch before wide white lines were added to the perimeter to create the octagonal shape. White lines and a frame bordered with hyphens were added on top of the layered shapes.

As you work on a scale drawing or plan, you can set grids to achieve uniform sizing and alignment while placing graphics on a page. The floor plan shown in figure 6.21 was developed by first setting the grid at the width of the aisles and then changing the grids for each scaled shape. The final location of some pieces was not on either of these scales, however, so the grid settings were turned off before final placement of these pieces.

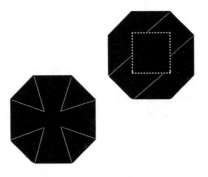

Fig. 6.20.

An octagon created with grids, a circle, and white lines.

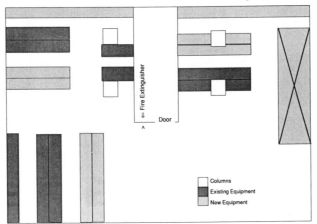

PRELIMINARY FLOORPLAN — Warehouse Storage System

Fig. 6.21.

A floor plan made by using grids.

Do not forget to use Ventura's column and margin guides as visible grids against which you align graphics. Although graphics do not snap to these grids, the grids can be helpful as guides to precise alignment.

Placing Graphics

In this chapter you have seen how to draw and shape graphics on the page. When you need to repeat graphics in a chapter, you have several options:

- Use the Show On All Pages command to repeat the graphic on every page in the set.

- Use the Show on This Page command to prevent the graphic from repeating on all pages

- Use a repeating frame to designate the facing pages to display the graphic and to suppress the frame and its graphics from view on selected pages.

- Copy the graphics into place by copying the graphic control frame or the graphics.

To show a graphic on all pages, first select the graphic. Then open the Graphic menu and choose Show On All Pages. The graphic (or set of graphics if more than one is selected) displays in the same position on every page in the chapter. The graphic appears even on pages added later with the Chapter menu Insert/Remove Page command. You can change the graphics on inserted pages without affecting the look of the graphics on pages that were created by Ventura to hold the contents of a multipage source text file. In figure 6.22, the lines, box, and text format instructions were automatically copied to every page by selecting the graphics and choosing Show On All Pages from the Graphic menu. The graphics on the inserted pages were selected, and the Show on This Page command was chosen. Then the text tool was used to change the contents of each box as appropriate for each page.

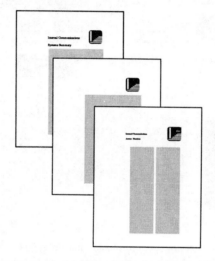

Fig. 6.22.

Customizing a graphic on every page.

By comparison, if you change a graphic on a page automatically created by Ventura, the change is reflected on all the pages holding the same source text file. To set the location of a graphic differently for facing pages, tie the graphics to a frame drawn on the page rather than to the page itself. Then set the frame as a repeating frame.

Graphics set to repeat with the Graphic menu Show On All Pages command display dark patterned squares as handles. Repeating graphics tied to the page appear in the same position on each page. When you need to mirror the positions on facing pages, you can tie the graphic to a frame drawn on the page and use the Repeating Frame command from the Frame menu to change the positions on left and right pages. Besides alternating positions, repeating frames also cause layered graphics to maintain the proper order as they appear on pages.

If you create an illustration to be repeated throughout a publication (or on all the left or all the right pages), you can make the graphic control frame a repeating frame.

Using a repeating frame causes layered graphics to appear in the correct order on each page. As explained in Chapter 7, you create a repeating frame by choosing the frame and selecting Repeating Frame from the Frame menu. When you use repeating frames to position graphics on consecutive or alternating pages, you have the option of selecting the frame and hiding it from view on selected pages.

Efficiency Tip

Using Repeating Frames for Repeating Graphics

If the same graphic (or set of graphics) appears in the same relative position on several pages, make the graphic control frame on the page a repeating frame. In the REPEATING FRAME dialog box, select Left & Right to "mirror" the contents of the frame on alternating pages. Using a repeating frame as a graphic control frame lets you hide the graphic on selected pages and maintain the proper order in layered shapes on alternating pages (see fig. 6.23).

To move a repeating frame that is part of a header or a footer, first choose the Page menu Turn Header Off or Turn Footer Off command. Select the frame and choose the Repeating Frame command from the Frame menu. If you choose For All Pages: Off, the frame is no longer a repeating frame, and you can make changes. Then reset the Repeating Frame command and choose the Turn Header On or Turn Footer On command again.

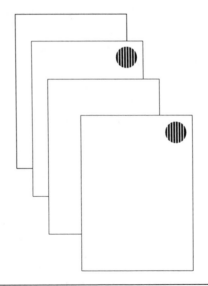

Fig. 6.23.

A repeating graphic control frame used to create shapes on alternate pages.

Using Box Text

Ventura actually provides two ways for you to place text in boxes: adding a frame with the Frame function or using the box text tool of the Graphic function. You have more flexibility with framed text because you cannot set Margins & Columns or use

Load Text/Pictures with box text. Box text is often used for forms and graphics call-outs, however. When you type new text into an empty frame or into a box text area, the text is stored in the caption file (CAP) created by Ventura for the chapter.

Efficiency Tip

Spell-Check Copy Created as Box Text

If you use a dictionary program to check the spelling in source text files, you should spell-check the CAP file after Ventura creates it. Be sure that the file remains an ASCII file. Do not add or delete any carriage returns or the text will appear in the wrong position in the chapter.

The box text tool is similar to the two-dimensional Graphic tools, except that you can type text into box text shapes. Box text is similar to frame text except that box text has no margins, always overlaps all text and graphics on the page, and can be only one column wide. You can assign line and fill attributes to box text.

To create box text, do the following:

1. Select a frame and choose the Graphic function.

2. Select the box text tool. As you move into the work area, the cursor changes to a cornered Te. When you click the mouse button, the cursor changes to a pointing hand.

3. Draw the box as large as necessary. As with all the graphics shapes, you can use the handles to resize the box later.

4. When you release the mouse button, an end-of-file marker appears in the frame to indicate the end of the text to be typed in the box.

5. Use the Line Attributes and Fill Attributes commands to set the box outline and fill pattern.

Typing and formatting box text is the same as typing and formatting text in frames. Chapters 4 and 5 explain these techniques in detail. To type text into the box, click the Text function and place the I-beam cursor immediately preceding the end-of-file marker. Then type the text you want in the box.

Ventura automatically creates a paragraph tag named Z_BOXTEXT when you draw the box. This tag has the same attributes as the Body Text tag in the current style file. You can change the typeface, size, and style of Z_BOXTEXT by retagging the text with any existing tag name or assigning a new tag. The tag name Z_BOXTEXT appears in the sidebar when three conditions are met:

1. Generated Tags: Shown is active in the SET PREFERENCES dialog box from the Options menu.

2. The sidebar is displayed (see the Options menu).

3. The Paragraph function is active.

You set the interline-spacing value for the Box Text tag in the SPACING dialog box under the Paragraph menu. This value establishes a grid for the placement of text typed in boxes, just as Body Text establishes the baseline for text placed on pages and in frames. See Chapter 5 to learn more about the use of the text grids Ventura offers.

Making Callouts for Illustrations

As explained in Chapter 9, you should use Ventura to type all descriptive text in imported graphics so that your publication is consistent. Graphics programs sometimes have limited typestyle selections; when you resize graphics, the type sizes in the graphics are resized too.

You may want to label the graphics you create or import with box-text callouts. You can create a box of the correct size and draw lines to parts of the graphic. Use the following procedure.

1. Use the Graphic selector to select the frame holding the desired figure.

2. Select the box text tool and move the cursor into the work area.

3. Click the mouse and draw the first box. If you want to change the default attributes of the box, open the Graphic menu and select the appropriate Attribute commands. Click Save To in the dialog boxes where you change the defaults.

4. Press the Shift key as you draw the next graphic so that the drawing tool is ready to draw again when you release the mouse button. The attribute defaults will apply to all boxes you add unless you change the attributes.

5. After you draw all the boxes, use the line tool to draw a line from any position on the graphic to its descriptive box.

6. Choose Line Attributes in the Graphic menu to choose the thickness and end style of the line. To apply the same attributes to all the lines, click Save To before closing the LINE ATTRIBUTES dialog box.

7. Repeat step 5 to draw the rest of the callout arrows.

8. After you position all boxes and callout arrows, choose the Text function and enter text in each box. Work with box text in the same way you enter, edit, and format text in a frame.

Making Layouts with Boxes of Text

Box text is useful for forms with complex arrangements of text and white space, especially forms having more blank space than text. If the form has more text than you want to type with Ventura's text tool, you have two choices:

- Design the form with frames on the page and import the text into the frames.

Making Arrows for Callouts

The line tool allows you to draw a line in any direction. When you use the line tool to draw callout arrows, start on the figure and draw back to the box-text callouts.

In figure 6.24, all four arrows were made with the same line-ending settings in the LINE ATTRIBUTES dialog box. After you draw the first arrow, open the Graphic menu and select the Line Attributes command to choose End Style. The left column is the style for the beginning of the line. The right column of styles defines the end of each line. Click Save To to set the default. Each line you draw from the figure to a callout box displays a similar arrow.

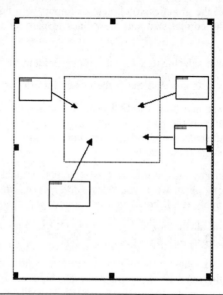

Fig. 6.24.

Frame with arrows to callouts.

- Start the form in Ventura with box text. Type a word or two that you can use to identify the box of text. After the boxes are drawn with short identifying labels, save the chapter file and quit Ventura. Use your word processor to edit Ventura's CAP file for the chapter and type the text for each paragraph. When you edit the CAP files, do not change the number of hard carriage returns in the files. Save the file as an ASCII file.

You can design and print small quantities of sequentially numbered forms, such as job control forms and invoices, using two techniques. First, you can use the AUTO-NUMBERING dialog box, discussed in Chapter 4:

1. Enter a tag name (@NUMBER, for instance) at Level 1 in the AUTO-NUMBERING dialog box. If you can use the Body Text tag to define the number, the source file will be smaller because you do not need a tag name for each paragraph (see step 3).

2. Use the Paragraph menu commands to size and position the number and specify Page Break: After.

3. In the source file, for each page you want to print, place one paragraph with the tag name created in step 1.

4. Create the form in Ventura, using repeating graphics of box text for all information that appears on each page. The chapter will contain a page for each form, but the graphic and boxed text placed on the first page are stored only once on the disk.

5. Load the source file onto the page.

Ventura inserts consecutive numbers each time the tag named in the AUTO-NUMBERING dialog box appears in the file.

The second technique for creating sequentially numbered forms is less complicated.

1. In a source file, place one paragraph return for each page you want to print. Tag the paragraph with a unique tag name.

2. Create the form in Ventura, using repeating graphics of box text for all information that appears on each page. Also add a frame in the position of the page number. Then load the source file into the frame. The chapter will contain a page for each form, but the graphics and box text placed on the first page are stored only once on the disk.

3. In the source file, place one paragraph with the tag name for each page you want to print.

4. In the Text function, click the I-beam cursor in the page number frame and choose Ins Special Item (Ctrl-C) from the Edit menu. Choose Cross Ref (F6) and select Page #.

You can create different page-number positions for left and right pages by creating this frame in two positions and using the For All Sides: Left and For All Sides: Right options in the REPEATING FRAME dialog box, as explained in Chapter 7.

See the examples in Chapter 16 for different ways to create forms.

── *Efficiency Tip*

Using Grid Settings To Create Forms with Typewriter Spacing

To create a form to be filled in with a typewriter, use box text and the GRID SETTINGS dialog box. First, set the vertical grid to typewriter spacing (12 points for single-spacing, 24 points for double-spacing). Then draw each box. When the Grid Settings are on, each box you draw aligns with the next. If the form has page-wide lines for entering information with a typewriter, create a tab with interline spacing at 12 or 24 points and a right leader tab set at the right margin.

Importing Graphics Files

Ventura's Graphic tools are often sufficient to add graphics enhancements to a publication—especially if the design of the publication uses rules, columns, text, and white areas to define the graphic impression of the piece. Heavily illustrated publications, however, usually incorporate graphics drawn in painting and drawing programs or graphics scanned into a compatible format. Ventura's Graphic tools produce object-oriented graphics (refer to "Object-Oriented Graphics," in this chapter, for definitions). Other graphics created by different drawing, painting, and scanning programs can be imported into Ventura in various formats with the Load Text/Picture command.

Placing graphics, whether created in Ventura or imported, is similar to placing text on a page. You can place graphics and text on pages or in framed areas. In Chapter 4 of this book, you see how to place text on pages, letting a file flow from page to page. Most publication designs, however, place graphics at designated positions. For this reason, you often create a frame on the page to tie the graphic, or set of graphics, to a specific position.

You can scale and crop imported graphics in Ventura, but you cannot change their line thicknesses or patterns with Graphic menu commands. Usually, you edit a graphic with the program used to create it. You can use Ventura's graphic shapes to overlay or hide sections of an imported graphic, and you should use Ventura's Graphic tools to annotate illustrations with captions and pointers.

In this section, you learn about the graphics programs and file formats Ventura reads: how to load graphics with the File menu and how to use the Frame and Edit menus to size, crop, and move imported graphics.

Types of Graphics Ventura Imports

To meet different needs, Ventura imports four kinds of graphics. Object-oriented (or vector graphics) and PostScript graphics load into Ventura as line art. Bit-mapped graphics and scanned artwork (bit-mapped images and gray-scale images) load into Ventura as image files. With these four formats, you can create publications containing designs created with CAD programs, newsletters with graphs created in compatible spreadsheets, and magazines containing pictures scanned from photographs, along with many other types of illustrated materials. With all the options for importing graphics into Ventura, you can produce high-quality graphics for many types of documents.

Object-Oriented Graphics

Object-oriented graphics are composed of separate objects—such as boxes, lines, and ellipses—that can be moved independently. Ventura's built-in graphics are object-oriented, and you can import object-oriented graphics from other programs. Object-oriented programs also are called *vector graphics* because the lines and patterns you see are actually stored as mathematical formulas for the vectors that compose the image. Ventura refers to object-oriented graphics as line art. A vector, shown in figure 6.25, is a line defined by a starting point, a directional angle, and a length.

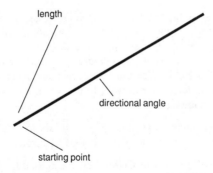

Fig. 6.25.

A vector.

Drafting programs, drawing programs, spreadsheet graphics, and several clip-art programs create object-oriented graphics (see fig. 6.26). You can import vector graphics produced by dozens of programs as long as the format is compatible with the standard formats listed in table 6.1.

Fig. 6.26.

Two graphics imported from Harvard Graphics.

Table 6.1
Graphic Formats and Extensions Compatible with Ventura

Line Art	Image
AutoCAD = SLD	GEM/HALO DPE = IMG
CGM = CGM	PC Paintbrush = PCX
DXF* = GEM	MacPaint = PNT
PostScript = EPS	
GEM = GEM	
HPGL = HPG	
Lotus = PIC	
Macintosh PICT = PCT	
Mentor Graphics = **	
(ASCII files)	
MS Windows = WMF	
NAPLPS VideoShow = PIC	

*DXF formats require a utility disk conversion before loading.

Line art and images stored in any format other than GEM are converted by Ventura in a copy of the original file. Ventura saves line art formats as GEM files and image format files as IMG files. Whenever a source file is converted from one format to another, you may see different results in Ventura, especially with regard to colors, fonts, and rotated text. Check the Ventura reference materials to determine whether specific limitations apply to features you want to use when preparing graphics source files. The following are examples:

- Bit-mapped images, rotated text, and gray or colors in PICT files do not translate during the conversion to Ventura's GEM format.

- All fonts convert to Helvetica in CGM files; background colors in CGM files do not convert. If the source program does not use standard CGM color mapping, the colors displayed in Ventura do not match those in the source program. The conversion of patterns is based on GSS CGI definition.

The capabilities of your printer may also influence imported graphics. Because vector graphics are defined mathematically, they can be smoothed during the printing process to create crisp line art and provide fill patterns. When you have the choice, use object-oriented (vector graphics) line art to produce the highest-quality image. Line art graphics consume less disk space than bit-mapped graphics but are not suitable for photographs.

Encapsulated PostScript Format

Although Ventura cannot stretch fonts or fill outline fonts with patterns, the PostScript language can. PostScript also has graphics capabilities that Ventura does not. You can load a file written in PostScript, called an *Encapsulated PostScript* (EPS) file, into Ventura as a graphic. You can create EPS format files using drawing programs or by direct coding in the PostScript programming language. Unless the EPS file contains a TIFF image or a Windows metafile (WMF) description of the image, when you place the image in Ventura you see only a box reserving the space for the graphic. If you use a program that creates a screen image as well as the encapsulated code (such as Adobe's Illustrator program on the Macintosh), when you place the EPS file in Ventura, you can see the graphic and scale or crop it as you would any other graphic. The display EPS graphic is a low-resolution version of what will print. The on-screen image may not show all elements of the original EPS file, but they will print.

EPS files can be printed only on a PostScript printer unless the file contains either a TIFF or Windows MetaFile (WMF) description. In Chapter 8, you see how to use the PostScript driver to print a file of a Ventura page. This file can also be loaded into a frame as an EPS file.

Several auxiliary programs provide the capability to take screen shots of other programs in operation. In general, the makers of Ventura do not recommend that you use RAM-resident programs (like screen-capture utilities) with Ventura. As you can see by many of the figures in this book, however, screen-shot programs *can* be used to capture pictures of Ventura's operations. Check with the vendors whose products you are considering, in order to verify the compatibility of their programs with Ventura.

You also can use Ventura to make a reduced page image that prints on PostScript printers. First, print the page to a file using the Set Printer Info command on the Options menu and the To Print command on the File menu. (Printing to a file is discussed in Chapter 8.) Ventura translates the contents of the page (both text and graphics) to instructions that are interpreted when you print. When you load Ventura-created PostScript files (choose PostScript as the image format), all you see is a large letter X on the screen.

The formats that Ventura supports represent hundreds of source programs. You should experiment with your programs to see whether any of your usual features produce results that do not translate into Ventura. As Ventura and other software vendors release new programs, experiment to determine whether the level of compatibility with Ventura changes.

Efficiency Tip

Primary Sources of EPS Files

You can use Adobe Illustrator or Cricket Draw on a Macintosh to create graphics and save them in Encapsulated PostScript format (IBM Windows version). Then you can telecommunicate or network the EPS file as text to a PC and place the graphics in Ventura.

Bit-Mapped Graphics

Bit-mapped graphics are patterns of dots, or pixels, rather than mathematical formulas. This type of graphic comes from a paint-type program such as GEM, Publishers Paintbrush Plus, HALO DPE, or MacPaint. Bit-mapped images also come from a scanner that produces digitized graphics with a GEM or PCX extension. Figure 6.27 shows a bit-mapped graphic drawn with HALO DPE.

Fig. 6.27.

Imported bit-mapped graphic.

Because bit-mapped images are composed of dots rather than whole objects, bit-mapped images cannot be broken easily into separate elements like boxes, circles, or lines. When a circle is drawn on top of a square, for example, the dots composing the circle actually replace the dots composing the square in the area where the two objects overlap.

Bit-mapped images are not smoothed like vector graphics when printed. Bit-mapped graphics are therefore considered inferior to vector graphics for most line art. Bit-mapped images, however, are superior for scanned images and for "fine art" images calling for air-brush effects. Ventura's LOAD TEXT/PICTURE dialog box refers to bit-mapped graphics as Image files.

Use Object-Oriented Graphics When Possible

Use object-oriented graphics rather than bit-mapped graphics whenever possible. Bit-mapped graphics have a jagged appearance, require large amounts of disk space, and take much longer to print.

When you require bit-mapped graphics, do not include text in the file in the source program. Place the graphics portion in Ventura and use Ventura's box text tool with text and tagging tools to add captions and labels.

In general, graphics look best displayed on the same system configuration that created them. Some bit-mapped graphics may seem distorted on the screen, but they print well if the original graphic was not distorted. A graphic created on equipment using a Hercules Graphics Card, for example, may look distorted when Ventura places it on equipment with an EGA graphics card or a different monitor.

Scanned Images

Scanned images are bit-mapped or gray-scaled images. Scanned graphics or photographs have changes in colors or tone (as opposed to black-and-white line art). A gray-scale image uses shades of gray to represent these tone changes. To print gray shades on a black-only printer (a laser printer or typesetting machine), you must create a halftone. The halftone converts the gray shades to patterns of black dots, varying the amount of white space between the dots to approximate different shades of gray. If no white space is left between dots, the image is black. A combination of more dots than white space appears as a dark gray, and more white space than dots appears as a light gray.

Halftones are used in newspaper printing, where you can see the patterns of dots because of low-resolution offset printing. In a four-color magazine, the dots creating tones are less evident because of the high resolution of the printers. Three-hundred-dots-per-inch laser printers, however, render a rather coarse-grained printed image that may be suitable for internal or informal communications.

Scanners that cannot produce gray-scale images vary the amount of white space between each square of 16 pixels to simulate a halftone dot. This halftone simulation is called *dithering*. Some scanners can produce gray-scale, or TIFF (Tagged Image File Format), images. These images must be converted to a halftone to print on a black-only printer. The Image Settings command from the Frame menu lets you control the conversion to halftone for gray-scale images (see "Image Settings" in this chapter).

If you know that the final images are to be printed on a laser printer, scan the images at 300 dpi to match the potential of the laser printer. Choosing higher resolutions creates larger files that can be printed only by printers capable of matching the resolution. When high-quality output is warranted, you can further improve images scanned at resolutions higher than 300 dpi by printing the final product on a high-resolution printer. Some new laser printers print at resolutions greater than 300 dpi; typesetters print at greater than 1,200-dpi resolution. If high-quality reproductions are required, check the scanning software you are using to see whether gray-scale scanning is supported. Gray-scale scanning requires nearly four times the storage that dithered scanning uses.

Remember that when you want to include photographs in a publication, you should use film prints (black-and-white glossies are preferred) rather than photocopies or other printed reproductions to create the scanned image. If you scan illustrations made of dots, the printed image from Ventura has a moire pattern that shows how the two grids of dots overlay one another.

When you import a scanned image, you may notice horizontal and vertical lines running through the image. These lines represent the edges of the 16-pixel squares. You can adjust the scaling of the image slightly (by a point or less, depending on the size of the frame) to remove the lines. Sometimes, you do not need to adjust the scaling because the printed image does not show the lines. The only way to tell, however, is to print, experiment, and print again. Later in this chapter, you learn how to use the SIZING & SCALING dialog box or the mouse to adjust the scaling of a graphic.

Efficiency Tip

Improving Scanning Resolution

If your scanner offers a choice of resolutions, choose the one that matches your printer's resolution, unless you are scanning a gray-scale image. The image may seem rough on low-resolution screens but should look better when printed (see fig. 6.28). Often, scanning at a high resolution and reducing to half size in Ventura decreases the size of each dot and of the white space between dots, thus "tightening up" the image.

Scanned 3.5 by 4.5 photo

Fig. 6.28.

A reduced scanned image.

You can save scanned images in the IMG format created by the scanning program or in one of the paint-type formats that Ventura supports. Ventura supports scanners that convert images to GEM image, HALO DPE, or ZSoft's PC Paintbrush. When loading scanned pictures (images), choose the PC Paintbrush format in the LOAD TEXT/ PICTURE dialog box.

Scanned images are stored at their original resolution, so scanned image files may be quite large. As with all graphics source files that Ventura assembles into a publication, the original file is not changed.

Efficiency Tip

Scan Only the Image You Need

A bit-mapped file is large, and Ventura saves the entire source file even if you use only part of it. To save disk space, then, scan only the area of the image needed in your publication.

Troubleshooting Tip

Don't Exceed the Memory of the Graphics Buffer

When using bit-mapped graphics, you may exceed the available memory in Ventura's graphics buffer. If you exceed the memory, Ventura looks on the hard disk for more memory, thus slowing the sizing and scaling functions. Select Publisher Info on the Desk menu and click the words Ventura Software, Inc. The diagnostic status box appears. The Graphics Buffer Size shows the number of bytes Ventura can handle before using the hard disk. If you avoid using images larger than the graphics buffer, sizing, scaling, and moving images are much faster.

The Load Text/Picture Command

Use the Load Text/Picture command to bring in graphics created in other programs. The entire graphics file is placed in Ventura as a single graphics object, regardless of how large the graphic is or how many different objects are in the original source file. In many cases Ventura changes fonts to Helvetica or Times Roman if the graphic includes text, regardless of the font settings specified by the graphics program.

When you import files in GEM format, Ventura works with that file, and tracks how you crop, size, and scale the image in the chapter file. When the original GEM image is used again, it is displayed in each chapter as you set up the image for that chapter. This method permits you to place frequently used images in a directory common to many publications. Each chapter displays its version of the original from the single stored file.

Ventura uses the GEM format for object-oriented graphics but accepts files in certain other formats and converts them to GEM when loading. In these cases, the loading process creates a second file with the same name and a new extension: GEM or IMG.

Make sure that you have enough disk space to store both the original source file and the Ventura GEM or IMG file on the specified disk. Refer to table 6.1 for names of some programs that convert to GEM as they are imported into Ventura.

To load files created by object-oriented graphics programs, display the LOAD TEXT/ PICTURE dialog box. Select Line-Art and the correct format. Only files with the extension of the selected format appear in the list of file names (see fig. 6.29). To load files created by bit-mapped graphics programs, select Image and the format. Only files with the IMG extension appear in the directory (see fig. 6.30).

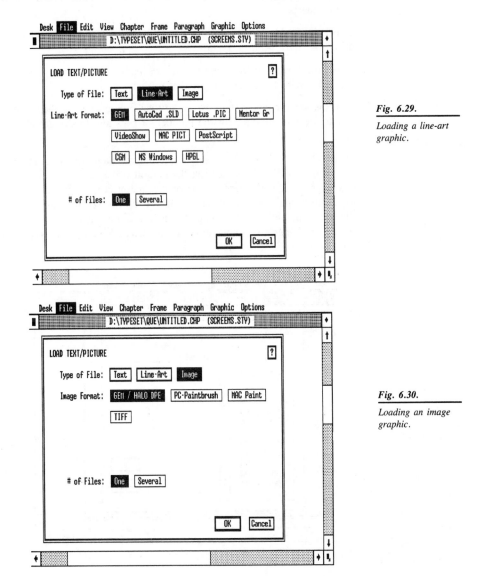

Fig. 6.29.

Loading a line-art graphic.

Fig. 6.30.

Loading an image graphic.

To place graphics from other programs on a page in Ventura, follow these steps:

1. Select or create a frame for the graphic.

2. Use the Ruling Box Around command from the Frame menu to define the rules around the frame.

3. In the RULING BOX AROUND dialog box, set Width: Frame, Color: Black, and Pattern: Solid. Choose fractional points as the measurement unit; for Height of Rule 1, enter the size of the rule around the box.

4. Select the Load Text/Picture command from the File menu. Select Type of File: Line Art or Image.

5. Select the format of the graphic you are loading. The dialog box shows only files with the extension for that format.

6. If in the same chapter, you use more than one graphic in the same format, select Several for the number of files and load them all at once. Click OK.

7. In the ITEM SELECTOR dialog box, find the name of the graphics file you want (see fig. 6.31). Check the default drive, directory and file extension on the Directory line of the dialog box. Use the scroll bars to scroll through the list of names. If you do not see the name of the file you want, click the backup button in the top left corner of the screen to change to another directory or drive. You also can type a new file, drive, or directory name.

Fig. 6.31.

Selecting a graphics file to import.

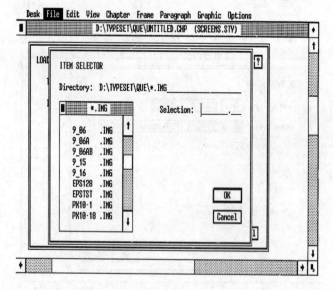

8. Once you find the name of the file you want to place, highlight it and click OK. If you are loading several files, the ITEM SELECTOR dialog box appears again. When you have loaded all the files you want, click OK in the ITEM SELECTOR dialog box.

9. If you loaded more than one file to the assignment list, use the Frame cursor to select a frame; then choose the picture file name from the list in the sidebar. The picture is now in the frame, and the file name is displayed in the current selection box below the sidebar.

You can store graphics source files in the same or separate disks and directories. Ventura finds the files by reading the instructions stored in the chapter file. For this reason, always use the Options menu Multi-Chapter command to copy all files to a disk (see Chapter 3). If you copy the publication to another disk, Ventura finds and copies the graphics file and resets the chapter file pointers to the new location. If Ventura cannot find the file when you print or reload the publication, the program continues loading the chapter file after you click OK in the displayed prompt box. After the chapter is loaded, you can load the graphics source file again.

Efficiency Tip

Using Chapter Pointers for Illustrated Periodicals

In Chapter 7, you learn how to use the Edit menu to remove files from the assignment list and save the frame as a template. If you repeat a graphic, such as a sales chart, with new information in each issue of a publication, leave the file attached to the frame. When you import the graphic for the next issue, make sure that the graphic has the same file name as the preceding issue's graphic file. Ventura loads the new graphic when you open the chapter. Because the pointers in Ventura's CHP file point to the names and locations of files rather than duplicating the contents of files, when you change the content of the source file, the updated version appears in the chapter.

To remove or move a graphic from a frame, select the Frame function and use the crossbar cursor to select the desired frame. To remove the file, choose the Remove Text/File command from the Edit menu. Type the name and extension of the file you want to remove or accept the default name by clicking OK. Click List of Files to remove the file from the chapter. Click Frame to remove the graphic from the frame but leave it in the assignment list. When you remove the graphics source files from the frame, any sizing or scaling settings remain with the frame. You don't need to remove a graphic from a frame to speed screen display or printing time. Use the Hide Pictures command from the Options menu.

Other Ways To Import Graphics

You can import some graphic formats not directly supported by the LOAD TEXT/ PICTURE dialog box if you use a Ventura utility program. Actually, if you have an illustration or need to make one, Ventura and the array of compatible programs and scanners on the market can help you import almost any image into your publications. The following sections describe two of these programs.

Utility Disk Conversions

Conversion utilities that convert DXF file formats to GEM and text file formats to PCX are provided with Ventura. You can use a utility program like SideKick Plus to save a screen to a file, convert it to a PC Paintbrush file, and import it into Ventura as a graphic. This technique saves most text and rules exactly as they appear on the screen. This method does not, however, convert reverse video or boldface type. The file you are converting cannot be more than 25 lines long, and the procedure does not work with a Hercules card. The new file has the same name as the original with the extension PCX.

To convert a SideKick file, or one created by another background utility, use the file TXTTOPCX found on the Ventura Utilities disk. Once the program is copied to the hard disk directory where the file to be converted resides, type the following on a DOS command line and press Enter:

TXTTOPCX filename /%

Use the letters in the following chart to replace the X in the command with the code for the monitor that was used to create the file:

A = AT&T 6300 or Xerox 6065

O = Color card or EGA card with color monitor

C = EGA card with enhanced monitor

M = EGA card with monochrome monitor

Several of the vendors listed in the Appendix offer screen-shot utilities that save files in IMG formats compatible with Ventura.

The Windows Clipboard

Images created in a Windows application can be saved in that program to a Clipboard in a Metafile format (with the WMF extension). These Windows Clipboard Metafiles can be loaded as graphics source files. First, use DOS to copy CLIP2VP.EXE from the Ventura Utilities disk into the Windows directory on your system. You then can choose the MS Windows option for Line-Art Format in the LOAD TEXT/PICTURE dialog box. You must know how to use the program where you created the image as an application under Windows in order to perform the following procedure.

After you copy CLIP2VP.EXE into the Windows subdirectory, choose CLIP2VP.EXE from the Windows Executive and shrink the program where you capture the image, making sure to set the Clipboard for Windows Metafile format. After you cut or copy the image to the Clipboard, expand the CLIP2VP icon and choose the Save As command to name the file. Name the file without an extension (the extension WMF is automatically added). Then close the program and the CLIP2VP application. After you start Ventura (from Windows or DOS), you can load the graphics source file as line art in Windows Metafile format. The image displays in Ventura as it appears in the graphics source file.

Working with Imported Graphics

Loading a graphic into Ventura can be a one-step process. If the graphic in the source file is the size you want on the page, simply load the graphic into a frame drawn to the correct size. Most graphics source files, however, require further manipulation, either to enlarge or reduce the graphic or to crop out white space or other graphics also contained in the source file.

When you load a graphics source file on a page, the image has the same length and width as in the source file (unless the source file is larger than the Ventura page). When you load a graphics source file into a frame, however, Ventura scales the graphic to fit the frame. Unlike text files loaded into Ventura, the original graphics file for each type of source graphic remains unchanged. The sizing and scaling instructions are stored with the frame, where you can set values for padding around the outside of the frame. You also can use the frame's margins and columns, as described in this section.

You learn in Chapter 7 how to caption frames containing source files from other programs. The focus in this chapter is on loading, sizing, scaling, and positioning graphics source files.

Changing Image Settings

TIFF (Tagged Image File Format) files are scanned images that contain gray shades instead of halftone dots that simulate gray shades. You must convert these gray shades to a halftone in order to print them on a printer or typesetting machine that can print only black (see "Scanning Images," in this chapter). If you are importing TIFF files and printing to a PostScript printer, you use the IMAGE SETTINGS dialog box under the Frame menu to control the conversion from gray shades to a halftone. You can alter the settings to produce different effects and levels of quality; however, you should use the defaults for most work.

Gray-tone images converted with the default dot pattern give the most realistic representation of an image. The Halftone Screen Type gives you the option of changing that pattern to create a special effect. The choices are dot (Default), Line, Ellipse, or Custom (set in the PS2.PRE file).

The Lines Per Inch setting is different from the Line option under Halftone Screen Type. Dots in a halftone are arranged in lines across the image. Offset printers define gray patterns (called screens) by the number of lines of dots that fit into an inch. The more lines per inch, the higher the resolution. Low-resolution newspapers use halftones that are 50–85 lines per inch, and higher quality black-and-white printing calls for a 120–133 lines-per-inch halftone. Set Lines Per Inch at 60 for 300 dpi (laser) printing, at 90 for 1,200 dpi typesetters, and 150 for 2,540 dpi typesetters.

Halftone Screen Angle should be set at 45 degrees for most purposes, but you can improve the appearance of some images and create special effects with others by changing the screen angle.

To set the image settings,

1. Select the frame that contains the image.

2. Open the IMAGE SETTINGS dialog box under the Frame menu.

3. Use Halftone Screen Type: Default (dot pattern) or select another.

Sizing and Scaling Imported Graphics

Use the Sizing & Scaling command on the Frame menu to reduce or increase the width and height of an image and to move images left, right, up, and down inside the frame.

Use the commands at the top of the SIZING & SCALING dialog box to set the position and size of frames on the page (see fig. 6.32). In the middle of the dialog box, the Picture Scaling option and three options beneath it relate to the graphic contents placed in frames with the Load/Text Picture command. These three options are Aspect Ratio, X Crop Offset, and Y Crop Offset. You cannot choose any of these options until a graphics source file is loaded into the active frame.

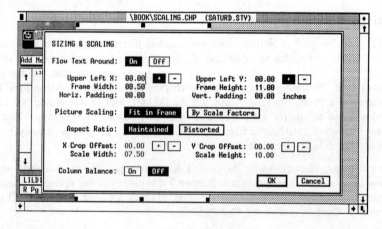

Fig. 6.32.

The SIZING & SCALING dialog box.

Picture Scaling offers two options. The Fit in Frame option scales an entire image to fit in the frame, based on the width of the frame. By Scale Factors allows you to define the exact size of the image. If you scale a picture larger than the frame size, only a portion appears in the frame (see fig. 6.33).

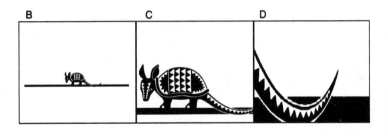

Fig. 6.33.

Scaling and cropping a graphics image.

Aspect Ratio: Maintained holds the height-to-width ratio of the original image (see fig. 6.33A). The width is the determining factor; the program calculates the height of the image in ratio with the width changes (see fig. 6.33B). With Picture Scaling set to By Scale Factors and Aspect Ratio set to Maintained, you can enlarge the size of an image in a frame to the size of the original (see fig. 6.33C). Click By Scale Factors and accept the Scale Width measurement Ventura provides.

Aspect Ratio: Distorted fills the frame with the image, changing the height-to-width ratio as necessary (see fig. 6.33D). You can use this choice with Fit in Frame to scale quickly if the frame shape is the same as the graphics shape and distortion is minimal. In most cases, however, distorted images are not acceptable.

Scale Width and Scale Height control the size of the image. If the original image size is larger than the frame, only the upper left corner of the image is seen in the frame. For easier scaling, you may want to change the unit of measure (in the top half of the dialog box to the right of Vert. Padding).

Efficiency Tip

Using an Image in Its Original Size

Use Picture Scaling: By Scale Factors if you want the printed image to be the same size as the scanned image. Click By Scale Factors and make no changes in the measurements.

Cropping Imported Graphics

Cropping trims off unnecessary parts of an image before printing. The best method is to crop a graphic in the graphics program before loading it into Ventura and use Ventura's cropping for fine-tuning. You cannot crop a graphic until you scale it with the SIZING & SCALING dialog box. Sometimes Ventura is unable to calculate the size of an imported graphic, and the graphic is larger than the frame. The Sizing & Scaling option allows you to reduce the graphic to fit the frame. The X Crop Offset values on the dialog box move the image left and right; the Y Crop Offset values move the image up and down in the frame (see fig. 6.34).

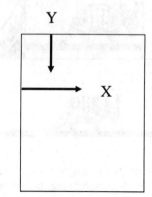

Fig. 6.34.

X and Y cropping.

In the upper half of the SIZING & SCALING dialog box, Frame Width and Frame Height appear. In the lower half of the box you can change the size of the graphic with Scale Width and Scale Height. If you use Fit in Frame, you can change only the width. If you use By Scale Factors, you can change both measurements.

To crop a graphics source file with the Sizing & Scaling command from the Frame menu, do the following:

1. Select the frame containing the desired graphics source file. Then click Sizing & Scaling from the Frame menu. Select Picture Scaling: By Scale Factors and leave the default Aspect Ratio: Maintained (again see fig. 6.32).

Because you are maintaining the ratio, you can change only Scale Width. This measurement is the width of the entire image needed to fill the frame with the cropped portion of the image. The height changes to match the ratio.

2. To crop three inches off the left and one inch off the top of the image, set inches as the measurement unit. For X Crop Offset, enter *03.00* + (plus); for Y Crop Offset, enter *01.00* + (plus). This command moves the picture to the left three inches and up one inch. A minus (−) after each value moves the image three inches to the right and one inch down.

Ventura stores the cropping, sizing, and scaling instructions with the chapter. The original unchanged image remains in the source directory. You always have the option of returning to the original full-size image by loading the image into a new frame.

Efficiency Tip

Quick-Cropping Imported Images

Once you enter the Scale Width, you can crop the image without entering exact amounts for the crop offsets. Use the following steps to do this.

1. Position the cursor anywhere in the frame. Hold the Alt key and press the mouse button. The cursor appears as an open hand (see fig. 6.35).

Fig. 6.35.

Cropping with the mouse.

2. While holding the Alt key and the mouse button, move the image in any direction until the area you want to print appears in the frame. When the image is positioned correctly, release the mouse button.

Efficiency Tip

Speeding the Display

You have probably noticed that Ventura repaints the entire screen each time a change is made. Graphics slow the repainting process considerably. After you have placed all graphics, choose Hide Pictures from the Options menu. The graphics are still in place but gray lines appear in the frames. If the graphics are hidden at printing time, Ventura reminds you that the chapter contains a hidden picture and asks whether you want to print hidden pictures.

Positioning and Reducing Imported Graphics

Usually, you want white space between the outside edges of the graphic and the frame. You can use a large amount of white space inside the frame edges to reduce the graphic. With the frame selected, use the Margins & Columns command from the Frame menu. To have the same amount of white space on all sides of the graphic, enter the same value for top, bottom, left, and right margins. Use a larger amount for any of these margins to offset the graphic or compensate for an odd shape.

Unless you are creating a special effect, you should have white space between the outside edges of the graphics frame and the text surrounding the frame. Use padding in the Frame menu SIZING & SCALING dialog box to insert white space around the outside of the frame. For Vert. Padding, insert the amount of white space you want both above and below the frame. For Horiz. Padding, enter the amount of white space you want on both the left and right sides of the frame.

Troubleshooting Tip

Graphic Doesn't Appear in the Frame

Sometimes when you load an Image file, nothing appears in the frame. The graphic may be loaded, but the part of the image that appears in the frame has no texture, or dots, and so appears blank. Use the technique illustrated in the Efficiency Tip "Quick-Cropping Imported Images" to move the picture into view.

Chapter Summary

Now that you know the alternatives available for adding graphics to a page, you can make decisions about whether to use Ventura or another program to create graphics. Chapter 7 takes you through all the steps involved in laying out a publication, incorporating the information you learned in Chapters 3 through 6 and providing tips about using Ventura's tools during the layout process. Chapter 11 offers more specific advice about making design specifications for graphics from diverse sources.

7

Creating Full-Page Layouts

You are ready now to use Ventura in the page-layout process. This chapter takes you through all the steps involved in building full-page layouts. The chapter begins by showing you how to start a new project with the naming of a new style file. The chapter continues with a discussion of how you further define the page layout, complete with headers and footers, text, and graphics.

Chapter 3 gives a glimpse of parts of the page-layout process. These parts are more fully described in this chapter. Chapters 4 through 6 explain how you can use other programs to prepare text and graphics and how you can bring the text and graphics into Ventura. You learn that you should do as much editing as possible in a word processor before starting to build a Ventura publication and that you should use other programs to create complex graphics. Chapters 4 through 6 also describe using Ventura's tools to create text and graphics.

This chapter begins by explaining how to start a new Ventura project and continues with the following steps:

- Entering page-layout specifications in the PAGE SIZE & LAYOUT dialog box

- Specifying standard layout elements on the page

- Using the Chapter menu to set up headers, footers, and page and chapter numbering

- Using the Frame menu to set up captions for figures and tables and number them consecutively

- Arranging text and graphics on a page

- Editing text and graphics in Ventura

These steps are described from the production perspective. The beginning assumption is that the design specifications for the publication are known already and that your

265

task is to build the publication according to the specifications. In Chapter 11, basic design principles are discussed and some of these same steps are reviewed from the designer's perspective. Part III of this book (Chapters 12 through 16) provides examples of how the basic design principles have been applied in examples of Ventura publications.

Starting a New Chapter

When you start Ventura from DOS, the publisher's window opens into an untitled chapter displayed in the format set by the active style file. The *active style file* is the one that was used in the preceding session. If you have been working on another chapter file and are ready to create a new one, use the New command to begin a new untitled chapter. When you start a new chapter, you can use the style file named at the top of the window, load a different style file with the Load Diff. Style command, or create a new style file with the Save As New Style command. If you decide to use the active style file, remember that the changes you make have an effect on all chapters using that style file.

Unless you are deliberately using a single style file with several projects (or sharing it with several users in a network installation), you start most projects by naming a new style file. A project may have several style files if individual chapters in the project reflect substantial changes in page layout. You learn more about arranging chapters in publications and accommodating changes in design later in this chapter and in Chapter 11. Following is a summary of the procedure used to start a new project and style file:

1. Start Ventura from DOS or use the New command from the File menu to clear the work area. Ventura leaves active the style file from the preceding chapter file but displays the name of the chapter as UNTITLED.CHP.

2. Use the Save As New Style command from the File menu to copy the active style and rename the copy. You may also use the Load Diff. Style command to load another existing style file. (If you modify the active style file, any other chapters using the file are also affected).

3. Use the Save As command from the File menu to rename the untitled chapter.

As you progress with Ventura, you will develop unique style files to satisfy individual requirements. You can use the style files that come with Ventura as a starting point, making changes to suit your purposes. To ''borrow'' a desired copy of a style file, use Load Diff. Style to load the sample file; then use Save As New Style to copy it with a new name.

Efficiency Tip ————————————————————————————————

Avoid Unintentional Changes to Style Files

When you start Ventura, the program loads the style file used in the last session. Any changes you make to that style file affect the current chapter and any other chapter using the same style file. Unless you intend to alter the active style file, use one of the following File menu commands to avoid changing the active file:

- Use Save As New Style to make a copy of the active style file.

- Use Load Diff. Style to select a different style.

- Use Open Chapter to open a formatted project into view.

The two basic components used in the development of a design are the page itself and the items you place on the page. A blank page in the work area shows the design set by the active style file. Ventura copies several style files to the TYPESET directory during program installation.

When you want to borrow a copy of a sample chapter and related source files for experimentation, remember first to make a copy of the project by using the Multi-Chapter command from the Options menu. (If you unintentionally modify Ventura's style files, you can use Multi-Chapter Copy All to copy a sample chapter and related files from the Examples disk provided with the program.) Copying projects is discussed in Chapter 3.

These sample files have names indicating the type of document, number of columns, and paper orientation they control. Each file name starts with an ampersand (&) followed by an abbreviation of the style of document it controls. The following chart summarizes the sample style files:

Type	File Name	Description
Book	&BOOK-P1.CHP	One-column portrait
	&BOOK-P2.CHP	Two-column portrait
Brochure	&BRO-L2.CHP	Two-column landscape
	&BRO-P3.CHP	Three-column portrait
Invoice	&INV-P1.CHP	One-column form with line items
Listing	&LSTG-P2.CHP	Two-column portrait
Letter	&LTR1-P1.CHP	One-column portrait
Magazine	&MAG-P3.CHP	Three-column portrait
Newsletter	&NEWS-P2.CHP	Two-column portrait
	&NEWS-P3.CHP	Three-column portrait
Phone directory	&PHON-P2.CHP	Two-column portrait
Press release	&PREL-P1.CHP	One-column portrait with lead-in paragraph
Proposal/Report	&PRPT-P1.CHP	One-column portrait
	&PRPT-P2.CHP	Two-column portrait

Type	File Name	Description
Table	&TBL-P1.CHP	One-column portrait for financial tables
	&TBL2-L1.CHP	One-column landscape for text tables
Technical documentation	&TCHD-P1.CHP	5.5-by-8 one-column portrait
	&TDDC-P1.CHP	8.5-by-11 one-column portrait
Viewgraph	&VWGF-L1.CHP	One-column landscape
	&VWGF-P1.CHP	One-column portrait

Ventura also provides a style file named DEFAULT.STY. This file is a good starting point when you intend to define tag names differently from those included with Ventura's example styles. Starting with the original DEFAULT style file is like starting with a blank sheet of 8.5-by-11-inch paper with 1-inch margins. On one hand, no special effects are embedded in paragraph tags or command options. On the other hand, you must name and define the tags, paper size and orientation, base page margins, columns, and rules. If you use DEFAULT.STY frequently for new projects, rename it as #DEFAULT.STY so that it is always listed fist in the ITEM SELECTOR dialog box.

Before you use a Ventura style file as the starting point for a new project, open the sample chapter in the TYPESET directory to see how the styles defined in that file look on the page. The related files for each example have the same root names and different extensions (CHP, STY, TXT). In addition to sample chapters for the styles listed, the chapter file named SCOOP includes source text and graphics files in a three-column portrait layout. Use the Show Tabs & Returns command in the Options menu when you review the sample files to see how the source files were prepared for Ventura production.

Many design elements are stored as part of the chapter file rather than as command settings in the style file. Therefore, when you want to modify or reuse a project, you load the *chapter* file for the project. Ventura automatically loads the style file and the source files for the selected chapter file. In Chapter 11 you learn how to use a chapter file as a template in repetitive projects or in projects with precise design specifications.

Efficiency Tip

Using a Sample Chapter for Quick Starts

When you're in a pinch and need to get a project out quickly, you can use Ventura's sample chapters as design templates. Load the sample chapter fitting your basic design parameters into the work area. Then use the File menu's Save As New Style command to name and send a copy of the style file to your project's directory. Use the File menu Save As command to copy and rename the chapter. Remove the sample source files—before you make any changes—using the Edit menu's Remove Text/File command. (The source files in the work area are the originals, not copies.)

Load the new source files, using Load Text/Picture from the File menu. Press Ctrl-S to save the changes to the new project file.

Entering Page-Layout Specifications for the Base Page

Ventura sets up a base page to define the page size, margins, and columns that prevail throughout the chapter. In this section you learn how to use the Chapter menu Page Size & Layout command and the Margins & Columns and Sizing & Scaling commands from the Frame menu to establish the design of the base page. The parameters for the base page are stored in the style file. You can use the `Print Stylesheet` option in the UPDATE TAG LIST dialog box under the Paragraph menu to create a table of the settings used to define the base page. Figure 7.1 shows the base page settings for Ventura's DEFAULT.STY.

C:\TYPESET\DEFAULT.STY

Base Page Settings

Page Size & Layout	Orientation:	Portrait
	Paper Type & Dimension:	Letter, 8.5 x 11 in.
	Sides:	Double
	Start On:	Right Side
Auto-Numbering	Level 1:	[*Body Text,1]
Margins & Columns	# of Columns:	1
Settings For Left Page		
	Top:	01.00 inches
	Bottom:	01.00 inches
	Left:	01.00 inches
	Right:	01.00 inches
	Widths/Gutters—1:	06.50 inches
Settings For Right Page		
	Top:	01.00 inches
	Bottom:	01.00 inches
	Left:	01.00 inches
	Right:	01.00 inches
	Widths/Gutters—1:	06.50 inches
Sizing & Scaling	Flow Text Around:	On
	Upper Left X:	00.00 inches

	Upper Left Y:	00.00 inches
	Frame Width:	08.50 inches
	Frame Height:	11.00 inches
Vertical Rules	Settings For Left Page	
	Inter-Col. Rules:	On
	Width:	0.007 inches
	Rule 1 Position:	00.00 inches
	Rule 1 Width:	0.000 inches
	Rule 2 Position:	00.00 inches
	Rule 2 Width:	0.000 inches
	Settings For Right Page	
	Inter-Col. Rules:	On
	Width:	0.007 inches
	Rule 1 Position:	00.00 inches
	Rule 1 Width:	0.000 inches
	Rule 2 Position:	00.00 inches
	Rule 2 Width:	0.000 inches
Frame Background	Color:	White
	Pattern:	Hollow

Fig. 7.1.

Output for base page of DEFAULT.STY.

The base-page settings Ventura generates when you use the `Print Stylesheet` option (described in Chapter 5 and shown in fig. 7.1) provides a summary of many of the commands stored as settings in the style file. As you saw in Chapter 5, the style file also controls the tag settings established with the Paragraph menu commands, the width table named in the SET PRINTER INFO dialog box (from the Options menu), and the AUTO-NUMBERING, FOOTNOTE SETTINGS, and CHAPTER (DEFAULT) TYPOGRAPHY SETTINGS dialog boxes (except for the `Widows` and `Orphans` options). As you proceed through the page-layout process in this chapter, you see how each of these features affects the overall project design.

To begin a new project, either use the Load Diff. Style command to load a style file with settings matching the intended page size and orientation or establish the settings in an existing style file by opening the PAGE LAYOUT dialog box from the Chapter menu. If you are altering an existing style file, set `Orientation` to `Portrait` or

Landscape, and set Paper Type & Dimension to one of the available options. Also choose whether to print the chapter for binding as a two-sided publication, and establish whether the first page of the chapter is a left or right page.

The settings for Page Size & Layout are stored in the style file. The margins, columns, and location (Upper Left X and Upper Left Y as set in the SIZING & SCALING dialog box under the Frame menu) set for the base page are also stored in the style file. All these procedures are discussed in this chapter.

Before making selections in the PAGE LAYOUT dialog box, plan the design of your document: the page size, orientation, and margins may affect the design specifications for the text and graphics. Figure 7.2 shows how the settings in the PAGE LAYOUT dialog box affect a page. Double-sided facing pages are displayed in the figure. The dimensions of the paper are outlined in dotted lines. The Orientation: Portrait option was chosen.

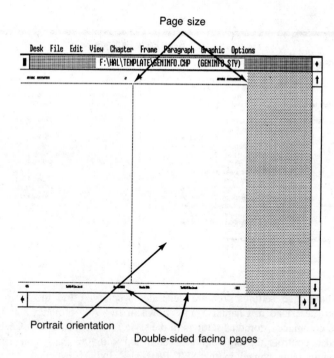

Fig. 7.2.

How the PAGE LAYOUT dialog box entries affect the page in the work area.

At any time during the production process, you can change the Page Size & Layout command options. Keep in mind, however, that you can have only one setting for each dialog box option in a chapter. Changing the orientation of the page or the page size drastically changes page design. The following sections explain how to set the page layout as you build a Ventura chapter.

Setting Page Orientation

The Orientation options on the PAGE LAYOUT dialog box are Portrait (vertical) and Landscape (horizontal). Changing the Orientation option affects the width and length of the columns, gutters, and margins of the base page. The most common orientation and paper dimensions (or page size) for business documents are 8.5 by 11 inches, portrait. Figure 7.3 shows a few variations. The variations listed correspond to the labels in figure 7.3.

a. An 8.5-by-11-inch page with Portrait orientation, printed one sheet per page

b. An 8.5-by-11-inch page with Landscape orientation, printed one sheet per page

c. An 11-by-17-inch tabloid page with Portrait orientation, printed four sheets per page

d. An 11-by-17-inch page with Landscape orientation, printed four sheets per page

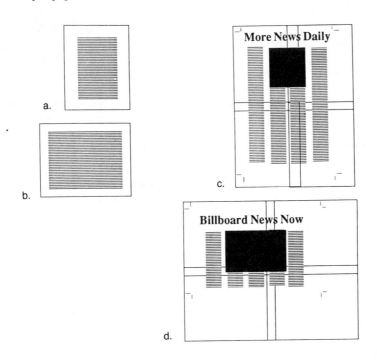

Fig. 7.3.

Examples of page size and orientation settings.

Specifying the Paper Size

Seven predefined standard paper sizes are available for the Paper Type & Dimension option in the PAGE LAYOUT dialog box. The measurements to the right correspond to the selected page size and cannot be altered. Ventura's list of paper sizes includes five standard American paper sizes and two European standards (see table 7.1). Custom paper sizes are set through the Sizing & Scaling command of the Frame menu.

Table 7.1
Measurements for Standard Paper Types in Ventura

Paper Type	Dimension
A4	21 cm by 29.7 cm
B5	17.6 cm by 25 cm
Broad Sheet	18 by 24 inches
Double	11 by 17 inches
Half	5.5 by 8.5 inches
Letter	8.5 by 11 inches
Legal	8.5 by 14 inches

The page size you specify does not have to match the measurements for the sheets of paper you load into your laser printer. For example, when you click Half (5.5-by-8.5-inch dimension), Ventura centers the image on letter-size paper in your printer. You can click Double to design pages up to 11 by 17 inches in size. If you have selected Double, another dialog box appears when you choose To Print from the File menu. On this dialog box, you can choose to print the page at an 8.5-by-11-inch reduction of the original page (if you have a PostScript printer) or to print the page in four sections that overlap. The Broad Sheet option (18 by 24 inches) offers the same printing reduction option for PostScript laser printers but (for certain typesetting—not laser—printers) prints the page in strips that require manual pasteup.

When you choose one of Ventura's standard page sizes that is smaller than the paper in your printer, Ventura centers the image on the paper. You can turn on the Crop Marks option, using the To Print command from the File menu; Ventura automatically creates crop marks to indicate the final trim size of the page (see fig. 7.4).

Crop marks, if you choose to print them, serve as reference points for positioning, when the publication is mass-produced at an offset printer. Crop marks also can be useful as a trim guide when each publication is printed in final form on the laser printer.

If you are creating a document that is not one of Ventura's standard page sizes, you use the Sizing & Scaling command from the Frame menu to establish the dimensions of a custom page and position it on the paper. Crop marks for custom page sizes print automatically when you choose the Crop Marks option at print time.

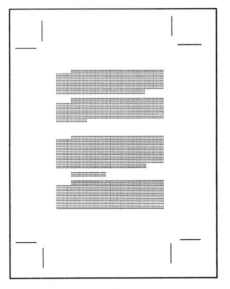

Fig. 7.4.

Printing crop marks around page layouts that are smaller than the paper in the printer.

Creating Custom Page Sizes

Ventura's seven different paper sizes can be printed in both portrait and landscape orientation (refer to table 7.1). You also can define a custom page size (for example, 5 by 7 inches) to accommodate unique design specifications.

To define a custom page size, first (in the PAGE LAYOUT dialog box) establish the orientation and choose a paper type and the dimension closest to the size of the custom page. Then select the base page in the work area as the active frame and open the SIZING & SCALING dialog box from the Frame menu. This dialog box offers controls for sizing and positioning frames. Use the Frame Width and Frame Height options to specify the width and length of the custom page size. To establish the position of the final trimmed page on the paper in your printer, set the Upper Left X and Upper Left Y options.

When you use the Frame menu's SIZING & SCALING dialog box to define a custom page size, you can move or resize the frame only by modifying the settings in the dialog box. (You cannot grab the handles to manipulate the frame.) Crop marks automatically print around the perimeter of the frame when you set Crop Marks: On using the To Print command from the File menu. The placement of the crop marks is illustrated in figure 7.5.

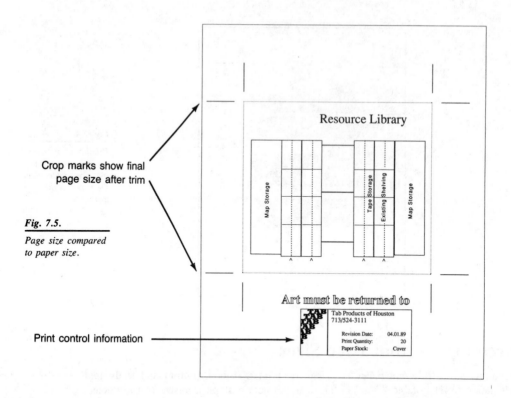

Crop marks show final
page size after trim

Fig. 7.5.

*Page size compared
to paper size.*

Print control information

Specifying a Page Size Larger than the Final Trim Size

The page size is often the same size as the publication once it is mass-produced, bound, and trimmed. You can, however, specify larger page sizes for special layouts. For the document shown in figure 7.5, the Paper Type & Dimension option in the PAGE LAYOUT dialog box is set to Letter, although the pages are trimmed later to 5 by 5 inches. The page was selected as the active frame and sized through the Frame Width and Frame Height options of the SIZING & SCALING dialog box. The location of the page in the work area was set with the X and Y coordinates in the same dialog box. In another frame placed on the page in figure 7.5, the area beyond the 5-by-5-inch layout area is used to print project control information, registration marks, and instructions to the printer.

If you are preparing a page smaller than letter size but will be printing and trimming it yourself, you can use a more efficient way to position the custom page on the paper. Usually when you trim centered copy to the finished size, you must trim all four sides. You can set up your custom page to be trimmed on just two sides by using this procedure:

1. Using the Frame function, select the base page.

2. Open the SIZING & SCALING dialog box from the Frame menu and use the `Frame Width` and `Frame Height` options to specify the width and length of the custom page size. Leave the `Upper Left X` and `Upper Left Y` options at zero, causing the upper left corner of the sheet of paper to be the upper left corner of your custom page.

3. Close the dialog box by clicking OK, and see the boundaries of the new page size in the work area.

When you print the file, choose `Crop Marks: On` from the PRINT INFORMATION dialog box on the File menu. Ventura will automatically print crop marks, but only one will print on the page (see fig. 7.6). Use these crop marks to trim the bottom and right edges of the page.

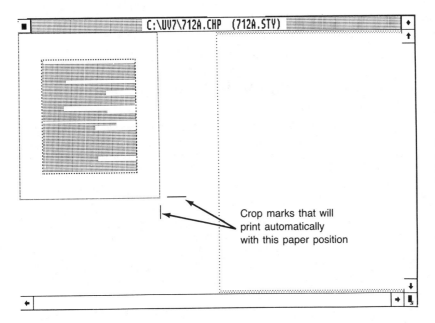

Fig. 7.6.

Custom page positioned for more efficient trim.

Crop marks that will print automatically with this paper position

---

Efficiency Tip

Creating Crop Marks for Custom Page Sizes

Ventura automatically prints crop marks for custom page sizes if three conditions are met:

1. The custom page size is defined by selecting the base page and changing the `Frame Width` and `Frame Height` settings in the SIZING & SCALING dialog box on the Frame menu.

2. Crop Marks: On is selected in the PRINT INFORMATION dialog box on the File menu before printing.

3. The custom page is positioned and printed on a paper size large enough for the crop marks to show.

Once you set the paper size and orientation, using the PAGE LAYOUT dialog box, you set the boundaries for text and graphics on the page by using the Frame function. If you are building a page layout to hold a multiple-page document, begin by setting the page and column margins as described in the next section. If you are building a page layout for a form or brochure, you can use the margins, columns, and rules set for the base page as a visible grid against which you place other frames and graphics. Column and margin guides display only on pages; frames placed on pages can have margins and columns, but guides for them do not display. Graphic shapes do not have margins or columns, but text typed in box text graphics can be positioned away from the perimeter of the box by using the Paragraph menu's Alignment and Spacing commands.

Setting Page and Column Margins

Margins reflect the limits used for text and column settings on pages and in the frames placed on pages. Margins are measured from the edges of the page—that is, from the page size (or frame size) defined in the Frame menu's Frame Width and Frame Height options in the SIZING & SCALING dialog box. The area within the page margins is sometimes called the *image area* of a publication. Make sure that the margins are within the image area of your target printer. Chapter 11 shows how to plan a layout when the design calls for elements to print outside the image area.

The margins and columns set for pages can be different from those set for frames added to the page and for frames Ventura automatically creates for headers, footers, and captions (see fig. 7.7). If you set the margins for the base page before you use the Headers & Footers or Footnote Settings commands, Ventura uses the same settings for the right and left margins of these frames. If you set the margins for a frame used to hold an illustration, Ventura provides the same right, left, top, and bottom margins for the caption frame created when a caption is set up using the ANCHORS & CAP-TIONS dialog box.

You can change the position of text within a frame by changing the margins of the frame or by using the Paragraph menu Alignment and Spacing commands. Settings for Above, Below, In From Left, and In From Right options in the SPACING dialog box determine where text falls within margins. Remember to click the Copy to Fac-ing Page option to copy the In From Left and In From Right settings in the SPAC-ING dialog box in order to reverse these settings if paragraphs indent differently on left and right pages.

You can further control spacing between the top margin of a page or frame and the first line of text from the CHAPTER TYPOGRAPHY SETTINGS dialog box on the Chapter menu and the FRAME TYPOGRAPHY SETTINGS dialog box on the Frame

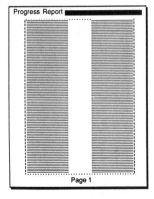

Fig. 7.7.

Columns and margins defining the limits of the text area and excluding running headers and footers.

menu. The Move Down To 1st Baseline By option gives you two choices. If you choose Cap Height, the space between the top margin and the baseline of the first text is equal to the tallest capital letter on the first line. If you choose Inter-Line, the space between the top margin and the baseline of the first text is equal to the inter-line Spacing for that tag. The CHAPTER TYPOGRAPHY SETTINGS dialog box sets the value for the chapter. You can override this default for a selected frame in the FRAME TYPOGRAPHY SETTINGS dialog box. You should choose Inter-Line for multiple-column documents to ensure that text aligns across columns.

Settings for Horz. Alignment, Vert. Alignment, and Text Rotation in the ALIGNMENT dialog box also affect the position of text in the frame. The instructions you set with the Paragraph menu commands prevail through all chapters using the style file named at the top of the window. Alignment for box text is set with the Paragraph menu because box text graphics do not have margins.

Any frame margins other than the base-page margins are saved with the chapter file, not the style file. Although to achieve the same effects you must set custom margins in each frame in a chapter, tags affect all chapters using the same style file.

Once you select the page in the work area as the active frame, you can set the margins and columns for the page. The settings you choose prevail for any pages that Ventura creates as you load a source text file onto the base page. If you use the Insert/Remove Page command from the Chapter menu to insert a new page, you can establish new margin and column settings for the inserted page and any clones created when you load a multiple-page source text file onto the inserted page. See "Setting Column Guides" in this chapter for a detailed description of using the MARGINS & COLUMNS dialog box. To learn more about mixing page styles in a chapter, see the section called "Overriding the Page Style" in this chapter.

Working with Double-Sided Publications

Choosing Sides: Double in the Chapter menu PAGE LAYOUT dialog box does not cause the printer to print on both sides of the paper. Instead, Sides refers to whether the final pages will be for a double-sided document (a book, newsletter, or manual) or a single-sided document (a letter, ad, form, or formal report). Although you can change from Single to Double at any time, using Double for single-sided documents has some advantages. (See the Efficiency Tip "Using the Double-Sided Option for Single-Sided Publications" in this chapter.)

In a double-sided publication, the inside page margin is often wider than the outside margin; this allows for binding. Double-sided documents need two sets of margins: one for even-numbered (left) pages and one for odd-numbered (right) pages. Ventura automatically adjusts the margin settings in the Frame menu MARGINS & COLUMNS dialog box when you choose Paper Type: Double. You need only to specify the measures for either page (Left or Right) as the Settings For option and click Copy To Facing Page. Ventura automatically reverses the margins and applies them to the facing pages. To see the settings, select a facing page as the Settings For and notice that the left and right margins have been changed accordingly. To reverse custom *column* settings on facing pages, however, you must select the page from Settings For and type the column values.

Headers and footers in double-sided layouts may or may not use the same text on facing pages. You may want to print the page number and revision date on all right pages, and the title and logo on all left pages. When the header or footer text for the left and right pages is the same, but the position for the text is reversed, Ventura sets the adjustment when you activate the Copy To Facing Page option. For example, you can cause the page number in a footer to always print at the outside edge of a double-sided design. To do so, set the right page number at the Right option and then click Copy To Facing Page to cause the left page to display the page number as the Left option.

Header and footer text typed in the dialog box stores in the CHP file for the chapter. When you need to establish a new header or footer in a chapter, you can also place frames on the selected pages and create custom headers. Header and footer text typed into frames placed on the page is stored in the CAP file for the chapter, along with all other text typed into empty frames. These two approaches to capturing header information are further discussed in "Placing Headers and Creating Custom Headers" later in this chapter.

Efficiency Tip ───

Controlling Left-Hand and Right-Hand Page Positions

When you prepare a double-sided document, be sure to include every page, including blank left pages used to "pad" the document so that new sections or chapters start on right-hand pages. Use the Insert/Remove Page command from the Chapter menu to insert blank pages. Supplying a numbered page for blank pages is also helpful for the people who print, copy, or bind the document. Be aware that if you insert or delete one page in a double-sided document, chaos will ensue when all pages after that page change from right to left pages and vice versa. You must add two pages to a double-sided chapter, even if one is blank, and you must replace a deleted page with a blank page in the chapter.

Use the Update Counters command on the Chapter menu to reset the page numbers when inserting pages, or when you intentionally depart from the default numbering sequence of pages.

By choosing the Facing Pages View command from the View menu, you can see pages that face each other in double-sided publications. You can set up a double-sided document as single-sided if the copy is centered on the page and the headers and footers are identical. Usually, however, you should use the Facing Pages View option for documents that print on two sides and turn off the Facing Pages view when you want to work on one page at a time.

Laying out and rearranging elements on pages can be quicker when you can see two pages at once. In the reduced view shown when you choose Facing Pages View, two pages fit into the work area side by side. You can "greek" the type to reduce screen redrawing time. *Greeking* means that lines rather than characters appear on the screen to simulate the position of type elements. To greek the type on-screen, use the Set Preferences command from the Options menu and select Text to Greek: All. Set the header tags (or any other tag that does not affect pagination) as a larger font than will be used at final print to serve as reference points in the greeked text. If you need to edit text, learn to use the mouse and the Ctrl-key shortcuts to zoom from Facing Pages view to Normal or Enlarged view. Unfortunately, however, you cannot use a Ctrl-key shortcut to return to the reduced Facing Pages view; you must use the mouse.

Efficiency Tip

Using the Double-Sided Option for Single-Sided Publications

When building long single-sided documents, reduce the time you spend turning pages on-screen by setting up the document as a double-sided document and viewing facing pages as you work. If the copy is centered on the page (the right and left margins are equal), you can leave the chapter as a double-sided layout when you print the final pages. If the left and right margins are not equal, change the Sides option in the PAGE LAYOUT dialog box to Single before printing.

Determining the Maximum Number of Pages Per Chapter

The number of paragraphs in a chapter determines Ventura's page-number limit per chapter. On a system with 640K of memory, Ventura can store 8,000 paragraphs in one chapter. To put that ceiling into perspective, a letter-size page with 0.5-inch margins on all sides containing a 1,000-byte paragraph that is 10-point type on 12-point leading has only one inch of white space left to fill at the bottom. Ventura has the potential of storing 8,000 paragraphs of similar length. Although each paragraph can be up to 8,000 bytes, Ventura recommends that you plan that each paragraph in tabular material hold no more than 4,000 or 5,000 bytes.

Most text-based publishing projects yield paragraphs of considerably less than 8,000 bytes. In database publishing projects, however, the technique you use to end lines without ending a paragraph creates paragraphs that might exceed the maximum size. In those types of projects, insert a paragraph return at least every 4K or 5K. Paragraphs and alternative line endings are described in more detail in Chapter 5.

Ventura lets you work with large chapter files, but operations perform faster with smaller files. Turning pages or making text edits that carry over to subsequent pages is slow in long files. If you divide a long chapter into separate files, you can work faster. Another advantage of breaking up files is that you can specify different running headers and footers for each file. Pages usually contain the running headers and footers and can be changed only by adding a new page (using the Insert/Remove Page command from the Chapter menu). When you split a chapter into sections, you can override the default numbering systems so that the sections appear as one chapter when printed.

When you're deciding how many pages a file should contain, consider also the size in bytes of the final publication. You want to be able to back up your publications on floppy disks for storage and transportation purposes. Therefore, files must be less than 330K for 5.25-inch, single-sided, low-density disks or less than 730K for 3.5-inch double-density disks. Files need to be less than 1.2M for 5.25-inch high-density disks and less than 1.4M for 3.5-inch high-density disks. If you are sending a file to a service bureau, be sure to ask which disks the bureau accepts.

You can start a document with any page number up to 9,999. You can change the starting page number of the chapter or set up the chapter for automatic numbering across chapters by using the Multi-Chapter command from the Options menu. Ventura then shifts all the page numbers in the chapter to match the new sequence. ("Numbering Chapters and Pages Automatically," later in this chapter, tells you how to break a chapter into two sections, restart numbering in the middle of a chapter, and number multiple chapters.)

Setting the Target Printer

As you add fonts and printers, deciding which printer and width table to use for final printing becomes part of the page-layout process. Each printer (and each set of fonts that you add to Ventura) shapes letters and symbols on the page differently. The width of each character (for each typeface and size) is used to adjust the position for letters and symbols so that the line, paragraph, and page endings you see on the screen match the printed page. The instructions for this process are stored in a file called a width table.

The Device Name option on the SET PRINTER INFO dialog box opened from the Options menu shows which printer is currently the target printer. The top line of the dialog box shows the printer width table used to create the file named in the Width Table option (see fig. 7.8). If the width table named matches the printer selected as Device Name, the word Ultimate displays at the end of the top line. Ultimate means that the printed page includes characters and letters that are shaped, sized, and spaced to the printer's ultimate potential.

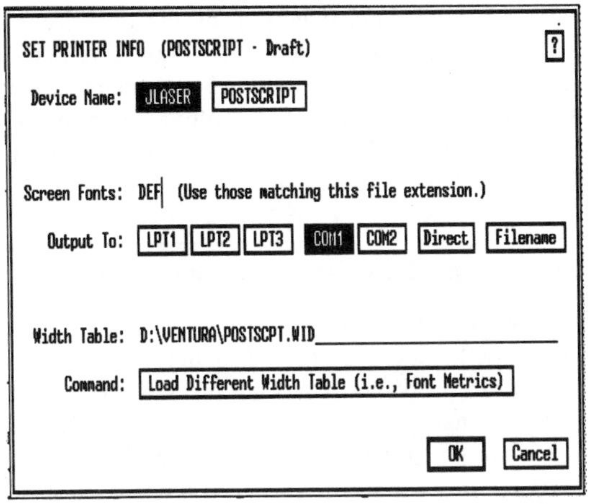

```
┌─────────────────────────────────────────────────────────┐
│  SET PRINTER INFO  (POSTSCRIPT · Draft)            [?]   │
│                                                           │
│  Device Name:  [JLASER]  [POSTSCRIPT]                     │
│                                                           │
│                                                           │
│  Screen Fonts:  DEF| (Use those matching this file extension.) │
│                                                           │
│  Output To:  [LPT1][LPT2][LPT3][COM1][COM2][Direct][Filename] │
│                                                           │
│                                                           │
│  Width Table:  D:\VENTURA\POSTSCPT.WID_____      │
│                                                           │
│  Command:  [Load Different Width Table (i.e., Font Metrics)] │
│                                                           │
│                                        [ OK ] [Cancel]   │
└─────────────────────────────────────────────────────────┘
```

Fig. 7.8.

The SET PRINTER INFO dialog box.

Suppose that you are designing a project for final printing with a typeface you don't own. You can purchase and add the printer font as described in Chapter 8, or you can find a service bureau to print your formatted files. When you adopt either of these approaches, use the SET PRINTER INFO dialog box and click Load Different Width Table. Select the Width Table from the ITEM SELECTOR dialog box that appears. You can add width tables to this list with the installation program (when you add a new type of printer) or by merging a width table for newly acquired fonts with the width table used for the printer (see Chapter 8).

A single width table can contain spacing, height, and kerning information for many different fonts. If you have more than one type of printer available (for example, a low-resolution printer for drafts and a higher-resolution printer for final copy), check the SET PRINTER INFO dialog box to confirm that the current width table is the one you intend to use with the style file for the chapter. You can change width tables during production, but the line, paragraph, and page endings may change to accommodate the change in the character instructions for each printer.

As you select alternative device names, Ultimate changes to Draft when the Width Table option does not match the Device Name option. Draft output does not shape the individual characters on the page properly, but can prove useful if you want to see the same line, page, and paragraph endings on both a low-resolution printer and a higher-resolution printer. Changing printers and width tables is further discussed in Chapter 8.

Specifying Page Elements

When you begin a session or select the New command from the File menu, Ventura loads UNTITLED.CHP and the style file that you used in the last session. The page size, margins and columns, and orientation are determined by the active style file. A blank page is in view.

You can begin building a chapter immediately using the Load Text/Picture command to bring in text and graphics from other programs. You can also begin the chapter using Ventura's built-in Graphic and Text tools. In well-planned projects, the definition of the page design is ongoing, so all pages conform to an overall grid system. At any time, you can return to the PAGE LAYOUT dialog box from the Chapter menu and change the options that define the page design.

Efficiency Tip

Changing the Page Settings during Production

If you are fine-tuning the design of a publication as you build the chapter, you can make changes in the page settings to see how the changes affect the pages in the work area. Remember to save your work when you are pleased with the results so that you can experiment, abandon changes if you want, and recover the last version saved. The changes you make affect all the pages created using the original settings.

A design layout is only partially set by the style file in use. Frames, margins, columns, and rules set for frames placed on pages influence the design of a publication substantially. All settings for any frame other than the base page are stored as settings in the chapter file; settings for the base page are stored in the active style file for that chapter. Because both the style file and the chapter file have an impact on the appearance of pages, use copies of both files when you want to create another publication based on an established design.

Figure 7.9 shows some of the elements that are placed on a page. The areas defined for these elements form a grid that defines the pages in the chapter. The grid system includes nonprinting column guides to mark the boundaries for margins and columns, running headers and footers, and patterns and rules which further define the design of the layout. You can turn off headers and footers on selected pages and set text and text alignment within the headers and footers to be different for facing pages. Remember that frames and graphics can be set to repeat on all pages. You can hide and turn off repeating elements when individual pages depart from the overall design.

When you insert blank pages within a chapter, the page settings for the new pages are the same as the settings for the page where you initiated the Insert/Remove Page command. In double-sided layouts, the new page takes on the appropriate right or left page settings and repetitive elements. (See the Efficiency Tip ''Controlling Left-Hand and Right-Hand Page Positions'' in this chapter.)

As discussed in ''Setting Page and Column Margins'' in this chapter, you can change page margins and columns on inserted pages without affecting the pages from which the pattern was copied. You can hide repeating frames and remove, rearrange, or add new repeating frames as you load files to new page patterns. Double-sided publications can have independent settings for tags placed on facing left and right pages for the headers, footers, margins, column widths, vertical rules, and temporary margins. In each chapter, however, you are limited to one setting for each of these Chapter menu commands: Page Size & Layout, Chapter Counter, and Automatic Numbering.

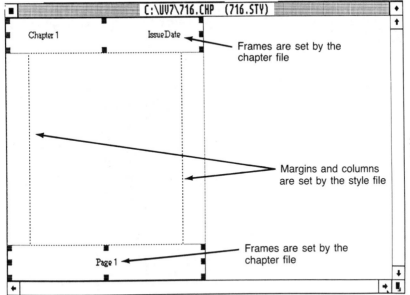

Fig. 7.9.

Page elements.

You can set page margins, columns, rules, sizes, and background of the page using either the Frame or Graphic function. Choose the page as the frame by clicking a Frame or Graphic tool near the edge of the work area, outside any other frames or graphic shapes. Handles display around the perimeter of the selected page and may be either black (Frame function) or gray (Graphic function). Any settings you make in the Frame menu dialog boxes affect the selected page and any pages patterned after it.

Creating Pages

The base page in a chapter actually serves as a guide to define where repeating elements appear on the chapter pages. The margin and column guides and the rules around and between columns make up the basic elements of the imaginary grid that marks the page. Professional designers, however, often use much more elaborate grid systems, defining weights and measurements that precisely determine where and how each line of copy is treated. The principle in designing a grid for the pages is to identify all the basic elements appearing routinely throughout the document. Ventura's methods of tagging text help you achieve consistency when matching design specifications that relate to the appearance of copy in the work area.

Figure 7.10 shows some examples of grid systems used in a book, a newsletter, and a brochure. Chapters 11 through 16 provide examples of grids used in various publications, including those shown in figure 7.10.

The following sections describe how to use the Frame and Chapter menu commands to set up a base-page grid system. Although you can define pages (and pattern others after them) that do not share the same characteristics as the base page, each chapter has only one base page; the settings for the first page in the chapter become the base-page settings in the style file generated with the Print Stylesheet command (refer to fig. 7.1).

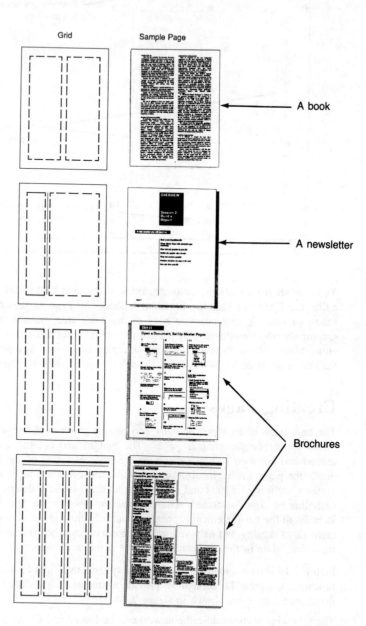

Grid   Sample Page

A book

A newsletter

Brochures

Fig. 7.10.

Examples of grids and their uses.

Setting Column Guides

You use the Margins & Columns command from the Frame menu to define one to eight columns for a page or frame. (You can set more than eight columns to a page using one of the techniques described in the section "Overriding the Page Style.") When you open the MARGINS & COLUMNS dialog box with the first page in a chapter selected as the active frame, you set the page margins and column widths and gutters for the base page (see fig. 7.11).

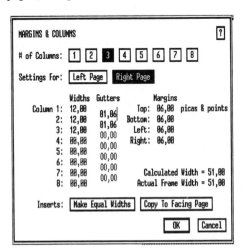

Fig. 7.11.

The MARGINS & COLUMNS dialog box.

A *margin* is white space between the text and the edge of the page. A *gutter* is white space between columns. A *column* is the width of text. The *actual frame width* is the size of the frame currently selected. The *calculated width* is the total of the left and right margins and the columns and gutters that you defined for the page or frame.

The MARGINS & COLUMNS dialog box is used to set the margins and columns of the base page or of frames placed on the page. This dialog box also controls the margins of header, footer, and footnote frames. Running headers, running footers, and footnotes must be a single column across the page, although text can be positioned at left, center, and right tabs, which gives the effect of three columns.

When you create a page, you first set the margins for the page. If all columns on the page are the same width, select the number of columns and enter the first gutter width in the MARGINS & COLUMNS dialog box. Ventura splits the width of the frame into equal columns separated by equal gutters between the margins you set. If you change the number of columns, Ventura updates the Column and Calculated Width options. If you change the left or right margin, Ventura calculates new Column and Calculated Width values.

You can enter different sizes for each column and gutter, and you can specify a different number of columns for the Left and Right pages. Ventura updates the Calculated Width option as you adjust settings for each page so that you can verify that the Calculated Width matches the Actual Frame Width.

Once the columns are set for the current page, click Copy To Facing Page in the dialog box for double-sided layouts. Select the opposite page as the Settings For option, and modify the column widths when you need to mirror (rather than just copy) column settings on facing pages.

Note that if you choose 1 from the # of Columns option, the first column measurement displays as black and all other column and gutters widths display as gray zeros. When you have set columns of unequal widths, you can click Make Equal Widths, and Ventura recalculates the column width, using the values for the first gutter and the left and right margins.

Figure 7.12 shows examples of layouts in which the columns are unequal, so custom columns need to be defined. In the examples, all the gutters measure the same, but the number and width of the columns vary. Rules add a graphic effect to two of the layouts. You use the VERTICAL RULES dialog box on the Frame menu to set the vertical rule in the first example by specifying Inter-Col. Rules: On. In the second example, you set the rule between the columns using the Rule 1 Position and Rule 1 Width options. Create the frame around the third column and use the Frame menu's Ruling Box Around command to define the outline and the Sizing & Scaling command to set Flow Text Around: Off. By designating the frame as a repeating frame, the layout can include multiple pages. In the third example, a repeating frame is added over the top half of the second column, turning Flow Text Around: On for the new frame.

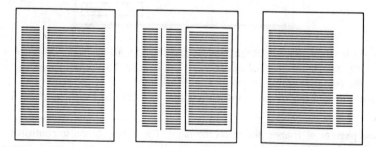

Fig. 7.12.

Examples of documents with custom column settings.

After setting the page size, orientation, margins, columns, and printed rules, use the Chapter Typography command to balance the text in the columns, as described in the next section.

Balancing Text in Columns

When *pouring text* (that is, putting text into a column), Ventura fills each column before going to the next column. If the text does not completely fill the last page, use the publishing tradition of dividing the copy evenly between the columns. In other words, balance the columns. Using the Chapter Typography command from the Chapter menu, you can turn Column Balance: On for the chapter. The FRAME TYPOGRAPHY SETTINGS dialog box from the Frame menu defaults to the chapter settings, but you can turn Column Balance: Off for text in individual frames. You cannot turn Column Balance: On for a frame unless the option is turned on for the chapter.

Ventura does not vertically justify (add space between lines in a column) to balance the columns, although the Profession Extension does offer a vertical justification option. If an odd number of lines exists, the left column is longer, following another publishing tradition of leaving the left column longer than the right when the number of lines is not equal.

If your project contains tags that are defined as Overall Width: Frame-Wide (in the ALIGNMENT dialog box from the Paragraph menu), you must turn Column Balance: On. An example of a Frame-Wide tag is a headline spreading across more than one column of text that is below the tag. Column Balance: On slows formatting speed, so turn off this option for the chapter when formatting and turn it on before printing. Or turn on Column Balance for the chapter and turn it off for all frames except those that require balanced columns.

The three SETTINGS dialog boxes are easily confused. The CHAPTER TYPOGRA-PHY SETTINGS dialog box controls settings for the chapter. The FRAME TYPOG-RAPHY SETTINGS and Paragraph menu's TYPOGRAPHY SETTINGS dialog boxes default to but can override those settings. Figures 7.13, 7.14, and 7.15 show these dialog boxes.

Fig. 7.13.

The CHAPTER TYPOGRAPHY SETTINGS dialog box.

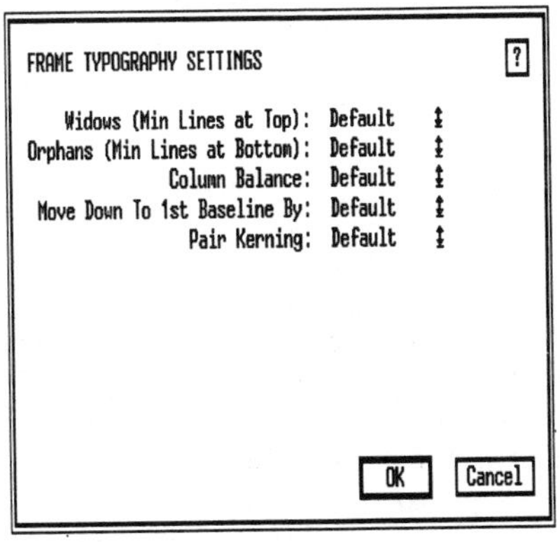

Fig. 7.14.

The FRAME TYPOGRAPHY SETTINGS dialog box.

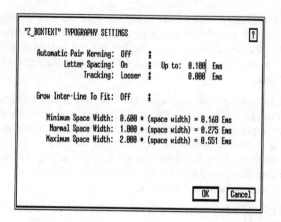

Fig. 7.15.

The Paragraph menu's TYPOGRAPHY SETTINGS dialog box.

Controlling Where Paragraphs Break with Widows and Orphans

Widows and orphans describe single lines of text separated from the rest of the paragraph by a column break, a page break, or an illustration. An *orphan* is the first line of a paragraph that is left behind when the rest of the paragraph continues to the next column or page. A *widow* is the last line of a paragraph that is at the top of a column or a page.

Letting single lines remain isolated from the rest of a paragraph is considered bad form. Some editors consider the first or last two lines of a paragraph to be widows or orphans and insist on keeping at least three lines of a paragraph together.

The Widows and Orphans options in the Chapter menu CHAPTER TYPOGRAPHY SETTINGS dialog box sets the minimum number of lines kept together for the entire chapter. The FRAME TYPOGRAPHY SETTINGS dialog box defaults to the chapter settings but lets you override the chapter settings for selected frames (again see fig. 7.14). Both these commands control the number of lines left at the bottom of a column or carried over to the next column. See "Fitting Copy," later in this chapter, for hints on correcting problems that can occur when you avoid leaving widows and orphans in text.

Kerning

Kerning allows you to make fine adjustments to the space between certain pairs of letters and is discussed in detail in Chapters 5 and 9. Although you can kern manually between any characters, Ventura stores kerning information for hundreds of pairs in the width table and will kern these characters for you. First, set Pair Kerning: On in the CHAPTER TYPOGRAPHY SETTINGS dialog box on the Chapter menu. Ventura then will kern text in any tag that has set Automatic Pair Kerning: On under the Paragraph Typography command on the Paragraph menu. The Pair Kerning setting in the FRAME TYPOGRAPHY SETTINGS dialog box on the Frame menu defaults to the chapter setting, but you can turn off kerning for a selected frame (again see fig. 7.14). If you select Pair Kerning: Off in the CHAPTER TYPOGRAPHY SET-TINGS dialog box, you override all kerning specified with the TYPOGRAPHY SET-TINGS dialog box from the Paragraph menu or the FRAME TYPOGRAPHY SETTINGS dialog box from the Frame menu. No type is kerned, but the tag settings are not changed. To re-enable kerning in all appropriately tagged paragraphs, select Pair Kerning: On. Turning Pair Kerning: Off in the chapter speeds redrawing of the screens but may change the position of text.

Placing Headers and Footers on the Page

Above the top margin and below the bottom margin of every chapter page is the area Ventura uses to place automatically created headers and footers. In manuscript-based publishing, Ventura's header and footer features automatically number pages incrementally and place constant text on the pages (see fig. 7.16). As more text is loaded onto pages, more pages are created and numbered automatically.

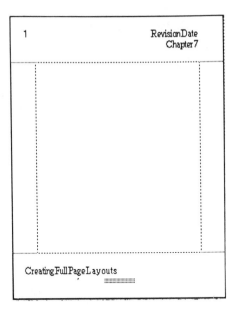

Fig. 7.16.

Running headers and footers outside the page margins.

You can use headers and footers to incorporate page numbers and chapter numbers in a maximum of two lines of text for each automatically created frame. Double-sided publications can have different header and footer text for left and right pages. All the text you type in the HEADERS & FOOTERS dialog box is stored in the chapter file. Therefore, when you use headers and footers, carefully proof the contents after each text change. You should not use an external program to check the spelling of dialog-box text placed in Ventura's CHP files.

When you are working with a publication that is relatively consistent in the number of pages per issue, you may want to use frames placed on the pages rather than automatic headers and footers. Once you set the contents in frames, you can update the text in the chapter's caption (CAP) file with a word processor's search and replace features. Manual headers and footers offer more flexibility than automatic headers and footers but are suitable only for projects where the number of pages is relatively consistent. Later in this chapter, you see how to number pages automatically without using headers and footers and how to set custom headers and footers in frames.

Caution: If you edit or spell check a CAP file, do not change the number of paragraph returns in the file and be sure to save the file as an ASCII file. For more information on the contents of caption files, see Chapter 3.

Ventura automatically creates a repeating frame when you use the Headers & Footers command from the Chapter menu. At the same time, Ventura generates a tag, Z_HEADER or Z_FOOTER. All Z tags have the default attributes of body text, but you can define a Z tag as you do any other tag with one exception: Alignment is controlled by the HEADERS & FOOTERS dialog box, not by the alignment definition in the tag. The Z tag appears in the list of tags only if you choose the Generated Tags: Shown option in the SET PREFERENCES dialog box from the Options menu.

The text in all automatically created paragraphs in a chapter is actually only one paragraph. Ventura separates the lines of text with a line break and aligns the text on left, right, and center tabs. You change the spacing between lines in a header by increasing the value of the interline spacing in the SPACING dialog box from the Paragraph menu. The interline value adjusts automatically as you change font sizes for the Z_HEADER tag if you have set Auto-Adjustments to Styles or Both in the SET PREFERENCES dialog box from the Options menu.

Follow this procedure to create a header or a footer:

1. Use the Headers & Footers command and click Left Page Header, Right Page Header, Left Page Footer, or Right Page Footer.

2. Click Usage: On to create a header or footer for the entire document. If you have selected Double as the page-layout option, click Copy To Facing Page from the Inserts options at the bottom of the dialog box if you want facing pages to be mirror images.

3. Select Left, Center, or Right to define the alignment for your copy. You can type two lines of text for each alignment, and you can use all three alignments. If you need more than two lines of copy in headers and footers, use the technique described in "Setting Custom Headers and Footers," in this chapter.

To edit the text of automatically generated headers and footers, you must return to the HEADERS & FOOTERS dialog box. If you don't want the headers and footers to appear on a certain page, click the Turn Header Off or the Turn Footer Off command from the Chapter menu when the page is active. The page number in the current selection box at the base of the sidebar indicates the current page. The Turn Header Off or Turn Footer Off setting stays with the *page number* (as it appears in the current selection box at the bottom of the sidebar) even if you move text from page to page. For this reason, wait until the end of a production cycle to turn off headers or footers for specific pages.

If you click the Inserts option boxes at the bottom of the HEADERS & FOOTERS dialog box, Ventura inserts chapter or page numbers into the header or footer. Place the Text cursor on the Left, Center, or Right alignment line and click any box from the Inserts options. The characters [P#] or [C#] appear on the alignment line but are replaced with a page or chapter number when printed.

When you click 1st Match as an Inserts option, [‹tag name›] appears on the alignment line. Replace the words tag name with the tag name you want Ventura to search for and insert as the header or footer. If Ventura doesn't find that tag name on the page, the program looks on previous pages for the copy last tagged with that tag name. Last Match inserts the last copy with that tag name on the page. This option is usually used to set up index-style headers and footers for directories and does not work if text is in a frame drawn on the page.

Text attributes are codes that you enter into text or some dialog boxes to change the style, point size, or font of words within paragraphs. You can enter text attributes on any of the alignment lines for any element of the headers and footers (see Chapter 4). The Text Attr. option in the HEADERS & FOOTERS dialog box works the same way as in all other dialog boxes. When you click the Text Attr. option, an end code (‹D›) is inserted. Backspace over the ‹D›, insert the attribute you want, and close the bracket. With headers and footers, however, you need to be sure to click Text Attr. again to include an ending code (‹D›) on each line or the setting will prevail throughout the header.

Numbering Chapters and Pages Automatically

The UPDATE COUNTERS dialog box in the Chapter menu allows you to set up to four counters that automatically number pages, chapters, tables, and figures. Page numbers and chapter numbers that appear in the header or footer are set here. You can restart the incremental numbering of pages or chapters at any time by choosing either the Initial or This counter and setting the Update Method to Previous Number + 1 or Restart Number.

The Renumber option from the MULTI-CHAPTER OPERATIONS dialog box on the Options menu renumbers pages across chapters. Before creating a table of contents or index, all chapters, pages, tables and figures must be renumbered. You can select Initial Page, Initial Table, or Initial Figure and choose Update Method: Previous Number + 1 for each chapter to cause Ventura to number pages consecutively across separate chapters. To actually renumber the chapters after setting the counters, choose the Options menu and the Multi-Chapter command. Add the chapters to be numbered to the MULTI-CHAPTER OPERATIONS dialog box and name the publication. If a chapter is highlighted, the Renumber option appears gray. Click anywhere in the dialog box to deselect the chapter. Then choose Renumber, and Ventura renumbers all chapters in the window in the order that they are listed.

A chapter is sometimes so large that you must split it into two files with your word processor. You can break a file into two chapters and use the Update Counters command to continue numbering across both chapters.

Use this procedure to split a chapter into two files:

1. Go to the top of the page that will be the first page of the second file. Choose a logical place to break the file—but it must be the beginning of a paragraph. At the top of this page, type a marker to search for with your word processing program—for example, *XXXX*.

2. Save the chapter under a new name—for instance, 1.CHP. The page-layout settings are the same, so use the same style file for both documents.

3. Use the Remove Text/File command from the Edit menu to remove the text name from the assignment list and save the chapter again.

4. Use your word processor to search for the marker, remove it, and split the text into two files: TEXT1 and TEXT2.

5. Load 1.CHP and use the Load Text/Picture command from the File menu to load TEXT1. Check the last page to be sure that the chapter ends as you had planned, and use the Save command. Because you are working with two sections of a single chapter, do not add a blank page if the first section ends on an odd number.

6. Use the Save As command to save the chapter as 2.CHP. Remove TEXT1 from the assignment list and load TEXT2. Use the Save command.

7. Use the Update Counters command from the Chapter menu to choose Which Counter: This Page and Update Method: Previous Number + 1. Use the Save command.

8. Use the MULTI-CHAPTER OPERATIONS dialog box from the Options menu to create a PUB file that contains the two chapters in the correct order. Choose Renumber.

You can restart page numbering and change the numbering format on any page in a chapter. For example, you can number an introduction in lowercase Roman numerals; then at page *xi*, you can restart the counter at 1 and use Arabic numerals. To do this, go to page 11 and use the Update Counters command from the Chapter menu. Select Number Format options.

The page number in the current selection box at the base of the sidebar and the page numbers you enter in the TO PRINT dialog box are the page numbers in relation to the entire chapter. This number is not necessarily the page number that appears on that page when you print the page. These chapter-assigned page numbers remain constant and always indicate your position from the first page of the chapter, regardless of the numbering systems in use. If you want to print a page number in a position other than those described in the preceding paragraph, you can use the INSERT SPECIAL ITEM dialog box position page and chapter numbers. That technique is described in the Efficiency Tip "Numbering Pages Using a Frame" in this chapter. The process is actually only semiautomatic because you first must place a frame wherever you intend to insert a page or chapter number.

Positioning Graphics

In theory, the way you create a page layout is first to place graphics on the page. Then, before going on to a new page, you fit the text around those graphics. You complete each page before you go on to the next. In practice, however, this procedure isn't always the best way for you to create page layouts. For example, to make sure that the text fits the number of pages allowed, you may want to place all the text first, leave space for the graphics, and position the graphics later. Or suppose that you are working with a brochure that uses graphics as the primary communicators. You may want to position all the graphics in the publication first and wrap the text around the graphics afterward.

The following sections describe some of the graphics techniques that Ventura allows.

Efficiency Tip

Placing Large Graphics from Other Programs

If you know that a graphic is much larger than the position reserved on the page, position the frame for the graphic to reserve the space, set up the other pages, and size or crop the graphic later.

Adding Graphic Elements to Pages

In addition to containing text, pages can include graphics (created in Ventura or imported from other programs) that repeat on all, or most, of the pages in a publication. Horizontal and vertical rules, which add a graphic element in many page designs, are added in a variety of ways. You can add other graphic shapes and images with Ventura Graphic tools or by loading graphics source files.

Remember that Ventura offers several ways to make different types of graphics appear in a chapter:

- *The VERTICAL RULES dialog box on the Frame menu.* You can place rules between all columns on a page and in two additional positions on the page. Vertical rules are interrupted by text that is tagged as frame-wide or column-wide and crosses the rules.

- *The RULING LINE ABOVE, RULING LINE BELOW, and RULING BOX AROUND dialog boxes on the Frame menu.* These rules are inside the frame, and you can define up to three rules in three different heights (weights) above, below, or around a frame. Frame rules overlap text unless you adjust a paragraph's tag or the frame's margins to accommodate the rules. You can import text or graphics into a frame.

- *The REPEATING FRAME dialog box on the Frame menu.* You can use this feature to cause the frame and its contents to appear on successive pages that are created automatically. (Repeating frames, however, do not repeat text in the frames when part of the text in the source file is placed on the base page first.)

- *The RULING LINES ABOVE, RULING LINES BELOW, and RULING BOX AROUND dialog boxes on the Paragraph menu.* Paragraph rules increase the amount of space between paragraphs and should be set so that Overall Height in the dialog boxes is an even multiple of body text, to enable the automatic alignment of text at a uniform baseline on a multiple-column page.

- *The box text tool from the Graphic function.* You can create one custom rule around a box and type text into it. You cannot import text files or graphics into the box.

- *The FOOTNOTE SETTINGS dialog box on the Chapter menu.* You can set the height and width of a rule between text and footnotes at the bottom of a page.

- *Ventura's Graphic tools.* You can place horizontal, vertical, or diagonal rules of varying heights. You can use these tools with the Show/Hide On All Pages and Show/Hide On This Page commands on the Graphic menu.

You can suppress all or part of the page elements when you use one of the techniques described in the following text. After you set up the page size and layout of the margins and columns, you are ready to begin working on the elements that appear on most pages. Use the Load Text/Picture command from the File menu to bring in graphics and text from other programs. To load more than one source file at a time to the sidebar, click # of Files: Several in the LOAD TEXT/PICTURE dialog box. As you select each file, Ventura returns to the ITEM SELECTOR dialog box for you to select another file. Click OK when you are finished.

You also can use Ventura's built-in text and Graphic tools to create graphics, as described in Chapter 6. Graphics can be drawn on pages, repeated automatically, and suppressed individually. If the graphic is in the same position on all pages, select the graphic and choose Show On All Pages from the Graphic menu. To hide the graphic on a page, select the graphic and choose Hide On This Page from the same menu.

If the graphic is in a different position on left- and right-hand pages, add a frame in position on a right-hand page. Place the graphic in the frame, select the Repeating Frame command on the Frame menu, and select For All Pages: Right. Repeat for the left-hand page. To hide the graphic on a page, select the graphic frame on that page and select On Current Page: Hide This Repeating Frame in the REPEATING FRAME dialog box. See "Hiding Page Elements" in this chapter for more information.

Any time two frames are placed on top of one another, you select the top frame when you click the mouse; you select the frame underneath when you hold the Ctrl key while you click the mouse. The name of the frame you have selected is displayed in the current selection box of the sidebar. When you want to work with a graphic you have placed in an area also occupied by another frame, make sure that the proper frame is selected and then make any necessary adjustments (see ''Layering Graphics'' in this chapter).

Wrapping Text around Graphics

You wrap text around graphics by selecting the frame and then displaying the SIZING & SCALING dialog box from the Frame menu. Set Flow Text Around: On. The best approach may be for you to build each page completely before going on to the next page.

Ventura wraps text around irregular shapes when you define the boundaries of the shape with frames (see fig. 7.17). To flow text around a shape, follow these steps:

1. Load the text onto the page or into a frame set up for the text.

2. Add a frame to hold the source graphics file, and open the Frame menu's SIZING & SCALING dialog box to select Flow Text Around: Off.

3. Load the graphics source file into the frame.

4. Use the Turn Line Snap On command to aid in adding a frame that is one line deep. Use the SIZING & SCALING dialog box to select Flow Text Around: On.

5. Use Copy and Paste to add as many frames as needed to cover the graphic where text should not flow.

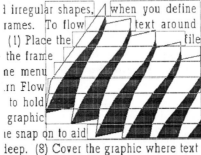

Fig. 7.17.

Wrapping text around shapes with irregular edges.

Handling Figure and Table Captions

Ventura has powerful features to help you number, caption, and position illustrations. Although you can type text in frames added beside illustrations as a caption technique, do so only when you have a small number of illustrations to label. Otherwise, use the Anchors & Captions command from the Frame menu to label and number tables and figures within the chapter.

Use the following steps to set a caption:

1. Use the Anchors & Captions command to name and label each illustration and to number tables and figures.

2. Select the reference point in text with the I-beam cursor and use the Edit menu's Ins Special Item command to select Frame Anchor. In the INSERT/EDIT ANCHOR dialog box, the last anchor name entered in the ANCHORS & CAPTIONS dialog box appears as the Frame's Anchor Name. Be consistent when assigning anchor names; if you need to type a different anchor name, it must match the name in the ANCHORS & CAPTIONS dialog box for that frame.

3. Use the Re-Anchor Frame command from the Chapter menu to make sure that all illustrations have moved with the reference point in text.

Figure 7.18 shows an illustration and a caption anchored to a reference point in the text.

Fig. 7.18.

Illustration and its anchor reference point in the text.

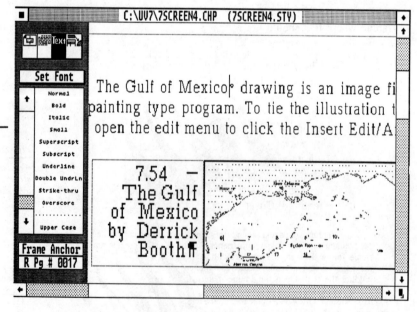

To set up a caption using the Anchors & Captions command, do the following:

1. Select the frame holding the illustration using the Frame cursor; then choose the Anchors & Captions command from the Frame menu (see fig. 7.19).

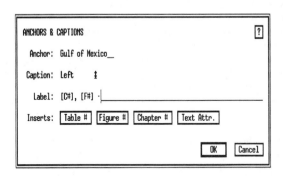

Fig. 7.19.

The ANCHORS & CAPTIONS dialog box.

2. Beside the Anchor option type the name you will use to tie the illustration to a specific point in text. The name must be exactly the same name you type later using the Ins Special Item command from the Edit menu to define the illustration's reference point in the text.

3. Choose where the caption is to print relative to the illustration. In figure 7.19, Below is chosen. Ventura stores the text tagged as Z_CAPTION in the CAP file for the chapter.

4. At the Label option, type the caption for the illustration; for instance, you may enter the word *Figure* or *Table* here. This label will print in the caption frame. Keep the label short because you can edit this information only from the ANCHORS & CAPTIONS dialog box. The text added in this step is stored in the CHP file, tagged as Z_LABELFIG.

5. To number the illustration, position the cursor beside Label where the number is to appear and select which Inserts option applies to the illustration. You can choose a chapter number in addition to a table or figure number. Any periods or hyphens between these inserts must be typed manually (see fig. 7.19). After doing this, you don't need to worry about typing those words or numbers in place. The text entered as the Label is stored in the CHP file.

6. If you have more copy to add to this caption, click OK to return to the work area where you see the caption frame positioned beside the illustration.

7. Use the Text function to type any additional copy. If the caption frame is not large enough, change to the Frame function and use one of the handles along the outside of the caption frame to increase the size of the illustration. You can change the size of both frames by using one of the handles along the border shared by both frames.

8. Ventura defaults to Previous Number + 1 and arabic Number Format, but you can use the Update Counters command from the Chapter menu to select Restart Number or change the Number Format default from arabic to any of the choices shown.

Ventura tags all captioned text with a Z_CAPTION tag. If you did not insert a number, Ventura's generated tag for the caption is Z_LABELCAP. If you insert a Table #, the tag is Z_LABELTBL; if you inserted a Figure #, the tag is Z_LABELFIG. Any text added to the caption frame is tagged Z_CAPTION. If you choose Generated Tags: Shown in the SET PREFERENCES dialog box, the new tag names are shown in the sidebar.

Efficiency Tip

Numbering Pages by Using a Frame

Most of Ventura's page-numbering features work only when you place text on the page or in the automatic header and footer frames that Ventura creates. You can, however, use the Ins Special Item command on the Edit menu to number pages. Add a frame in the position you want the page number to appear. Using the Text function, click the I-beam cursor in the frame and choose the Ins Special Item command (Ctrl-C). Choose Cross Ref (F6) and select Page #. Using the Frame function, select the frame and choose the REPEATING FRAME dialog box on the Frame menu to make this a repeating frame For All Pages: Left & Right. You can create a different page number position for left and right pages by using the For All Pages: Left and For All Pages: Right options in the REPEATING FRAME dialog box.

Tying Illustrations to Text References

The ANCHORS & CAPTIONS dialog box is used to tie the caption to the frame, but the Ins Special Item command on the Edit menu is used to place a reference point, or *anchor*, in the text. The anchor ties the illustration to a related point in the text.

To anchor an illustration to a point in text, first position the Text I-beam at the desired point in the text. From the Edit menu, click Ins Special Item (Ctrl-C) and select Frame Anchor (F5) (see fig. 7.20). Ventura defaults to print the graphic on the same page in all cases but also allows you to specify whether the position should be above, below, or on the same line as the text reference. (See Chapter 4 for more information about anchors.) Ventura displays an appropriate notation in the source text. When you set the anchor in the dialog box as Fixed, On Same Page As Anchor or as Relative, Automatically At Anchor, the notation that appears in the text is ‹$&Anchor Name›. For an anchor set as Relative, Below Anchor Line, the notation is ‹$&Anchor Name[v]›; for Relative, Above Anchor Line, the notation in text is ‹$&Anchor Name[ˆ]›.

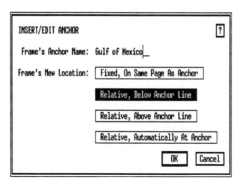

Fig. 7.20.

The INSERT/EDIT ANCHOR dialog box.

Once anchors are set in the text and in the ANCHORS & CAPTIONS dialog box, you use the Re-Anchor Frames command from the Chapter menu to position captioned illustrations close to the referenced text points. After you re-anchor frames, check the new positions if you used Above or Below as the caption option in the ANCHORS & CAPTIONS dialog box. In those cases, Ventura places the caption in the top and bottom margins of the page when the reference point is close to either extreme. You can move the illustration by selecting the frame and using the Frame crossbar cursor to adjust the position.

When you use Ventura's features to manage the captions and numbering sequences of illustrations, you choose from one of three approaches (in each case, you start by choosing the Anchors & Captions command from the Frame menu):

- When the captions are short, use the Label option in the ANCHORS & CAPTIONS dialog box to type the caption. Select the table, figure, or chapter number insert that you want to use. (This information is stored in Ventura's CHP file.)

- When the captions are longer than 80 characters, you can type more text in the caption frame, using the Text I-beam and the Frame function handles to expand the space of the caption frame.

- When the captions are long, type an identifying word in the caption frame and use your word processor to expand the text. This procedure is useful if you have many illustrations to caption.

You can choose from the three preceding techniques when typing captions for illustrations. In the second and third cases, you can spell check the contents of the caption file with an external dictionary as long as you are careful to do the following:

1. Always save CAP files as ASCII files.

2. You see the text from all box text, framed text, and caption frames when you load the CAP file as a word processing document. Do not delete or add any returns in the file. If you do, text from the CAP file appears in the wrong frames in the Ventura chapter.

Ventura does not recognize a non-ASCII file as a CAP file and uses the returns to position the captions.

Overriding the Page Style

A few design specifications cannot have alternative settings within the same chapter. Page Size & Layout settings, for instance, cannot be mixed in one style file. Other predominate design factors that have only one setting are the grid established by the interline spacing of the Body Text tag, headers and footer formats, Auto-Numbering settings, and Footnote Settings. Although you can change the options for each of these during production, each change you make establishes a new default that affects the entire chapter.

Most other design elements can be overridden in a variety of ways. In the sections that follow, you see how to create alternative effects in the design of a publication by doing the following:

- Setting columns and margins in frames

- Inserting and removing pages

- Hiding page elements

- Setting custom headers and footers

Setting Columns and Margins in Frames

You may have one or more pages that don't fit the design established by the master grid of the style-file and page-layout settings. The first and last pages of a newsletter, for instance, usually do not fit the master grid of the inside pages. Alternatively, you may want a different header or footer for certain pages, or you may need more columns than the eight Ventura allows per page. An example of each of these follows. All three examples shown work best if the copy to fit the new page margins is in a separate file.

To change margins and columns, follow these steps:

1. Go to the page that requires new columns or margins. This page can be at any location in the chapter. Use Turn Line Snap On from the Options menu if you are concerned with the even alignment of text you place in the frame with other text on the page. Select Turn Column Snap On to cause the new frame to align on a column guide.

2. Add a new frame in the area where you need to override the settings set by the style file. Change the margins, columns, rules, or background of the added frame as needed. (Remember column and margin guides do not display in frames you add to the page.)

3. While the frame is selected, choose Flow Text Around: On from the SIZING & SCALING dialog box. Use the Load Text/Picture command from the File menu to load the new file into the selected frame.

If you want a different header or footer to repeat on pages,

1. Set up the text in a frame.

2. Use the REPEATING FRAME dialog box from the Frame menu to choose whether the frame should repeat on left, right, or both types of pages (see ''Setting Custom Headers and Footers'' in this chapter).

To place more than eight columns on a page, you can place frames by following the next steps. Use this technique when creating large documents that exceed Ventura's maximum of 725 line elements per frame. You can avoid exceeding the maximum by adding frames. Many of the limits on the program are avoided with the Professional Extension, which supports EMS memory. See Chapters 2 and 10 for more on the Professional Extension.

1. Set the page with at least two columns.

2. Load a text file to the page.

3. Add a frame, covering one of the columns. Set the frame in place with both Turn Column Snap On and Turn Line Snap On (accessed through the Options menu) so that each frame aligns precisely with the next. Leave the top and bottom margins in the frame set to zero and set the number of columns for the frame.

4. Load the same text file that is on the page into the new frame.

5. Open the REPEATING FRAME dialog box from the Frame menu to make this a repeating frame.

Text loaded into repeating frames doesn't repeat from page to page. Instead, Ventura adds text to the repeating frame where the text on the page left off. If you are formatting data with leader tabs, you need to increase the number of repeating frames in use. Each frame must be precisely the same size.

Inserting and Removing Pages

You use the Insert/Remove Page command from the Chapter menu to insert and delete chapter pages. Once the INSERT/REMOVE PAGE dialog box is open, choose the position for the new page (before or after the current page) by clicking either option in the dialog box. Ventura inserts the new page and lets you set new page margins and columns as well as vertical rules and frame background.

To override the current page margins, columns, vertical rules, or frame backgrounds, follow these steps:

1. Go to the page that requires new page margins.

2. Use the Insert/Remove Page command from the Chapter menu and choose the Insert New Page, Before Current Page option from the dialog box. Ventura creates and inserts a new page.

3. Set up the new margins, columns, rules, or frame background for the inserted page.

4. Use the Load Text/Picture command to load the new file onto the page. Ventura creates new pages until the entire file has been loaded. The

original pages continue after the last page of the inserted file; however, they may change from odd-numbered to even-numbered pages.

If a chapter file already has a text file poured onto the pages, the only way you can insert and pour a new text file onto the pages is to use the Insert/Remove Page command. If you try to insert a second file on the last page of a chapter file, the second text file replaces the first text file in the chapter file.

Ventura has three methods that you can use to force a left (even-numbered) page to become a right (odd-numbered) page: you can insert a blank page in front of the left page; you can create a tag with Page Break: Before/Until Right using the Breaks command on the Paragraph menu; or you can make each section a separate file if the publication consists of many sections. If you choose the third method, you should end each section with an even-numbered page and start each section with an odd-numbered page.

The Remove Current Page option in the INSERT/REMOVE PAGE dialog box always refers only to the current page. You cannot delete a page until you remove source files from the frames by using the Remove Text/File command from the Edit menu. After removing the source file from the frame or list, you can remove the current page. To do this, select a frame and press the Del key. If the frame contains framed text, the text is erased. If the frame contains a source file named in the assignment list, deleting the frame leaves the document's name available as an item in the list. You cannot remove more than one page at a time.

Hiding Page Elements

You can use Ventura's Show and Hide commands in the Options menu to hide some or all pictures in a chapter to speed screen redrawing. If you want to speed the draft-print process, you can choose to hide pictures when you print the chapter; the frames that contain pictures will print solid black. A dialog box appears telling you This chapter has at least one hidden picture and asking you whether you want to print all hidden pictures or keep them hidden.

To hide repeating frames placed on pages, select the frame on the page where you do not want the repeating frame to appear. Then open the REPEATING FRAME dialog box from the Frame menu. For the On Current Page option, select Hide This Repeating Frame. If the frame still appears, click anywhere in the work area and the frame will disappear. Ventura-drawn graphics can also be tied to a repeating frame and therefore individually suppressed on selected pages in the same way.

To hide on an individual page a graphic that is set to show on all pages, you can add either a frame or another graphic to cover the portion you do not want to use. You can hide the top, bottom, or sides of a source graphic by using the cropping features described in Chapter 6. Another way to create a similar effect is to set the margins of the frame holding the graphics to measurements that hide the portion of the graphic you do not want to see.

Header and footer frames are suppressed from displaying and printing in a different way. Rather than hide a header or footer, select the Turn Header On/Off or Turn Footer On/Off commands from the Chapter menu to suppress the element on an individual page. Solid white frames do not hide elements in headers or footers. When you need to cover an element in an automatically created header, you must first select the header as the graphic control frame and then place a graphic shape over the element. To make the shapes obscure the elements, choose the Fill Attributes command from the Graphic menu and choose the White, Solid, and Opaque options. Every other header or footer in the chapter will also be obscured.

Note: Test the capability of your printer to support opaque and transparent shapes by printing the chapter called CAPABILI.CHP in the TYPESET directory.

Efficiency Tip

Suppressing Headers and Footers

If you do not want automatic headers or footers printed on selected pages within a chapter, you have two choices:

- Use the Insert/Remove Page command from the Chapter menu to create a new page. Select Turn Header Off and Turn Footer Off from the same menu. The inserted page is blank, and the text continues flowing on the next page.

- Select Turn Header Off or Turn Footer Off in the Chapter menu for that page.

An inserted page remains blank until you place a source file on it, and the page maintains a relative location in the chapter file. If the pages before an inserted page expand or contract, the inserted page moves accordingly. Turning a header or footer off, on the other hand, creates an instruction that stays with the numbered page. For example, turning the header off on page 3 and adding two pages in front of page 3 causes page 5 to print without a header.

If you do want chapter headers, footers, and page numbers printed on blank pages, create a new tag. Call this tag Page Break. From the Paragraph menu select the Alignment command and choose Center (so that you can spot these tags easily). Then select the Breaks command and choose Page Break: After and Keep With Next: No. This procedure creates a tag containing no text—just a page break. Insert one page-break tagged paragraph on the last page of the chapter that has text; insert another tagged paragraph on the blank page. These tagged paragraphs then force page breaks and create one blank page.

Setting Custom Headers and Footers

Ventura's header and footer features place up to two lines of constant text in repeating frames that default to appear on every page in a chapter. Occasionally, design specifications call for custom headers and footers because of the limits (summarized shortly) on automatic headers and footers.

Use the Headers & Footers command from the Chapter menu to create automatic headers and footers whenever possible because the Page #, Chapter #, and Copy To Facing Page options make the process easier. However, some restrictions to automatic headers and footers exist:

- Headers and footers can be only one-column wide with copy that is flush left, flush right, or centered.

- Headers and footers for single-sided publications must use the same text on every page. Double-sided publications can have different text for left and right pages.

- Pages created with the Insert Page command use the same header and footer dialog boxes as the other pages in the chapter.

- Headers and footers each cannot exceed two lines in length.

- Headers and footers can be placed only over and under the text on the page, not in the margins beside the text on the page.

- Headers and footers cannot be copied to the Clipboard for use in another chapter.

- Spelling programs cannot be used to check the contents of automatic headers and footers because the text is stored in the CHP file for the chapter.

To overcome any of the limits of the automatic headers and footers, you can place frames on the page using one of two techniques:

1. Create a frame and designate it as a repeating frame if you want the same header or footer text to repeat through the chapter.

2. Create a frame and copy and insert it as often as needed if the header or footer text in the frame changes as the pages change. Once you set the first frame, use the Clipboard to copy the frame to each new page. Ventura places the frame in precisely the same place that it appeared on the page from which it was copied. For this reason, reposition frames on left and right pages if any position other than centered was originally set. Any time you modify the contents or the characteristics of the frame, the modification appears only on the page where the frame is placed.

You can create repeating frames to add headers and footers manually by using the following technique:

1. Create a frame by clicking the Frame function's Add New Frame button.

2. Add any text to the frame and place the I-beam cursor in the text where you want the page or chapter number to appear.

3. Open the Edit menu and choose Ins Special Item (Ctrl-C). Select Cross Ref (F6) and select either Page # or Chapter #.

4. Make this frame a repeating frame by using the Repeating Frame command on the Frame menu.

Ventura's headers and footers are designed to place text above or below the margins of a page. You can set custom margin settings in automatic headers, therefore changing the point at which a header or footer begins and ends within the margins. But you cannot position page numbers adjacent to text on the page by using this dialog box. You can, however, use the INSERT SPECIAL ITEM dialog box to insert automatically formatted page numbers that increase in regular increments and print in the left and right margins. (See the Efficiency Tip "Numbering Pages by Using a Frame" in this chapter.)

Developing Efficient Procedures

You have learned that you can set for a single page margins and columns that also govern succeeding pages of text and graphics. You have learned how to insert pages with the same page measurements and how to define the margins and columns of a new page in the chapter. You also have learned how to hide repeating frames on individual pages. Chapters 3 through 6 explain how you can place text and graphics on the pages, using the Load Text/Picture command or Ventura's Text and Graphic functions. When you're actually assembling a chapter, however, studying various methods or sequences of operations is helpful before you decide on the one that suits you best. The following sections provide some helpful hints for efficient use of Ventura.

Starting with a Blank Page

After you define the characteristics of the page as described in the preceding sections of this chapter, you can begin placing text and graphics on each page. This section takes you through the typical sequence involved in that procedure.

If your design specification limits you to one or two variations in margins and columns, make the base page match the predominate specification.

If your design specification uses different margins and columns, choose from the following approaches to match the specification:

- Use the Add New Frame button when you are making changes to individual pages in the chapter. Activate the Frame function and click Add New Frame, located at the top of the sidebar. Draw a frame the size of the new margins and columns you want for that page.

- Use the Insert/Remove Page command from the Chapter menu when several consecutive pages hold a source file with margin and column settings different from the balance of the chapter.

- Separate different layouts into different chapter files.

Although you can set several different page styles in one chapter, mixing page styles is an advanced technique that solves problems such as how to produce a cover page for a report. Adding a new frame solves the problem, as does using separate chapters for the different styles of pages. You may want to mix page styles, however, for chapters that are repeatedly updated and reissued, as in the case of newsletters. Then you have only one set of tags and files to maintain. To learn more about mixing page styles in one chapter, see "Overriding the Page Style" earlier in this chapter.

Efficiency Tip

Starting a Page in the Reduced View

Start building each page in the chapter by working in the Reduced view (Ctrl-R), letting the column and line snaps help you place frames. Text and graphics from other programs can be poured into frames quickly and reviewed later. To type or edit text or to draw graphics with Ventura's tools, change to Normal view (Ctrl-N). Change to Enlarged view (Ctrl-E) to work with small type (eight points or less) and to align graphics and text precisely.

After you have specified the margins and columns for the base page, you place text and graphics on the page. The general guidelines follow.

Set the Body Text tag to match the typeface and line spacing specifications for the project. As you place source files, the bulk of the text fills approximately the same number of pages as in the final version of the chapter. Attach tags for the other standard paragraphs in the chapter, such as major headings and subheads. Before you begin setting tag specifications in multiple-column layouts, decide whether you intend to use Ventura's automatic adjustments to spacing values as you change the size of fonts. Set the Auto-Adjustments option to No in the SET PREFERENCES dialog box to control spacing and achieve even alignment of text on multiple-column pages. Work in Reduced view at first to lay out the entire page. Then change to Normal view to make fine adjustments.

Use the Turn Column Snap On/Off command from the Options menu (described shortly) to help you position frames vertically against column edges. Use the Turn Line Snap On/Off command from the Options menu (also described shortly) to align frames along an invisible horizontal grid set at the value of body-text interline spacing.

Use the Grid Settings command from the Graphic menu to define an invisible crosshatch grid in a selected frame to help you position box text and Ventura-drawn graphics.

To place illustrations on pages, draw the frame for the image slightly larger than the final image. Select the frame and load the source file, using the LOAD TEXT/PICTURE dialog box. (The image you load must be in one of the compatible formats listed in the dialog box.) You can adjust the size of the image in the frame by changing the size of the frame. You use the Remove Text/File command from the Edit menu to remove graphics files from frames and the assignment list. In Chapter 6 you see how to convert text and Ventura pages into images. You cannot, however, use the File Type/Rename command from the Edit menu to convert graphics files.

If you need to move or crop an illustration within the frame sized with the framing handles, open the SIZING & SCALING dialog box from the Frame menu. Note the scale width that Ventura calculated as the reduction size. Then click By Scale Factors and change the Scale Width measurement back to the one Ventura calculated when you sized the frame. Click OK to return to the work area where you now can use the mouse to size and crop the illustration. Select the illustration frame with the Frame cursor. Then hold down the Alt key while you click and drag the illustration into position with the gloved hand displayed.

As you use the mouse to crop illustrations, Ventura updates crop measurements in the SIZING & SCALING dialog box. If you need to be more precise than the resolution of your screen allows, adjust the values in the dialog-box options after you let Ventura show you the estimated values.

Add captions for illustrations by selecting the frame that holds the illustration and then click the Anchors & Captions command from the Frame menu. Ventura automatically creates an auxiliary frame to hold the text of the illustration's caption in the position you select from the Caption option. Using the ANCHORS & CAPTIONS dialog box and tying illustrations to reference points in text are described in ''Tying Illustrations to Text References'' in this chapter.

Verify that the page elements are appropriate for the current numbered page. Format special characters and phrases in paragraphs by using the Text function.

Save your work often. Press Ctrl-S or click Save from the File menu to execute the Save command.

The most efficient approach you can use to build a publication varies with the type of publication you are producing and your own personal preferences. In some cases, you assemble all the elements for a single page at a time, refining every detail of that page before going on to the next page. In other cases, you quickly position all or part of the elements on each page, working through the entire layout once before going back and making fine adjustments. More tips on positioning text and graphics are in the sections that follow.

Place the longest file as the source file on the pages and then reserve space for other articles by drawing frames. Select a frame and then load a document into the frame, placing one file at a time. Ventura shows you when you have reached the end of a file by displaying an end-of-file marker in the frame. If a source file is to continue in another frame, select the frame and then click the name of the file in the assignment list.

Efficiency Tip

Look for the End-of-File Marker

If you have chosen Show Tabs & Returns from the Options menu, a hollow box appears as an end-of-file marker for each source file. When placing text in a frame that may not hold an entire file, look for the end-of-file marker. Finding the marker is faster than reading text to locate the end of the source file.

You can use the Go to Page command from the Chapter menu to turn through an article quickly. You can open the dialog box by pressing Ctrl-G. When you use the Insert Page command, you can load a separate source file onto the page. The pages needed to hold the file are automatically added to the chapter.

Efficiency Tip

Creating Thumbnails of Page Designs

Designers sometimes want to see a reduced version of certain pages on one sheet, called a *thumbnail,* to view the overall design elements or to check certain facing pages. Although Ventura does not have a feature that allows you to create thumbnails of designs with text flowing from page to page, you can create reduced layouts that have text and graphics.

For example, if you want to reduce a letter-size document 30 percent, do the following:

1. Use the Save command from the File menu to save the chapter file.

2. Choose the Page Size & Layout command from the Chapter menu.

3. Select Double from the Paper Type & Dimension options on the PAGE LAYOUT dialog box. Click OK.

4. Choose the To Print command from the File menu. Select the pages you want to print and the paper tray containing letter-size paper. Then click OK.

5. Click Shrink from the dialog box that appears asking how to print this oversized sheet on the paper you have loaded.

If you want to reduce a letter-size document 50 percent, follow the preceding steps but change the Paper Type & Dimension option to Broad Sheet. After printing, use either the Abandon command from the File menu or the Page Size & Layout command to change the Paper Type & Dimension option back to Letter.

Changing the Views of a Page

The View menu lists keyboard shortcuts and four different views that you can use on any page:

Facing Pages view	Facing Pages view is available only if Double is chosen on the PAGE LAYOUT dialog box from the Chapter menu. This view allows you to look at two pages that face each other when printed. If you have used the Options menu to specify that type is to be greeked, the screen is redrawn faster.
Reduced view	Reduced view allows you to view the placement of elements on one page.

Normal view	Normal view gives you an actual-size view of the page that represents type sizes as they appear when printed. This view is the most accurate.
Enlarged view	Enlarged view gives you a double-size view of the page. This view is used for precise placing of frames, editing text, and viewing pictures.

The View menu also gives the keyboard shortcuts for each view.

Efficiency Tip

Reducing Screen Redrawing Time

If you use Reduced view or Facing Pages view, redrawing time decreases. Generally, however, you cannot use these views for editing. The more faces you choose to be greeked on-screen (using the Set Preferences command from the Options menu), the faster the screen is redrawn.

If you have imported graphics into your file, use the Hide Pictures command from the Options menu, unless you are positioning the graphics. Gray screened lines appear rather than the graphic, and redrawing time is greatly reduced. You may hide selected pictures or all pictures in a chapter. To see only one picture, select Hide All Pictures, select the one you want to see, and choose Show All Pictures. Only the selected picture appears.

Efficiency Tip

Zooming an Area into View

While you are reviewing a chapter in the Reduced view or Facing Pages view, you can use the mouse to zoom a particular area into a larger view. Position the Frame, Paragraph, Edit, or Graphic cursor over the area you want to enlarge and press Ctrl-N or Ctrl-E to zoom the area in Normal or Enlarged view, respectively.

Turning Pages

You can move from page to page in a chapter file when you press the PgUp and PgDn keys. Press Home to turn to the first page or press End to turn to the last page in a chapter. The Go to Page command from the Chapter menu offers the fastest way to turn to specific page numbers. When you select this command (or press Ctrl-G), the GO TO PAGE dialog box opens with the cursor positioned by the Selected Page option so that you can type the page number you want (see fig. 7.21). Ventura defaults to fill the Selected Page value with the current page value. Be sure to overstrike both numbers if you are turning to a page starting with a number different from the selected page's number. You can stop pages from turning by pressing the Esc key.

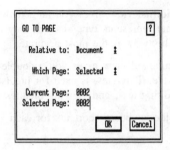

Fig. 7.21.

*The GO TO PAGE
dialog box.*

In a multiple-file document, you can choose Relative to: File, and the page you select is relative to that file only. Before you choose the Go to Page command from the menu, you must select a frame containing the article you want. Then select the Go to Page command and click one of the Which Page options to turn to the desired pages of the selected file.

Efficiency Tip

Turn Pages Faster by Going from Last Page to First Page

Go to Page turns pages faster when moving backward than when moving forward. When making changes on a large document, begin at the last page and use Go to Page to move to the next page that needs editing. After all changes, choose Reduced view, set all text to greek except the heading size (for reference), and use PgDn to scan all pages in the file before printing.

Using Nonprinting Guides

Nonprinting guides include all the various dotted and dashed lines that appear on-screen but not on the printed page. (Some monitors may not show these lines correctly.) These guides include page margins and column guides (see fig. 7.22). The column and margin guides show only on base pages and not on frames drawn on the pages. The horizontal lines shown in figure 7.22 represent the invisible grid Ventura establishes to align the baselines of text. To align frames on this horizontal grid, click Turn Line Snap On from the Options menu. These guides also include the *ruler guides*, dotted lines in the ruler area showing the cursor position. You also can move the ruler's zero point from the left margin to any position on the page. For more information on the zero point, see "Changing the Zero Point" later in this chapter.

Ruler guides are useful for positioning objects on a page. Ruler guides do not affect the width of text (as column guides do) or the length of text (as the bottom page margin does).

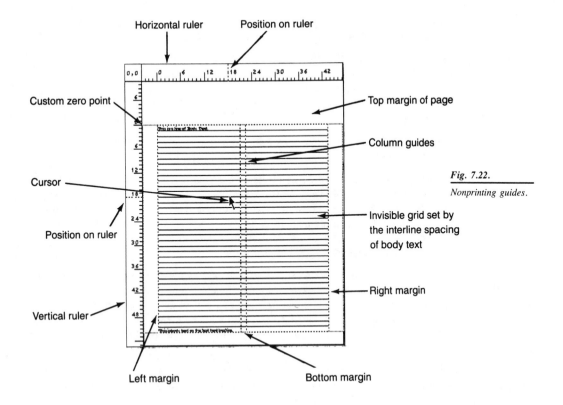

Horizontal ruler   Position on ruler

Custom zero point

Top margin of page

Column guides

Cursor

Fig. 7.22.

Nonprinting guides.

Position on ruler

Invisible grid set by
the interline spacing
of body text

Right margin

Vertical ruler

Left margin   Bottom margin

Using Column Snap and Line Snap

Ventura offers four grids (although three of the grids have only a single dimension) to help control the placement of elements on the page. Only two of the grids are ever displayed in the work area, although the effect of each grid is obvious when you enable the appropriate commands.

The Body Text and Box Text tags establish independent baselines for the alignment of text. Body Text aligns text on the page, and Box Text aligns text placed in boxes added with the Graphic box text tool. Both of these grids remain invisible throughout production. The effect of either grid is seen when you use the Turn Line Snap On command from the Options menu.

The alignment of text within a box of text drawn with the Graphic box text tool depends on the Box Text tag's line-spacing value. Activate the Show Generated Tags command in the Options menu to see this tag in the sidebar. If the box text must align on the same baselines as text on the pages or in other frames, make box text line-spacing values an even multiple of body text line-spacing values.

Use the Turn Column Snap On command from the Options menu when you want to align frames along column boundaries as you add the frames. When this command is enabled, the frame snaps into position on the closest vertical column guide. Frames already in place do not snap to the column guides unless you select and move the frames with the crossbar cursor.

Use the Turn Line Snap On command to line up frames vertically in increments of the line spacing set for body text. This feature is extremely useful when you want to align objects quickly and precisely, especially when you are working in Reduced view or Facing Pages view.

Sometimes, you may prefer to work with both snap effects turned off. For example, when you want to position frames freely without regard for the grids.

Ventura-drawn graphics can be controlled by a grid that is inactive by default. You can set separate units of measure for horizontal and vertical elements forming the crosshatch grid. You may choose to establish only a horizontal or only a vertical grid by setting the other measurement to zero. When you turn off the grid settings, the measurements remain set but are inactive until you turn on the grid settings. Each frame can have independent graphic grid settings.

The graphic grid is the only crosshatch grid feature available in Ventura. The graphic grid is enabled when you click the Graphic function and then open the GRID SETTINGS dialog box from the Graphic menu. You can enable the grid before you draw graphics to control precisely the size and position of each element. You may choose to enable the grid after you draw the graphics and move the graphics into positions on the grid.

You can draw a perfect square or circle by pressing the Alt key while drawing with the Graphic tools. To control the size, you can enter the width (or diameter) as the horizontal setting on the graphic grid. The grid setting controls the size of the graphic, and the Alt key ensures that the graphic will be perfectly square or round. The graphic grid, however, is disabled while you use the Alt key. To overcome this problem, draw the graphic to size using the graphic grid; then hold down the Alt key and click the lower right handle on the graphic. The graphic will snap to perfect proportions.

The invisible graphic grid begins at the edge of the page as defined by the Upper Left X, Upper Left Y, Frame Height, and Frame Width settings in the SIZING & SCALING dialog box for the active frame. You can set several alternative grids for the same page by adding frames to establish different grid settings. For more information on the graphic grid, see Chapter 6.

Efficiency Tip

Using Margin and Column Guides as Visible Grids To Design Display Ads, Forms, and Charts

Set margins, columns, and gutters for the page to create a grid you can see as you create a complex layout. Frames align along the column guides if you choose Turn Column Snap On, but graphic shapes and box text do not. Turn on the graphic grid to align graphics and box text. Remember, with frames you can use the SIZING & SCALING dialog box to size frames precisely, but you cannot set a default for all frame backgrounds or ruling lines. By contrast, each graphic tool can have a default line and fill pattern. Boxed and framed text can be tagged to align vertically at the top, middle, or bottom of each area. When you no longer need to see the page grid, click Hide Column Guides to clean up the view.

Using the Rulers To Position Objects

With the Show/Hide Rulers command from the Options menu, you can show or hide the horizontal and vertical rulers at the top and left of the screen. You use these rulers to help place frames and graphics on a page or to check the measurement of a placement. Select Show Rulers to display the rulers when they are hidden. When you click the command, it toggles between Show and Hide.

The on-screen position of the pointer or of an object being moved is indicated by dotted markers on the rulers (see fig. 7.23). These markers can be especially helpful when you align objects or draw a frame or graphic to exact size. As you saw in Chapter 6, you also can use the GRID SETTINGS dialog box to create Ventura-drawn graphics of uniform sizes using the rulers.

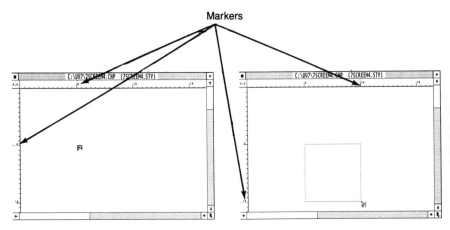

Markers

Fig. 7.23.

Markers on the rulers showing position and size of elements.

The following sections explain how to choose the unit of measure and how to change the zero point for the rulers.

Choosing the Unit of Measure

The Set Ruler command from the Options menu lets you set which unit of measure is displayed on the rulers. You may choose to work with one unit of measure throughout the production, or you may want to switch among the different measures as you open various dialog boxes. For example, if you use picas to set margins, columns, and indent specifications, set the ruler to Picas to check the alignment of text. When you want to check the position of a frame on the page, set the ruler to Inches and set the measurement in the Frame menu's SIZING & SCALING dialog box to inches.

The increments displayed along the rulers vary, depending on the size of the page layout and the active view: Facing Pages, Reduced, Normal, and Enlarged. The rulers show finer increments of measure in the Enlarged view than in the Reduced view.

Changing the Zero Point

The *zero point* is where the top and left rulers intersect and begin measurement. The zero point is at the top left corner of the page in all views. Before you can change the zero point, the rulers must be visible. If the rulers are not visible, click Show Rulers from the Options menu.

You can change the zero point in one of two ways: you can enter the exact position in the SET RULERS dialog box, or you can click the 0,0 in the box at the upper left corner of the work area. Drag the mouse and zero point to the new zero-point location on the page (the dotted-line markers on the rulers help you position the zero point). The measures on the rulers then shift to the new zero point, as shown in figure 7.24.

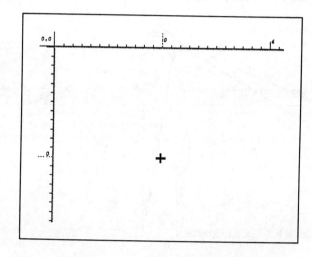

Fig. 7.24.

The measures on the rulers shifted to the new point.

When you move the zero point on one page, the new position appears on every page of the publication.

Efficiency Tip

When To Move the Zero Point

When you want to measure the size of an object or area, move the zero point. When you want to set tabs, move the zero point to the edge of the frame because tab positions are set relative to the distance from the edge of the frame. Because the ruler counts both left and right from the zero point, you can center objects in a frame quickly by changing the zero point to the exact center of the frame. When you want to position an object relative to other objects on the page, keep the zero point at the top left corner of the page.

Fitting Copy

Chapters 4 and 5 explain how to place text on pages and change the format or type specifications. However, these chapters did not tell you how to make the text actually fit the space allowed. During the page-layout process, you will find that copy fitting can be a major problem. What do you do when the text for a 4-page newsletter runs to 4.5 pages? How do you make a table of numbers fit a defined area on the page? How can you force two columns to bottom out at the same measure when the columns consist of different text sizes? The best way is to estimate the number of characters before you load text into Ventura. (Chapter 9 explains two methods of estimating characters.)

To fit copy into a column or onto a defined number of pages when you cannot edit the copy, you can change the length of the text in a column, using any of the following techniques:

- Change the margins.

- Change the column widths.

- Change the gutter width.

- Make the frames smaller or larger.

The most direct methods that you can use are to change the margins of the page or resize the frame. For example, if the text of a four-page price list is two to three lines too long, you might decide to add one line of text to each column by decreasing the bottom margin measurement or by dragging the frame handles to extend below the bottom page margin.

If you have strict standards about making text meet the bottom margins or your extra text is too long to make fit by extending the bottom margin, you may need to use one of the approaches described next. Remember, however, that if you set the widows and orphans at any value other than 1, as described earlier in this chapter, you must always visually review a publication to see whether an unacceptable amount of blank space has been left at the base of a column.

One way for you to change the amount of space that the text occupies is to change the text width, set by the margins and columns (setting margin and column measurements is described earlier in this chapter). This technique is fine for copy fitting when you use Ventura to establish design specifications or when you have to make copy fit on a certain number of pages. For publications that must match precise design specifications, however, changing the width or size of the text is the least accepted method of fitting copy.

A better approach is to change the Inter-Line (or *leading*) option in the SPACING dialog box from the Paragraph menu. Ventura allows you to alter the interline spacing in fractional points that are not noticeable to the naked eye but can make several lines' difference in copy that fits on a page. If you use small increments, this method is the least disruptive to the basic design of publications that are single-sided and formatted in a single column. Changing the value of interline spacing without regard for the baseline grid, however, results in an unbalanced alignment of text placed on multiple-column or facing pages.

If changing Inter-Line spacing does not shorten text enough and you have a Post-Script printer, you can decrease point sizes in half-point increments. For instance, you can change 10-point Body Text to 9.5-point, using the FONT dialog box from the Paragraph menu. The difference in size probably will be unnoticeable, and it allows you to reduce other settings on the Paragraph menu. Reduce line spacing settings in the SPACING dialog box by fractional points and increase the Tracking setting in the TYPOGRAPHY SETTINGS dialog box by one-hundredths.

Efficiency Tip

Change Leading To Fit Copy in Single-Column Formats

To change the leading in a chapter, first select a paragraph of body text with the Paragraph cursor and then choose the Spacing command from the Paragraph menu. Change the Inter-Line spacing option to affect the amount of space within a paragraph; change the Inter-Paragraph measurement to affect the amount of space left between consecutive paragraphs formatted with the same tag names. You also can change the spacing in the Above and Below options.

If you are trying to fit a table of tabbed entries into a space of a specific width, you can change the tabs and, if necessary, the type size. To fit a tabbed table into a space of a set length, you can adjust the leading or space between similar paragraphs, as described previously.

Copy fitting in multiple-column and facing-pages layout usually requires that you employ techniques other than adjusting margins and line spacing. You should change spacing values for a tag as a copy-fitting aid only when you are careful to keep all the tag's values equal to a multiple of the body text's line spacing. Remember that the frame's top and bottom margins, as well as the overall height of ruling lines, also affect the position of a paragraph on the page relative to the baseline established by the Body Text tag.

In both multiple-column and single-column layouts, you can adjust the tracking controls in the TYPOGRAPHY SETTINGS dialog box from the Paragraph menu. This feature controls the space between letters and should be adjusted only in fine increments. A change to tighter tracking of one-third of an em can lessen the number of lines in a paragraph. You may want to adjust tracking in a tag used to format only those paragraphs where copy fitting is a problem. When you want to make a long document fit a specific number of pages, experiment with tighter or looser tracking for the Body Text tag. For more information on the use of the TYPOGRAPHY SETTINGS dialog box, see Chapters 5 and 9.

Another technique you can use to control copy fitting in multiple-column projects involves adding space. When you don't have enough copy to fill a page, consider adding a quotation in a frame to complement the design of the page. When you have a small amount of space to fill, you can add white space on the page in two ways:

- Add a new tag and paragraph with a value equal to the amount of space you want to add. Using this technique is the same as adding two carriage returns with a typewriter to produce double-spaced text.

- Add a blank frame, choosing Flow Text Around: On option in the SIZING & SCALING dialog box.

White space is an important component in the design of a page. Both preceding techniques add white space for fine-tuning adjustments and should not be used until the final copy-editing stages. You should use Ventura's horizontal and vertical paragraph-spacing values, frame padding, and frame and page margins and columns to establish settings that can prevail throughout the production process to make the design consistent and the layout process expedient.

Changing point size and spacing settings to make copy fit is a tedious process that may cause lines in different columns to be placed at slightly different positions and therefore look unbalanced on the page. For suggestions on how to fit copy before the page-layout stage, see the discussion of fitting copy in Chapter 9.

Using the Clipboard To Reposition Text and Graphics

You can use the Edit menu's commands to cut, copy, and paste text and graphics as you develop a chapter. These commands affect only the items (whether text, graphic, or framed areas) selected at the time you invoke the command. As with all the menus and dialog boxes, you cannot choose the commands in gray. Ventura prompts you if you inappropriately try to use one of the shortcuts to the Clipboard commands.

In Chapters 3 through 6, you learned how to select and edit text and graphics. The steps are summarized again here because they are an integral part of the page-layout process. You can select groups of frames that include both text and graphics by holding the Shift key as you click the pointer on several frames.

Selecting Frames with the Pointer Tool

You select frames with the Frame cursor, text with the Text I-beam, and graphics with the Graphic pointer. When you want to select a framed collection of text and graphics, you need only to select the frame. Once you have made a selection, you can cut to remove the selection, copy to make a copy of the selection for use, or paste the selection into place.

Use one of the following techniques to select and deselect desired frames:

- Put the Frame cursor over the desired frame and click once to select the frame. If the handles do not display as expected, the object may be overlaid by other frames. You can select frames below the top layer by holding the Ctrl key as you click. For more than two layers, continue holding the Ctrl key and clicking until the desired graphic is selected. Remember that *all* frames and graphics attached to a frame move with that frame.

- Hold the Shift key as you click several different frames, one at a time. Using this procedure, you may select more than one frame from the same page at a time; the frames do not have to be adjacent.

- To deselect an object from a selected group of frames, hold the Shift key and click that object.

- To select graphics, first select the graphic control frame and then press Ctrl-Q to select all the graphics attached to that frame. (The graphic control frame is the frame that was active when you chose the Graphic function and then used the Graphic tools.) You can deselect from the selected set by pressing Shift and clicking on a selected graphic. You use the Send to Back or Bring to Front commands from the Graphic menu to ''dig out'' objects drawn with the Graphic tools, as described in ''Layering Graphics,'' in this chapter.

Selecting Text with the Text Tool

To select text with the Text tool, place the Text I-beam immediately preceding the first character in the desired selection, click and hold the mouse button, and drag to the end of the desired selection before you release the mouse button. Alternatively, you can place the cursor to the left of the first character, click the character, move to the right of the last character, and then press Shift and click. The selected text is displayed in reverse video.

Reversing All Changes Made since the Last Save

A good reason exists to save your work after you reach a point where you are pleased with the results. After you save, you can use the File menu Abandon command to undo unsuccessful experiments. Before you experiment with a change to the design of text, graphics, tags, or pages, click the Save command from the File menu. Then experiment. If you don't like the results, you can click the Abandon command and then OK to go back to the last point saved. If you have not used the Save or the Save As commands since the last time you used the Open Chapter command, you restore the publication to the condition it was in before you opened it.

You can save your backup files by using the Set Preferences command from the Options menu. Click the Keep Backup Files: Yes option from the SET PREFER-ENCES dialog box. Ventura saves the last copies of the style file, chapter, and source files with the same names, except the first character of each file's extension changes to a dollar sign ($). Think of these backups as production backups that allow you to find the last generation of a file if a power or equipment failure occurs during production. (See Chapter 3 for information on how to archive publications from the fixed disk to ·floppy disks and for information on how to set up directories and back up publications for various types of projects.)

Efficiency Tip

Use the Save and Abandon Commands

Save your documents often while you are working. Doing so enables you to use the Abandon command to reverse your most recent changes. You can use the Ctrl-S shortcut to save the file quickly.

Using Cut, Copy, Paste, and the Backspace Key

The Cut, Copy, and Paste commands from the Edit menu affect all the frames and graphics selected with the pointer tool or the phrases of text selected with the Text I-beam.

Both the Cut (or the Del key) and Copy (or Shift-Del) commands put the selected frame, text, or graphic on the Frame, Text, or Graphic Clipboard. These clipboards are storage areas; the contents are not visible. The Cut command removes the selected frame or text from the page. The Copy command leaves the frame or text on the page and puts a copy of the selected area on the appropriate Clipboard. The Clipboards are temporary storage areas that are active while you are working; the contents of the Clipboards are overwritten the next time you use the Cut or Copy command. All the Clipboards are erased when you leave Ventura.

When you use the Cut or Copy command and inadvertently lose Clipboard contents that you needed to keep, you can retrieve the lost Clipboard contents only by invoking the Abandon command. This command reloads the file as it looked when you last used the Save command. If you save your file frequently, you won't have to redo many of the changes you made.

The Clipboards remain active throughout each Ventura session. For example, suppose that you use the Graphic function to draw something. Then you copy the graphic to the Graphic Clipboard and open another publication without leaving Ventura. With the Paste command, you can pull the graphic from the Clipboard onto the page in the new publication.

Efficiency Tip

Preserving the Clipboard Contents

When you specifically do not want to replace the contents of the Text Clipboard, position the Text cursor and use the backspace key to delete text. If you do not mind that text on the Clipboard is overwritten, use the Cut command and let the Clipboard serve as a temporary backup for later retrieval of the objects.

Retrieving Objects with the Paste Command

With the Paste command (or the Ins key), you can retrieve what you last cut or copied to the Clipboard and place the contents on the page. Ventura pastes from the Text Clipboard if the Text function is activated, from the Frame Clipboard if the Frame function is activated, and from the Graphic Clipboard if the Graphic function is activated. To paste from the Text Clipboard, activate the Text function, position the Text cursor where the text should appear, click once to activate the cursor, and press the Ins key. To paste from the Frame or Graphic Clipboard, select the Frame or Graphic function and press the Ins key. The frame or graphic is inserted on the new page at the same position it occupied on the page before cutting. You can move the object anywhere on the new page.

When objects are first pasted onto the page, the objects remain selected. That is, you can see the handles of the pasted graphics and text. If you are pasting a group of objects, you can move the objects as a group by dragging the entire selection immediately after pasting it onto the page. If you click the pointer off the selection, the pasted object is no longer selected.

You can use the Paste command to move selected objects from page to page or from chapter to chapter if you complete the related cut-and-paste operation before you quit Ventura. To move graphics or text from another program into Ventura, you must use the Load Text/Picture command. If you have copied the Windows Clipboard converter, CLIP2VP.EXE, from the Ventura Utilities disk to the WINDOWS directory, you can use the Windows option under Line-Art Format in the LOAD/TEXT PICTURE dialog box. This option allows you to load Windows metafile pictures (WMF) created from any Windows application that places line art metafiles on the Windows Clipboard. (See Appendix G of the *Xerox Ventura Publisher Reference Guide*.)

Efficiency Tip

Making a Visible Clipboard on the Last Page of a Chapter

You can ensure consistency in a document by creating a page of examples and storing it as the last page of a chapter. As the production team needs one of these elements, they copy and paste it into position, resizing and editing if necessary. This page may contain line and fill attributes for graphics, a frame with an attached formatted caption, a text frame, or a frame for graphics with margins and padding (white space inside and outside) already set. Once all elements are placed in the chapter, use the Insert/Remove Page command to delete this last page.

Efficiency Tip

Sending Instructions and Callouts to the Production Team

When you want to convey comments or instructions to the production team, embed the comments in the source files and tag the paragraphs with a special tag name just for comments. You can set the comments apart with a larger point size, a color setting for the text, or with rules to draw attention to the comment as the pages are reviewed on-screen during production. Once the comment is dealt with, the production team selects the text and paragraph mark with the text cursor and then cuts the copy from the page.

Using tag names to identify paragraphs for cutting also enables you to embed in the source file any callout or caption you want to accompany the text. Instead of typing the copy into frames or box text graphics placed on the page, the production team can cut the text to the Clipboard and paste it to its new location.

Layering Graphics

Ventura is a three-dimensional system in a particular sense: in addition to placing objects next to each other, you can layer objects on top of each other. Usually, the first object placed in a series becomes the bottom layer; the last object is the top layer. You may often want to change the order of the layers; you can do so by using the Send to Back command and the Bring to Front commands from the Graphic menu. You also can work through the stack by pressing Ctrl and then clicking to select objects below the top object.

The Send to Back command sends a specific object to the bottom layer in a series. In figure 7.25, for example, the lighter oval is sent behind the darker oval. You can use this command to shade boxes in the background for a particular area. Chapter 6 illustrates how you can use this command and the Cut and Paste commands to create drop-shadowed boxes.

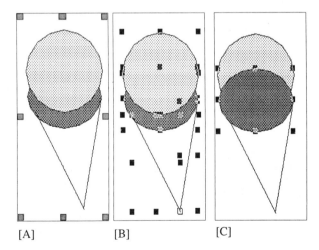

[A] [B] [C]

Fig. 7.25.

Using the Send to Back command.

The Bring to Front command makes a selected object come to the top layer, in front of any other unselected objects. When you arrange a series of objects, you may find this command a useful alternative to the Send to Back command.

The Bring to Front command is especially useful when you are dealing with more than two layers of objects. When only two objects are layered, you can select the top one by clicking it with the pointer. Then you use the Send to Back command to uncover the object below.

When you move frames or graphics, the text or graphic automatically becomes the top layer on that page. You may need to use the Send to Back command to return the text or graphic to the proper order, even though you did not use the Bring to Front command.

Chapter Summary

This chapter took you through the sequence of steps followed when building any publication with Ventura. You opened a new publication; set up the underlying elements and nonprinting margins, columns, and invisible grids; and used the guides and grids to arrange text and graphics on each page.

Chapters 3 through 7 present all the commands and steps required for a complete production cycle except for the printing and design processes. The next chapter explains the process of printing the publication. Part II offers basic guidelines to help you design your own publications, and Part III provides examples of publications that have been designed for efficient production, as well as for usefulness and pleasing appearance.

8

Printing

Your ultimate goal in the production process is to print your publication on a high-resolution printer. Sometimes this output becomes the distribution copy or copies. More often, the output becomes the camera-ready pages from which photocopying or offset printing equipment reproduces the document. Pages ready for black-and-white or color reproduction can be printed from computers equipped with Ventura and from computers connected to high-resolution printers that are not necessarily equipped with Ventura.

If you use only the fonts delivered with Ventura and a single printer, printing is a simple, straightforward procedure. You use the File menu to open the chapter and then select the To Print command, choosing the options you want. When you want to print more than one chapter at a time, you use the Options menu Multi-Chapter command and select the To Print command to choose the options you want.

In this chapter, you learn how to set the print options for a single chapter and how to print several chapters from a single print request. You learn how to test your printer's potential; you also learn how to select one type of printer for drafts and another printer for final copies. You see how the Device Name, Output To, and Width Table options in the SET PRINTER INFO dialog box are reflected in the File menu's PRINT INFORMATION dialog box. You also learn how to add and use new fonts and how to merge new font width tables with one of the width tables Ventura provides. Before you begin printing, you need to know the different printers and fonts installed on your system and the way to access them.

Knowing and Choosing Printers and Printer Fonts

The printing devices available for personal computers fall into six broad categories: character printers, plotters, dot-matrix printers, ink-jet printers, laser printers, and phototypesetters. Of these devices, only laser printers and phototypesetters are normally used for the final printing of a Ventura publication. One reason is that laser printers and phototypesetters can print at much higher resolutions than dot-matrix printers and ink-jet printers.

The term *laser* is not the distinguishing feature between laser printers and phototypesetters; typesetters also use laser technology to create the image on the drum. The

323

primary difference between laser printers and phototypesetters is the method used to lay the image on the paper. Laser printers work the way most photocopiers work. The laser printer places electrostatic charges on a drum, the charges are transferred to the paper, and the paper picks up black (or color) toner in the pattern of the charges. Phototypesetters also lay a pattern of charges on the paper, but the image is set on photosensitive paper and then developed by a chemical process.

Understanding the Two Kinds of Fonts

Ventura's capability to use two kinds of fonts—bit-mapped and outline—increases your choices of printers and fonts. Printers using bit-mapped fonts use a printer control language to interpret the instructions for each font. Outline (or curve-fitting) fonts, on the other hand, are formed and scaled by applying a mathematical formula to the typeface outline. An illustration of each type of font is included in Chapter 9.

Bit-mapped fonts are used for screen and printer fonts. Characters are stored as a pattern of dots (bits) for each size, style, and orientation available. Each combination is saved in a separate font file and displays and prints solid characters. If you create a document using Times Roman Medium in four different sizes, for example, you use four fonts. Printers such as the Hewlett-Packard LaserJet Plus, LaserJet II, and Laser-Jet 2000 can use bit-mapped fonts downloaded to the printer before or during a Ventura session. Bit-mapped fonts take up more memory because each dot of a character, rather than just the outline, is described.

Outline fonts are just that—font outlines that the printer interprets and prints as solid or hollow shapes. The character is formed from that outline at print time, making these fonts more flexible than bit-mapped fonts. Many PostScript printers maintain several typeface outlines as resident fonts because outline fonts consume less space than bit-mapped fonts. You can add to your system outline printer and screen fonts that are compatible with both PostScript and non-PostScript printers.

With both font types, each letter printed on the page is created by a series of individual dots. Typesetters print more dots per inch than do laser or dot-matrix printers and therefore have higher resolution. Projects undertaken with Ventura can be printed on dot-matrix, PostScript, and Interpress™ printers and typesetters, including the following:

- Apple LaserWriter, LaserWriter® Plus, and other PostScript printers including TI Omnilaser, DEC Print Server 40, IBM 4216, QMS PS 800, 1200, and 2400 laser printers

- Allied Linotronic 100, 200, and 300 typesetters

- Compugraphic 9400-PS

- Varityper 4200P and 4300P

- Hewlett-Packard LaserJet, LaserJet Plus, LaserJet II, and LaserJet 2000 laser printers

- Xerox 4045 laser printer

- Printers compatible with the JLaser board

- AST TurboLaser, Cordata, NEC, Printware, Tegra, and other laser printers

- Interpress 2.0 printers including the Xerox 4050, 8700, and 9700 printers

- Epson, IBM ProPrinter, and Toshiba dot-matrix printers

- Xerox 4020 color ink jet printer

The Appendix of this book provides a list of product names and company addresses. New printing products offering faster throughput, higher resolution, color originals, and larger selections of typefaces are continually becoming available.

Before designing publications with Ventura, you should become familiar with the capabilities of your printer. Not every printer can take advantage of all Ventura's features (for example, reverse type, white lines, transparent overlapping images, rotated text, gray characters, and gray scale illustration). Some printers produce higher-resolution graphics and text than other printers. The list of fonts available with printers also varies. Generally, you should design your publications with the final-copy printer in mind.

Deciding about Installed Printers

Different types of printers have different capabilities. Interpress printers, for example, can print very close to the edge of a page, but other printers leave at least .25 inch of white space around the edge of the paper. With some printers, you may need to adjust the Paragraph menu's Spacing Above and Below options for headers and footers in sample chapter files to position headers and footers within the image area for the printer. Other printers may require that you adjust frame margins and columns to center a page within the image area. Many laser and dot-matrix printers do not support printing white text on black backgrounds and cannot obscure an element by covering it with an opaque shape. PostScript printers support both these features but cannot print transparent overlapping graphic shapes. The graphic on the bottom will always be obscured.

Efficiency Tip

Know Your Printer's Capabilities

Print the file CAPABILI.CHP, from the TYPESET directory, to check your printer's capabilities. CAPABILI.CHP is a one-page chapter that shows whether fill patterns and graphics are transparent, which font sizes are available, and how close your printer prints to the paper's edge. If you have more than one printer available, select an alternative using the Device Name option in the SET PRINTER INFO dialog box. To select the width table for that printer, click Load Different Width Table in the same dialog box, and Ventura will display a list of width tables in the ITEM SELECTOR dialog box. (See "Using the SET PRINTER INFO dialog box" in this chapter.)

Appendix F of the *Xerox Ventura Publisher Reference Guide* includes a summary of the features and limitations of several Ventura-compatible printers, along with special installation and cabling recommendations.

PostScript printers print shapes, lines, and text in shades of gray, as well as outlined and rotated text. When you use a PostScript printer to print CAPABILI.CHP as described in the preceding tip, the Colored Text options print in shades of gray if the default prologue is used. If Ventura's alternative PostScript prologue, PS2.EFF, is used, however, the printed Colored Text results look different, as explained in the following paragraph.

Ventura sends the PostScript prologue (PS2.PRE), stored in the VENTURA directory, to the printer before printing a file. If the alternative PostScript prologue, PS2.EFF, is named PS2.PRE in the VENTURA directory, fonts tagged as the colors yellow and cyan print as rotated text, magenta prints as outlined text, and green prints as shaded text. None of these options, however, will appear as such on the screen. Adding the alternative prologue provided by Ventura is discussed in the Efficiency Tip "Printing Typeface Outlines" in Chapter 9. You do not have to use the alternative prologue to rotate text, however, because Text Rotation is an option in the ALIGNMENT dialog box.

By comparison, non-PostScript printers do not print text or graphic lines in shades of gray and cannot use the ALIGNMENT dialog box's Text Rotation option or font colors to print rotated or outlined text. Another distinction between PostScript and non-PostScript printers is the capability of PostScript printers to increment characters in half points and set custom point sizes. Non-PostScript printers print only the discrete point sizes listed in the FONT SETTINGS dialog boxes.

You can install up to six printers with Ventura. You need install only one of each type listed at the beginning of this chapter. During installation, the printer driver and font files are copied from the floppy disk to the hard disk. (A *driver* is software that translates information sent from your computer into a form the printer can recognize.) Ventura comes with many printer drivers, which are listed as options when you run the VPPREP program provided on the Application disk.

Make sure that you first install the type of printer you intend to use for final printing. Then install the draft printers or printers that are not used as often. The first printer installed is more important than the others because Ventura copies that printer's width table as a new file called OUTPUT.WID. OUTPUT.WID is the default width table Ventura uses. You can change the Width Table option with Load Different Width Table in the SET PRINTER INFO dialog box. When the width table matches the printer you select, the SET PRINTER INFO dialog box shows Ultimate as the print quality. If the width table does not match the type of printer, the word Draft displays at the top of the dialog box (see fig. 8.1).

Choosing High or Low Resolution

One difference among printers is the resolution in which they print. *Resolution* is a measure of the density in which text and graphics are printed and is usually specified in dots per inch (dpi). Many laser printers print 300 dpi, and a few are capable of printing 600 to 1,000 dpi. This resolution is high compared to 9-pin dot-matrix printers, which print 120-by-144 dots per inch (24-pin printers like the IBM ProPrinter print 180-by-180 dpi). Typesetting equipment, however, prints 1,200 or 2,400 dpi.

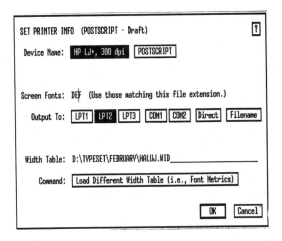

```
SET PRINTER INFO (POSTSCRIPT · Draft)                        [?]
Device Name:  [HP LJ+, 300 dpi] [POSTSCRIPT]


Screen Fonts: DEF  (Use those matching this file extension.)
   Output To:  [LPT1] [LPT2] [LPT3] [COM1] [COM2] [Direct] [Filename]


Width Table:  D:\TYPESET\FEBRUARY\HALIJ.WID_____

   Command:   [Load Different Width Table (i.e., Font Metrics)]


                                          [OK] [Cancel]
```

Fig. 8.1.

The SET PRINTER INFO dialog box with Draft *displayed.*

The higher the resolution, the smoother the appearance of the edges of text and graphics. The lower the resolution, the greater the jaggedness of the edges. Some printers have a range of resolution settings, as shown in table 8.1. Most printers can print pages of text at higher resolutions but may encounter problems when an inadequate amount of printer memory is available for printing graphics or mixing several fonts on a page. Choosing a lower-resolution printer driver impairs the resolution of bit-mapped fonts, but the trade-off may be necessary for selected pages. You also can make pages less complex to avoid printer memory errors by disabling kerning, letter spacing, and tracking and by using fewer variations in fonts or fewer and smaller graphics.

Table 8.1
Resolutions of Apple, HP, and Linotronic Printers

Printer	Resolution Settings
LaserJet	Pictures and graphics at 75 dpi; text at 300 dpi
LaserJet Plus	150 or 300 dpi
Linotronic 100	1,200, 900, 600, or 300 dpi
Linotronic 300	635, 1,270, or 2,540 dpi
Compugraphic 9400-PS	2,400 dpi
Varityper 4200P	1,200 dpi
Varityper 4300P	1,200 or 2,400 dpi

For HP LaserJet series printers and the Xerox 4045, you can install 150- and 300-dpi printer drivers to help overcome printer memory limitations. You add the alternative printer drivers using the VPPREP program provided on the Ventura Application disk.

Using Built-in Fonts

Another major difference among printers is the number of built-in fonts. As described in Chapter 9, some printers have no built-in fonts, and others offer only a few. A font that is built into the printer is always available and is listed as a Resident font in the ADD/REMOVE FONTS dialog box. Resident fonts speed the printing process but require printers to have enough memory to store the individual font files. The Post-Script width table contains font information for additional typeface families, which you can purchase. Therefore, if you have a PostScript printer you may have more fonts listed as Resident on the ADD/REMOVE FONTS dialog box than your printer actually supports.

When you select a typeface that is not resident on your printer, Ventura changes the word at the bottom of the Style list box in the ADD/REMOVE FONTS dialog box from Resident to Download to indicate that the font must be downloaded (sent) to the printer during the printing process. Downloading during printing leaves the maximum amount of printer memory available for processing but increases the printing time. Later in this chapter you learn how to add fonts and download fonts to the printer before you start Ventura.

The standard HP LaserJet printer has one built-in font (12-point Courier). If the Hewlett-Packard F cartridge is loaded in the printer and the HPF.WID table is named as the source width table, you can also use Dutch and Swiss in a selection of sizes (see table 8.2). The characters printed are a subset of the international character set delivered with Ventura. You can print the CHARSET.CHP file from the TYPESET directory to see which Alt key and numeric-keypad combinations create symbols supported by the standard HP LaserJet printer. The symbol character set supported by most other printers is not included on the F cartridge.

With the HP LaserJet Plus and Series II printers, Ventura downloads four typefaces in a variety of sizes and styles. More faces, sizes, and styles may be downloaded if the printer has adequate memory. The Apple LaserWriter also has four resident typefaces, although each typeface is available in any size between 1 and 254 points in a variety of styles (normal, boldface, italic, and boldface italic). (See the Efficiency Tip "Making PostScript Fonts Print Larger than 254 Points," in this chapter, to learn how to make Ventura print PostScript fonts larger than 254 points.) Seven additional typefaces are built in as resident fonts on the LaserWriter Plus and many other PostScript printers.

For each printer, Ventura includes three typefaces with which you can print the international character set delivered with the program. The character set is made up of all the letters and numbers you can type from the keyboard and also includes many special characters and symbols made when you type three digits from the numeric keypad while holding down the Alt key. Serif (Dutch or Times), sans serif (Swiss or Helvetica), and Courier (nonproportional) typefaces are available in a selection of sizes and styles (see table 8.2).

Table 8.2
Built-In Printer Fonts

Printer	Fonts and Sizes
PostScript printers	Times, Helvetica, Courier, and Symbol (all sizes, several styles)
Advanced PostScript printers Linotronic 100, 200, & 300	Times, Helvetica, Courier, Symbol, Avant Garde, Bookman, New Century Schoolbook, Helvetica Narrow, Palatino, Zapf Chancery, and Zapf Dingbats (all sizes, several styles)
Compugraphic 9400-PS	Includes 73 fonts
Varityper 4200P and 4300P	Includes 35 fonts
LaserJet Cartridge F	Dutch 8 and 10 normal Swiss 14 bold Courier 12 normal
LaserJet Plus Series II, & Series 2000	Courier 10 medium, bold; and 12 normal, medium Swiss 6 normal Swiss and Dutch 8, 10, 12 normal; 10, 12 bold, normal italic; and 12, 14, 18 and bold Symbol 10 normal
Color Ink Jet	Swiss and Dutch 8 and 10 normal; 10 bold, normal italic; 14 normal, bold, normal italic; and 18, 20, 28, 36 bold
Xerox 4045	Swiss 6 normal Swiss and Dutch 8, 10, 12 normal; 10 and 12 bold, normal italic; and 14, 18, 24 bold Courier 12 normal Symbol 10 normal
Interpress	Titan 10 normal, bold, normal italic, bold italic; and 12 normal, bold Modern 6, 8, 10, 12, 14, 18, 24, 30, 36 normal, bold, bold italic, normal italic Classic 6, 8, 10, 12, 14, 18, 24 normal, bold, normal italic Symbol 6, 8, 10, 12, 14, 18, 24 normal, bold, normal italic

Besides the international character set, Ventura provides another character set that is often referred to as the *mathematical*, or *symbol*, character set. To print these characters, Ventura provides the Symbol typeface to enable selected printers (see table 8.2) to print from this collection of Greek letters, pointing arrows, and other noncharacter symbols. Many models of PostScript printers also print the Dingbat typeface, which is another collection of bullets, icons, and other decorative symbols. Appendix E in *Xerox Ventura Publisher Reference Guide* includes a table of each of the character sets supported by Ventura.

Screen fonts are used to display on-screen the letters, numbers, and symbols seen on the printed page. The screen font files are different from the corresponding printer fonts because printers and monitors have different resolution capabilities. Most font foundries provide screen fonts compatible with CGA, EGA, and VGA monitors; but if a specific screen font is not loaded, Ventura substitutes one of the generic screen fonts loaded during program installation and scales the font to size during printing. In the case of the Zapf Dingbats typeface, Ventura displays a character from the international character set (unless you add screen fonts for Dingbats) but prints a Dingbat when you use an advanced PostScript printer. Having a screen font that matches the printer font is helpful for accuracy, especially when you use kerning or a unique typeface to achieve a particular effect. See Chapter 9 for more on matching screen fonts to printer fonts.

Using Downloadable Fonts

In addition to the fonts that come with your printer, you can add to your collection by buying *downloadable fonts* on floppy disks. These fonts are sometimes called *soft fonts* because they are not hard-coded into chips in the printer or into the printer font cartridge but are stored on your computer's hard disk. Downloadable fonts can be downloaded (sent) to your printer as you print or can be downloaded to the printer before you begin a Ventura session.

You can purchase downloadable fonts from printer manufacturers or software developers. Font vendors make both bit-mapped and outline fonts that are downloadable and Ventura-compatible. Adobe Systems is one of the primary sources for downloadable PostScript fonts. Bitstream® is another popular source of downloadable fonts for Hewlett-Packard, PostScript, and compatible printers. You can use downloadable fonts to add to the fonts supported by your printer, and you also can use downloadable fonts when you prepare files for printing from systems that do not have Ventura loaded. Refer to "Copying Fonts to Your Hard Disk" later in this chapter to add to the printer fonts provided with Ventura.

Using Commands That Affect Printing

Three Ventura commands from different menus play a significant role in printing. The Set Printer Info command from the Options menu provides options for changing the current printer, the width table, and the port. The Page Size & Layout command from the Chapter menu sets the orientation and page size for printing. The To Print command from the File menu governs the specifics of the printing operation, such as the number of copies printed, the starting page, and the range of pages. The following sections describe these commands more fully.

When you design and produce any publication, one of the first decisions you make is which printer and fonts to use for the final camera-ready pages. In many cases, you use the same printer for the entire production sequence, from early proofs to final masters. In fact, most installations probably use only one printer or one type of printer, even if more printers are available. As you progress with Ventura and undertake new types of projects, however, you are likely to want to add printer fonts and screen fonts to augment those delivered with Ventura or your printer.

Using the SET PRINTER INFO Dialog Box

You change the current printer selection, the width table, and the printer port in the SET PRINTER INFO dialog box opened from the Options menu (see fig. 8.2).

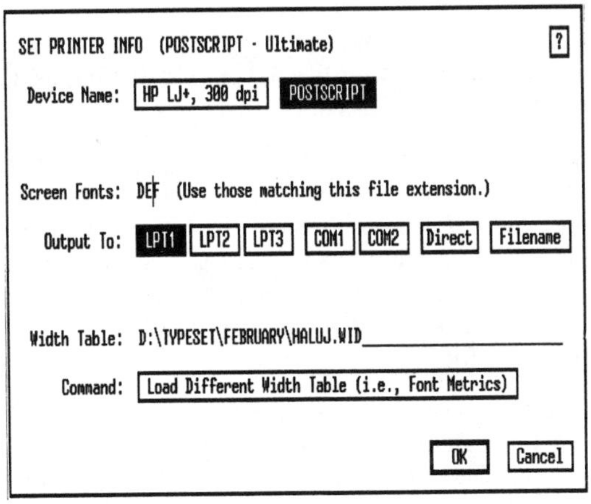

Fig. 8.2.

The SET PRINTER INFO dialog box with Ultimate *displayed.*

The Device Name option in this dialog box displays the currently selected printer and up to five other printer drivers installed on your system. When the Width Table named in the SET PRINTER INFO dialog box matches the printer selection in Device Name option, the word Ultimate displays after the name of the source width table (again see fig 8.2). Ultimate indicates that the shapes of characters on the page are formed by a width table that matches the fonts used by the named device. If the word Draft appears, the active width table does not match the targeted printer, and line and page endings are set according to the fonts used by a different type of printer.

Choosing the Output Printer

If your system has only one printer and Ventura's basic fonts, you never need to change the options in the SET PRINTER INFO dialog box. Ventura customizes the default options for the printer, port, width table, and screen fonts when you install the program. If your system has more than one type of printer, you change from one printer to another by using the Options menu's Set Printer Info command.

To select a different type of printer, choose an alternative from those listed after Device Name on the SET PRINTER INFO dialog box. When you change to another printer, you also must decide whether to load a version of that printer's width table or keep the one you have been using. Switching between different types of printers in the middle of a project to print proof copies is fine if you use the width table for the final printer. If you use the draft printer's width table for interim proof copies, line and page endings may differ from the final printing.

Choosing the Destination of the Output

When you change from one printer to another, Ventura highlights in the Output To option of the SET PRINTER INFO dialog box the port specified for that printer during installation. Typically, LPT1, LPT2, or LPT3 are parallel ports; COM1 and COM2 are serial ports. If your system has only one communications port but you use two different printers, you may need to change the cable connections each time you change printers.

Besides changing the specified port with the Output To option, you can choose one of the two other Output To options: Direct or Filename.

Direct refers to a direct cable connection, not a serial or parallel port. This option is used for the JLaser controller board, the AST TurboLaser, or the Cordata laser printer. These devices work off controller boards installed in your computer. Cables connect these controller boards directly to the printer. Ventura creates a bit map of each page and sends it directly to the printer. This technique delivers printed pages quickly but renders the Output To: Filename option inactive because each page in a chapter individually represents a 1M file.

If your Output To selection is Filename, Ventura sends the publication to a file rather than a printer. Before printing, Ventura displays a new screen, prompts you to name the file, and automatically adds the extension C00. If you use the Options menu's Multi-Chapter command to print to more than one file, the first file has the extension C01, the second C02, and so on. Printing to a file creates a very large file because all downloaded fonts are also placed in the file (see "Moving a Project to Another System for Printing" in this chapter).

Choosing the Printer Width Table

The width table you choose when working with a chapter file is stored with the style file. When you retrieve the chapter file, the style file looks for and uses that width table. The Set Printer Info command from the Options menu gives you the option to change width tables as you switch between printers or collections of printer fonts. See the Efficiency Tip "Printing Drafts on Laser and Matrix Printers" for instances when you do not want to change the width tables to match the printer you are using.

Ventura copies a width table to the VENTURA directory for each printer type installed. The width table assigns the space allowed for each alphabetic character, number, and symbol in a given font. Ventura uses the width table to decide all line endings, hyphenations, and page breaks. Always use the width tables for your *final* output device while you are in the page-review stages of production. Because the final device's width table is often used to print drafts, Ventura does not automatically load the matching width table when you choose a new printer.

Efficiency Tip

Printing Drafts on Laser and Dot-Matrix Printers

If you print drafts of a project on one type of printer and then switch to another for final printing, the line endings and page breaks will probably change. To avoid this, always use the width table for the final output device. When printing on the draft device, the characters will not match the final output but the line endings will.

Each font installed or added needs an entry in a width table (the WID files). Font vendors usually supply width tables that you merge with the width table Ventura provides for your printer. Chapter 9 discusses using as few fonts as possible for documents. For repetitive projects that use few fonts, create a new width table with just those fonts. Later in this chapter, you learn how to add and remove fonts from width tables and how to save new width tables.

Using the PAGE LAYOUT Dialog Box

The Page Size & Layout command from the Chapter menu opens a dialog box containing two options that directly affect printing: Orientation and Paper Type & Dimension (see fig 8.3). These options and the Sides and Start On options are usually set when you begin the page-layout process. Chapter 7 discusses the options fully, but the summary of the options that follows shows how the settings affect printing. Page layout options store as settings in the style file.

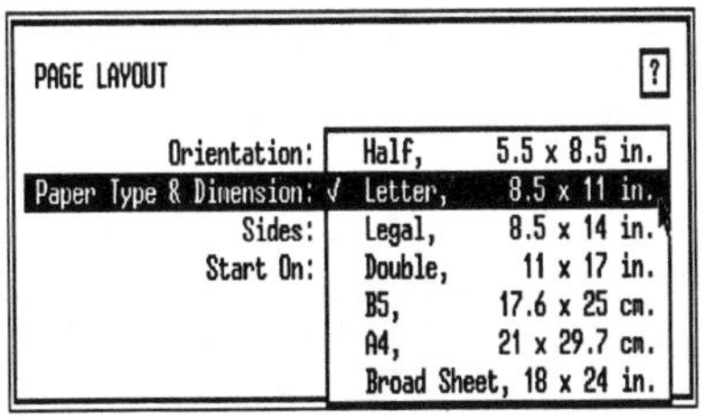

Fig. 8.3.

The PAGE LAYOUT dialog box with Paper Type & Dimension *open.*

Orientation determines whether the copy is positioned on paper that is narrower in width than length (portrait) or narrower in length than width (landscape). You can choose either Portrait or Landscape orientation for any Paper Type.

The Paper Type & Dimension option refers to the paper size. Half is half of letter size; Double is double letter size, and B5 and A4 are standard paper sizes in Europe. Broad Sheet refers to sheets larger than 11 by 14 (up to 18 by 24), which certain typesetters print in strips for paste-up. When you select a paper type, Ventura posts the dimensions of the paper type selected. See "Printing Parts of Oversized Pages" in this chapter for information about printing on paper smaller than the layout in the publisher's window.

The Sides option does not make your printer print on both sides of a page; it refers to whether a style file should be set for single or double (facing) pages. When a document is offset printed on both sides, the inside margin of each page should be larger than the outside margin to allow for drilling holes or binding. If you set Sides: Double, you save time by setting up the margins, headers, or footers for only one page. Ventura then "mirrors" these measurements for the facing page. To use the Facing Pages view to see more than one page at a time, you must set Sides: Double. (See Chapter 7 for other reasons for using Double.)

You use the Start On option to control the starting page. If you select double-sided pages, you can specify that the first page of the document be a left or a right page. Remember that odd-numbered pages should appear on the right page of publications with facing pages.

Printing a Chapter

If you use more than one printer or if you want to use fonts other than the built-in printer fonts, specify the desired printer and width table in the SET PRINTER INFO dialog box (described in previous sections of this chapter). You also use this dialog box to redirect printing from one communication port to another and to request Ventura to print a file to disk rather than to the printer. Once you have established the printer, port, and width table settings in the SET PRINTER INFO dialog box, use the File menu To Print command to initiate a print request for the chapter loaded into view.

When you select the To Print command, the PRINT INFORMATION dialog box appears. The following section explains this dialog box more fully.

The PRINT INFORMATION Dialog Box

Use the PRINT INFORMATION dialog box in the production process to print both preliminary and final copies of your document. This dialog box appears when you choose To Print from the File menu or Multi-Chapter from the Options menu. With this dialog box you can choose which pages and how many copies to print, which paper tray to use, the collation order, and instructions to print crop marks or spot color overlays (see fig 8.4).

Troubleshooting Tip

Printing and Saving

As you print a large bit-mapped image, printer or electrical malfunctions may force you to reboot your computer. When you reboot, you lose all changes made to your document since the last save. Before issuing the To Print command, therefore, always save your chapter if you have made any changes you intend to keep. If the file changes are an experiment with a new technique, save the file under a temporary name and keep the original version until you have seen the printed results.

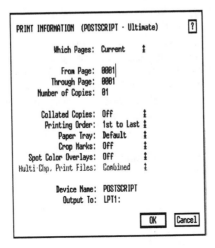

Fig. 8.4.

The PRINT INFORMATION dialog box accessed from the File menu.

The first option in the PRINT INFORMATION dialog box is Which Pages. This option allows you to choose All, Selected, Left pages only, or Right pages only; you can also leave active the default value Current to print only the page in view. The Selected setting lets you enter specific page numbers in the From Page and Through Page options.

Efficiency Tip

Two-Sided Printing

If you are producing final output rather than camera-ready art for offset printing, you can print double-sided copies with some laser printers. (Some printers tend to smear or burn the toner when paper is reinserted for printing.) If your printer properly feeds and prints paper on two sides, you can set up the print instructions in the PRINT INFOR-MATION dialog box. Select Which Pages: Right and set Printing Order: 1st to Last. After the right-sided pages are printed, reload the printer with the printed pages. Select Which Pages: Left and set Printing Order: Last to 1st.

Note: Some printers eject pages face up and some face down. This difference determines whether you reload the pages face up or face down. It also determines whether you print Right pages 1st to Last and Left pages Last to 1st, or vice versa.

If you use the Multi-Chapter command under the Options menu to print more than one chapter, you must have the same number of left and right pages in each chapter. If a chapter ends on a right page, you must insert a blank left page at the end. Sometimes this blank page contains the text *This page intentionally left blank*. To center this text on the page, create a tag called Blank Page with Page Break: Before & After and Vert. Alignment: Center under the Paragraph menu. If the chapter has a header, footer, or repeating frame, turn it off for this page, from the Chapter menu.

Ventura retains the print option settings you enable when you click OK to print, and keeps these settings until you change them in the PRINT INFORMATION dialog box.

Use the Number of Copies option when you want more than one copy of each page printed. This option is closely tied to the Collated Copies option. After you specify the number of copies to be printed, set Collated Copies: On or Off. Setting Collated Copies: On sorts the copies automatically but often involves significantly longer printing time. If you print five copies with Collated Copies: Off, the printer processes each page only once and prints five copies of page 1, then five copies of page 2, and so on. With Collated Copies: On, the printer reprocesses the image for each sheet of paper printed and prints one complete copy of the entire publication before printing the next copy (see fig. 8.5). This option is handy when you want to review the first complete copy while the other copies are printing, or if you are print-ing several final copies for distribution.

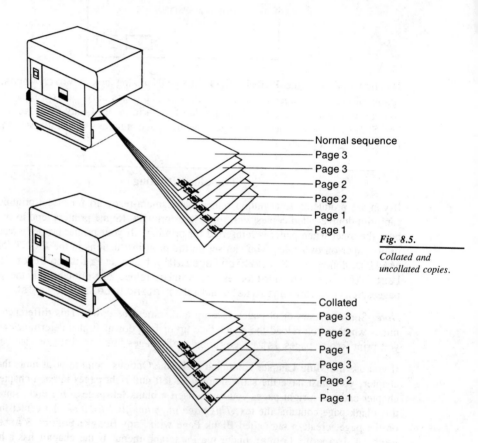

Normal sequence
Page 3
Page 3
Page 2
Page 2
Page 1
Page 1

Collated
Page 3
Page 2
Page 1
Page 3
Page 2
Page 1

Fig. 8.5.

Collated and uncollated copies.

The Printing Order option controls the order in which the pages are printed. Ven-tura can print a document from the first to the last page or vice versa. If you choose Last to 1st, the document takes longer to print; but if your printer ejects pages face up, you may save time rearranging the pages manually (see fig. 8.6).

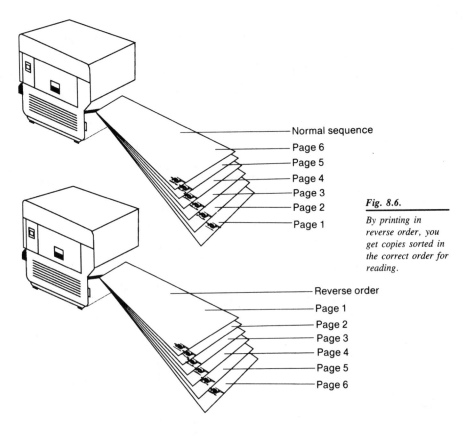

Normal sequence
Page 6
Page 5
Page 4
Page 3
Page 2
Page 1

Fig. 8.6.

By printing in reverse order, you get copies sorted in the correct order for reading.

Reverse order
Page 1
Page 2
Page 3
Page 4
Page 5
Page 6

Efficiency Tip

Save Time When Printing Multiple Copies

You can save time when printing more than one copy of a file by printing to a file and using the DOS COPY command to send that file to your printer. With this method the hard disk will send the file to the printer faster. In addition, if you choose, for instance, Number of Copies: 20, Ventura prints only one copy to the file and includes an instruction to print the file 20 times. When you print 20 copies directly from Ventura, the display is frozen until all 20 copies have been printed. (See "Creating a Print File" in this chapter for more information.)

Paper Tray: Default is used if your printer has only one paper tray. Alt #1 and Alt #2 are for printers with more than one paper tray. Select Manual if you want to hand-feed the paper one sheet at a time. (Some printers automatically feed a sheet of paper placed in the single-sheet slot.)

Efficiency Tip

Improving the Look of Reproduced Copies

Two simple practices can help you improve the look of final pages reproduced from laser-printed originals. The first is to use laser paper stock intended for producing camera-ready originals. The second is to have the print shop slightly reduce the originals.

The `Multi-Chp. Print Files` option is gray unless you are using the Multi-Chapter command from the Options menu and are printing to a file. The two options, Combined and Separate, allow you to combine all chapters in one print file or, because print files are usually large, print each chapter to a separate file. (See "Copying Files with the Multi-Chapter Command" in this chapter.)

If you set `Crop Marks: On`, Ventura automatically positions trim marks around the edge of the page. The offset printer uses the crop marks to position the copy for each page when printing more than one page at a time (see fig. 8.7). Crop marks are not printed if the document page size is the same or larger than the paper size. (The page size is determined by the SIZING & SCALING dialog box; paper size is set in the PAGE LAYOUT dialog box.) See Chapter 7 to learn how to position crop marks as trim marks and how to place crop marks around a portion of a page.

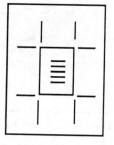

Fig. 8.7.

*Printing
crop marks.*

Ventura 2.0 supports printing spot color overlays. Each color enabled in the DEFINE COLORS dialog box will be printed on a separate sheet. The name of the color prints at the top of each page, and the text and graphics print in black. When you prepare this type of camera-ready artwork, select the Define Color command from the Paragraph menu and disable any colors not used. If you use color on only selected pages, first print the chapter with `Spot Color Overlays: Off` in the PRINT INFORMATION dialog box. Then set `Spot Color Overlays: On`, and each color enabled will print.

Note: Ask your print shop whether color overlays are more economical than designating spot color with nonreproducible pencils on the final pages. Many shops may not require that you provide separate master pages for each color.

Faster Printing of Draft Copies

Choose a lower resolution for printing draft copies if your printer offers the option. With lower resolution, your draft copies print faster. If you work with a PostScript printer, you can cut printing time by overriding automatic kerning in the CHAPTER TYPOGRAPHY dialog box (although doing so may affect line endings). Remember to reset chapter kerning to On when you reach the final print stages. Speed printing even more by selecting Hide All Pictures from the Options menu before issuing the print request. Hidden pictures do not print unless you instruct Ventura to print them. If you want to see some of the graphics on the draft copy, hide all the pictures and then select the frames containing those you want to print. Once selected, use the Show This Picture command on the Options menu and then initiate the print request.

The two options displayed at the bottom of the PRINT INFORMATION dialog box, Device Name and Output To, reflect the settings specified in the Options menu SET PRINTER INFO dialog box. (If the printer or port shown is not correct, click Cancel and open the SET PRINTER INFO dialog box to change the setting.) When Filename displays as the Device Name, a new dialog box opens when you click OK and Ventura asks you to name the print file. Print files can be used to minimize the amount of time your computer is tied up printing and can also be used to print from systems not configured with Ventura. Printing to files is discussed in more detail later in this chapter.

Troubleshooting Hints

After you complete your entries in the PRINT INFORMATION dialog box and click OK, a new dialog box appears to display the printing status (see fig. 8.8). The screen and mouse freeze until all pages are formatted. Ventura first loads the printer driver and then loads the printer fonts.

```
PRINTING CHAPTER/PUBLICATION...

Loading Printer Fonts
```

Fig. 8.8.

Printing-status display while Ventura is loading fonts.

As Ventura begins formatting the pages before sending them to the printer, another box appears. This box shows the number of the page currently printing and tells you that you can press Esc to stop printing (see fig. 8.9).

Erratic or unexpected results during printing may be caused by many factors. You can stop printing at any time by pressing Esc. Printing stops after the current page is printed. Because Ventura writes files to the hard disk during printing operations,

Fig. 8.9.

Printing-status display while Ventura is printing.

```
┌─────────────────────────────────────────────────┐
│ ┌─────────────────────────────────────────────┐ │
│ │                                             │ │
│ │        PRINTING CHAPTER/PUBLICATION...      │ │
│ │                                             │ │
│ │      Printing Page #, (Press ESC to stop):  │ │
│ │                                             │ │
│ │                    0010                     │ │
│ │                                             │ │
│ └─────────────────────────────────────────────┘ │
└─────────────────────────────────────────────────┘
```

always make sure that at least 500K of space is available before you initiate a print request. Inadequate amounts of hard disk space and random-access memory can result in problems when printing. Solutions to other types of printer problems are described in the following paragraphs.

Ventura prompts you to check connections between the computer and the printer when you initiate a print request that cannot be completed. If you use a printer that has worked previously, you may simply need to change the Output To option in the SET PRINTER INFO dialog box to one appropriate for the printer. When you install a new printer, self-test the printer and then test the printer with Ventura. If you use a serial communications port, check to see that the DOS MODE command in the AUTO-EXEC.BAT file in the root directory contains these statements:

    mode lpt1: = com1:

    mode com1:96,e,7,1,p

The printer does not print from Ventura, DOS, or other installed programs. In this case, improper cables are a likely suspect. Check Appendix F in the Ventura reference manual for cable specifications and part numbers.

PostScript printer problems. Version 23 of PostScript for the Apple LaserWriter below Version 2 was shipped with a bug that can cause problems when you print documents of 20 pages or more on some Apple LaserWriters. To overcome the problem, copy the PostScript prologue file named PS1.PRE from the POSTSCPT directory of the Utilities disk to the VENTURA directory on your hard disk. Ventura sends the patch to the printer each time you print a chapter, along with the file named PS2.PRE. If you have problems printing with other types of PostScript printers, verify that the software version is compatible with the printer by checking with the vendor of your printer or with Xerox. You may need to upgrade either Ventura or PostScript to resolve the problem.

The letters seem improperly shaped, or large gaps of white space appear between words. Check the top of the PRINT INFORMATION dialog box to see whether Draft or Ultimate appears. Remember that Ventura uses a width table compatible with the printer type named in parentheses to shape letters on the printed page. When the Device Name option shows that a dissimilar type of printer is selected, line and page endings on-screen match those on the printed page, but draft pages may be difficult to read or proof.

The letters are properly shaped but gaps between words and letters are too great. Use the PARAGRAPH TYPOGRAPHY dialog box options described in Chapter 5 to adjust the settings for letter and word spacing. If you have changed the word spacing and decide that you do not like the effect, load the default style file in the TYPESET directory to find and reenter the original word-spacing values.

Printing Parts of Oversized Pages

Ventura has two Paper Type & Dimension options available on the PAGE LAYOUT dialog box, that allow you to print an oversized page on 8.5-by-11-inch paper: Double and Broad Sheet. If you select Paper Type & Dimension: Double (11-by-17 inches) and then select To Print, a second dialog box appears before printing begins (see fig.8.10).

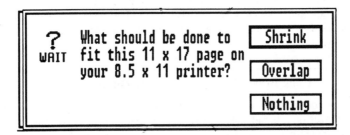

Fig. 8.10.

Dialog box for printing an 11-by-17-inch page.

If your printer prints an 11-by-17-inch sheet or if final output is on a Linotronic type-setter using 12-inch-wide paper, choose Nothing from this dialog box. If you choose Shrink, Ventura reduces the entire page to fit on an 8.5-by-11-inch page. Shrink works only on PostScript printers, however. If you choose Overlap, Ventura prints the layout on four 8.5-by-11-inch pages, which you can use as a proof or to paste up into one 11-by-17-inch sheet, as shown in figure 8.11.

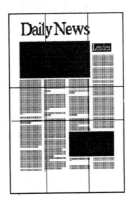

Fig. 8.11.

Overlapping pages to produce an 11-by-17-inch proof or paste-up copy.

Any time the dimensions for your layout exceed 11-by-17 inches, you can select the Broad Sheet setting in the PAGE LAYOUT dialog box. When the Broad Sheet setting is enabled and you are ready to print, another dialog box appears, as shown in figure 8.12. The program prompts you to specify how to print the oversized page on an 8.5-by-11-inch sheet.

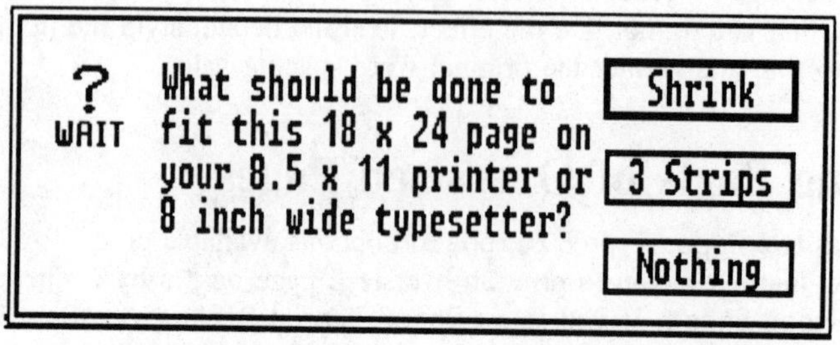

Fig. 8.12.

Dialog box for printing an 18-by-24-inch page.

```
?     What should be done to     ┌─────────┐
WAIT  fit this 18 x 24 page on   │ Shrink  │
      your 8.5 x 11 printer or   ┌──────────┐
      8 inch wide typesetter?    │ 3 Strips │
                                 ┌─────────┐
                                 │ Nothing │
```

As already mentioned, if you choose Shrink and have a PostScript printer, Ventura reduces the entire page. Certain typesetting machines print the page in three vertical strips 24 inches long, which you can paste up as one page before printing. The 3 Strips option is not for use with laser printers. If your printer prints 18-by-24-inch sheets, choose Nothing.

Efficiency Tip

Using Broad Sheet Pages To Lay Out Small Type

Suppose that you want to use very small point sizes in a chapter. Try working in larger point sizes on a broad sheet page on the screen. Then, if you have a PostScript printer, use the Shrink print option to print the chapter on 8.5-by-11-inch paper. Because the 18-by-24-inch broad sheet is roughly two times the size of an 8.5-by-11-inch sheet, it's easiest to double the printed point sizes you want. For instance, use 8-point text and 14-point heads if you want to print 4-point text with 7-point heads.

Moving a Project to Another System for Printing

Ventura provides two ways for you to move a publication from one system to another:

- Use the print file feature to create a copy of the file to print on other systems where Ventura may not be installed.

- Use the Multi-Chapter command to combine all the chapter files in a publication so that the publication can be edited and printed on another system equipped with Ventura.

The following sections explain both these procedures.

Creating a Print File

Printing to a file usually creates a large file because it contains all instructions to the printer embedded within the chapter's text. However, this useful option simplifies and speeds up production by enabling you to

- Print a Ventura project on a laser printer or typesetter that does not have the latest version of Ventura

- Transfer Ventura files through telecommunications to another location

- Allow more than one computer to output Ventura documents on the same printer

- Speed printing 20 to 50 percent by using the DOS COPY command to print Ventura print files

- Set up more than one file to print during lunch or at night

- Archive a project that never changes but must be sent to other locations for regular output (such as display ads sent to several retail locations for PostScript typesetter output)

- Alter the print file to take advantage of PostScript capabilities that Ventura does not support, such as printing characters larger than 254 points and condensing and spreading font characters

- Produce a file that you can load into Ventura as an illustration

You cannot edit a print file in Ventura. If you want to edit a chapter, you must open the chapter, make the changes, save the changes, and then print the chapter to a file again. Because the print file is an ASCII file, however, you can edit some parts of it using your word processor. Any changes made in a print file have no effect on other files associated with the chapter. The danger is that if you don't understand the Post-Script language, knowing what to change in a print file can be difficult.

Efficiency Tip

Making PostScript Fonts Print Larger Than 254 Points

You can print fonts larger than 254 points on a PostScript printer by changing the numbers used to set the font in the print file created for the chapter. In the following example, the search function of a word processor was used to locate the text enclosed in parentheses on the first line, and the font size was changed to 756 points in the second line of code. The results produce the letter *R* filling a printed page and displaying as 254 points on-screen.

```
450 2014 33 0 (R)fjt
/txscale 75600 3 mul 72 div def /tyscale 75600 3 mul 72 div
```

Because Ventura 2.0 supports PostScript's capability to scale fonts by discrete increments both horizontally and vertically, be sure to change both aspects of the size in the numbers following *txscale* and *tyscale*.

Use the following procedure to create a print file for a single chapter or for a publication composed of several chapters. Because the print file can be quite large, be sure you have enough free disk space before printing. Once the print file is created, use the DOS COPY command to send the print file to the printer.

1. Open the chapter in Ventura.

2. Complete all edits and save the document as you would normally, using the Save command from the File menu.

3. With the chapter still open, choose Set Printer Info from the Options menu.

4. In the SET PRINTER INFO dialog box, select Filename for the Output To option (refer to fig. 8.1). (This option is not available for JLaser, Cordata, and AST Turbo Lasers because the size of the print file is too large for storage on floppy disks.)

5. Because Filename tells Ventura to print only to a file rather than to a printer, the width table should already match the printer. If you must change the width table, click Load Different Width Table (refer to fig. 8.1) to choose an alternative table from the ITEM SELECTOR dialog box that opens (see fig. 8.13). After choosing the appropriate width table, click OK to close the ITEM SELECTOR dialog box. Remember that if you change width tables at this point, line endings in your chapter may change.

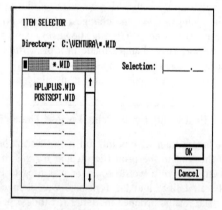

Fig. 8.13.

The width table ITEM SELECTOR dialog box.

6. Choose To Print from the File menu, and select the pages you want to print.

7. A new dialog box appears; Ventura prompts you to name the file to which you are printing. Ventura automatically adds the extension C00 to the file name (see fig. 8.14). Before you type the file name, you can change the Directory option (by using the backup button or by clicking the Directory line, pressing Esc to clear the line, and then typing the destination).

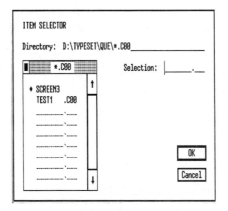

Fig. 8.14.

*Naming a
disk file.*

8. If you are using the Multi-Chapter command to print more than one
   chapter that will eventually be copied to a floppy disk, choose Multi-
   Chp. Print Files: Separate when the PRINT INFORMATION
   dialog box appears (see fig. 8.15). Ventura will print each chapter to a
   separate file, which is easier to copy to floppy disks than one huge file.
   The first chapter will have the extension C00, the next chapter the
   extension C01, and so on.

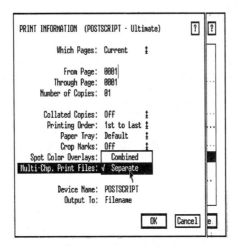

Fig. 8.15.

*The PRINT
INFORMATION
dialog box accessed
from the Multi-
Chapter command
from the Options
menu.*

Efficiency Tip

Print to the Hard Disk To Save Printing Time

Although the file you are printing will eventually be copied to a floppy disk, it will
print faster to the hard disk. Print the file to a hard disk. Then exit Ventura and copy
the C00 file(s) from the hard disk to a floppy disk with the DOS COPY command.

Once the print file is on a floppy disk, you can carry the disk to the computer with the desired printer. You can also telecommunicate the C00 file from one computer to another.

To print the C00 file from a floppy disk to a printer connected to the computer through a parallel printer port, insert the floppy disk into drive A or B and type the following command at the DOS prompt:

COPY A:<*filename*>.C00 LPT1:

or

COPY B:<*filename*>.C00 LPT1:

If your printer is a Xerox 9700, use the XPRINT utility provided with your printer instead of using the DOS COPY command. If you use a serial printer, you must type the following two instructions before using the COPY command:

MODE LPT1:=COM1:
MODE COM1:96,N,8,1,P

If you use a PostScript printer to print a print file, you must also copy the DTR.TXT file from the POSTSCPT directory on the Utilities disk to the printer, using the following statement:

COPY A:\POSTSCPT\DTR.TXT LPT1:

You need to copy the DTR.TXT file only once unless you also use other programs that establish protocols other than DTR for the printer. The symptoms of this type of problem are that the printer prints only a few pages at a time, or perhaps none at all, after you have used the printer with another program. If this happens, copy the DTR.TXT file to the printer again.

Efficiency Tip

Printing Long Files While You Are Working

Some of your files may take a long time to print. To work while these long files are printing, use the Set Printer Info command to change the Output To option to Filename. After you print the document to a file, take it to another computer and use the DOS COPY command to send the file to the printer, freeing your computer screen for other tasks. If you have only one computer, you can use the COPY command to send the file to the printer after you finish your work session.

Print files can also be used to capture an image of a Ventura page that you want to use in another chapter. The file that Ventura creates when you print to a file name using the PostScript width table is similar to an Encapsulated PostScript (EPS) file. A true EPS file is created using the PostScript language and can take advantage of many PostScript capabilities that Ventura does not support. (Ventura accepts this file because it isn't really an EPS file.) You can load the file into another Ventura document, using the Load Text/Picture command from the File menu. Select PostScript for the Line-Art Format option. The image itself does not appear on-screen; instead, a large *X* shows in the frame. When you print the document, however, the captured image prints. One limitation is that you cannot load a file created with a style file set for Orientation: Landscape into a chapter set for Orientation: Portrait.

Copying Files with the Multi-Chapter Command

Before you can print or copy a publication consisting of more than one chapter file, you must use the Multi-Chapter command from the Options menu to create a publication. This publication should include all relevant files: the table of contents, all chapters, and the index.

If you have not already created the publication for the project, you can start with an untitled chapter in the publisher's window. To create a publication with multiple chapters, follow these steps:

1. Select Multi-Chapter from the Options menu.

2. The MULTI-CHAPTER OPERATIONS dialog box appears (see fig. 8.16). Select Add Chapter to open the ITEM SELECTOR dialog box.

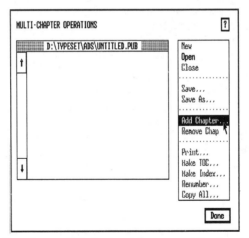

Fig. 8.16.

The MULTI-CHAPTER OPERATIONS dialog box.

3. Select the first chapter file you want in your publication (usually the cover page or table of contents) and click OK. Ventura collects all the files associated with that chapter file and displays the name of the CHP file in the chapter list.

4. Select Add Chapter for each chapter until you have loaded all the chapters for this publication in the proper order for printing.

   If you select chapters in the wrong order, you can rearrange them. Position the mouse cursor on the name of the chapter that is out of order (see fig. 8.17). Hold down the left mouse button and drag the title into the proper position.

Fig. 8.17.

*Reorganizing
chapters in a
publication.*

5. After you have loaded all chapters, use the Save As command from the
MULTI-CHAPTER OPERATIONS dialog box to assign a name to the
publication. Ventura adds the PUB extension and returns to the MULTI-
CHAPTER OPERATIONS dialog box. The publication file contains only
pointers for the directory location and names of all chapters in this
publication.

6. If you are copying the chapters to a floppy disk, click the Copy All
option. When the COPY ALL dialog box appears, the new PUB file and
its location appear on the PUB or CHP line (see fig. 8.18). If you need
to change the destination, click the PUB & CHPs line, press Esc, and type
the new destination. If all files are going to the same destination, click
Make All Directories the Same As the First. If this is all you will
be doing with Multi-Chapter commands, click Done.

7. To print the publication, click Print in the MULTI-CHAPTER
OPERATIONS dialog box and choose the settings in the PRINT
INFORMATION dialog box that appears; the chapters will print in the
order listed. If you are printing to a file, Multi-Chp. Print Files is
enabled when the PRINT INFORMATION dialog box appears, giving
you two choices. If you choose Combined, all chapters will print in one
file. If you choose Separate, each chapter will print in a separate file
with the first having the extension C00, the second C01, and so on. If
you are printing to a file, another dialog box will appear asking you to
name the output file.

A service bureau can use the print file instead of bringing up the publication and printing from the screen. A good precautionary technique, however, is to copy the publication (not in a print file) to a floppy disk and send it, too. If a page has a problem in
the print file, the original files are available to print that one page without waiting for
a corrected floppy disk to arrive. As noted in the Efficiency Tip ''Making PostScript
Fonts Print Larger than 254 Points,'' you can search for and make minor edits to print
files, using your word processor.

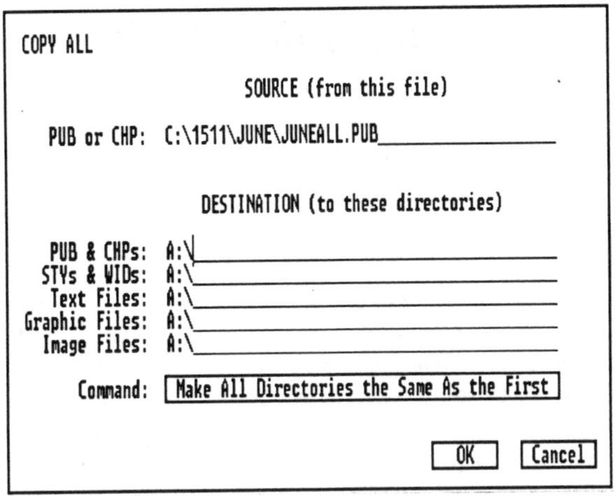

```
COPY ALL

                         SOURCE (from this file)

    PUB or CHP:  C:\1511\JUNE\JUNEALL.PUB_____


                      DESTINATION (to these directories)

      PUB & CHPs:  A:_____
      STYs & WIDs: A:_____
       Text Files: A:_____
    Graphic Files: A:_____
      Image Files: A:_____

         Command:  [ Make All Directories the Same As the First ]


                                      [   OK   ]  [ Cancel ]
```

Fig. 8.18.

Copying the entire publication to a floppy disk.

Performing Multi-Chapter Operations

Once you have created a publication, you can open that publication from the menu in the MULTI-CHAPTER OPERATIONS dialog box; then you can make a table of contents or an index or renumber all pages after editing. You must select a publication created with the Multi-Chapter command or else Ventura informs you that the publication is not in the proper format to be loaded. Check to make sure that you are loading the publication from the correct drive and directory. Creating a publication does not change a chapter file; publication files "point to" chapters in the same way that each chapter file points to the location of the width, style, and source files.

The Multi-Chapter command offers the most reliable way to copy files for two reasons. First, if more storage area is required Ventura prompts you to continue archiving with a new disk. Second, the process updates the pointers to source files and to the files Ventura uses to complete a project's layout.

Note: Always use the Options menu Multi-Chapter Copy All option to copy Ventura files—never the DOS COPY command—for two reasons. First, Ventura may store files associated with a chapter file in different directories, depending on which directories are named in the ITEM SELECTOR dialog boxes. Although you may be able to track down the files for copying, the most reliable way to change Ventura's pointers to these files is to create an updated copy (using Copy All) of the project's chapter file.

The second reason is that when you use Copy All to copy to a particular drive, Ventura changes the pointers to refer to the new location. When you use the DOS COPY command to copy files, the pointers in the CHP file are not changed. Ventura indicates which files cannot be found when you load a chapter file, and Ventura attempts to display the project by substituting style and width files. (See Chapter 7 for a troubleshooting hint on changing the file pointers with a word processor.)

Adding New Printers and Fonts

The next sections explain how to add a new printer driver to your system, how to copy fonts to the hard disk, how to download soft fonts to the printer, and how to download fonts "permanently" to your printer.

Adding a New Printer

To connect a new printer to your system or format pages for a printer you do not have, you must use the VPPREP program and rerun part of the installation to install the appropriate printer driver. When the program asks Are you installing this version for the first time? answer N. Ventura inquires which monitor, mouse, printer, and ports you use. You have to provide answers only for the monitor, mouse, and new printer prompts. All previously installed printers (up to a total of six) may remain on the system for use with Ventura.

Copying Fonts to Your Hard Disk

The first step involved in loading printer fonts is to copy them to your hard disk. (For information about loading screen fonts, see Chapter 9.) All fonts provided with Ventura already have width tables. If the font vendor does not provide a width table, you can use a utility provided by Ventura to create one. Then you must merge one of the tables Ventura provides (or one you have created) with the new font's width table. You cannot merge width tables intended for use with dissimilar printers. (See "Choosing the Printer Width Table" earlier in this chapter to learn how Ventura uses width tables.)

Efficiency Tip

Keep Width Tables as Small as Possible

You can reduce the size of a width table by removing from a copy of the width table installed for your printer any fonts you do not use. Small width tables leave more space available for processing, send fewer instructions to the printer, and consume less archive disk space than larger tables. Always, however, leave either 10-point Helvetica (or Swiss) or 10-point Times (or Dutch) in each width table; Ventura requires at least one of these for reference.

Ventura's width tables include all the fonts listed in table 8.2. You do not have to create a width table if you load one of the PostScript typefaces listed in Appendix K of *Xerox Ventura Publisher Reference Guide*. If you use other typefaces, you must add a width table for the new fonts. Appendix K also includes instructions for creating a new width table.

To load printer fonts onto your hard disk, do the following:

1. Copy the fonts to the correct directory. The following instructions assist you in the placement of fonts.

Copy to the VENTURA directory all HP LaserJet Plus, JLaser, Cordata, AST TurboLaser, and Xerox 4045 fonts and width tables (files with the extension WID). If you load JLaser or Cordata fonts, use the DOS RENAME command to change the font extension to B30. If you load AST TurboLaser fonts, change the font extension to W30. If you load Xerox 4045 fonts, change the font extension to XFN.

Copy to the PSFONTS directory all PostScript fonts (you may have to create this directory). If the PostScript fonts are in ASCII format, change the font extension to PFA. If the PostScript fonts are not in ASCII format, change the extension to PFB. For example, if you install a PostScript ASCII file (rather than a binary file), change

filename.extension

to

filename.PFA

Use the DOS RENAME command to change file names. If you load PostScript fonts, skip steps 2 through 5. The Ventura PostScript width table includes the most commonly used PostScript typefaces. However, the file name for each font you install must match the font name in the PostScript width table. The Ventura PostScript file name is given in Appendix K of the *Xerox Ventura Publisher Reference Guide.*

2. If the width table for another printer appears in the SET PRINTER INFO dialog box, select Load Different Width Table (refer to fig. 8.1). Ventura displays a new dialog box listing all width tables (refer to fig. 8.13). Select the printer width table from those displayed in the ITEM SELECTOR dialog box that appears and click OK.

3. Choose the Add/Remove Fonts command from the Options menu. The file name at the top of the screen should be the name of the width table you loaded (see fig. 8.19).

4. Click Save As New Width Table, which saves the existing width table in case you need to recover the original. The name of the new width table appears at the top of the dialog box.

5. Click Merge Width Tables, and select the width table for the new fonts. Ventura combines the two width tables. The new fonts now appear in the dialog box.

6. Select each font you loaded, making sure that Download appears at the bottom of the Style list window. This word toggles between Download and Resident. Download means that the font is stored on the hard disk rather than in the printer. Be sure to follow this procedure for each PostScript typeface you add (see ''Downloading Soft Fonts to the Printer'' in this chapter).

7. If you don't want to keep one of the fonts you loaded, select that font and click Remove Selected Font.

8. After you have correctly loaded all fonts, you can choose the original width table that you stopped using in step 4. Click Save As New Width Table.

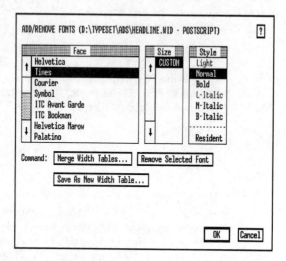

ADD/REMOVE FONTS (D:\TYPESET\ADS\HEADLINE.WID · POSTSCRIPT)

Face	Size	Style
Helvetica	CUSTOM	Light
Times		Normal
Courier		Bold
Symbol		L·Italic
ITC Avant Garde		N·Italic
ITC Bookman		B·Italic
Helvetica Narow		
Palatino		Resident

Command: [Merge Width Tables...] [Remove Selected Font]

[Save As New Width Table...]

[OK] [Cancel]

Fig. 8.19.

The ADD/REMOVE FONTS dialog box.

Downloading Soft Fonts to the Printer

Before you design a large publication that calls for downloadable fonts, experiment a little with the fonts. To use downloadable fonts, you must download them from your hard disk to the printer before you print the page or publication. This section describes the difference between permanent and temporary downloading and explains how to download fonts. Chapter 9 offers more information about using different fonts.

Some printers (such as the HP LaserJet and Xerox 4045) allow you to download new fonts to your printer "permanently" instead of downloading from the hard disk at the beginning of each job (temporarily downloading). This capability saves printing time but uses more printer memory. This downloading is not really permanent, however, because the downloaded fonts are erased when the printer is turned off. The only truly permanent fonts are hard-coded into the chips in the printer or the printer's font cartridges, but these fonts by definition are not downloadable; they reside in the printer's ROM or cartridge.

The printer manufacturer or font vendor provides a utility to download fonts. Use the Options menu Add/Remove Fonts command to disable Ventura's automatic font downloading. In the ADD/REMOVE FONTS dialog box, the last item in the Style option is Download if the fonts are stored on your hard disk and Resident if the fonts are stored on your printer.

To download fonts "permanently" to your printer, do the following:

1. Choose the Add/Remove Fonts command from the Options menu.

2. In the Face, Size, and Style list boxes, select the fonts you want to download to the printer.

3. Resident and Download are toggles at the bottom of the Style list box. When you click Download, Resident appears.

4. Repeat steps 2 and 3 for each font in a family that you want permanently downloaded.

Some printers—PostScript printers, for instance—can print any size of a specific typeface and style once the font is downloaded. Other printers require that each combination of size, typeface, and style be downloaded as a separate font. To use the entire family in the Palatino typeface on a PostScript printer, for example, you need to download four different styles: normal, boldface, italic, and boldface italic. For design suggestions (and other production considerations when choosing fonts for publications) and a discussion of type families, see Chapter 9.

Most printers can handle no more than 16 soft fonts per page and 32 soft fonts per publication. (Even this maximum depends on the size of the font because larger fonts take up more space.) When the printer finishes printing the publication, temporarily downloaded fonts are cleared from the printer's memory. Printing is slower with temporarily downloaded fonts because the fonts are downloaded each time the publication is printed. Temporarily downloaded fonts have the advantage of releasing printer memory space when the font is not being used.

—— Efficiency Tip

Automatically Downloading Fonts

You can use a batch file or lines of instructions in your AUTOEXEC.BAT file to download fonts to your printer at the start of your work session. If you use the batch-file method, you need to turn on your printer a few minutes before you start the batch file so that the printer is ready to receive the fonts.

Batch downloading is advisable if you normally use the same number and style of fonts, as for company letters or publications that always use a specified type style. Be sure to use the ADD/REMOVE FONTS dialog box to disable Ventura's automatic font downloading for these fonts. Before deciding whether to use batch files to download fonts to the printer, experiment a little with downloading fonts.

Because permanently downloaded fonts remain in the printer's memory until you turn it off, publications are printed more quickly. The amount of printer memory remaining for processing each page, however, is limited by the number of fonts downloaded. In particular, you may have problems printing pages with graphics when several fonts are permanently downloaded.

To download fonts automatically to a HP LaserJet Plus, LaserJet Series II, or compatible printer before using Ventura, use the HPDOWN program on the Ventura Utilities disk. If your printer has at least 1M of memory and is connected to LPT1, you can speed printing considerably by following these steps:

1. Use your word processor to create a file with no blank lines, called HPLJPLUS.CNF in the VENTURA directory.

2. Store all fonts to be downloaded in the same file. The first line of this file must contain the disk drive and directory.

3. For each line thereafter type *PERMFONT* followed in parentheses by the font ID number (name the first font 1, the second font 2, and so on); a blank space; and the file name of the font—for example,

```
HPFONTS(C:\FONTS)
PERMFONT(1 TMSN3010.SFP)
PERMFONT(2 TMSN3012.SFP)
PERMFONT(3 TMSB3010.SFP)
PERMFONT(4 TMSB3012.SFP)
```

4. Save this file as an ASCII file and copy the HPDOWN.EXE file from the Utilities disk to the VENTURA directory.

5. Type *hpdown*. The fonts are copied to the printer connected to LPT1.

6. Load Ventura and open the ADD/REMOVE FONTS dialog box from the Options menu. Change each font you named in the file from Download to Resident by clicking the word Download at the bottom of the Style list box. Ventura knows that those fonts are stored in the printer and won't send them with each file. If you make a mistake, click Resident to change that font back to Download.

7. Click Save As New Width Table to save these changes under a new name if you won't download regularly. If you want to download these fonts each work session, save the width table under the same name and include the HPDOWN statement in your AUTOEXEC.BAT file.

Efficiency Tip

Erasing Fonts To Free Printer Memory

When you download fonts at the beginning of the day, you may run into memory problems when printing pages with graphics. If the pages with graphics do not use the downloaded fonts, you can flush the fonts out of the printer's memory by turning off the printer. When you turn the printer back on, print the pages with graphics first before permanently downloading the fonts again.

To shorten printing time, download fonts to the HP LaserJet Plus and Series II printers before you load Ventura instead of downloading the fonts as each chapter prints. Such downloading consumes much of the printer's memory, however, and you may get an out-of-memory message if you use several fonts or have graphics in your file.

PostScript fonts you add need to be listed in a CNF file called POSTSCPT.CNF. The VENTURA directory contains a sample file that you can modify or copy to use as a pattern for new CNF files you create. The file contains the name of the directory where you store the fonts and includes three codes you can change to match your configuration.

[I]

If you compare figure 8.20 with the POSTSCPT.CNF file stored in your VENTURA directory, you will notice a few changes. For example, the directory name in the figure has been changed to access a directory called NEWFONTS. The *eoftype* code was changed from PC to MAC to suppress the printing of Apple's end-of-file ^D codes on a network. The *imgtype* code was changed from FAST to COMPACT to create smaller files, although they may take longer to print. *Coltype* was changed from COLOR to GREY, and all the fonts except the new ones installed were removed.

```
psfonts(C:\NEWFONTS\)
eoftype(MAC)
imgtype(COMPACT)
coltype(GREY)
font(NewCenturySchlbk-Roman,20,M,TEXT,RES)
font(NewCenturySchlbk-Italic,20,I,TEXT,RES)
font(NewCenturySchlbk-Bold,20,B,TEXT,RES)
font(NewCenturySchlbk-BoldItalic,20,BI,TEXT,RES)
```

Fig. 8.20.

A modified POSTSCPT.CNF file.

You can keep multiple CNF files if you rename the one you want to use as POST-SCPT.CNF before you start Ventura. See Appendixes F and K of *Xerox Ventura Publisher Reference Guide* to add fonts that are not listed in the sample CNF file.

Chapter Summary

The printing process can be simple if you use only the fonts built into your printer. If you want to add downloadable fonts for your publications, the process involves several steps outside of Ventura before you can use the fonts when formatting your publication. The number of different fonts you can use in one chapter (or style file) is limited by the amount of memory in the printer and the size of the fonts you download.

If you have only one printer in your office, workshop, or studio, and you use only the fonts hard-coded in your printer, the printing process is straightforward. You select the To Print command from the File menu and set the options you want. If you have more than one printer installed with Ventura, you can use the SET PRINTER INFO dialog box from the Options menu to select the printer. Ventura changes to the port that was specified for that printer during the installation procedure.

The quality and appearance of the printed page depend on both the capability of your printer and the excellence of your design. In Chapter 9, you learn more about selecting fonts to enhance the quality of your publications.

II

Designing and Producing Different Types of Publications

Includes

Typography

Using the Professional Extension

Ventura Publisher as a Design Tool

9

Typography

D esigners and typographers have unique ways of describing a document's text in terms of fonts, leading, kerning, and letter spacing. In this chapter, you learn how to view a Ventura publication in these terms and how to set up your design specifications by using Ventura's menus. You learn how to estimate the amount of text that fits on each page and how to make fine adjustments in design specifications so that you can fit copy into a defined space.

This chapter also explains what fonts are available for each printer and how you can add new fonts to the menus. After reading this chapter, you will see the importance of knowing the fonts, sizes, and styles available for your printer before you begin the design process. In fact, you should become thoroughly familiar with your printer's capabilities and limitations. Avoid being shocked at the last minute by discoveries of what your printer cannot do. Ventura provides a sample chapter called CAPABILI.CHP, short for capabilities, in the TYPESET subdirectory. Load and print this chapter to discover the potential of your printer. If you have more than one printer available, use the Set Printer Info command from the Options menu to change printers and compare their potentials.

Understanding Fonts

The word *font* comes from the French word *fondre*, which means to melt or cast. The term once referred literally to the trays of cast metal letters that printers used to compose a document. Each tray or font included all letters of the alphabet for a specific typeface, style, and size combination. For example, one tray held only 10-point Times italic letters, another tray held only 10-point Times bold, and so on. A font, then, was a particular composite of size, typeface, and style. The word *font* has the same meaning in Ventura's Font command and dialog box.

In more recent times, *font* has been defined more loosely to mean the name of a typeface, such as Times or Helvetica. This definition makes sense for the new computer fonts, such as the PostScript language fonts, that are based on formulas. Each letter of the alphabet is cast, or designed, only once to define the shape of the letter. This information is then stored as a complex curve-fitting equation. A printer using a programming language like PostScript or Interpress to create text can produce a typeface of any size for which the printer "knows" the shape of each letter. When creating design specifications for type in a Ventura publication, you must be specific about the type of printer as well as the fonts (typefaces, sizes, and type styles).

The next sections discuss in more detail the basic elements of a font: typeface, size, and style.

Typeface

In the traditional sense, a *typeface* is a family of type with the same basic shape for each letter. The Times typeface, for example, encompasses all sizes and styles of type that are variations of the same design for each letter of the alphabet. Typefaces are broadly grouped into two kinds, serif and sans serif, examples of which are shown in figure 9.1. The word *serif* refers to the fine cross strokes across the ends of the main strokes of a letter (across the top and bottom of the *h* or the *p*, for example). *Sans serif* means letters without serifs.

Times is a serif typeface.

Helvetica is a sans serif typeface.

Typefaces are often distinguished on another scale as either body-copy typefaces or display typefaces. *Body-copy* typefaces are commonly used for text, especially for the main body of a document, and are legible in small point sizes. *Display* typefaces, on the other hand, are used primarily in display ads and logos, headings in documents, and headlines in newsletters. Display typefaces can be ornate and are usually larger than 12 points. Figure 9.2 shows examples of both body-copy and display typefaces.

Fig. 9.2.

Display type and body-copy type.

Body type can be as small as 9 points.

Body type can be as large as 12 points.

Display typefaces

are usually designed for larger sizes.

When used on computers and laser printers, typefaces are frequently divided into another pair of categories: bit-mapped fonts and curve-fitting (outline) fonts (see fig. 9.3).

Bit-mapped fonts, which are printed as patterns of dots, may appear jagged at the edges when you print them (the way the screen fonts appear on your screen). Some bit-mapped fonts are designed to be printed at higher resolutions and when produced on a laser printer, can look as good as curve-fitting fonts. Bit-mapped fonts are hard to scale to different sizes with a formula method of scaling, so the font designer must develop a different set of designs for each size.

You can use Bitstream's Fontware Installation Kit, included with early shipments of Ventura 2.0, to add new bit-mapped fonts or create new sizes for those installed on your system. Stored as a pattern of dots, these fonts usually take up a great deal of storage space on the hard disk and require more printer memory as a page is being printed.

 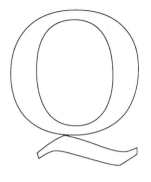

Fig. 9.3.

Bit-mapped font (left) and curve-fitting (outline) font (right).

Curve-fitting fonts are defined by curve-fitting mathematical formulas. These typefaces can be scaled to any size or made boldface or italic by changing a few variables in the formulas that define the shapes of the letters. PostScript is one example of a curve-fitting language used to produce curve-fitting fonts. Choosing PostScript fonts when printing with a PostScript printer or typesetter ensures a smooth finished product. Fonts stored as formulas take up less space in the printer's memory than do bit-mapped fonts, so you can download more of the curve-fitting fonts at one time.

You can use any font that your printer supports, even though Ventura may not provide a matching screen font. Later in this chapter you learn how to add screen fonts when you want to see on-screen the same typefaces you see on the printed page. Chapter 8 discusses how to add printer fonts and access them by merging one of Ventura's width tables with the table provided with the new fonts.

Efficiency Tip

Printing Typeface Outlines and Rotated Text with PostScript Printers

The PostScript file PS2.EFF, on the Utilities disk, enables you to print typeface outlines, gray, and rotated text. Before you install the alternative to the PostScript printer prologue, rename the default file (PS2.PRE in the VENTURA directory) to PS2.SAV for later use. Then copy PS2.EFF from the POSTSCPT directory on the Utilities disk to the VENTURA directory on your hard disk. Name the copy PS2.PRE. After you start Ventura, choose the FONT dialog box `Color: Magenta` option to print outlines around typefaces instead of solid letters (the outlines do not display on the screen). The `Cyan` option prints the selected text as 90-degree rotated text (not shown on-screen), the `Yellow` option prints the selected text as 260-degree rotated text (not shown on-screen), and `Green` prints text as a shade of gray. If you select the `Text Rotation` option from the ALIGNMENT dialog box under the Paragraph menu, text rotation is shown on-screen.

Size

Type size is measured in points. The point system derives from the French word *poindre*, meaning to prick. A point was the smallest possible mark that a printer could make on a page—about 1/72 inch. An inch, then, contains approximately 72 points. A type's point size is usually the measurement of the full height of the lowercase letters from the top of the ascender to the bottom of the descender. The *ascender* is the stem that points up on some lowercase letters, such as *h*, *l*, and *k*. The *descender* is the stem that points down on some lowercase letters, such as *j*, *g*, and *y*. Because the actual shape of each letter of a typeface is determined by the original designer, the true vertical measurement of any one letter can vary slightly among different typefaces.

You can change the point size of selected characters by selecting the characters with the Text cursor and holding the Shift key while moving the up arrow or the down arrow. With a PostScript printer, Ventura produces any size of type from 1 to 254 in half-point increments. These half-point increments are not to be confused with the fractional points found in many of Ventura's dialog boxes. The fractional point measurement allows you to make spacing adjustments in 100th of a point increments. Non-PostScript fonts can be sized in the available size fonts.

Another common measurement in typesetting is the *pica*. An inch contains 6 picas, and each pica contains 12 points (for a total of 72 points to the inch). This measuring system is used by Ventura's type-specifying dialog boxes (when you select points and picas as the unit of measure) and in the SET RULER dialog box (accessed from the Options menu), used to set the unit of measure shown on the rulers. Picas are normally used to define horizontal and vertical distances on the page and not to define type size, even if you describe type larger than 12 points. A 1.5-inch measure on the page is 9 picas, for example, but a 1.5-inch high character is 108 points.

Do not confuse the printer's or typesetter's horizontal measurement in picas with *pitch*, a horizontal measurement on a letter-quality printer. Pitch—usually 8, 10, or 12—gives the number of characters that fit in an inch. The horizontal pica measurement has nothing to do with the number of characters per inch, which varies depending on the size of the type, the typeface, the actual characters used in the words, and the letter spacing.

Designers who need to fit copy or match previously printed type sizes often further distinguish typefaces by two other measures, cap height and x height. *Cap height* is the height of a typeface's uppercase letters. Because a capital letter has no descender (except in some ornate styles), a 10-point capital letter does not measure 10 points. Usually, the capital letter's height is two-thirds of the point size. The letters in figure 9.4 were set as 36-point letters from an assortment of typefaces. Note the differences between cap heights. The *x height* is the size of the lowercase *x* and the bowls, or rounded portions, of other lowercase letters such as *e*, *c*, and *d*.

Body copy is usually set between 9 and 12 points in size, with headlines generally larger. Business cards and classified ads can be smaller, in 7-point or 8-point sizes. Text smaller than 6 points is difficult to read in most typefaces and is rarely used.

The FONT dialog box, shown in figure 9.5, displays sizes and styles for each typeface in the width table you specify in the SET PRINTER INFO dialog box. If you have chosen the PostScript width table, the word Custom rather than individual point sizes appears under Size in the FONT dialog box (see fig. 9.6). You can type any point size, in half-point increments, from 1 to 254 as a custom size.

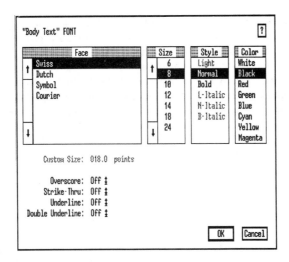

AyAyAyAyAyAy*Ay*

Fig. 9.4.

Letters with the same nominal size that look different in different typefaces.

"Body Text" FONT   [?]

Face	Size	Style	Color
Swiss	6	Light	White
Dutch	8	Normal	Black
Symbol	10	Bold	Red
Courier	12	L-Italic	Green
	14	N-Italic	Blue
	18	B-Italic	Cyan
	24		Yellow
			Magenta

Custom Size: 018.0 points

Overscore: Off ‡
Strike-Thru: Off ‡
Underline: Off ‡
Double Underline: Off ‡

[OK] [Cancel]

Fig. 9.5.

The FONT dialog box showing settings for a non-PostScript printer.

"Body Text" FONT   [?]

Face	Size	Style	Color
Helvetica	CUSTOM	Light	White
Times		Normal	Black
Courier		Bold	Red
Symbol		L-Italic	Green
Palatino		N-Italic	Blue
CenturySchlbook		B-Italic	Cyan
Zapf Chancery			Yellow
Zapf Dingbats			Magenta

Custom Size: 018.0 points

Overscore: Off ‡
Strike-Thru: Off ‡
Underline: Off ‡
Double Underline: Off ‡

[OK] [Cancel]

Fig. 9.6.

The FONT dialog box showing settings for a PostScript printer.

Most non-PostScript printers do not have all point sizes available in each typeface. If a point size is not available in the printer width table you have specified, that size displays in gray rather than black in the Size list of the FONT dialog box. In Chapter 8, you learn how to add printer fonts to width tables so that more sizes, faces, and styles are available.

Usually, you want to use the sizes and styles supported by your printer and width table. You can use other options if, for example, you are creating documents to be printed on a laser printer or typesetter at another location. You may specify a Post-Script device as your target printer, choose fonts of any size and face, and use a dot-matrix printer or other non-Postscript device for drafts. When you print these draft documents, the printer either converts the fonts to ones it supports or prints them as bit-mapped fonts.

Ventura loads width tables during program installation for the printers you select. You can add a width table by rerunning part of Ventura's VPPREP program, even though the type of printer you select is not connected to your system. New width tables are created when you select different types of printers or collections of printer fonts using the Load Different Width Table option in the SET PRINTER INFO dialog box. Use the width table for the printer you intend to use for final copy during page layout. This choice allows you to see the line and paragraph endings as they will appear in final print. Refer to Chapter 8 to learn more about moving a document to another system for printing and about adding width tables and printer fonts to the collection delivered with the program.

Style

The third basic element of the traditional font is style. Styles listed in the Paragraph menu's FONT dialog box include Normal, Bold, and Italic. Figure 9.7 shows some examples of different type styles. As discussed in Chapter 5, a Set Font button is displayed on the left of the screen when you use the Text function. You can use this button to change the style of selected letters or phrases. (The Text function also allows you to underscore, overscore, superscript, subscript, strikethrough, and change the capitalization of individual letters and phrases in paragraphs.) You can choose any of the attributes shown in the Text function's assignment list after you select the text with the editing cursor. Remember that style changes made with the Text function embed bracketed codes in the source file to override settings established by paragraph tags.

As is the case with size, not all printers support all the styles shown on the Ventura menus. The styles unavailable with your printer display in gray in the FONT dialog box. With a PostScript printer, you can print all sizes of any face and style that your printer supports and any size for the faces and styles that you have added.

You can use the ATTRIBUTE OVERRIDES dialog box from the Paragraph menu to add underscores, double underscores, overscores, and strikethroughs to all text in a paragraph. You also can adjust the size and position of superscripts and subscripts and small caps with this dialog box.

Changing the Default Font

Chapter 5 explains how to change type specifications using the Font command from the Paragraph menu. This chapter examines the FONT dialog box in terms of the

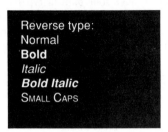

Black type:
Normal
Bold
Italic
Bold Italic
SMALL CAPS

Reverse type:
Normal
Bold
Italic
Bold Italic
SMALL CAPS

Fig. 9.7.

Examples of type styles available on a PostScript printer.

typefaces and fonts listed there. You can change the default font and add or remove fonts to or from the list in the dialog box.

The default font is defined by the Body Text tag in the style file you are using. This font determines the appearance of new text typed into a file with the Text function. The default font also defines unformatted text placed in Ventura from a word processing file. The default font for the Ventura-generated Z tags (box text, captions, headers, and footers) matches the Body Text tag in the active style file.

To change the default font during a work session, click the Paragraph function. Then select a paragraph that is tagged as Body Text. Use the commands under the Paragraph menu to change the characteristics of the Body Text tag.

Using Printer Fonts

As mentioned throughout this chapter, the fonts available with Ventura vary from printer to printer and from installation to installation. Essentially, three types of printer fonts exist, each font with its own method of installation. These three types are built-in fonts, cartridge fonts, and downloadable fonts. Each of these types of fonts is described briefly in the following sections.

Efficiency Tip

Know Your Printer

If you do not know whether a particular typeface or size is installed on your printer, refer to the FONT dialog box. Any non-PostScript typeface or size displayed in gray is not installed on the target printer. If you have set up PostScript as your printer option, however, you can enter any point size from 1 to 254, in half-point increments (again see fig. 9.6). Although many PostScript font names are displayed in the FONT dialog box, you can print only those stored on your hard disk or in your printer.

Built-In Printer Fonts

Built-in printer fonts are installed by the manufacturer of your printer. They are always available for any document. Ideally, every font should be built into the printer. Unfortunately, however, fonts take up memory, so most printers have a limited selection of built-in fonts.

Most PostScript printer models have four built-in typefaces: Times, Helvetica, Courier, and Symbol—primarily Greek and mathematical symbols—(see fig. 9.8). Many other printers supporting the PostScript language offer the same choices (see table 8.2, "Built-In Printer Fonts". You can print each of these in any size or style listed in the FONT dialog box.

Fig. 9.8.

The Apple LaserWriter's four built-in typefaces.

Times
Helvetica
Courier
Symbol: Σψμβολ

Newer PostScript printers add several more typefaces as built-in fonts: Avant Garde, Bookman, New Century Schoolbook, Helvetica Narrow, Palatino, Zapf Chancery, and Zapf Dingbats—all symbols—(see fig. 9.9). You can print these fonts, except Zapf Dingbats, in any size or style listed in the FONT dialog box. Zapf Dingbats can be printed in all sizes but only in normal style.

Fig. 9.9.

The Apple LaserWriter Plus's 11 built-in typefaces.

Times
Helvetica
Helvetica Narrow
Courier
Symbol: Σψμβολ
Avant Garde
Bookman
New Century Schoolbook
Palatino
Zapf Chancery
Zapf Dingbats: ✳✧☆✦

Times and Helvetica typefaces are built into PostScript typesetters. All other typefaces are downloaded as the pages are printed. Unless you use fonts permanently downloaded to a hard disk attached to the typesetter, the amount of memory in the typesetter limits the number of typefaces that you can download at one time.

Cartridge Fonts

Similar to built-in fonts, cartridge fonts are coded into computer chips. Cartridge fonts are built into removable cartridges rather than hard-wired into the printer itself. The number of fonts available for a specific document depends on the cartridge installed in the printer when the document is printed.

The Hewlett-Packard LaserJet Plus I and II are cartridge printers. If you do not insert a cartridge into the printer, the default font is 12-point Courier. Early models of the LaserJet printers do not have enough memory to accommodate downloaded fonts. The Hewlett-Packard LaserJet Plus and HP II are also cartridge printers, but their expanded memory enables Ventura to download additional fonts to them.

Downloadable Fonts

Downloadable fonts differ from built-in and cartridge fonts in one significant aspect: because downloadable fonts are not hard-coded into hardware, they take up memory space (RAM) when downloaded to the printer. (Chapter 8 explains how to install downloadable fonts.)

Ventura supports downloadable fonts sold by various manufacturers listed in the appendix of this book. For example, at this writing, Adobe Systems, Inc., offers a wide range of downloadable fonts for PostScript printers. Bitstream also makes downloadable fonts for both PostScript and non-PostScript printers.

Efficiency Tip

Shorten Printing Time

Downloading fonts at the beginning of each print job lengthens print time. If time is a concern, stick to the built-in fonts on your printer.

You can use the ADD/REMOVE FONTS dialog box to disable automatic font downloading. Some printers (the LaserJet Plus Series II, for example) provide instructions to download fonts to the printer "permanently" rather than download from the hard disk at the beginning of and during each print job. What really happens is that you download a font to RAM in the printer before printing begins. This type of downloading saves printing time but uses more memory. The downloading is not truly permanent, because the fonts are erased when you turn off the printer. (See Chapter 8 for more information on downloading fonts.)

Matching Screen Fonts and Printer Fonts

Many printer fonts that you can purchase separately and add to your printer also provide matching screen fonts. Ventura manages printer fonts in the width table but keeps each screen font as a separate file in the VENTURA directory. Ventura is delivered with screen fonts for serif (Times or Dutch), sans serif (Helvetica or Swiss) and Symbol typefaces in the following font sizes, based on the monitor you specify during installation:

CGA (640×200) screen fonts
    Swiss and Dutch 10, 14, 18, 36
    Courier and Symbol 12

EGA (640×350) screen fonts
    Swiss and Dutch 8, 9, 10, 11, 12, 14, 18, 20, 24, 36
    Courier and Symbol 12

VGA (640×480) screen fonts
    Swiss and Dutch 6, 7, 8, 9, 10, 11, 12, 14, 16, 18, 20, 22, 24, 28, 36, 48
    Courier 12, 20, 24
    Symbol 12

The Ventura Professional Extension is delivered with the screen fonts listed under VGA and also includes Swiss and Dutch 48 and 72 and Symbol 8, 10, and 24 for equations.

If you choose a printer font that does not have a matching screen font, Ventura substitutes the closest match from the available screen fonts. Ventura scales the screen fonts to match the size selected for printing. In the scaling process, you lose some of the clarity and definition of the typeface on the screen but not on the printout. To ensure that lines and paragraphs end at the same positions on-screen and on printed pages, adjust the space between words on-screen.

In the case of Adobe's Zapf Dingbats, Ventura substitutes the character on-screen with the equivalent value from the International character set, but prints the specified Dingbat if you have an advanced PostScript printer. Xerox's Ventura reference guide, Appendix E, shows the Dingbat symbols. If your printer supports other fonts and you need to see on-screen the same typefaces, styles, and space between words as you see on paper, you must add screen fonts to match the printer fonts. This process is described in the following section.

Adding Screen Fonts

Even if you use just one printer and the fonts provided with Ventura, you may want to add screen fonts to match the zoom views Ventura offers. For instance, to see 10-point text properly shaped in Enlarged view, you must add a 20-point screen font. Keep in mind that Ventura scales existing fonts to size only when the actual size is not available. But if you often work with 12-point type, for example, it may be helpful to add a 6-point screen font. When you switch to Reduced view, Ventura uses an actual screen font, not a scaled-down version of a larger font, to create the page in view. Small point sizes reside in files that do not take much space, but large font sizes consume considerably more memory.

Adding Additional Screen Fonts To Speed Full-Screen Displays

Another reason to add screen fonts is to minimize the time Ventura takes to redraw screens on full-page displays. If you select VGA as your display during installation, Ventura automatically uses high-resolution screen fonts with a VGA extension. If you are willing to sacrifice on-screen clarity for 40 percent to 60 percent faster screen redraws, use the VPREP program to select an EGA display. The screen will repaint faster using the lower-resolution EGA screen fonts.

1. Insert the Application disk into drive A, type *A:VPREP*, and press Enter. When the program asks Are you installing for the first time? answer N.

2. Follow the program prompts and choose any EGA option as your display.

3. Use the SET PRINTER INFO dialog box from the Options menu to change the Screen Fonts option from VGA to EGA.

Ventura now chooses lower-resolution screen fonts for display. To change back to high-resolution displays, change the Screen Fonts option back to VGA.

You can add as many as 700 screen fonts with a maximum size of 35K each. If, however, a collection of screen fonts (those with the same file extension) is larger than 68K, the screen fonts compete for the same memory used to hold chapter source files. In addition, Ventura loads all screen fonts with the extension specified in the SET PRINTER INFO dialog box. This procedure can slow loading time.

Although storing 700 screen fonts may be unusual, all screen fonts could have the same extension. For this reason, you should assign a unique extension to rarely used fonts, fonts used with a particular printer, or fonts used on a specific project. If a recurring newsletter requires only a few fonts, for instance, give these fonts an NSL extension. When you work on the newsletter, specify NSL as the screen font in the SET PRINTER INFO dialog box and only those fonts will be loaded.

Each set of fonts identified by a unique extension must include Ventura's Helvetica and Times Roman files for 10, 14, 18 and 36 points. All screen fonts must be—or must be converted to—Ventura format. Fonts for higher- and lower-resolution displays can be used in the same set—just name the font files with the same extension. Be careful not to add fonts that duplicate those you already have; different font vendors may give the same fonts different names, and Ventura may not know which to use.

Most font products come with instructions for making and adding fonts compatible with Ventura. Use the following procedure to convert standard Adobe fonts from ABF format to Ventura format:

1. Copy the Adobe font files to the VENTURA directory or to the VPFONTS directory. Assign file extension ABF. (All fonts to be grouped in a collection must reside in the same directory.)

2. Copy the ABFTOFNT.EXE program from the POSTSCPT directory on the Utilities disk to the font directory on your hard disk.

3. Use the DOS CHANGE DIRECTORY command (cd\<directory name>) to change to the directory where the fonts are located. Type the following at the DOS prompt to convert the file formats:

   ABFTOFNT *.ABF

   During the conversion, the file extensions are changed to PSF.

4. Use the DOS RENAME command to change the PSF extension to one matching your font-naming conventions.

Some font vendors provide installation programs that allow you to copy the printer fonts, width table, and screen fonts into Ventura's directories after you enter your display type, output device, and the font sizes you want loaded. Once you complete the font vendor's installation program, you must use Ventura to create a new printer width table by merging the vendor's table with a Ventura width table. You learn to add printer fonts and create new printer width tables in Chapter 8.

After you add new screen fonts, Ventura knows how to display them. You cannot, however, print the publication in that font unless you also install the font on the printer. A screen font is a bit-mapped font. It is not the same as the font used by the printer. Typically, you install screen fonts at the same time you install printer fonts, but you may want to install only the printer font.

You use the Load Different Width Table option in the SET PRINTER INFO dialog box to activate printer fonts. To match the printer fonts to a set of screen fonts, type the file extension of the screen fonts in the Screen Fonts option of the SET PRINTER INFO dialog box. If you don't add a screen font when you add a new font to your printer, Ventura uses an existing screen font to get the nearest match to the printer font. The word spacing on the screen may look incorrect, but the line and page endings are correct, and the final printed page will show accurate letter spacing. Refer to Chapter 8 to see how to add printer fonts and width tables.

Efficiency Tip

Installing Screen Fonts for a Second Printer

If you use your own draft printer and take the document to another system with a different printer for final printouts, install the screen fonts for the final printer. This way you can see a more accurate on-screen version of how the final pages will print. This method is especially helpful when you prepare documents for service-bureau processing.

Removing Screen Fonts

Removing screen fonts is as simple as changing the font's extension or deleting the individual screen font files from the VENTURA directory. Removing screen fonts, however, does not reduce the amount of memory reserved for them. (Check the Screen Font option on the DIAGNOSTIC dialog box to see the amount of space reserved for screen fonts in your configuration.) Remember that Ventura recognizes as active only the screen fonts with file extensions matching the letters typed in the SET PRINTER INFO dialog box Screen Font option. Never remove all the screen-font files that Ventura loaded during program installation.

Planning Your Design Specifications

The first decision you must make in the design process is to determine the type of printer you will use for final production of the document. In addition, you must know the type of font cartridge you have or which downloadable fonts you can use. When you have this information, you can list all the different fonts available for use in your design specifications.

The next step is to list the fonts to be used in a particular publication. You should limit the number of fonts to be used for both aesthetic and practical reasons. The best designs use only a few fonts on each page. In addition, some printers cannot handle more than a few fonts per page or per cartridge. A third factor in determining the number of fonts is the number of text elements used in the document. For example, elements that need differentiation in a book may include the following:

- Chapter openings, section openings, or feature article headlines
- Folios
- Different levels of headings or headlines
- Body copy
- Figure captions
- Labels within figures
- Footnotes
- Special sections, such as sidebars, summaries, and tables

The type-specification process involves merging the two lists: the list of the fonts available or that you want to use, and the list of the different elements within the document (see fig. 9.10).

If you come from an office environment in which all publications are printed on a letter-quality printer, you may find the comparatively wide range of fonts confusing. If so, you can approach the type specification of a document in two ways.

The fastest way to acquire a sense of design and develop good design specifications is to study and imitate published works that are similar in structure to your document. Match your design specifications as closely as possible to those of published documents. In other words, select fonts that are similar to those used for headings, body copy, and captions in the published document. You do not have to match the typefaces exactly, but try to substitute typefaces in the same category (serif or sans serif;

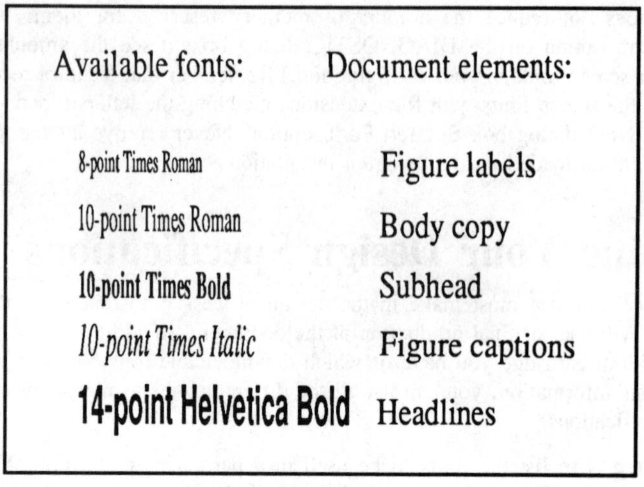

Fig. 9.10.

Beginning the type-specification process.

Available fonts:	Document elements:
8-point Times Roman	Figure labels
10-point Times Roman	Body copy
10-point Times Bold	Subhead
10-point Times Italic	Figure captions
14-point Helvetica Bold	Headlines

Efficiency Tip

Print a Type Sample Sheet

The CAPABILI.CHP file shows whether your printer can print white type on black boxes or can support transparent graphics, and shows how close to the paper edge your printer can print. This sample chapter also shows whether the selected printer prints paragraphs as shades of gray or prints font outlines and rotated text.

CAPABILI.CHP was created with a serif font and illustrates the sizes between 6 and 72 points that are available on your printer in that font. If you are not familiar with the different typefaces in the FONT dialog box, or if you do not know which ones your printer supports, make and print sample copies of CAPABILI.CHP, using each of the Face options in the FONT dialog box. Figure 9.11 shows type samples.

Fig. 9.11.

A type sample sheet.

We offer...
Times

8 9 10 11 12 14 18 24

Bold
Italic
Bold Italic

Helvetica

8 9 10 11 12 14 18 24

Bold
Italic
Bold Italic

Reverse type (all fonts)

roman, italic, or boldface; and so on). Part III of this book shows examples of documents with different type specifications and Ventura's example chapters include several well-designed samples.

A second approach to creating type specifications is to study the underlying principles followed by designers and typographers. Some of these guidelines are listed here:

1. Do not use more than two typefaces in a document. Usually, one typeface should be serif, the other sans serif. Use variations in size and style to distinguish different elements.

2. Use variations in size rather than boldface type to distinguish different heading levels. Too many bold headings on a page can distract the reader. One common exception to this rule is the lowest heading level, which may be boldface in the same size and typeface as the body copy.

3. In body copy, use the italic style rather than underscores. (Underscored text is a convention developed for use in documents printed on letter-quality printers that cannot print italic type.)

4. Use all capital letters as a deliberate design strategy rather than as a way to show emphasis or to differentiate heading levels. Studies have shown that a string of capital letters is difficult to read. Use variations in size rather than all caps text to differentiate headings. One common exception to this rule occurs when the list of available fonts is too limited to accommodate all heading levels. In this case, you can use all capital letters to distinguish between two heading levels in the same font.

Few documents can follow all these guidelines without making exceptions, the most common of which have been mentioned here. One mark of a good designer is knowing when and how to break the rules.

Ventura's Typography commands give the designer a large measure of control over the appearance of a document. The Chapter Typography command under the Chapter menu controls kerning, column balance, the number of lines allowed for widows and orphans, and the space from the top margin to the baseline of the first text for the entire chapter. The Frame Typography command under the Frame menu defaults to the Chapter settings but allows you to override any of these settings for a selected frame. The Paragraph Typography command under the Paragraph menu controls spacing between letters and words and allows Ventura to change leading when characters within a paragraph change size (as in equations).

Choosing Automatic or Forced Leading

The term *leading* originated at the same time that the words *font* and *serif* were introduced. Leading once referred literally to thin strips of metal (lead) that were inserted between lines of type to add vertical space in a column or a tray of set type. Thus, the reference to 2 points of leading indicated that a strip of metal, 2 points thick, was to separate each line of text from the next. If the size of the text was 10 points, adding 2 points of leading yielded a total of 12 points for each line of text. With the advent of computerized typesetting equipment and its accuracy, typesetters began measuring leading from the base of one line of type to the base of the line below it. For example, a type specification of 10/12 Times Roman calls for 10-point Times Roman letters with 12 points of leading from baseline to baseline. Ventura uses this same technique to measure leading. In Ventura, however, leading is called Inter-Line spacing in the SPACING dialog box.

You can take advantage of Ventura's automatic leading feature by choosing the Set Preferences command from the Options menu and setting Auto-Adjustments: Styles. Then, when you change the point size in the FONT dialog box, the leading automatically changes also—to a value approximately 20 percent greater than the point size.

The Auto-Adjustments option has two other options: " and - -. These options allow you to control whether a word processors' inch marks are converted to two opening and two closing quotation marks or are left as they are for a document that requires inch marks and whether two hyphens are converted to an em dash. In addition to choosing either of these options, you can choose None or Both (see fig. 9.12).

Fig. 9.12.

The SET PREFERENCES dialog box.

The Body Text tag's interline spacing value forms the basis for an invisible grid to which Ventura adheres when setting text on the page. Although you cannot see the grid, you can see the effect of the grid when you choose Turn Line Snap On in the Options menu and move a frame from one location to another on the page.

Ventura automatically increases space between lines if you increase the size of a font or change the position of any character within a line. Select Paragraph Typography from the Paragraph menu and specify Grow Inter-Line To Fit: On in the TYPOG-RAPHY SETTINGS dialog box.

To cause text to begin on the first baseline measured from the top of a column, set Move Down To 1st Baseline By to Inter-Line. (The option is located in the CHAPTER TYPOGRAPHY SETTINGS dialog box under the Chapter menu.) Alternatively, you can set the global default for the chapter to Move Down To 1st Baseline By: Cap Height to cause ascenders and capital letters to abut the top of the column. Set the option to Inter-Line when you use multiple font sizes in multicolumn layouts to help achieve even alignment of text on a uniform baseline.

Variations between the cap heights or x heights of different typefaces may affect your choice of leading. For example, when a design includes a typeface with a small x height, such as Times, you can use tighter leading without losing legibility. A typeface with a large x height, such as Avant Garde, needs leading at least 20 percent greater than the point size (the default for automatic leading in Ventura) in order to be readable.

If you are familiar with the traditional typesetting environment, you are probably accustomed to specifying the exact leading as well as the type size. Generally speaking, the use of automatic leading is a production convenience rather than a design principle. You can turn off Ventura's automatic leading feature by setting the Auto-Adjustments option in the SET PREFERENCES dialog box to None. Or you can override automatic leading by changing the interline spacing in the SPACING dialog box (accessed from the Paragraph menu) after you change the point size.

When you let Ventura set the interline spacing (leading), the program also automatically sets proportionate amounts for the space above and below paragraphs. Like interline leading, paragraph spacing values also change automatically when you change the point size of the paragraph tag. If you are designing a publication that has more than one column on a page, develop type specifications based on the interline spacing (leading) of body text. As detailed in Chapter 5, the even alignment of text across columns depends on the values you set in several different commands:

- The height and top and bottom margins of the page or frame (Frame menu, MARGINS & COLUMNS dialog box)

- Space above, below, and between paragraphs, as well as space between lines (Paragraph menu, SPACING dialog box)

- Rules above or below paragraphs (Paragraph menu, RULING LINES ABOVE and RULING LINES BELOW dialog boxes)

The leading for any line is usually determined by the largest characters in that line. You can let Ventura adjust leading as you change font sizes in tags, and you can let Ventura automatically override leading to accommodate larger fonts in paragraphs tagged with smaller settings. The capability to size selected text using the Text function and FONT dialog box has been made more expedient with Ventura 2.0.

Interactive font selection lets you specify a point size for selected text without opening a dialog box or setting a tag. Just select the desired text, hold the Shift key, and tap the up or down arrow. Because PostScript printers print typefaces in any point size, each tap on an arrow key changes the size one point. (You can set half points when you select the text and then choose the Set Font button with the Text function). With non-PostScript printers, each tap on an arrow key changes the font to the next available size. The next available size depends on the fonts in the active width table. Use the Grow Inter-Line To Fit option from the Paragraph Typography command to increase interline spacing automatically when a font size larger than the default for the paragraph is embedded in the text. The interline spacing set for the tag does not change, but the oversized text is spaced so that it does not overstrike text on the preceding line.

Another exception to setting leading values based on the largest character is when you use large initial caps in a layout. The technique is commonly referred to as *drop caps*; Ventura refers to it as a big first character. When you use Ventura's SPECIAL EFFECTS dialog box to set the font specifications for an initial cap, the leading remains uniform within the body of the paragraph.

Figure 9.13 shows two examples of 10-point text on 12-point leading and a 36-point big first character. If you choose Space for Big First: Normal, Ventura aligns the top of the big first character with the top of the first line of body text and indents the number of lines needed for the character to fit. Space for Big First: Custom allows you to determine the number of indented lines, and the baseline of the big first character aligns with the baseline of the last indented paragraph line.

Fig. 9.13.

Ventura's alignment options for drop caps.

This is a 24 point Helvetica Big First Char. with Space For Big First: Normal. Ventura automatically aligns the top of the character with the top of the first line of text and calculates the number of lines to indent.

This is a 24 point Helvetica Big First Char. with Space For Big First: Custom. You set the number of lines to indent and Ventura aligns the baselines of the First Char. and the last indented line of text.

You may need to adjust the first character position because of cap height variations (explained under "Size" at the beginning of this chapter). You also may want to adjust position depending on whether the first character of text is a character with an ascender. There are two ways to fine-tune positioning of the big first character, but both will probably take experimenting. You can use Set Font Properties in the SPECIAL EFFECTS dialog box to increase the point size. Begin with a 2-point increase and see whether that forces alignment. You also can use the Shift option in the same dialog box. Change the measurement value to the right of Shift to fractional points. Then enter *2* points and choose whether to shift the character up or down.

Mixing Typefaces

As stressed in the design guidelines listed earlier in this chapter, you should use only one or two typefaces—usually a serif and a sans serif—in a single publication. You then can vary the size and style to differentiate elements in the text. You will find that using only one typeface streamlines the production process. Limiting the number of fonts in a width table, as described in Chapter 8, also frees memory that can be used to hold source documents during production.

One element of each font is its style—normal, bold, or italic (see ''Style'' earlier in this chapter). Ventura's method of formatting text allows you to assign a type style either to paragraphs of copy (using the FONT dialog box) or to selected words within paragraphs (using the Text function, as discussed in Chapter 5). When you change the font settings in the FONT dialog box from the Paragraph menu, you globally change all similarly tagged paragraphs. Figure 9.14 shows how a design change in the typeface can affect the appearance of body text.

Globally change the default values of Body Text to see the effect of a change in type specifications. This is Helvetica 12-point.

Globally change the default values of Body Text to see the effect of a change in type specifications. This is Helvetica 11-point, set on the default leading (14.40 fractional points) for 12 point type

Globally change the default values of Body Text to see the effect of a change in type specifications. This is Times 12-point.

Globally change the default values of Body Text to see the effect of a change in type specifications. This is Times 11-point type, set at the default leading (14.40) for 12-point type.

Fig. 9.14.

Comparison of body text tags.

Changing the typeface in the FONT dialog box, however, does not change any attributes that you attached to segments of the paragraph with the Text function. These attributes (such as bold, italic, underscore, overscore, superscript, subscript, strike-through, and change of capitalization) remain attached to the text. For example, you can decide to change all the body text in a chapter from Times to Helvetica by altering the body text tag specifications. But if you used the Text function to set attributes around phrases in a paragraph, you cannot globally override the settings unless you change the attribute codes with a word processing program.

Kerning Headlines and Titles

A document's headlines and titles should stand out from the body copy. As mentioned previously, you can use size rather than boldface or all caps to emphasize these elements. With large display type, however, you often find that letters appear to have too much space between them. If you have a PostScript printer, you will need to *kern* the type for a more professional appearance.

Kerning refers to fine adjustments made to the spacing between certain pairs of letters to give the overall text a balanced appearance. Tracking, as set in the Paragraph menu's TYPOGRAPHY SETTINGS dialog box, controls the spacing between all letters in a paragraph. As explained in Chapter 5, apparent excess space between two letters, in some instances, is an optical illusion caused by the angles of the two adjacent letters. For example, the edges of the capital A have a slope opposite to the capital V. When the letters A and V are adjacent in a word, as in KNAVE, the space between the A and the V appears to be much wider than the spaces between any of the other letters (see fig. 9.15).

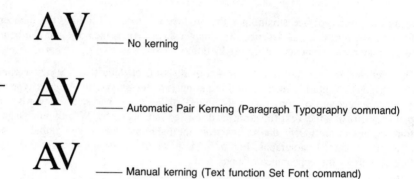

No kerning

Automatic Pair Kerning (Paragraph Typography command)

Manual kerning (Text function Set Font command)

Fig. 9.15.

An example of necessary kerning: between the letters A and V.

Setting Automatic Kerning with Tags

Ventura provides kerning tables with all PostScript fonts but not for other printers. Ventura also can use kerning tables provided by other font vendors. (Not all font vendors supply kerning tables, so be sure that you check for availability.) Kerning tables list the pairs of characters that usually need to be moved closer together as well as the adjustment needed for each pair.

When you set Automatic Pair Kerning: On in the TYPOGRAPHY SETTINGS dialog box, Ventura looks for and uses the kerning tables if Pair Kerning: On is set as the chapter default in the CHAPTER TYPOGRAPHY SETTINGS dialog box. You cannot change kerning amounts in any of the Paragraph menu dialog boxes; you can simply turn pair kerning on or off.

You can make minor kerning adjustments character-by-character with the Set Font button under the Text function (see "Kerning Manually"). If you are interested in adding kerning instructions for pairs of letters to a width table, consult Appendix K of the Ventura reference guide for the discussion of the VFM file. The process is complex but can be used to add up to 1,000 pairs to a width table used with Ventura.

Set the Pair Kerning: On option in the CHAPTER TYPOGRAPHY dialog box to enable kerning in paragraph tag and frame settings. If you want to override tags set in a frame, set the CHAPTER TYPOGRAPHY SETTINGS dialog box option On but set the FRAME TYPOGRAPHY SETTINGS Pair Kerning option Off.

You can use the On-Screen Kerning option in the SET PREFERENCES dialog box (accessed from the Options menu) to show kerning on-screen. If you want all point sizes kerned on-screen, select All. If you select one of the point sizes, Ventura kerns only sizes above that point size. On-Screen Kerning: All or None has no effect on the printed output, but showing kerning on-screen slows screen redrawing time. Because kerning involves fine adjustments often lost on a low-resolution printer or screen, you should generally leave the On-Screen Kerning option set to None. Click On-Screen Kerning: All if you want to check positions when fitting copy and want to see the effect of kerning on a particular line before printing. Kerning instructions applied with one of the manual techniques always display kerned text on-screen.

Kerning Manually

If your printer doesn't support automatic kerning, or certain characters need more kerning than the kerning tables have given, you can manually adjust the space between letters in two ways. The simplest way is to use Ventura's interactive kerning technique to see the kerning effects on-screen.

To make kerning adjustments between two or more characters, select the letter(s) with the Text tool. Then press the Shift key and press either the left-arrow key to tighten or the right-arrow key to loosen the space to the right of the selected letter(s). If you have selected more than one letter, the space to the right of each letter is changed.

Alternatively, you can select the letter(s) you want to kern and click the Set Font button to open the FONT SETTING FOR SELECTED TEXT dialog box. If you select Tighter and enter an amount, the space after the selected character(s) is reduced by that amount. Kerning in Ventura is measured in percentages of an em space. However, Ventura uses the @ symbol as the measure of an em rather than the capital letter *M* in the font. The value you enter to the right of Kern is a percentage of the width of an @ sign. Because screen resolution is limited and you must print and check each adjustment individually when kerning manually, use manual kerning only in specific cases. For example, study a printed draft of the document and examine headlines for pairs of letters that appear to need more kerning. (Kerning is also discussed in Chapter 5.)

If you adjust kerning manually in Ventura and then reopen your source file, you see the kerning formulas in the text. If you used the FONT SETTING FOR SELECTED TEXT dialog box to kern, the formula appears differently than if you kerned interactively. In the first instance, Ventura adds a text attribute for the active font in that dialog box between the opening bracket and the percent sign and adds a *D* between the percent sign and the closing bracket.

Manual kerning instructions are placed in the source text file as bracketed codes. The syntax is an opening angle bracket, a percent sign, a minus sign (to set the kerning tighter), the percent of an em used to move the letter, and a closing angle bracket. Remember that Ventura uses the size of the @ character in the current font as the measure of an em.

In the following example, the letter *A* was moved 14 percent of a single em space closer to the W, and the letter V was moved 8 percent of a single em space closer to the A using these instructions embedded in the source file:

    W<%-14>A<%-8>VE<%0>

Chapter 5 discusses entering text attributes and coded instructions in a word processing file so that Ventura can convert them when you load the file. Setting up kerning in a word processing file, as shown in figure 9.16, is accurate but time-consuming (unless you use the same formula often and can store the formula in your word processor).

Fig. 9.16.

*Kerning commands
in a word processing
file.*

```
<%-11>RAVE<%0>;        Made all the letters tighter

<%62>RAVE<%0>;         Made all the letters looser

RA<M%100>V<D%0>E       The A was selected and a value of one em was set
                       to move the E away from the V)
```

Store a Kerning Formula in Your Word Processor

Sometimes words that occur frequently in your publications—a logo, for instance—need kerning corrections. For rapid, uniform, and repetitive use, store the word and its kerning text attributes in a glossary on your word processor. Whenever you use that word, you can insert the word and all its kerning commands.

Handling Captions

In any document, you should treat similar items consistently, including labels within figures and figure titles or captions. Consistency can be difficult to achieve when you bring figures into Ventura from other programs. Can each graphing program match the fonts used in figures from other drawing packages? Can you scale the figure larger or smaller after it is in Ventura? You must specify how to handle captions, figure titles, and figure labels in each different program used as a source of illustrations for the document.

Even if you type all graphics captions as part of Ventura text and format them using a tag, you still must specify the font you want to use for labels within the figures. Additionally, you may need to account for type-size changes that result when you shrink or enlarge a figure in Ventura. As explained in Chapter 6, when you change the size of a graphic imported from another program, you also change the size of the type used in that graphic. Graphics are often imported oversized because reduction of the graphic in Ventura tightens up or improves the appearance of the lines or dots. If you know that an imported figure is to be reduced by 50 percent, the type that accompanies that figure should be twice as large as the type in the final document. To handle labels and titles within illustrations, refer to the discussion of box text in Chapter 6. Ventura's caption feature, designed to place captions above, below, or beside framed illustrations, is discussed in Chapter 7.

Type Figure Labels and Captions in Ventura

To ensure consistency, enter all figure labels, titles, and captions directly in Ventura. Both the box text and caption features allow you to keep these elements with the illustration, as described in Chapters 6 and 7.

Fitting Copy within a Defined Space

Copy casting is one of the steps in the broader task of copy fitting: the process of making the text fit into a limited number of pages or column inches. In this section, you learn how to cast copy—estimate how much copy will fit on a page or how many pages the final manuscript will fill when printed—and how to fine-tune the type specifications (the word, letter, and line spacing) to make copy fit. Because copy casting is normally based on body text only (without headings), the process is one of estimation and is not exact. Chapter 7, "Creating Full-Page Layouts," explains several methods of fitting the final copy into a predefined area, such as a column, a page, or a specific number of pages, when you work in Ventura.

Choosing the Method of Copy Casting

Traditionally, professional designers have approached the problems of copy casting from two angles. First, based on the design specifications, a designer may estimate how many words (or characters) will fill the allotted space. Magazine editors use this approach when they ask authors to write articles of a specified word length. Second, a designer can study the completed text, estimate how much space the written text fills, and then make adjustments to the design if necessary to force the text to fit a specified area. The following sections elaborate on the methods of copy casting.

Estimating the Number of Pages from a Disk File

The quickest way to estimate how many pages a certain document fills is to load the file onto the page of an untitled chapter, with the design set by the style file you intend to use. Set the characteristics for the Body Text tag to the anticipated settings, and then press the End key to go to the last page of the publication.

Efficiency Tip

Quickly Abandon a Test Document

If you placed a file in Ventura for estimating purposes only, just click the New or Quit command in the File menu and choose to abandon the changes when prompted whether you intend to save the chapter.

When the amount of actual text differs significantly from the amount of text required, you can force the copy to fit by adjusting the margins in Ventura, either before or after you place the text. Changing the margins after you place the text works if all the text is placed on the page and is not in individual frames added to the page. As another option, you can edit the copy to shorten or lengthen the text to the desired length.

Estimating the Number of Characters You Want

Estimating the number of characters you need to fill a certain number of pages is a little more involved than simply estimating the number of pages a given manuscript fills. Because Ventura sets in the style file both the image area's boundaries (margins and columns) and the bulk of the typographic settings, you can experiment with alternate design specifications by simply loading different style files to a sample chapter file. You can use one of Ventura's sample chapter files, or you can create your own style file after placing a sample text file on the page or in a frame on the page. The trick to keeping this technique simple is to make sure that the sample source text and style files contain the same tag names. As you look at each design, place in the file a marker (a word or a character you will look for later with a word processor) to indicate where in the text the allotted space ends.

Once you have decided on the design to be used, use a word processor to check the number of characters needed to fill the space. Remember to adjust the number of characters if your sample source files are longer than the measured area. You may need to copy and paste the text from the original file into a temporary file if you marked an ending point before the end of the source file.

Using a Typecasting Reference Book

One useful traditional technique for casting copy is to refer to a typecasting reference book. Such a book, available at most bookstores, shows examples of text in various sizes and with different leadings. From these examples, you can choose the look you want for your body copy. Also provided is the average number of characters per pica for each font. You can get the character count from the word processing program or by estimating the number of characters per page or per line of printed copy. You also may use a type gauge to measure the type against a specific column width and length to estimate the number of lines of final copy. To determine the number of lines per inch at various leadings, you can use a second measuring guide or gauge. The sequence of calculations goes something like this:

1. Select a font to be used for the text.

2. In the typecasting reference book, look up the average number of characters per pica for that font.

3. Determine the number of characters in the word processing file.

4. Divide the total number of characters by the average number of characters per pica to estimate the total number of picas required by the text.

5. Divide the total number of picas by the column width in picas to estimate the total number of lines of final copy.

6. Look up the number of lines per inch for the leading you plan to use.

7. Divide the total number of lines by the number of lines per inch to estimate the number of inches of final copy.

8. Divide the number of inches of final copy by the number of inches per page to estimate the total number of pages.

Because this method of casting copy or estimating length is tedious and has a wide margin for error, many typesetters use one of the following two methods for setting dummy text.

Setting Dummy Text: Method 1

With the first method, typesetters lay out one or two sample pages, using stock type samples, and estimate the number of characters that will fit on a page. Often, the character count is converted to an estimated number of words to be assigned to an author. You can use this technique with Ventura as well. The steps for this method follow:

1. Type one paragraph exactly 100 characters long.

2. Set the type in the specified font.

3. Duplicate the paragraph as many times as necessary to fill the column or page.

4. Count the number of paragraphs required to fill the column or page and multiply that number by 100 to estimate the character count per page.

5. Multiply this number by the number of pages to determine the maximum character count for the document.

6. Divide this number by 5, depending on the writing style, to estimate the number of words needed to fill the allocated pages (with an average of 5 characters per word).

Setting Dummy Text: Method 2

Another quick method of fitting copy is to make your own typecasting reference pages: create a 100-character paragraph of text and set it in the exact width that you plan to use in the document. Set copies of the same paragraph in different sizes or with different leading, and measure the depth of each variation (see fig. 9.17). You can roughly estimate the total number of column inches for the document using the following formula:

$$\frac{\text{inches per 100 characters} \times \text{number of characters in text files}}{100}$$

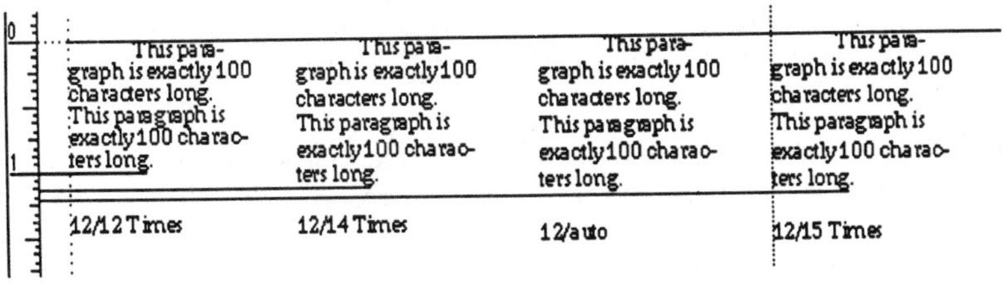

This paragraph is exactly 100 characters long. This paragraph is exactly 100 characters long.	This paragraph is exactly 100 characters long. This paragraph is exactly 100 characters long.	This paragraph is exactly 100 characters long. This paragraph is exactly 100 characters long.	This paragraph is exactly 100 characters long. This paragraph is exactly 100 characters long.
12/12 Times	12/14 Times	12/auto	12/15 Times

Fig. 9.17.

12-point Times font with different leading specifications.

Neither copy-casting technique absolutely guarantees that copy will fit the space allowed. You still must do final copy fitting directly in Ventura, but you can employ many techniques to assist in this task. Besides changing margins, column sizes, gutter widths, and leading, you also can affect how copy fits with changes in alignment, hyphenation, and word and letter spacing. These techniques are described in the following sections.

Changing the Type Specifications To Fit Copy

After casting copy with one or more of the methods described in the preceding sections, you may decide to change the type specifications for a document to make the text fit a prescribed number of pages or column inches. Besides the obvious solutions—changing the type size or typeface—you can affect the amount of space required by the text by changing subtle specifications such as the column width, letter spacing, and line spacing in fine increments.

Adjusting the Column Width

If you are accustomed to traditional typesetting techniques, you probably have specified text in terms of the width of each column. When you define the number of columns for the pages and frames of a publication, you either enter the width of the columns or let Ventura divide the space between the margins evenly.

Here is one rule of thumb for determining the optimum width of text: The best line or column width is equal to 60 characters of the specified font, style, and size. Lines that are too long are hard for the reader to follow; the lines also need extra leading to improve legibility. Columns that are too narrow (much shorter than 30 characters in line length) have awkward line breaks and too much hyphenation. You should not use justification on short line lengths.

Adjusting the Leading

The results of copy casting can be significantly affected by the choice of leading. When you set the Auto-Adjustments: Styles option on the SET PREFERENCES dialog box, Ventura's automatic leading feature inserts an interline spacing value that is 20 percent greater than the size of the font selected for the paragraph. Once you set an above, below, or interparagraph spacing value, the auto-adjustment feature also increases and decreases those amounts proportionately. When you produce a single-column layout, you can satisfactorily use automatically adjusted leading for all but the larger fonts. If you are planning a multicolumn layout, set Auto-Adjustments: None after you establish the interline spacing for body text so that you have control over all spacing for other tags you add.

For a complete discussion of controlling the even alignment of text on the invisible grid determined by body text's interline spacing, see Chapter 5.

Adjusting Hyphenation and Justification

In casting copy, you can fit more text on a page when hyphenation and justification are turned on. Normally, Ventura hyphenates text automatically when you choose a hyphenation dictionary in the ALIGNMENT dialog box from the Paragraph menu. Hyphenated text takes up less space than unhyphenated text. Likewise, justified text tends to take up less space than unjustified text because the justification process can reduce the space between words; unjustified text has standard spacing between words and letters.

Justified text usually calls for hyphenation, especially when the columns are narrow, because justified text without hyphenation tends to have more rivers. *Rivers* are wide areas of white space that run through several lines of type and are caused by forced spacing between words. Figure 9.18 provides some examples of both justified and unjustified text.

Justified text requires less space than text which is not justified. Justified text requires less space than text which is not justified. Justified text requires less space than text which is not justified.

Justified text requires less space than text which is not justified. Justified text requires less space than text which is not justified. Justified text requires less space than text which is not justified.

Fig. 9.18.

Examples of justified and unjustified text.

Controlling Word and Letter Spacing

If you think that you can improve your document's appearance by reducing the spacing between words, you should first consider the tradeoffs. If you allow wide spacing between words and letters, the rivers of white space may seem wide in justified text, but fewer words are hyphenated. Text with narrow spaces between characters and words requires frequent hyphenation to achieve a uniform right margin. Unless you have some special effects in mind, you should leave Ventura's defaults for word spacing alone. Generally speaking, changing word spacing is the last resort in copy fitting.

When necessary, however, you can help fit justified text into a specific space by adjusting the spacing between words and letters. Use the Letter Spacing option in the Paragraph menu's TYPOGRAPHY SETTINGS dialog box to adjust spacing between letters in a word in justified text.

In justification, letter spacing adds space between the letters of words in order to force text to the right margin. You may have noticed an extreme instance in a narrow newspaper column with only one word on a line. Sometimes the space between letters is the same as the space between words in the rest of the copy. This amount of letter spacing is too much for body text.

Figure 9.19 illustrates how Ventura displays lines with too much space between words. To see loose lines, choose Show Loose Lines from the Options menu. Changing letter spacing is one way to improve loose lines. You also can correct some loose lines by inserting a discretionary hyphen (press Ctrl-hyphen) at some point in the first word on the second or third loose line. The right box in figure 9.19 shows that although two lines were improved through forced hyphenation, one line still exceeds the maximum set for the space between words. Copy editing is the best way to improve the final loose line's appearance.

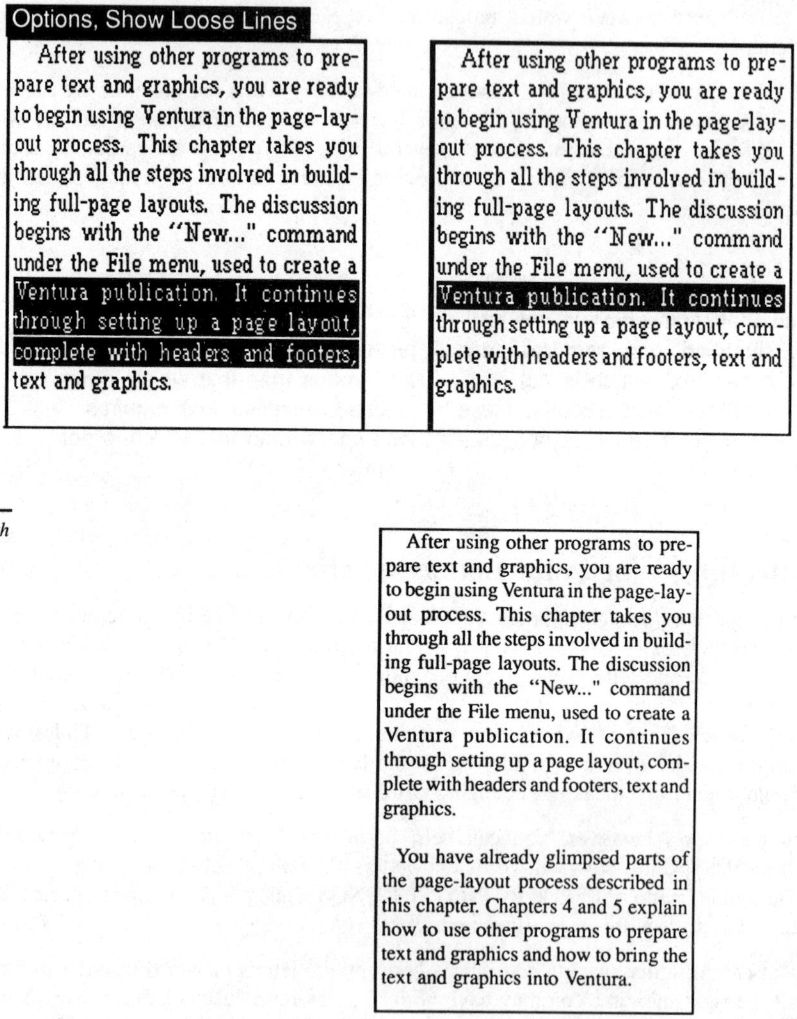

Options, Show Loose Lines

After using other programs to prepare text and graphics, you are ready to begin using Ventura in the page-layout process. This chapter takes you through all the steps involved in building full-page layouts. The discussion begins with the "New..." command under the File menu, used to create a Ventura publication. It continues through setting up a page layout, complete with headers and footers, text and graphics.

After using other programs to prepare text and graphics, you are ready to begin using Ventura in the page-layout process. This chapter takes you through all the steps involved in building full-page layouts. The discussion begins with the "New..." command under the File menu, used to create a Ventura publication. It continues through setting up a page layout, complete with headers and footers, text and graphics.

Fig. 9.19.

Display of lines with too much space.

After using other programs to prepare text and graphics, you are ready to begin using Ventura in the page-layout process. This chapter takes you through all the steps involved in building full-page layouts. The discussion begins with the "New..." command under the File menu, used to create a Ventura publication. It continues through setting up a page layout, complete with headers and footers, text and graphics.

You have already glimpsed parts of the page-layout process described in this chapter. Chapters 4 and 5 explain how to use other programs to prepare text and graphics and how to bring the text and graphics into Ventura.

The default minimum, normal, and maximum space width values control spacing between words. These ranges are given as percentages of normal space for the font. Most publishers are likely to accept Ventura's defaults for these settings rather than change them. You may want to change these settings for a deliberate design strategy in special publications, such as advertisements and brochures.

Efficiency Tip

Use Tracking instead of Kerning for Body Text

Letter spacing between all characters in a paragraph is controlled by tracking (see fig. 9.20). Kerning, however, controls spacing only between certain pairs of characters. For this reason, use tracking instead of letter spacing to tighten or loosen body text. Also the results of automatic kerning are displayed only when you set On-Screen Kerning: On in the SET PREFERENCES dialog box, but tracking results are shown at all times.

TIDAL WAVES   I l l u s t r a t i o n s

After using other programs to prepare text and graphics, you are ready to begin using Ventura in the page-layout process. This chapter takes you through all the steps involved in building full-page layouts. The discussion begins with the "New..." command under the File menu, used to create a Ventura publication. It continues through setting up a page layout, complete with headers and footers, text and graphics.

You have already glimpsed parts of the page-layout process described in this chapter. Chapters 4 and 5 explain how to use other programs to prepare text and graphics and how to bring the text and graphics into Ventura.

After using other programs to prepare text and graphics, you are ready to begin using Ventura in the page-layout process. This chapter takes you through all the steps involved in building full-page layouts. The discussion begins with the "New..." command under the File menu, used to create a Ventura publication. It continues through setting up a page layout, complete with headers and footers, text and graphics.

You have already glimpsed parts of the page-layout process described in this chapter. Chapters 4 and 5 explain how to use other programs to prepare text and graphics and how to bring the text and graphics into Ventura.

Fig. 9.20.

Examples of loose and tight tracking.

Efficiency Tip

Leave On-Screen Kerning Off unless Checking Spacing for Automatic Kerning

With On-Screen Kerning: On in the SET PREFERENCES dialog box, redrawing the screen takes longer. This setting is used only to show the effects of the automatic kerning as set in the Paragraph menu's TYPOGRAPHY SETTINGS dialog box, because the results of manual kerning, interactive kerning, and tracking are visible on-screen at all times.

Access the TYPOGRAPHY SETTINGS dialog box from the Paragraph menu and set Letter Spacing: On. This option tells Ventura, if the maximum and minimum spacing between words does not fill a justified line, add space between the letters up to the value shown to the right of Letter Spacing: On. This value is specified in percentages of the @ sign in the same point size. Don't enter a whole @ as the maximum space width unless you are creating special effects.

Tracking offers another method for controlling how copy fits in an area. Tracking moves every letter within paragraphs either farther apart or closer together, depending on the option you select. Tightening and loosening letters in paragraphs with tracking renders a printed effect similar to kerned paragraphs or kerned letters within paragraphs, but tracking affects every letter in a tagged paragraph. In contrast, pair kerning affects specific pairs of letters. Both techniques (alone or together) can be used to create subtle differences that make a document look professional.

The cumulative effect of tighter tracking can also decrease the number of pages in a long document. You control the amount of adjustment by setting the TYPOGRAPHY SETTINGS Tracking option Looser or Tighter and specifying the amount in fractions of the width of a whole @ sign in that point size.

For more information on tracking, kerning, and letter spacing, see Chapter 5.

Chapter Summary

This chapter provides information about fonts and copy casting in order to help you design your publications for Ventura. The chapter examines some of the issues involved in choosing fonts for a publication and in working with built-in and downloadable fonts. You learned how to fit copy into a defined space and how to estimate the amount of space required before you place the text on the page in Ventura.

The next chapter offers more tips on the overall design of a publication, including developing an underlying grid structure and setting up template files, which make large projects proceed efficiently.

10

Using the Professional Extension

The Professional Extension is an optional extension of Ventura Publisher Version 2.0. This new add-on brings to Ventura features commonly associated with dedicated publishing systems. Because the Professional Extension supports Extended Memory Specification (EMS), this program speeds document access time and eliminates the memory barrier that previously limited document length (and sometimes resulted in the Frame Too Complex to Format error message). The Professional Extension adds a vertical justification feature, commonly used in newspaper and magazine production. This add-on program simplifies the production of tables, formulas, equations, and symbols. With it, you can automatically cross-reference other pages, sections, chapters, captions, figures, and tables, and insert a predefined variable at specified points. The Professional Extension includes a 130,000-word hyphenation dictionary, which you can customize by adding still more words.

These features are described in this chapter, along with explanations of the advantages of using each feature and examples of common uses of each.

Equipment Requirements

The Professional Extension requires approximately 600K additional bytes of hard-disk space beyond the space required by the Ventura Publisher Version 2.0 base product. The EDCO hyphenation dictionary requires an additional 1.2M bytes of disk space plus 1.2M bytes of extended RAM memory and another 256K bytes of extended RAM memory (if your document is large) for a total of 1.5M bytes of EMS memory. Installing the EDCO hyphenation dictionary is optional. If you do not install the dictionary, Ventura still can hyphenate by using the algorithms available with Version 2.0.

The installation procedure for the Professional Extension is the same as for the Version 2.0 base product. If you have already installed the base product, installing the Professional Extension does not remove that version. You run Ventura 2.0 by typing *VP*, or you run the Professional Extension and Ventura by typing *VPPROF*.

If you plan to run Ventura only with the Professional Extension, you can save disk space by deleting the following files from the VENTURA directory after you install the Professional Extension: VP.APP, VP.OVR, VP.RSC, and VP.STR. You also can delete the VP.BAT file in the root directory to avoid accidentally trying to run Ventura Publisher without the Professional Extension.

Extended memory specification (EMS) memory is not required to run the Professional Extension without the hyphenation dictionary, but EMS memory is highly recommended. No special procedures are required to make Ventura Publisher use the EMS memory if it is installed in your computer. If you do use EMS memory, at least 144K bytes must be available before you start Ventura Publisher; otherwise, no EMS memory will be used.

After you have installed the Professional Extension, you are ready to explore its features. The hyphenation feature is one of the most frequently used, followed by cross-referencing.

Hyphenation

The EDCO hyphenation dictionary provides hyphenation for 130,000 English words. As already mentioned, the optional dictionary installation requires an additional 1.2M bytes of disk space plus 1.2M bytes of extended memory. If you do not install the dictionary or if you have installed the dictionary on the hard disk but do not have enough extended memory, Ventura still hyphenates by using the English-hyphenation algorithms available with Version 2.0.

To find out which method of hyphenation your program is using, choose the Alignment command from the Paragraph menu to display the ALIGNMENT dialog box. The hyphenation setting is displayed as USENGLSH if the algorithms are being applied or USDICT if the EDCO dictionary is installed and you have sufficient EMS memory. Most users find the EDCO dictionary superior to the algorithms because of the number of words contained in the EDCO dictionary and the fact that EDCO can hyphenate longer words.

Choosing the Method of Hyphenation

If the dictionary is installed and you have sufficient memory, you can switch between the hyphenation dictionary and the algorithm. First, in the VENTURA directory make a copy of the USENGLSH.HY1 file and name the copy USENGLSH.HY2. You can then apply this hyphenation algorithm to selected text. Select a paragraph or series of paragraphs; then choose the Alignment command from the Paragraph menu. Choose USENGLSH.HY2, which is displayed as an option in the ALIGNMENT dialog box.

If dictionary hyphenation is selected for any paragraph (that is, if USDICT is the hyphenation option displayed in the ALIGNMENT dialog box), any word needing hyphenation is first compared to the contents of the EDCO dictionary. If the word is not found in the dictionary, the word is checked against the standard prefixes and suffixes dictionaries (ENGLISH.PFX and ENGLISH.SFX files in the Ventura directory). If the word still cannot be hyphenated, you can switch to the algorithm method for that paragraph or edit the dictionary, as described in the next section.

Looking Up Words and Editing the Dictionary

The Professional Extension comes with two utilities that let you look up the hyphenation of a word or edit the hyphenation dictionary (to add or delete words or to change the hyphenation for specific words).

You use the utility called CHKWORD to see how a word is hyphenated in the dictionary. To use the utility, type *CHKWORD* at the DOS prompt. The CHKWORD utility displays the name of the currently loaded dictionary and the status of the prefix and suffix files and then prompts you for a word. If the word you type is in the dictionary, the word is displayed with valid hyphenation points shown as hyphens and invalid hyphenation points as tildes. (Invalid hyphenation points are those eliminated by the M, B, and E parameters, described in the next section.) You can enter other words to check their hyphenation, but you cannot change the hyphenation through CHK-WORD. To exit the CHKWORD utility, press Enter without typing a new word.

To edit the dictionary, you first use your word processor to type a list of the words you want changed. Enter a carriage return at the end of each word (that is, type only one word on each line) and insert hyphens in each word where hyphenation points are allowed. Each word must be immediately preceded by one of the following codes, with no intervening spaces:

+ A plus sign adds the word to the dictionary.

= An equal sign changes the hyphenation points of an existing word.

! An exclamation point deletes the word from the dictionary.

You need not insert hyphens in the words to be deleted, and the list of words need not be in alphabetical order.

When you have completed your list, save the file as ASCII text and give the file any name you wish, such as NEWTERMS. Then run the DUPD utility.

Before you run the DUPD utility to insert the edits in the dictionary, you must load the dictionary into memory. You load the dictionary by starting the Professional Extension and then quitting the program. (See "Clearing Memory" to learn how to verify that the VPPROF.BAT file is set up to keep the dictionary in memory.) You also must be sure that the hard disk has enough free space to store the original dictionary and the updated version (that is, an additional 1.2M bytes).

Once these two requirements are met, you can merge the update file with the main dictionary. At the DOS prompt, type *DUPD* followed by the name of the ASCII file with the changed terms: *DUPD newterms*, for instance.

The Professional Extension creates a new updated dictionary, and a copy of the original dictionary is saved on disk.

The two dictionaries of prefixes and suffixes are in ASCII format and may be edited with any word processor. Prefixes or suffixes need not be stored in alphabetical order in these files, although maintaining files is easier if you do keep the entries in order. If you edit these files, you must reload the dictionaries into memory by rebooting your computer and then running the Professional Extension.

Changing Hyphenation Controls

When the EDCO hyphenation dictionary is installed, an additional line of text is automatically added to the VPPROF.BAT file in the root directory. This line reads

    DRTLCFG -M6 -B2 E3 -AA -PC:\VENTURA\DICT\

This line defines the default parameters for hyphenation as follows:

M Specifies the length (minimum number of characters) of the shortest word that will be checked against the dictionary. The default minimum is six characters. Words of five or fewer characters will not be hyphenated.

B Specifies the minimum number of characters allowed before a hyphen is inserted. The default value is two; a hyphen never separates the first character of a word from the rest of the word.

E Specifies the minimum number of characters allowed to follow a hyphen. The default value is three; a hyphen never separates the last two characters of a word from the rest of the word.

A Specifies how apostrophes are counted in calculating word length. AA sets the default for the language in use. AE treats the apostrophe as the end of the word, and AC treats the apostrophe as a normal character. AA is the same as AE for the English dictionary.

P Specifies the path for the dictionary directory. The default is to install the dictionary in the DICT subdirectory of the VENTURA directory. Note that the path name ends with a backslash.

Using any word processor, you can edit the VPPROF.BAT file as ASCII text and change these parameters. Be sure to separate parameters with a space. Do not put a space after the hyphen associated with any parameter, and be sure to save the changed text as ASCII only. To put the changed values into effect, you must reboot your computer and restart the Professional Extension.

Clearing Memory

Normally, the 1.2M-byte English dictionary is loaded from disk into EMS memory only once—when you first boot your system and start the Professional Extension. When you quit Ventura Publisher, the dictionary remains in memory; therefore, when you restart Ventura Publisher a second time, the process is much faster. You can clear the memory by rebooting the computer if you want the memory to be available for other applications.

To change the default so that the memory is automatically cleared every time you quit Ventura Publisher, edit the VPPROF.BAT file as ASCII text (using any word processor). When you open the VPPROF.BAT file, you find the following line, added by the Professional Extension installation:

DLOAD ENGLISH

This line loads the English dictionary into memory when you start the Professional Extension. To clear the memory every time you quit the Professional Extension, add the following two lines to the end of the VPPROF.BAT file:

CD \VENTURA\DICT
DLOAD -U

Be sure to save the VPPROF.BAT file as ASCII text.

Cross-Reference Features

The Professional Extension lets you cross-reference a page number, chapter number, figure number, table number, section number, caption, or variable text. For instance, suppose that you add the text *See figure 10.4*. The cross-reference feature automatically updates that reference if the figure is moved or the figure numbers change. Cross-references and their required markers are set up through the options under the Ins Special Item command's pop-up menu, shown in figure 10.1.

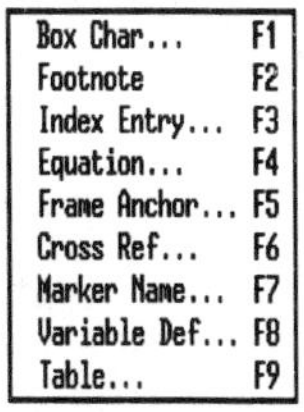

Box Char...	F1
Footnote	F2
Index Entry...	F3
Equation...	F4
Frame Anchor...	F5
Cross Ref...	F6
Marker Name...	F7
Variable Def...	F8
Table...	F9

Fig. 10.1.

The Ins Special Item pop-up menu.

The cross-reference feature is a valuable tool when you are developing a long document that will go through extensive editing or updating, with changing references to figures or sections. You also can use this feature in magazines, newspapers, and newsletters to generate *Continued on page. . .* and *Continued from page. . .* cross-references when articles jump pages. You can use the variable-text cross-reference to customize a document like a proposal by inserting specific client names, or you can customize a lease contract by changing names and addresses and terms. This feature is also used to insert the current page number or chapter number on a page.

Inserting the Current Page Number or Chapter Number

The most common use of cross-referencing is to add the current page number or chapter number to a page. Of course, you can create the chapter number by typing it as ordinary text on the opening page of a chapter; but by using the cross-referencing feature to generate the chapter number, you can access other Ventura features, such as referencing the current chapter from another chapter and automatic chapter renumbering when a chapter is added or deleted. This feature is the same as the Insert Cross Reference command reached through the Edit menu in Version 2.0, but the procedure is slightly different with the Professional Extension.

To insert the current page number or chapter number on a page, first select the Text function and insert the text cursor at the location where you want the page or chapter number to appear. Then follow these steps:

1. Choose Ins Special Item from the Edit menu (or use the keyboard shortcut, Ctrl-C).

2. Select Cross Ref from the pop-up menu (or press the F6 function key).

3. In the dialog box, select Refer To: P# to insert the current page number or Refer To: C# to insert the current chapter number (see fig. 10.2). Leave the At The Name line blank. Press the Return key or click OK to close the dialog box.

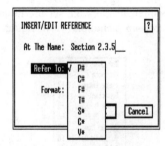

Fig. 10.2.

The INSERT/EDIT REFERENCE dialog box with a pop-up menu.

Marking a Reference Location

Besides referencing a page number or a chapter number, you can reference figure numbers, table numbers, section numbers, captions, or variable text. To create these references, you must first use the cross-referencing feature to mark any elements to which you wish to refer. You can mark places within the text, or you can mark a frame.

To insert a marker in the text, first select the Text function and insert the text cursor at the location where you want the marker to appear. Then follow these steps:

1. Choose Ins Special Item from the Edit menu (or use the keyboard shortcut, Ctrl-C).

2. Select Marker Name from the pop-up menu (or press the F7 function key).

3. In the dialog box shown in figure 10.3, enter a marker name. You can use upper- and lowercase letters here, but the case is ignored when the label is referenced from elsewhere.

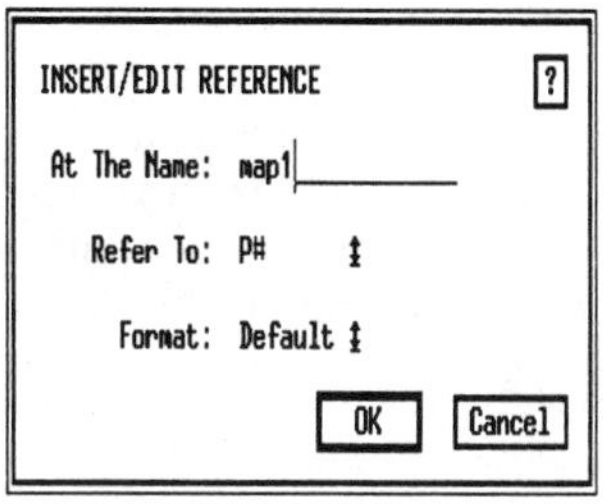

Fig. 10.3.

The INSERT/EDIT REFERENCE dialog box for inserting a marker.

To mark a frame, first select the Frame function and select the frame you want to mark.

1. Choose the Anchors & Captions command from the Frame menu.

2. In the dialog box, enter the anchor name. As with text markers, you can use upper- and lowercase letters here, but the case is ignored when the label is referenced from elsewhere.

Efficiency Tip

Keep a Log of All Marker Names as You Create Them

Keep a running log of all marker names, anchor names, and caption names as you create them. You will need to use the exact spelling and spacing when you refer to these names from elsewhere in the manuscript.

Creating a Variable

Besides inserting cross-references to page numbers, chapter numbers, figure numbers, table numbers, or section numbers, you can set up variable text, which is inserted wherever you cross-reference the name of the variable in the text. Suppose, for example, that you have a standard proposal you use when bidding on new work. You create a variable called Client and another called AcctRep. Initially, you designate the variable text for Client to be *ABC Company* and the variable text for AcctRep to be *J.*

Higgins. Wherever you set up a cross-reference to Client in the text, the phrase *ABC Company* is inserted automatically, and wherever you cross-reference the variable name AcctRep, the phrase *J. Higgins* is inserted. Later, when developing a new proposal for another client named Beta Inc., which will be handled by account representative R. Webster, you can change the text assigned to these variable names once, and the text automatically changes throughout the document when you use the Multi-Chapter command to renumber the chapter (as described in the next section).

The results of using this feature are similar to those of a global search-and-replace operation with a word processor, but by changing the text for each variable only once, you have the effect of performing many simultaneous global searches, and you can change the text in many chapters at once. This feature can be used to insert the current date, a revision number, an address or phone number, or any other text that routinely appears throughout a document but changes with different versions of the document. You should anticipate, however, that globally replacing one phrase with another of a different length may result in different line breaks, column breaks, and page breaks throughout the document. Ventura handles these adjustments automatically, but you should review the page layouts before printing the final copy.

To define a variable, first select the Text function and insert the text cursor at the location where you want to store the variable definition. This location can be the cover page or first page of the document, if all the variables are listed there as part of the document design, or the location may be at the end of the document on a page that you always print but do not distribute to all readers. Then follow these steps:

1. Choose Ins Special Item from the Edit menu (or use the keyboard shortcut, Ctrl-C).

2. Select Variable Def from the pop-up menu (or press the F8 function key).

3. In the dialog box, enter a variable name. You can use upper- and lowercase letters here, but the case is ignored when the name is referenced from elsewhere.

4. Finally, type the substitute text associated with that variable name and press Return or click OK to close the dialog box.

The variable text will be inserted wherever you insert a cross-reference to the variable name, as described in the following section.

Later, you can change the variable text, and the text will automatically change throughout the document when you use the Renumber option under the Multi-Chapter command, as described in the next section.

Creating a Cross-Reference

Once you have used the Ins Special Item command to mark a reference location or the Anchors & Captions command to mark a frame, you can cross-reference these locations from other parts of the document. To insert a cross-reference, first select the

Text function and insert the text cursor at the location where you want the marker to appear. Then follow these steps:

1. Choose Ins Special Item from the Edit menu (or use the keyboard shortcut, Ctrl-C).

2. Select Cross Ref from the pop-up menu (or press the F6 function key).

3. In the dialog box, enter the name of the frame or the text label on the At The Name line. You need to match the spelling of the name you typed when setting the marker or variable name, but you need not match the case (capitalization).

4. On the Refer To line, select the type of reference you want to create:

Page number	P#
Chapter number	C#
Figure number	F#
Table number	T#
Section Number	S*
Caption Text	C*
Variable Text	V*

    If you select one of the # options, such as P#, you can specify the format for the number on the format line or select Default to use the currently defined format.

    When you click OK to close the dialog box, no text appears in the cross-reference.

5. To activate the cross-reference feature, choose the Multi-Chapter command from the Options menu. Create a publication that contains all the chapters which are part of the publication (see Chapter 4 for a description of using the Multi-Chapter command). Then, in the MULTI-CHAPTER dialog box, select Renumber to update all cross-references in the text. You must go through this last step even if your document is composed of only one chapter.

The cross-references created in this way are updated automatically whenever the page numbers, chapter numbers, figure numbers, table numbers, or section numbers are changed by adding, deleting, or moving parts within a chapter and then renumbering through the Multi-Chapter command. The Renumber command also inserts new or changed variable text throughout the document.

Efficiency Tip

Renumber Just before Printing a Document

Because renumbering a document takes time, restrict the number of times you use the Renumber command during document production. Rather than renumber every time you create a new cross-reference—so that you can see the cross-reference in the text immediately—wait until you are ready to print a draft of the document.

Limit the Number of Printings

Another good idea is to restrict the number of times you print a document during production. Sometimes, a good deal of time lapses between the time you enter new edits from a marked manuscript and the next time you—or anyone—will actually read the new draft. Frequently, a last-minute review of the printout brings a few more edits or afterthoughts after you have entered the edits from the marked manuscript. To avoid still another printing, wait to print until just before a proofreading or copy editing session, instead of printing just after entering new edits from a marked manuscript.

Editing a Cross-Reference

You are sure to find occasions when you need to edit a cross-reference. To change a cross-reference, marker name, or variable definition, first select the Text function, and then work through these steps:

1. Choose Show Tabs & Returns under the Options menu. These normally hidden characters are displayed in the text on each page. Cross-reference markers are displayed as small circles in the text.

2. Place the cursor immediately to the left of the marker to be edited. The words Marker Name, Reference, or Variable Def. will appear in the current selection box. If you did not position the text cursor immediately in front of the marker (that is, if a space intervenes and the marker identification is not displayed), you can use the text-cursor arrow keys to move the cursor forward or back until these words appear.

3. Choose Edit Special Item from the Edit menu (or use the keyboard shortcut, Ctrl-D).

4. A dialog box appears, appropriate to the type of marker you have selected, and you can change the name of the marker or variable definition, as explained in the sections describing each marker type.

5. Use the Renumber command to update all references.

The Table Function

The Professional Extension adds a table function to the features of Ventura Version 2.0. A table is any text formatted in rows and columns. (Here the term *column* indicates tabular format, rather than the multicolumn page layouts used in newspapers and magazines.) Projects as diverse as financial statements, calendars, price lists, and mailing lists can be handled easily and efficiently with this feature.

You can type tables in a word processor, or you can type them directly into Ventura. The Professional Extension package also includes an external utility that lets you take information from any spreadsheet or database and import that information as a Ventura table. You can set up a table with rows and columns and edit the format of the rows and columns as required for your table. Because the table is treated as one object, you can move it with text. You also can create column headings or titles to move with the table if it contains multiple pages of information.

Tables that have short passages of text can be typed directly in the Professional Extension. When you want to load files from word processors, spreadsheets, or databases, you use the Table function to format the layout of the files you load with the Prn to Table option in the LOAD TEXT/PICTURE dialog box. Because of the extended memory support offered with the Professional Extension, you can load longer documents, such as databases, without exceeding the program's capacity.

Inserting and Creating Tables

The Table function is located below the four 2.0 publishing functions, in a new addition button. When you activate the Table function, a corresponding assignment list with table commands is presented, as shown in figure 10.4.

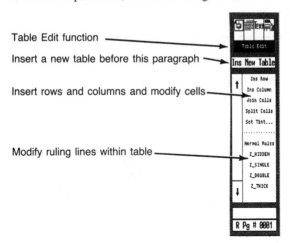

Table Edit function

Insert a new table before this paragraph

Insert rows and columns and modify cells

Modify ruling lines within table

Fig. 10.4.

The Table Edit commands.

Click the button labeled Table Edit to insert a table. The table cursor is displayed as a small cross in the work area. Place the cross between two paragraphs where you want the table to appear. When you click the mouse, a small horizontal bar displays at the point of the cursor. Click the Ins New Table addition button to open the INSERT/EDIT TABLE dialog box.

You also can insert a table from the Text function by choosing Ins Special Item from the Edit menu. The shortcut keys are Ctrl-C and F9 to choose Table. The INSERT/EDIT TABLE dialog box appears.

The features in the INSERT/EDIT TABLE dialog box, shown in figure 10.5, allow you to create a basic table. After the table is created, you use the Edit menu and commands from the assignment list to customize your table. The features in the INSERT/EDIT TABLE dialog box are described next.

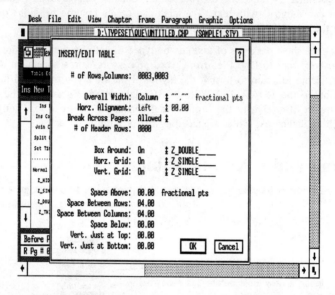

Fig. 10.5.

The INSERT/EDIT TABLE dialog box.

First, in the # of Rows,Columns line, you type the number of rows. Then press the Tab key and enter the number of columns. You can add rows and columns later by using the insert commands from the assignment list. All the rows and columns are the same size, but you can customize individual cells later from the assignment list and Table Edit commands.

The Overall Width line is where you control the flow of the table within column or margin boundaries. If you choose Column from the pop-up menu of this option, the table automatically conforms to the column setup of the page. Choosing Custom allows you to set the width of the table up to the width of the page. This feature sets the overall width of the entire table. To set width values for individual columns, choose Change Column Width in the Edit menu (described later).

Horz. Alignment controls the horizontal alignment on the page. Choosing Custom from the Overall Width pop-up menu requires that you set the horizontal alignment. You can choose left, center, right, or Custom Indent. The table is treated like a separate paragraph, and this feature aligns the table on the page or column.

Break Across Pages works like the Breaks feature for paragraphs. If you choose Allowed from the pop-up menu, the table will be broken if it falls at the end of a page. If a break is unacceptable, choose No, and the entire table will be moved to a new page. Do not choose No for long tables that cannot fit on a page.

The # of Header Rows option allows you to continue the titles in a table across multiple pages without retyping. The # of Header Rows option acts like a header feature to the table.

Specifying Box Around: On places a box around the entire table. Three automatic tags are created on the Box Around line: Z_DOUBLE, Z_SINGLE, and Z_THICK. You can give another name to a tag by typing the new name in place of the default name. Set these tags by choosing a tag and setting any of the line attributes from any of the ruling line features in the Paragraph function.

The Horizontal Grid (Horz. Grid) option places lines between the rows in the table. You can remove lines from individual cells by using the Join feature, which is discussed in the section "Editing Tables." The widths of the lines are controlled by tags, like the rules in the Box Around option.

The Vertical Grid (Vert. Grid) option places lines between the columns in the table. You can override this feature for individual cells during the editing phase.

The Space Above option works on the table exactly like the space-above command works with paragraphs. The space is added above the entire table, between it and the preceding text.

Space Between Rows adds space between rows in the table.

Space Between Columns adds space to the left of the columns. This added space separates text in the columns.

Space Below operates exactly like Space Above except Space Below adds space after the table and before text following the table.

Vert. Just at Top justifies the table vertically on the page starting at the top. Tables are treated like individual paragraphs. Details about vertical justification are covered in the section "Setting Automatic Vertical Justification."

Vert. Just at Bottom justifies the table vertically on the page starting at the bottom. See also the section on vertical justification.

Editing Tables

Once the table is defined through the INSERT/EDIT TABLE dialog box, you can select and edit specific portions of the table. Just as when you are editing sections of text, you use the mouse to mark, or select, the portion of the table you want to edit. The steps for marking and editing a table are as follows:

1. Activate the Table Edit function by clicking that button, at the left of the screen.

2. Place the table cursor at the beginning of the portion of the table you want to edit.

3. Drag the mouse to the lower right of the portion of the table you want to edit.

4. Release the mouse button. The area will be surrounded by a gray line.

You may now choose any of the commands from the assignment list or Edit menu. You can

- *Cut, Copy, and Paste Rows and Columns*. Change every cell in the table using Edit Table Settings in the Edit menu.

- *Add new columns or rows*. Place the table cursor anywhere in the table and choose Ins Row or Ins Column from the assignment list.

- *Change column widths*. Choose any cell or group of cells and then choose Change Column Width from the Edit menu. You can also change the widths with the mouse by pressing and holding the Alt key while you move the column with the mouse.

- *Apply attributes to cells*. Mark a cell or group of cells and choose an attribute or attributes from the assignment list. You can join cells, set colors and tints, or override the default ruling lines between cells.

- *Tag a cell independently from other cells to change the formatting and alignment of the text*. You can add special leader characters and other special effects.

Moving and Copying Rows and Columns

Create the basic table and then edit it as follows:

1. Choose the Table Edit function.

2. Select the rows or columns you want to cut or copy.

3. Choose Cut Row/Column from the Edit menu to cut and copy the row or column from the table. The marked section is cut or copied to the Clipboard, depending on your response to the Cut/Copy Rows or Columns prompt.

4. Move the pointer to the line between the rows or columns where you want to insert the portion of the table in the Clipboard. The line between the rows or columns can be selected even if it is hidden.

5. Choose Paste from the Edit menu.

6. Answer the prompt asking whether you want to insert the table portion between rows or between columns. You can also mark and cut or copy the entire table. When you choose to cut an entire table, you receive a warning prompt. You can continue or cancel the operation if that is not what you intended.

Adding Rows and Columns

As mentioned previously, you can add rows or columns to your table at any time. Follow these steps:

1. Choose the Table Edit function.

2. Mark the point where you want to insert the row(s) or column(s).

3. Choose Ins Row or Ins Column from the assignment list. You will see a prompt asking whether you are sure. One row or column is added unless you mark multiple rows or columns. For example, if you mark four rows and choose insert rows, the Professional Extension adds another four rows. Rows and columns are added above the marked row or to the left of the marked column.

Changing Column Widths

You can change the width of a column or columns in two ways:

1. Mark the column and choose Set Column Width from the Edit menu.

   or

2. Press and hold the Alt key while you move the column border by dragging the mouse.

The TABLE COLUMN WIDTHS dialog box, shown in figure 10.6, is much like the TAB SETTINGS dialog box. The marked column number is in the Column Number box. You can change the column number by clicking on the arrows on either side of the Column Number box.

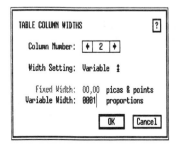

Fig. 10.6.

The TABLE COLUMN WIDTHS dialog box.

You use a pop-up menu to choose a width setting of Fixed or Variable for each column in the table. The fixed width sets the column to the width you enter on the Fixed Width line.

A variable width column is proportionately sized from the remaining space after all fixed width columns are set. The variable widths are determined by the Variable Width settings for the table. Each Variable Width setting is compared to the other

Variable Width settings for all columns in the table. For example, a column with a Variable Width setting of 2 gets twice as much space as a column with a setting of 1. You can set all columns to have the same width by giving them all the same number.

The best method is to set the narrowest column and then set all others to a multiple of this amount. You can also use percentages, but make sure that they total to 100: for example, a 10 percent column, two 30 percent columns, and two 15 percent columns. Ventura looks at the overall width of the table and creates the columns accordingly.

Applying Attributes and Making Other Modifications

The Table function allows you to apply any of the attributes in the assignment list to any cells or blocks of cells in the table. Mark the areas first and choose the attribute(s) from the assignment list.

You also can make changes to the size of cells and the appearance of the rules between cells.

In many tables, some cells are larger than others. To create larger cells within a table, mark a group of cells and choose the Join Cells attribute in the assignment list. All rules dividing the group of marked cells are hidden to create one large cell. If you join cells containing text, only the text in the upper left cell of the group is displayed. You can choose Split Cell to undo a Join command.

To change rules between cells in a table, first mark the rule by dragging the mouse. Then choose the appropriate rule from the assignment list. You also can select entire cells or groups of cells and change the rules by choosing from the assignment list.

Customizing Rule Tags

You can create special rule tags that will be placed in the assignment list. For example, to create a dashed rule to be used in a table, follow these steps:

1. In the Paragraph function, choose Generated Tags: Shown in the SET PREFERENCES dialog box.

2. Select the rule tag you want to change or to use as a pattern to create a new rule line attribute. For example, choose Z_SINGLE from the assignment list.

3. Choose Add New Tag and name the new rule line tag DASHES.

4. DASHES now replaces Z_SINGLE in the current selection box.

5. Choose Ruling Line Above from the Paragraph menu.

6. In the RULING LINES ABOVE dialog box, choose Dashes: On, Dash width: 3, and Dash spacing: 2.

7. Set the Table Rule List line to Shown (if the option is not already selected as the normal default) so that the new tag will be shown in the attribute list. Then press Return or click OK to close the dialog box.

8. Choose Table Edit and mark a line in the table with the mouse. If you do not see the new tag in the assignment list, scroll with the scroll bar.

9. Click on the new tag name—DASHES; the marked line assumes the new attribute.

Tagging Cells

The default tag for all cells is Table Text. You can create new tags just as you do for any text. To save tag space, you can mark text with the mouse and use the SET FONT box for changing fonts in a table. For specifications that will be applied more than once, however, you should create tags. If you set Grow Inter-Line To Fit to On in the Paragraph Typography command's dialog box when setting large fonts, spacing between lines will automatically be adjusted to accommodate the larger text.

The Alignment command on the Paragraph menu is more frequently used in setting up table tags than in normal text tags. The alignment settings especially useful for tables are Horizontal Alignment, Vertical Alignment, Text Rotation, and In from Right to Decimal.

The horizontal and vertical alignment options let you put text in corners of cells, to either side, or in the center. You can align numbers from the right edge of a column by choosing Horizontal Alignment: Decimal and specifying the distance numerically next to the In from Right to Decimal option. Rotated text allows you to place text so that the lines run vertically along a cell. You should limit the vertical height of the text to be rotated or the cell will grow with a long entry. You should not try to edit rotated text. Turn off rotation to edit the text and then rotate it again. Use line breaks instead of paragraph breaks (Ctrl-Enter) to help break long lines of rotated text.

Modifying the Entire Table

At times you may want to change something about an entire table. Follow these steps to modify an entire table:

1. Choose the Table Edit function.

2. Mark any portion or all of the table and choose Edit Table Settings from the Edit menu. You can use a shortcut by pressing Ctrl-D.

3. The INSERT/EDIT TABLE dialog box appears, and you can make changes that affect the entire table.

Points To Remember

- Line breaks using Ctrl-Enter are a quick way to move text down in a cell. You can use Space Above, but this command affects all tagged text. You can move text by setting the spacing attributes between rows and columns in the Table Edit function.

- Breaks and special effects are not used with tables. It is best to leave table text breaks set to Set Line Break: Before and Keep With Next: No.

- You can set tabs within cells if required, but the Table Edit function eliminates the need to set tabs. The Auto-Leader option in the TAB SETTINGS dialog box is useful for filling empty cells with lines.

- When using the Attribute Overrides command, you can define line attributes that can be assigned to selected text. Line Width: Margin-Wide causes any line attribute to extend across the entire cell.

- Using the Define Colors option, you can define a color that can be applied to any cell in a table. Choose Apply Tint from the assignment list in the Table Edit function.

- The ruling line commands in the text tags add ruling lines above text in addition to the lines in the table. Do not get these ruling lines confused with the rules separating cells of a table. See the steps describing how to set up default rules for tables.

Loading a Source File as a Table

The Professional Extension includes a utility program that can read PRN files from 1-2-3, TXT files from dBASE, and similar formats from other spreadsheets or databases. The only requirement is that the text file created by your spreadsheet or database be formatted with at least two spaces between columns in a spreadsheet or fields in a database.

If a blank cell is found, the text is shifted to fill the void. This movement throws off your table alignment.

To load text from a spreadsheet or database into a Ventura Publisher table, follow these steps:

1. Use the spreadsheet or database application to create on disk a PRN file or a TXT file holding the data. You may need to adjust the column width settings in your spreadsheet to ensure that all columns are separated by at least two spaces. When converting data from a database,

be sure that each field length is at least two characters longer than the longest entry in that field. If the fields are not long enough, you must use the REPORT TO FILE command (in dBASE) or use custom code to produce a text file with at least two spaces between fields in every record.

2. Start the Professional Extension, and open the document into which you want to insert the data as a table.

3. Select the Text function, and place the cursor at the location in the text where you want to insert the data.

4. Choose Load Text/Picture from the File menu.

5. In the dialog box, select PRN to Table, and select Destination: Text Cursor. Then click OK to close the dialog box.

6. In the next dialog box showing a list of the files on disk, select the PRN or TXT file that you created with the spreadsheet or database application.

The file is converted into a table and saved as a new disk file with the extension TBL at the end of the new file name. You can edit the table as you edit any text and set up table parameters (explained in the previous sections of this chapter). Any changes made to the data in Ventura Publisher are reflected in the TBL file, but the original PRN file remains unchanged.

Vertical Justification

Vertical justification is the process or result of forcing the text in all columns across a page or throughout a document to end at the same point—usually the bottom margin. Normally, you may expect text to flow naturally to the bottom margin, but many factors can prevent this flow. Some of these factors may be insufficient text to fill the columns, different type specifications for headings and body copy across columns, widow and orphan controls forcing lines to next column, the Keep With Next option of the Breaks command on the Paragraph menu forcing lines to the next column, and forced page breaks and column breaks.

For many documents, these other considerations override the desire to force text to bottom out on each page; and you will find that most business reports, ads, forms, and brochures do not force vertical justification. Most newspapers and magazines, on the other hand, require vertical justification by tradition and by design. In these cases, the Professional Extension offers the vertical justification feature, which adds small increments of space between lines of text in order to force short columns to fill down to the bottom margin of the page or frame. Figure 10.7 shows a page before and after the vertical justification process.

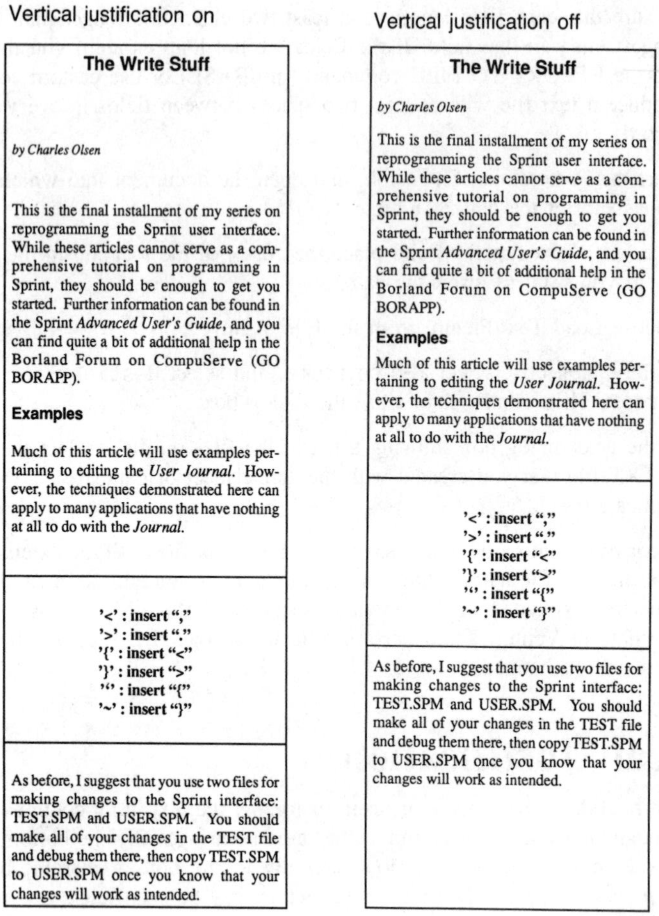

Vertical justification on

Vertical justification off

The Write Stuff

by Charles Olsen

This is the final installment of my series on reprogramming the Sprint user interface. While these articles cannot serve as a comprehensive tutorial on programming in Sprint, they should be enough to get you started. Further information can be found in the Sprint *Advanced User's Guide*, and you can find quite a bit of additional help in the Borland Forum on CompuServe (GO BORAPP).

Examples

Much of this article will use examples pertaining to editing the *User Journal*. However, the techniques demonstrated here can apply to many applications that have nothing at all to do with the *Journal*.

```
'<' : insert ","
'>' : insert "."
'{' : insert "<"
'}' : insert ">"
''' : insert "{"
'~' : insert "}"
```

As before, I suggest that you use two files for making changes to the Sprint interface: TEST.SPM and USER.SPM. You should make all of your changes in the TEST file and debug them there, then copy TEST.SPM to USER.SPM once you know that your changes will work as intended.

The Write Stuff

by Charles Olsen

This is the final installment of my series on reprogramming the Sprint user interface. While these articles cannot serve as a comprehensive tutorial on programming in Sprint, they should be enough to get you started. Further information can be found in the Sprint *Advanced User's Guide*, and you can find quite a bit of additional help in the Borland Forum on CompuServe (GO BORAPP).

Examples

Much of this article will use examples pertaining to editing the *User Journal*. However, the techniques demonstrated here can apply to many applications that have nothing at all to do with the *Journal*.

```
'<' : insert ","
'>' : insert "."
'{' : insert "<"
'}' : insert ">"
''' : insert "{"
'~' : insert "}"
```

As before, I suggest that you use two files for making changes to the Sprint interface: TEST.SPM and USER.SPM. You should make all of your changes in the TEST file and debug them there, then copy TEST.SPM to USER.SPM once you know that your changes will work as intended.

Fig. 10.7.

Columns before and after vertical justification.

In vertical justification, space is added in the following sequence:

1. Space is first added between frame borders and the surrounding text—up to the maximum allowed for each frame (as specified through dialog box entries described in the following sections).

2. If the text does not reach the bottom margin after the first sweep, space is added between paragraphs or between tables and paragraphs—up to the maximum allowed for each paragraph or table.

3. If the text does not reach the bottom margin after the first two sweeps, space is added between lines of text—up to the maximum allowed.

If these three sweeps still do not yield vertical justification, no justification is implemented for the page. This limitation prevents the creation of very loose pages at the end of a chapter or before a forced page break. You can intervene further by either changing the global settings for maximum space allowed or changing the settings for selected individual frames, style sheet tags, or tables.

In all cases, the space is increased incrementally and evenly down the whole column so that the space added throughout the column is evenly distributed between all frames, paragraphs, tables, or lines until the maximum is reached. This procedure never moves text across page boundaries.

Setting Up Vertical Justification throughout a Chapter

The Chapter Typography command is used to set vertical justification on or off for the whole chapter. If vertical justification is turned on, the Chapter Typography menu lets you specify the maximum amount of space that can be added around any frame on the page. In most cases, you can achieve perfect vertical justification simply by using the Chapter Typography command to turn on vertical justification. Set Vertical Justification Within Frame to Feathering and Vertical Justification Around Frame to Movable, and let the defaults for spacing around frames, paragraphs, lines, and tables handle the rest. The defaults and other alternatives are described here and in the following sections.

To set up vertical justification for a chapter, choose the Chapter Typography command. The dialog box displays options for widow and orphan control, column balance, and pair kerning. (These options are available with Version 2.0 and described in Chapter 5.) In addition, the Professional Extension adds five more options for vertical justification (see fig. 10.8).

```
CHAPTER (DEFAULT) TYPOGRAPHY SETTINGS        ?

           Widows (Min Lines at Top):  3        ‡
      Orphans (Min Lines at Bottom):  3        ‡
                   Column Balance:  Off      ‡
         Move Down To 1st Baseline By:  Cap Height ‡
                      Pair Kerning:  On       ‡
         Vert. Just. Within Frame:  Feathering ‡
         Vert. Just. Around Frame:  Moveable  ‡

              Vert. Just. Allowed:  000.0  %
                 At Top of Frame:  00.00  fractional pts
              At Bottom of Frame:  00.00

                                    [ OK ]  [Cancel]
```

Fig. 10.8.

The CHAPTER (DEFAULT) TYPOGRAPHY SETTINGS dialog box.

Vert. Just. Within Frame offers three vertical justification alternatives on a pop-up menu: Off, Feathering, or Carding. When this setting is Off, no vertical justification takes place in the chapter—regardless of any other settings for frames, paragraphs, or tables. When Feathering is selected, space is added incrementally between frames, paragraphs, lines, and tables (as described in the preceding paragraphs) until the text reaches the bottom of the column. When you choose Carding, space is added in multiples of Body Text interline spacing.

The purpose of the Carding option is to maintain alignment between baselines of text across columns—a requirement of some newspapers and magazines. However, this alternative works only if you have already set up all style sheet tags to enable this kind of alignment. One way of doing this is to make sure that the spacing around all headings and captions is set up in the style sheet tags in multiples of body text interline spacing, and to make every vertical justification setting in the CHAPTER TYPOGRAPHY, FRAME TYPOGRAPHY, PARAGRAPH TYPOGRAPHY, and INSERT/EDIT TABLE dialog boxes a multiple of body text interline spacing.

The Vert. Just. Around Frame setting determines how space is added around frames on a page. Two alternatives appear on the pop-up menu: Fixed and Moveable. If you select Fixed, each frame remains in position and space is added below the frame. If you select Moveable, the frame is moved down to add space above the frame, and extra space is also added below the frame. The recommended setting is Moveable, unless your frames are aligned across columns or otherwise positioned carefully by intentional design.

As described earlier in this chapter, the amount of space added during the vertical justification process is determined by the maximum settings made through the CHAPTER TYPOGRAPHY, FRAME TYPOGRAPHY, and PARAGRAPH TYPOGRAPHY dialog boxes. The Vert. Just. Allowed setting globally increases or decreases the maximum amounts allowed for vertical justification on each page. For example, if the maximum space allowed for vertical justification below a frame is 10 points, and you set Vert. Just. Allowed to 120 percent, the maximum space attempted for vertical justification below a frame will be 12 points.

The At Top of Frame and At Bottom of Frame settings determine the maximum amount of space allowed in adjusting the space above and below a frame, between the frame and the preceding or following text. This amount is added to whatever amount has also been set as vertical padding for the frame (top and bottom frame margins). By default, these options are normally set to an amount equal to body text interline spacing.

Overriding Vertical Justification for Selected Frames

The Frame Typography command offers the same options as the Chapter Typography command and lets you override the global settings for selected frames. You can turn off vertical justification for a selected frame or change the maximum space allowed in vertically justifying the frame text. You can also turn vertical justification on or off for new pages inserted within a document.

To override the Chapter Typography settings for a selected frame, first choose the Frame function and select the frame or inserted page you want to change. Then choose the Frame Typography command under the Frame menu. To change vertical justification for text placed within the frame, change Vert. Just. Within Frame and Vert. Just. Allowed. To change the amount of space added around a frame, change Vert. Just. Around Frame and specify the amounts At Top of Frame and At Bottom of Frame.

If the frame on a new inserted page is selected and changed, the changed settings affect all additional pages that are created automatically when more than one page of text is flowed onto the new page.

Setting Up Vertical Justification by Tag

The Paragraph Typography command displays a dialog box with options for kerning, tracking, and interword space adjustments, which are available in Version 2.0 and described in Chapter 5. If you have installed the Professional Extension, three more options are added to the dialog box. These options let you specify the maximum amount of space that can be added above or below a paragraph or between lines in a paragraph, as shown in figure 10.9. These settings can be different for each style sheet tag. For example, a common practice is to allow the most space to be added around headings and allow little or no space to be added between lines of body text.

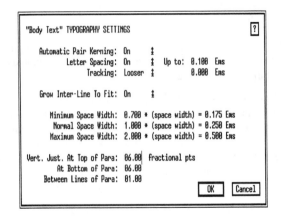

Fig. 10.9.

The TYPOGRAPHY SETTINGS dialog box.

By default, the Vert. Just. At Top of Para and At Bottom of Para are set equal to the paragraph spacing settings for body text. If body text space above and below are both set to zero, the default values for vertical justification will be set to body text interparagraph space. If interparagraph spacing for body text is set to zero, the default for all tags will be set to zero for vertical justification, in which case you may want to override the default for heading tags.

Adjusting the space between lines within a paragraph is the last step in the process of vertical justification. Normally, the space allowed for adjusting between lines is set to zero in the Between Lines of Para option. If you wish to override this setting for body text, you should not allow more than 10 percent of body text interline spacing. Heading tags can have a larger allowance for interline space adjustments.

As described in ''Inserting and Creating Tables,'' the Insert/Edit Table command lets you specify the maximum amount of space to be added above and below a selected table. These settings are not tied to a style sheet tag, and they can be different for each table.

Equations in Text

A principle feature of the Ventura Publisher Professional Extension is the interactive creation of complex mathematical and scientific equations that use Greek characters and other special mathematical symbols. Before the introduction of the Professional Extension, such equations were possible using the Symbol font, but the time consumed arranging the figures and symbols was completely unrealistic. With the Professional Extension, you can enter coded text at your keyboard, watch the equation develop on-screen, and then place the equation in context in your file.

Equations are elegant expressions used by mathematicians and technologists. Equations represent the reduction of complex thought processes into an arrangement of conventional symbols that can be read, interpreted, and used by others who are familiar with the symbols and conventions used. The most famous equation, and perhaps the most elegant reduction, was Einstein's life's work on the general theory of relativity, which he reduced to $E = mc^2$. Such a compact reduction, which can easily be accommodated in a line of text, is all too rare. Most equations are complex matrixes or profound strings with several decks. The Professional Extension, however, has removed the problems of setting equations. They can be set directly in Ventura, or the author can set up the equations in the text file by adding the commands and style sheet tags needed for automatic formatting in Ventura.

The Professional Extension uses strings of pseudo-English commands and some easily remembered conventional characters to describe the equation—just as a mathematician might describe a formula for a nonmathematical person. For example, the word *sqrt* produces the square root symbol, and the word *sup* creates a superscript. You enter the string of words and characters at the keyboard, and they are displayed on a special intermediate screen that has a ledger line. The program then interprets the input in the space below. You can edit the equation immediately or later.

You also can enter the string of pseudowords in text. Ventura's automatic vertical justification ensures that even the most complex multideck formulas can reside in text form, demanding very little time for copy fitting when brought to pages.

Creating Equations

The rigidity of the basic interline spacing of the body text cannot normally accommodate interspersed equations, so the spacing must be allowed to "grow" in paragraphs that contain equations. This flexibility allows the page layout to absorb the embedded patterns that will be produced.

This flexibility is achieved by the following steps:

1. With the Ventura file open, open a new text file.

2. Change to Paragraph tagging.

3. Highlight the text you want to manipulate.

4. Under the Paragraph menu, choose Typography Settings.

5. In the TYPOGRAPHY SETTINGS dialog box, change the `Grow Inter-Line To Fit` option to `On`.

6. Change to the Text function.

7. Set the cursor at the location where an equation is to be displayed.

8. On the Edit menu, select Ins Special Item (or press Ctrl-C). Then press F4 to select the equation generator.

The equation screen appears (see fig. 10.10). It consists of a blank screen with two rules running across the top of the screen. Press Ctrl-C to see a help menu.

Try typing $a + b$, and see the result:

a+b

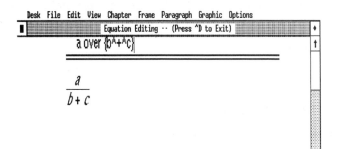

Fig. 10.10.

The equation screen.

Now type

sqrt { a sup 2˜ +˜ b sup 2}

for the result shown in figure 10.11.

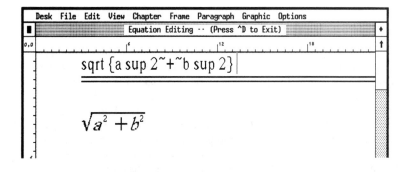

Fig. 10.11.

Results of typing sqrt { a sup 2˜ +˜ b sup 2}.

The pseudoword *sqrt* is one of the basic commands and signifies a square root sign. Another command is *sup*, signifying superscript. The tilde (˜) is another frequently used diacritical mark. The tilde adds space between characters in the equation; with just a space between the symbols, no space is created in the formula. Finally, the braces { } produce a delimited grouping, or boundary, around any parts of the expression.

To insert the assembled equation into text, hold down Ctrl while you press D. This command causes the program to exit from the equation screen and place the generated expression in text at the desired location.

Efficiency Tip

Using Fixed Spaces To Indent Equations

Because attributes, such as Center, or Right do not always produce the desired results for equations, always use Left or Justified alignment for body text. If the equation is deep and complex, insert a colon at the point in text where the equation will appear; press Return for a new line; then insert the equation. You can indent the equation as far as necessary along the line by pressing Ctrl-Shift-M to add em quads for the best indention. Quads are a printer's term for em spaces used to position a line flush on a margin. Now, press Return for a new line and continue with the rest of the text in the paragraph.

Numbering Equations

If the copy being set contains several equations in each chapter, some conventions call for the equations to be numbered sequentially in parentheses at the right margin on the line where the equation appears. The text then refers to each equation by the parenthetical numbers.

To set these equation numbers in unjustified text, enclose the equation string between $<\$E >$, followed by a tab and then the number (in parentheses) in its correct sequence.

$<\$Ex+y>$ (3)

The tagged value of the first tab should be Set Right with the value of the right margin. Text that is tagged as justified cannot be given tabbing values.

The easiest method for aligning a few equation numbers in justified text is by quadding the line from the end of the equation until the parenthetical number is closely aligned with the right margin of the page or column. To quad with nonprinting em spaces, use Ctrl-Shift-M. For closer adjustment, use en spaces or thin spaces. En spaces are produced with Ctrl-Shift-N, and thin spaces (one-third of an em) are produced with Ctrl-Shift-T. Obviously, this method is more time-consuming than using tabs. Use it only when you have no alternative to justified body text. When parenthetical numbers appear on every page of the document, a quicker method is to make a formula number tag with no line break, flush right, and cross-referenced. The number jumps to the formula line if typed in the text file immediately after the tagged formula.

If the equation needs editing, move the cursor along the line to the left of the equation to be edited and watch for the word EQUATION to appear in the current selection box.

Select Edit Special Item in the Edit Menu, (or use the shortcut Ctrl-D) to display the equation screen with the pseudostring on the ledger line and the resulting formula set up below. Edit the equation, and then press Ctrl-D to complete the edit.

If the equation changes in length during the editing process, you will have to realign the parenthetical number if you are using justified text.

Formatting Equations

Equations do not need special style sheets; equations are set by the instructions added to the source files as you type equations in the work area. Any tag used in a style file can be used to set the format of a paragraph where an equation occurs.

On some printers the superscript and subscript characters may not be pleasingly aligned. To adjust, choose the Typography command from the Paragraph menu and select Attribute Overrides to obtain more a favorable size, height, and location of the superscript and subscript characters. Adjust only the paragraph affected by the required changes.

Do not use tabs within equations, but use the tilde (˜) or the circumflex, or caret, (ˆ) to add space between characters. Both diacritical marks create spaces of similar size.

A valuable secondary feature of the equation-setting facility is Xerox Ventura Publisher's capability to handle common fractions. This addition to the program is very useful, for although some fonts from third-party vendors have a sprinkling of common fractions, such as 1/3, 1/2, and 3/4 in their extended ASCII character set, Ventura Publisher does not address them.

In earlier editions of Ventura, a compromise was possible by building a macro to use superscript and subscript numbers together with a forward slash; the method was cumbersome and extremely time-consuming.

Version 2.0 changes all that. You simply write the fraction in text, and the program sets the fraction accurately. Use the same command as for equations, for example, <$E1/2> to set the fraction one-half. If the fraction is preceded by whole numbers, set it as <$E12 3/4> separating the whole numbers from the fraction by a single space. Failure to use a space results in the whole numbers being set as part of the fraction.

Typographical convention divides common fractions into two designs: *em fractions* and *en fractions*. Em fractions are generated automatically by Version 2.0, using a sloping fraction bar between numbers. Em fractions are employed for simple fractions, such as 1/2, 1/3, or 3/4. Em fractions are also used in stock quotations. They are generated in text with ½ or at the console with 1/2. Conventional en fractions have a horizontal crossbar and are used when the denominator is a large number, such as

9/64th, or when a string of fractions is being added together. En fractions are generated in text with commands: `size 6 9 over 64` produces $\frac{9}{64}$ and `size 6 13 over 1000` produces $\frac{13}{1000}$. Generating en fractions at the console is similar. The `size` command changes the point size of the numbers immediately following, in this case to 6 points. The `size` command is canceled when a tilde or caret is used in the string. PostScript printers can scale type in half-point increments, so the `size` command can be something like 4.5 in order to get a good fit of type to text. Non-PostScript printers, however, use fixed bit-mapped characters, and 6-point Swiss or Helvetica is the smallest allowable type that can be used.

If subsequent editing is required after the file has been brought inside the page, invoke the Edit function by placing the cursor over the tiny degree mark immediately preceding the fraction; then press Ctrl-D. If the degree mark is not showing, move the cursor over the line until the word EQUATION appears in the current selection box; then press Ctrl-D.

The elements of the fraction now appear on the ledger line, and the result appears below. Add the necessary space between the whole numbers and the fraction or edit the figures in the fraction, and watch for a second or so until the result appears. After you are satisfied, press Ctrl-D to return the edited version into the text.

Fractions can be set directly from the keyboard by using the Ins Special Item command and selecting Equation. Enter the whole number; press the space bar once; then enter the fraction, separating the numerator from the denominator by a forward slash (/). If the result below the ledger line is correct, press Ctrl-D to insert the fraction into the text.

Learning the Rules

As with even the simplest of spoken languages, you must observe a few basic rules of syntax and avoid using reserved natural words when you are setting equations. These special words are listed in the documentation of the Professional Extension.

The rules of the equation language are limited to three:

1. A space must be included before and after each command. Use the tilde (˜) to make a full space. Use two or more tildes to make even bigger spaces. A thin space can be made with the caret, or circumflex accent, sign (ˆ).

   Failure to introduce a tilde or ˆ before and after a command results in the command word's appearing as text in the expression.

2. Ordinary spaces written in the pseudostring are not printed. $X + Y$ will appear as $X+Y$. Be sure that you have a tilde or ˆ before and after each character requiring spacing. These special characters are the plus and minus signs and the equal sign.

3. Almost all commands in the pseudostring modify whatever follows:

   x sup 2 modifies the 2 so that it becomes a superscripted attachment of X

But there are a few exceptions. These exceptions are the commands for diacritical marks, which modify the preceding expression (for example, *xyz bar* ensures that the characters *xyz* are below a bar line).

All diacritical marks (for example, ˜ ˆ ‗) affect the following:

1. Any character

2. Any special word

3. Any group of characters not separated by a space

4. Any matter placed inside braces { }

Efficiency Tip

Enclose Expressions with Tildes; Add Spaces between Elements

Setting equations in text could not be more simple than the method used in the Professional Extension. But newcomers usually forget that each expression must be enclosed by spaces created by either a ˜ or a ˆ. Make a habit of entering a ˜ instead of pressing the space bar and following the expression with a ˜ before pressing the space bar (for example, ˜ +˜, or x˜ =˜ 1).

Similarly, you must have a conventional space separating each element in the expression (for example, *xsup2* must be separated with spaces: *x sup 2*)

On the following pages are examples of equations and text extracted from an early scientific text book on microwave technology. The first example is the edited text from a word processor as it would be submitted by the author. The equation strings delimited by the <$E > convention are highlighted (see fig. 10.12). The second example is the printed result after the Professional Extension has introduced the copy into a formatted style sheet having all the attributes tagged for the correct body text (see fig. 10.13).

The steps for producing equations are as follows:

1. Select the Text function.

2. Select On for Grow Inter-Line To Fit in the Paragraph menu TYPOGRAPHY SETTINGS dialog box.

3. Select Ins Special Item in the Edit Menu, or press Ctrl-C.

4. Select Equation from the pop-up menu, or press F4.

5. Follow these logical steps of interpretation:

    a. Enter the first expression, followed by a space.

    b. Enter the command, followed by a space.

    c. Enter the next expression.

    d. Enter a diacritical mark.

```
@SIDEHEAD = An example of setting equations directly in text
Cayley-Hamilton's Theorem.<197> The characteristic equation
of a matrix was defined by Eq. (10) of Sec. 12.3.
<MI>Theorem 7.<D><197>Every matrix satisfies its
characteristic equation. To prove this, let the
characteristic equation of P be
< >< >< >< >< ><$Ep sup n~+~c sub 1 p sup n-1~+~<193>~=~0>
and let the <MI>n<D> roots of this equation be <MI>pk. Form
the matrix
< >< >< >< >< ><$Eroman bold M~=~{roman bold P} sup n~+~c
sub 1 {roman bold P} sup n-1~+~ . . .~+~c sub n>
Any <MI>n<D>th-order vector can be expanded in terms of
eigenvectors a<MIV>k<D> of P.
Let
< >< >< >< >< >< ><$Eroman bold a~=~sum from k d sub k {roman
bold a} sub k> ,
Then
< >< >< >< >< ><$Eroman bold Ma~=~sum from  k ((d sub k (p
sub k sup n)~+ ~c sub 1 (p sub k sup( n -1)) . . .~+~c sub n
)) (roman bold a) sub k>
The expression in parenthesis on the right of this equation
vanishes. Therefore
< >< >< >< >< ><$Eroman  bold M roman bold a~=~0>
for any vector a. Therefore M = 0, and P satisfies its
characteristic equation, which proves the theorem.
The spur or trace of a matrix is defined as the sum of its
diagonal elements. The last theorem needed for discussion to
follow will now be stated.
<MI>Theorem 8<D>.<197>The spur of a matrix P is equal to the
sum of its eigenvalues <MI>p<MIV>k<D>. Let the
characteristic equation of P be
< >< >< >< >< ><$Ep sup n~+~c sub 1 p sup n-1~+~<193>~=~0> .
The sum of the roots of the polynomial is equal to
<MI>c<MV>1. The characteristic equation is the expansion of
det (P <197><MI> p<D>|). In the expansion of the
determinant, the coefficient multiplying <$Ep sup n-1> is
<$Esum from n P sub nn> . Therefore
< >< >< >< >< ><$Esum from n P sub nn~=~ sum from k ^p sub k>
```

Fig. 10.12.

*Text coded to yield
equations.*

e. Enter operator ($+$, $-$, $\times$, $/$).

f. Enter a diacritical mark.

g. Enter additional expressions and modifiers, following the same progression.

Consult the Professional Extension documentation for a complete summary of the equation commands. The documentation also contain charts showing the special characters and symbols and the commands to produce these characters and symbols.

Chapter Summary

By now you should have a good idea of the advantages of the features added by the Professional Extension, along with basic guidelines as to when and how to apply these features. As noted in this chapter, you have limited hyphenation and cross-referencing with the Version 2.0 base product, but the base product offers no convenient alternatives to the features offered by the Professional Extension for building tables, achieving vertical justification, and creating equations. Furthermore, the Professional Extension's capability to access EMS memory lets you work faster and import large database files that cannot be handled by the base product. The Professional Extension is a worthwhile investment for anyone who expects to use even one of its added features.

An example of setting equations directly in text

Cayley-Hamilton's Theorem.— The characteristic equation of a matrix was defined by Eq. (10) of Sec. 12.3.

Theorem 7.—Every matrix satisfies its characteristic equation. To prove this, let the characteristic equation of **P** be

$$p^n + c_1 p^{n-1} + \ldots = 0$$

and let the n roots of this equation be pk. *Form the matrix*

$$\mathbf{M} = \mathbf{P}^n + c_1 \mathbf{P}^{n-1} + \ldots + c_n \tag{1}$$

Any nth-order vector can be expanded in terms of eigenvectors a_k of P.

Let

$$\mathbf{a} = \sum_k d_k \mathbf{a}_k \tag{2}$$

Then

$$\mathbf{Ma} = \sum_k d_k (p_k^n + c_1 p_k^{n-1} \ldots + c_n) \mathbf{a}_k \tag{3}$$

The expression in parenthesis on the right of this equation vanishes. Therefore

$$\mathbf{Ma} = 0$$

for any vector **a**. Therefore $\mathbf{M} = 0$, and **P** satisfies its characteristic equation, which proves the theorem.

The spur or trace of a matrix is defined as the sum of its diagonal elements. The last theorem needed for discussion to follow will now be stated.

Theorem 8.—The spur of a matrix **P** is equal to the sum of its eigenvalues p_k. Let the characteristic equation of **P** be

$$p^n + c_1 p^{n-1} + \ldots = 0 \tag{4}$$

The sum of the roots of the polynomial is equal to c_1. The characteristic equation is the expansion of det $(\mathbf{P} - pI)$. In the expansion of the determinant, the coefficient multiplying p^{n-1} is $\sum_n P_{nn}$. Therefore

$$\sum_n P_{nn} = \sum_k p_k \tag{5}$$

Fig. 10.13.

Results of the code shown in figure 10.12.

11

Ventura Publisher
as a Design Tool

Ventura, a tremendous design tool in many ways, is outstanding in at least three respects:

- You can use Ventura to sketch rough ideas for designs to be reviewed with the rest of your team or your client. (The term *client* can include managing editors, publication department managers, or end-user groups—anyone with whom the designer must share decisions.)

- You can use the structure Ventura provides through style file tags, to organize specifications for the production team.

- You can create *template* systems to ensure that all parts of a publication follow the same specifications.

This chapter deals with elements that must be considered in any document design and with tips about using Ventura as a design tool. The design considerations are presented in the sequence you follow in Ventura when building a document from scratch. You first see how to use Ventura to develop a series of different design ideas for a project. Then, you learn what goes into a template system so that you can create a series of publications with the same design. Finally, you learn how the designer can work ahead of the production team, sketching the layout of each page of the publication before the text and graphics from other programs are placed on the pages. Desktop publishers often play all these roles. If you are the designer, production team, author, and editor, you can learn how to follow the steps of all these professionals.

In practice, some of these steps may be done first on paper instead of at the computer; in fact, designers on some teams may never touch the computer. Whether you—as the designer—are simply writing out the design specifications or actually setting up the master template, you should know how Ventura works before making your specifications.

Traditionally, a designer becomes involved in production only after the writing is complete or well under way. If the project team is small, however, and the authors are willing, many typographic design specifications can be incorporated in the text during the writing stage. If you plan the design ahead of time, for instance, you can let the authors know how to apply attributes to text and how to code paragraphs that have

421

formats different from the settings for body copy. Other design details, such as the page size and margins, can be decided later, after the writing but before the text is placed in Ventura. In other words, you can wait to develop some design specifications until you learn what text and graphics are required for the publication.

This chapter shows you how to prepare your design specifications in terms of Ventura's commands and capabilities.

Creating Design Alternatives

You can use Ventura to create a series of quick "comps" of different designs for a publication before deciding on the final design. A designer's *comp* is a comprehensive layout of a design idea, usually done by hand with pencils, rulers, and colored pens. Sketching out your ideas with Ventura instead of using pencil and ruler offers three advantages:

- Copying and moving elements on a page is easy if you are working on a single design.

- Making copies of the first design and modifying it to create alternative designs is an efficient design practice.

- Showing clients crisp text and graphics elements printed on a high-resolution printer makes an effective presentation.

Identifying the Essential Elements

One of the steps in the design process is to identify the essential elements of the publication to be created. Suppose that you are creating a newsletter. Although the production manager views the elements in terms of articles that must be written by various authors, the designer uses another perspective to view the newsletter. The designer may list the newsletter's design elements as follows:

- Page size and margins
- Base page grid structure
- Running heads and running feet
- Two different page formats (right and left)
- A number of heading levels
- Several types of graphics

In addition, this particular publication may include one or more of the following special considerations or constraints affecting the design:

- Feature articles requiring special placement
- Sidebars distinct from the rest of the text on a page

For this proposed publication, you can use Ventura as a design tool and let the program's built-in text and graphics features create representations of your basic design elements. You need not know the exact text or contents of the publication to rough out a design idea. You can use dummy text for headlines or headings, frames filled with horizontal lines for body copy, and black or gray boxes for figures. Use shaded boxes to show where graphics are to be placed, for example, and crop marks to show the page size. To enhance the design, you can use ruled lines. Figure 11.1 shows how design ideas for the chapters of a book can be handled in Ventura's terms.

You also may type *greek* text to show the position and size of text on a page. The phrase *greek text*, in this case, refers to text used to represent the font, but not the content, of the text on a page. Typesetters use standard block paragraphs called greek, but the text looks more like Latin (''Lorem ipsum dolor sit ...''). This use of the term *greek* differs slightly from that used to describe the appearance or display of text in the Reduced view command, in which small fonts are displayed as gray bars—not as readable text. You can determine the point size below which text is greeked using the SET PREFERENCES dialog box.

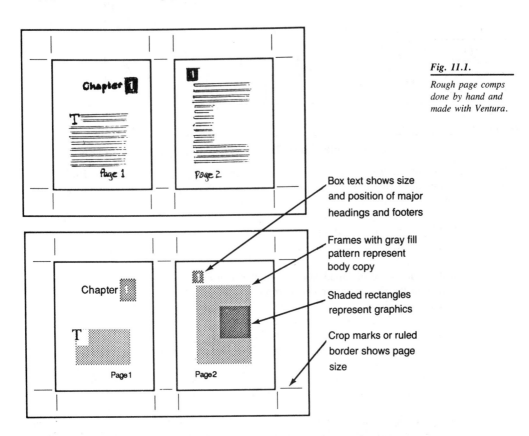

Fig. 11.1.

Rough page comps done by hand and made with Ventura.

Box text shows size and position of major headings and footers

Frames with gray fill pattern represent body copy

Shaded rectangles represent graphics

Crop marks or ruled border shows page size

Once you create the basic elements of your publication, you can modify the design or rearrange the elements on the page to develop variations. Instead of creating a different Ventura chapter to represent each design idea, you can use one design chapter to create and show many pages of different design variations (see fig. 11.2). You can also do the following:

- Create representations of all the basic design elements once and store them on the first page of the design chapter (in fig. 11.2, these include the chapter number, text copy, and the page number)

- Add a new page for each new design variation

- Use the Copy and Paste commands to duplicate the design elements onto new pages

- Add new tags (that is, change type specifications for the existing tags and save them under new names) to selected text as needed to represent each new design

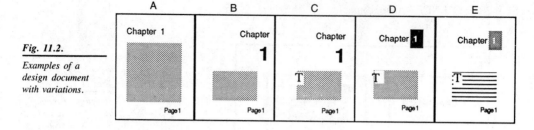

Fig. 11.2.

Examples of a design document with variations.

Use Horizontal Lines To Represent Body Copy in a Design

To represent body copy as horizontal lines (see fig. 11.2E), use the Ruling Line Below command in the Paragraph menu to set the Body Text tag to have a ruling line below each paragraph. Set the Width option to Column to set the ruled lines to column width, and insert a height of 0.5 points for the rule. Then insert carriage returns to fill frames with "dummy" body copy.

If the trim size of the publication is smaller than 8.5 by 11 inches, you can use a solid border in the design document to represent the edges of the pages. This border lets you see how the final pages will look when trimmed (see fig. 11.3). In the final publication, however, you should use crop marks rather than solid lines to indicate the edges of the paper. Otherwise, the solid lines may show in the final publication—especially if the pages are to be folded into signatures before being trimmed. (A *signature* is a single sheet of paper on which are printed an even number of pages [usually 16 or 32]. The pages are arranged so that the paper can be folded and trimmed to create a booklet or a small section of a larger document.)

After a design idea is chosen, the designer translates that idea into the specifications for Ventura and the other programs used to construct the parts of the publication. Ideally, the designer then sits down at the computer with Ventura and builds the basic template system for the final publication, as explained in Chapter 7.

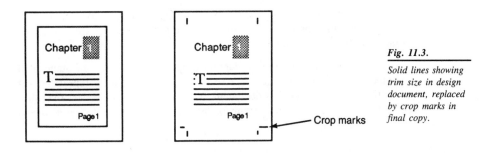

Crop marks

Fig. 11.3.

Solid lines showing trim size in design document, replaced by crop marks in final copy.

Using a Chapter To Build a Template

Whenever you start a new publication, you must go through a certain series of steps and commands to set up the pages before you begin placing text and graphics from other programs. In traditional terms, you define the design specifications for the publication. In Ventura, you make selections in the PAGE LAYOUT dialog box and use various commands on the Frame menu to set up margins, column guides, and other elements on the page.

A *template* is a Ventura chapter that embodies the basic design specifications (see fig. 11.4). The basic grid system for each page appears on the template. The template also includes common elements that are to appear within the publication in specific locations or at repeated intervals. A template is set up with a style file and all the defaults are tailored to match the design specifications for the publication.

Fig. 11.4.

Ventura templates.

Benefits of Using Templates

Using a template system offers several important benefits: A template system saves repeated setup steps, forces you to think ahead, embodies design, enforces consistency, and simplifies the page layout process.

Saves Repeating Setup Steps

One major benefit of using a template system is that the decisions and actions described in this chapter are executed only once during the production cycle, instead of once for every new file that makes up the full publication. Whenever you start a new project, you must complete a certain number of steps and commands to set up the pages before you begin typing text, drawing illustrations, or placing text and graphics from other programs into a page layout. In computer terms, you define the margins, the page size, the number of columns, and the default settings (for font, line weight, paragraph alignment, and so on).

Templates save time in large production projects by "capturing" some of the steps required to set up a new document so that you don't have to repeat the same steps every time you start a similar document. You can save hours or days over the life of a project by using a template system for large publications or any series of documents that share the same design.

Efficiency Tip

Use Ventura's Example Chapters for a Quick Start

Choose one of Ventura's example chapter files (stored in the TYPESET subdirectory) similar to the publication you are creating. Save the file under a new name, and modify the settings as needed.

You should develop a template system for any publication project that requires more than one CHP file. Chapters of books, reports, and manuals can be cloned from the first CHP file by loading that chapter and saving it (using the Save As command) under a new name. Then replace the original source files with those appropriate for the new chapter. Newsletters and magazines are candidates for template systems in which a CHP template is opened and saved under a new name for each issue of the publication. Shorter documents such as price lists, menus, ads, and brochures are candidates for template systems if you produce several documents with the same or similar layouts.

Forces You To Think Ahead and Embodies Design

It's a good idea to "think out" the design of your document before you make your initial page setup. The first step in thinking out a production plan is to list the design specifications to be applied throughout a publication. Whenever possible, design specifications should be "captured" in the template system.

Aside from the practical advantages of saving time and providing a disciplined approach to producing a document, a template system can serve the function of preserving the aesthetic intent of a design. By incorporating as many of the design specifications as possible into an electronic template, the production group is aided in preserving the "look" the designer intended.

Enforces Consistency and Simplifies Page Layout

A good designer always applies the rule of consistency. In the past, the designer enforced consistency by issuing lists of standards and printing blue lines as grid guides on the final page layout boards. In electronic publishing, you can enforce consistency by working with electronic templates to enforce a grid system and apply type specifications. You can set up guidelines for elements such as ruled line lengths and weights, fill patterns, tab settings, paragraph alignment, indentations, bullet sizes and styles, and in-figure labels. You can control the spacing above and below a figure and the spacing between a graphic and the frame that contains it. All these specifications are set once and then done automatically in Ventura.

A good template system can help simplify the page layout process by providing guides that help the layout artist arrange elements on each page. Ventura displays column guides and other frame margins (similar to blue lines) on-screen. Style files ensure that all type specifications are consistently and efficiently applied throughout the publication or series of publications sharing the same design.

Defining the Basic Standards for Your Publication

Before you lay out your page grid, you should define the basic defaults and standards to be used in the publication. These defaults and standards include defining the page size and orientation, establishing the margins, turning column balance on or off, setting up a width table for the fonts to be used, and choosing a unit of measure. The specifications are stored with the template publication and preserved in all files cloned from the template.

In the following sections, notice that these standards are discussed in the sequence in which they appear as you build a template. You must specify page size and orientation in the PAGE LAYOUT dialog box, and you must set margins on the page before you add elements to any page for a particular publication design.

Ventura's powerful style file is used to set typographic characteristics for copy elements used in your layout. The style file controls widow and orphan lines, ensures that headings stay with text, and makes sure that certain elements always start on a right page. You can specify, for example, that a heading flow across more than one column in multicolumn formats, ensure consistent spacing between articles, and specify that the top of the first capital letter in copy begin exactly at the top margin of a page.

Defining the Page Layout

You define the paper size and orientation through the PAGE LAYOUT dialog box when you open a new chapter (see fig. 11.5). By setting these standards in a template, you ensure that all other files cloned from that template have the same page-size and orientation settings.

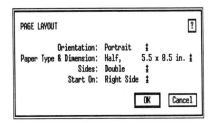

Fig. 11.5.

The PAGE LAYOUT dialog box

Most publications have the same page size for all sections, but the orientation of the pages may vary from section to section. You may have a set of appendixes with financial reports that must be printed Orientation: Landscape to accommodate many columns of numbers. In this case, set up two templates: one for all Orientation: Portrait pages and one for all Orientation: Landscape pages.

The page size is usually the same as the final publication after it is mass produced, bound, and trimmed, such as a 5.5-by-8.5-inch booklet defined by Paper Type: Half in the PAGE LAYOUT dialog box (again see fig. 11.5). You also can specify that you are printing on 8.5-by-11-inch paper, for example, and use that setting as the board size to design a smaller layout. In this case, you use the Sizing & Scaling command to set the base page as a 6-by-9-inch layout positioned at Upper Left X: 1.25 and Upper Left Y: 1.00, as in figure 11.6. Crop marks (when enabled just before printing) automatically print in position. You also can use a larger page (8.5 by 11 inches) than the final design (6 by 9 inches), and add graphic lines as crop marks before printing. (See "Creating Custom Page Sizes" and "Creating Custom Crop Marks" in Chapter 7.)

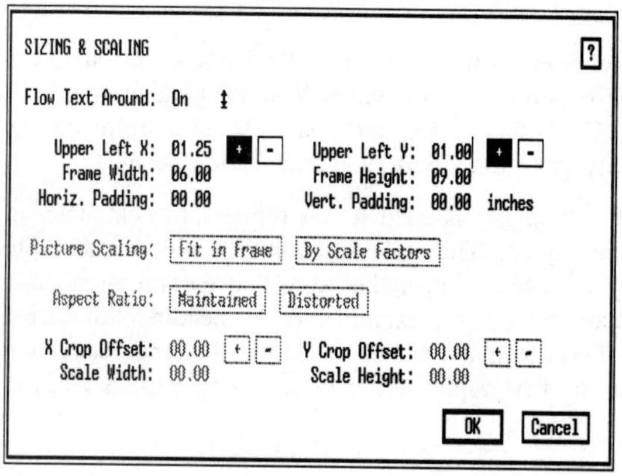

Fig. 11.6.

6-by-9-inch booklet page, with the base page defined as 6 by 9 and printed on 8.5-by-11-inch paper with automatic crop marks.

```
SIZING & SCALING                                              [?]

Flow Text Around:  On  ‡

        Upper Left X:  01.25  [+][-]    Upper Left Y:  01.00  [+][-]
         Frame Width:  06.00             Frame Height:  09.00
       Horiz. Padding: 00.00             Vert. Padding: 00.00  inches

      Picture Scaling:  [Fit in Frame] [By Scale Factors]

        Aspect Ratio:  [Maintained] [Distorted]

       X Crop Offset:  00.00  [+][-]    Y Crop Offset:  00.00  [+][-]
        Scale Width:  00.00             Scale Height:  00.00

                                              [ OK ]  [Cancel]
```

The margins for the base page are defined in the MARGINS & COLUMNS dialog box from the Frame menu. These margins apply throughout a chapter. If your publication prints on both sides, specify Sides: Double and Ventura automatically mirrors right margins on left pages.

In long projects, each section of the publication using a different design should have a separate template, that is, a separate CHP file (see fig. 11.7). For margin and column changes that affect only a few pages, you can use one page design and change individual pages with one of two methods: You can use the Insert/Remove Page command on the Chapter menu to add a new page and set new column settings, or you can add a frame to the page and set new column settings for that frame. (See "Overriding the Page Style" in Chapter 7.)

The margins do not necessarily define the limits of the text and graphics that appear on a page. Ventura lets you place text and graphics in frames that are positioned beyond the margins. The side margins determine the width of the column guides. The

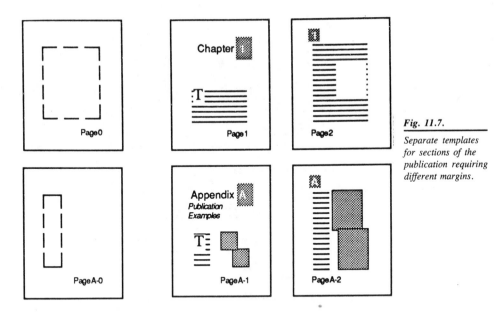

Fig. 11.7.

Separate templates for sections of the publication requiring different margins.

bottom margin determines where text stops flowing when placed in a column. Elements that can fall outside the margins are ruled lines around pages, vertical and horizontal rules that are part of the design, and running heads and feet (see fig. 11.8).

In designing pages with text or graphics that are to be printed close to the page-size (paper-size) boundaries, you must make sure that your printer can print these areas, especially when you create designs that "bleed" across the inside margins or outer edges of the final publication. Most printers cannot print at the extreme edges of the page (see fig. 11.9).

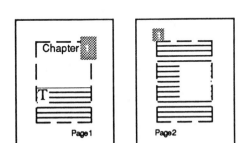

Fig. 11.8.

Margins do not limit all text and graphics.

Setting Up a Width Table

As you begin to build your template, you should first decide which fonts you will use. Make this selection once by defining the target printer and the width table with the Options menu Set Printer Info command (see "Setting the Target Printer" in Chapter

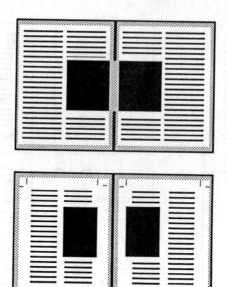

Fig. 11.9.

Designs cannot "bleed" to the paper's edges.

7). From then on, all publication files cloned from this template have the same printer specifications.

Selecting a Unit of Measure and Displaying Rulers

If you make all your design specifications in the same unit of measure, you can set up the template so that the ruler displays the same unit of measure in all files made from the template. Use the Options menu's Set Ruler command to do this (see fig. 11.10). If you give your specifications in two or more different measures (inches for margins but picas for copy depth, for instance), select the unit of measure in which you prefer to view the horizontal and vertical ruler lines.

Fig. 11.10.

Setting the unit of measure in the template.

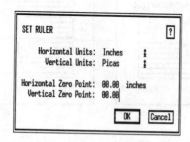

The zero point of the rulers (0,0) can serve as a production aid. Whenever possible, you should make the position of the zero point on the page a part of the design specifications. Normally, this reference point is the top left corner of the page, but your design specifications may require a different zero point. Figure 11.11 shows the zero point in the middle of a two-page spread. You also can move the zero point to the left and top margins of a 6-by-9-inch page on 8.5-by-11-inch paper.

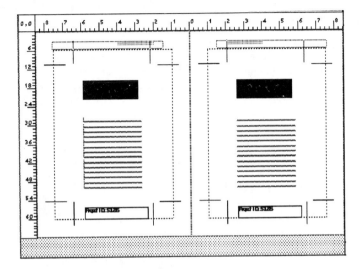

Fig. 11.11.

Design specifications in reference to the zero point.

Setting Up the Style File

Any new text typed in Ventura and any placed text files automatically take on the template's default settings for the Body Text tag. Also, the Options menu Line Snap command takes on the interline spacing set for Body Text. Set the type specifications for the Body Text tag to match the font, alignment, and spacing settings that are used most often. Set up additional tags as required by the design specifications. Remember that you can override a tag's settings in Text mode by setting the font for selected text with the Set Font button.

The designer can use Ventura's style file to control how much space is between figure captions and the text following, how much space is between text and ruled lines, and whether or not a headline crosses all columns on a page. Having a style file ensures consistent spacing in the publication and helps speed the production process.

To control space between articles in a newsletter, for instance, use the Spacing command on the Paragraph menu to set the spacing above each headline. To control space between a figure caption and copy below it, use the Spacing command to set the spacing below each figure caption.

Creating a Base-Page Grid

The best publication designs are based on base-page grids that position elements throughout the chapter. The nonprinting grid lines that display on-screen include page margins and column guides. The grid established for the baseline of text is invisible, but the effect is evident when you move frames on the page. The base-page grids have nothing to do with the Graphic menu's Grid Settings command, which sets up separate grids for each frame used to control graphics. (Graphic grids are covered in more detail in Chapter 6, and the text grid is covered in Chapter 5. Chapter 7 explains how to use grids when you are setting up page layouts.)

Simple grid structures involving one, two, or three columns are relatively easy to work with; but complex grids offer more design possibilities (see fig. 11.12). Variety in a one-column grid structure, for example, can be achieved by varying the type specifications and paragraph alignment indentations. A two-column grid structure adds the possibility that graphics and text can expand to full-page width on selected pages. A three-column grid offers at least three page variations.

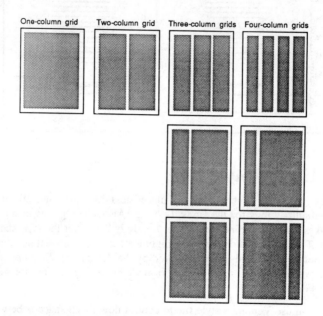

Fig. 11.12.

Grid structures showing design possibilities.

You can set up an evenly spaced grid structure with Ventura's Margins & Columns command and then adjust the column guides to view different effects. To set up the grids shown in the first column of figure 11.13, for example, select # of Columns: 3 and click Make Equal Widths to divide the page in thirds. Make a note of the width Ventura sets for each width and gutter. Next, select # of Columns: 2 and enter the column width derived from the three-column settings for only one of the columns and the gutter and click OK. Ventura automatically sizes the other column to fill the remaining space. The second and third columns of figure 11.13 show the same technique applied to a four-column grid. (See ''Setting Column Guides'' in Chapter 7 for more information.)

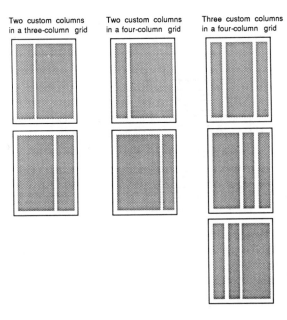

Two custom columns in a three-column grid

Two custom columns in a four-column grid

Three custom columns in a four-column grid

Fig. 11.13.

Adjusting column widths to create custom grid settings.

Efficiency Tip

Columns as Grid Markers

You can set the space between columns to zero (see fig. 11.14) and use the Frame menu's Margins & Columns command to help divide the page into equal parts. This procedure results in a visible grid of vertical guides. Then add frames on each page to create the guides you want to use to define the text.

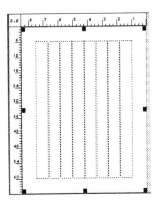

Fig. 11.14.

Using columns with no space between as grid markers.

Documents with the same grid on every page are much easier to produce than documents using variations of the grid. A common variation, the mirror-image page layout, is particularly difficult to handle (see fig. 11.15). Individual page layout is not difficult, but chaos ensues if you have to insert or delete a page after the publication is laid out. When you work with mirror-image designs, the best rule of thumb is to insert or delete an even number of pages to keep intact all the subsequent page layouts.

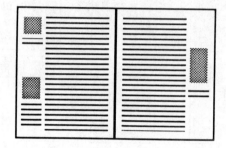

Fig. 11.15.

Mirror-image page design.

Publications with complex grid systems require the designer's attention throughout the production cycle. That attention is especially important for magazines and newsletters that incorporate various sizes of display ads. The designer can work ahead of the production team to specify where ads are to be placed and how articles jump from one page to another.

Efficiency Tip

Build a Page Layout Like a Painting

A publication does not have to be built from front to back, page by page. You can construct a publication in layers, just as painters work on canvas. The painter first pencils the rough outline on the canvas and then gradually adds layers of paint.

In Ventura, the basic grid system is the painter's penciled sketch. You can use shaded boxes to reserve certain areas for planned graphics and particular articles. The text and graphics that you bring in from other programs to replace the place holders are like the painter's gradually added layers of paint.

During both the design and production phases, you can work on views of facing pages for double-sided publications. Working on both pages can be advantageous when you want to consider the overall impact of the open publication or when you want to create graphic images that bleed across one page to the other.

The designer may be called in once more after the Ventura publication goes to production. (Refer to Chapters 3 through 8 for the production process following the design step.) The final design activities are described in the following paragraphs.

Identifying Common Text and Graphics Elements

Most of the text and graphics for a publication probably will be brought in from other programs. Some elements, however, are repeated throughout the publication. In a template, these repeated elements can appear on the base page and in some individual frames.

Elements that appear in the same position on every page belong on the base page and in the running head and running foot frames. Although you position the running head and running foot frames with the correct type specifications and alignment and you use Ventura's automatic page-, section-, and chapter-numbering features, the text of the running heads and running feet usually changes in each CHP file. When you clone the template, one of your first steps is to change the text of the running head and running foot.

In addition to the elements that belong on every page, other elements may be repeated irregularly but frequently throughout the publication. You can create these items just once and store them on the base page. Whenever you need one of the repeated elements, you can duplicate it with the Copy and Paste commands.

For example, you can use the base page to store a graphics symbol that appears at the end of every article in a newsletter or magazine. Create the graphic and select Show On All Pages on the Graphic menu. When you reach the end of an article, you copy the graphic and paste it at the end of the article. The copied graphic is automatically set as Show On This Page, and the original still appears on all pages. To create standard box text blocks or display ads in sizes that are too large to store on the base page, see "Using a Clipboard Page To Store Graphics Standards for a Chapter" in this chapter.

Adding Standard Elements to Individual Pages

Besides the elements positioned or temporarily stored on the base page, your publication may contain elements that appear predictably on certain numbered pages. The template for a newsletter, for example, should include the banner or logo for the first page (see fig. 11.16). If all issues of the newsletter are always the same length, you may be able to predict the positions of the masthead, subscription information, and other permanent features. You also can add place holders for the headline text for feature articles that start on the first page.

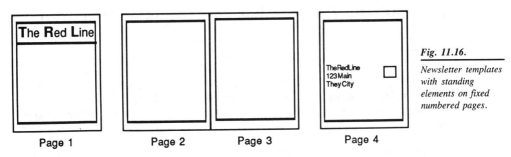

The Red Line

TheRedLine
123 Main
TheyCity

Page 1   Page 2   Page 3   Page 4

Fig. 11.16.

Newsletter templates with standing elements on fixed numbered pages.

Using a Clipboard Page To Store Graphics Standards for a Chapter

The designer sets standards for all graphics elements in the publication. Samples of these elements can be stored as a Clipboard Page on the last page in the template. The production personnel can copy and paste these elements to the Frame, Text, or Graphics Clipboard as needed. All elements on the Clipboard Page are stored in the CAP file, and the page should be deleted when it is no longer needed. Standards stored on the Clipboard Page can include

- Spacing above and below graphics frames
- Spacing between a graphic and its frame
- Thickness of rules around graphics frames
- Definition of a standard callout

To control spacing above and below graphics frames, create a frame of any size on the Clipboard Page. Set line thickness (using the Frame menu's Ruling Box Around command) and set Vert. Padding (using the Frame menu's Sizing and Scaling command) to define the border of white space between text and the frame. As the frame is resized, the white space around it remains the same.

To control spacing between a graphic and its frame, create a frame of any size on the Clipboard Page. Set line thickness (using the Frame menu's Ruling Box Around command) and set the margins and columns (from the Frame menu) to define the border of white space needed inside the frame. As the frame is resized, the white space between the graphic and the frame remains the same.

To create a standard callout, select Box Text from the Graphic menu and set the line attributes for the thickness of the ruled boxes around the callouts. Draw a line using the graphics line tool and set the line attributes for Thickness and End Style. After the graphic is positioned, the line direction can be altered as needed.

Determining the Number of Templates Required

You already have seen that a separate template file is required for each unique page size and orientation. In addition, you can use templates to handle any other essential differences in sections of your publication. When the basic format of running heads and feet changes between major sections of a publication, for example, you may need more than one template (see fig. 11.17). On the other hand, if the only difference between sections is the number of columns, which can be handled by adding a frame, one template may suffice.

As a general rule, create separate templates if either of the following conditions occurs:

- Page size varies
- Page orientation changes

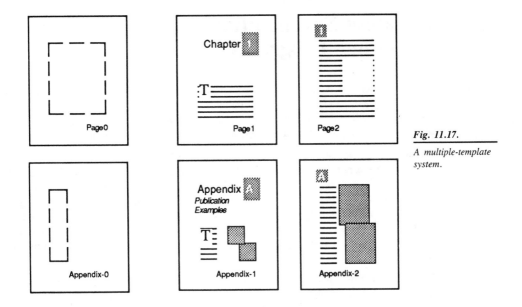

Fig. 11.17.

A multiple-template system.

Adding Instructions for Working with the Template

If the person designing the template is not the same person who uses it in production, the template designer should list the steps necessary for working with the template. The steps can be simple—serving primarily as reminders of each step. A designer may list the following instructions for the current issue of a newsletter:

1. Open the template and immediately save it under a new name.

2. Remove any source files not appropriate for the new template.

3. Change the running heads and feet on the page.

4. Change the volume and date information on the first page, below the newsletter banner.

5. Place the table of contents on the first page before placing the feature article.

6. Continue placing text and graphics as specified for the current issue.

7. Delete these instructions.

To catch the attention of the production staff, you can type instructions directly on the template's page or on the first page. The production person can delete the instructions after reading them.

Creating Specifications for Other Programs

Chapter 9 presents most of the necessary considerations for selecting fonts for different text elements. You can put these specifications directly into your Ventura style file for the template. Line widths and fill patterns can be set as default values in the Ventura template. These items also can be stored as defined elements on the page or applied in the graphics programs used to create the content of the publication.

A designer should have a good idea of the number and sources of graphic elements that go into the publication. Knowing the capabilities and limitations of the available programs, the designer must specify how each illustration is to be treated. What are the size limitations or preferences for the figures, for example? If you follow a grid system, each figure's width must match the increments allowed by the grid. A two-column grid allows two figure widths (one-column or full-page width); a three-column grid allows three different figure widths; a four-column grid allows four widths; and so on.

The designer must answer other questions. What fonts, styles, and sizes are used in illustrations and captions? Are the figures to be enlarged or reduced during page composition? Are photographs and other special illustrations to be pasted up by hand or scanned into the computer? You can simply write out these specifications, or you can use the programs that create the graphics to create figure templates just as you use Ventura to create publication templates.

Your design specifications for body copy, captions, and figure titles should include directions for paragraph alignment (left, right, justified, or centered) and spacing between paragraphs. The designer must consider convenience and speed of production. Many formats can be handled by style file tags in Ventura. Other formats require special treatment and may slow the production process. You can generate a printout of the style file to see the typographic settings associated with each tag by using the Paragraph menu Update Tags command.

Going beyond Ventura

For some publications, the final pages for distribution are printed on a laser printer. In most cases, however, you make multiple copies with a photocopier or an offset printer.

After the final pages of the publication are printed on a high-resolution printer, some final preparation still may be required before the pages are ready to be reproduced. This preparation can include manual pasteup of figures that cannot be produced on the computer, photograph markup for halftone processing, and tissue overlays to specify multiple-color printing.

Some artwork may be impossible to render with the computer—a photograph or original artwork featuring fine charcoal or airbrush techniques, for example. In such a case, leave space for the special artwork on the Ventura page and paste photostats of the artwork by hand on the final version before making multiple copies of the publication.

If you have to paste up many elements, you may want to lay all the pages on *boards*: heavy white paper that keeps the pages flat and prevents pasted-down elements from peeling up.

If you use photographs, you can scan them into the computer and then place them on the Ventura page (see Chapter 6). Alternatively, the print shop can use a camera to create *halftones*. A halftone is composed of dots, like a scanned image; but most scanned images are saved at low resolutions (between 72 and 300 dpi) whereas halftones have many more dots per inch.

You should check with your print shop before you set up pages for halftones. To save time, you can use solid black boxes to reserve space for photographs on Ventura pages (as shown in fig. 11.18). Otherwise, you can use a scanned image of the photograph to indicate the exact size and cropping required.

Ventura Printout

Photograph

Halftone

Negative

Fig. 11.18.

Handling photographs.

Negative Page Image with Photo stripped in

Final Printed Page

Scanned Images versus Photographs

If the final publication is to be printed on a porous paper such as newsprint, a 300-dpi scanned image can look as good as a photographic halftone.

If the final publication is to be printed on glossy paper, 300-dpi scanned images may be too coarse for the final product. You still can scan, place, scale, and crop your Ventura image to show the camera operator how to handle the original photograph (see fig. 11.19).

Fig. 11.19.

Using a scanned image to hold the place of a halftone in the final production.

Ventura Printout

8-by-10 Inch Photo

Tissue Overlay

If the publication is to be printed in more than one color, you can use one of two methods to prepare the pages for the print shop. If the areas printed in each color do not overlap, you can manually overlay tissue paper on the page and mark the colors to be used on the tissue (see fig. 11.20). Alternatively, you can print an individual page for each color enabled in the DEFINE COLORS dialog box by setting Spot Color Overlays: On and Crop Marks: On when you print. If you print on a page larger than the size of your document, the name of the color and the registration marks print at the top of each page. In Chapter 7, you saw how to add custom crop marks when Ventura's automatic crop marks are inappropriate.

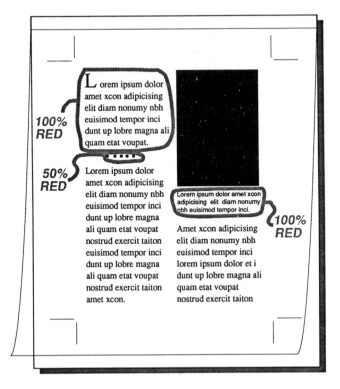

Fig. 11.20.

Tissue overlays indicate the colors to be used.

Chapter Summary

In Chapters 3 through 11, you have learned all the steps needed to produce a Ventura publication. In particular, this chapter offers tips for designing a publication using Ventura's tools. The next part of the book provides examples of publications produced with Ventura. You can find notes about how the principles given in Chapters 3 through 11 were applied in each publication.

III

Examples of Publications Created Using Ventura Publisher

The chapters in Part III present examples of publications created with Ventura. These documents illustrate specific applications of the procedures and principles covered throughout this book and demonstrate the wide range of designs possible with Ventura Publisher. You can develop your own design ideas with the help of the sample pages, sample templates, and style file tags provided with many of the examples. Whether you need to create a business report or a brochure, the examples in Part III help you get started.

Each chapter in Part III covers different types of documents. Each chapter discusses design principles and production tips relevant to that type of document. Then the chapter describes several examples of documents collected from a wide variety of sources. Production steps, style file tags, and other topics are covered for each example. The designer, production staff, and client or sponsor for each example is given.

Includes

Creating Reports, Books, and Manuals

Designing and Producing Newsletters,
Magazines, and Newspapers

Creating Overhead Transparencies, Slides, and Handouts

Creating Brochures, Fliers, and Display Ads

Forms

12

Creating Reports, Books, and Manuals

▼

I n this chapter, you learn some specific design and production ideas that apply to reports, manuals, and books. Whether you are producing a 300-page text-book, a 30-page business proposal, or a 3-page list of illustrated steps for a pro-cedures manual, these publications share many characteristics. These publications are usually longer than the documents in the categories presented in the following chapters. The full publication normally is composed of several chapter (CHP) files, so these types of documents are good candidates for template systems. Even if your document uses the same running heads and running feet throughout all sections, dividing the material into several CHP files still makes good sense in many cases. In this chapter, you find tips on when and why to divide a document into several files.

Another common characteristic shared by these documents is size. Most business reports and many manuals are published in 8.5-by-11-inch format. Books fre-quently have smaller dimensions, and this chapter shows you how to prepare a document for smaller finished page sizes.

The publications in this category have similar formats. These documents usually have a one-column format, although some have a second smaller column for headings, captions, and figures. Traditionally, most business reports are single-sided documents; manuals and books are usually double-sided documents. In this chapter, you learn how and when to use Ventura's single-sided, double-sided, and facing-page options.

This chapter focuses on the specific design and production ideas that apply to the types of documents just described. You can apply the same design principles and production tips to any publication in the general category of long publications made of several sections or chapters. You see how the general design principles and production tips have been applied to the examples (see fig. 12.1).

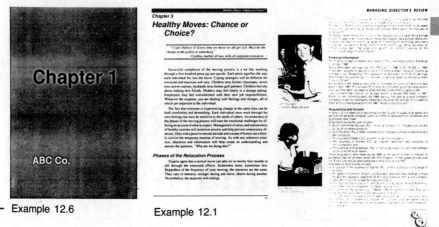

Fig. 12.1.

Examples of the publications in this chapter.

Example 12.6

Example 12.1

Example 12.2

Example 12.3

Example 12.4

Example 12.5

Design Principles

Design principles developed by book designers can be applied to business reports and manuals. Because reports and manuals are long publications, for example, effective use of white space and running heads makes the documents more attractive and easier to use. The design principles presented in these examples range from tips on creating the design, to page layout, to choice of typefaces. By applying these principles, you can produce publications with a professional appearance, uncluttered and unified in design.

Many of these principles apply to all types of publications, not just those in this chapter. Their applications to reports, books, and manuals are described generally in this section.

Don't be afraid of white space.

White space is any area of a page that does not have text or graphics. The principle of allowing white space in the basic design applies to any document but is worth special mention in this chapter because this principle has not been applied to most publications of the types presented. Traditionally, business reports are produced with the same margin settings as those used for letters, memos, minutes, and agendas, instead of being designed specifically to allow white space on the pages. Books usually have minimal white space—leaving only enough room at the edges for the reader's thumbs to hold the book open without covering the text.

Perhaps in the interest of cutting printing costs, contemporary books tend to have smaller margins (less white space) than the classic proportions (shown in fig. 12.3). More white space in the design usually means more pages. Depending on the content of the book and the way it is to be used, however, you can increase the apparent white space without increasing the total number of pages by using a smaller size of type, a different typeface, or tighter leading. Figure 12.2 shows the relative amount of space required if you lay out the same text in different grids and fonts. You can often produce the effect of more white space on a page without actually reducing the amount of text or increasing the number of pages. The effect of increased white space is a more attractive and readable publication.

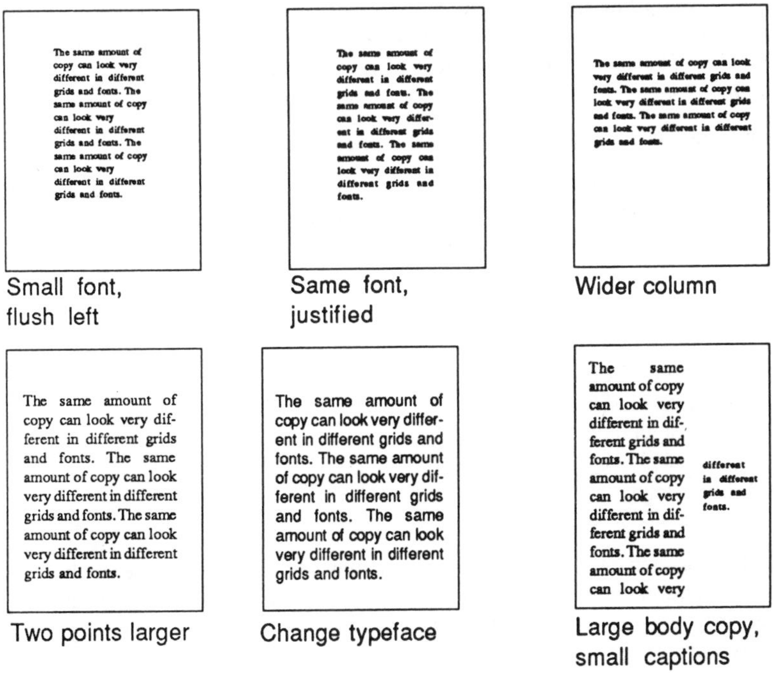

Small font,
flush left

Same font,
justified

Wider column

Two points larger

Change typeface

Large body copy,
small captions

Fig. 12.2.

The same amount of copy in different grids and fonts.

Use a grid system.

The traditions of book design and production are older than any of the other principles discussed in this book. Gutenberg's Bible, for instance, shows traces of the grid system he used to lay out his pages. A few decades later, a book named *De Divina Proportione*, written by Fra Luca Pacioli and illustrated by Leonardo da Vinci, applied the rules of classic proportion to book design. Contemporary designers still study this master work and apply the same principles in new book designs. Later still, Renaissance designers used basic geometry and rules of proportion to design books (as well as buildings, rooms, and paintings). One classic method of defining the margins of a book is shown in figure 12.3. As you can see, the facing pages are crossed with a pattern of straight lines in order to determine the margins.

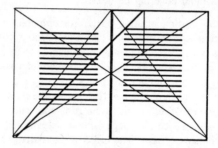

Fig. 12.3.

The classic proportions for book designs.

You can use many methods for deriving grids based on classic proportions, and you also can develop the grids for your publications by imitating similar documents that you admire. The point is that the underlying grid for your publication merits some forethought. Chapter 11 and the examples in this chapter show how Ventura's page feature lets you lay out a grid system for a publication.

Use only one or two different typefaces in a document.

As explained in Chapters 9 and 11, the type-specification process involves listing each element of the document that requires type specifications. For reports, books, and manuals, the list may include the following:

- Body text
- Header
- Footer
- Chapter or section titles
- One or more subhead levels
- Figure captions
- Figure labels
- Table headings
- Table data

Each of these elements may be subdivided into several other elements that require more type specifications. In the running feet, for example, you may want the page number in boldface type and the section name in italic. The majority of book designers, however, follow the guiding principle of simplicity in design. If you study other published works, you see that most books use only one or two different type-faces with variations in size and style used sparingly. The best approach in designing your first report is to imitate the type specifications used in professionally designed documents similar to yours, such as the examples shown in this chapter. Once you become familiar with the underlying design principles, you can easily design your own long documents.

Apart from the design principle of simplicity, one reason for having few type changes in a Ventura publication is that some laser printers are limited to 8 fonts per page or per publication. Some of the examples that follow show how as many as 14 different elements can be distinguished by 8 or fewer fonts.

Table 12.1 shows some of the typefaces commonly used in these types of documents. You can see that the more decorative typefaces such as ITC Machine and Zapf Chancery are not recommended for the publications in this chapter and that the list of type-faces commonly used in books and manuals is much more limited than the list for business reports.

Use all capitals (uppercase text) as a deliberate design strategy rather than as a method for emphasizing text or showing a heading.

Table 12.1
Typefaces Commonly Used in Reports, Books, and Manuals
(Y = used, N = not used)

Typefaces	Reports	Books	Manuals
ITC American Typewriter	Y	N	N
ITC Avant Garde	Y	N	Y
ITC Bookman	Y	N	Y
Courier	N	N	N
ITC Friz Quadrata	Y	N	Y
ITC Galliard	Y	Y	Y
ITC Garamond	Y	Y	Y
Glypha	N	N	Y
Goudy Old Style	Y	Y	Y
Helvetica	Y	Y	Y
ITC Korinna	Y	N	Y
ITC Lubalin Graph	Y	Y	Y
ITC Machine	N	N	N
ITC New Baskerville	Y	Y	N
New Century Schoolbook	Y	Y	Y
Optima	Y	Y	Y
Palatino	Y	Y	Y
ITC Souvenir	Y	Y	Y
Times	Y	Y	Y
Trump Mediaeval	Y	Y	Y
ITC Zapf Chancery	N	N	N

If you are accustomed to letter-quality printers, you probably have used uppercase type to add emphasis or to distinguish headings. Uppercase letters can still be a part of your deliberate design strategy (as in Examples 12.2 and 12.3 for selected headings) or when other size or style variations are not possible. Do not use uppercase letters, however, just because ''that's the way the author typed it.'' Long headings can be hard to read when the text is all uppercase. Consider changing all-capital headings to uppercase and lowercase letters and setting them in boldface or italic.

Use running heads and running feet to help readers find topics.

This principle is applicable to any long document—including magazines—but the rule is a mandate in reference books and manuals. Besides the page number, you should include the section or chapter name in the running heads or running feet. Place the names near the outer edges of the pages for easy reference. This principle is applied in three of the examples in this chapter.

Treat all figures consistently in the fonts, line weights, and fill patterns you use.

In the past, business-report figures came from a single source: one spreadsheet program on a dot-matrix printer, or a team of one illustrator and one typesetter. Consistency becomes a more important issue when you use Ventura to assemble graphics from many different sources, such as a spreadsheet program, a drawing program, and Ventura's built-in graphics tools. Some figures may be used full-size in the final document, but others may need reducing or enlarging in Ventura. To keep line weights consistent in the publication, you may want to use heavier lines in the drawing program if the figure is to be scaled smaller in Ventura, or use lighter-weight lines if the figure is to be scaled larger. If possible, choose fill patterns that are common to all the graphics programs you use.

Be sure that your final figures have consistent type specifications. You can standardize captions by making them a part of the word processing text files instead of the graphics files. For labels in your figures, you may need to establish standards for the fonts to be used in your drawing program. If your report includes many graphs, for example, and your spreadsheet program has fewer available fonts than Ventura, you may want to match the fonts in all your images to the spreadsheet graphics. Another alternative is to import only the graphic elements themselves from outside programs and add all text directly in Ventura. (This technique is demonstrated in an example in Chapter 14.)

Be sure that the space between text and graphics is the same for all figures.

When a graphic fills a frame that abuts text, you can adjust the margin settings for the graphic frame to define the exact space from the graphic to the edge of the frame. This technique is applied in Example 12.3. If the graphic is created through Ventura's Graphic function, the graphic is not confined by the frame's margins or borders. Then you can use the Vert. Padding option in the SIZING & SCALING dialog box under the Frame menu to control spacing outside the frame between text and the frame. This technique is described in Chapter 11 and applied in Example 12.2.

Because strict standards for positioning graphics may slow the production schedule by requiring meticulous adjustments, you may not want rigid standards. You should, however, know and declare your ideal standards for positioning and your limits of tolerance. Your specification may be as simple as "Use vertical padding as the minimum amount of space above and below frames," or "Roughly center the graphic between the adjacent text blocks," but even these simple guidelines are worth stating explicitly. Don't assume that graphics fall naturally into place.

Text on each page should bottom out to margin.

Book designers have traditionally followed the principle that the text on every page should end at exactly the same vertical position. This goal is easy to accomplish for books that are primarily body copy without graphics or subheadings—like the traditional Victorian novel. The principle becomes increasingly difficult to apply if your document incorporates complicating factors such as the following:

- Subheadings within each chapter or section
- Figures
- Footnotes
- Tables that cannot be broken across pages
- Limitations for widows and orphans

You can change the space around figures to make small adjustments in the length of the text on a page. In many documents, however, you find that it is impossible to bottom out all pages to the same point. Alignment can be especially tricky if you follow the common conventions regarding *widows* and *orphans*. These terms are used to describe the situation in which one line of a paragraph is separated from the rest of the paragraph by a page break or a column break (see Chapter 7).

In some documents, you may plan ragged bottom margins as a deliberate design strategy. In general, however, let Ventura's frame margins define the maximum length of the text. As shown in the following examples, Ventura's bottom margin is not the same as the limits of text on the page layout: in these examples, the running heads and feet always fall outside the page margins that are defined for the page frame.

Let the same graphic elements carry the theme throughout the document.

As explained in Chapter 11, Ventura's page can include graphic elements that appear on every page, such as shaded boxes and ruled lines. You also can use graphics to set off headings in the text and to highlight important points. You can see how common graphic elements (black boxes, ruled lines) are applied in every example shown here. In many published books, the cover design has no relation to the inside page layouts; but a common graphic theme is often used on the cover as well as inside pages of business reports, catalogs, directories, annual reports, and other documents. This technique is applied in Examples 12.2, 12.4, and 12.6.

Production Tips

The production tips in this chapter can be applied to any long document composed of several sections or chapters. The tips help you produce your publications more quickly and efficiently than you might do without following these suggestions. The tips range from creating separate templates for different sections to preparing text in a word processor before you start Ventura.

Many of these tips apply to other types of publications, such as the newsletters described in Chapter 13 and the brochures described in Chapter 15. The application to reports, books, and manuals is described generally in this section.

Make each section or chapter a separate chapter (CHP) file.

Even if your document has the same underlying page throughout (that is, the underlying page does not change for each chapter or section), several good reasons exist for breaking a long document into smaller parts and saving each as a separate file:

- Small files are faster to work with—faster to save and faster to print.

- You must make separate CHP files of any sections requiring a different page orientation because you cannot mix portrait and landscape pages in one CHP file. An appendix with tables of figures may require a landscape format, for example, but the rest of the document appears in portrait format.

- You may want to start with a different page grid for different sections of the book (see the following tip).

- When the document is divided into several chapter files, you can set different running heads or running feet for each section, making an easy reference for readers.

- If your document is long or includes many graphics, you may want to break the document into sections to keep file sizes small enough to fit a backup of all files related to that CHP on one floppy disk.

- If different sections of the document are to be completed at different times, but not necessarily in sequence, you can begin each new section when it is ready. In this way, you can have different sections of the publication in different stages of the production process.

- You can divide the Ventura production tasks among several people on the production team.

- If a file is damaged, you lose only part of the work you have done.

This production practice of dividing a document into parts is especially pertinent to the long publications in this chapter and is more rarely applied in the shorter publications described in Chapters 13 through 15.

Build a template for all sections.

If the final document is to be composed of several CHP files, build a master-template file from which all the other files are cloned; then use the Multi-Chapter command in the Options menu to link all related CHP files into a single publication (PUB) file. Chapter 11 offers suggestions for building template systems. You see how those ideas are applied in each template used in the examples in this chapter.

If you expect to update sections of the document periodically without reprinting the entire book, include section numbers in the page-numbering system and let each section start with page 1.

This useful production trick may conflict with design ideas and the offset printer's preferences, but using section numbers as part of the page-numbering system (1-1, 1-2, 1-3,...2-1, 2-2, and so on) is the best way to handle frequently changed "living" documents, such as procedures manuals. Ventura's automatic page-numbering feature cannot handle letter suffixes added to inserted pages (23a, 23b, 23c, for instance); but in a single section you can number all pages sequentially with a compound page number that includes a fixed section number and a changing suffix (23.1, 23.2, 23.3). If chapters are linked in a single PUB document, you can use the Page Counter command to force each chapter to start with page 1. Example 12.1 uses compound page numbers.

This tip should be applied only to manuals updated frequently. Generally speaking, the best practice is to number all pages consecutively in a document. You can specify the starting-page number for each section in the Page menu's PAGE COUNTER dialog box, or you can use Ventura's Multi-Chapter command from the Options menu to string together several CHP files and number all pages sequentially.

Do all text editing in advance, using a word processing program.

This method of preparation is described in Chapters 4 and 5 and has been set as a goal throughout this book. Ideally, to simplify Ventura production, perform all copy editing in a word processing program that offers global searches, spelling checks, scrolling shortcuts, and other features not included in Ventura. Use Ventura primarily for formatting the text.

Examples

The examples in this chapter have been selected to demonstrate a variety of formats and to illustrate various applications of the design principles and production tips described in the previous sections. As noted in those sections, not all the principles and tips that apply to books can be demonstrated in these few examples, but the design principles not specifically applied here are shown in some of the examples in the chapters that follow. The six examples presented in this chapter are as follows:

12.1. A One-Column Book with Ruled Lines

12.2. A One-Column Annual Report with Graphics in the Margins

12.3. A One-Column Periodical with Side-By-Side Subheads and Body Text

12.4. A One-Column Report with Graphics Running Heads

12.5. A Two-Column Report with Custom Ruling Lines

12.6. Section Cover Pages for a Manual

Example 12.1: A One-Column Book with Ruled Lines

Design: Jane Hudson
Production: Docuset
Client: Smart Moves

The book in this example is designed to be especially economical in using white space and maximizing the character count per page (therefore minimizing the page count for the entire document). This design can be applied to any long document.

This book is set up to be printed in 6-by-9-inch page size, set in one column with body text indented from the left margin. Ruling lines are used to set off the opening text elements in each chapter. Figure 12.4 shows the final printout of two pages.

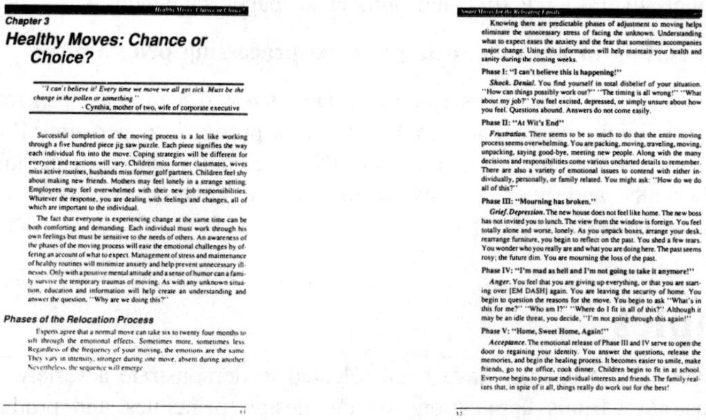

Fig. 12.4.

Final pages of one-column book with ruled lines.

Design Principles for a One-Column Book with Ruled Lines

This publication follows a simple one-column grid structure and adheres to the general design principles described at the beginning of this chapter. Two principles are especially well illustrated here.

Use only one or two different typefaces in a document. This publication uses only two typefaces: Times and Helvetica. Variety is attained by applying these typefaces in various sizes and styles, such as 14-point bold italic and 10-point bold italic.

Use running heads and running feet to help readers find topics. This publication positions both these design elements for easy reference and also sets up compound page numbers. Each chapter starts with page 1, and the chapter number is shown with the page number.

Template for a One-Column Book with Ruled Lines

Figure 12.5 shows the page for the template. The frame of the running feet is set with a ruling line above; the frame that appears as the header is actually a repeating frame set with white type on a black frame background pattern. Crop marks were generated with the Sizing & Scaling command to set the underlying frame to 6 by 9 inches and choosing Crop Marks: On in the PRINT INFORMATION dialog box.

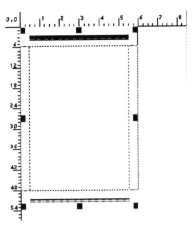

Fig. 12.5.

The template for one-column book with ruled lines.

Efficiency Tip

Capabilities of PostScript Printers

The examples in this book were completed on systems using PostScript printers. These printers have capabilities that most other printers (the HP LaserJet, for example) do not have. These features include the following:

- Access to all sizes of each font for which a width table exists

- Capability to print reverse type and white boxes and lines

- Capability to handle full-page graphics at high resolution

If you do not use a PostScript printer, some of these examples may not work in the ways described. However, you may be able to find alternative methods for achieving similar results.

Style File Tags for a One-Column Book with Ruled Lines

Set up the following tags in the style file:

Tag Name	Feature
Chapter Number	14-point bold italic Helvetica
Chapter Title	24-point bold italic Helvetica, indent 3 picas, first line outdent 3 picas

Quotation	10-point italic Times, indent 3 picas, first line indent 6 picas, ruling lines above: line 1, 1-point wide, space below 0.5 point; line 2, 0.5-point wide
Quotation Credit	10-point Times, right alignment, ruling lines below: line 1, 0.5-point wide, space below 0.5-point; line 2, 1-point wide, space below 2 picas
Body Text	10-point Times, indent 3 picas, first line indent 6 picas, space below 0.5 pica
Heading 1	14-point bold italic Helvetica
Header Text	10-point bold italic Times, right alignment, white text, black ruling line above 14-point wide, space below rule 3 is − 12 points (a minus value, resulting in white text on top of black line), white ruling line below 1-point wide
ZFooter	10-point Times, ruling line above

Production Steps for a One-Column Book with Ruled Lines

To create the design for the one-column book with ruled lines, follow these steps:

1. Prepare text in a word processing file.

2. To create the first chapter, start a new Ventura CHP publication. Set the margins and column guides on the page, the footer as a frame with a ruling line above, and the header as a repeating frame with the chapter title in white type on a black ruling line background, as shown in figure 12.5.

3. Use the Page Counter command to set page numbers to start with 1 in this CHP chapter and in all later chapters created through the Multi-Chapter command (step 7). Set up the style file as described in the preceding section.

4. Working in Reduced view, place or load the text for this chapter on the page.

5. Starting at the beginning of the document, label the text with the tags defined in the style file. Notice that the ruled lines above the quotation at the opening of each chapter are part of the tag for quotations, and that the ruled lines below the quotation are part of the tag for quotation credits.

6. To start a new chapter, save this chapter under a new name, remove the old source files, and load source files for the new document. Use the Headers & Footers command to edit the footer for each CHP file. Edit

the repeating frame text of the header to reflect the new chapter information.

7. Use the Multi-Chapter command to link all chapter files together as a single PUB file.

Example 12.2: A One-Column Annual Report with Graphics in the Margins

Design: Graphicor
Production: Hilton Trevis with Punch Line Holdings
 and Graphicor
Client: Punchline

The design in this example is elegantly simple and can be applied to many publications. An annual report may seem to be a specialized publication because of its extensive financial tables, but the basic design can be used for any publication that links tabular material, text, and graphics. This particular annual report is set up to be 20 pages long, in one column of 9-point Helvetica type. Figure 12.6 shows the final printouts of three pages.

Fig. 12.6.

Pages of one-column annual report with graphics.

Design Principles for a One-Column Annual Report with Graphics in the Margins

This publication follows the design principles discussed in this book. The following principles are especially relevant to this publication:

Don't be afraid of white space. The page grid is set up to allow wide margins for white space.

Use only one or two different typefaces in a document. All the tags use Helvetica type of different sizes and styles (such as boldface and italic).

Use all uppercase text as a deliberate design strategy. The page headers in this document are set up as all uppercase text. The headers are short enough to maintain readability in uppercase, so the uppercase style promotes the reference function of headers and also contributes to a visually attractive page.

Be sure that the space between text and graphics is the same for all figures. The space between graphics and text is controlled by using a rectangle as a spacing guide.

Let the same graphic elements carry the theme throughout the document. In this publication, ruled lines are used as a common graphic theme throughout.

Template for a One-Column Annual Report with Graphics in the Margins

Figures 12.7 and 12.8, respectively, show the MARGINS & COLUMNS dialog box and the template page. The box of ruled lines at the outside margin of each page is set up as a repeating frame that contains a series of 2-point carriage returns. The carriage returns are set up with a tag that creates a ruling line below, which is the width of the frame.

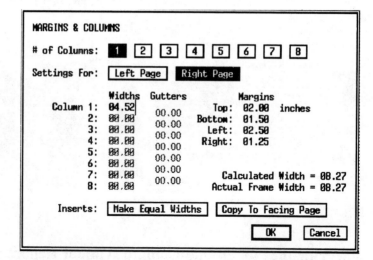

Fig. 12.7.

The MARGINS & COLUMNS dialog box for one-column annual report with graphics.

Style File Tags for a One-Column Annual Report with Graphics in the Margins

Set up the following tags in the style file:

Tag Name	Feature
Section Title	14-point bold italic Helvetica, right aligned
Body Text	9-point Helvetica
Subhead	12-point bold Helvetica

Page Number   36-point bold italic Helvetica, right aligned

Ruled Frame   2-point Helvetica, ruled line below, frame width

Ten additional tags were created for 2-, 3-, 4-, 5-, and 6-column tabular material: a Column Headings tag and Table Data tag are needed for each type of table. The headings on center columns are boldface, but the data on flush-left columns (text entries) and on flush-right columns (numbers) is normal (not bold).

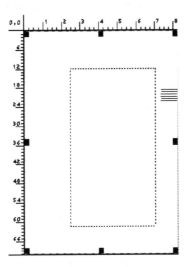

Fig. 12.8.

The template for one-column annual report with graphics.

Production Steps for a One-Column Annual Report with Graphics in the Margins

To create the one-column annual report with graphics in the margins, follow these steps:

1. Prepare text in a word processing file.

2. Start a new Ventura publication and set the margins and column guides on the page as shown in figures 12.7 and 12.8.

3. Working in Reduced view, place all text on the page.

4. On page 1 of the document, set up a Clipboard Page, as described in Chapter 11, to which you attach the following graphic elements:

   • Page numbers as box text over the frame of ruled lines

   • Black boxes to mark where photographs are to be dropped in

   • Box text for captions to each photograph

5. Copy the frame created in step 4 to subsequent pages and position elements on each page, using a spacing guide. The tips in this section give extra guidance for completing this step.

Use Vertical Padding for Consistent Spacing between Text and Graphics

To control spacing between text and the black rectangles that serve as photo windows, use the Vert. Padding option in the SIZING & SCALING dialog box under the Frame menu. This option allows you to insert white space above and below the frame.

Copying One Frame for Repeated Use

You can save time by drawing one frame containing two box text elements (a page number and a caption) and a black rectangle the size of the photographs. If most photographs are the same size, you can use the black rectangle to ensure consistency. You can also resize the black rectangle or box text as needed; remember that the vertical padding and caption tag are already built in.

You can use this technique whenever all the elements associated with the graphics frame are the same size wherever they appear. In this example, all the page numbers have the same tag in box text, and all the photographs in this report are the same size; therefore, all the captions are the same width of box text.

After you draw the frame with the box text elements and rectangle, follow these steps:

1. Copy that frame and paste it on each page, using the Copy Frame and Paste Frame commands. Paste the frame onto all pages first. Then go back to page 1 and lay out each page as described in step 2.

2. Position the page number and change the text of the page number as appropriate. Also, select and position the black box and caption. Doing so is one step if the black box and caption were correctly positioned in relation to each other when you set up the first frame (before copying it to all pages). You can delete the box and caption if no photos appear on a page, or copy and paste the box and caption if additional photos appear on a page.

The Clipboard Page prints as a page of the chapter. Unless you want the page, therefore, always delete the Clipboard Page when you finish a page layout.

Example 12.3: A One-Column Periodical with Side-by-Side Subheads and Body Text

Design: Jan White
Production: Gary Shepherd
Client: Sandia National Laboratories

The publication in this example is actually the in-house newsletter for a company that uses a wide range of computers and computer applications. The newsletter keeps employees informed of new developments and tips about the various computer systems and applications used. This document is included in this chapter on books and reports—rather than Chapter 13, on newsletters and magazines—because the document is 60 pages long and uses a design that can be applied to many long publications, such as books and reports.

Design Principles for a One-Column Periodical with Side-by-Side Subheads and Body Text

This format uses a one-column grid and follows the design principles discussed throughout this book. The following principles are especially relevant to this publication:

Don't be afraid of white space. The format positions all heads and subheads in a wide left margin and indents all body text to create white space on the pages.

Use only one or two different typefaces in a document. All the tags use Dutch type of different sizes and styles (such as boldface).

Use all uppercase text as a deliberate design strategy. The major headers in this document are set as all uppercase text. The all uppercase style distinguishes the major headings from subheads and also contributes to a visually attractive page.

Be sure that the space between text and graphics is the same for all figures. The space between graphics and text is controlled with graphics frame margins.

Figure 12.9 shows the final printout of one page.

Production Tricks for a One-Column Periodical with Side-by-Side Subheads and Body Text

The primary trick in making this publication easy to produce is in the handling of the headings and body text. If you view the format as a two-column format, you spend hours adjusting headings to match corresponding body text whenever you edit the text. Alternatively, you may set the Body Text tag to flush-left first line, with a right tab for subheads and a left tab for the first line of normal text; indent all subsequent lines; and type subheads as part of the body text. You then have to scroll through the document in the Text function, however, and select and change the font of each subhead one by one. The best solution—and the one used here—is to set the Subhead tag with no line break after, to force subheads to print alongside the body text. The Body Text tag is set with a left indent. Figure 12.10 shows the possible solutions.

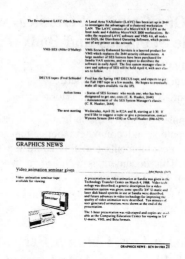

Fig. 12.9.

One page of one-column periodical with side-by-side subheads and body text.

Text as formatted with tags:

Article Title

                              Subhead
Text related to this heading.

Page layout:

Text as formatted with tags:

Article Title

Subhead   Text related to this
               heading.

Page layout:

Text as formatted with tags:

Article Title

Subhead   Text related to this
              heading.

Page layout:

Fig. 12.10.

Three ways of handling side-by-side subheads and body text.

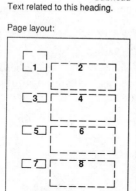

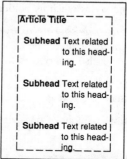

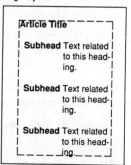

Worst Solution: Format titles flush left, subheads flush right, and body text flush left, then create separate frames for each title or subheading heading and the text related to each heading.

Acceptable Solution: Format body text flush left with a hanging indent, right tab set for subheadings, then select each subheading individually and Set Font to bold in Text Function.

Best Solution: Format subheads and body text with separate tags, no line break after subhead, body text indented from left.

Template for a One-Column Periodical with Side-by-Side Subheads and Body Text

Figures 12.11 and 12.12 show the MARGINS & COLUMNS dialog box and the template page.

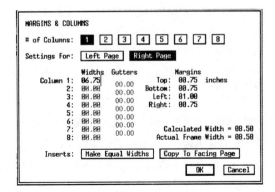

Fig. 12.11.

The MARGINS & COLUMNS dialog box for one-column periodical with side-by-side subheads and body text.

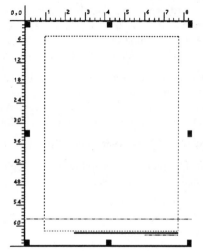

Fig. 12.12.

The template for one-column periodical with side-by-side subheads and body text.

Style File Tags for a One-Column Periodical with Side-by-Side Subheads and Body Text

Set up the following tags in the style file:

Tag Name	Feature
Section Title	18-point Dutch, ruling line above 7.98 points wide, ruling line below 0.24 points wide, space above line 1.98 points
Article Title	14-point Dutch, ruling line below, no line break after (side-by-side with author text)
Author	8-point Dutch, right alignment
Subhead	10-point bold Dutch, column wide, right aligned, indent 3.92 inches from right (to allow subheadings to line-wrap), no line break after (side-by-side with Body Text, aligning with first line of multiple-line headings)

Body Text	10-point Dutch, indented 3 inches from left
Bullet Text	10-point Dutch, indented 3.14 inches from left, first line outdent 0.14 inch
ZFooter	10-point Dutch, ruling line above 1.98 points wide, space below rule 1.98 points

Production Steps for a One-Column Periodical with Side-by-Side Subheads and Body Text

To create a one-column periodical with side-by-side subheads and body text, follow these steps:

1. Prepare text in a word processing file. In this case, the text is collected from many different writers using a wide variety of word processors or text editors. Collect and format text in ASCII by typing style file tags into the ASCII text before loading the text into Ventura.

2. Start a new Ventura publication and set the margins and column guides on the page as shown in figures 12.11 and 12.12. Use the Headers & Footers command to set up the footer text with embedded codes for changing fonts. In this case, the footer is typed as follows:

   GRAPHIC NEWS: SCN 04 1988 <FOO2BP012>[P#]<D>

   The codes used in this footer are as follows (see Chapter 4 for more on embedded codes and special symbols):

   FOO2 is the code for Helvetica
   B is the code for boldface
   P012 is the code for the point size
   [P#] indicates the page number
   <D> indicates to resume the normal font for this tag

   The normal font, the ruling line, and the right alignment of the footer are handled by the ZFOOTER tag.

3. Working in Reduced view, place all text on the page.

4. Check the format of the text, starting from the beginning of the document, to verify that the style file tags were set correctly in the ASCII text files. Add a frame to the inside margin for graphics as needed.

Efficiency Tip

Use Graphic Frame Margins To Control Space between Graphics and Text

When a graphic fills a frame that abuts the text, you can adjust the margin settings for the graphic frames to define the exact space from the graphic to the edge of the frame. In figure 12.13, graphic frames that appear in the wide left margin are positioned immediately below the headings and abut the left margin of body text. The top and right margins are set to 0.25 inch. In the SIZING & SCALING dialog box, set Flow Text Around: Off.

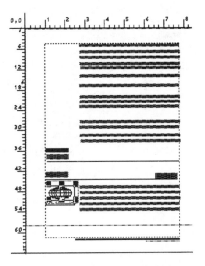

Fig. 12.13.

Top and right margins of the graphic frame are set to 0.25 inch.

Example 12.4: A One-Column Report with Graphics Running Heads

Design: Grace Moore
Production: Emily Rosenberg
Client: Venture Development Services

The report used in this example is designed to accommodate relatively simple text formatting in a one-column grid that maximizes white space by using wide margins. The text is also more readable because of the short line length that results from the wide margin settings. This same design can be applied to any business report; the generous running heads (16-point Times with a graphics background) make this design especially applicable to relatively short reports composed of many short sections.

This design, however, probably is not good for a reference manual or training guide without considerable expansion of the style file tag settings to accommodate a wider variety of subheads and other visual aids. Books and long reports probably do not use running heads as large as the ones in this report, but a similar design could be used on chapter or section opening pages, with a narrower top margin on subsequent pages.

This limited-distribution report is reproduced in 8.5-by-11-inch format with portrait orientation. The grid and graphic elements on the inside pages are designed to carry out a theme that originates with the report cover's design (see fig. 12.14). The final document—one in a series of documents to be published over time—is stored as one CHP file. The text is made up of one source file for each section, a mailing list of names and addresses, and a text file of captions for full-page figures. The figures, not shown here, are reprints of articles from other sources and are pasted in manually.

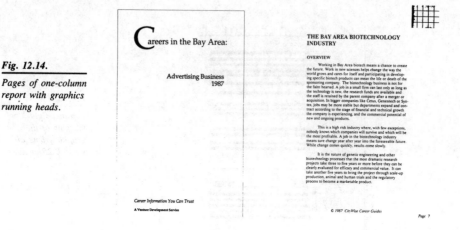

Fig. 12.14.

Pages of one-column report with graphics running heads.

Efficiency Tip ———————————————————————

Caution: Always Obtain Written Permission To Reprint

When you include information or excerpts from other published works, as in Example 12.4, be sure to obtain written permission from the publisher of the work you want to use.

Design Principles for a One-Column Report with Graphics Running Heads

All the design principles described at the beginning of this chapter are applied in this report. The two principles that are especially well illustrated by this example are repeated and described here.

Don't be afraid of white space. In this report, the left and right margins are 2.25 inches and the top margin is 2.5 inches. The running heads and running feet extend beyond these margins to give each page the feel of a full-page grid with a great deal of white space. The relatively short length of each line of text makes the copy easy to read.

Let the same graphic elements carry the theme throughout the document. A gray rectangle crossed with white (reverse) lines is used on the cover, and a smaller gray box with white lines is repeated in the top right corner of every page, as a background for the running heads.

Template for a One-Column Report with Graphics Running Heads

In final form, this document is double-sided. Because the margins, heads, and feet are identical on every page of the report, it requires only one set of running heads and feet; the publication is set up in Ventura as a one-sided document.

The wide margins define the limits of the text placed from word processing files. The template page includes the graphic that appears in the upper right corner of every page (see fig. 12.15).

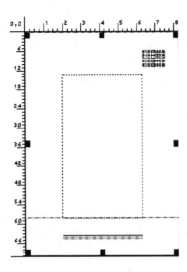

Fig. 12.15.

The template for a one-column report with graphics running heads.

Style File Tags for a One-Column Report with Graphics Running Heads

The normal default for body type specifications—flush left 12-point Times—holds for this publication. The first line of each paragraph is indented by pressing the tab key in the original word processing file. Instead of stripping out these tabs and using the Alignment command to indent the first line, the Body Text tag specifies that the first tab be set at 0.25 inch. Because the author had originally inserted a blank line between paragraphs, the designer decided to let this convention stand instead of using the Spacing command to set the space between paragraphs. The following list of tags shows that only four different type specifications are used in the publication.

Set up the following tags in the style file:

Tag Name	Feature
Header Text	16-point bold italic Times, right aligned
Heading	18-point bold Times

Byline   12-point italic Times

Body Text   12-point Times, first line indented with a tab stop set at
                0.25 inch

Production Steps for a One-Column Report with Graphics Running Heads

Use the following steps to produce this publication once the page is set up as shown in figure 12.15.

1. Type and format text files in the word processing program. Set all text flush left and indent each paragraph by pressing the tab key. Press Enter twice between paragraphs. Create a separate text file for each section. Store the files in the subdirectory for this report.

2. Open the Ventura template document for this series of reports, and modify the page and cover page to reflect the new report name. Save the modified template under the new report name. (For more information, see Chapter 7.)

3. Working in Reduced view, place text for the first section on the page frame. Add a new page to start each new section until all text is placed (consult Chapter 4).

4. Return to the beginning of the document, format headings and bylines with the style file tags, and add frames or whole pages to open spaces for figures. In the frame, type the name of the figure to be pasted up (the figure name is covered by the manual pasteup on the final boards). Add the chapter titles as box text over the graphic in the upper right corner of each page. (See Chapters 6 and 7 for full details.)

5. Return to the beginning of the documents and, working in Normal view, review each page on-screen. Adjust the placement of the figure frames added in step 4 wherever necessary.

Preparation of a One-Column Report with Graphics Running Heads for Reproduction

All graphics are pasted by hand into page areas reserved for the graphics. All figures are enlarged or reduced photographically to fit the space before pasting. These limited-run reports are reproduced on xerographic equipment at a light setting so that the cut edges of the pasted figures do not show.

Example 12.5: A Two-Column Report with Custom Ruling Lines

Design: Zeta Type
Production: Christopher M. Glazek
Client: Walden Capital Partners

The report in this example is composed of approximately 20 investment listings, each sharing the same repeated format. This same design can be applied to many reference or listing formats. This report is set up using tags that arrange the frame-wide or column-wide text in a two-column, custom format. Figure 12.16 shows the final printout of one page.

Fig. 12.16.

Page of two-column report with custom ruling lines.

Style File Tags for a Two-Column Report with Custom Ruling Lines

Set up the following tags in the style file:

Tag Name	Feature
Company Name	16-point Helvetica condensed, frame width, ruling line above with custom settings:
	Height: 10.02 points
	Custom width: 1.98 points
	Space above Rule 1: 69.0 points
	Space below Rule 3: Minus option
Category	12-point Times, frame width, flush right
Tabular Heads	9-point bold Helvetica condensed, frame width, center tabs every 1.5 inches
Tabular Data	9-point Times, frame width, same tabs as Tabular Heads

Col. 1 Head	9-point Helvetica, column width, indented 2 picas
Col. 1 Data	10-point Helvetica, column width, indented 3 picas
Description Head	9-point Helvetica, column width, flush left, starts new column
Update Head	9-point Helvetica, column width, flush left
Body Text	10-point Times, column width, indented 2 picas, tab set at 4 picas for paragraph indent when needed for second paragraph

Production Steps for a Two-Column Report with Custom Ruling Lines

To create this design, follow these steps:

1. Prepare text in a word processing file, tagging the paragraphs with the following tags (for more information, see Chapters 4 and 5):

   Company Name
   Category
   Tabular Heads
   Tabular Data
   Col. 1 Head
   Col. 1 Data
   Descriptive Head
   Update Head
   Body Text

2. Start a new Ventura publication, and set the margins and column guides on the page. Load the style file as described in the preceding section.

3. Working in Reduced view, place all text on the page.

4. Starting at the beginning of the document in the Text function, scroll through and use the Set Font button to set each company's city and state in 14-point italic Helvetica Condensed.

Example 12.6: Section Cover Pages for a Manual

Design: Based on corporate logo
Production: TechArt
Client: Intelligence Knowledge
Engineering

The section, or chapter, cover pages in this example are created as a single-sided publication with a repeated graphic. Each page of the publication contains only the new section or chapter name as box text. The cover pages are printed without page numbers and are inserted between the sections of the final document. This example is provided to show a simple technique for producing a series of cover pages using the same basic design. You can apply this technique to any publication using graphics cover pages for sections.

Each cover page shows the product logo on a gray background. An example of a cover page from this publication is shown in figure 12.17. Because these pages contain only a few words of text, most of the design principles mentioned at the beginning of this chapter are not applicable.

Fig. 12.17.

A section cover page for a manual.

Production Tricks for Section Cover Pages for a Manual

These cover pages are prepared for printing on 8.5-by-11-inch paper, but they are to be part of a document trimmed to 6 by 9 inches. The pages, therefore, can accommodate the bleed from the larger paper and show crop marks as well. Because the design bleeds beyond the edges of the paper, the underlying frame is larger than the final 6-by-9-inch trim size, and the crop marks are added as graphic elements to the underlying frame. If the final pages were to be 8.5 inches by 11 inches, the page size selected in this dialog box should be even larger to accommodate the bleed. (As explained in Chapter 11, *bleed* describes pages on which the inked area runs beyond the trimmed edges of the final document.)

This document is single sided because all the pages are right pages, even though the larger document into which they are inserted is double-sided. The MARGINS & COLUMNS dialog box settings used for the template are shown in figure 12.18.

The template page includes the logo and the gray background, originally scanned from existing artwork (see fig. 12.19). Crop marks created as graphic elements on the page show the printer where to trim the printed covers.

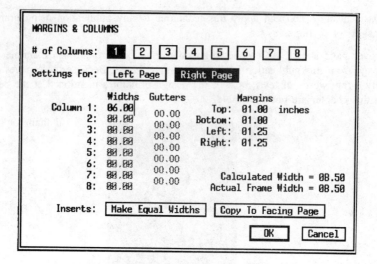

Fig. 12.18.

The MARGINS & COLUMNS dialog box for section cover page for a manual.

Fig. 12.19.

The template for section cover page for a manual.

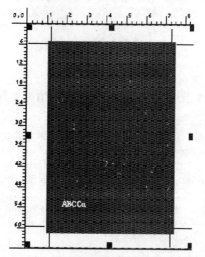

Production Steps for Section Cover Pages for a Manual

The design steps for the cover page are simple:

1. Load the scanned background design on the page of the template, and type the text for the first section title as box text.

2. Go through each cover page using the Copy Graphic and Paste Graphic commands to copy the title box text from the first cover to each subsequent page. Change the text to reflect the new section names.

Preparation of Section Cover Pages for a Manual for Reproduction

All the pages call for a bleed at the edges (see fig. 12.20). Usually, this design means that the color must be printed beyond the trim area. The pages with bleeds, therefore, should be delivered to the offset printer as a set separate from the rest of the document. Include a note stating that the pages call for bleed. Pages like these are often handled separately because larger paper and more cuts are required than for other pages. Page numbers outside the bleed area indicate where each page is to be inserted into the finished document.

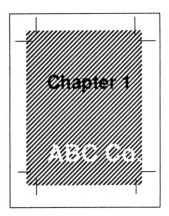

Fig. 12.20.

A page with crop marks and bleed.

Chapter Summary

This chapter presents general descriptions and specific applications of the design principles and production tips that apply to long documents, such as books, manuals, and reports. After studying the examples in this chapter, you should be better equipped to design your own long documents, set up the templates, and implement efficient production procedures. If you are still new to Ventura and long document production, remember to take a small portion of text through the entire production cycle before finalizing the full cycle of production steps for your project plan.

Finally, beware of setting tight production deadlines, or trying to predict the completion date, for your first few production projects with Ventura—assuming that you have this luxury, of course!

13

Designing and Producing Newsletters, Magazines, and Newspapers

N ewsletters, magazines, and newspapers have become so much a part of our daily lives that they are often taken for granted. The design and layout are expected to be inviting, and the information to be presented clearly. Both readers and publishers of these documents share an interest in special touches, which complicate the production process. To achieve an attractive publication, the publisher must often kern headlines, wrap text around graphics, and vary page layouts. At the same time, producers of magazines, newsletters, and newspapers face more deadline pressure than any other type of publisher. The demand for efficiency in production techniques, therefore, is especially important.

Following are four characteristics that distinguish newsletters, magazines, and newspapers from other types of publications:

- The publications use at least two columns, usually more, in the underlying grid. The number of columns can change from page to page.

- The flow of text for a single article or story can jump from one page to another several pages away.

- The documents are usually produced as a series. A document of the same basic format and length is produced at regular intervals.

475

- The documents often call for special layouts that may involve kerning headlines, wrapping text around graphics, or pasting display ads from one Ventura document into another.

These and other characteristics involve their own special design and production problems and practices. This chapter explains and illustrates these special concerns. When you understand the underlying principles, you can apply the suggestions in this chapter to other types of documents, too.

Figure 13.1 shows examples of publications described in this chapter.

Fig. 13.1

Examples of publications.

Ventura can be a tremendous help and time-saver when you create newsletters and similar publications. After you have a good design for a newsletter, for example, you can use the master chapter file (CHP) for every issue. You do not need to re-create formats. As discussed in Parts I and II of this book, Ventura also eases typesetting chores, such as kerning, wrapping text, and using different typefaces.

Design Principles

The design principles that apply to newsletters derive from the long traditions of newspaper and magazine publishing. Because these publications are relatively short, the design is particularly important. You need to convey information in a limited space and in an uncluttered, attractive format. The principles stressed in this chapter address these needs. The principles range from the number of typefaces and the use of ruled lines to considerations of margins and the provision of ample white space.

This section provides a general description of the application of design principles to newsletters, magazines, and newspapers. In the "Examples" section, the principles are illustrated. Keep in mind, however, that some of these principles apply to *all* types of publications, not just those mentioned in this chapter.

Use only one or two different typefaces in a document.

Magazines and newsletters often use many more typefaces than do the business reports, books, and manuals shown in the preceding chapter, especially when the magazine or newsletter includes display ads. The basic principle of simplicity, however, remains the best guide. Table 13.1 shows some of the typefaces commonly used in magazines and newsletters. In these publications, display ads often contain a wide variety of typefaces, but headlines and body copy use only one or two.

Table 13.1
Typefaces Used in Magazines and Newsletters
(Y = used; N = not used)

Typefaces	*Newsletters*	*Magazines*
ITC American Typewriter	Y	N
ITC Avant Garde	Y	N
ITC Benguiat	Y	Y
ITC Bookman	Y	Y
Courier	N	N
ITC Friz Quadrata	Y	Y
ITC Galliard	Y	Y
ITC Garamond	Y	Y
Glypha	Y	Y
Helvetica	Y	Y
ITC Korinna	Y	N
ITC Lubalin Graph	Y	Y
ITC New Baskerville	Y	Y
New Century Schoolbook	Y	Y
Optima	Y	Y
Palatino	Y	Y
ITC Souvenir	Y	Y
Times	Y	Y
Trump Mediaeval	Y	Y

Use variations in the grid to help distinguish different sections of the magazine.

You have probably seen how some newsletters and magazines distinguish sections by giving them different grid structures. (See Chapter 11 for a full discussion of grid systems.) Figure 13.2 shows an example. The main feature begins on a facing-page spread. A graphic, the story title, and one column of text fill the left page. The feature continues on the right page with three columns of text. Another variation might be to have letters to the editor occupying three columns and articles occupying two columns. Example 13.6, described later in this chapter, uses this technique to differentiate the first page from inside pages.

Fig. 13.2.

Varying the grid structure to distinguish sections.

Use ruled lines to help set off the grid of the pages.

In addition to using margin and column guides as grid lines to help lay out your pages, you can use Ventura's ruled lines to enhance the appearance of the pages. Designers, for example, often drop vertical rules between columns of text. The use of horizontal rules to separate articles is demonstrated in Examples 13.1, 13.2, 13.3, 13.5, and 13.6.

All columns on all pages should bottom out to the same point.

This rule is applied more strictly in magazines than in most newsletters or other documents. As mentioned in the preceding chapter, the problems associated with column alignment are compounded when you add subheadings in an article, have strict rules about the spacing around graphics and between paragraphs, and do not allow widows and orphans. You may need to adjust the space around headings and figures to force columns to meet the bottom margin.

On the other hand, a ragged bottom margin, as shown in figure 13.3, allows more flexibility in copy fitting. The ragged margin is better than an even margin that stops above the bottom of the grid. Example 13.1 shows bottom alignment and provides production tips for copy fitting.

Don't be afraid of white space.

Applications of this principle vary greatly. Some magazines—*The New Yorker*, for instance—fill every column completely with small type. This kind of design can be attractive and functional; it produces the greatest number of words in the fewest number of pages. Good designers can make this design work. But if you are just beginning to learn the ins and outs of page layout, you should follow the rule of allowing some white space on pages. In the examples in this chapter, you see that white space occurs primarily around article titles and subheads. This practice is common in newsletters and newspapers.

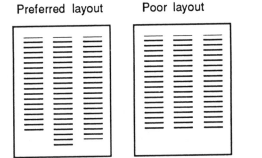

Preferred layout   Poor layout

Fig. 13.3.

Deliberately making a bottom margin ragged.

Provide estimates of the number of characters per column for contributors and editors.

Providing character-count estimates is something that most professional editors do as a matter of course when they make an assignment. These estimates help eliminate many problems that arise when you begin to lay out the pages. You need to plan or estimate the amount of space you want to allocate for the text of each article and let the type specifications for the article determine the number of words that fit in the space. Chapter 9 describes methods of counting characters and casting copy before placing the text in Ventura.

Production Tips

In this chapter, the emphasis is on documents laid out in several columns and using figures of varying widths. The production tips presented in this section are applicable to these kinds of publications and cover all stages of production from building the publication to getting it ready to take to a printer. You learn when to use a drawing program to create banners, for example, and when and where to place a table of contents. You can find tips for handling documents with many illustrations and for scaling figures and pictures to column widths. The tips also tell you how to adjust spacing in multicolumn publications and how to get your publication ready for the printer.

Although this section describes how the tips are applied generally to newsletters, magazines, and newspapers, many tips in this chapter also apply to other types of publications. In the "Examples" section later in the chapter, the pertinent tips are specifically applied to some examples.

If you need type larger than that shown in the FONT dialog box and have a PostScript printer that supports large sizes, use a draw program to create a banner.

The largest type you can specify directly in Ventura is 254 points (for PostScript fonts) or the largest font in the currently loaded width table (for non-PostScript printers). If your banner calls for larger type and you use a PostScript printer, you can change font specifications in a print file and print type as large as the page. (The technique to print type larger than 254 with PostScript printers is explained in Chapter

8). You also can create the banner by using a draw program. Place the banner as a graphic in Ventura and scale the image to a larger size. You can stretch text from a draw file to any size and get good results. If your printer cannot handle large type sizes, however, try the next technique.

If your printer cannot handle large type sizes, use a scanned image or a paint figure for the banner.

If you use a width table that does not have large display type, you can create a banner by scanning large type set on another system or by using large type in a paint file. The scanned image provides the best quality printout if you save the image as a high-resolution image, as was done in figure 13.4. In either case, you probably need to clean up the image pixel-by-pixel to get smooth edges. The results are always of lower quality than images produced with a true laser font. (For examples of scanned and paint-type graphics, see Chapter 6; for examples of bit-mapped characters, see Chapter 9.)

Fig. 13.4.

Using a scanned image for a newsletter banner.

If your publication includes a contents list that varies in length, you should place or type the list before filling the rest of the page.

Rather than situate long articles on the pages first, type or place those elements that you cannot continue on subsequent pages. The table of contents is just one example of this kind of element. You do not need to know the exact page numbers when you first type the table of contents, but you do need to know the number of articles appearing in the issue and the lengths of the titles.

The contents list in figure 13.5, for example, must be placed before the rest of the page is laid out. In this chapter, you learn how three other publications—Examples 13.3, 13.5, and 13.6—deal with a list of contents that must fit on one page or in one column.

Use a spacing guide to position text and graphics and to adjust the space between articles.

Precise spacing is especially important in newsletters and magazines. See Chapter 11 for a description of using frame margins as spacing guides for graphics loaded into frames and using the vertical padding option to control spacing between text and half-tones or graphics. To control spacing around graphics drawn with Ventura's tools,

Length of Contents must be determined before start of lead article

Fig. 13.5.

The contents list on the first page of a newsletter.

place them in a frame set with vertical padding or use rectangles as spacing guides. In this chapter, you see frame margins used as spacing guides in Examples 13.2 and 13.4.

Scale pictures and figures to precise column widths.

A picture can span more than one column, but all pictures should conform to the grid lines. A picture, for example, can be one column, two columns, or three columns wide in a three-column grid design but should not be one and a half columns wide unless your grid is designed to accommodate this variation. Figure 13.6 shows a page of figures that range from one-half column wide to two columns wide.

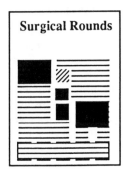

Fig. 13.6.

An example of varying the size of figures within the grid.

Pages with several figures look best if the edges of the figures are aligned with other pictures or headlines.

Figure 13.7 provides examples of various layouts that follow or violate this guideline. The pages on the left position figures by making one edge of each figure align horizontally or vertically with the edge of another figure on the page. The pages on the right do not follow this rule. As a result, the pages on the right lack balance and look haphazard.

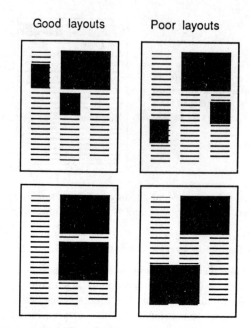

Good layouts   Poor layouts

Fig. 13.7.

*Aligned figures
versus unaligned
figures.*

Use black boxes or frames to reserve space for photographs where the printer is to drop in halftones.

When offset printers prepare plates for pages that require halftones (see Chapter 11), the preparers usually black out the space on the camera-ready copy so that the camera creates a clear window in the negative. You can save the printer this extra step by using black boxes or frames with black backgrounds to reserve space for halftones. The camera-ready master pages are printed directly from Ventura in black images on white paper. The offset printer prepares the photographic negative; the print image is transparent on a black background. The plate made from the negative has a raised or chemically treated surface that picks up ink from the roller and lays the ink on the paper. The plate is a mirror image of the final page.

Efficiency Tip

Talk to Your Printer before Preparing Final Camera-Ready Pages

If you are not familiar with the offset-printing process, find out the form your printing service prefers for camera-ready pages. Also find out how the printing charges can change if you do more or less of the preparation yourself.

Use white boxes to reserve space for line art to be pasted in before copy is sent to the printer.

The printer wants to lay halftones on transparent windows in the negative (created by black boxes or frames on the camera-ready page), but the paste-up artist usually wants to paste down figures on a white background. Figure 13.8 shows how you can type the name or number of each figure in the space reserved for the figure. To draw the white box to size, use Ventura's box text feature, setting `Line Attributes: None` and `Fill Attributes: White Solid Opaque`. Type the figure label in the box for the paste-up artist.

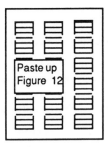

Fig. 13.8.

Identifying figures for the paste-up artist.

Use a template for all issues.

The template systems for newsletters and magazines can be elaborate compared to those for most other types of documents. In some of the examples that follow, you see how comprehensive a template can be. Chapter 11 provides a full discussion of template systems.

Use pull-out quotes to extend copy that falls short of filling the assigned space.

Pull-out quotes are short sentences excerpted from the text, printed in larger type, and set off from the rest of the page by boxes or lines (see fig. 13.9). Magazines and newsletters frequently use pull-out quotes to fill space and to emphasize points from the article. A pull-out quote usually is set four to six points larger than the body copy.

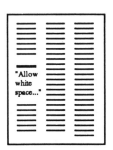

Fig. 13.9.

Using pull-out text quotes to fill space or emphasize specific text.

To help estimate how much space a pull-out quote requires, use a formula based on your type specifications. First, multiply the number of lines in the quote by the spacing per line. Then add this result to the amount of space you want above and below the quote, including ruling lines. The sum equals the number of points of vertical measurement needed for a pull-out quote of that length.

Following are some estimates based on 16-point type with 18-point leading, allowing .25 inch for a ruled line above the pull-out quote:

Number of Lines in Quote	Number of Inches Added
1	0.50
2	0.75
3	1.00
4	1.25
5	1.50

Use tracking to make fine adjustments in copy fitting.

Several copy-fitting techniques are described in Chapter 9, but the quickest way to shorten the number of inches (or feet) of text is to tighten tracking. To tighten tracking, select a paragraph of Body Text and open the PARAGRAPH TYPOGRAPHY dialog box from the Paragraph menu. Set Tracking:Looser, up to .009 EMs.

When you have a PostScript printer, you can change the point size of Body Text by a half-point. Half-point changes in type size pass the untrained eye and can make a considerable difference in the number of printed lines.

You should not adjust leading (interline spacing) in multicolumn layouts, unless you adhere to the rule stressed in Chapter 5. To achieve uniform baselines across columns when you mix different font sizes and rules on the same page, all spacing values (above, below, interline, interparagraph), rules, and margins must be integer multiples of the value of the Body Text's interline spacing. Changing leading in single-column layouts can be a quick way to affect how text fits into a given area.

Try not to let articles span more than one chapter (CHP) file.

The limit to the number of pages you can have in one chapter file is 999 pages, as defined by Ventura. For practical reasons, however, you usually set a much lower limit during production. If you build a long magazine in several CHP files, try to keep each article within one chapter (even if the article jumps pages in that chapter). Divide the publication into chapters at points where one section ends and the next section begins, as shown in figure 13.10.

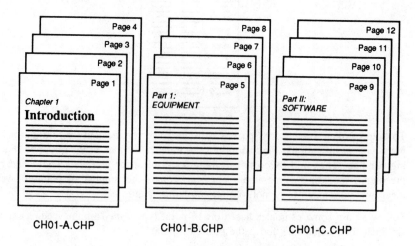

Fig. 13.10.

Dividing publications into chapters (CHP files).

CH01-A.CHP   CH01-B.CHP   CH01-C.CHP

The idea is to keep each text file (from the word processing program) in one Ventura file rather than start the text in one CHP file and continue it in a second Ventura CHP file. If you cannot confine the text file to one file, you must divide the original text file into two Ventura text files. If you divide the original text file, the blocks between documents are not linked, and edits that shorten or lengthen the text on the last page of the first CHP file do not cause text to flow to or from the first page of the second CHP file.

Examples

This chapter contains six examples of newsletters, magazines, and tabloids to help explain the design principles, production steps, and disk-file organization for different kinds of Ventura publications. Following is a list and brief description of these examples:

13.1. A 16-Page Newsletter with Strict Rules for Column Breaks

13.2. A Four-Page Newsletter Prepared for Two-Color Printing

13.3. A 24-Page Newsletter with Three Grid Variations

13.4. A Tabloid Newsletter Prepared for Two-Color Printing

13.5. A 12-Page Newsletter with Pull-Out Quotes and Fillers

13.6. Four Pages from Two Magazines

Example 13.1: A 16-Page Newsletter with Strict Rules for Column Breaks

Design: Elizabeth Smith
Production: Kevin Price
Client: Orrick, Herrington & Sutcliffe

The 16-page newsletter in this example is designed for ease of production by a group of contributors who have primary responsibilities unrelated to publishing. The trick is that the newsletter always contains the same set of features, each of which is always the same size and occupies the same relative position on the pages.

The techniques used here can be applied to any publication regularly produced by a group whose primary function is *not* publishing. Such publications include newsletters produced by volunteer staff, house communications produced by administrative staff, and event calendars produced by educational institutions and seminar agencies.

This newsletter, produced by a law firm, uses a two-column format and routinely presents an essay on one topic related to a field of law of interest to the firm's clients. The contents always follow the same basic formula:

- A list of contents (varying in length), always appears on page 1.

- A masthead containing information about the publisher always appears on page 1.

- A feature article or essay about one topic (4,000 to 6,000 words in length), always starts on page 1 and continues uninterrupted to page 14 (minimum) or 16 (maximum).

- An essay about secondary topics (300 to 2,000 words in length), sometimes follows the main essay.

- A list of the partners and associates who handle the topics discussed, always appears on the last page.

- A form for ordering more copies of this newsletter or other newsletters on other topics, always appears on the last page.

Figure 13.11 shows how some of these basic elements are laid out in one issue.

Fig. 13.11.

Two pages of the newsletter.

Using the same format for every issue enables each contributor to know exactly how many words to write.

Design Principles for a 16-Page Newsletter

The design principles listed at the beginning of this chapter are applied in this newsletter. Four of those principles have been applied in a way that intentionally simplifies the production process. Because the producers of the newsletter are not professional publishers, these principles are especially important.

Use only one or two different typefaces in a document. This newsletter uses only one typeface, Palatino, in five fonts (see ''Style File Tags for a 16-Page Newsletter''). The relatively short list of tags used to format new articles each issue helps simplify the production of the newsletter.

Use ruled lines to help set off the grid of the pages. Horizontal ruled lines are used to set off standing elements such as the contents list, the masthead information, and all titles.

Provide estimates of the number of characters per column for contributors and editors. For this newsletter, the length of each feature is standard. The total newsletter is 48,000 characters, or about 8,000 words. Before beginning an assignment, a writer knows how long the text should be. The editor's primary concern is that the finished article not exceed the expected word count. If an article is too short, the editor can fill the extra space by adding space around headings.

All columns on all pages should bottom out to the same point. This general rule is rigidly applied in this publication.

Production Tip for a 16-Page Newsletter

The production tip offered here can be applied to any publication for which a primary goal is simplicity in the production process.

If your publication includes a contents list that can vary in length, you should place or type the list before filling the rest of the page. The contents list on page 1 is typed without specific page numbers and positioned before the first article is positioned.

Using the Chapter menu CHAPTER TYPOGRAPHY dialog box, set `Column Balance: On` to force all columns to bottom out at the same point on each page.

The Template for a 16-Page Newsletter

Settings in the MARGINS & COLUMNS dialog box are as follows: 2 columns of equal width with a 1.5-pica gutter, top and bottom margins of 1 inch, left and right margins of .75 inch. The template, shown in figure 13.12, is set up with one page and uses a simple 2-column format. The first page of the template contains a standing banner and masthead as well as dummy text for the table of contents. Page 16 contains the list of partners and the mailing label area. A list of production steps is stored on page 1 for easy reference.

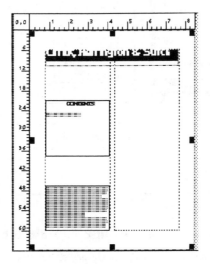

Fig. 13.12.

Template for the 16-page newsletter.

Additional tags are used to format the masthead, list of partners, and response form, but these formats are set up once in the template with standing text. They do not have to be reapplied for each issue. For this reason, the additional tags are given names that start with X so that they fall at the end of the tag list. More frequently applied tags appear at the top of the list, as shown in figure 13.13.

Style File Tags for a 16-Page Newsletter

Set the following tags in the style file:

Tag Name	Feature
Banner	36-point Palatino, white type on black frame background
Issue Title	24-point Palatino, ruling line below
Section Title	14-point Palatino bold, space added above
Subhead	12-point Palatino bold, ruling line above
Body Text	12-point Palatino, justified, indented first line

Fig. 13.13.

Tag list with frequently used tags at the top.

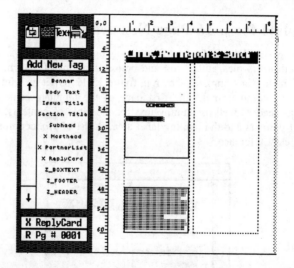

Efficiency Tip

Sorting Tag Names

Ventura sorts tag names alphabetically. Assign tags names that automatically sort frequently used tags to the top of the list.

Production Steps for a 16-Page Newsletter

As an aid for the producers of this quarterly newsletter, the following steps appear on page 1 of the template. You easily can adapt these steps to any publication of this type.

1. Collect all text files on disk. The target character count is 48,000 for the entire newsletter, or about 8,000 words, excluding the standing items on

pages 1 and 16 of the template. The "Contents" are in a separate file always named CONTENTS.DOC.

2. Open the TEMPLATE.CHP file for this newsletter, set up as shown in figure 13.12. Save the template with a new name that includes the volume and issue number. If the volume number is 1 and the issue number is 4, for example, name the file VOL1-04.CHP.

3. On page 1, change the issue identification below the banner.

4. When the template is cleared after an issue, leave the file CONTENTS.DOC in the table of contents frame and the masthead, banner, list of partners, and mailing information in their frames. The next month's copy, therefore, is in place and needs only page numbers.

5. Load the lead article on the page frame, scroll through each column, formatting text with tags from the style file.

6. If additional articles follow the lead article, add new frames for each additional text file. Load and format each text file.

7. If the final text is too long or too short to fit the 16 pages allowed, change the space above and below headings and subheads to shrink or expand the text. If the copy still does not fit, change the interline spacing of the Body Text tag to a value between 12 and 13.2 points (12/12 and 12/13.2).

8. Update the page numbers in the table of contents on page 1.

9. Before printing the final master copy, print the newsletter on a laser printer for proofing. Be sure that the Editorial Review Board or the appointed director sees a copy before it is sent to the print shop.

10. Print the newsletter on a typesetter. Send the camera-ready pages to the printer. Specify type, color, weight of paper, and the number of copies.

Example 13.2: A Four-Page Newsletter Prepared for Two-Color Printing

Design: Zeta Type
Production: Christopher M. Glazek
Client: United Way

This four-page newsletter has a page size of 8.5 by 11 inches and is based on a three-column grid. Figure 13.14 shows the newsletter's first and last pages.

The banner is pasted up on two acetate overlays that are part of the camera-ready copy for this newsletter each month. The offset print shop drops in photographs and half-tones, but all other elements are created in Ventura.

Fig. 13.14.

The first and last pages of the newsletter.

Production Tips for a Four-Page, Two-Color Newsletter

Many production tips are applied in this example, including the following:

Because each article is placed in a separate frame, spacing between articles is controlled by the placement of the frames.

Scale pictures and figures to precise column widths.

Use vertical padding to control the space above and below the black boxes or frames where the printer is to drop in halftones.

Notice that the banner is 72 points. Although a PostScript printer can accommodate this size, other printers cannot. In this example, the banner is created on another system and pasted up manually.

You can apply the production tips provided here to any newsletter or newspaper, particularly publications consisting of many different articles, figures, and photographs. The steps that specifically address two-color printing are applicable to any two-color publication; you also can adapt the tips for three-color and four-color jobs.

The Template for a Four-Page, Two-Color Newsletter

Settings in the MARGINS & COLUMNS dialog box are as follows: 3 columns of equal width with 1.5-pica gutters; top, left, and right margins of 3 picas, and a bottom margin of 5 picas. The template, shown in figure 13.15, is set up with a three-column underlying page to display column guides as a grid throughout the publication, but all text and graphics are in frames added to each page. The first page contains one frame with standing text that is part of the banner, plus dummy text for the current volume, issue, and date. Page 4 contains a standing in-house ad and mailing label area.

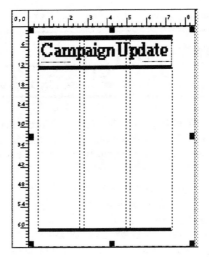

Fig. 13.15.

Template for the four-page, two-color newsletter.

Style File Tags for a Four-Page, Two-Color Newsletter

Set up the following tags in the style file:

Tag Name	Feature
Banner	10-point Palatino (typed in all caps), flush-right tab at right margin, ruling lines below 2 picas, width of frame (applied to text above and below the larger, pasted-up banner text, such as address, volume, issue, date)
Title 1	12-point Helvetica bold (typed in all caps), width of frame, ruling line below 0.25 point, width of text
Title 2	24-point Helvetica italic, space below 1.5 picas
Title 3	18-point Helvetica italic, space below 1.5 picas
Body Text	10-point Palatino, first-line indent 1 pica
Bullet	Same as Body Text with overall indent of 1 pica, first-line outdent to margin, tab at 1 pica
Caption	10-point Palatino italic

As an alternative to formatting the banner text (for the date, as shown in fig. 13.16) with a right tab, you can set up two tags:

Address	10-point Palatino (typed in all caps), flush left, no line break after (to force side-by-side with Vol/date)
Vol/date	10-point Palatino (typed in all caps), flush right, ruling lines below 2 picas, width of frame

UNITED WAY OF THE BAY AREA

Fig. 13.16.

A close-up of the banner.

Campaign Update

410 BUSH STREET   SAN FRANCISCO   CALIFORNIA   94108   VOLUME VIII   ISSUE II   NOVEMBER 4, 1987

You may prefer this method if you are loading the address and date information from a text file for each issue (instead of editing dummy text in the template) and if the word processing files always have the date typed on a line separate from the address information (see fig. 13.17).

Fig. 13.17.

The address and volume/date typed on separate lines.

```
@Address=UNITED WAY OF THE BAY AREA
@Banner=Campaign Update
@Address=410 BUSH STREET SAN FRANCISCO CALIFORNIA      94108
@Vol/date=VOLUME VIII ISSUE II NOVEMBER 4, 1987
```

Production Steps for a Four-Page, Two-Color Newsletter

To create the newsletter, follow these steps:

1. Open the TEMPLATE.CHP file for this newsletter. Save the template, using a new name that includes the volume number and issue number. If the volume number is 1 and the issue number is 4, for example, name the file VOL1-04.CHP.

2. On page 1, change the issue identification below the banner.

3. Draw the frame for each story as wide as the number of columns required by the story—use the display of the page margins as a guide in adding new frames. Page 1 includes two stories in two frames, for example: one three-column frame contains the lead story and a second two-column frame with a ruled line above it contains the second story. Page 2 is composed of three frames for stories, two caption frames, plus three frames that serve as windows for photographs that the offset print shop is to drop in. The frame layouts are shown in figure 13.18.

   As an alternative, you can draw individual frames in each column and link one story through several frames or columns. In this case, however, you must also draw a separate frame for the lead article titles, which run across all three columns of the page.

4. Position frames with black backgrounds as windows for photographs. Figure 13.19 shows frames that serve as place holders for photographs that the offset printer drops in as photographic halftones. The frame

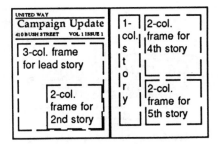

Fig. 13.18.

Frame arrangement on two pages.

Work with as Few Frames as Possible

As a general rule, try to work with as few frames as possible and use tags to vary text from column-wide to frame-wide. For every frame you add, you add time used to adjust the size and alignment of the frame and open dialog boxes for margins, columns, and ruling lines. A more efficient method is to draw one frame for a story on a page and let overlaid frames force text to wrap around graphics and other stories or sidebars.

margins of the black windows on the page serve as spacing guides, controlling the amount of space between photographs and the adjacent text as long as all frames abut.

After you set the frame background and vertical padding for the first frame, use the Copy and Paste commands to create the others and resize them.

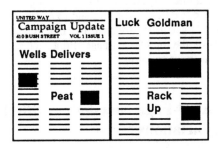

Fig. 13.19.

Page printed with black boxes as windows for halftones to be dropped in by the offset printer.

5. The pages printed from the CHP file are pasted onto boards; the acetate overlays are registered with page 1, and tissue overlays on each page indicate the color separations to be executed by the offset printer (see fig. 13.20). The final delivery to the print shop includes photographs keyed to the windows on each page.

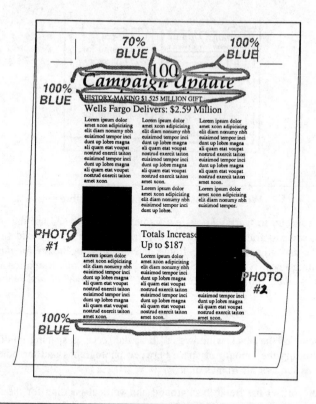

Fig. 13.20.

Tissue overlays identify photographs to be dropped in and indicate color to the offset printer.

Efficiency Tip

Color Separations with Ventura

You can print individual frames for each color enabled in the REFINE COLORS dialog box by setting `Spot Color Overlays: On` and `Crop Marks: On` when you print. If you are printing on a larger page size than the final size of your document, the name of the color prints on the top of each page. Print each file with registration and crop marks by turning on these options.

Example 13.3:   A 24-Page Newsletter with Three Grid Variations

Production: Susie Rich
Client: LaserJet Journal (Hewlett-Packard)

This 24-page newsletter is similar to the preceding example in that it has a page size of 8.5 by 11 inches and is based on a three-column grid. This example, however, demonstrates three simple variations of the grid. Figure 13.21 shows page 1 and page 3 of the newsletter. The banner is pasted up on two acetate overlays that are part of the camera-ready copy for this newsletter each month. The offset printer drops in photographs and halftones, but all other elements are created in Ventura.

Fig. 13.21.

Two pages of the newsletter.

The Template for a 24-Page Newsletter with Three Grid Variations

Settings in the MARGINS & COLUMNS dialog box are as follows: 3 columns of equal width with 1.5-pica gutters, top margin of 9 picas, bottom margin of 6 picas, left and right margins of .75 inch. The template, shown in figure 13.22, is set up with a three-column page and a ruling line at the top and the bottom. All text and graphics are in frames added to each page. The first page contains one frame with standing text that is part of the banner plus dummy text for the current issue date, and two frames loaded with the same items in each issue: graphics clips and the table of contents. Each new section is represented by a unique page set up with the section title as header text and a ruling line below the header frame at the top of the page.

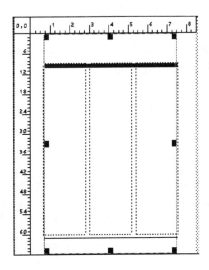

Fig. 13.22.

Template for the 24-page newsletter.

Style File Tags for a 24-Page Newsletter with Three Grid Variations

Set up the following tags in the style file:

Tag Name	Feature
Logo	12-point Zapf Humanist italic, centered, ruling line above and below
Price	11-point Zapf Humanist bold, left-aligned, no line break after
Table	11-point Zapf Humanist bold, centered, no line break after
Date	11-point Zapf Humanist bold, right-aligned, frame-width ruling line below
Feature Name	11-point Zapf Humanist bold, no line break after (to force side-by-side with page number), ruling line above, space above varies, space below 1 pica
Page Number	11-point Zapf Humanist bold, right-aligned
Subtopics	Same as body text, indented 0.25 inch
Heading 1	11-point Zapf Humanist bold
Heading 2	10-point ITC Garamond bold
Body Text	10-point ITC Garamond

Production Steps for a 24-Page Newsletter with Three Grid Variations

After the text is typed, each article and the table of contents are stored as separate text files. Use the following steps to produce the newsletter:

1. The table of contents must fit the page length allowed on page 1. To force the contents list to bottom out to the page margin, adjustments are made to the Space Above setting of the Feature Name tag. If you have Ventura's Professional Extension, set Vert Just. Within Frame: On in the CHAPTER TYPOGRAPHY dialog box under the Chapter menu. Ventura adjusts leading automatically to ensure exact copy fitting. Figure 13.23 shows a close-up of the table of contents with the tags identified.

2. The left column of the cover is created as a graphic and loaded into the column-wide frame.

3. Text for each section is stored as a separate file. When text is placed on the underlying page prepared for each section, Ventura adds pages as needed to handle the full text file. Figure 13.24 shows how using separate underlying pages works.

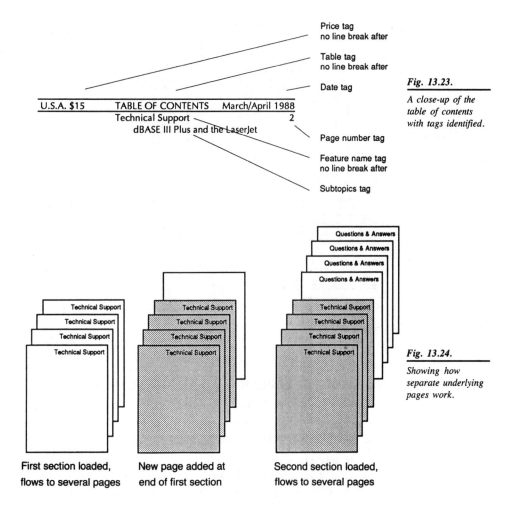

Price tag
no line break after

Table tag
no line break after

Date tag

Fig. 13.23.

A close-up of the table of contents with tags identified.

U.S.A. $15   TABLE OF CONTENTS   March/April 1988
Technical Support   2
dBASE III Plus and the LaserJet

Page number tag

Feature name tag
no line break after

Subtopics tag

Questions & Answers
Questions & Answers
Questions & Answers
Questions & Answers

Technical Support
Technical Support
Technical Support
Technical Support

Technical Support
Technical Support
Technical Support
Technical Support

Technical Support
Technical Support
Technical Support
Technical Support

Fig. 13.24.

Showing how separate underlying pages work.

First section loaded,
flows to several pages

New page added at
end of first section

Second section loaded,
flows to several pages

4. If an article fills only part of the last page in its section, a sidebar or filler is added to the page, or the text jumps to a frame added at the bottom of another section (see fig. 13.25). Frames added for jumps have a gray ruling line at the top, set with the Ruling Line Above command from the Frame menu. If you have Ventura's Professional Extension, you can create a cross-reference using the Ins Special Item command on the Edit menu. The Professional Extension offers a cross-referencing feature that can be used to insert ''continued to'' and ''continued from'' and reference the appropriate page numbers for articles that jump pages.

5. The pages printed from the Ventura CHP file are pasted onto boards; the acetate overlays are registered with page 1, and tissue overlays on each page indicate the color separations that the offset print shop is to execute (see Chapter 11).

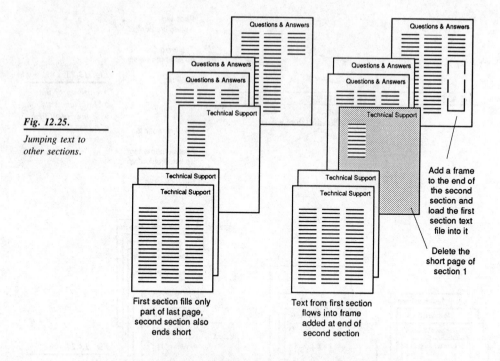

Add a frame to the end of the second section and load the first section text file into it

Delete the short page of section 1

First section fills only part of last page, second section also ends short

Text from first section flows into frame added at end of second section

Example 13.4: A Tabloid Two-Color Newsletter

Design: ZETA
Production: ZETA
Client: The Surgery Center

The newsletter in this example uses a five-column grid. The tabloid-size (11-by-17-inch) pages are printed in sections on 8.5-by-11-inch paper for the editing reviews; the final camera-ready pages are printed full size on a Linotronic 300 typesetter. Each month, the banner is pasted up on the camera-ready copy. Other elements to be printed in the two colors are separated by the offset print shop rather than printed on separate sheets of paper from Ventura.

The left half of figure 13.26 shows the layout of the first page with spaces reserved for photographs ranging from one-half column wide to two columns wide. The right half of figure 13.26 shows the same page after the photographs are dropped in.

Design Principles for a Tabloid Two-Color Newsletter

All the design principles described at the beginning of this chapter are applied in this page layout. Some principles, however, are particularly well illustrated. The tabloid makes effective use of white space and variations in the grid. Estimates of character counts are essential for this kind of production.

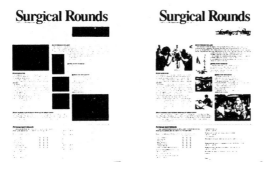

Fig. 13.26.

Page 1 of the newsletter before and after the photographs are dropped in.

Use variations in the grid to help distinguish different sections of the newsletter. The page shown in figure 13.26 provides a good example of grid variations: the basic grid is five columns; text ranges from two to three columns wide, and graphics (mostly photographs) vary from one-half column to two columns wide. These grid variations help differentiate sections, maintain the reader's interest, and, when applied to several pages of a publication, can accommodate a wide variety of formats.

Don't be afraid of white space. White space is achieved primarily by leaving a great deal of space between the banner and the first line of text. The page layouts are further opened with the use of a ragged-right margin for text and generous spacing between columns and between text and figures.

The Template for a Tabloid Two-Color Newsletter

Settings in the PAGE LAYOUT dialog box are as follows: Orientation: Portrait, Paper Type: Double (11-by-17-inch paper). Not all laser printers can handle the narrow inside and outside margins (0.33 inch); some printers force a minimum margin of 0.5 inches. The template is set up initially with two pages—the first and last pages. Additional pages are added when needed.

The template for this complex design is an essential production aid for each issue (see fig. 13.27). The page is set up in five columns of equal width with .25-inch gutters. The top margin is set at 1.5 inches; the bottom margin is 1 inch; the left and right margins are .33 inch. Page 1 of the template includes the banner and a questionnaire. Page 2 includes the mailing label. All other text and graphics are in frames added to each page.

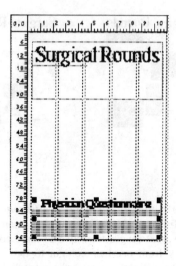

Fig. 13.27.

*Template for the
tabloid newsletter.*

Style File Tags for a Tabloid Two-Color Newsletter

Set up the following tags in the style file:

Tag Name	Feature
Banner	10-point Times italic, set in box text (used for subheading below pasted-up banner)
Heading	12-point Helvetica Condensed bold with big first character (an option under the Special Effects command from the Paragraph menu), flush left, frame wide. The first character is 24 points, the default for 12-point text.
Body Text	10-point Times, indent first line, frame wide
Question Title	14-point Helvetica Condensed bold with big first character, flush left, frame wide
Question Text	10-point Times, indent first line, column wide

Additional tags are required for each different line of tab settings in the questionnaire. See Chapter 16 for detailed explanations of forms.

Production Steps for a Tabloid Two-Color Newsletter

A number of people are involved in the production of this newsletter at different stages of the process; they use the following steps to produce the publication:

1. The copywriter writes the text to meet the precalculated total number of words. (See Chapter 9 for a description of copy casting.)

2. The editorial staff edits the text before passing the disk file, along with the photographs, to the production group.

3. The production staff loads the text file into Ventura and formats the text, using Ventura's style-file tags.

4. The production staff positions each frame for text and places black frames where photographs are to be printed.

5. A senior editor reviews the first printouts of the composed pages. These pages are printed in pieces on 8.5-by-11-inch paper, using the Print command's option to print overlapping output sheets. If the copy is too short or too long, the production team sends the page back to the editors for copy changes. The designer also makes notes to the production staff if any headlines need to be kerned manually.

6. The final pages are printed full size on a Linotronic 300 typesetter.

7. The final full-size typeset pages are marked for the printer. Tissue overlays identify elements printed in different colors and show where halftones of the photographs must be stripped in (see fig. 13.28). The photographs supplied to the printer may need to be marked for sizing and cropping. Individual pages for each color enabled in the REFINE COLORS dialog box can be printed by setting Spot Color Overlays: On and Crop Marks: On when you print.

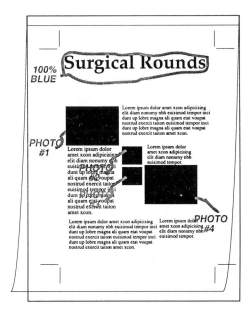

Fig. 13.28.

Using tissue overlays to show the printer how to separate the image for color printing and drop-in photos.

Example 13.5: A 96-Page Journal Compiled from Many Sources

Production: Charles Heinekel
Client: HAL-PC User Journal

This monthly newsletter is prepared by volunteer editors, contributors, and production assistants for a large, nonprofit professional association. All text is delivered on disk from a wide variety of word processing applications. Assembling this material into finished camera-ready pages requires nearly a full week each month. Figure 13.29 shows two pages of the journal.

Fig. 13.29.

Two pages of the journal.

Production Tips for a 96-Page Journal

Because of the size of this monthly journal, regular contributors are encouraged to code files to speed the production process. Because body text needs no tag, feature titles and bylines are consistent for all articles. Because Ventura supports a multitude of word processing programs, formatting consists mainly of bold and italic. If files must be submitted in ASCII format, Ventura's text-attribute codes (<B>=bold, <I>=italic and <D>=return to normal font) are available for writers willing to insert them.

The Template for a 96-Page Journal

Settings in the MARGINS & COLUMNS dialog box are as follows: 2 columns of equal width with a 2.5-pica gutter, top margin of 4.5 picas, bottom margin of 4 picas, left and right margins of 3 picas. The template, shown in figure 13.30, is set up with a two-column page. Each new section is represented by a unique page already set up with the section title as header text at the top of the page and the section number in gray box text in the outside margin.

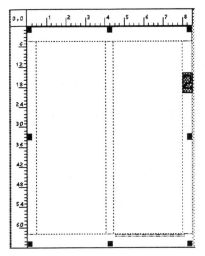

Fig. 13.30.

Template for the 96-page journal.

Style File Tags for a 96-Page Journal

Set up the following tags in the style file:

Tag Name	Feature
Feature Title	24-point Palatino bold, ruling line below, frame wide
Byline	14-point Palatino bold italic, flush right, frame wide
Subtitle	14-point Palatino bold, flush left, frame wide
Body Text	10-point Palatino, justified
Heading 1	12-point Helvetica bold
Heading 2	10-point Helvetica bold

Additional tags are available as needed for individual ads on tabular material.

Production Steps for a 96-Page Journal

This journal consists of articles by a number of different authors. Unlike in-house newsletters where all contributors use the same computer system, this journal is assembled from a wide range of sources. Following are the steps used to create this journal:

1. If the disk files and telecommunicated files for the text are not already formatted, the production volunteers convert the files to ASCII text files and do all formatting in Ventura. If the files already are formatted in one of the word processing programs Ventura supports, production places the files directly in Ventura to preserve bold and italic character formats.

Efficiency Tip

When To Request ASCII Text Files

For the best and most efficient results, you want authors to use a word processor that Ventura supports, preferably the same word processing program that the production team uses. Otherwise, ask the authors to save their files as text-only (ASCII) files. Then let the production team format the text with a word processor that Ventura supports. Ask authors to enter the Ventura tags (or abbreviations that you can expand by using global search and replace commands) directly in the text files to mark the headings. (The authors can use @Feature Title =, @ Heading 1 =, and @ Heading 2 =, for example, and end each title or heading with a new line that starts with @ Body Text.) Some ASCII files need double carriage returns to separate paragraphs. Tabs should be stripped out, and the first lines of paragraphs should be indented. Left margins are discouraged in ASCII files, because they can create unpredictable results.

2. Text from each author is stored as a separate file. When the text of the first article in a section is placed on the page prepared for that section, Ventura automatically adds pages as required to handle the full text file. Subsequent articles are added in new frames, starting at the end of the first article in each section, as shown in figure 13.31. If an article fills only part of the last page in its section, a sidebar or filler is added to the page. A series of sample page layouts is shown in figure 13.32. The first article in each section starts a new underlying page.

Fig. 13.31.

Adding pages to accommodate the full text file.

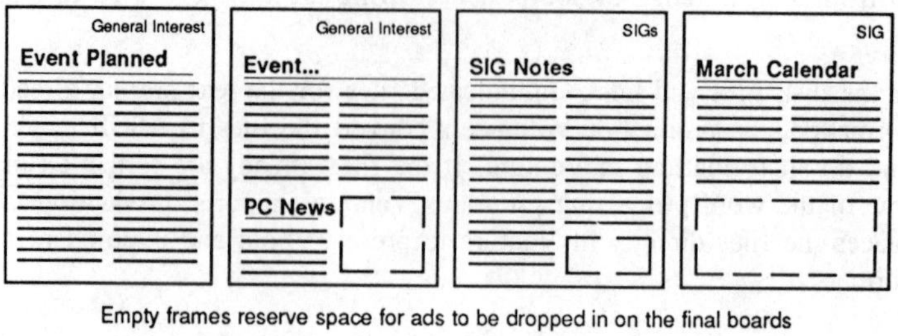

First article loaded into page

New frame added for other articles

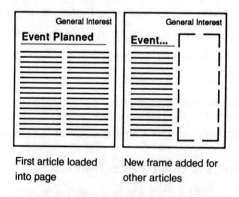

Fig. 13.32.

A series of sample page layouts.

Empty frames reserve space for ads to be dropped in on the final boards

3. Frames are added as space holders for ads to be pasted in manually. The frame margins are used to control spacing between text and graphics.

4. The table of contents must always fit the page length on page 1. To force the table of contents to bottom out to the page margin, adjustments are made to the Space Above setting of the Contents Headings tag. With the addition of Ventura's Professional Extension, this frame can be set with Vert Just. Within Frame: On in the CHAPTER TYPOGRAPHY dialog box under the Chapter menu. Ventura adjusts leading to ensure that the contents fill the entire frame.

Example 13.6: A 12-Page Newsletter with Pull-Out Quotes and Fillers

Production: Information Network
Client: ArmaDilla News (ARMA)

This 12-page newsletter has an 8.5-by-11-inch page size. The first page is based on a three-column grid; inside pages are laid out in a two-column grid. The banner is pasted up on an acetate overlay that is part of the camera-ready copy for this newsletter each month. Other elements to be printed in the two colors are separated by the offset print shop, rather than printed on separate sheets of paper from Ventura. Figure 13.33 shows pages excerpted from the newsletter.

Fig. 13.33.

Two pages of the newsletter.

The Template for a 12-Page Newsletter with Pull-Out Quotes and Fillers

Settings in the MARGINS & COLUMNS dialog box are as follows: 6 columns of equal width, a 2.5-pica gutter, top margin of 1.67 inches, bottom margin of .67 inch, left and right margins of .5 inch. The template is shown in figure 13.34. All text and graphics are in frames added to each page, with each frame extending across two, three, or four columns of the underlying frame. The first page contains one frame with dummy text for the current volume, issue, and date, which is part of the banner; standing text for the copyright; plus frames positioned for the lead article and the contents list. The last page includes a standing house ad and mailing label information.

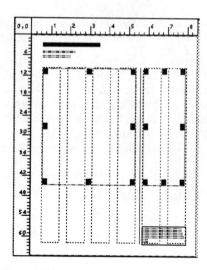

Fig. 13.34.

Template for the newsletter with pull-out quotes and fillers.

Style File Tags for a 12-Page Newsletter with Pull-Out Quotes and Fillers

This newsletter uses a large number of different tags for the contents list, an index on the last page, events lists, and tabular material. This example, however, focuses on the six tags that appear in articles:

Tag Name	Feature
Top Quote	14-point Helvetica bold italic, indented 2 picas from the right column edge and 6 picas from the left
Article Title	18-point Helvetica bold, ruling line above frame wide
First Paragraph	12-point Palatino, big first character
Body Text	12-point Palatino, first-line indent
Pull Quote	14-point Helvetica, ruling lines below, column wide
Filler	12-point Palatino italic, ruling line above
Quote Source	12-point Palatino, flush right

Production Steps for a 12-Page Newsletter with Pull-Out Quotes and Fillers

Use the following steps to produce this newsletter:

1. Open the TEMPLATE.CHP file for this newsletter. Save the template, using a new name that includes the volume number and issue number. If the volume number is 1 and the issue number is 4, for example, name the file VOL1-04.CHP.

2. On page 1, change the issue identification below the banner.

3. Build each page by adding frames and loading the text for each article. Format the text, using Ventura's tags.

4. Pasted-up display ads, pull-out quotes, and fillers are used to complete the page if an article falls short of filling a whole page or a series of whole pages. Pull-out quotes and filler text are loaded in frames laid on top of the article text. Empty frames are used to hold places for ads to be pasted in manually. In figure 13.35, you can study the frame layout for page 5 and see the results in the finished page.

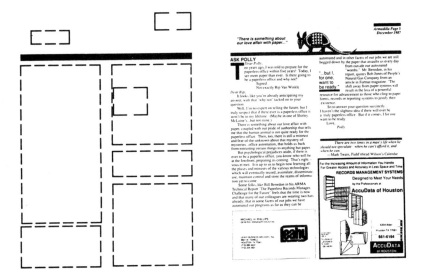

Fig. 13.35.

The frame layout and the finished page.

5. The table of contents must fit in one column on page 1. If the list is too long, adjustments are made to the spacing after the contents tags are set up in the style file.

6. The pages printed from the Ventura CHP file are pasted on boards; the acetate overlays are registered with page 1, and tissue overlays on each page indicate the color separations to be executed by the offset print shop. (See Chapter 11 for a description of tissue overlays.) The final delivery to the print shop includes photographs keyed to the windows on each page.

Chapter Summary

The examples presented in this chapter show many variations in production methods. The short newsletter with a relatively simple format and relaxed standards is easy to produce by a team whose primary function is *not* publishing. The tabloid-size newsletter, on the other hand, involves complex grid variations and strict production standards applied by a team of professionals. The design and production tips provided at the beginning of the chapter and illustrated by the examples give you a good overview of what is involved in producing a newsletter, magazine, or newspaper. You can apply these ideas to your own publications.

14

Creating Overhead Transparencies, Slides, and Handouts

Desktop publishing usually is associated with books, reports, newsletters, and magazines; but Ventura also is an excellent tool for creating presentation materials. You can develop tables and graphs in other programs, place them in Ventura, and then add captions and topic summaries with Ventura's text tools. To produce overhead transparencies, you can use a laser printer to print the images on clear acetate. If you want 35mm slides for a presentation, you can print the images on paper and then photograph the printed sheets.

Some examples presented in this chapter are designed specifically for use as overhead transparencies or slides (see fig. 14.1). Other examples are designed as printed handouts, but all examples share the following characteristics:

- Presentation materials consist of a series of similar parts.

- The items are primarily graphics; words usually appear in a large type font.

- Each item requires some extra touches in Ventura, that are not possible in the graphics programs that create the graphs and diagrams.

Design Principles

The design principles that apply to presentation materials are derived from a mixture of basic design traditions, advertising guidelines, principles of training theory, and techniques of projecting images for an audience. The principles emphasized in this chapter concern the selection and sizes of typefaces, the amount and content of text, and the sizes of the images themselves.

509

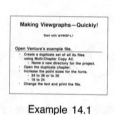

Example 14.1

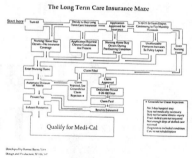

Example 14.2

Fig. 14.1.

Examples from the documents in this chapter.

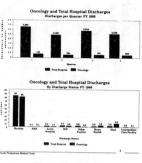

Example 14.3

Example 14.4

Several guidelines are dictated by the dimensions of the final product; for instance, slides are usually 35mm by 25mm. Other guidelines are borrowed from the advertising industry because the best presentation materials are similar to billboards and display ads. The application of these principles to presentation materials is described generally in this section. In the "Examples" section, the same principles are demonstrated in specific examples.

Select only one or two typefaces. Keep headings of the same level the same size. Keep similar text on all images in the same typeface.

This guideline is difficult to follow when graphics images come from different programs with different fonts. The number of fonts available in your spreadsheet graphing program is probably smaller than the number available in your drawing program. Ventura probably has more fonts than either your spreadsheet or drawing program. Before you make the final specifications for a set of presentation materials, you should know all the font options of the programs you use, as well as which fonts your printer can handle. Consult Chapters 9 and 11 for additional suggestions for controlling type specifications when images are drawn from several sources. Table 14.1 shows the typefaces commonly used in presentation materials.

On each overhead transparency or slide, try to limit the text to 25 words or fewer.

The number *25* is somewhat arbitrary. You set different limits for different purposes; but brevity generally increases effectiveness. Billboard designers follow a rule of not

Table 14.1
Typefaces Used in Tables, Graphs, and Overhead Transparencies
(Y = used; N = not used)

Typefaces	Graphs	Overheads/Slides
ITC American Typewriter	Y	Y
ITC Avant Garde	Y	Y
ITC Bookman	Y	Y
ITC Friz Quadrata	N	Y
ITC Galliard	Y	Y
ITC Garamond	Y	Y
Glypha	Y	N
Goudy Old Style	N	Y
Helvetica	Y	Y
ITC Korinna	Y	N
ITC Lubalin Graph	Y	Y
ITC Machine	Y	Y
New Century Schoolbook	Y	Y
Optima	Y	Y
Palatino	Y	Y
ITC Souvenir	N	Y
Times	Y	Y
Trump Mediaeval	Y	Y
ITC Zapf Chancery	N	Y

exceeding 7 words if possible—and billboards have a strong impact. You also may have seen the other extreme and had difficulty reading and understanding slides and overhead transparencies with too many words in small type.

You may decide that your limit is 50 words per page—or more, especially if the text is on a page to be handed out rather than projected on a screen. The important point is to recognize that these materials require special attention to word count and point size.

Give graphs descriptive titles or captions.

Your graph titles or captions should include enough information to be meaningful. The graph title "1987 Income," for example, conveys little information. Create more descriptive titles and captions, like those used in newspapers and magazines. The caption, "1987 Income Shows Increased Widget Sales Relative to Other Categories," for example, enables viewers to understand the purpose of the graph.

For images to be projected as slides or overhead transparencies, use large point sizes for text.

For overhead transparencies, one rule of thumb is that the image on the paper (not the projected image) should be easy to read from approximately 10 feet away (see fig. 14.2). For most audiences, this rule means that important words should be set no smaller than 36 or 24 points.

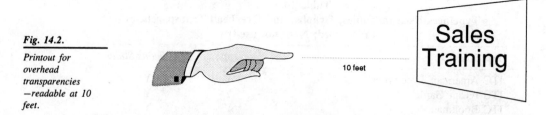

Fig. 14.2.

Printout for overhead transparencies —readable at 10 feet.

For slides, an image on 8.5-by-11-inch paper should be easy to read from 7 feet away (see fig. 14.3). This rule means that the text is 18 or 24 points in size, slightly smaller than the text on overhead transparencies.

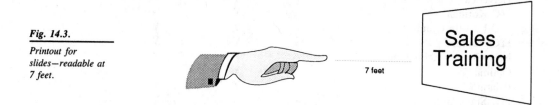

Fig. 14.3.

Printout for slides—readable at 7 feet.

For overhead transparencies, fit all images into a 7-by-9-inch area.

This rule applies particularly to framed overhead transparencies because a transparency frame usually has a 7.5-by-9.5-inch window (see fig. 14.4). You can set the margins of an 8.5-by-11-inch page to confine the text and graphics to a 7-by-9-inch area.

Fig. 14.4.

Overhead transparency proportions.

The 7-by-9-inch ratio is a good guide to follow even when the images are not framed. Viewing conditions may restrict some people in the audience from seeing the edges of the overhead, but the center of the image is visible to everyone in the room. If you want the option of using the same visual material in both slides and transparencies, these measurements also approximate the 24mm-by-35mm proportions used in slides. Another advantage of these presentation sizes is that your graphics images benefit from being surrounded by white space.

For materials to be made into slides, set all images within an area of approximately 3:2 proportions.

Frames for 35mm slides have a 35mm-by-24mm clear window. You should design your graphics—especially slide images with a ruled border—within this 3:2 proportion. If you do not use 35mm film for your slides, you must calculate the right proportions based on the final size of your slide window. Use the following formula to do this:

$$\frac{\text{slide width}}{\text{slide height}} = \frac{\text{Ventura image width}}{\text{Ventura image height}}$$

If you decide to use a width of seven inches for your images, for example, you can calculate the proportional height with this formula:

$$\text{Ventura image height} = \text{Ventura image width} \times \left(\frac{\text{slide height}}{\text{slide width}}\right)$$

If possible, design all the images in a series so that they use the same page orientation—choose either Portrait or Landscape in the PAGE LAYOUT dialog box.

Consistency makes the production steps easier than mixing portrait and landscape pages in a series. If the material being presented is not consistent in orientation, you must develop the presentation materials in two or more different Ventura chapter (CHP) files.

Production Tips

The production tips in this chapter are specifically applicable to presentation materials projected on a screen for an audience. The tips provide ways to produce material easily for high-quality results. By observing these tips, you frequently can eliminate one or more steps in the entire production process, thereby increasing efficiency and decreasing time spent in production.

The reasons for applying these tips are described generally in this section. Some tips are repeated with the examples, accompanied by explanations of their specific applications to that example.

Use automatic page numbering to number the set in sequence.

You can use Ventura's automatic page-numbering feature to number the images used in a presentation. In this way, you can easily find the images in the Ventura document when you want to update selected materials. If you do not want the numbers to show when you project the images, use a small point size (12 points or less) and place the page numbers at the bottom of the image area (see fig. 14.5). This trick is used in all the examples in this chapter.

If the sequence changes for particular presentations, or if some presentations are shortened by omitting selected images, you can still use the automatic page-numbering feature to number the master set and print alternate numbers as box text in the same small font on each page.

Fig. 14.5.

Automatic page numbering for a set of presentation materials.

If you use a laser printer for the final output, use a gray screen rather than solid black areas for the best projection image.

If your printer's toner cartridge is at its peak performance, you can get truly solid black areas on special laser paper. Even with a good cartridge, however, black areas may print unevenly when you print directly on acetate sheets for transparencies. This unevenness is exaggerated when the image is projected. You can reduce the effects of uneven toner by using gray fill patterns instead of black (see fig. 14.6).

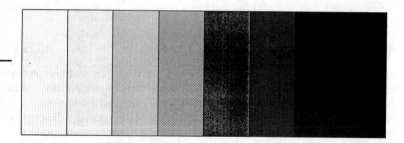

Fig. 14.6.

Comparison of printed black and gray areas.

To create overlays, copy the complete image on several pages, then delete portions of the image from each page.

To create a set of overhead transparencies with overlays, first create the whole image on one page. Copy the complete image to subsequent pages—one for each overlay. Then go back to the first page and delete the image parts that appear on the overlays. On each following page, delete all parts of the image except what appears on that specific overlay. An example of a set of overlays is shown in figure 14.7.

You can achieve a similar effect when you prepare slides. Build the full image first, then copy the complete image to subsequent pages. Keep the full version on the last page in the series, and delete selected elements from each page preceding the full image (see fig. 14.8).

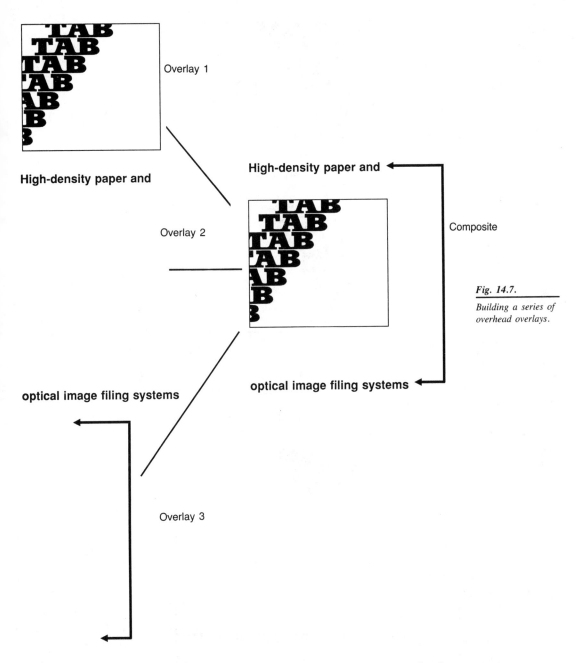

High-density paper and

Overlay 1

High-density paper and

Overlay 2

Composite

Fig. 14.7.

Building a series of overhead overlays.

optical image filing systems

optical image filing systems

Overlay 3

To summarize, pages in a series of overlays for overhead transparencies do not repeat the same elements, but each page in a series of slides repeats elements from the previous pages and adds new elements.

Slide 1

High-density paper and

Slide 2

optical image filing systems

High-density paper and

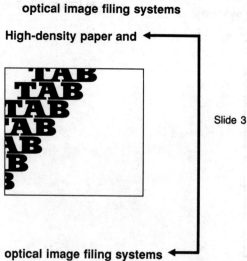

Slide 3

optical image filing systems

Examples

The examples used in this chapter have been selected to demonstrate a variety of formats and to explain various applications of the general design principles and production tips discussed in the preceding sections. The four examples presented here are the following:

14.1. A Viewgraph

14.2. A Flow Chart

14.3. A Series of Graphs

14.4. An Organization Chart

Example 14.1: A Viewgraph

Design: Modify &VWGF-L1 by Ventura

Training tools and presentation materials can be turned out quickly when you use a Ventura sample chapter as a starting point. Example 14.1 shows a viewgraph created by using the sample chapter file called &VWGF-L1, which is supplied with the program.

Production Steps for Creating Viewgraphs from a Sample Chapter

Make copies of Ventura's sample files when you want to create templates for new projects. This practice ensures that the sample files remain intact. The method used to produce the viewgraph shown in figure 14.9 does not alter in any way the sample files that are delivered with the program. Ventura provides two viewgraph samples, one in portrait and the other in landscape orientation. You can use either as a starting point, depending on the type of viewgraphs you want to produce.

The steps you need to take are summarized in figure 14.9, and the details are presented in the following steps:

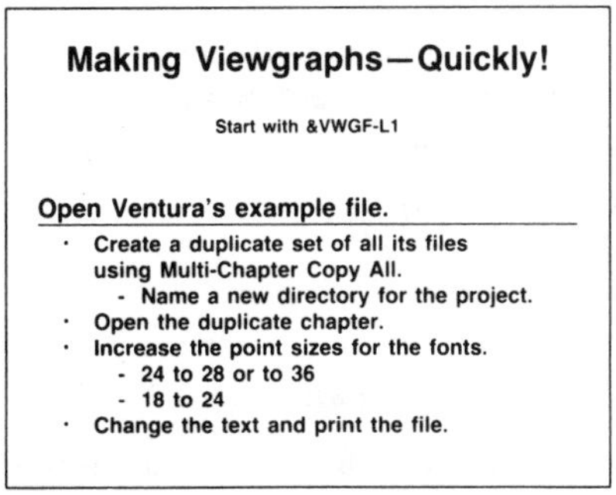

Making Viewgraphs—Quickly!

Start with &VWGF-L1

Open Ventura's example file.
- · Create a duplicate set of all its files
  using Multi-Chapter Copy All.
  - - Name a new directory for the project.
- · Open the duplicate chapter.
- · Increase the point sizes for the fonts.
  - - 24 to 28 or to 36
  - - 18 to 24
- · Change the text and print the file.

Fig. 14.9.

A viewgraph created by modifying the sample supplied with Ventura.

1. Begin by opening the viewgraph (titled &VWGF-L1 or &VWGF-P1) from the TYPESET directory. (If you are concerned that the sample stored in the TYPESET directory has been altered inappropriately, you can open the sample chapter from the examples disk provided with the program.)

2. Once you have the sample chapter on-screen, use the MULTI-CHAPTER OPERATIONS dialog box opened from the Options menu to select the Copy All command.

3. In the COPY ALL dialog box that opens, type a directory name for the project on the PUB & CHPs file destination line (use any directory other than TYPESET), and click Make All Directories the Same As the First to copy the destination for the other files. Once the directories are set, click OK to start the copy process. The Copy All command makes directories and copies files all in one step.

4. When the copy process is completed, click Done to return the work area to the screen.

5. Notice that the title line at the top of the work area reflects that the sample chapter is still in view. Instead of changing that chapter, use the Open Chapter command on the File menu to display the ITEM SELECTOR dialog box, where you can turn to the project directory and select the duplicate chapter you just made.

6. Any changes you now make to the style, source, or chapter files will not affect the samples stored in the TYPESET directory. If you want to rename the chapter file in the new directory, use the Save As command. If you want to rename the Style file, use the Save As New Style command. If you want to rename the source text file, use the Edit menu File/Type Rename command. The Save As and Rename commands make copies of the files, rather than rename the originals.

7. Change the point sizes for the tags you will use to larger point sizes. 18 points is often too small for overhead transparencies and should be changed to 24 points. Use point sizes ranging between 24 and 36 points to make the viewgraph more readable.

8. Add a ruling box around the page by selecting the page as the frame, and then opening the Frame menu's RULING BOX AROUND dialog box. Set the Rule Above Line 1 at 0.5 inch, and then set ruling line values and space between rules to complement your text.

Example 14.2: A Flow Chart

Design: Reyna Cowan
Production: Reyna Cowan
Client: Bonnie Burns

This flow chart is composed entirely of box text, white rectangles, and lines drawn with Ventura's Graphic tools (see fig. 14.10).

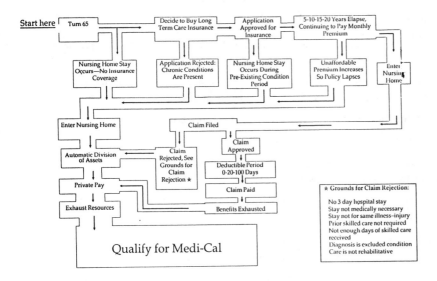

Fig. 14.10.

Printout of the flow chart.

Developed by Bonnie Burns 3/88
Design and Production, SF HICAP

Production Tips for a Flow Chart

The rectangles for the box text were created and arranged on the page to fill the available space. Outlines of the box text rectangles were used as guides in drawing the actual lines of the flow chart with the line tool. The box text rectangles have no fill, but do have line attributes measuring 0.25 points; lines for the arrows are 1 point thick. White rectangles hide unwanted lines (see fig. 14.11).

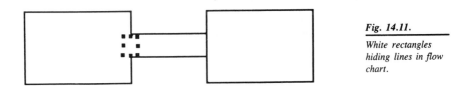

Fig. 14.11.

White rectangles hiding lines in flow chart.

Efficiency Tip

Making Straight Lines

To draw a perfectly straight horizontal, vertical, or 45-degree angle line, press the Alt key while drawing the line. If you move the cursor to the right or left, the line snaps in 45-degree increments.

If you want to straighten a line that has been drawn, position the graphic selector over an end handle while you press the Alt key.

Production Steps for a Flow Chart

You can create the flow chart entirely in Ventura. Use the Graphic function box text and line tools and the following procedure:

1. Use the Grid Settings command to set up a grid 2 picas by 2 picas (the smallest distance between elements of the diagram).

2. Select the base page, to which you can attach the boxes of text.

3. Activate the Graphic function and choose the box text tool.

4. Set Line Attributes to create 0.25-point black lines. Set the Fill Attributes to White and Opaque.

5. Type the text into the boxes. Select and rearrange the boxes, as needed, to fit the space.

Efficiency Tip

Lay Out Elements before Drawing Lines

When you are creating a diagram or chart with a set number of elements, lay out the elements first; then draw the connecting lines.

6. Select the line tool and use the Alt key constraint to draw ''paths'' between the box text elements. Each path is composed of two parallel lines—one for each side of the path.

7. Select the rectangle tool and set Line Attributes to None; set Fill Attributes to White and Opaque. Then draw white rectangles to cover parts of the box text borders where the paths connect (again see fig. 14.11).

8. Select the line drawing tool, and draw the first line. Set the Line Attributes and click Save To to update the defaults with the settings.

9. Each time you draw a line, press the Shift key (so that the line tool will stay enabled once you release the mouse button) and the Alt key (to make the line stay straight).

Example 14.3: A Series of Bar Graphs

Design: Zeta Type
Production: Christopher M. Glazek
Client: Pacific Presbyterian Medical Center

This series of bar graphs was composed using 1-2-3, GEM Draw, and Ventura Publisher (see fig. 14.12). Both the method used and one alternative technique, which can be used if you do not have a graphing or drawing application, are described in this section. The production tips for this example can be applied to any bar graph.

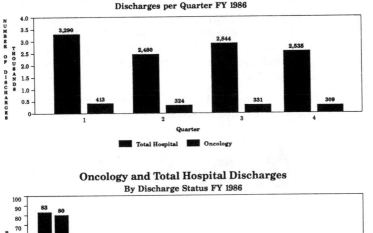

Fig. 14.12.

A series of bar graphs.

Design Principles for a Series of Bar Graphs

All the design principles described at the beginning of this chapter are applied in this report. The choice of typefaces and the size of the type are especially important in these transparencies.

Select only one or two typefaces. Keep headings of the same level the same size. Keep similar text on all images in the same typeface. In this example, the choice of fonts in the spreadsheet graphing program is the limiting factor. The text created by the graphing application was stripped out in GEM Draw, and the graphic loaded into Ventura shows only the bars and legend rectangles. The axes labels, bar labels, legend text, and graph titles are typed in Ventura in fonts not available in the graphing program.

For images to be projected as slides or overhead transparencies, use large point sizes for the text. As mentioned in the preceding paragraph, the graphing program's titles are not large enough. Ventura's tools are used to add text to get the larger type sizes required for presentations.

Production Tips for a Series of Bar Graphs

The bars in these graphs were generated with a spreadsheet graphing program. The PIC files created in 1-2-3 were opened in GEM Draw, where the text labels and axes were deleted (see fig. 14.13). The modified bar graphs were then brought into Ventura, where the axes labels, bar labels, legend text, graph titles, and captions were added with Ventura's box text tool.

Note: When you import graphs from Windows applications (such as Excel), the text is always dropped and must be added in Ventura.

Fig. 14.13.

Bars, stripped of text and axes, when first placed in Ventura.

Troubleshooting Tip

Test One Graph before Generating Many

Create one sample graph with the graphing program and place the sample in Ventura to check the size and position of the image. Based on this test, refine the specifications used in the graph program (if your graph program lets you adjust final graph size or font sizes).

Production Steps for a Series of Bar Graphs

You use a spreadsheet, a drawing program, and Ventura to produce this series of graphs.

1. Create the graphs in a spreadsheet or graphing program.

2. Copy the PIC files to GEM Draw or another graphics program. In the graphics program, delete the text and labels from the graphs.

Now you are ready to transfer the graphs to Ventura.

3. Open a document and set up a page for the graphs.

4. Set the top and bottom margins at 1.25 inches and the left and right margins at 1.50 inches on a letter-size base page, with a landscape orientation (see fig. 14.14). The margin settings confine the image to an area of 6 by 8 inches—well within the 7-by-9-inch limit recommended for transparencies.

5. Activate the Graphic function and use the rectangle tool to draw a box on the base page. Specify that the box have Fill Attributes of None and Line Attributes set for a 0.25-point wide border. All bar graphs in this presentation will be adjusted to fit within these borders, which also serve as the axes.

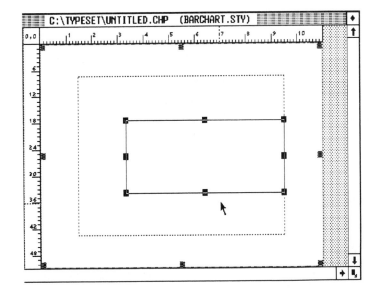

Fig. 14.14.

The page for bar graphs.

6. Add a new frame for the graphs; use the Load Text/Picture command to import the graphs into Ventura. Adjust the size and position of the frame to align the bars with the axes.

7. Use the box text tool to write the text of the legend, positioned to match the legend boxes from the graphing program. The box text is attached to the graphics frame created in step 6.

8. Also with the box text tool, add the titles of the graph.

Another method of creating these bars is to use Ventura's rectangle tool to draw them. Use this technique only if you already have a printed version of the bars or have sketched out the graph in the correct scale.

Example 14.4: Organization Chart

Design: Linda Mercer
Production: Information Network
Client: AISP Houston

These overhead transparencies were created by loading a chart from an external program into frames drawn on two Ventura pages (see fig. 14.15). Graphic box text was placed over each element so that Ventura's fonts could be used to print the final product.

Production Steps for an Organization Chart

The charting program worked quickly with a list of names and positions to draw the organization chart. All the shadowed boxes and lines were added automatically, as the

Fig. 14.15.

Organization chart.

chart was viewed in that program. The fonts, however, did not match the type specifications set forth by the designer until the chart was loaded into Ventura. The solution follows these steps:

1. Create the organization chart using a charting or graphic program and save it in a format compatible with Ventura.

2. Use the Load Text/Picture command and place the file in two frames on separate pages (see fig. 14.16).

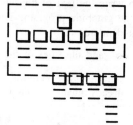

Fig. 14.16.

Original chart was too large for one page.

3. Select each frame and press the Alt key as you hold down the mouse button to pan part of the chart into view.

4. Use the box text tool to overlay the text in each cell of the organization chart. Abbreviate the text if necessary to fit the 14-point Helvetica font into the small boxes.

5. Give the box a solid white fill (to hide the text imported with the chart) but no border. Type the text in Ventura, setting the font name, size, and style with Z_BOXTEXT or any other tag you choose.

If you do not have a drawing application, you can use an alternative approach: Create the entire chart with Ventura's graphics tools. In this case, the box text elements still have an opaque white fill, but the border is set to 1 point black. Then use the rectangle tool to create other boxes with black solid fill. Choose Send to Back from the Graphic menu to create the drop shadows.

Cloning Complex Objects

When you want to create a series of identical objects, each composed of several elements—such as box text elements with black rectangles as drop shadows—create one entire composite first. Then copy and paste both elements as a unit (see fig. 14.17).

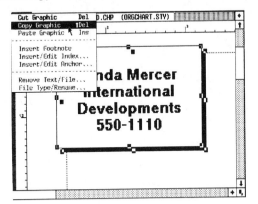

Fig. 14.17.

Copying a two-part object.

Chapter Summary

Transparencies, slides, and handouts are used frequently in almost all business settings. With Ventura, you can create effective presentation materials in less time and at less expense than with other methods. As demonstrated in the examples in this chapter, you have few limitations to the formats you can use. You can combine formats in any way necessary. You also can save the files so that you can use the same templates whenever you need to create new transparencies.

15

Creating Brochures, Fliers, and Display Ads

Throughout most of this book, the focus has been on multiple-page publications that repeat the same basic page elements on every page and use the same type specifications for the entire document. In this chapter, you learn how to use Ventura to produce one-page brochures, fliers, and display ads (see fig. 15.1). The brochures, fliers, and display ads discussed in this chapter appear in a wide variety of forms, but they share three important characteristics:

- The documents are promotional materials.

- The documents are usually only one or two pages long in a Ventura file.

- The documents are often a nonstandard size; the final pages may be trimmed and folded.

Brochures come in a wide variety of sizes but most frequently are designed to fit on 8.5-by-11-inch paper folded into three panels. Brochures may also be designed as four (or more) 8.5-by-11-inch pages printed on 11-by-17-inch paper and folded in half. These formats are economical because they are standard paper sizes (the formats don't require special paper trims after printing), and after being folded they fit neatly into standard business envelopes.

Design Principles

The design principles in the preceding chapters generally apply to the publications in this chapter, but you are likely to find more exceptions to the rules in this category—brochures, fliers, and ads—than in any other. Some of the common exceptions are described in this section to give you an idea of how and why brochures, fliers, and ads can break the rules.

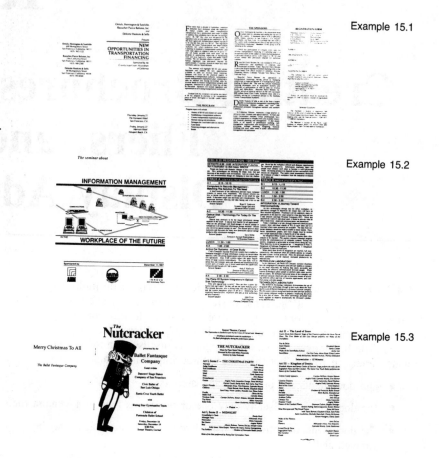

Example 15.1

Fig. 15.1.

Examples of brochures, fliers, and display ads.

Example 15.2

Example 15.3

Keep text to a minimum.

Following this guideline can be difficult when you work with small formats. When designing a small brochure, ad, or flier, most people tend to include as much information as possible about the product or service. Too many words in an ad, however, can make the final image uninviting. Readers simply may not read text printed in a small point size. By choosing your words carefully, you can get a few important points across and still draw the reader to call or come to the event or store.

The choice of font sets the tone of the piece.

Brochures, ads, and fliers often use decorative or unusual typefaces for headings and sometimes for body copy as well. Different typefaces can convey a sense of seriousness, elegance, or frivolity. If you are not sure how typefaces affect the reader, you probably should stay with traditional typefaces rather than experiment with more decorative ones. For instance, Example 15.1 is a brochure for an event presented by firms in the fields of law, investment banking, and accounting; this brochure calls for the more serious, traditional tone of a serif font like Palatino.

Use only one or two different typefaces in a document.

Almost any font can be used in a brochure, flier, or ad, but the same rule applies here as with all other publications: use only one or two typefaces. The use of too many fonts in a small space causes the brochure, ad, or flier to look busy and detracts from the message. You see how this rule is applied in most of the ads described in Example 15.4.

Don't be afraid of white space.

If you skim through any magazine, you are likely to find several full-page ads that leave most of the page blank. These ads are extreme examples of this principle, but these ads usually make their points well. Sometimes, you may deliberately violate this principle, however. Examples 15.1 and 15.3 use small point sizes for the type in order to gain white space.

Use all capital letters as a deliberate design strategy rather than a method for emphasizing text or showing a heading.

Avoid using all uppercase letters in long blocks of text. Remember that all uppercase text can be difficult to read, especially in sentences.

On the other hand, use all uppercase letters instead of a larger point size in order to make a few words stand out on the page. You also can use uppercase instead of changing the typeface for a head. Example 15.2, for example, uses uppercase for the title and figure captions on the front cover. Uppercase text has the greatest impact if the words or phrases are short. The appearance of uppercase text often can be improved if you manually kern the spaces between certain pairs of letters. (Refer to Chapters 5 and 9 for information about kerning.)

A good alternative to all capital letters is *small caps*. Type the text in all uppercase letters and set the first characters of capitalized words in a larger point size. This technique is applied in Example 15.1.

Production Tips

Many production tips that improve productivity when you produce long documents are irrelevant for one-page documents like those described in this chapter. Other production tips are unique to one-page brochures, ads, and fliers. This section lists some production tips for you to keep in mind for documents like these.

Compensate for ragged-right text by setting unequal right and left margins.

The need for a balanced appearance is evident in these examples. Because of the ragged-right text, the right margin may appear to be different from the left. You can compensate for this visual difference by using a wider left margin setting (or a narrower right margin).

For ads containing mostly graphics with little text, add text to the page after you position the graphic.

In many ads, the graphic fills most of the available space. As a result, the position of the graphic is the most important factor of the page layout. Text is frequently short and to the point. You can save a great deal of time by positioning the graphic before you place the text. Changing the text to fit the graphic is much easier than trying to change the graphic to fit the text.

If your ad includes a border, use a ruling box around the frame for the ad rather than a graphic rectangle. This technique gives more precise dimensions.

If you use a border in your ad, use the Ruling Box Around command from the Frame menu to create the border (instead of drawing a border with the rectangle tool). If the border is to match the dimensions of the ad precisely, simply set the size of the frame to the precise dimensions of the ad with the Sizing & Scaling command. If the border is to be inside the dimensions of the ad, set the outside margins of the ad as the Space Above Rule 1 in the RULING BOX AROUND dialog box.

If your ad includes a border, set narrower margins inside the border than the margins between the edge of the page and the border.

A border should be an integral part of the entire design. If the margins inside the border are larger than those outside, the final result is not as attractive or unified as it should be.

Examples

Many readers find that the examples in this chapter are the most useful in the book because one-page brochures, fliers, and ads are used frequently. With Ventura, you easily can produce short brochures, ads, and fliers and add variations with only a few additional steps. The examples in this chapter range from a three-fold brochure to a series of one-page ads. Some examples use scanned images or drawn graphics; others rely entirely on type. Following are the examples in this chapter:

15.1. A Three-Fold Brochure

15.2. A Large-Format Event Brochure

15.3. A Two-Fold Program with 10 Tags

15.4. Display-Ad Designs

Example 15.1: A Three-Fold Brochure

Production: Kevin Price
Client: Orrick, Herrington & Sutcliffe

This brochure is designed to be printed on 8.5-by-11-inch paper and folded into thirds (see fig. 15.2). The third panel is perforated at the fold and includes a registration form for the event. The cover and outside panels allow for a great deal of white space to draw the reader's attention to the text on those pages. The inside pages, by contrast, are dense with text; large initial capital letters help break up the panels. The initial capital letters also support the tone of this piece, which has a long tradition and is reminiscent of classical manuscripts.

Fig. 15.2.

A three-fold brochure.

The Template for a Three-Fold Brochure

The template is set up with one page and uses a simple three-column format in landscape orientation (see fig. 15.3). The first page contains the panels that fall on the outside of the folded brochure; the second page contains the inside panels. The outside panels are already set up with dummy box text representing elements that appear in the same position on every brochure. The third inside panel is set up with a standing registration form.

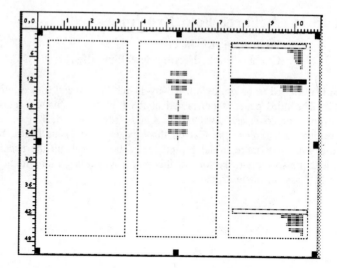

Fig. 15.3.

Template page for the three-fold brochure.

Style File Tags for a Three-Fold Brochure

Set up the following tags in the style file:

Tag Name	Feature
Presenters	14-point Palatino, right aligned
Event Title	24-point bold Palatino, right aligned, ruling line above and below, column wide
Sponsor and Dates	12-point italic Palatino, right aligned
Headings	14-point bold Palatino, centered, ruling line below, space added below
Drop Cap	9-point Palatino, big first character (36 points), justified, space added below
Body Text	9-point Palatino, indented first line, justified, space added below

Remember that the large first character for the Drop Cap tag is set up with the Set Font Properties option of the Special Effects command.

Six additional tags are required for the registration form on the third inside panel. (Examples of forms are described in Chapter 16.)

Production Tricks for a Three-Fold Brochure

The production tricks offered here can be applied to any publication that must fit precisely on a few pages.

Know Your Folds

Before setting up the template for a folded brochure, make a physical folded model of the brochure and write the panel number or contents on each panel. Then unfold the model and see how the panels fall on the full-size sheet (see fig. 15.4).

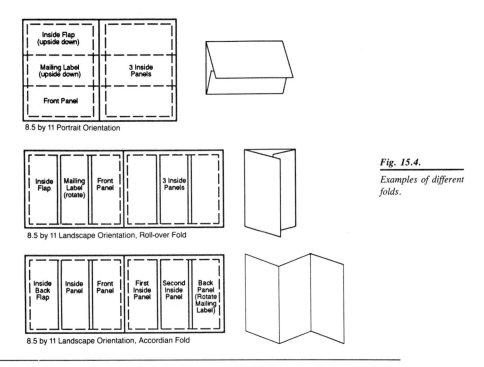

Fig. 15.4.

Examples of different folds.

Provide estimates of the number of characters per column for contributors and editors. Providing these estimates is possible when the design is determined before the writing begins. In this case, the same design is applied to all brochures produced by this firm. The character count for the inside panels is estimated initially, but when headings are added, the final count may change. Fine adjustments can be made to the line spacing to make the final copy fit.

Production Steps for a Three-Fold Brochure

Use the following procedure to create a three-fold brochure:

1. Write the copy using a word processing program, check it, and save it to a file. The target character count for the inside panels is 6,000 (about 1,000 words).

2. Open a new CHP file for this brochure. Set up the file and set the style file tags as listed earlier in this discussion. Save the document twice:

once as TEMPLATE.CHP (to be used when creating other similar brochures) and again with a name that includes the event date, such as JAN-EVNT.CHP.

3. On page 1, change the dummy box text to reflect the title, dates, and sponsors of the current event. Type the event title with soft returns at the ends of lines; that is, let automatic word wrap occur or press Ctrl-Enter to insert line breaks. The soft returns keep the ruling lines set for this tag from appearing between the lines of the title.

4. Place the text on page 2. Scroll through each column, formatting text with tags from the style file described earlier.

5. If the final text is too long or too short to fit in the two columns allowed, change the Headings tag with the Spacing command to alter the space above and below headings. This alteration should shrink or expand the text. If the copy still does not fit, change the leading (interline spacing) of the Body Text tag to a value between 9 and 11. If you use Ventura's Professional Extension, you can turn on vertical justification for this frame; Ventura automatically changes the spacing to fit the copy in the frame.

6. Edit the text of the registration form to reflect the current event's dates, location, and contact name.

7. Before printing the final master copy, print the brochure on a laser printer for proofreading. Make sure that the sponsors (or their appointed director) see a copy before the brochure is sent to the print shop.

8. Print the brochure on a laser printer, mark tissue overlays for spot color, and send the camera-ready pages to the printing company (see fig. 15.5). Alternatively, if several tissue overlays are required, you can use Ventura's Spot Color Overlay print feature to make individual sheets for each color that is enabled and used. Specify type, second color, weight of paper, and number of copies.

9. Use the Multi-Chapter command to copy the Ventura files for this issue to an archive disk named NEWS. Delete from the hard disk the text file for the two inside panels.

Example 15.2:   A Large-Format Event Brochure

Production: Information Network
Client: ARMA (American Records
Management Association)

This seminar announcement is printed on oversized sheets of paper, trimmed to 11 by 21 inches, and folded. The Ventura document is designed as four full 8.5-by-11-inch page layouts plus a 4-by-11-inch registration form (produced as the fifth page of the seminar document). The logos were available as photostats (film copies of the original artwork) and pasted up manually on the final camera-ready boards. All other graphics were produced with Harvard Graphics (see fig. 15.6).

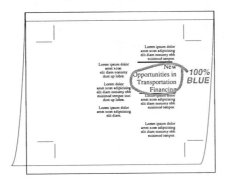

Fig. 15.5.

Using tissue overlays to show the printer how to separate the image for color printing.

Fig. 15.6.

A large-format event brochure.

The Template for a Large-Format Brochure

The template is set up with one page and uses a two-column format (see fig. 15.7).

Style File Tags for a Large-Format Brochure

Set up the following tags in the style file:

Tag Name	Feature
Seminar Title	30-point Helvetica bold, flush right
Cover Text 2	18-point Times italic bold
Cover Text 3	12-point Helvetica bold

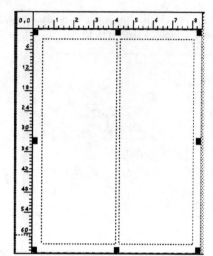

Fig. 15.7.

Template page for a large-format brochure.

Cover Text 4	12-point Helvetica
Heading 1	16-point Helvetica bold, indent .125 inch, left tab at 1.125 inches, white text, 18-point wide black ruling line above, space below rule 3 is −14 points (a minus value, resulting in white text on top of black line), column wide
Heading 2	16-point Helvetica bold, indent .125 inch, white text, 18-point wide black ruling line above, space below rule 3 is −14 points (a minus value, resulting in white text on top of black line), frame wide, space added below
Subhead 1	16-point Helvetica bold, left tab at .875 inch, ruling line above and below, column wide
Body Text	10-point Times, indent first line, justified, right tab at 3.5 inches, column wide
Speaker	10-point Times, left aligned, indent first line, right tab at 3 inches

Production Tricks for a Large-Format Brochure

Provide estimates of the number of characters per column for contributors and editors. Providing this estimate is possible when the design is determined before the writing begins. In this case, the text was collected first from the sponsor and various speakers.

Then the design was developed to accommodate a large number of characters. The text was edited to match the estimated number of characters that fit on the two large inside panels. Fine adjustments were made to the spaces above and below the headings to make the final copy fit.

Efficiency Tip

Keep the Number of Tags to a Minimum

Use as few tags as necessary to format the text. In this example, the Subhead 1 tag has a ruling line above. Tag the session title, always on the next line, as Subhead 1, and the ruling line above will complete the rules above and below the session number text. Because Body Text is justified and tabs are ignored in justified alignment, a separate tag must be set for the session speaker credit (see fig. 15.8).

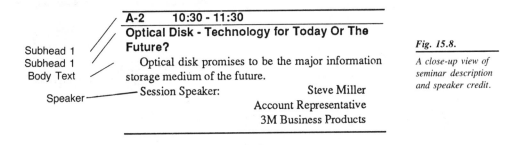

Fig. 15.8.

A close-up view of seminar description and speaker credit.

Production Steps for a Large-Format Brochure

1. On pages 1 and 4, type all text as box text.

2. Also on pages 1 and 4, load the graphics into individual frames. To scale the graphics proportionally to fit the frames, use the Sizing & Scaling command and set Picture Scaling: Fit in Frame and Aspect Ratio: Maintained.

3. On page 2, place the consolidated text file on the page so that the text flows automatically into two columns. Then apply the tags to format the text in Ventura. If the final text is too long or too short to fit in the two columns allowed, change the space above and below headings to shrink or expand the text. If the copy still does not fit, change the leading of the Body Text tag.

4. On page 3, add and load four individual two-column frames with the rest of the text (see fig. 15.9).

5. Lay out the registration form, front and back, on page 5 of the document (see fig. 15.10). Use the Edit menu's Ins Special Item command to add check boxes to the form. If you have a PostScript printer, set Text Rotation: 90 in the ROTATION dialog box for all

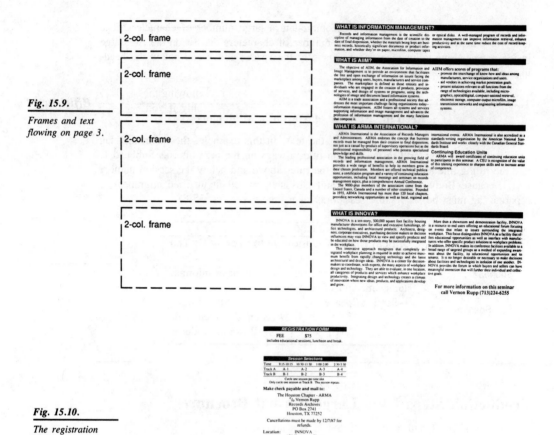

Fig. 15.9.

Frames and text flowing on page 3.

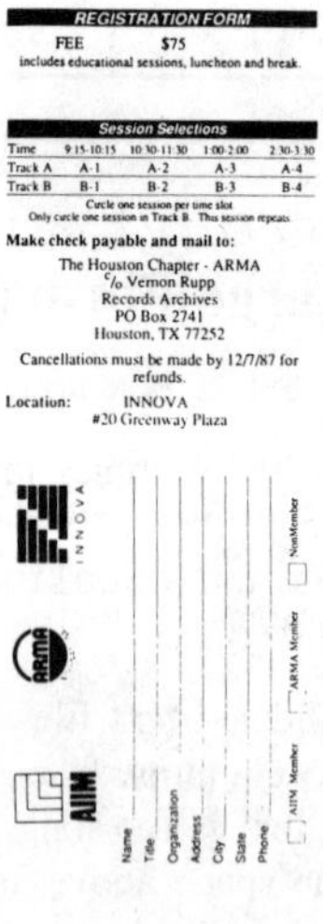

Fig. 15.10.

The registration form.

tags on the registration form and they will be in position without the cutting and pasting that is described in step 6. (See Chapter 5 for more on the rotated alignment feature.)

6. On the final camera-ready boards, cut and rotate the name-and-address form and paste up the registration form and the logos on page 1 and on the registration form.

Scanned Images or Manual Pasteup

If you already have a logo as camera-ready artwork on film, you can manually paste the artwork on the final pages printed on the laser printer or typesetter. Using this method is faster than cleaning up a scanned version of the logo or drawing the logo in a graphics application. Using a scanned image is more efficient only if you use the same logo many times

Example 15.3: A Two-Fold Program with 10 Tags

Design: J. Meyer
Client: Ballet Fantasque Company

This program for a performance of *The Nutcracker* is designed to be printed on 8.5-by-11-inch sheets and folded in half. One characteristic of programs like this is that they use many more tags per page than an average book, report, or brochure shown in previous examples. Ten tags are required to format the text on the inside pages (see fig. 15.11).

Fig. 15.11.

Four pages from the two-fold program.

The production tips offered here can be applied to any booklet format in which one Ventura page becomes two final pages or to publications using similar tabbed layouts, such as event programs and menus.

The Template for a Two-Fold Program

The template is set up with one page and uses a two-column format (see fig. 15.12). Because two final pages are arranged on each Ventura page, you add page numbers as text to each page instead of using a header or footer with automatic page numbering.

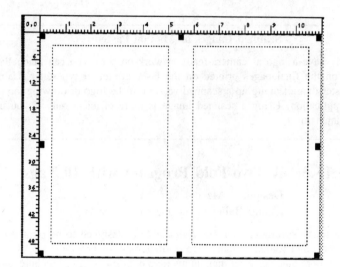

Fig. 15.12.

Template page for the two-fold program.

Efficiency Tip

Know Your Signature

Before laying out any publication for which one page is folded to create two final pages, decide whether you want to lay out the panels sequentially or in the order required for final printing. If you arrange the panels in sequential order—as you may have to do if you want to flow a single text file sequentially through all the panels—you (or the offset printer) must cut up the panels and paste them in a different order for the final camera-ready boards (see fig. 15.13). If you arrange the panels in the offset printer's sequence, you cannot view facing pages as you work (see fig. 15.14).

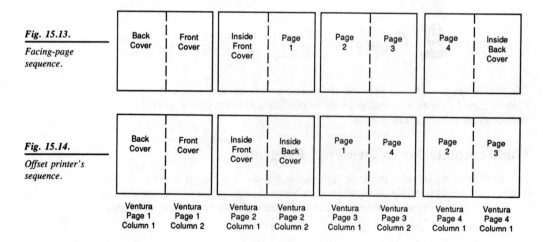

Fig. 15.13.

Facing-page sequence.

Fig. 15.14.

Offset printer's sequence.

If you use the offset printer's sequence, the first page contains the panels that become the front and back covers. The second page contains the panels that become the inside front and back covers. The third page becomes pages 1 and 4, and the fourth page becomes pages 2 and 3. The single text file can be loaded on the underlying frame to flow sequentially because the panels that are out of sequence (the back cover and the final page 4) are reserved for advertising. Force text to skip these columns by using a column break tag or by adding frames over the page frame (see fig. 15.15).

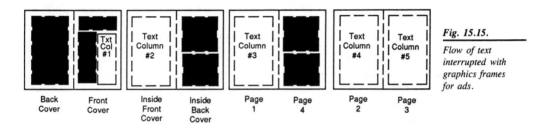

Fig. 15.15.

Flow of text interrupted with graphics frames for ads.

Style File Tags for a Two-Fold Program

Set up the following tags in the style file:

Tag Name	Feature
10 Center	10-point, centered
10 Left	10-point, left aligned, right tab with leaders set at 4.25 inches
12 Center	12-point, centered
14 Center	14-point, centered
14 Left	14-point, left aligned
18 Center	18-point, centered
24 Center	24-point, centered
24 Left	24-point, left aligned
72 Left	72-point, left aligned
Body Text	18-point

Many other tags are required for the display ads themselves. Display ads are described in Example 15.4.

Use Type Specs as Tag Titles

When working with a large number of tags, you find that identifying the differences in the type specifications in the tag name is helpful, as has been done in this example. If you list the type size in the first characters of the tag name, the tags are grouped by size in the style file window.

Use Your Word Processor To Format Text Whenever Possible

Many tags in Example 15.3 have the same point size and alignment but differ in weight (normal, bold, italic). Use a Ventura-compatible word processor to format bold and italic type. This strategy allows you to set tags only when the point size or alignment changes.

Production Steps for a Two-Fold Program

The first step is to create the text of the program with a word processor. The graphics image on the front cover is scanned from printed artwork. Use the following steps to produce the program:

1. Use box text to position the text on the back cover and the title on the front cover.

2. Load the rest of the text on the front cover into a frame. Format all text with the tags you set up earlier.

3. Scan the graphics image on the cover from printed artwork. Rotate the image in a graphics program and load the image into a frame in Ventura.

4. Beginning on page 2, continue the text file from page 1 into the underlying frame. The text automatically flows through the columns on four pages. Notice that the Body Text tag set type at 18 points. This setting forces the text to fill the total number of columns needed for the *final* booklet pages. As the appropriate tags are applied, the text shrinks gradually to fill only four columns. The extra space created with the larger point size remains to use as needed. Where frames are drawn over the text to make space for display ads, the text flows into the next available column.

5. Create the ads in Ventura using scanned images for all graphics. Follow the techniques described in Example 15.4.

Use a Large-Size Body-Text Tag at First To Force Extra Pages

You can set the Body Text tag to a large text size to force a certain number of pages to flow from the current page. Then change the Body Text tag to the size needed for the final version. After you apply the Body Text tags needed for the final version, the extra space created from the larger point size remains for you to use as needed. If you follow this procedure, the text has a predetermined path to follow and shrinks (when smaller type specs are applied) and expands (when graphics are dropped in and when larger type specs are applied). Figure 15.16 shows the space available when you initially set a large body-text size. If you don't follow this procedure and use the Insert Page command instead, you actually will create a new page and will have to repeat the steps of selecting the new base page and loading it with text (see fig. 15.17).

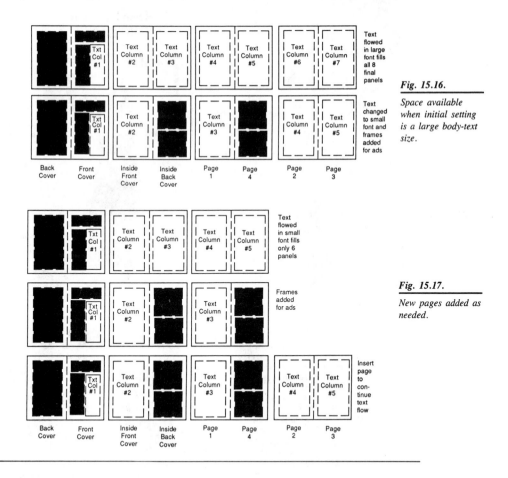

Fig. 15.16.

Space available when initial setting is a large body-text size.

Fig. 15.17.

New pages added as needed.

Example 15.4: Display-Ad Designs

Production: India Currents and J. Meyer
Client: Various

This example demonstrates the use of Ventura to produce display ads (see fig. 15.18). You can apply the recommendations about using special paper for the final printout to any ad or publication that is manually pasted on larger pages or boards. The production tips offered here can be applied to any format composed primarily of graphics and box text—display ads, posters, and one-page fliers, for example.

On The Occasion Of Christmas
December 25, 1987
Noon to 7:00 p.m.
SPECIAL HOLIDAY MENU
Featuring Roast Tom Turkey, Honey Glazed Virginia Ham
and Roast Prime Rib of Beef au jus
$22.00 per person plus tax and gratuity
Children's Menu for our guests under twelve $12.50
Reservations: 646-1706

MONTEREY PLAZA
THE GRAND HOTEL ON THE BAY

City Celebration, Inc. and
Grants for the Arts of the San Francisco Hotel Tax Fund
present

1988 San Francisco
ETHNIC DANCE
Festival

10th Anniversary Season!

Herbst Theatre
June 3, 4, 10, 11 & 12
All shows 8 pm
Except June 12 (2 pm)

26 dance companies
and 4 soloists, including:
Chitresh Das Dance Company
June 3, 8 pm
Mythili Kumar (soloist)
June 11, 8 pm
Abhinaya School of Dance
June 12, 2 pm

Herbst Theatre Tickets
Adults $16 & $13
Children $13 & $10
Sponsor $25

Charge by Phone:
(415) 552-3656
or STBS in Union Square

Fig. 15.18.

*Printouts of a series
of display ads.*

PRINCE INDIA
RESTAURANT

Authentic North Indian Cuisine
BUFFET LUNCH Mon-Sat
$5.95 11 a.m.-2:00 p.m.
**SUNDAY CHAMPAGNE
BRUNCH**
**12:00-2:30 p.m. $7.95
children $4.50**

DINNER 7 days a week
5:00 p.m.-9:30 p.m.

*6830 Village Parkway (next to
McDonald's), Dublin, CA 94568*

(415) 829-7944
Catering & Takeout Available

LOWEST FARES, BEST SERVICE AT

SAI TRAVELS

Established Since 1982

*With blessings from
His Holiness
SAI BABA of SHIRDI*

IATA   ARC
SINGAPORE AIRLINES   Pan Am.

- *Bargain Fares to India, Pakistan,
  Bangladesh, Sri Lanka, and Nepal*
- *Visitors' Medical Insurance*
- *Super-low Fares to Europe
  London from $519*

(408) 720-8944
SUNNYVALE
1026 E. El Camino Real
Sunnyvale, CA 94087

(415) 657-1724
FREMONT - NEWARK
39949 Duffel Plaza, Newark, CA 94560
(Across from Newark Hilton)

Production Tricks for Display-Ad Designs

Use the rulers as guides to draw a new frame the exact size of the ad. Then use the Sizing & Scaling command to check the exact height and width of the frame. Make adjustments in the SIZING & SCALING dialog box as needed.

Use the Margins & Columns command to define the margins as the distance between the border around the ad and the text and graphics inside the ad (see fig. 15.19). Use the Ruling Box Around command to define the border. (You can define up to three ruled lines of various thicknesses and intervals.)

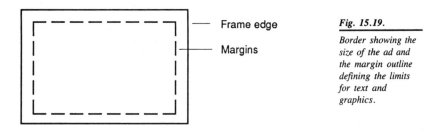

— Frame edge

— Margins

Fig. 15.19.

Border showing the size of the ad and the margin outline defining the limits for text and graphics.

Efficiency Tip

Designing a Series of Ads

Use the following procedure if you are designing a series of ads the same size but in a separate document (that is, if you're not laying out individual ads directly on the pages of the publication). Display the MARGINS & COLUMNS dialog box and define the margins of the base page to be equal to the size of the ads, including the border. Use the lines of the margins as guides to draw the frame that contains each ad.

Compose the ad using box text, Ventura-drawn graphics, and graphics from other sources. You can set up a style file and apply tags to the box text, or you can select the Text function and use the Set Font button to format the text.

Efficiency Tip

Use Scanned Images of Logos

Use scanned images of existing logos as placeholders for artwork to be pasted up manually. Alternatively, use scanned images as the final artwork instead of reproducing a logo exactly with a drawing program. Although, technically, you can draw the same logo with a graphics program and set the text in Ventura, hours of fine-tuning may be necessary for you to get the computer version to match the proportions and positioning of the actual logo.

Efficiency Tip

Put Text That You Need To Align Vertically in One Box

You don't need to draw a different box for text each time the font changes. A single box can have lines of text set in different fonts. You can align text easily by putting several lines in one box rather than positioning individual box-text elements. Use the Alignment and Spacing commands to adjust the position of the text inside the box. If you use Ventura's Professional Extension, you can change the spacing to fit the copy in the box. In figure 15.20, the ad is composed of one box-text element formatted with all text centered.

Fig. 15.20.

An ad composed of one box-text element plus graphics.

Efficiency Tip

Clone Box Text To Clone Type Specifications

If you need several box-text elements that share the same type specifications, create the first one and then copy and paste the box-text element to create additional text. Edit each copied box as needed. This procedure was used to create the three columns of information in figure 15.21.

Fig. 15.21.

A cloned and edited box-text element used to create similar blocks.

**Use Graphics Applications To Create Complex Borders,
Graphics, and Rotated Text**

Use Ventura's Graphics tools for simple lines, rectangles, and ovals, but use a graphics application for graphics composed of multiple lines and layered objects. You can use the `Rotate Text` option in the ALIGNMENT dialog box to rotate text at an angle. Figure 15.22 incorporates some of these elements.

Fig. 15.22.

*Rotated text and
graphics from a
graphics application.*

Use Scanned Images of Photos for Position Only, To Show Scale and Crop

Use scanned images of photographs as placeholders for halftones to be dropped in by the offset printer. The scanned image is marked *For Position Only* and serves as a guide to the offset printer in scaling and cropping the actual halftone of the photograph.

Preparation for the Reproduction of a Series of Varied Display Ads

Ads to be sent to other publications for insertion should be printed on a Linotronic typesetter or photostated. If you are sending laser-printer output, use laser paper or coated stock to get the best black image and to provide the best surface for pasteup. These special papers are available from most well-stocked paper-supply houses. Some stocks are designed to be printed on one side and waxed (for pasteup) on the other.

If you are using regular bond paper, include a note that the camera-ready copy you are delivering is on regular bond paper. Otherwise, a production staff unfamiliar with laser printing may think that you are delivering a photocopy instead of an original. (This common misunderstanding should occur less frequently in the future as more production departments use laser printers.)

Use Black Boxes To Insert Windows for Halftones

Use black boxes as placeholders for halftones to be dropped in by the offset printer. The photo in figure 15.23, for example, is set up as a black box in the Ventura layout. The black box causes a clear window in the negative where the halftone is to be dropped in. If the black is maximum black, the box serves as a guide to the offset printer in scaling the actual halftone of the photograph.

Fig. 15.23.

Using black boxes as windows for photographs.

LOWEST FARES, BEST SERVICE AT

LOWEST FARES, BEST SERVICE AT

SAI TRAVELS

SAI TRAVELS

Established Since 1982

Established Since 1982

With blessings from His Holiness SAI BABA of SHIRDI

- *Bargain Fares to India, Pakistan, Bangladesh, Sri Lanka, and Nepal*
- *Visitors' Medical Insurance*
- *Super-low Fares to Europe London from $519*

With blessings from His Holiness SAI BABA of SHIRDI

- *Bargain Fares to India, Pakistan, Bangladesh, Sri Lanka, and Nepal*
- *Visitors' Medical Insurance*
- *Super-low Fares to Europe London from $519*

(408) 720-8944
SUNNYVALE
1026 E. El Camino Real
Sunnyvale, CA 94087

(415) 657-1724
FREMONT - NEWARK
39949 Duffel Plaza, Newark, CA 94560
(Across from Newark Hilton)

(408) 720-8944
SUNNYVALE
1026 E. El Camino Real
Sunnyvale, CA 94087

(415) 657-1724
FREMONT - NEWARK
39949 Duffel Plaza, Newark, CA 94560
(Across from Newark Hilton)

Chapter Summary

The examples in this chapter demonstrate the wide variety of formats possible with Ventura. In addition, the examples show some innovative uses of pages and repeating frames in the development of a design series. You also have learned some of the tricks involved in preparing final camera-ready boards that include pasted-up elements.

16

Forms

Among all the documents suited to desktop publishing, one category that benefits particularly from Ventura Publisher's ruling lines feature is forms. In this classification are included any printed document specifically designed to collect information that is entered by hand or by a conventional typewriter.

As a group, forms have three common elements that merit special treatment during production:

- Forms rely heavily on tab settings and ruling lines to format the text.

- Forms usually include ruled lines and special characters (such as square boxes) as functional parts of the document rather than as design elements only.

- Forms often require a mix of frames and box text elements with side-by-side text or multiple columns in a relatively small space.

What this last point suggests is that setting up the basic page layout for a 1-page form or questionnaire can take as long as setting up the page layout for a 200-page book with the same format throughout. This fact is true of forms no matter what production methods you use. Because forms break the text area into several blocks and require a mastery of Ventura's tab setting and ruling line features, forms take longer per page than almost any other format (see fig. 16.1).

Example 16.1

Example 16.2

Example 16.3

Fig. 16.1.

Forms from this chapter.

Design Principles

Although most of us have never tried to design a form, we tend to think that we know good form design by virtue of having filled out hundreds of forms. The fact is that good form design is difficult and time-consuming. The principles of form design are based on a long history of filling out forms and on the experiences of people who have had to work with poorly designed forms. These principles are routinely applied by the professionals who design most of the forms we fill out as a part of normal business in an information-oriented society.

Because form layouts can be challenging, typesetting systems have been designed exclusively to produce forms; the designs of the forms are handled by the system's boilerplate formats. In the past, therefore, a business needing forms worked with a printing firm that specialized in form design and production. With Ventura, however, you can design and produce your own forms in less time and with less expense than is possible using traditional production methods.

Generally speaking, when you design a form, you should follow all the basic design principles recommended throughout this book. Four design principles specific to forms are stressed in this chapter.

Let the sequence of fields follow the expected sequence of entry.

This principle seems obvious, but the point is worth mentioning. Don't put so much emphasis on the aesthetic appearance of the forms that you interfere with the natural sequence of entries and so create a form that cannot be used efficiently. If the entries on the form will at any time be typed into a computer, for example, the sequence of entries on-screen should match the sequence of entries on the form itself.

The most common reason for violating this guideline is a practical one rather than a designer's whim: the database entry screen does not follow the sequence on the paper form because the two forms are designed for different purposes or different "audiences."

Clearly associate each label with its entry area.

Again, this principle may seem obvious, but we all have had the experience of wondering whether a simple label like *Name* is intended for the blank line above or below the label, as demonstrated in figure 16.2.

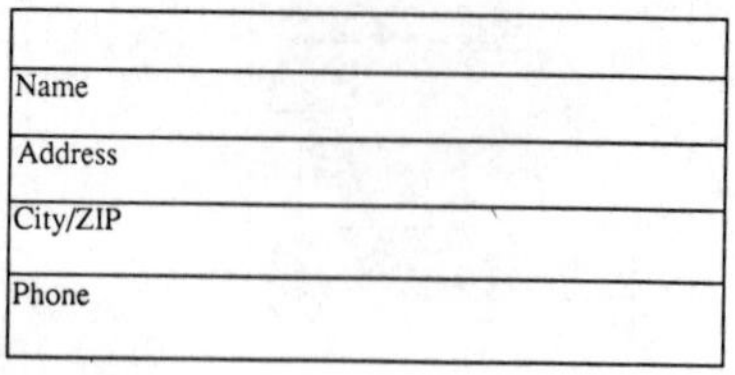

Fig. 16.2.

This form leaves a question as to where the name is to be entered.

Name
Address
City/ZIP
Phone

Allow enough room for hand-written entries.

Allow at least three-eighths-inch depth for each entry that will be written by hand (except multiple-choice entries and check marks).

Match line spacing to carriage returns for forms that are filled in using a typewriter.

If by any chance the form may be completed on a typewriter, use the typewriter's standard spacing of six lines per inch.

Production Tricks

Forms can make particular use of two features in Ventura: tab leaders and ruling lines. Without these features, the form-designing process can be painstaking and tedious.

Use Ventura's style file tags to create ruled lines for entries.

One of Ventura's strengths is its capability to associate ruled lines and tab leaders with text through the tag specifications. This feature is especially useful in form design of the type demonstrated in Examples 16.1 and 16.2, where ruled lines separate areas on the form and tab leaders draw lines for hand-written entries.

Use a symbol font rather than draw graphics boxes for columns of check mark selections.

If you need to insert a check box or a filled box at the start of a line on a form, choose the Special Effects command on the Paragraph menu, select Bullet, and then select the type of box. When you need several boxes on the same line, you can insert them at tab positions by using the Edit menu's Ins Special Item command and then choosing Hollow or Filled box characters. Shadowed boxes (used in Example 16.1), check marks, and other symbols also can be inserted as text rather than as graphics elements when you use a symbol font. A symbol font (Zapf Dingbats, for instance) is a set of special characters—such as bullets, boxes, stars, diamonds, and other symbols —that can be set as a part of the text. Boxes and symbols inserted as text shift as you edit the text file. Boxes added as graphic shapes, however, may need to be repositioned manually every time you change the form.

Examples

The following examples demonstrate the wide range of approaches possible for form designs.

16.1. A Form Using Tab Leaders as Entry Lines

16.2. A Form Using Box Text and Ruled Lines in Tags

16.3. A Form Composed of Duplicate Frames

Example 16.1. A Form Using Tab Leaders as Entry Lines

Production: The Zeta Group
Client: Bottled Water Study

This form consists of a page with seven frames. All text is typed in a single word processing file and formatted in Ventura using ruling lines to form black backgrounds for reverse type and tab leaders for entry lines (see fig. 16.3).

Fig. 16.3.

Form using tab leaders as entry lines.

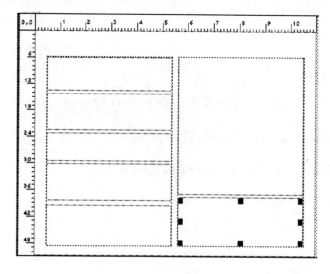

Template for a Form Using Tab Leaders as Entry Lines

The page layout orientation is landscape. The page is set up as two columns with margins that outline the grid for the form. Text is loaded into the seven other frames that are overlaid on the page as shown in figure 16.4. Each frame has a ruling box around it.

Fig. 16.4.

Base page column guides overlaid with seven frames.

Style File Tags for a Form Using Tab Leaders as Entry Lines

Nearly 20 different tags are used to build this form, but they can be described in three categories:

Tag Category	Settings
Section headings	10-point bold Helvetica white text, indented 3 points
	1-pica wide ruling line above (frame wide)
	− 11 points as the space below line 3 (a minus value, resulting in white text on top of black line as shown in figure 16.5—see Chapter 5 for a detailed explanation of this effect)
Lines with ruled lines for entries	Set up with tabs that use an underscore as a tab leader. Lines that fall under this category are shown in figure 16.6
	A different tag is set for each line requiring different tab settings
Lines with check boxes	Set up with tabs for alignment of the boxes as shown in figure 16.7 (which are set in a symbol font)
	Separate tags are required for the headings of each column of check boxes

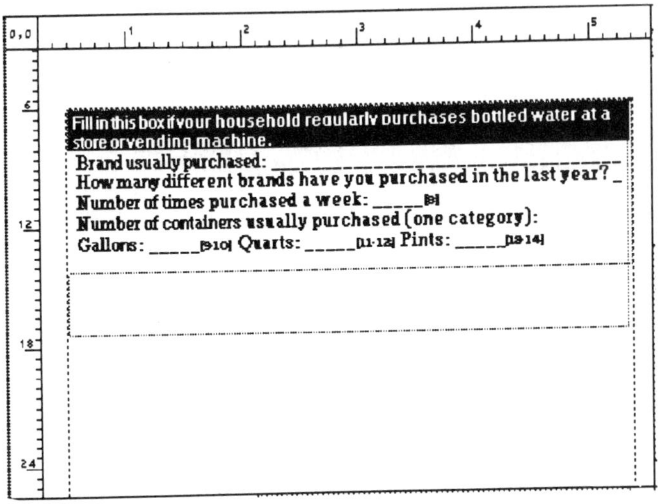

Fig. 16.5.

Close-up of two-line heading.

Fig. 16.6.

*Lines that use tabs
with underscores as
tab leaders.*

Name of company which delivers: _____[15]
How did you first hear of that company? _____[16-17]
Number of times delivered per month: _____[19-20]
Number of gallons delivered each time: _____[21-22]

Fig. 16.7.

*Lines that use tabs
to align a symbol
font as check boxes.*

Household Shopping Patterns:

Which of the following statements apply to your household? Check all that apply.

Statement	Applies	Does Not Apply
We prefer name brands.	❑ [38-1]	❑ [-2]
We avoid products that contain additives or preservatives.	❑ [39-]	❑
We prefer sodium-free/salt-free products.	❑ [40-]	❑
We avoid plastic food containers in favor of glass.	❑ [41-]	❑
Labels are important sources of information about bottled water.	❑ [42-]	❑

Define all tags while you are working—after the text is loaded as body text into all frames.

Production Steps for a Form Using Tab Leaders as Entry Lines

As mentioned, all text is created in a word processor, imported, and then formatted in Ventura.

1. Type the text in a word processor, inserting tabs followed by the angle bracket codes Ventura uses to interpret box characters. For example, when you load the file shown in figure 16.8 to a chapter, the characters <$B0> will print as box characters set in the same size and font as the rest of the paragraph.

2. Print a draft of the form to use for copy proofing and as a visual guide for the tab stops you will have to set in Ventura (see fig. 16.8).

3. Load the text into the seven frames laid out as shown in figure 16.4.

Fig. 16.8.

*Draft printed from
word processor
shows boxes as
<$B0>.*

```
Type of bottled water dispensed (check one of fill in
other):
<$B0> Spring water [24-1]     <$B0> Purified water [24-2]
Other:

Please check the types of bottled water you usually drink
and write in the brands you usually order of each type:

<$B0> Drinking water [25-1]     Brand:_____[26-27]
<$B0> Mineral water [25-2]      Brand:_____[28-29]
<$B0> Seltzer [25-3]            Brand:_____[30-31]
```

Scroll through the text in enlarged view and work through steps 4 through 6, setting tags as appropriate and creating new tags as needed for new line formats.

4. Insert a hard carriage return at the end of the first line, if necessary, to force two-line headings to have a black ruling line behind both lines of text.

5. Select the square-bracketed numbers and set them 2 points smaller than the normal text.

6. Adjust the length of each frame as necessary to accommodate the text for each section. Select Turn Line Snap On in the Options menu to leave uniform amounts of space between the frames. The adjustments you make to the size of the frames snap to uniform increments of the baseline grid set for the chapter. (The grid is established by the value you set for Body Text's interline spacing.)

7. If your printer supports Zapf Dingbats, you can print shadowed boxes by typing the angle bracket code *<113>* in your text file wherever you want a check box. Once you load the file to Ventura, select the symbol that appears and change the font (using Set Font) to Symbol.

Example 16.2.   A Form Using Box Text and Ruled Lines in Tags

Production: Davis Ford Publications
Client: Southern Comfort of Vero Beach

This 5.5-by-8.5-inch invoice form is designed to be offset-printed 2-up on 8.5-by-11-inch paper (that is, the offset printer prints two forms on each sheet of paper and cuts the printed sheets in half). The form is composed entirely of box text. The company logo is pasted up manually on the final camera-ready boards. Figure 16.9 shows the form as printed by Ventura, before the logo is added.

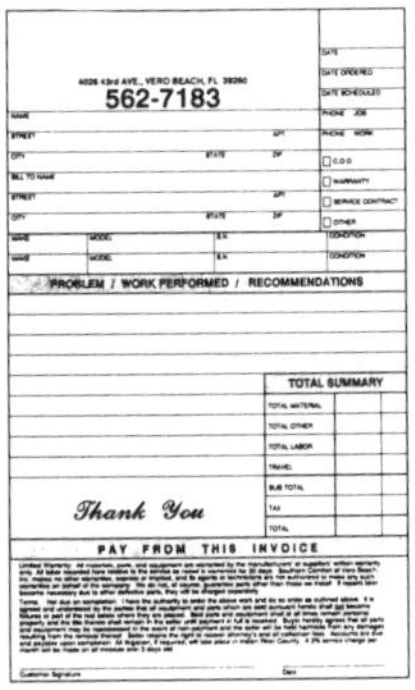

Fig. 16.9.

Printout of form using box text.

Template for a Form Using Box Text and Ruled Lines in Tags

The document is set up as a single invoice printed on 8.5-by-11-inch paper, with Paper Type & Dimension in the PAGE LAYOUT dialog box set at Half (5.5 by 8.5 inches). The margins of the base page are set at .25 inch on all sides, and the column width is set to be 5 inches wide. Because the size of the page is 5.5 by 8.5 inches, Ventura's crop marks can be printed automatically on the 8.5-by-11-inch paper.

Style File Tags for a Form Using Box Text and Ruled Lines in Tags

Eight basic tags are required for the style file:

Tag Name	Settings
Address	8-point bold Helvetica, centered
Phone	14-point bold Helvetica, centered
Section Titles	12-point bold Helvetica, centered
Entry below Label	8-point Helvetica, indented 3 points, ruling line above, tabs set at 15 and 20 picas
Entry beside Label	8-point Helvetica, indented 3 points, ruling line below, tab set at 1 pica
Thank You	14-point bold Commercial Script, centered
Terms	6-point Helvetica, indented 3 points, space added below
Signature	6-point Helvetica, indented 3 points, two tabs

Production Steps for a Form Using Box Text and Ruled Lines in Tags

As mentioned, this form is composed entirely in Ventura, using the box text tool. The form consists entirely of box text elements.

1. Draw the box text elements roughly in their relative positions as shown in figure 16.10, without text at first—adjustments to size and position will be made as text is added.

2. Start with the box text areas where text will require the tightest fit, and fill each box with text, formatting the tags as listed. Start with the top right corner of the form, where the width is determined by the length of the words *Service Contract* plus the check box that goes with these words (see fig. 16.11).

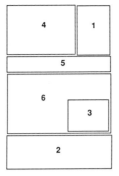

Fig. 16.10.

Rough box text layout and sequence of development.

Fig. 16.11.

Close-up of top of form (boxes 1 and 4), graphics boxes and tags identified.

Efficiency Tip

Start with the Hardest

In constructing a form or a page of many frames or box text elements of different sizes, always start with the frame that has the tightest fit or the widest text requirements. All other areas can be developed to fit the space remaining after the critical areas have been defined.

Next, you set two tags for the entry area labels.

3. Set the Entry below Label tag with the settings listed in the preceding section. This single tag accommodates a variety of formats (see figs. 16.11 and 16.12).

4. Set the Entry beside Label tag with the settings listed in the preceding section, to accommodate four entries that are tabbed in to fit graphics boxes (again see fig. 16.11).

5. Position titles as separate box text elements with shaded background.

6. Do the second critical area in this form, the Terms box at the bottom of the form. This box must be large enough to accommodate all the text in 6-point Helvetica.

7. Do the Total Summary area, where the box must be wide enough to accommodate 4-digit, hand-written numbers. Create the Total Summary area as a box text element added on top of the larger box for the description.

8. Set the Signature and Date lines with one tab: the flush-left tab where the word *Date* is positioned (see fig. 16.12).

Fig. 16.12.

Close-up of bottom of form.

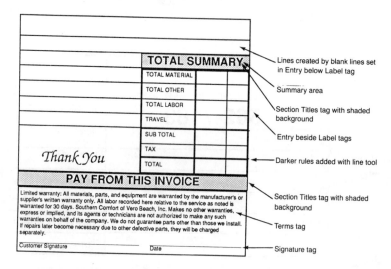

To get the ruled lines that mark where the hand-written signature and date go, you can follow one of two methods. You can add another tag to the style file, setting up three tab stops: the first and third tabs having underscores as leaders, the second tab having the same position as the tab for *Date* in the line below. This method is the cleanest and most typographically correct.

A second method—slightly faster but just as effective—is the "white box" technique. The trick is to create only one tag for the Signature and Date text and give the tag a ruling line above. You can overlay part of the ruling line above with a white box to create the separation between the two entry lines (see fig. 16.13). (The laser printer must support white boxes in order for this technique to work.) The drawback of this method is that you need to align the white box as close as possible to the tabbed word *Date* without covering any part of the printed character *D*.

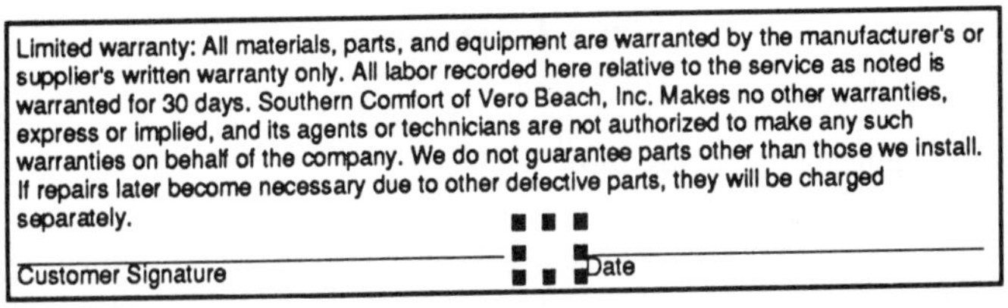

Fig. 16.13.

Ruling line overlaid by white box.

9. Add dark lines to the Total Summary area by using the line tool.

10. Paste up the company logo on the final camera-ready boards.

An alternative method for creating this form is to use one tag with no ruling lines and type the underscore character to draw the lines. The drawback with this approach is that some fonts print a series of underscores as dashed lines rather than solid lines.

Example 16.3. A Form Composed of Duplicate Frames

Production: Davis Ford Publications

This form is composed of five sets of identical entries—all requesting information about an applicant's present and prior employment (see fig. 16.14). The area is created once and then copied and pasted four times.

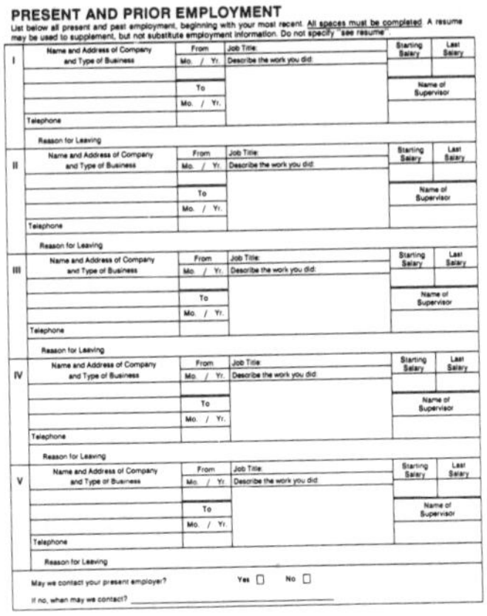

Fig. 16.14.

Printout of form.

Style File Tags for a Form Composed of Duplicate Frames

Only four tags are needed for this form:

Tag Name	Settings
Form Name	18-point bold Helvetica
Instructions	9-point Helvetica
Center Head	9-point Helvetica, center in frame, ruling line below
Body Text	9-point Helvetica, indent 3 points, tabs at 0.25, 3.75, 4.25, 4.75, and 5.25, ruling line below

Production Steps for a Form Composed of Duplicate Frames

The base page outlines the full form area, with 0.33-inch margins on all sides. Before starting to build the repeating entry areas, you set up the frames.

1. Create the top and bottom frames, and make the vertical measure the smallest possible to accommodate the text.

2. Use the vertical ruler line as a guide for dividing the area between the top and bottom frames into five equal parts, and draw one frame the depth of one-fifth of the layout area.

3. Add to the frame eight box text elements, roughly laid out with the first section marker to the left (see fig. 16.15).

4. In the first box, type the section number. In the second box, type the two-line heading and let the width of the frame force the automatic text wrap. This way, the Center Head tag will create a ruling line below the second line only.

5. Set other tags as shown in figure 16.15: Center Head (also used for From, To, Mo. / Yr., Starting Salary, Last Salary, and Name of Supervisor), and Body Text (Telephone, Reason for Leaving, Job Title, and Describe. . .). The sequences of ruled lines are composed of carriage returns set with the Body Text tag.

6. Use the tab settings of the Body Text tag to indent *Reason for Leaving* and the two lines in the bottom frame.

7. Use tabs to position the Yes/No entries, and insert the check boxes as box characters using the Ins Special Item command under the Edit menu.

8. Copy and paste the frame four times to create the five entry areas, as shown in figure 16.14. Because all the box text is linked to one frame, all the text is moved with the Copy Frame command.

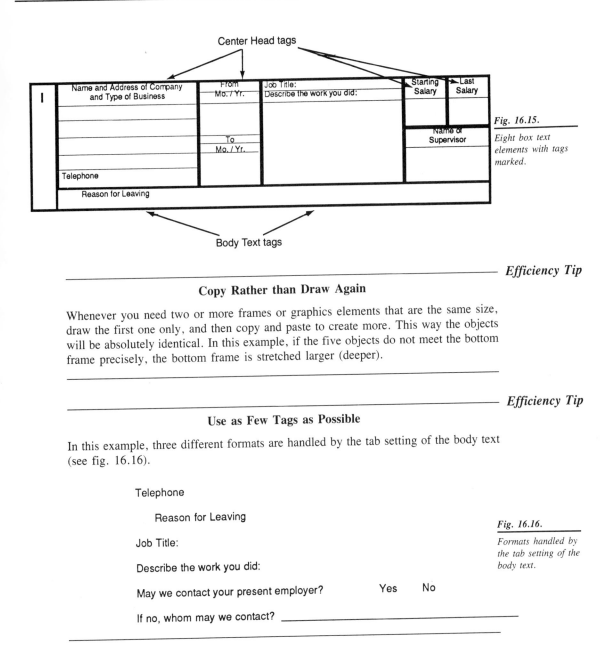

Center Head tags

	Name and Address of Company and Type of Business	From Mo. / Yr.	Job Title: Describe the work you did:	Starting Salary	Last Salary

Telephone

To Mo. / Yr.

Name of Supervisor

Reason for Leaving

Body Text tags

Fig. 16.15.

Eight box text elements with tags marked.

Copy Rather than Draw Again

Whenever you need two or more frames or graphics elements that are the same size, draw the first one only, and then copy and paste to create more. This way the objects will be absolutely identical. In this example, if the five objects do not meet the bottom frame precisely, the bottom frame is stretched larger (deeper).

Use as Few Tags as Possible

In this example, three different formats are handled by the tab setting of the body text (see fig. 16.16).

Telephone

Reason for Leaving

Job Title:

Describe the work you did:

May we contact your present employer?   Yes   No

If no, whom may we contact? _____

Fig. 16.16.

Formats handled by the tab setting of the body text.

Summary of Part III

Part III of *Using Ventura Publisher*, 2nd Edition, illustrates Ventura's wide range of uses and helpful features for producing professional documents. Whether your publishing projects are large or small, Ventura has the capabilities to produce high-quality published documents that just a few years ago could be produced only by professional designers and typesetters. Ventura's Professional Extension program extends the capabilities of Ventura 2.0 and offers methods that make publishing long documents, spreadsheets, or databases even less time-consuming. See Chapter 10 of this book to learn how the Professional Extension uses computer memory beyond 640K to allow you to work with source files larger than those handled expediently by 2.0. The Professional Extension also offers features to take care of many tasks you encounter when laying out illustrated and technical manuscripts, directories, catalogs, and numeric listings.

With Ventura, professional quality is available to individuals; businesses; and non-profit, educational, and government organizations. You may be producing books and manuals or single-page fliers and ads. Part III helps you with each stage—designing, creating, and printing the professional documents you need for your job. We hope that the examples in this section of the book will get you started toward making Ventura a true publishing tool.

Appendix

Hardware and Software Vendors

This appendix lists many products compatible with Ventura for the IBM XT and compatibles and vendors who sell these products. The products include fonts, graphics, drawing programs, painting programs, scanners, graphics cards and monitors, input devices, output devices, and other software. In each category, items are listed alphabetically by product. The addresses were accurate at the time this book was printed.

Scanners

Abaton, AST
MicroTek Lab, Inc.
16901 South Western Avenue
Gardena, CA 90247

Abaton Technology
48431 Milmont Drive
Fremont, CA 94538

Advanced Vision Research
2201 Qume Drive
San Jose, CA 95131

AST TurboScan™
AST Research, Inc.
2121 Alton Avenue
Irvine, CA 92714

AT&T®
AT&T Computer Systems Division
650 E. North Belt
Houston, TX 77067

Canon® IX-12
Canon USA
One Canon Plaza
Lake Success, NY 11042

Canon® IX-12
Dest Corporation
1202 Cadillac Court
Milpitas, CA 95035

ConoVision™ 1600
Conographic Corporation
17841 Fitch
Irvine, CA 92714

Crystal Scan
Taxan Corp.
18005 Cortney Court
City of Industry, CA 91748

Datacopy 220, 230, 730, 830, 830i
Datacopy Corporation
1215 Terra Bella Avenue
Mountain View, CA 94043

Hewlett-Packard ScanJet™
Hewlett-Packard Company
8020 Foothills
Roseville, CA 95678

IGX 7000 Imagesetter
Itek Graphix Corp.
Composition Systems Division
34 Cellu Drive
Nashua, NH 03063

KEE for 386
IntelliCorp
5215 North O'Connor Boulevard, Suite 1030
Irving, TX 75039

LM-300, 301, LS-300
Princeton Graphics Systems, MLP
601 Ewing Street, Building A
Princeton, NJ 08540

Ricoh SS-30, IS-30, MR-2
Ricoh of America
1360 Post Oak Boulevard
Houston, TX 77056

RM-1541
Relisys
320 South Milpitas Blvd.
Milpitas, CA 95035

RS312
Ricoh Corporation
3001 Orchard Parkway
San Jose, CA 95134

Scantek
Scantek Video Inc.
366 West Olive Avenue, Suite 5
Sunnyvale, CA 94068

T-Scan
Videotex Systems Inc.
8499 Greenville Avenue, Suite 205
Dallas, TX 75231

Graphics Cards and Monitors

2Page Display Systems & (640×480)
Verticom, Inc.
545 Weddell Drive
Sunnyvale, CA 94089-2114

Amdek® Color 722
Amdek Corporation
2201 Lively Boulevard
Elk Grove Village, IL 60007

AST-VGA, TurboVision, 1800,
560 Soft/Hard Enhanced
AST Research, Inc.
2121 Alton Avenue
Irvine, CA 92714

AT&T
AT&T Computer Systems Division
650 E. North Belt
Houston, TX 77067

Casper MC54
TW Casper Corp.
3012 Lawrence Expressway
Santa Clara, CA 95051

Color Graphics Card
Xitron
1428 East Ellsworth
Ann Arbor, MI 48108

COMPAQ® Color Monitor (CGA or EGA)
COMPAQ Computer Corporation
20555 FM 149
Houston, TX 77070

Conographic ConoVision™
Conographic Corporation
17841 Fitch
Irvine, CA 92714

DBM Magna - 4
DBM
634 Georgia Avenue
Palo Alto, CA 94043

Enhanced Color Display & VGA Monitors
International Business Machines Corporation
1133 Westchester
White Plains, NY 10604

FastWrite VGA
Video Seven Inc.
46335 Landing Parkway
Fremont, CA 94538

LaserView™ Plus
Sigma Design, Inc.
46501 Landing Parkway
Fremont, CA 94538

MicroVitec
1943 Providence Court
College Park, GA 30337

Mitsubishi XC-1410C
Mitsubishi Electronics America, Inc.
991 Knox Street
Torrance, CA 90502

Moniterm Viking®
Moniterm Corporation
5740 Green Circle Drive
Minnetonka, MN 55344

MultiSync II
NEC Home Electronics USA Inc.
1255 Michael Drive
Wood Dale, IL 60191-1094

Nanao 8042S
Nanao
23510 Telo Avenue #5
Torrance, CA 92505

Page Manager 100
Vermont Microsystems
11 Tigan Street
P.O. Box 236
Winooski, VT 05404

PC's Limited EGA Monitor
PC's Limited
1611 Headway Circle, Building 3
Austin, TX 78754

PGS HX-12, HX-12E, HX-9, HX-9E,
SR-12, SR-12P, MAX-12
Princeton Graphics Systems, MLP
601 Ewing Street, Building A
Princeton, NJ 08540

Quadram Quadchrome Enhanced Display
Quadram Corp.
One Quad Way
Norcross, GA 30093

Qubie Basic Time HR31 350
Qubie
Dept. P
507 Calle San Pablo
Camarillo, CA 93010

RE-1475
Relisys
320 South Milpitas Blvd.
Milpitas, CA 95035

Spectrum, Super EGA & VGA
Genoa Systems
73 East Trimble Road
San Jose, CA 95131

SummaSketch Plus, SummaSketch Professional
Summagraphics Corporation
777 State Street Extension
Fairfield, CT 06430

Tatung CM-1380-F
Tatung Co. of America
2850 El Presidio Street
Long Beach, CA 90810

The Genius R, 2TM, MC TM
Micro Display Systems Inc.
1310 Vermillion Street
P.O. Box 455
Hastings, MN 55033

Thomson CM 4350
Thomson Consumer Products Corp.
5731 W. Slauson Avenue #111
Culver City, CA 90230

TI Professional
Texas Instruments
Data Systems Group
P.O. Box 809063 H-860
Dallas, TX 75080

TVGA8800
Trident Microsystems, Inc.
321 Soquel Way
Sunnyvale, CA 94086

VEGA VGA
Video Seven Inc.
46335 Landing Parkway
Fremont, CA 94538

WY-700™
Wyse Technology, Inc.
3571 North First Street
San Jose, CA 95134

Xerox® Full Page Monitor
Xerox Corporation
101 Continental Boulevard
El Segundo, CA 90245

Input Devices

Felix
Lightgate
6202 Christie
Emeryville, CA 94608

LogiMouse®
Logitech, Inc.
805 Veterans Boulevard
Redwood City, CA 94063

Microsoft® Mouse
Microsoft Corporation
16011 NE 36th Way
Redmond, WA 98073

PC Mouse™
Mouse Sytems™ Corporation
2600 San Thomas Expressway
Santa Clara, CA 95051

Protocol Converts
Xitron
1428 East Ellsworth
Ann Arbor, MI 48108

Output Devices: Printers and Printer Drivers

720 IQ LasersImager
Printware
1385 Mendota Heights Road
St. Paul, MN 55120

Apple® LaserWriter® and LaserWriter Plus
Apple Computer, Inc.
20525 Mariani Avenue
Cupertino, CA 95014

AST TurboLaser®/PS-Plus 3
AST Caminconn
2121 Alton Avenue
Irvine, CA 92714

Canon USA
One Canon Plaza
Lake Success, NY 11042

CAP Card (Canon & Ricoh Printer Driver)
Laser Master Corp.
7156 Shady Oaks Road
Eden Prairie, MN 36689

*Color Printer & Background Charge
  Laser Printers*
Texas Instruments
Data Systems Group
P.O. Box 809063 H-860
Dallas, TX 75080

Compugraphic Converter
Puter Group
1717 West Beltline Highway
Madison, WI 53713

Conodesk
Conographic Corporation
17841 Fitch
Irvine, CA 92714

Cordata Technologies™, Inc.
275 East Hillcrest Drive
Thousand Oaks, CA 91360

Crystalprint
Qume Corporation
6133 Bristol Parkway, Suite 280
Culver City, CA 90230

Express, Laserpro
Office Automation Systems, Inc.
9940 Barnes Canyon Road
San Diego, CA 92121

GB 112
Hercules Computer Technology
921 Parker Street
Berkeley, CA 94710

Genicom 5010
Genicom Corporation
One Genicom Drive
Waynesboro, VA 22980

Genesis Laser Imagesetters
Tegra
900 Middlesex Turnpike
Billerica, MA 08121

GoScript
LaserGo
9235 Trade Place, Suite A
San Diego, CA 92126

Grafplus
Jewell Technologies
4740 44th Avenue S.W., Suite 203
Seattle, WA 98116

Hewlett-Packard LaserJet™,
*   Series II Laser Printer*
Hewlett-Packard Company
8020 Foothills
Roseville, CA 95678

IBM ProPrinter™
International Business Machines Corporation
1133 Westchester
White Plains, NY 10604

JLaser Plus
Tall Tree Systems
2585 East Bayshore Road
Palo Alto, CA 94303

Kyocera F-100A, F-2010, F-3010
Kyocera Unison Inc.
3165 Adeline Avenue
Berkeley, CA 94703

LaserPort
DP-Tek, Inc.
245 N. Hydraulic
Wichita, KS 67214

Linotronic™ 100/300
Linotype Corp.
425 Oser Avenue
Hauppauge, NY 11788

Linotype 202 Driver
Edco Services Pubset
12410 North Dale Mabry Highway
Tampa, FL 33618

LZR 2665, 1260
Dataproducts Corp.
6200 Canoga Avenue
Woodland Hills, CA 91365

MegaBuffer
Advanced Vision Research
2201 Qume Drive
San Jose, CA 95131

MT910 Laser Printer, Universal Publishing Sys.
Mannesman Tally
8301 South 180th Street
Kent, WA 98032

PostScript® Printer, AST TurboLaser®
AST Research, Inc.
2121 Alton Avenue
Irvine, CA 92714

Printer Driver
Chelgraph Limited
Berkeley Court, High Street
Cheltenham, Gloucestershire GL52 6DA
England

Printware Inc.
1385 Mendota Heights Road
St. Paul, MN 55120

PS 810
QMS, Inc.
One Mangum Pass
Mobile, AL 36689

QMS ColorScript 100
QMS Inc.
One Magnum Pass
Mobile, AL 36618

VBS 9030
Victor Beitner Systems
1111 Finch Avenue West, Suite 357
Downsview, Ontario M3J 2E5
Canada

Ventura Publisher to 202
Xitron
1428 East Ellsworth
Ann Arbor, MI 48108

Vepset
Mumford Micro Systems
P.O. Box 400
Summerland, CA 93067

VT600 Plain Paper Typesetter
Varityper
1 Mount Pleasant Avenue
East Hanover, NJ 07936

Xerox® 4045 & Color Ink Jet
Xerox Corporation
800 Long Ridge Road
P.O. Box 1600
Stamford, CT 06904

Fonts

Bitstream® Fontware™
Bitstream Inc.
Athenaecum House
215 First Street
Cambridge, MA 02142

CES
509 Cathedral Parkway #10-A
New York, NY 10025

Conofonts
Conographic Corporation
17841 Fitch
Irvine, CA 92714

Downloadable Postscript Fonts
Image Club Graphics
#206-19th St. NE
Calgary, Alberta T2E 7A2
Canada

Fontographer
Altsys Corp.
720 Avenue F #108
Plano, TX 75074

GEM™ Presentation & Publication Apps.
Digital Research Inc.
60 Garden Court, Box DRI
Monterey, CA 93942

Glyphix
SWFTE International
P.O. Box 219
Rockland, DE 19732

Hot Type
Victor Beitner Systems
1111 Finch Avenue West, Suite 357
Downsview, Ontario M3J 2E5
Canada

HP & Bitstream Font Editor & Font Pack
SoftCraft
16 North Carroll Street 500
Madison, WI 53703

Outline to Bit Map Converter
Laser Master Corporation
7156-7160 Shady Oak Road
Eden Prairie, MN 55344

PostScript® Typeface
Adobe Systems, Inc.
1870 Embarcadero Road
Mountain View, CA 94303

Professional Series
Font Factory
P.O. Box 5429
Kingwood, TX 77325

ProFont Editor
FontCenter
509 Marin Street #227
Thousand Oaks, CA 91360

Publisher's Type Foundry
ZSoft Corporation
450 Franklin Road, Suite 100
Marietta, GA 30067

SoftCraft Inc.
16 N. Carroll Street, Suite 500
Madison, WI 53703

Xitron Image Processor Products
Xitron
1428 East Ellsworth
Ann Arbor, MI 48108

VP/Fonts, VP/Tabs, VP/Saddle, VP/Base
Laser Edge
360 17th Street #203
Oakland, CA 94612

VS Library of Fonts
VS Software
P.O. Box 6158
Little Rock, AR 72216

Weaver Graphics
Fox Pavillion Box 1132
Jenkinstown, PA 19046

Wilkes Publishing Corporation
25251 Paso del Alicia
Laguna Hills, CA 92653

Graphics/Design Drawing Programs

AutoCAD®
Autodesk, Inc.
2320 Marinship Way
Sausalito, CA 94956

CadKey®, CadKey 3®
Micro Control Systems, Inc.
27 Hartford Turnpike
Vernon, CT 06066

Corel Draw
Corel
1600 Carling Avenue
Ottawa, Ontario K1Z 8R7
Canada

Decorative Dropcaps
ProGraf
P.O. Box 270987
Houston, TX 77277

DP Graphics
IMSI
1299 Fourth Street
San Rafael, CA 94901

Dynamic Graphics, Inc.
6000 North Forest Park Drive
Peoria, IL 61614-3592

GEM™ Presentation & Publication Apps.
Digital Research, Inc.
60 Garden Court, Box DRI
Monterey, CA 93942

Genus
11315 Meadow Lake
Houston, TX 77077

Genesis
Tegra
900 Middlesex Turnpike
Billerica, MA 08121

GoldMind Publishing
12155 Magnolia Avenue, Suite 3-B
Riverside, CA 92503

HALO DPE™
Media Cybernetics, Inc.
8484 Georgia Avenue #200
Silver Spring, MD 20910

Harvard™ Graphics
Software Publishing Corp.
1901 Landings Drive
P.O. Box 7210
Mountain View, CA 94039

Hercules RamFont
Hercules Computer Technology, Inc.
921 Parker St.
Berkeley, CA 94710

HotShot® Graphics
SymSoft Corporation
444 First Street
Los Altos, CA 94022

Image Club Graphics
206-2915 19th Street NE
Calgary, Alberta T2E 7A2
Canada

LaserCad
AI Systems
2450 East 7000 South
Salt Lake City, UT 84121

Microsoft® Windows Paint
Microsoft Corporation
16011 NE 36th Way
Redmond, WA 98073

PC CAD Programs
Mentor Graphics Corporation
1940 Zanker Road
San Jose, CA 95112

PC Paintbrush® +
ZSoft Corporation
450 Franklin Road, Suite 100
Marietta, GA 30067

PC Quik-Art, Inc.
394 South Milledge Avenue #200
Athens, GA 30606

Publisher's PicturePak
Marketing Graphics, Inc.
4401 Dominion Boulevard #210
Glen Allen, VA 23060-3379

Quality Analyst
Northwest Analytical
520 NW Davis
Portland, OR 97209

Screen Slots
Jewell Technologies
4740 44th Avenue S.W., Suite 203
Seattle, WA 98116

SLED
VS Software
P.O. Box 6158
Little Rock, AR 72216

T-Scan
Videotex Sustems Inc.
8499 Greenville Avenue, Suite 205
Dallas, TX 75231

Versacad Design
Versacad Corp.
2124 Main Street
Huntington Beach, CA 92648

Video Show
General Parametrics
1250 9th Street
Berkeley, CA 94710

Ventura Add-Ons

Designer Stylesheets
BCA/Desktop Designs
P.O. Box 2191
Walnut Creek, CA 94595

Desktop Publishing Associates
140 Bentley Street, Suite 3
Markham, Ontario L3R 3L2
Canada

Ventura Publishers Users Group
16160 Caputo Drive
Morgan Hill, CA 95037

VPToolbox
Ventura Publishers Users Group
16160 Caputo Drive
Morgan Hill, CA 95037

VP Toolbox 3.0
SNA Inc.
P.O. Box 3662
Princeton, NJ 08543

Will-Harris Designer Disks
Daniel Will-Harris
P.O. Box 480265
Los Angeles, CA 90048

XVP/TABS
The Laser Edge
360 17th Street, Suite 203
Oakland, CA 94612

Glossary

Alignment. The positioning of lines of text on a page or in a column: aligned left (flush left, ragged right); centered; aligned right (flush right, ragged left); or justified (flush on both the left and right).

Ascender. The portion of a lowercase letter that rises above its main body. Technically, only three letters of the alphabet have ascenders: *b*, *d*, and *h*. Uppercase letters and the lowercase letters *f*, *k*, *l*, and *t* also reach the height of the ascenders. See also **Descender**.

ASCII. America Standard Code for Information Interchange. ASCII format files can be saved and read by most database, spreadsheet, and word processing programs, making ASCII an ideal format for information exchange. These files include all the characters of the text itself (including tabs and carriage returns) but not the non-ASCII codes used by some applications to indicate character and paragraph formats.

Assignment list. The list of files, tags, or attributes that can be transferred to the selected frame, paragraph, or text. Shown in the sidebar on the left side of the screen.

Attribute. The style used to enhance readability of text. Typical attributes include boldface and italic. Font changes assigned to selected text are also considered attributes. Examples of font attributes include 14 point, blue, and kern.

Bad break. Term used to refer to line breaks that hyphenate words incorrectly or separate two words that need to stay together (such as *Mr. Smith*), and to page breaks and column breaks that result in widows or orphans. See also **Orphans/widows**.

Baseline. The lowermost point of letters, not including descenders. For example, the baseline of a line of text would be the lowermost point of letters such as *a* and *x*, excluding the lower edges of *p* and *q*.

Base page. The page-size initial frame defined by the Page Layout command. You can place additional frames on top of this page, including graphics that you want repeated on every page in a publication.

Binding margin. The additional space added to the side of the page to allow for binding the pages together.

Bit map. A graphic image or text formed by a pattern of dots. PC Paint, GEM Paint, and PC Paintbrush documents are bit-mapped graphics, as are scanned or digitized images. The higher the number of dots, the greater the resolution and the sharper the image. Low-resolution images are sometimes called *paint-type* files, and they usually have a lower number of dots per inch (dpi) than high-resolution scans do.

Bleed. Term used to describe the part of a printed image that extends to the trimmed edge of the sheet or page.

Blue lines. Term used to describe one type of preliminary test printing of a page to check the offset printer's plates. This test printing is done using a photochemical process (instead of printers' inks) that produces a blue image on white paper.

Blue pencil/blue line. Traditionally, a guide line that is drawn using a blue pencil or printed in light blue ink on the boards used for pasting up a page layout manually. The blue ink is sometimes called *non-repro* blue because it is not picked up by the camera when a page is photographed to make plates for offset printing. A blue line functions much like the on-screen margin and column guides Ventura displays to help you position text and graphics; these lines do not appear when the page is printed.

Board. A sheet of heavyweight paper or card stock onto which typeset text and graphics are pasted manually. See also **Blue pencil/blue line**.

Body copy. The main part of the text of a publication, as distinguished from headings and captions. See also **Body text** and **Body type**.

Body text. The style file tag initially assigned to text as the text is imported into Ventura from a text file. Also, refers to the body copy. See also **Body copy**.

Body type. The type (font) used for the body copy. Generally, fonts that are used for body copy, as distinguished from display type.

Boilerplate. See **Template**.

Box text. A box created using the Graphic function that contains text. Box text will not flow around frames and can have graphics (such as arrows) attached directly to it. Box text is often used to make tables and callouts.

Box text tool. The Graphic tool you use to create text.

Break. The flow of text from one paragraph to the next. Normally each paragraph continues directly below the preceding paragraph or (if no more room is left on this column or page) continues at the top of the next column or page (line break).

Brochure. A folded pamphlet or small booklet.

Bullet. A circle, square, or other symbol before an indented paragraph or line that is used to highlight items in a list.

Callout. The text used to point out and identify parts of an illustration. Also, headings that appear in a narrow margin next to the body copy. See also **Pull-out quotation**.

Camera-ready art. The complete pages of a publication assembled with text and graphics, and ready for reproduction. Literally refers to the pages that are ready to be photographed as the first step in the process of making plates for offset printing. See also **Mechanicals** and **Offset printing**.

Caps and small caps. Text in which letters that are normally lowercase are set as uppercase letters smaller than the normal capitals in a font. In Ventura, you can achieve this effect by setting initial capitals to a larger point size.

Captions. Descriptive text identifying photographs and illustrations. See also **Callout**.

Carriage return. A line break that you enter by entering a carriage return (pressing the Return or Enter key) at the end of a line or paragraph. Sometimes called a *hard carriage return* to distinguish it from the *soft carriage returns* that occur because of automatic wordwrap at the right margin of a page or the right edge of a column.

Chapter. A combination of text and picture files, formatted with a style file. In Ventura, a CHP file consists of pointers to each of these files, along with instructions on how to combine them on-screen or on the printer.

Click. To press and release a mouse button quickly.

Clipboard. A part of computer memory that temporarily stores the text or graphics that are cut or copied using the commands under the Edit menu. The Paste command brings the contents of the Clipboard onto the page. The Clipboard can hold one text block, one picture, and one graphic—independent of each other—at any given time.

CNF file. Contains the directory location and names of fonts for the printer width table of the same name.

Collated copies. Printed in order, with the first page on top of the stack that comes out of the printer. An option on the PRINT INFORMATION dialog box. Multiple copies are grouped into whole copies of the publication under this option.

Color separations. The films needed to create plates for multicolor offset printing. In four-color printing, separate films are created for magenta, cyan, yellow, and black inks. Using Ventura, you can print a separate page for each color by choosing Spot Color Overlay On: from the TO PRINT dialog box. In two- or three-color printing, if the colors are not overlapping, you also can use a tissue overlay to indicate colors to the offset printer.

Column guides. The nonprinting dotted vertical lines that mark the left and right edges of the columns within a frame on the screen.

Column rules. Vertical lines drawn between columns using Ventura's Vertical Rules command under the Frame menu.

Comp. Traditionally, a designer's "comprehensive" sketch of a page design that shows the client what the final page will look like when printed. Usually a full-size likeness of the page, the comp is a few steps closer to the final than a *pencil rough* and can be composed using ink pens, pencils, color markers, color acetate, pressure-sensitive letters, and other tools available at art-supply shops. Using Ventura, a comp can look like the finished product, with typeset text, ruled lines, and shaded boxes created in Ventura directly; the comp can be used as a starting point in building the final document.

Continued line. See **Jump line**.

Continuous tone. Describes an illustration or photograph, black-and-white or color, that consists of many shades between the lightest and the darkest tones and that is not broken up into dots. Continuous-tone images usually need to be converted into dots, either by scanning or by half-toning, in order to be printed in ink or on a laser printer.

Copy fitting. A method used to determine the amount of copy (text) that will fit in a given area on a page or in a publication, using a specified font. Also, to make copy fit on a page in Ventura by adjusting the line spacing, word spacing, or letter spacing.

Corner style. See **Rounded-rectangle tool**.

Crop. To trim the edges from a graphic, to make it fit a given space or to remove unnecessary parts of the image. When a graphic image is cropped in Ventura, the portions not displayed in the document are still stored in the original image file.

Crop marks. Lines printed on a page to indicate where the page will be trimmed when the final document is printed and bound. Ventura prints these marks if the base page size is smaller than the paper size and Crop Marks: On is set in the PRINT INFORMATION dialog box.

Default. The program's initial setting of a value or option. Default settings usually can be changed by the operator.

Descender. The portion of a lowercase letter that hangs below the baseline. Five letters of the alphabet have descenders: *g*, *j*, *p*, *q*, and *y*. See also **Ascender** and **Baseline**.

Deselect. To cancel the current selection by choosing another or by clicking on a blank area of the pasteboard.

Desktop publishing. The use of personal computers and software applications such as Ventura Publisher to produce camera-ready publications.

Dialog box. A window or full-screen display that appears in response to a command that calls for setting options.

Digitize. To convert an image to a system of dots that can be stored in the computer. See also **Scanned image files**.

Dingbats. Traditionally, ornamental characters such as bullets, stars, and flowers used by printers to decorate a page or as special characters within the text. The laser font Zapf Dingbats includes many of these traditional symbols as well as some new ones.

Directory. A grouping of files on disk. Each directory can have subdirectories.

Display type. Type used for headlines, titles, headings, advertisements, fliers, and so on. Display type is usually a large point size (several sizes larger than body copy) and can be a decorative font.

Dot-matrix printer. A printer that creates text and graphics by pressing a matrix of pins through the ribbon onto the paper. These impact printers usually offer lower resolution (dots per inch) than non-impact laser printers.

Dots per inch (dpi). See **Resolution**.

Double sided. A term describing a publication that will be reproduced on both sides of the sheets of paper. The front side of a page has an odd-numbered page, and the back side has an even-numbered page. To print on both sides, specify Sides: Double in the PAGE LAYOUT dialog box. See also **Facing pages**.

Drag. To hold down the main mouse button, move the mouse until it is positioned where you want it, and release the button.

Draw-type files. See **Object-oriented files**.

Drop-down menu. A list of commands that is displayed when you select a menu word. In Ventura, the menu titles appear on the menu bar along the top of the screen, and the menu commands ''drop down'' in a list below the title selected.

Dummy publication. Traditionally, a pencil mock-up of the pages of a publication, folded or stapled into a booklet, that the offset printer uses to verify the correct sequence of pages and positioning of photographs. See also **Template**.

EDCO dictionary. The Professional Extension includes the 130,000-word EDCO dictionary for complete and professional hyphenation. 1.2M of EMS is required to store the EDCO dictionary.

Ellipse. A regular-shaped oval. The shape that is created with Ventura's circle drawing tool, as distinguished from irregular ovals, which are egg-shaped.

Ellipsis. Series of three dots in text (. . .), used to indicate that some of the text has been deleted (usually from a quotation). Ellipses also appear on the menus with every Ventura command that opens a dialog box.

Em. Traditionally, a unit of measure equal to the width of the letter M in the current point size. An em dash is the same width as an em space. Ventura uses the width of the @ character in the current point size to define an em.

EMS memory. If you have installed an Expanded Memory Specification board or chip on your computer, Ventura uses any available EMS memory for portions of the system software. Using EMS memory frees conventional memory and enables you to work on longer documents. By storing a document in EMS memory, the Professional Extension dramatically speeds performance. 8M of unused EMS, for example, enables you to work on a 6.5M chapter.

En. One half the width of an em. Identifies the width of an en dash or an en space. See also **Em**.

Enter key. A key you press to break a line when the text tool is active. Usually has the same effect as the Return key. See also **Carriage return**.

Extension. The part of the file name after the period. For instance, the extension in the file name NEWS.CHP is CHP. Extensions used by Ventura to differentiate between different types of files include STY (style file), CHP (chapter), PUB (publication), WID (width table), CAP (caption), VGR (graphic), and INF (information).

Facing pages. In a double-sided publication, the two pages that face each other when the publication is open. Facing pages have an even-numbered page on the left and an odd-numbered page on the right.

Feathering. Adding an even amount of space between all lines on a page or column to force vertical justification.

Figure space. A space the width of a numeral in the current point size. A figure space is used to hold space in a table to keep numbers aligned.

File. A unit of information stored on disk. Different types of information are stored in files with different extensions. The different file types recognized by Ventura include style (STY), chapter (CHP), publication (PUB), width table (WID), caption (CAP), and graphic (VGR).

Filter. A method of determining which files will be selected for a particular operation. Filters are often called "wild card" characters. The asterisk (*) indicates that any set of characters can be displayed; the question mark (?) indicates that any single character can be displayed in that position. For instance, *.STY will display any file name with the extension STY. GRAB????.IMG will display all eight-character file names starting with the letters GRAB and having the extension IMG.

Flush. Aligned with, even with, coming to the same edge as. See also **Alignment**.

Flush right (or right-justified). Text in which lines end at the same point on the right margin. Opposite of ragged right or left-justified. See also **Alignment**.

Folio. Page number on a printed page, often accompanied by the name of the document and date of publication. See also **Header** and **Footer**.

Font. One complete set of characters in the same face, style, and size—including all the letters of the alphabet, punctuation, and symbols. 12-point Times Roman is a different font from 12-point Times Italic, 14-point Times Roman, or 12-point Helvetica, for example. Screen fonts (bit-mapped fonts used to display text accurately on the screen) can differ slightly from the printer fonts (outline fonts used to describe fonts to the laser printer) because of the difference in resolution between screens and printers.

Font metric. The width and height information for each character in each font. This information is stored in a width table.

Footer. One or more lines of text that appear at the bottom of every page. In Ventura, the footer is entered through the Headers & Footers command under the Page menu, and formatted with embedded codes or by changing the ZFOOTER tag in the style file. The footer frame can be adjusted using any of the commands under the Frame menu. Also called "running footer" or "running foot." See also **Folio**.

Footnote. Explanatory information at the bottom of the page, that is referenced in the body copy on the same or succeeding pages.

Format. The page size, margins, and grid used in a publication. Also, the character format (font) and paragraph format (alignment, spacing, and indentation).

Frame. A rectangular box used to hold text or pictures. Base pages are special frames that Ventura automatically creates as needed to accommodate all text in a file.

Frequency. See **Lines per inch**.

GEN file. Ventura creates source files with a GEN extension when you create a table of contents or index with the Multi-Chapter command or when you print the stylesheet with the Update Tags command.

Generic font. A screen representation of alphanumeric characters, which may not reflect what the printed characters will look like.

Graphic. A line, box, or circle drawn with Ventura, or an illustration placed in a Ventura publication from another application.

Graphic grid. An invisible grid set from the Graphic menu. When you draw or move Ventura's graphics, they snap to the measurement.

Graphic selection tool. The tool used most often to select and manipulate text and graphics. When this tool is selected, the pointer looks like an arrow.

Gray scale. Some scanners produce images that are shades of gray instead of a bit-mapped image that simulates gray. Ventura converts gray-scale images to a halftone to print them on a black-only printer. (See "Image Settings" in Chapter 6.)

Greek text. Traditionally, a block of text used to represent the positioning and point size of text in a designer's comp of a design. Standard greek text used by type-setters actually looks more like Latin: "Lorem ipsum dolor sit amet. . . ."

Greeking. The conversion of text to symbolic bars or lines that show the position of the text on the screen but not the alphanumeric characters. Used to increase screen drawing speed when the text is too small to be legible. Greeking does not affect what is printed. Text is usually greeked in Ventura's Reduced view, and small point sizes may be greeked in closer views on some screens. You can specify the point size below which text is greeked through the Set Preferences command under the Options menu.

Grid. The underlying design plan for a page. In Ventura, the grid is composed of a series of nonprinting horizontal and vertical lines (margins, column guides, and frame edges).

Guide. A type of nonprinting line that appears as a dotted line on the screen. Nonprinting lines include margin guides, column guides, and frame edges.

Gutter. The inside margins between the facing pages of a document. Also, the space between columns. In some word processors, the gutter measure is entered as the difference between measures of the inside margin and the outside margin.

Hairline. The thinnest rule possible—generally 0.25 point. (Some laser printers do not support hairline rules.) See also **Ruling line**.

Halftone. The conversion of continuous-tone artwork (usually a photograph) into a pattern of dots or lines that look like gray tones when printed by the offset printing press.

Handles. The eight small black rectangles that surround a selected frame, line, rectangle, or circle drawn with Ventura's drawing tools. You can drag the handles to change the size of the selected frame.

Hanging indent. The first line of a paragraph that extends to the left of the rest of the lines in the same paragraph. A hanging indent also can be used to create headings that are set to the left of the body copy.

Hard carriage return. See **Carriage return**.

Hard disk. Disk storage that is built into the computer or into a piece of hardware connected to the computer. Capable of storing much more information than a removable *floppy disk*.

Header. One or more lines of text that appear at the top of every page of a document. In Ventura, the header is entered through the Headers & Footers command under the Page menu, and formatted with embedded codes or by changing the ZHEADER tag in the style file. The header frame can be adjusted using any of the commands under the Frame menu. The header is also called ''running header'' or ''running head.'' See also **Footer** and **Folio**.

Headline. The title of an article in a newsletter, newspaper, or magazine. Often shown in a large type size.

Highlight. To visually differentiate a selection on the screen. Usually, highlighting reverses the normal appearance of the selected text, graphics, or options (for example, black text on a white background will appear as white text on a black background).

Hyphenation. The method of dividing words over two lines to achieve better word spacing on each line. Hyphenation can be achieved in two ways: (1) Ventura automatically hyphenates text (based on its dictionary) as the text is placed or typed on the page if automatic hyphenation has been activated through the Alignment command under the Paragraph menu; (2) Ventura also recognizes hyphens that have been inserted by the word processing program.

I-beam. The shape the pointer assumes when you select the text tool.

Icon. A functional graphic representation of a tool, file, or command displayed on a screen.

Image. A picture that is composed of individual dots. Usually created with a "paint" program or with a scanner.

Image area. The area of a page inside the margins where you put most of the text and graphics.

Increment. The distance between tick marks on the rulers.

Indentation. Positioning of the first line or the subsequent lines of a paragraph to the right of the left column guide (to create a left indent), or positioning the right margin of the paragraph to the left of the right column guide (to create a right indent), relative to the other text on the page.

INF file. Contains the most recent display settings for Show/Hide Pictures, Rulers, and Set Preferences under the Options menu. An INF file also contains the style file name, active function, and dialog box settings for loading chapter, style, and source files from the last work session.

Insertion point. The blinking vertical bar indicating where you will type or paste text.

Inside margin. The margin along the binding edge of the page. For single-sided publications, the inside margin is always the left margin. For double-sided publications, the inside margin is the left margin of a right-hand (odd-numbered) page, and the right margin of a left-hand (even-numbered) page. See also **Gutter**.

Interline spacing. The space between lines in a paragraph. Also called "leading."

Interpress. A language used to describe how to print a page that consists of both text and pictures. This description is completely independent of the printing device. Therefore, the page can be printed on any printer or typesetter that uses Interpress, and the page will be printed at the full resolution that each printer or typesetter can produce.

Invert. See **Reverse**.

Italic. Letters that slope toward the right, as distinguished from upright, or Roman, characters.

Jump line. Text at the end of part of an article on a newsletter, magazine, or newspaper page, indicating on what page the article is continued. Also, the text at the top of a continued article, indicating from where the article is continued.

Justified text. Text that is flush at both the left and right edges. See also **Alignment**.

Kern. To adjust the spacing between letters, usually to move them closer together. See also **Kerning**.

Kerning. The amount of space between letters, especially certain combinations of letters that must be moved close together in order to create visually consistent spacing between all letters. For example, the uppercase letters *AW* may appear to have a wider gap between them than the letters *MN* unless a special kerning formula is set up for the *AW* combination.

Landscape printing. The rotation of a page design to print text and graphics horizontally across the longer axis of the page or paper (usually 11 inches). In Ventura, `Orientation: Landscape` is an option in the PAGE LAYOUT dialog box. See also **Portrait printing**.

Laser printing. Term used to describe printing with one of the toner-based laser printers that are available for PCs. These printers use laser technology to project an intense light beam with a narrow band width (1/300th of an inch in 300-dots-per-inch printers) to create the charge on the printer drum that picks up the toner and transfers it to the paper. Some typesetters also use laser technology in conjunction with their photochemical processing, but these devices are usually referred to as phototypesetters rather than laser printers.

Layout. The process of arranging text and graphics on a page. Also, a sketch or plan for the page. Also, the final appearance of the page. In platemaking, a sheet indicating the settings for the step-and-repeat machine.

Layout grid. See **Grid**.

Leaders. Dotted or dashed lines that fill the space between tab settings. Ventura offers two types of tab leaders, plus a custom leader option, through the Tab Settings command under the Paragraph menu.

Leading. Historically, the insertion of thin strips of metal (made of a metal alloy that included some proportion of lead) between lines of cast type to add space between the lines and to make columns align vertically. In modern typography, the vertical spacing between the baselines of two lines of text. In Ventura, leading is called interline spacing and is entered in points on the SPACING dialog box under the Paragraph menu. As an example of the terminology used in describing line spacing, 12-point Times with one point of leading would be considered "one-point leaded" type, or 12-point Times with 13-point leading, or "12 on 13 Times." The type specs are sometimes written as "12/13 Times."

Letter spacing. The space between letters in a word. Also, the practice of adding space between letters. Letter spacing can be adjusted through `Automatic Kerning` and `Tracking` options in the TYPOGRAPHIC CONTROLS dialog box under the Paragraph menu. In Ventura, unjustified text has fixed letter spacing, and justified text has variable letter spacing that is adjusted within the limits entered in the TYPOGRAPHIC CONTROLS dialog box. See also **Kerning** and **Word spacing**.

Ligatures. Character combinations that are often combined into special characters in a font. For example, some downloadable fonts come with the combinations *fi* and *fl* as special characters.

Line art. Traditionally, a drawing that does not contain any halftones. In computer terms, a picture that is stored as a mathematically defined object. Any picture not produced using a "paint" program or scanner is probably line art.

Line break. The end of a line of text that is created by automatic wordwrap and hyphenation. See also **Carriage return**.

Line drawing tool. The tool you use in Ventura to draw a straight line in any direction.

Line length. The horizontal measure of a column or a line of text.

Line spacing. See **Leading**.

Lines per inch. Spacing between the rows of dots in a halftone is defined by the number of lines per inch, or frequency. The higher the number of lines, the greater the resolution. (See ''Image Settings'' in Chapter 6 for suggested settings for laser printers and phototypesetters.)

List box. The area in a dialog box that lists options from which to choose.

Load text. To place a text file into a frame.

Logo. A company trademark. Also, the banner on the front cover of a magazine or newsletter.

Margin. Traditionally, the distance from the edge of the page to the edge of the layout area of the page. In Ventura, the page size and the margins for the whole document are set through the base page attributes, and each added frame can have its own margins. The margins in Ventura should define the limits of text that is placed in columns on the page, with headers, footers, and column rules outside the margins.

Margin guides. The dotted, nonprinting lines near the borders of frames on the screen that mark the margins of each frame as specified in the MARGINS & COLUMNS dialog box under the Frame menu.

Masthead. Section of a newsletter or magazine giving the title and details of staff, ownership, advertising, subscription dates, and so on. Sometimes used to describe the banner or wide title on the front of a magazine, newsletter, or newspaper. See also **Logo**.

Measurement system. The units you choose using the Set Ruler command under the Options menu: inches, centimeters, or picas. You can enter a value into a dialog box in any unit of measure—regardless of the current Set Ruler selection—by clicking on the units that are displayed in the dialog box.

Mechanicals. Traditionally, the final pages or boards with pasted-up galleys of type and line art, sometimes with acetate or tissue overlays for color separations and notes to the offset printer. See also **Camera-ready art**.

Memory. The computer's temporary storage of information while you are working (also called *RAM*, for *random-access memory*). You copy the contents of memory onto disk using the Save command or the Save As command, both under the File menu.

Menu bar. The area at the top of the publication window that lists the menu titles.

Moire pattern. An undesirable grid pattern that can result when two transparent dot-screen fill patterns are overlaid, or (sometimes) when a bit-mapped graphic with gray fill patterns is reduced or enlarged.

Negative. A reverse image of a page, produced photographically on a clear sheet of film, as an intermediate step in preparing plates for offset printing from camera-ready mechanicals.

Nonbreaking space. A special character inserted between two words so that they cannot be separated by a line break.

Normal View. A command under the View menu that shows a page in the publication window at approximately the same size the page will print, depending on the characteristics of your screen display.

Object-oriented files. Draw-type files that consist of a sequence of drawing commands (stored as mathematical formulas). These commands describe graphics (such as mechanical drawings, schematics, charts, and ad graphics) that you would produce manually with a pencil, straightedge, and compass. Usually contrasted with paint-type files or bit maps. See also **Bit map**.

Offset printing. The type of printing done using a printing press to reproduce many copies of the original (which is printed on a laser printer in Ventura). The press lays ink on a page based on the raised image on a plate created by photographing the camera-ready masters.

Orientation. The page position: portrait or landscape. Portrait orientation means that the text runs horizontally across the narrower width of the page and the columns run down the longer length of the page. Landscape orientation means that the text runs horizontally across the wider measure of the page. See also **Landscape printing** and **Portrait printing**.

Orphans/widows. The first line of a paragraph is called an *orphan* when the line is separated from the rest of the paragraph by a page break. The last line of a paragraph is called a *widow* when the line is forced onto a new page by a page break and separated from the rest of the paragraph. Most publishers consider widows and orphans bad page breaks (or column breaks). The term *widow* is also used to describe bad line breaks that occur when the last line of a paragraph has only one word, especially when it falls at the bottom of a column or page.

Outdent. Text on the first line of a paragraph that prints to the left of the left paragraph margin.

Outline font. A printer font in which each letter of the alphabet is stored as a complex mathematical formula, as distinguished from bit-mapped fonts, which are stored as a pattern of dots.

Outside margin. The unbound edge of a publication. For single-sided publications, the outside margin is the right margin. For double-sided publications, the outside margin is the right margin of right-hand (odd-numbered) pages, and the left margin of left-hand (even-numbered) pages.

Overhead transparency. An image printed on clear acetate and projected onto a screen for viewing by an audience.

Overlay. A transparent acetate or tissue covering a printed page, where color indications and other instructions to the offset printer are written. Also, an overhead transparency that is intended to be projected on top of another transparency.

Oversize publication. A publication with a page size larger than standard paper size. See also **Page size**, **Paper size**, and **Tile**.

Padding. The white space between the outside of a frame and the text that surrounds the frame.

Page size. The dimensions of your publication as set up in the PAGE LAYOUT dialog box, or by changing the size of the base page through the Sizing & Scaling command under the Frame menu. Page size can differ from paper size. See also **Paper size**.

Paint-type file. See **Bit map**.

Paper size. Each size of paper a printer can print on. Standard sizes are letter (8.5 by 11 inches), legal (8.5 by 14 inches), double (11 by 17 inches), and European A4 (8.27 by 11.69 inches) and B5 (6.93 by 9.84 inches).

Paragraph. Any line or lines of text ended by pressing the Enter key. A single letter, word, or line is considered a paragraph if the Enter key is pressed at the end.

Paste. The act of moving text or a picture from the Clipboard to the page.

Pasteup. See **Mechanicals**.

Phototypesetting. Producing a page image on photosensitive paper, as when documents are printed on a PostScript phototypesetter. This process is sometimes referred to as *cold type* to distinguish it from the older method of casting characters, lines, or whole pages in lead (*hot type*).

Pica. A unit of measure equal to approximately 1/6 inch, or 12 points. Use the Set Ruler command under the Options menu to select picas as the unit of measure for the ruler lines and dialog box displays.

Picture. Any drawing or illustration that is placed in a frame. A picture can be either an image or line art.

Pixel. The smallest unit on a computer screen display. Monitors can have different screen resolutions, or pixels per inch, as well as different overall sizes (total number of pixels).

Point. A standard unit of measure for type, measured roughly from the top of the ascenders to the bottom of the descenders in a line of type. A point is the smallest unit of measure in typographic measurement. If you have a PostScript printer, Ventura enables you to set type in half-point increments and set spacing in hundredths of a point, called fractional points. Twelve points are in a pica and 72 points are in an inch. A point equals 1/12 pica, or 1/72 inch. See also **Pica**.

Pointer. The on-screen icon that moves when you move the mouse.

Pop-up menu. When you click the setting beside some dialog box options, a sub-menu of choices pops up. When you choose Pop Up Menu Symbols Shown with the Set Preferences command on the Options menu, a symbol appears beside options with pop-up menus.

Port. The connection point in the computer for peripherals such as a printer or mouse.

Portrait printing. The normal printing orientation for a page: horizontally across the shorter axis of the page (usually, 8.5 inches). In Ventura, Orientation: Portrait is an option in the PAGE LAYOUT dialog box. See also **Landscape printing** and **Orientation**.

PostScript. A page-description language, developed by Adobe Systems Incorporated, that is used by the Apple LaserWriter and other high-resolution printers and typesetters. PostScript is used to describe how to print a page that consists of both text and pictures. This description is completely independent of the printing device. Therefore, the page can be printed on any printer or typesetter that uses PostScript, and the page will print at the full resolution that each printer or typesetter can produce.

Prepress proofs. Proofs made using photographic techniques. Sometimes called "blue lines." See also **Blue lines** and **Press proofs**.

Press proofs. A test run of a color printing job through the printing press to check registration and color. See also **Prepress proofs**.

Print area. The area of a piece of paper where a printer can reproduce text or graphics. The print area is usually smaller than the paper size.

Printer font. A bit-mapped or outline font that is installed in the printer or downloaded to the printer when a publication is printed. Usually distinguished from the screen font that is used to display the text on the screen. See also **Font**.

Proofread. To read a preliminary printout of a page to check for spelling errors, alignment on the page, and other features that are not related to the technical accuracy of the content.

Proofs. See **Prepress proofs**, **Press proofs**, and **Blue lines**.

Proportional spacing. The different amount of space given to each character in a font. When proportionally spaced, the letter *i* gets less space than the letter *w*.

Publication. A combination of chapter (CHP) files linked together through Ventura's Multi-Chapter command. Each chapter file can have its own set of text, picture, and style files.

Pull-out quotation. Quotation extracted from a newsletter or magazine article and printed in larger type in the column, often blocked off with ruled lines.

Ragged right. Text in which lines end at different points near the right margin. Distinguished from flush right (justified) text. See also **Alignment**.

RAM. See **Memory**.

Rectangle tool. The tool you use to create squares and rectangles with square corners (as opposed to rounded corners).

Resolution. The number of dots per inch used to represent alphanumeric characters or graphic images. High-resolution images have more dots per inch and look smoother than low-resolution images. The resolution of images displayed on the screen is usually lower than the resolution of the laser printout. Laser printers print 300 dots per inch or more; typesetters print 1,200 dots per inch or more.

Reverse. The opposite of a text's or graphic's normal appearance on the printed page. Normally, text and graphics are black on a white background; when reversed, they are white on a black background.

Right justified. See **Flush right** and **Alignment**.

Roman. Upright text styles, as distinguished from italic (slanted) styles. Sometimes used to refer to Normal style in Ventura's ADD/REMOVE FONTS dialog box, in contrast to Bold or Italic.

Roughs. Traditionally, the preliminary page layouts done by the designer using pencil sketches to represent page design ideas. Also called ''thumbnails.''

Rounded-rectangle tool. The tool you use to draw squares and rectangles with rounded corners.

Rulers. Ventura's electronic rulers, one across the top of the publication window and one down the left side. Rulers show measures of the page layout in inches, picas, or centimeters. Use the Show Rulers command under the Options menu to display the rulers. Use the Set Ruler command to select the unit of measure displayed on the ruler lines and dialog box displays. Increments (tick marks) on the rulers depend on the size and resolution of your screen, and the view (Normal, Reduced, or Enlarged view).

Rules. Black lines added to the page—for example, between columns—to enhance the design or readability of the publication. Rules can be horizontal or vertical, and of varying lengths and widths.

Ruling line. Any border or line associated with text (through Paragraph menu commands) or with frames (through Frame menu commands).

Runaround. See **Text wrap**.

Running heads and feet. See **Header** and **Footer**.

Sans serif. Typefaces without serifs, such as Helvetica and Avant Garde. See also **Serif**.

Scale. To increase or decrease the size of a picture.

Scanned-image files. Bit-mapped files created with hardware that digitizes images (converts a two- or three-dimensional image to a collection of dots stored in the computer's memory or on disk). If the image is scanned as gray-scales, Ventura converts the image to a halftone before printing.

Scanner. A device that converts an image on paper into a computer image.

Screen. A pattern of dots used to print shades of gray on a black-only printer (laser or offset). Usually identified as a percentage: a 100-percent screen is solid black, and a 10-percent screen is light gray.

Screen font. See **Font**.

Screen type. When printing to a PostScript printer a TIFF or PostScript image with gray-scale information, you can change the appearance of the image by changing the pattern of the halftone from the default dot pattern to ellipses, lines, or a custom pattern.

Script fonts. Type designed to look like handwriting or calligraphy—for example, Zapf Chancery.

Scroll bar. The gray bars on the right side and the bottom of the publication window, which you use to move horizontally or vertically in the publication window. Every scroll bar has a scroll box and scroll arrows at each end. List boxes in dialog boxes also can have scroll bars for viewing a long list of files or options.

Select. To click or drag the mouse to designate where the next action will take place.

Serif. Line crossing the main stroke of a letter. Typefaces that have serifs include Times, Courier, New Century Schoolbook, Bookman, and Palatino. See also **Sans serif**.

Shade pattern. See **Screen**.

Signature. In printing and binding, the name given to a printed sheet of (usually) 16 pages after it has been folded.

Single sided. A term describing a publication that will be reproduced on one side only of each sheet of paper. To print on single sides, specify Sides: Single in the PAGE LAYOUT dialog box.

Size. To make a graphic smaller or larger on a page by dragging the handles.

Small caps. See **Caps and small caps**.

Snap-to. An option in Ventura that makes frame or graphic borders adhere to a predetermined grid. This feature is useful for accurately aligning text and graphics.

Soft carriage return. See **Carriage return**.

Spot color. Any color(s) that appears on a page in addition to the base color.

Style. One of the variations within a typeface, such as Roman, bold, or italic.

Style file. A file (stored separately from the text) that controls the typographic format of the text.

Tag. The format applied to a particular paragraph.

Template. A Ventura CHP file containing only the layout grid and boilerplate text and graphics for a periodical or book. Serves as the starting point for creating many similar documents, such as issues of a newsletter. Variable items—text and graphics that are not common to all chapters or issues—are added to the template document and saved under another name so that the template document remains unchanged.

Text box. The area in a dialog box where you type text.

Text-only file. Text created with another application and then saved without any type specifications or other formatting. See also **ASCII**.

Text wrap. Automatic line breaks at the right edge of a column or the right margin of a page. (See also **Carriage return**.) Also, the ability to wrap text around a graphic on a page layout.

Thin space. A space the width of a period.

Thumbnails. See **Roughs**.

Tick marks. Marks on the rulers defining increments of measure.

TIFF file. Tagged Image File Format files contain images in shades of gray instead of using dots to simulate gray. When printing a TIFF file to a PostScript printer, you can specify the pattern, resolution, and angle of the halftone. (See "Image Settings" in Chapter 6.)

Tile. The portion of the page in an oversize publication that is printed on a single sheet of paper. To make a complete page, you must assemble and paste together the tiles. See also **Oversize publication**.

Toggle switch. An on-off command. Used to describe cases in which the same command is invoked to turn a feature on and off.

Tones. The shades of a photograph or illustration that is printed as a series of dots. Each tone is a percentage of black. The smaller the percentage, the lighter the tone.

Tracking. Decreasing or increasing the amount of space between letters in a word.

Transparency. See **Overhead transparency** and **Overlay**.

Typeface. A single "type family" of one design of type in all sizes and styles. Times and Helvetica are two different typefaces, for instance. Each typeface has many fonts (that is, sizes and styles). Sometimes the terms *typeface* and *font* are used interchangeably.

Typeset. The act of producing a document on a typesetting machine. Ventura can produce documents that have "near typeset" quality on a laser printer or on a PostScript typesetter.

Txscale. The width of a character along the horizontal axis, as defined in a PostScript file.

Tyscale. The height of a character along the vertical axis, as defined in a PostScript file.

Uppercase. See **Caps and small caps**.

Vector graphics. See **Object-oriented files**.

Vertical justification. The adjustment of the spacing between lines of text (leading) in fine increments in order to make columns and pages end at the same point.

VGR file. Stores the elements drawn with Ventura's graphic tools.

View. The size of the page as it appears in the publication window, based on selections under the View menu. The smallest view (Reduced view) shows a complete page or two facing pages; the largest view (Enlarged view) shows text and graphics at twice the size they will print.

White space. Empty space on a page, not used for text or graphics.

Widow. The last line of a paragraph left at the top of a new column or page. See also **Orphans/widows**.

Width table. A Ventura file that contains font metric information.

Wild card. See **Filter**.

Word spacing. The space between words in a line or a paragraph. See also **Kerning** and **Letter spacing**.

Wordwrap. The automatic adjustment of the number of words on a line of text in order to match the margin settings. The carriage returns that result from automatic wordwrap are called *soft carriage returns* to distinguish them from the *hard carriage returns* that result when you press the Enter key. See also **Text wrap** and **Carriage return**.

Wrap. See **Text wrap** and **Wordwrap**.

WYSIWYG. "What You See Is What You Get" (pronounced "wizzywig") describes systems such as Ventura that display full pages on-screen with text and graphics. Some systems are more WYSIWYG than others in the accuracy of the display.

X-height. A distinguishing characteristic of a font. The height of lowercase letters that do not have ascenders or descenders (such as *x*, *a*, and *c*). Also called the body of the type.

Zero point. The intersection of the 0 points on the two rulers. When you start Ventura, the zero point is located at the intersection of the left and top margins. You can reposition the zero point.

Index

H

I

T